DISCARD

Y0-DBO-597

DISCARD

NIXON

PASADENA CITY COLLEGE

JUN 1 9 19

LIBRARY

The Third Year of His Presidency

PASADENA CITY COLLEGE

JUN 5 1972

LIBRARY

CONGRESSIONAL QUARTERLY

1735 K STREET, N. W., WASHINGTON, D. C.

Congressional Quarterly Inc.

Congressional Quarterly Inc., an editorial research service and publishing company, serves clients in the fields of news, education, business and government. It combines specific coverage of Congress, government and politics by Congressional Quarterly with the more general subject range of an affiliated service, Editorial Research Reports.

Congressional Quarterly was founded in 1945 by Nelson and Henrietta Poynter. Its basic periodical publication was and still is the CQ *Weekly Report,* mailed to clients every Saturday. A cumulative index is published quarterly.

The CQ *Almanac,* a compendium of legislation for one session of Congress, is published every spring. *Congress and the Nation* is published every four years as a record of government for one presidential term.

Congressional Quarterly also publishes paperback books on public affairs. These include the twice-yearly *Guide to Current American Government* and such recent titles as *Candidates '72, Dollar Politics* and *China and U.S. Foreign Policy.*

CQ Direct Research is a consulting service which performs contract research and maintains a reference library and query desk for the convenience of clients.

Editorial Research Reports covers subjects beyond the specialized scope of Congressional Quarterly. It publishes reference material on foreign affairs, business, education, cultural affairs, national security, science and other topics of news interest. Service to clients includes a 6,000-word report four times a month bound and indexed semi-annually. Editorial Research Reports publishes paperback books in its fields of coverage. Founded in 1923, the service merged with Congressional Quarterly in 1956.

Book Service Editor: Robert A. Diamond
Contributors: Arlene Alligood, James W. Lawrence, Andrea W. Loewenstein, Carol Moore, Harry Van-Dernoot, Wayne Walker, Stanley L. Williams. Index: Linda Strassburg, Janet Sims. Book Researcher: Janice L. Goldstein.
Cover design: Howard Chapman, Art Director.

Library of Congress Catalog No. 72-77848
International Standard Book No. 0-87187-031-2

Copyright 1972 by Congressional Quarterly Inc.
1735 K Street, N.W., Washington, D.C. 20006

TABLE OF CONTENTS

Messages and Statements

734067

STATE OF UNION: DUAL PLEA FOR ACTION ON PAST REQUESTS

President Nixon broke with precedent Jan. 20 when he delivered two state-of-the-union messages to Congress—a 4,000-word speech tailored for national television and a 15,000-word document elaborating on the address.

It was the first dual state-of-the-union message ever delivered by a U.S. President. *(All direct quotations on this page and on the following page are from the expanded, 15,000-word message. Text of shorter message prepared for delivery to televised joint session of Congress, p. 3; text of expanded message, p. 6.)*

In the 15,000-word message, as well as in his televised address, Nixon urged Congress to act quickly on the "six great goals" he outlined in his 1971 message and to help formulate programs that would:

• Relieve "the burden of property taxes" and provide "both fair and adequate financing for our children's education—consistent with the principle of preserving the control by local school boards over local schools."

• Transfer the scientific and technological advances of the space and military programs to "creating new sources of clean and abundant energy; developing safe, fast, pollution-free transportation;...developing effective emergency health care systems which could lead to the saving of as many as 30,000 lives each year...."

Noting that 1972 is a presidential election year, Nixon called on the Democratic-controlled Congress to "keep the national interest first" and pass his proposals on welfare reform, revenue sharing, executive reorganization, environmental protection and national health insurance—all plans he submitted in 1971 and which have languished in Congress. *(Review of Nixon actions in 1971, p. 20)*

Nixon described the renewed dock strike as "extremely costly for the American people, particularly for the farmer for whom a whole year's income can hinge on how promptly he can move his goods." He asked Congress for passage of the Emergency Public Interest Protection Act, which he proposed in February 1970, to "give us the permanent machinery so badly needed for resolving future (transporation) disputes."

Foreign Affairs

As is traditional in state-of-the-union messages, Nixon devoted most of his time to domestic issues. But he did say that the war in Vietnam was winding down, that he had opened new lines of communication with Moscow and Peking and that U.S. defense spending will increase again in fiscal 1973 so that the United States could "negotiate from a position of strength."

He urged Congress to "act upon the fundamental aid reform proposals submitted by this administration in 1971."

Education-Property Taxes

Nixon committed himself to finding some solution to the growing problem involved in the financing of local school systems mainly through property taxes, which he described as "one of the most inequitable and regressive of all public levies."

Noting court decisions in California, Minnesota, Texas and New Jersey which held that the method of financing schools through property taxes was "discriminatory and unconstitutional," he promised legislative proposals on the subject later in 1972.

The administration is known to be considering a value-added tax, a form of federal sales tax that is in common use in Europe, as a new source of revenue that could be earmarked for aid to education and as a relief to property owners. He did not specify what his proposals would include, however.

The President said his Commission on School Finances, established in March 1970, has been studying the problem and he now has the Advisory Commission on Intergovernmental Relations working in the same area.

"Later in the year...," Nixon said, "I shall make my final recommendations for relieving the burden of property taxes and providing both fair and adequate financing for our children's education—consistent with the principle of the control by local school boards over local schools."

Desegregation. The President again called on Congress to approve his special revenue-sharing plan for education and enact "my $1.5-billion program of Emergency School Aid to help local school districts desegregate wisely and well."

Nixon's desegregation aid bill was approved in different forms by the House and Senate in 1971 and is tacked onto the higher education bill. It is, however, embroiled in a controversy over busing and has yet to go to conference.

He reaffirmed his opposition to "unnecessary busing for the sole purpose of achieving an arbitrary racial balance."

Science and Technology

The President said he would soon submit a special message to Congress suggesting ways to transfer some of the scientific and technological advances from the military and space programs to private industry. In recent years private industry had been calling for transfer of the benefits of space technology.

"Among these proposals will be an increase next year of $700-million in civilian research and development spending," he said, "a 15-percent increase over last year's level and a 65-percent increase over 1969."

As an example, Nixon said, "our outstanding capabilities in space technology should be used to help the

Department of Transportation develop better mass transportation systems. As has been said so often in the last two years, a nation that can send three people across 240,000 miles of space to the moon should also be able to send 240,000 people three miles across a city to work."

Initial efforts, he said, would include activities aimed at:

- Creating new sources of clean and abundant energy.

- Developing safe, fast, pollution-free transportation.

- Reducing loss of life and property from earthquakes, hurricanes and other natural disasters.

- Developing effective emergency health care systems which would lead to the saving of as many as 30,000 lives each year.

- Finding new ways to curb drug traffic and rehabilitate drug users.

The Economy

Nixon, crediting his 1971 wage-price control action, took an optimistic view of economic trends as 1972 started. *(1971 economic review, p. 26)*

But he said the 6-percent unemployment rate "is too high. I am determined to cut that percentage.... The budget I present to the Congress next week will be an expansionary budget—reflecting the impact of new job-creating tax cuts and job-creating expenditures."

But, he said, "I would emphasize once again...that our ultimate objective is lasting price stability without controls."

International Economics. "Just as we have entered a new period of negotiation in world politics," the President said, "so have we also moved into a new period of negotiation on the international economic front.

"We have already made important strides in this direction. The realignment of exchange rates which was announced last month represents an important step forward—but now we also need basic long-range monetary reform.... We have the opportunity to help bring a new economic order to the world."

Unfinished Business

Welfare Reform. The President declared that the first item of unfinished business for the 92nd Congress is welfare reform.

"I have now given prominent attention to this subject in three consecutive messages on the state of the union," he said. "The House of Representatives has passed welfare reform twice.... I urge the Senate Finance Committee to place welfare reform at the top of its agenda."

The Finance Committee resumed hearings on HR 1, the President's welfare reform measure, on the same day he delivered his message.

Revenue Sharing. Noting that the "financial crisis of state and local government is deepening," Nixon urged Congress to approve his revenue-sharing proposals.

The President first submitted his revenue-sharing plans to Congress in 1969. Sporadic hearings were held during 1971, but Congress has taken no action on any of the plans.

Message Origins

The Constitution (Article II, Section 3) provides that a President "from time to time give to the Congress information of the state of the union, and recommend to their consideration such measures as he shall judge necessary and expedient."

The annual message, as it was called through most of American history, or the state-of-the-union message, as it became known after 1945, owed its origin to the nation's first President. George Washington initiated a practice of appearing personally before Congress each year to assess national problems and prospects.

When Thomas Jefferson came to the White House in 1801, he ended what he considered a quasi-monarchial ceremony and substituted a written message to Congress.

The precedent of a written message—many of which were little more than short statements accompanying reports from executive departments—was followed until Woodrow Wilson delivered his first annual message in person in 1913.

Executive Reorganization. Because of its structure, the President said, "our federal government today is too often a sluggish and unresponsive institution, unable to deliver a dollar's worth of service for a dollar's worth of taxes."

He repeated his 1971 proposal to reorganize the seven existing federal departments into four dealing with human resources, natural resources, economic development and community development. Late in 1971, Nixon withdrew his plan to eliminate the Department of Agriculture and split its functions among the four new agencies.

Health Insurance. The President said his national health insurance legislation (HR 7741 and S 1623) is "essential to assure that no American is denied basic medical care because of inability to pay." He also proposed elimination of the $5.80 monthly Medicare fee.

The House Ways and Means Committee concluded hearings on HR 7741, along with several competing plans, late in 1971 and is expected to write its own bill. The Senate Finance Committee plans to hold hearings on the subject early in 1972.

Equal Rights for Women. Nixon did not mention a proposed constitutional amendment guaranteeing equal rights for men and women (H J Res 208) that was approved by the House in October.

But he did recommend that the jurisdiction of the Civil Rights Commission be expanded to include sex discrimination. Such a provision was deleted from the higher education bill (HR 7248) during House debate in November.

Rural America. In addition to repeating his request for a $1.1-billion revenue-sharing program for rural development, Nixon announced that he would "soon present a major proposal to expand significantly the credit authorities of the Farmers Home Administration, so that this agency...can also help spur commercial, industrial and community development in rural America."

STATE OF UNION TEXT I

Following is the text, as prepared for delivery to a joint session of Congress, of President Nixon's Jan. 20, 1972 State of the Union message.

Mr. Speaker, Mr. President, my colleagues in the Congress, our distinguished guests and my fellow Americans:

Twenty-five years ago I sat here as a freshman Congressman—along with Speaker Albert—and listened for the first time to the President address us on the State of the Union.

I shall never forget that moment. The Senate, the Diplomatic Corps, the Supreme Court, the Cabinet entered the chamber, and then the President of the United States. As all of you are aware, I had some differences with President Truman, as he did with me. But I remember that on the day he addressed that Joint Session of the newly-elected Republican Congress, he spoke not as a partisan but as President of all the people—calling upon the Congress to put aside partisan considerations in the national interest.

The Greek-Turkish aid program, the Marshall Plan, the great foreign policy initiatives which have been responsible for avoiding a world war for the past 25 years were approved by that 80th Congress, by a bipartisan majority of which I was proud to be a part.

1972 is before us. It holds precious time in which to accomplish good for this Nation. We must not waste it. I know the political pressures in this session of the Congress will be great. There are more candidates for the Presidency in this chamber today than there probably have been at any one time in the whole history of the Republic. There is an honest division of opinion, not only between the parties but within the parties, on some issues of foreign policy and domestic policy as well.

However, there are great national problems that are so vital they transcend partisanship. Let us have our debates. Let us have our honest differences. But let us join in keeping the national interest first. Let us join in making sure that legislation the Nation needs does not become hostage to the political interest of any party or any person.

There is ample precedent, in this election year, for me to present you with a huge list of new proposals, knowing full well that there could be no possibility that they could be enacted even if you worked night and day.

I shall not do that.

I have presented to the leaders of the Congress today a message of 15,000 words discussing in some detail where the Nation stands and setting forth specific legislative items on which I ask the Congress to act. Much of this is legislation which I proposed in 1969, in 1970, and to the First Session of this 92nd Congress last year, and on which I feel it is essential that action be completed this year.

I am not presenting proposals which have attractive labels but no hope of passage. I am presenting only vital programs which are within the capacity of the Congress to enact, within the capacity of the budget to finance, and which I believe should be above partisanship—programs which deal with urgent priorities for the Nation, which should and must be the subject of bipartisan action by this Congress in the interests of the country in 1972.

When I took the oath of office on the steps of this building just three years ago today, the Nation was ending one of the most tortured decades in its history.

The 1960s were a time of great progress in many areas. They were also a time of great agony—the agonies of war, of inflation, of rapidly rising crime, of deteriorating cities—of hopes raised and disappointed, and of anger and frustration that led finally to violence, and to the worst civil discord in a century.

To recall these troubles is not to point fingers of blame. The Nation was so torn in those final years of the 60s that many in both parties questioned whether America could be governed at all.

The Nation has made significant progress in these first years of the 70s.

Our cities are no longer engulfed by civil disorders.

Our colleges and universities have again become places of learning instead of battlegrounds.

A beginning has been made on preserving and protecting our environment.

The rate of increase in crime has been slowed—and here in the District of Columbia, the one city where the Federal Government has direct jurisdiction, serious crime in 1971 was actually reduced by 13 percent from the year before.

Most important—because of the beginnings that have been made, we can say today that the year 1972 can be the year in which America may make the greatest progress in 25 years toward achieving our goal of being at peace with all the nations in the world.

As our involvement in the war in Vietnam comes to an end, we must now go on to build a generation of peace.

To achieve that goal, we must face realistically the need to maintain our defenses.

In the past three years, we have reduced the burden of arms. For the first time in 20 years, spending on defense has been brought below spending on human resources.

As we look to the future, we find encouraging progress in our negotiations with the Soviet Union on limitation of strategic arms. Looking further into the future, we hope there can eventually be agreement on the mutual reduction of arms. But until there is such a mutual agreement, we must maintain the strength necessary to deter war.

Because of rising research and development costs, because of increases in military and civilian pay, and because of the need to proceed with new weapons systems, my budget for the coming fiscal year will provide for an increase in defense spending.

Strong military defenses are not the enemy of peace. They are the guardian of peace.

There could be no more misguided set of priorities than one which would tempt others by weakening America, and thereby endanger the peace of the world.

In our foreign policies, we have entered a new era. The world has changed greatly in the eleven years since President John F. Kennedy said, in his Inaugural Address, "We shall pay any price, bear any burden, meet any hardship, support any friend, oppose any foe, to assure the survival and the success of liberty."

Our policy has been carefully and deliberately adjusted to meet the new realities of the new world we now live in. We make only those commitments we are able and prepared to meet.

Our commitment to freedom remains strong and unshakable. But others must bear their share of the burden of defending freedom around the world.

This is our policy:

• We will maintain a nuclear deterrent adequate to meet any threat to the security of the United States or of our allies.

• We will help other nations develop the capability of defending themselves.

• We will faithfully honor all of our treaty commitments.

• We will act to defend our interests whenever and wherever they are threatened any place in the world.

• But where our interests or our treaty commitments are not involved our role will be limited.

• We will not intervene militarily.

• But we will use our influence to prevent war.

• If war comes we will use our influence to try to stop it.

• Once war is over we will do our share in helping to bind up the wounds of those who have participated in it.

I shall soon be visiting the Peoples Republic of China and the Soviet Union. I shall go there with no illusions. We have great differences with both powers. We will continue to have great differences. But peach depends on the ability of great powers to live together on the same planet despite their differences. We would not be true to our obligation to generations yet unborn if we failed to seize this moment to do everything in our power to insure that we will be able to talk about these differences rather than fight about them.

As we look back over this century, we can be proud of our Nation's record in foreign affairs.

America has given more generously of itself toward maintaining freedom, preserving peace and alleviating human suffering around the globe than any nation has ever done.

We have fought four wars in this century—but our power has never been used to break the peace, only to keep it; never to destroy freedom, only to defend it. We now have within our reach the goal of ensuring that the next generation can be the first generation in this century to be spared the scourges of war.

Here at home, we are making progress toward our goal of a new prosperity without war.

Industrial production, consumer spending, retail sales and personal income all have been rising. Total employment and real income are the highest in history. New home-building starts this past year reached the highest level ever. Business and consumer confidence have both been rising. Interest rates are down, and the rate of inflation is down. We can look with confidence to 1972 as the year when the back of inflation will finally be broken.

Good as this record is, it is not good enough—not when we still have an unemployment rate of six percent.

It is not enough to point out that this was the rate of the early, peacetime years of the 1960s, or that, if the more than 2 million men released from the Armed Forces and defense-related industries were still on their wartime jobs, unemployment would be far lower.

Our goal is full employment in peacetime—and we intend to meet that goal.

The Congress has helped to meet it by passing our job-creating tax program last month.

The historic monetary agreements we have reached with the major European nations, Canada and Japan will help meet it, by providing new markets for American products—and thus new jobs for American workers.

Our budget will help meet it, by being expansionary without being inflationary—a job-producing budget that will help take up the gap as the economy expands to full employment.

Our program to raise farm income will help meet it, by helping to revitalize rural America—and by giving to America's farms their fair share of America's increasing productivity.

We will also help meet our goal of full employment in peacetime with a set of major initiatives to stimulate more imaginative use of America's great capacity for technological advance, and to direct it toward improving the quality of life for every American.

In reaching the moon, we saw what miracles American technology is capable of achieving. Now the time has come to move more deliberately toward making full use of that technology here on earth, in harnessing the wonders of science to the service of man.

I shall soon send to the Congress a special message proposing a new program of Federal partnership in technological research and development—with Federal incentives to increase private research, and federally-supported research on projects designed to improve our everyday lives in ways that will range from improving mass transit to developing new systems of emergency health care that could save thousands of lives annually.

Historically, our superior technology and high productivity have made it possible for America's workers to be the most highly paid in the world, and for our goods still to compete in world markets.

Now that other nations are moving rapidly forward in technology, the answer to the new competition is not to build a wall around America, but rather to remain competitive by improving our own technology still further, and by increasing productivity in American industry.

Our new monetary and trade agreements will make it possible for American goods to compete fairly in the world's markets—but they still must compete. The new technology program will not only put to use the skills of many highly-trained American—skills that might otherwise be wasted. It will also help meet the growing technological challenge from abroad, and thus help to create new industries as well as creating jobs for America's workers in producing for the world's markets.

This Second Session of the 92nd Congress already has before it more than 90 major administration proposals which still await action.

I have discussed these in the written message that I delivered today.

They include our programs to improve life for the aging; to combat crime and drug abuse; to improve health services and to ensure that no one will be denied needed health care because of inability to pay; to protect workers' pension rights; to promote equal opportunity for members of minorities and others who have been left behind; to expand consumer protection; to improve the environment; to revitalize rural America; to help the cities; to launch new iniatives in education; to improve transportation, and to put an end to costly labor tie-ups in transportation.

They also include basic reforms which are essential if our structure of government is to be adequate to the needs of the decades ahead.

They include reform of our wasteful and outmoded welfare system—and substitution of a new system that provides work requirements and work incentives for those who can help themselves, income support for those who cannot help themselves, and fairness for the working poor.

They include a $17.6-billion program of Federal revenue sharing with the States and localities—as an investment in their renewal, and an investment of faith of the people.

They also include a sweeping reorganization of the Executive branch of the Federal Government, so that it will be more efficient, more responsive, and able to meet the challenges of the decades ahead.

One year ago, I laid before the opening session of this Congress six great goals.

One of these was welfare reform. That proposal has been before the Congress now for nearly two and a half years.

My proposals on revenue sharing, government reorganization, health care and the environment have now been before the Congress for nearly a year. Many of my other major proposals have been here as long or longer.

1971 was a year of consideration of these measures. Now let us join in making 1972 a year of action on them—action by the Congress, for the Nation and for the people of America.

In addition, there is one pressing need which I have not previously covered, but which must be placed on the national agenda.

We long have looked to the local property tax as the main source of financing for public primary and secondary education.

As a result, soaring school costs and soaring property tax rates now threaten both our communities and our schools. They threaten communities because property taxes—which more than doubled in the 10 years from 1960 to 1970—have become one of the most oppressive and discriminatory of all taxes, hitting most cruelly at the elderly and the retired; and they threaten schools, as hard-pressed voters understandably reject new bond issues at the polls.

The problem has been given even greater urgency by three recent court decisions, which have held the conventional method of financing schools through local property taxes discriminatory and unconstitutional.

Nearly two years ago, I named a special Presidential Commission to study the problems of school finance, and I also directed the Federal Departments to look into the same problems. We are developing comprehensive proposals to meet these problems.

This issue involves two complex and inter-related sets of problems: support of the schools, and the basic relationships of Federal, State and local governments in any tax reforms.

Under the leadership of the Secretary of the Treasury, we are carefully reviewing the tax aspects; and I have this week enlisted the Advisory Commission on Intergovernmental Relations in addressing the intergovernmental relations aspects.

I have asked this bipartisan Commission to review our proposals for Federal action to cope with the gathering crisis of school finance and property taxes. Later in the year, when both Commissions have completed their studies, I shall make my final recommendations for relieving the burden of property taxes and providing both fair and adequate financing for our children's education.

All of my recommendations, however, will be rooted in one fundamental principle with which there can be no compromise: local school boards must have control over local schools.

As we look ahead over the coming decades, vast new growth and change are not only certainties. They will be the dominant reality of our life in America.

Surveying the certainty of rapid change, we can be like a fallen rider caught in the stirrups—or we can sit high in the saddle, the masters of change, directing it on a course that we choose.

The secret of mastering change in today's world is to reach back to old and proven principles, and to adapt them, with imagination and intelligence, to the new realities of a new age.

This is what we have done in the proposals that I have laid before the Congress. They are rooted in basic principles that are as enduring as human nature and as robust as the American experience; and they are responsive to new conditions. Thus they represent a spirit of change that is really renewal.

As we look back at these old principles, we find them as timely as they are timeless.

We believe in independence, and self-reliance, and in the creative value of the competitive spirit.

We believe in full and equal opportunity for all Americans, and in the protection of individual rights and liberties.

We believe in the family as the keystone of the community, and in the community as the keystone of the Nation.

We believe in compassion toward those in need.

We believe in a system of law, justice and order as the basis of a genuinely free society.

We believe that a person should get what he works for—and those who can should work for what they get.

We believe in the capacity of people to make their own decisions, in their own lives and in their own communities—and we believe in their right to make those decisions.

In applying these principles, we have done so with a full understanding that our quest in the 70s is not merely for more, but for better—for a better quality of life for all Americans.

Thus, for example, we are giving a new measure of attention to cleaning up our air and water, and to making our surroundings more attractive. Thus we are providing broader support for the arts, and helping stimulate a deeper appreciation of what they can contribute to the Nation's activities and to our individual lives.

Nothing matters more to the quality of our lives than the way we treat one another—than our capacity to live respectfully together as a unified society, with a full and generous regard for the rights of others and the feelings of others.

As we recover from the turmoil and violence of recent years, as we learn once again to speak with one another instead of shouting at one another, we are regaining that capacity.

As is customary here, on this occasion, I have been talking about programs. These programs are important. But even more important than programs is what we are as a Nation—what we mean as a Nation, to ourselves and to the world.

In New York harbor stands one of the most famous statues in the world—the Statue of Liberty, the gift in 1886 of the people of France to the people of the United States. This statue is more than a landmark; it is a symbol—a symbol of what America has meant to the world.

It reminds us that what America has meant is not its wealth, not its power, but its spirit and purpose—a land that enshrines liberty and opportunity, and that has held out a hand of welcome to millions in search of a better and a fuller and above all, a freer life.

The world's hopes poured into America, along with its people—and those hopes, those dreams, that have been brought from every corner of the world, have become a part of the hope that we hold out to the world.

Four years from now, America will celebrate the 200th anniversary of its founding as a Nation.

There are some who say that the old Spirit of '76 is dead—that we no longer have the strength of character, the idealism, the faith in our founding purposes, that that spirit represents.

Those who say this do not know America.

We have been undergoing self-doubts and self-criticism. But these are the other side of our growing sensitivity to the persistence of want in the midst of plenty, and of our impatience with the slowness with which age-old ills are being overcome.

If we were indifferent to the shortcomings of our society, or complacent about our institutions, or blind to the lingering inequities—then we would have lost our way.

The fact that we have these concerns is evidence that our ideals are still strong: And indeed, they remind us that what is best about America is its compassion. They remind us that in the final analysis, America is great not because it is strong, not because it is rich, but because it is good.

Let us reject the narrow visions of those who would tell us that we are evil because we are not yet perfect, that we are corrupt because we are not yet pure, that all the sweat and toil and sacrifice that have gone into the building of America were for naught because the building is not yet done.

Let us see that the path we are traveling is wide, with room in it for all of us, and that its direction is toward a better Nation in a more peaceful world.

Never has it mattered more that we go forward together.

The leadership of America is here today, in this Chamber—the Supreme Court, the Cabinet, the Senate, the House of Representatives.

Together, we hold the future of the Nation, and the conscience of the Nation, in our hands.

Because this year is an election year, it will be a time of great pressure.

If we yield to that pressure, and fail to deal seriously with the historic challenges that we face, then we will have failed America. We will have failed the trust of millions of Americans, and shaken the confidence they have a right to place in their government.

Never has a Congress had a greater opportunity to leave a legacy of profound and constructive reform for the Nation than this Congress.

If we succeed in these tasks, there will be credit enough for all—not only for doing what is right, but for doing it the right way, by rising above partisan interest to serve the national interest.

If we fail, then more than any of us, America will be the loser.

That is why my call upon the Congress today is for a high statesmanship—so that in the years to come, Americans will look back and say that because it withstood the intense pressures of a political year, and achieved such great good for the American people, and for the future of this Nation—this was truly a great Congress.

(Text of expanded State of the Union message, next page)

TEXT OF NIXON'S STATE OF UNION ADDRESS II

Following is the text, as made available by the White House, of President Nixon's expanded and more detailed State of the Union message sent to Congress Jan. 20, 1972.

TO THE CONGRESS OF THE UNITED STATES:

It was just 3 years ago today that I took the oath of office as President. I opened my address that day by suggesting that some moments in history stand out "as moments of beginning," when "courses are set that shape decades or centuries." I went on to say that "this can be such a moment."

Looking back 3 years later, I would suggest that it was such a moment—a time in which new courses were set on which we now are traveling. Just how profoundly these new courses will shape our decade or our century is still an unanswered question, however, as we enter the fourth year of this administration. For moments of beginning will mean very little in history unless we also have the determination to follow up on those beginnings.

Setting the course is not enough. Staying the course is an equally important challenge. Good government involves both the responsibility for making fresh starts and the responsibility for perseverance.

The responsibility for perseverance is one that is shared by the President, the public, and the Congress.

• We have come a long way, for example, on the road to ending the Vietnam war and to improving relations with our adversaries. But these initiatives will depend for their lasting meaning on our persistence in seeing them through.

• The magnificent cooperation of the American people has enabled us to make substantial progress in curbing inflation and in reinvigorating our economy. But the new prosperity we seek can be completed only if the public continues in its commitment to economic responsibility and discipline.

• Encouraging new starts have also been made over the last 3 years in treating our domestic ills. But continued progress now requires the Congress to act on its large and growing backlog of pending legislation.

America's agenda for action is already well established as we enter 1972. It will grow in the weeks ahead as we present still more initiatives. But we dare not let the emergence of new business obscure the urgency of old business. Our new agenda will be little more than an empty gesture if we abandon—or even de-emphasize—that part of the old agenda which is yet unfinished.

Getting Ourselves Together

One measure of the Nation's progress in these first years of the Seventies is the improvement in our national morale. While the 1960's were a time of great accomplishment, they were also a time of growing confusion. Our recovery from that condition is not complete, but we have made a strong beginning.

Then we were a shaken and uncertain people, but now we are recovering our confidence. Then we were divided and suspicious, but now we are renewing our sense of common purpose. Then we were surrounded by shouting and posturing, but we have been learning once again to lower our voices. And we have also been learning to listen.

A history of the 1960s' was recently published under the title, *Coming Apart*. But today we can say with confidence that we are coming apart no longer. The "center" of American life has held, and once again we are getting ourselves together.

The Spirit of Reason and Realism

Under the pressures of an election year, it would be easy to look upon the legislative program merely as a political device and not as a serious agenda. We must resist this temptation.

The year ahead of us holds precious time in which to accomplish good for this Nation and we must not, we dare not, waste it. Our progress depends on a continuing spirit of partnership between the President and the Congress, between the House and the Senate, between Republicans and Democrats. That spirit does not require us always to agree with one another, but it does require us to approach our tasks, together, in a spirit of reason and realism.

Clear words are the great servant of reason. Intemperate words are the great enemy of reason. The cute slogan, the glib headline, the clever retort, the appeal to passion—these are not the way to truth or to good public policy.

To be dedicated to clear thinking, to place the interests of all above the interests of the few, to hold to ultimate values and to curb momentary passions, to think more about the next generation and less about the next election—these are now our special challenges.

Ending The War

The condition of a nation's spirit cannot be measured with precision, but some of the factors which influence that spirit can. I believe the most dramatic single measurement of the distance we have traveled in the last 36 months is found in the statistics concerning our involvement in the war in Vietnam.

On January 20, 1969 our authorized troop ceiling in Vietnam was 549,500. And there was no withdrawal plan to bring these men home. On seven occasions since that time, I have announced withdrawal decisions—involving a total of 480,500 troops. As a result, our troop ceiling will be only 69,000 by May 1. This means that in 3 years we will have cut our troop strength in Vietnam by 87 percent. As we proceed toward our goal of a South Vietnam fully able to defend itself, we will reduce that level still further.

In this same period, expenditures connected with the war have been cut drastically. There has been a drop of well over 50 percent in American air activity in all of Southeast Asia. Our ground combat role has been ended. Most importantly, there has been a reduction of 95 percent in combat deaths.

Our aim is to cut the death and casualty toll by 100 percent, to obtain the release of those who are prisoners of war, and to end the fighting altogether.

It is my hope that we can end this tragic conflict through negotiation. If we cannot, then we will end it through Vietnamization. But end it we shall—in a way which fulfills our commitment to the people of South Vietnam and which gives them the chance for which they have already sacrificed so much—the chance to choose their own future.

The Lessons of Change

The American people have learned many lessons in the wake of Vietnam—some helpful and some dangerous. One important lesson is that we can best serve our own interests in the world by setting realistic limits on what we try to accomplish unilaterally. For the peace of the world will be more secure, and its progress more rapid, as more nations come to share more fully in the responsibilities for peace and for progress.

At the same time, to conclude that the United States should now withdraw from all or most of its international responsibilities would be to make a dangerous error. There has been a tendency among some to swing from one extreme to the other in the wake of Vietnam, from wanting to do too much in the world to wanting to do too little. We must resist this temptation to over-react. We must stop the swinging pendulum before it moves to an opposite position, and forge instead an attitude toward the world which is balanced and sensible and realistic.

America has an important role to play in international affairs, a great influence to exert for good. As we have throughout this century, we must continue our profound concern for advancing peace and freedom, by the most effective means possible, even as we shift somewhat our view of what means are most effective.

This is our policy:

• We will maintain a nuclear deterrent adequate to meet any threat to the security of the United States or of our allies.

• We will help other nations develop the capability of defending themselves.

• We will faithfully honor all of our treaty commitments.

• We will act to defend our interests whenever and wherever they are threatened any place in the world.

• But where our interests or our treaty commitments are not involved our role will be limited.

• We will not intervene militarily.

• But we will use our influence to prevent war.

• If war comes we will use our influence to try to stop it.

• Once war is over we will do our share in helping to bind up the wounds of those who have participated in it.

Opening New Lines of Communication

Even as we seek to deal more realistically with our partners, so we must also deal more realistically with those who have been our adversaries. In the last year we have made a number of notable advances toward this goal.

In our dealings with the Soviet Union, for example, we have been able, together with our allies, to reach an historic agreement concerning Berlin. We have advanced the prospects for limiting strategic armaments. We have moved toward greater cooperation in space research and toward improving our economic relationships. There have been disappointments such as South Asia and uncertainities such as the Middle East. But there have also been progress we can build on.

It is to build on the progress of the past and to lay the foundations for greater progress in the future that I will soon be visiting the capitals of both the Peoples Republic of China and the Soviet Union. These visits will help to fulfill the promise I made in my Inaugural address when I said "that during this administration our lines of communication will be open," so that we can help create "an open world—open to ideas, open to the exchange of goods and people, a world in which no people, great or small, will live in angry isolation." It is in this spirit that I will undertake these journeys.

We must also be realistic, however, about the scope of our differences with these governments. My visits will mean not that our differences have disappeared or will disappear in the near future. But peace depends on the ability of great powers to live together on the same planet despite their differences. The important thing is that we talk about these differences rather than fight about them.

It would be a serious mistake to say that nothing can come of our expanded communications with Peking and Moscow. But it would also be a mistake to expect too much too quickly.

It would also be wrong to focus so much attention on these new opportunities that we neglect our old friends. That is why I have met in the last few weeks with the leaders of two of our hemisphere neighbors, Canada and Brazil, with the leaders of three great European nations, and with the Prime Minister of Japan. I believe these meetings were extremely successful in cementing our understandings with these governments as we move forward together in a fast changing period.

Our consultations with our allies may not receive as much attention as our talks with potential adversaries. But this makes them no less important. The cornerstone of our foreign policy remains—and will remain—our close bonds with our friends around the world.

A Strong Defense: The Guardian of Peace

There are two additional elements which are critical to our efforts to strengthen the structure of peace.

The first of these is the military strength of the United States.

In the last 3 years we have been moving from a wartime to a peacetime footing, from a period of continued confrontation and arms competition to a period of negotiation and potential arms limitation, from a period when America often acted as policeman for the world to a period when other nations are assuming greater responsibility for their own defense. I was recently encouraged, for example, by the decision of our European allies to increase their share of the NATO defense budget by some $1 billion.

As a part of this process, we have ended the production of chemical and biological weaponry and have converted two of our largest facilities for such production to humanitarian research. We have been able to reduce and in some periods even to eliminate draft calls. In 1971, draft calls—which were as high as 382,000 at the peak of the Vietnam war—fell below 100,000, the lowest level since 1962. In the coming year they will be significantly lower. I am confident that by the middle of next year we can achieve our goal of reducing draft calls to zero.

As a result of all these developments, our defense spending has fallen to 7 percent of our gross national product in the current fiscal year, compared with 8.3 percent in 1964 and 9.5 percent in 1968. That figure will be down to 6.4 percent in fiscal year 1973. Without sacrificing any of our security interests, we have been able to bring defense spending below the level of human resource spending for the first time in 20 years. This condition is maintained in my new budget—which also, for the first time, allocates more money to the Department of Health, Education, and Welfare than to the Department of Defense.

But just as we avoid extreme reactions in our political attitudes toward the world, so we must avoid over-reacting as we plan for our defense. We have reversed spending priorities, but we have never compromised our national security. And we never will. For any step which weakens America's defenses will also weaken the prospects for peace.

Our plans for the next year call for an increase in defense spending. That increase is made necessary in part by rising research and development costs, in part by military pay increases—which, in turn, will help us eliminate the draft—and in part by the need to proceed with new weapon systems to maintain our security at an adequate level. Even as we seek with the greatest urgency stable controls on armaments, we cannot ignore the fact that others are going forward with major increases in their own arms programs.

In the year ahead we will be working to improve and protect, to diversify and disperse our strategic forces in ways which make them even less vulnerable to attack and more effective in deterring war. I will request a substantial budget increase to preserve the sufficiency of our strategic nuclear deterrent, including an allocation of over $900 million to improve our sea-based deterrent force. I recently directed the Department of Defense to develop a program to build additional missile launching submarines, carrying a new and far mor effective missile. We will also proceed with programs to reoutfit our Polaris submarines with the Poseidon missile system, to replace older land-based missiles with Minuteman III, and to deploy the SAFEGUARD Antiballistic Missile System.

At the same time, we must move to maintain our strength at sea. The Navy's budget was increased by $2 billion in the current fiscal year, and I will ask for a similar increase next year, with particular emphasis on our shipbuilding programs.

Our military research and development program must also be stepped up. Our budget in this area was increased by $594 million in the current fiscal year and I will recommend a further increase for next year of $838 million. I will also propose a substantial program to develop and procure more effective weapons systems for our land and tactical air forces, and to improve the National Guard and Reserves, providing more modern weapons and better training.

In addition, we will expand our strong program to attract volunteer career soldiers so that we can phase out the draft. With the cooperation of the Congress, we have been able to double the basic pay of first-time enlistees. Further substantial military pay increases are planned. I will also submit to the Congress an overall reform of our military retirement and survivor benefit programs, raising the level of protection for military families. In addition, we will expand efforts to improve race relations, to equalize promotional opportunities, to control drug abuse, and generally to improve the quality of life in the Armed Forces.

As we take all of these steps, let us remember that strong military defenses are not the enemy of peace; they are the guardians of peace. Our ability to build a stable and tranquil world—to achieve an arms control agreement, for example—depends on our ability to negotiate from a position of strength. We seek adequate power not as an end in itself but as a means for achieving our purpose. And our purpose is peace.

In my Inaugural address 3 years ago I called for cooperation to reduce the burden of arms—and I am encouraged by the progress we have been making toward that goal. But I also added this comment: "...to all those who would be tempted by weakness, let us leave no doubt that we will be as strong as we need to be for as long as we need to be." Today I repeat that reminder.

A Realistic Program of Foreign Assistance

Another important expression of America's interest and influence in the world is our foreign assistance effort. This effort has special significance at a time when we are reducing our direct military presence abroad and encouraging other countries to assume greater responsibilities. Their growing ability to undertake these responsibilities often depends on America's foreign assistance.

We have taken significant steps to reform our foreign assistance programs in recent years, to eliminate waste and to give them greater impact. Now three further imperatives rest with the Congress:

• To fund in full the levels of assistance which I have earlier recommended for the current fiscal year, before the present interim funding arrangement expires in late February;

• To act upon the fundamental aid reform proposals submitted by this administration in 1971;

• And to modify those statutes which govern our response to expropriation of American property by foreign governments, as I recommended in my recent statement on the security of overseas investments.

These actions, taken together,will constitute not an exception to the emerging pattern for a more realistic American role in the world, but rather a fully consistent and crucially important element in that pattern.

As we work to help our partners in the world community develop their economic potential and strengthen their military forces, we should also cooperate fully with them in meeting international challenges such as the menace of narcotics, the threat of pollution, the growth of population, the proper use of the seas and seabeds, and the plight of those who have been victimized by wars and natural disasters. All of these are global problems and they must be confronted on a global basis. The efforts of the United Nations to respond creatively to these challenges have been most promising, as has the work of NATO in the environmental field. Now we must build on these beginnings.

America's Influence for Good

The United States is not the world's policeman nor the keeper of its moral conscience. But—whether we like it or not—we still represent a force for stability in what has too often been an unstable world, a force for justice in a world which is too often unjust, a force for progress in a world which desperately needs to progress, a force for peace in a world that is weary of war.

We can have a great influence for good in our world—and for that reason we bear a great responsibility. Whether we fulfill that responsibility—whether we fully use our influence for good—these are questions we will be answering as we reshape our attitudes and policies toward other countries, as we determine our defensive capabilities, and as we make fundamental decisions about foreign assistance. I will soon discuss these and other concerns in greater detail in my annual report to the Congress on foreign policy.

Our influence for good in the world depends, of course, not only on decisions which touch directly on international affairs but also on our internal strength—on our sense of pride and purpose, on the vitality of our economy, on the success of our efforts to build a better life for all our people. Let us turn then from the state of the Union abroad to the state of the Union at home.

The Economy: Toward A New Prosperity

Just as the Vietnam war occasioned much of our spiritual crisis, so it lay at the root of our economic problems 3 years ago. The attempt to finance that war through budget deficits in a period of full employment had produced a wave of price inflation as dangerous and as persistent as any in our history. It was more persistent, frankly, than I expected it would be when I first took office. And it only yielded slowly to our dual efforts to cool the war and to cool inflation.

Our challenge was further compounded by the need to reabsorb more than 2 million persons who were released from the Armed Forces and from defense-related industries and by the substantial expansion of the labor force.

In short, the escalation of the Vietnam war in the late 1960's destroyed price stability. And the de-escalation of that war in the early 1970's impeded full employment.

Throughout these years, however, I have remained convinced that both price stability and full employment were realistic goals for this country. By last summer it became apparent that our efforts to eradicate inflation without wage and price controls would either take too long or—if they were to take effect quickly—would come at the cost of persistent high unemployment. This cost was unacceptable. On August 15th I therefore announced a series of new economic policies to speed our progress toward a new prosperity without inflation in peacetime.

These policies have received the strong support of the Congress and the American people, and as a result they have been effective. To carry forward these policies, three important steps were taken this past December—all within a brief 2-week period—which will also help to make the coming year a very good year for the American economy.

On December 10, I signed into law the Revenue Act of 1971, providing tax cuts over the next 3 years of some $15 billion, cuts which I requested to stimulate the economy and to provide hundreds of thousands to new jobs. On December 22, I signed into law the Economic Stabilization Act Amendments of 1971, which will allow us to continue our program of wage and price restraints to break the back of inflation.

Between these two events, on December 18, I was able to announce a major breakthrough on the international economic front—reached in cooperation with our primary economic partners. This breakthrough will mitigate the intolerable strains which were building up in the world's monetary and payments structure and will lead to a removal of trade barriers which have impeded American exports. It also sets the stage for broader reforms in the international monetary system so that we can avoid repeated monetary crises in the future. Both the monetary realignment—the first of its scope in history—and our progress in readjusting trade conditions will mean better markets for American goods abroad and more jobs for American workers at home.

A Brighter Economic Picture

As a result of all these steps, the economic picture—which has brightened steadily during the last 5 months—will, I believe, continue to grow brighter. This is not my judgment alone; it is widely shared by the American people. Virtually every survey and forecast in recent weeks shows a substantial improvement in public attitudes about the economy—which are themselves so instrumental in shaping economic realities.

The inflationary psychology which gripped our Nation so tightly for so long is on the ebb. Business and consumer confidence has been rising. Businessmen are planning a 9.1 percent increase in plant and equipment expenditures in 1972, more than four times as large as the increase in 1971. Consumer spending and retail sales are on the rise. Home building is booming—housing starts last year were up more than 40 percent from 1970, setting an all-time record. Interest rates are sharply down. Both income and production are rising. Real out put in our economy in the last 3 months of 1971 grew at a rate that was about double that of the previous two quarters.

Perhaps most importantly, total employment has moved above the 80 million mark—to a record high—and is growing rapidly. In the last 5 months of 1971, some 1.1 million additional jobs were created in our economy and only a very unusual increase in the size of our total labor force kept the unemployment rate from falling.

But whatever the reason, 6 percent unemployment is too high. I am determined to cut that percentage—through a variety of measures. The budget I present to the Congress next week will be an expansionary budget—reflecting the impact of new job-creating tax cuts and job-creating expenditures. We will also push to increase employment through our programs for manpower training and public service employment, through our efforts to expand foreign markets, and through other new initiatives.

Expanded employment in 1972 will be different, however, from many other periods of full prosperity. For it will come without the stimulus of war—and it will come without inflation. Our program of wage and price controls is working. The consumer price index, which rose at a yearly rate of slightly over 6 percent during 1969 and the first half of 1970, rose at a rate of only 1.7 percent from August through November of 1971.

I would emphasize once again, however, that our ultimate objective is lasting price stability without controls. When we achieve an end to the inflationary psychology which developed in the 1960's, we will return to our traditional policy of relying on free market forces to determine wages and prices.

I would also emphasize that while our new budget will be in deficit, the deficit will not be irresponsible. It will be less than this year's actual deficit and would disappear entirely under full employment conditions. While Federal spending continues to grow, the rate of increase in spending has been cut very sharply—to little more than half that experienced under the previous administration. The fact that our battle against inflation has led us to adopt a new policy of wage and price restraints should not obscure the continued importance of our fiscal and monetary policies in holding down the cost of living. It is most important that the Congress join now in resisting the temptation to overspend and in accepting the discipline of a balanced full employment budget.

I will soon present a more complete discussion of all of these matters in my Budget Message and in my Economic Report.

A New Era in International Economics

Just as we have entered a new period of negotiation in world politics, so we have also moved into a new period of negotiation on the international economic front. We expect these negotiations to help us build both a new international system for the exchange of money and a new system of international trade. These accomplishments, in turn, can open a new era of fair competition and constructive interdependence in the global economy.

We have already made important strides in this direction. The realignment of exchange rates which was announced last month represents an important forward step—but now we also need basic long-range monetary reform. We have made an important beginning toward altering the conditions for international trade and investment—and we expect further substantial progress. I would emphasize that progress for some nations in these fields need not come at the expense of others. All nations will benefit from the right kind of monetary and trade reform.

Certainly the United States has a high stake in such improvements. Our international economic position has been slowly deteriorating now for some time—a condition which could have dangerous implications for both our influence abroad and our prosperity at home. It has been estimated, for example, that full employment prosperity will depend on the creation of some 20 million additional jobs in this decade. And expanding our foreign markets is a most effective way to expand domestic employment.

One of the major reasons for the weakening of our international economic position is that the ground rules for the exchange of goods and money have forced us to compete with one hand tied behind our back. One of our most important accomplishments in 1971 was our progress in changing this situation.

Competing More Effectively

Monetary and trade reforms are only one part of this story. The ability of the United States to hold its own in world competition depends not only on the fairness of the rules, but also on the competitiveness of our economy. We have made great progress in the last few months in improving the terms of competition. Now we must also do all we can to strengthen the ability of our own economy to compete.

We stand today at a turning point in the history of our country—and in the history of our planet. On the one hand, we have the opportunity to help bring a new economic order to the world, an open order in which nations eagerly face outward to build that network of interdependence which is the best foundation for prosperity and for peace. But we will also be tempted in the months ahead to take the opposite course—to withdraw from the world economically as some would have us withdraw politically, to build an economic "Fortress America" within which our growing weakness could be concealed. Like a child who will not go out to play with other children, we would probably be saved a few minor bumps and bruises in the short run if we were to adopt this course. But in the long run the world would surely pass us by.

I reject this approach. I remain committed to that open world I discussed in my Inaugural address. That is why I have worked for a more inviting climate for America's economic activity abroad. That is why I have placed so much emphasis on increasing the productivity of our economy at home. And that is also why I believe so firmly that we must stimulate more long-range investment in our economy, find more effective ways to develop and use new technology, and do a better job of training and using skilled manpower.

An acute awareness of the international economic challenge led to the creation just one year ago of the Cabinet-level Council on International Economic Policy. This new institution has helped us to understand this challenge better and to respond to it more effectively.

As our understanding deepens, we will discover additional ways of improving our ability to compete. For example, we can enhance our competitive position by moving to implement the metric system of measurement, a proposal which the Secretary of Commerce presented in detail to the Congress last year. And we should also be doing far more to gain our fair share of the international tourism market, now estimated at $17 billion annually, one of the largest factors in world trade. A substantial part of our balance of payments deficit results from the fact that American tourists abroad spend $2.5 billion more than foreign tourists spend in the United States. We can help correct this situation by attracting more foreign tourists to our shores—especially as we enter our Bicentennial era. I am therefore requesting that the budget for the United States Travel Service be nearly doubled in the coming year.

The Unfinished Agenda

Our progress toward building a new economic order at home and abroad has been made possible by the cooperation and cohesion of the American people. I am sure that many Americans had misgivings about one aspect or another of the new economic policies I introduced last summer. But most have nevertheless been ready to accept this new effort in order to build the broad support which is essential for effective change.

The time has now come for us to apply this same sense of realism and reasonability to other reform proposals which have been languishing on our domestic agenda. As was the case with our economic policies, most Americans agree that we need a change in our welfare system, in our health strategy, in our programs to improve the environment, in the way we finance State and local government, and in the organization of government at the Federal level. Most Americans are not satisfied with the status quo in education, in transportation, in law enforcement, in drug control, in community development. In each of these areas —and in others—I have put forward specific proposals which are responsive to this deep desire for change.

And yet achieving change has often been difficult. There has been progress in some areas, but for the most part, as a nation we have not shown the same sense of self-discipline in our response to social challenges that we have developed in meeting our economic needs. We have not been as ready as we should have been to compromise our differences and to build a broad coalition for change. And so we often have found ourselves in a situation of stalemate—doing essentially nothing even though most of us agree that nothing is the very worst thing we can do.

Two years ago this week, and again one year ago, my messages on the state of the Union contained broad proposals for domestic reform. I am presenting a number of new proposals in this year's message. But I also call once again, with renewed urgency, for action on our unfinished agenda.

Welfare Reform

The first item of unfinished business is welfare reform.

Since I first presented my proposals in August of 1969, some 4 million additional persons have been added to our welfare rolls. The cost of our old welfare system has grown by an additional $4.2 billion. People have not been moving as fast as they should from welfare rolls to payrolls. Too much of the traffic has been the other way.

Our antiquated welfare system is responsible for this calamity. Our new program of "workfare" would begin to end it.

Today, more than ever, we need a new program which is based on the dignity of work, which provides strong incentives for work, and which includes for those who are able to work an effective work requirement. Today, more than ever, we need a new program which helps hold families together rather than driving them apart, which provides day care services so that low income mothers can trade dependence on government for the dignity of employment, which relieves intolerable fiscal pressures on State and local governments, and which replaces 54 administrative systems with a more efficient and reliable nationwide approach.

I have now given prominent attention to this subject in three consecutive messages on the state of the Union. The House of Representatives has passed welfare reform twice. Now that the new economic legislation has been passed, I urge the Senate Finance Committee to place welfare reform at the top of its agenda. It is my earnest hope that when this Congress adjourns, welfare reform will not be an item of pending business but an accomplished reality.

Revenue Sharing: Returning Power to the People

At the same time that I introduced my welfare proposals 2-1/2 years ago, I also presented a program for sharing Federal revenues with State and local governments. Last year I greatly expanded on this concept. Yet, despite undisputed evidence of compelling needs, despite overwhelming public support, despite the endorsement of both major political parties and most of the Nation's Governors and mayors, and despite the fact that most other nations with federal systems of government already have such a program, revenue sharing still remains on the list of unfinished business.

I call again today for the enactment of revenue sharing. During its first full year of operation our proposed programs would spend $17.6 billion, both for general purposes and through six special purpose programs for law enforcement, manpower, education, transportation, rural community development, and urban community development.

As with welfare reform, the need for revenue sharing becomes more acute as time passes. The financial crisis of State and local government is deepening. The pattern of breakdown in State and municpal services grows more threatening. Inequitable tax pressures are mounting. The demand for more flexible and more responsive government—at levels closer to the problems and closer to the people—is building.

Revenue sharing can help us meet these challenges. It can help reverse what has been the flow of power and resources toward Washington by sending power and resources back to the States, to the communities, and to the people. Revenue sharing can bring a new sense of accountability, a new burst of energy and a new spirit of creativity to our federal system.

I am pleased that the House Ways and Means Committee has made revenue sharing its first order of business in the new session. I urge the Congress to enact in this session, not an empty program which bears the revenue sharing label while continuing the outworn system of categorical grants, but a bold, comprehensive program of genuine revenue sharing.

I also presented last year a $100 million program of planning and management grants to help the States and localities do a better job of analyzing their problems and carrying out solutions. I hope this program will also be quickly accepted. For only as State and local governments get a new lease on life can we hope to bring government back to the people—and with it a stronger sense that each individual can be in control of his life, that every person can make a difference.

Overhauling the Machinery of Government: Executive Reorganization

As we work to make State and local government more responsive—and more responsible—let us also seek these same goals at the Federal level. I again urge the Congress to enact my proposals for reorganizing the executive branch of the Federal Government. Here again, support from the general public— as well as from those who have served in the executive branch under several Presidents—has been most encouraging. So has the success of the important organizational reforms we have already made. These have included a restructured Executive Office of the President—with a new Domestic Council, a new

Office of Management and Budget, and other units; reorganized field operations in Federal agencies; stronger mechanisms for interagency coordination, such as Federal Regional Councils; a new United States Postal Service; and new offices for such purposes as protecting the environment, coordinating communications policy, helping the consumer, and stimulating voluntary service. But the centerpiece of our efforts to streamline the executive branch still awaits approval.

How the government is put together often determines how well the government can do its job. Our Founding Fathers understood this fact—and thus gave detailed attention to the most precise structural questions. Since that time, however, and especially in recent decades, new responsibilities and new constituencies have caused the structure they established to expand enormously—and in a piecemeal and haphazard fashion.

As a result, our Federal Government today is too often a sluggish and unresponsive institution, unable to deliver a dollar's worth of service for a dollar's worth of taxes.

My answer to this problem is to streamline the executive branch by reducing the overall number of executive departments and by creating four new departments in which existing responsibilities would be refocused in a coherent and comprehensive way. The rationale which I have advanced calls for organizing these new departments around the major purposes of the government—by creating a Department of Natural Resources, a Department of Human Resources, a Department of Community Development, and a Department of Economic Affairs. I have revised my original plan so that we would not eliminate the Department of Agriculture but rather restructure that Department so it can focus more effectively on the needs of farmers.

The Congress has recently reorganized its own operations, and the Chief Justice of the United States has led a major effort to reform and restructure the judicial branch. The impulse for reorganization is strong and the need for reorganization is clear. I hope the Congress will not let this opportunity for sweeping reform of the executive branch slip away.

A New Approach to the Delivery of Social Services

As a further step to put the machinery of government in proper working order, I will also propose new legislation to reform and rationalize the way in which social services are delivered to families and individuals.

Today it often seems that our service programs are unresponsive to the recipients' needs and wasteful of the taxpayers' money. A major reason is their extreme fragmentation. Rather than pulling many services together, our present system separates them into narrow and rigid categories. The father of a family is helped by one program, his daughter by another, and his elderly parents by a third. An individual goes to one place for nutritional help, to another for health services, and to still another for educational counseling. A community finds that it cannot transfer Federal funds from one program area to another area in which needs are more pressing.

Meanwhile, officials at all levels of government find themselves wasting enormous amounts of time, energy, and the taxpayers' money untangling Federal red tape—time and energy and dollars which could better be spent in meeting people's needs.

We need a new approach to the delivery of social services—one which is built around people and not around programs. We need an approach which treats a person as a whole and which treats the family as a unit. We need to break through rigid categorical walls, to open up narrow bureaucratic compartments, to consolidate and coordinate related programs in a comprehensive approach to related problems.

The Allied Services Act which will soon be submitted to the Congress offers one set of tools for carrying out that new approach

in the programs of the Department of Health, Education and Welfare. It would strengthen State and local planning and administrative capacities, allow for the transfer of funds among various HEW programs, and permit the waiver of certain cumbersome Federal requirements. By streamlining and simplifying the delivery of services, it would help more people move more rapidly from public dependency toward the dignity of being self-sufficient.

Good men and good money can be wasted on bad mechanisms. By giving those mechanisms a thorough overhaul, we can help to restore the confidence of the people in the capacities of their government.

Protecting the Environment

A central theme of both my earlier messages on the state of the Union was the state of our environment—and the importance of making "our peace with nature." The last few years have been a time in which environmental values have become firmly embedded in our attitudes—and in our institutions. At the Federal level, we have established a new Environmental Protection Agency, a new Council on Environmental Quality and a new National Oceanic and Atmospheric Administration, and we have proposed an entire new Department of Natural Resources. New air quality standards have been set, and there is evidence that the air in many cities is becoming less polluted. Under authority granted by the Refuse Act of 1899, we have instituted a new permit program which, for the first time, allows the Federal Government to inventory all significant industrial sources of water pollution and to specify required abatement actions. Under the Refuse Act, more than 160 civil actions and 320 criminal actions to stop water pollution have been filed against alleged polluters in the last 12 months. Major programs have also been launched to build new municipal waste treatment facilities, to stop pollution from Federal facilities, to expand our wilderness areas, and to leave a legacy of parks for future generations. Our outlays for inner city parks have been significantly expanded, and 62 Federal tracts have been transferred to the States and to local governments for recreational uses. In the coming year, I hope to transfer to local park use much more Federal land which is suitable for recreation but which is now underutilized. I trust the Congress will not delay this process.

The most striking fact about environmental legislation in the early 1970's is how much has been proposed and how little has been enacted. Of the major legislative proposals I made in my special message to the Congress on the environment last winter, 18 are still awaiting final action. They include measures to regulate pesticides and toxic substances, to control noise pollution, to restrict dumping in the oceans, in coastal waters, and in the Great Lakes, to create an effective policy for the use and development of land, to regulate the siting of power plants, to control strip mining, and to help achieve many other important environmental goals. The unfinished agenda also includes our National Resource Land Management Act, and other measures to improve environmental protection on federally owned lands.

The need for action in these areas is urgent. The forces which threaten our environment will not wait while we procrastinate. Nor can we afford to rest on last year's agenda in the environmental field. For as our understanding of these problems increases, so must our range of responses. Accordingly, I will soon be sending to the Congress another message on the environment that will present further administrative and legislative initiatives. Altogether our new budget will contain more than three times as much money for environmental programs in fiscal year 1973 as we spent in fiscal year 1969. To fail in meeting the environmental challenge, however, would be even more costly.

I urge the Congress to put aside narrow partisan perspectives that merely ask "whether" we should act to protect the environment and to focus instead on the more difficult question of "how" such action can most effectively be carried out.

Abundant Clean Energy

In my message to the Congress on energy policy, last June, I outlined additional steps relating to the environment which also merit renewed attention. The challenge, as I defined it, is to produce a sufficient supply of energy to fuel our industrial civilization and at the same time to protect a beautiful and healthy environment. I am convinced that we can achieve both these goals, that we can respect our good earth without turning our back on progress.

In that message last June, I presented a long list of means for assuring an ample supply of clean energy—including the liquid metal fast breeder reactor—and I again emphasize their importance. Because it often takes several years to bring new technologies into use in the energy field, there is no time for delay. According, I am including in my new budget increased funding for the most promising of these and other clean energy programs. By acting this year, we can avoid having to choose in some future year between too little energy and too much pollution.

Keeping People Healthy

The National Health Strategy I outlined last February is designed to achieve one of the Nation's most important goals for the 1970's, improving the quality and availability of medical care, while fighting the trend toward runaway costs. Important elements of that strategy have already been enacted. The Comprehensive Health Manpower Training Act and the Nurse Training Act, which I signed on November 18, represent the most far-reaching effort in our history to increase the supply of doctors, nurses, dentists and other health professionals and to attract them to areas which are experiencing manpower shortages. The National Cancer Act, which I signed on December 23, marked the climax of a year-long effort to step up our campaign against cancer. During the past year, our cancer research budget has been increased by $100 million and the full weight of my office has been given to our all-out war on this disease. We have also expanded the fight against sickle cell anemia by an additional $5 million.

I hope that action on these significant fronts during the first session of the 92nd Congress will now be matched by action in other areas during the second session. The Health Maintenance Organization Act, for example, is an essential tool for helping doctors deliver care more effectively and more efficiently with a greater emphasis on prevention and early treatment. By working to keep our people healthy instead of treating us only when we are sick, Health Maintenance Organizations can do a great deal to help us reduce medical costs.

Our National Health Insurance Partnership legislation is also essential to assure that no American is denied basic medical care because of inability to pay. Too often, present health insurance leaves critical outpatient services uncovered, distorting the way in which facilities are used. It also fails to protect adequately against catastrophic costs and to provide sufficient assistance for the poor. The answer I have suggested is a comprehensive national plan—not one that nationalizes our private health insurance industry but one that corrects the weaknesses in that system while building on its considerable strengths.

A large part of the enormous increase in the Nation's expenditures on health in recent years has gone not to additional services but merely to meet price inflation. Our efforts to balance the growing demand for care with an increased supply of services will help to change this picture. So will that part of our economic program which is designed to control medical costs. I am confident that with the continued cooperation of those who provide health services, we will succeed on this most important battlefront in our war against inflation.

Our program for the next year will also include further funding increases for health research—including substantial new sums for cancer and sickle cell anemia—as well as further increases for medical schools and for meeting special problems such as drug addiction and alcoholism. We also plan to construct new veterans hospitals and expand the staffs at existing ones.

In addition, we will be giving increased attention to the fight against diseases of the heart, blood vessels and lungs, which presently account for more than half of all the deaths in this country. It is deeply disturbing to realize that, largely because of heart disease, the mortality rate for men under the age of 55 is about twice as great in the United States as it is, for example, in some Scandinavian countries.

I will shortly assign a panel of distinguished experts to help us determine why heart disease is so prevalent and so menacing and what we can do about it. I will also recommend an expanded budget for the National Heart and Lung Institute. The young father struck down by a heart attack in the prime of life, the productive citizen crippled by a stroke, an older person tortured by breathing difficulties during his later years—these are tragedies which can be reduced in number and we must do all that is possible to reduce them.

Nutrition

One of the critical areas in which we have worked to advance the health of the Nation is that of combating hunger and improving nutrition. With the increases in our new budget, expenditures on our food stamp program will have increased ninefold since 1969, to the $2.3 billion level. Spending on school lunches for needy children will have increased more than sevenfold, from $107 million in 1969 to $770 million in 1973. Because of new regulations which will be implemented in the year ahead, we will be able to increase further both the equity of our food stamp program and the adequacy of its benefits.

Coping with Accidents— and Preventing Them

Last year, more than 115,000 Americans lost their lives in accidents. Four hundred thousand more were permanently disabled and 10 million were temporarily disabled. The loss to our economy from accidents last year is estimated at over $28 billion. These are sad and staggering figures—especially since this toll could be greatly reduced by upgrading our emergency medical services. Such improvement does not even require new scientific breakthroughs; it only requires that we apply our present knowledge more effectively.

To help in this effort, I am directing the Department of Health, Education and Welfare to develop new ways of organizing emergency medical services and of providing care to accident victims. By improving communication, transportation, and the training of emergency personnel, we can save many thousands of lives which would otherwise be lost to accidents and sudden illnesses.

One of the significant joint accomplishments of the Congress and this administration has been a vigorous new program to protect against job-related accidents and illnesses. Our occupational health and safety program will be further strengthened in the year ahead—as will our ongoing efforts to promote air traffic safety, boating safety, and safety on the highways.

In the last 3 years, the motor vehicle death rate has fallen by 13 percent, but we still lose some 50,000 lives on our highways *each year*—more than we have lost in combat in the entire Vietnam war.

Fully one-half of these deaths were directly linked to alcohol. This appalling reality is a blight on our entire Nation—and only the active concern of the entire Nation can remove it. The Federal Government will continue to help all it can, through its efforts to promote highway safety and automobile safety, and through stronger programs to help the problem drinker.

Yesterday's Goals: Tomorrow's Accomplishments

Welfare reform, revenue sharing, executive reorganization, environmental protection, and the new national health strategy —these, along with economic improvement, constituted the six great goals I emphasized in my last State of the Union address— six major components of a New American Revolution. They remain six areas of great concern today. With the cooperation of the Congress, they can be six areas of great accomplishment tomorrow.

But the challenges we face cannot be reduced to six categories. Our problems—and our opportunities—are manifold, and action on many fronts is required. It is partly for this reason that my State of the Union address this year includes this written message to the Congress. For it gives me the chance to discuss more fully a number of programs which also belong on our list of highest priorities.

Action for the Aging

Last month, I joined with thousands of delegates to the White House Conference on Aging in a personal commitment to make 1972 a year of action on behalf of 21 million older Americans. Today I call on the Congress to join me in that pledge. For unless the American dream comes true for our older generation it cannot be complete for any generation.

We can begin to make this a year of action for the aging by acting on a number of proposals which have been pending since 1969. For older Americans, the most significant of these is the bill designated H.R. 1. This legislation, which also contains our general welfare reform measures, would place a national floor under the income of all older Americans, guarantee inflation-proof social security benefits, allow social security recipients to earn more from their own work, increase benefits for widows, and provide a 5-percent across-the-board increase in social security. Altogether, HR 1—as it now stands—would mean some $5.5 billion in increased benefits for America's older citizens. I hope the Congress will also take this opportunity to eliminate the $5.80 monthly fee now charged under Part B of Medicare— a step which would add an additional $1.5 billion to the income of the elderly. These additions would come on top of earlier social security increases totalling some $3 billion over the last 3 years.

A number of newer proposals also deserve approval. I am requesting that the budget of the Administration on Aging be increased five-fold over last year's request, to $100 million, in part so that we can expand programs which help older citizens live dignified lives in their own homes. I am recommending substantially larger budgets for those programs which give older Americans a better chance to serve their countrymen—Retired Senior Volunteers, Foster Grandparents, and others. And we will also work to ease the burden of property taxes which so many older Americans find so inequitable and so burdensome. Other initiatives, including proposals for extending and improving the Older Americans Act, will be presented as we review the recommendations of the White House Conference on Aging. Our new Cabinet-level Domestic Council Committee on Aging has these recommendations at the top of its agenda.

We will also be following up in 1972 on one of the most important of our 1971 initiatives—the crackdown on substandard nursing homes. Our follow-through will give special attention to providing alternative arrangements for those who are victimized by such facilities.

The legislation I have submitted to provide greater financial security at retirement, both for those now covered by private pension plans and those who are not, also merits prompt action by the Congress. Only half the country's work force is now covered by tax deductible private pensions; the other half deserve a tax deduction for their retirement savings too. Those who are now covered by pension plans deserve the assurance that their plans are administered under strict fiduciary standards with full disclosure. And they should also have the security provided by prompt vesting—the assurance that even if one leaves a given job, he can still receive the pension he earned there when he retires. The legislation I have proposed would achieve these goals, and would also raise the limit on deductible pension savings for the self-employed.

The state of our Union is strong today because of what older Americans have so long been giving to their country. The state of our Union will be stronger tomorrow if we recognize how much they still can contribute. The best thing our country can give to its older citizens is the chance to be a part of it, the chance to play a continuing role in the great American adventure.

Equal Opportunity for Minorities

America cannot be at its best as it approaches its 200th birthday unless all Americans have the opportunity to be at their best. A free and open American society, one that is true to the ideals of its founders, must give each of its citizens an equal chance at the starting line and an equal opportunity to go as far and as high as his talents and energies will take him.

The Nation can be proud of the progress it has made in assuring equal opportunity for members of minority groups in recent years. There are many measures of our progress.

Since 1969, we have virtually eliminated the dual school system in the South. Three years ago, 68 percent of all black children in the South were attending all black schools; today only 9 percent are attending schools which are entirely black. Nationally, the number of 100 percent minority schools has decreased by 70 percent during the past 3 years. To further expand educational opportunity, my proposed budget for predominantly black colleges will exceed $200 million next year, more than double the level of 3 years ago.

On the economic front, overall Federal aid to minority business enterprise has increased threefold in the last 3 years, and I will propose a further increase of $90 million. Federal hiring among minorities has been intensified, despite cutbacks in Federal employment, so that one-fifth of all Federal employees are now members of minority groups. Building on strong efforts such as the Philadelphia Plan, we will work harder to ensure that Federal contractors meet fair hiring standards. Compliance reviews will be stepped up, to a level more than 300 percent higher than in 1969. Our proposed budget for the Equal Employment Opportunity Commission will be up 36 percent next year, while our proposed budget for enforcing fair housing laws will grow by 20 percent. I also support legislation to strengthen the enforcement powers of the EEOC by providing the Commission with authority to seek court enforcement of its decisions and by giving it jurisdiction over the hiring practices of State and local governments.

Overall, our proposed budget for civil rights activities is up 25 per cent for next year, an increase which will give us nearly three times as much money for advancing civil rights as we had 3 years ago. We also plan a 42 percent increase in the budget for the Cabinet Committee on Opportunities for the Spanish speaking. And I will propose that the Congress extend the operations of the Civil Rights Commission for another 5-year period.

Self-Determination for Indians

One of the major initiatives in the second year of my Presidency was designed to bring a new era in which the future for American Indians is determined by Indian acts and Indian decisions. The comprehensive program I put forward sought to avoid the twin dangers of paternalism on the one hand and the termination of trust responsibility on the other. Some parts of this program have now become effective, including a generous settlement of the Alaska Native Claims and the return to the Taos Pueblo Indians of the sacred lands around Blue Lake.

Construction grants have been authorized to assist the Navajo Community College, the first Indian-managed institution of higher education.

We are also making progress toward Indian self-determination on the administrative front. A newly reorganized Bureau of Indian Affairs, with almost all-Indian leadership, will from now on be concentrating its resources on a program of reservation-by-reservation development, including redirection of employment assistance to strengthen reservation economies, creating local Indian Action Teams for manpower training, and increased contracting of education and other functions to Indian communities.

I again urge the Congress to join in helping Indians help themselves in fields such as health, education, the protection of land and water rights, and economic development. We have talked about injustice to the first Americans long enough. As Indian leaders themselves have put it, the time has come for more rain and less thunder.

Equal Rights for Women

This administration will also continue its strong efforts to open equal opportunities for women, recognizing clearly that women are often denied such opportunities today. While every woman may not want a career outside the home, every woman should have the freedom to choose whatever career she wishes—and an equal chance to pursue it.

We have already moved vigorously against job discrimination based on sex in both the private and public sectors. For the first time, guidelines have been issued to require that Government contractors in the private sector have action plans for the hiring and promotion of women. We are committed to strong enforcement of equal employment opportunity for women under Title VII of the Civil Rights Act. To help carry out these commitments I will propose to the Congress that the jurisdiction of the Commission on Civil Rights be broadened to encompass sex-based discrimination.

Within the Government, more women have been appointed to high posts than ever before. As the result of my directives issued in April 1971 the number of women appointed to high-level Federal positions has more than doubled—and the number of women in Federal middle management positions has also increased dramatically. More women than ever before have been appointed to Presidential boards and commissions. Our vigorous program to recruit more women for Federal service will be continued and intensified in the coming year.

Opportunity for Veterans

A grateful nation owes it servicemen and servicewomen every opportunity it can open to them when they return to civilian life. The Nation may be weary of war, but we dare not grow weary of doing right by those who have borne its heaviest burdens.

The Federal Government is carrying out this responsibility in many ways: through the G.I. Bill for education—which will spend 2-1/2 times more in 1973 than in 1969; through home loan programs and disability and pension benefits—which also have been expanded; through better medical services—including strong new drug treatment programs; through its budget for veterans hospitals, which is already many times the 1969 level and will be stepped up further next year.

We have been particularly concerned in the last 3 years with the employment of veterans—who experience higher unemployment rates than those who have not served in the Armed Forces. During this past year I announced a six-point national program to increase public awareness of this problem, to provide training and counseling to veterans seeking jobs and to help them find employment opportunities. Under the direction of the Secretary of Labor and with the help of our Jobs for Veterans Committee and the National Alliance of Businessmen, this program

has been moving forward. During its first five months of operation, 122,000 Vietnam-era veterans were placed in jobs by the Federal-State Employment Service and 40,000 were enrolled in job training programs. During the next six months, we expect the Federal-State Employment Service to place some 200,000 additional veterans in jobs and to enroll nearly 200,000 more in manpower training programs.

But let us never forget, in this as in so many other areas, that the opportunity for any individual to contribute fully to his society depends in the final analysis on the response—in his own community—of other individuals.

Greater Role for American Youth

Full participation and first class citizenship—these must be our goals for America's young people. It was to help achieve these goals that I signed legislation to lower the minimum voting age to 18 in June of 1970, and moved to secure a court validation of its constitutionality. And I took special pleasure a year later in witnessing the certification of the amendment which placed this franchise guarantee in the Constitution.

But a voice at election time alone is not enough. Young people should have a hearing in government on a day-by-day basis. To this end, and at my direction, agencies throughout the Federal Government have stepped up their hiring of young people and have opened new youth advisory channels. We have also convened the first White House Youth Conference—a wide-open forum whose recommendations have been receiving a thorough review by the Executive departments.

Several other reforms also mean greater freedom and opportunity for America's young people. Draft calls have been substantially reduced, as a step toward our target of reducing them to zero by mid-1973. Already the lottery system and other new procedures, and the contributions of youth advisory councils and younger members on local boards have made the draft far more fair than it was. My educational reform proposals embody the principle that no qualified student who wants to go to college should be barred by lack of money—a guarantee that would open doors of opportunity for many thousands of deserving young people. Our new career education emphasis can also be a significant springboard to good jobs and rewarding lives.

Young America's "extra dimension" in the sixties and seventies has been a drive to help the less fortunate—an activist idealism bent on making the world a better place to live. Our new ACTION volunteer agency, building on the successful experiences of constituent units such as the Peace Corps and Vista, has already broadened service opportunities for the young—and more new programs are in prospect. The Congress can do its part in forwarding this positive momentum by assuring that the ACTION programs have sufficient funds to carry out their mission.

The American Farmer

As we face the challenge of competing more effectively abroad and of producing more efficiently at home, our entire Nation can take the American farmer as its model. While the productivity of our non-farm industries has gone up 60 percent during the last 20 years, agricultural productivity has gone up 200 percent, or nearly 3-1/2 times as much. One result has been better products and lower prices for American consumers. Another is that farmers have more than held their own in international markets. Figures for the last fiscal year show nearly a $900 million surplus for commercial agricultural trade.

The strength of American agriculture is at the heart of the strength of America. American farmers deserve a fair share in the fruits of our prosperity.

We still have much ground to cover before we arrive at that goal—but we have been moving steadily toward it. In 1950 the income of the average farmer was only 58 percent of that of his non-farm counterpart. Today that figure stands at 74 percent—not nearly high enough, but moving in the right direction.

Gross farm income reached a record high in 1971, and for 1972 a further increase of $2 billion is predicted. Because of restraints on production costs, net farm income is expected to rise in 1972 by 6.4 percent or some $1 billion. Average income per farm is expected to go up 8 percent—to an all-time high—in the next 12 months.

Still there are very serious farm problems—and we are taking strong action to meet them.

I promised 3 years ago to end the sharp skid in farm exports—and I have kept that promise. In just 2 years, farm exports climbed by 37 percent, and last year they set an all-time record. Our expanded marketing programs, the agreement to sell 2 million tons of feed grains to the Soviet Union, our massive aid to South Asia under Public Law 480, and our efforts to halt transportation strikes—by doing all we can under the old law and by proposing a new and better one—these efforts and others are moving us toward our $10 billion farm export goal.

I have also promised to expand domestic markets, to improve the management of surpluses, and to help in other ways to raise the prices received by farmers. I have kept that promise, too. A surprisingly large harvest drove corn prices down last year, but they have risen sharply since last November. Prices received by dairy farmers, at the highest level in history last year, will continue strong in 1972. Soybean prices will be at their highest level in two decades. Prices received by farmers for hogs, poultry and eggs are all expected to go higher. Expanded Government purchases and other assistance will also provide a greater boost to farm income.

With the close cooperation of the Congress, we have expanded the farmers' freedom and flexibility through the Agricultural Act of 1970. We have strengthened the Farm Credit System and substantially increased the availability of farm credit. Programs for controlling plant and animal disease and for soil and water conservation have also been expanded. All these efforts will continue, as will our efforts to improve the legal climate for cooperative bargaining—an important factor in protecting the vitality of the family farm and in resisting excessive government management.

Developing Rural America

In my address to the Congress at this time 2 years ago, I spoke of the fact that one-third of our counties had lost population in the 1960's, that many of our rural areas were slowly being emptied of their people and their promise, and that we should work to reverse this picture by including rural America in a nationwide program to foster balanced growth.

It is striking to realize that even if we had a population of one billion—nearly five times the current level—our area is so great that we would still not be as densely populated as many European nations are at present. Clearly, our problems are not so much those of numbers as they are of distribution. We must work to revitalize the American countryside.

We have begun to make progress on this front in the last 3 years. Rural housing programs have been increased by more than 450 percent from 1969 to 1973. The number of families benefiting from rural water and sewer programs is now 75 percent greater than it was in 1969. We have worked to encourage sensible growth patterns through the location of Federal facilities. The first biennial Report on National Growth, which will be released in the near future, will further describe these patterns, their policy implications and the many ways we are responding to this challenge.

But we must do more. The Congress can begin by passing my $1.1-billion program of Special Revenue Sharing for Rural Community Development. In addition, I will soon present a major proposal to expand significantly the credit authorities of the Farmers Home Administration, so that this agency—which has done so much to help individual farmers—can also help spur commercial, industrial and community development in rural America. Hopefully, the FHA will be able to undertake this work as a part of a new Department of Community Development.

In all these ways, we can help ensure that rural America will be in the years ahead what it has been from our Nation's beginning—an area which looks eagerly to the future with a sense of hope and promise.

A Commitment to Our Cities

Our commitment to balanced growth also requires a commitment to our cities—to old cities threatened by decay, to suburbs now sprawling senselessly because of inadequate planning, and to new cities not yet born but clearly needed by our growing population. I discussed these challenges in my special message to the Congress on Population Growth and the American Future in the summer of 1969—and I have often discussed them since. My recommendations for transportation, education, health, welfare, revenue sharing, planning and management assistance, executive reorganization, the environment—especially the proposed Land Use Policy Act—and my proposals in many other areas touch directly on community development.

One of the keys to better cities is better coordination of these many components. Two of my pending proposals go straight to the heart of this challenge. The first, a new Department of Community Development, would provide a single point of focus for our strategy for growth. The second, Special Revenue Sharing for Urban Community Development, would remove the rigidities of categorical project grants which now do so much to fragment planning, delay action, and discourage local responsibility. My new budget proposed a $300 million increase over the full year level which we proposed for this program a year ago.

The Department of Housing and Urban Development has been working to foster orderly growth in our cities in a number of additional ways. A Planned Variation concept has been introduced into the Model Cities program which gives localities more control over their own future. HUD's own programs have been considerably decentralized. The New Communities Program has moved forward and seven projects have received final approval. The Department's efforts to expand mortgage capital, to more than double the level of subsidized housing, and to encourage new and more efficient building techniques through programs like Operation Breakthrough have all contributed to our record level of housing starts. Still more can be done if the Congress enacts the administration's Housing Consolidation and Simplification Act, proposed in 1970.

The Federal Government is only one of many influences on development patterns across our land. Nevertheless, its influence is considerable. We must do all we can to see that its influence is good.

Improving Transportation

Although the executive branch and the Congress have been led by different parties during the last 3 years, we have cooperated with particular effectiveness in the field of transportation. Together we have shaped the Urban Mass Transportation Assistance Act of 1970—a 12-year, $10 billion effort to expand and improve our common carriers and thus make our cities more livable. We have brought into effect a 10-year, $3 billion ship construction program as well as increased research efforts and a modified program of operating subsidies to revamp our merchant marine. We have accelerated efforts to improve air travel under the new Airport and Airway Trust Fund and have been working in fresh ways to save and improve our railway passenger service. Great progress has also been made in promoting transportation safety and we have moved effectively against cargo thefts and skyjacking.

I hope this strong record will be even stronger by the time the 92nd Congress adjourns. I hope that our Special Revenue Sharing program for transportation will by then be a reality—so that cities and states can make better long-range plans with greater freedom to achieve their own proper balance among the many modes of transportation. I hope, too, that our recommendations for revitalizing surface freight transportation will by then be accepted, including measures both to modernize railway equipment and operations and to update regulatory practices. By encouraging competition, flexibility and efficiency among freight carriers, these steps could save the American people billions of dollars in freight costs every year, helping to curb inflation, expand employment and improve our balance of trade.

One of our most damaging and perplexing economic problems is that of massive and prolonged transportation strikes. There is no reason why the public should be the helpless victim of such strikes—but this is frequently what happens. The dock strike, for example, has been extremely costly for the American people, particularly for the farmer for whom a whole year's income can hinge on how promptly he can move his goods. Last year's railroad strike also dealt a severe blow to our economy.

Both of these emergencies could have been met far more effectively if the Congress had enacted my Emergency Public Interest Protection Act, which I proposed in February of 1970. By passing this legislation in this session, the Congress can give us the permanent machinery so badly needed for resolving future disputes.

Historically, our transportation systems have provided the cutting edge for our development. Now, to keep our country from falling behind the times, we must keep well ahead of events in our transportation planning. This is why we are placing more emphasis and spending more money this year on transportation research and development. For this reason, too, I will propose a 65 percent increase—to the $1-billion level—in our budget for mass transportation. Highway building has been our first priority —and our greatest success story—in the past two decades. Now we must write a similar success story for mass transportation in the 1970s.

Peace at Home: Fighting Crime

Our quest for peace abroad over the last 3 years has been accompanied by an intensive quest for peace at home. And our success in stabilizing developments on the international scene has been matched by a growing sense of stability in America. Civil disorders no longer engulf our cities. Colleges and universities have again become places of learning. And while crime is still increasing, the rate of increase has slowed to a 5-year low. In the one city for which the federal government has a special responsibility—Washington, D.C.—the picture is even brighter, for here serious crime actually fell by 13 percent in the last year. Washington was one of 52 major cities which recorded a net reduction in crime in the first nine months of 1971, compared to 23 major cities which made comparable progress a year earlier.

This encouraging beginning is not something that has just happened by itself—I believe it results directly from strong new crime fighting efforts by this administration, by the Congress, and by state and local governments.

Federal expenditures on crime have increased 200 percent since 1969 and we are proposing another 18 percent increase in our new budget. The Organized Crime Control Act of 1970, the District of Columbia Court Reform Act, and the Omnibus Crime Control Act of 1970 have all provided new instruments for this important battle. So has our effort to expand the federal strike force program as a weapon against organized crime. Late last year, we held the first National Conference on Corrections—and we will continue to move forward in this most critical field. I will also propose legislation to improve our juvenile delinquency prevention programs. And I again urge action on my Special Revenue Sharing proposal for law enforcement.

By continuing our stepped-up assistance to local law enforcement authorities through the Law Enforcement Assistance Administration, by continuing to press for improved courts and correctional institutions, by continuing our intensified war on drug abuse, and by continuing to give vigorous support to the principles of order and respect for law, I believe that what has

been achieved in the Nation's capital can be achieved in a growing number of other communities throughout the Nation.

Combating Drug Abuse

A problem of modern life which is of deepest concern to most Americans—and of particular anguish to many—is that of drug abuse. For increasing dependence on drugs will surely sap our Nation's strength and destroy our Nation's character.

Meeting this challenge is not a task for government alone. I have been heartened by the efforts of millions of individual Americans from all walks of life who are trying to communicate across the barriers created by drug use, to reach out with compassion to those who have become drug dependent. The federal government will continue to lead in this effort. The last 3 years have seen an increase of nearly 600 percent in federal expenditures for treatment and rehabilitation and an increase of more than 500 percent in program levels for research, education and training. I will propose further substantial increases for these programs in the coming year.

In order to develop a national strategy for this effort and to coordinate activities which are spread through nine federal agencies, I asked Congress last June to create a Special Action Office for Drug Abuse Prevention. I also established an interim office by Executive order, and that unit is beginning to have an impact. But now we must have both the legislative authority and the funds I requested if this office is to move ahead with its critical mission.

On another front, the United States will continue to press for a strong collective effort by nations throughout the world to eliminate drugs at their source. And we will intensify the worldwide attack on drug smugglers and all who protect them. The Cabinet Committee on International Narcotics Control—which I created last September—is coordinating our diplomatic and law enforcement efforts in this area.

We will also step up our program to curb illicit drug traffic at our borders and within our country. Over the last 3 years federal expenditures for this work have more than doubled, and I will propose a further funding increase next year. In addition, I will soon initiate a major new program to drive drug traffickers and pushers off the streets of America. This program will be built around a nationwide network of investigative and prosecutive units, utilizing special grand juries established under the Organized Crime Control Act of 1970, to assist state and local agencies in detecting, arresting, and convicting those who would profit from the misery of others.

Strengthening Consumer Protection

Our plans for 1972 include further steps to protect consumers against hazardous food and drugs and other dangerous products. These efforts will carry forward the campaign I launched in 1969 to establish a "Buyer's Bill of Rights" and to strengthen consumer protection. As a part of that campaign, we have established a new Office of Consumer Affairs, directed by my Special Assistant for Consumer Affairs, to give consumers greater access to government, to promote consumer education, to encourage voluntary efforts by business, to work with state and local governments, and to help the federal government improve its consumer-related activities. We have also established a new Consumer Product Information Coordinating Center in the General Services Administration to help us share a wider range of federal research and buying expertise with the public.

But many of our plans in this field still await congressional action, including measures to insure product safety, to fight consumer fraud, to require full disclosure in warranties and guarantees, and to protect against unsafe medical devices.

Reforming and Renewing Education

It was nearly 2 years ago, in March of 1970, that I presented my major proposals for reform and renewal in education. These proposals included student assistance measures to ensure that no qualified person would be barred from college by a lack of money, a National Institute of Education to bring new energy and new direction to educational research, and a National Foundation for Higher Education to encourage innovation in learning beyond high school. These initiatives are still awaiting final action by the Congress. They deserve prompt approval.

I would also underscore my continuing confidence that Special Revenue Sharing for Education can do much to strengthen the backbone of our educational system, our public elementary and secondary schools. Special Revenue Sharing recognizes the nation's interest in their improvement without compromising the principle of local control. I also call again for the enactment of my $1.5 billion program of Emergency School Aid to help local school districts desegregate wisely and well. This program has twice been approved by the House and once by the Senate in different versions. I hope the Senate will now send the legislation promptly to the conference committee so that an agreement can be reached on this important measure at an early date.

This bill is designed to help local school districts with the problems incident to desegregation. We must have an end to the dual school system, as conscience and the Constitution both require—and we must also have good schools. In this connection, I repeat my own firm belief that educational quality—so vital to the future of all of our children—is not enhanced by unnecessary busing for the sole purpose of achieving an arbitrary racial balance.

Financing Our Schools

I particularly hope that 1972 will be a year in which we resolve one of the most critical questions we face in education today: how best to finance our schools.

In recent years the growing scope and rising costs of education have so overburdened local revenues that financial crisis has become a way of life in many school districts. As a result, neither the benefits nor the burdens of education have been equitably distributed.

The brunt of the growing pressures has fallen on the property tax—one of the most inequitable and regressive of all public levies. Property taxes in the United States represent a higher proportion of public income than in almost any other nation. They have more than doubled in the last decade and have been particularly burdensome for our lower and middle income families and for older Americans.

These intolerable pressures—on the property tax and on our schools—led me to establish the President's Commission on School Finance in March of 1970. I charged this Commission with the responsibility to review comprehensively both the revenue needs and the revenue resources of public and non-public elementary and secondary education. The Commission will make its final report to me in March.

At the same time, the Domestic Council—and particularly the Secretaries of the Treasury and of Health, Education and Welfare—have also been studying this difficult and tangled problem. The entire question has been given even greater urgency by recent court decisions in California, Minnesota and Texas, which have held the conventional method of financing schools through local property taxes discriminatory and unconstitutional. Similar court actions are pending in more than half of our states. While these cases have not yet been reviewed by the Supreme Court, we cannot ignore the serious questions they have raised for our states, for our local school districts, and for the entire nation.

The overhaul of school finance involves two complex and interrelated sets of problems: those concerning support of the schools themselves, and also the basic relationships of Federal, State and local governments in any program of tax reform.

We have been developing a set of comprehensive proposals to deal with these questions. Under the leadership of the Secretary of the Treasury, we are carefully reviewing the tax aspects of these proposals; and I have this week enlisted the Advisory Commission on Intergovernmental Relations in addressing the intergovernmental relations aspects. Members of the Congress and of the executive branch, Governors, state legislators, local officials and private citizens comprise this group.

Later in the year, after I have received the reports of both the President's Commission on School Finance and the Advisory Council on Intergovernmental Relations, I shall make my final recommendations for relieving the burden of property taxes and providing both fair and adequate financing for our children's education—consistent with the principle of preserving the control by local school boards over local schools.

A New Emphasis on Career Education

Career Education is another area of major new emphasis, an emphasis which grows out of my belief that our schools should be doing more to build self-reliance and self-sufficiency, to prepare students for a productive and fulfilling life. Too often, this has not been happening. Too many of our students, from all income groups, have been "turning off" or "tuning out" on their educational experiences. And—whether they drop out of school or proceed on to college—too many young people find themselves unmotivated and ill equipped for a rewarding social role. Many other Americans, who have already entered the world of work, find that they are dissatisfied with their jobs but feel that it is too late to change directions, that they already are "locked in."

One reason for this situation is the inflexibility of our educational system, including the fact that it so rigidly separates academic and vocational curricula. Too often vocational education is foolishly stigmatized as being less desirable than academic preparation. And too often the academic curriculum offers very little preparation for viable careers. Most students are unable to combine the most valuable features of both vocational and academic education; once they have chosen one curriculum, it is difficult to move to the other.

The present approach serves the best interests of neither our students nor our society. The unhappy result is high numbers of able people who are unemployed, underemployed, or unhappily employed on the one hand—while many challenging jobs go begging on the other.

We need a new approach, and I believe the best new approach is to strengthen career education.

Career Education provides people of all ages with broader exposure to and better preparation for the world of work. It not only helps the young, but also provides adults with an opportunity to adapt their skills to changing needs, changing technology, and their own changing interests. It would not prematurely force an individual into a specific area of work but would expand his ability to choose wisely from a wider range of options. Neither would it result in a slighting of academic preparation, which would remain a central part of the educational blend.

Career Education is not a single specific program. It is more usefully thought of as a goal—and one that we can pursue through many methods. What we need today is a nationwide search for such methods—a search which involves every area of education and every level of government. To help spark this venture, I will propose an intensified Federal effort to develop model programs which apply and test the best ideas in this field.

There is no more disconcerting waste than the waste of human potential. And there is no better investment than an investment in human fulfillment. Career Education can help make education and training more meaningful for the student, more rewarding for the teacher, more available to the adult, more relevant for the disadvantaged, and more productive for our country.

Manpower Programs: Tapping our Full Potential

Our trillion dollar economy rests in the final analysis on our 88 million member labor force. How well that force is used today, how well that force is prepared for tomorrow—these are central questions for our country.

They are particularly important questions in a time of stiff economic challenge and burgeoning economic opportunity. At such a time, we must find better ways to tap the full potential of every citizen.

This means doing all we can to open new education and employment opportunities for members of minority groups. It means a stronger effort to help the veteran find useful and satisfying work and to tap the enormous talents of the elderly. It means helping women—in whatever role they choose—to realize their full potential. It also means caring for the unemployed—sustaining them, retraining them and helping them find new employment.

This administration has grappled directly with these assignments. We began by completely revamping the Manpower Administration in the Department of Labor. We have expanded our manpower programs to record levels. We proposed—and the Congress enacted—a massive reform of unemployment insurance, adding 9 million workers to the system and expanding the size and duration of benefits. We instituted a Job Bank to match jobs with available workers. The efforts of the National Alliance of Businessmen to train and hire the hard-core unemployed were given a new nationwide focus. That organization has also joined with our Jobs for Veterans program in finding employment for returning servicemen. We have worked to open more jobs for women. Through the Philadelphia Plan and other actions, we have expanded equal opportunity in employment for members of minority groups. Summer jobs for disadvantaged youths went up by one-third last summer. And on July 12 of last year I signed the Emergency Employment Act of 1971, providing more than 130,000 jobs in the public sector.

In the manpower field, as in others, there is also an important unfinished agenda. At the top of this list is my Special Revenue Sharing program for manpower—a bill which would provide more Federal dollars for manpower training while increasing substantially the impact of each dollar by allowing States and cities to tailor training to local labor conditions. My welfare reform proposals are also pertinent in this context, since they are built around the goal of moving people from welfare rolls to payrolls. To help in this effort, HR 1 would provide transitional opportunities in community service employment for another 200,000 persons. The Career Education program can also have an important long-range influence on the way we use our manpower. And so can a major new thrust which I am announcing today to stimulate more imaginative use of America's great strength in science and technology.

Marshalling Science and Technology

As we work to build a more productive, more competitive, more prosperous America, we will do well to remember the keys to our progress in the past. There have been many, including the competitive nature of our free enterprise system; the energy of our working men and women; and the abundant gifts of nature. One other quality which has always been a key to progress is our special bent for technology, our singular ability to harness the discoveries of science in the service of man.

At least from the time of Benjamin Franklin, American ingenuity has enjoyed a wide international reputation. We have been known as a people who could "build a better mousetrap"—and this capacity has been one important reason for both our domestic prosperity and our international strength.

In recent years, America has focused a large share of its technological energy on projects for defense and for space. These projects have had great value. Defense technology has helped us preserve our freedom and protect the peace. Space technology has enabled us to share unparalleled adventures and to lift our sights beyond earth's bounds. The daily life of the average man has also been improved by much of our defense and space research—for example, by work on radar, jet engines, nuclear reactors, communications and weather satellites, and computers. Defense and space projects have also enabled us to build and maintain our general technological capacity, which—as a result—can now be more readily applied to civilian purposes.

America must continue with strong and sensible programs of research and development for defense and for space. I have felt for some time, however, that we should also be doing more to apply our scientific and technological genius directly to domestic opportunities. Toward this end, I have already increased our civilian research and development budget by more than 40 percent since 1969 and have directed the National Science Foundation to give more attention to this area.

I have also reoriented our space program so that it will have even greater domestic benefits. As a part of this effort, I recently announced support for the development of a new earth orbital vehicle that promises to introduce a new era in space research. This vehicle, the space shuttle, is one that can be recovered and used again and again, lowering significantly both the cost and the risk of space operations. The space shuttle would also open new opportunities in fields such as weather forecasting, domestic and international communications, the monitoring of natural resources, and air traffic safety.

The space shuttle is a wise national investment. I urge the Congress to approve this plan so that we can realize these substantial economies and these substantial benefits.

Over the last several months, this administration has undertaken a major review of both the problems and the opportunities for American technology. Leading scientists and researchers from our universities and from industry have contributed to this study. One important conclusion we have reached is that much more needs to be known about the process of stimulating and applying research and development. In some cases, for example, the barriers to progress are financial. In others they are technical. In still other instances, customs, habits, laws, and regulations are the chief obstacles. We need to learn more about all these considerations—and we intend to do so. One immediate step in this effort will be the White House Conference on the Industrial World Ahead which will convene next month and will devote considerable attention to research and development questions.

But while our knowledge in this field is still modest, there are nevertheless a number of important new steps which we can take at this time. I will soon present specific recommendations for such steps in a special message to the Congress. Among these proposals will be an increase next year of $700 million in civilian research and development spending, a 15 percent increase over last year's level and a 65 percent increase over 1969. We will place new emphasis on cooperation with private research and development, including new experimental programs for cost sharing and for technology transfers from the public to the private sector. Our program will include special incentives for smaller high technology firms, which have an excellent record of cost effectiveness.

In addition, our Federal agencies which are highly oriented toward technology—such as the Atomic Energy Commission and the National Aeronautics and Space Administration—will work more closely with agencies which have a primary social mission. For example, our outstanding capabilities in space technology should be used to help the Department of Transportation develop better mass transportation systems. As has been said so often in the last 2 years, a nation that can send three people across 240,000 miles of space to the moon should also be able to send 240,000 people 3 miles across a city to work.

Finally, we will seek to set clear and intelligent targets for research and development, so that our resources can be focused on projects where an extra effort is most likely to produce a breakthrough and where the breakthrough is most likely to make a difference in our lives. Our initial efforts will include new or accelerated activities aimed at:

- Creating new sources of clean and abundant energy;
- Developing safe, fast, pollution-free transportation;
- Reducing the loss of life and property from earthquakes, hurricanes and other natural disasters;
- Developing effective emergency health care systems which could lead to the saving of as many as 30,000 lives each year;
- Finding new ways to curb drug traffic and rehabilitate drug users.

And these are only the beginning.

I cannot predict exactly where each of these new thrusts will eventually lead us in the years ahead. But I can say with assurance that the program I have outlined will open new employment opportunities for American workers, increase the productivity of the American economy, and expand foreign markets for American goods. I can also predict with confidence that this program will enhance our standard of living and improve the quality of our lives.

Science and technology represent an enormous power in our life—and a unique opportunity. It is now for us to decide whether we will waste these magnificent energies—or whether we will use them to create a better world for ourselves and for our children.

A Growing Agenda for Action

The danger in presenting any substantial statement of concerns and requests is that any subject which is omitted from the list may for that reason be regarded as unimportant. I hope the Congress will vigorously resist any such suggestions, for there are many other important proposals before the House and the Senate which also deserve attention and enactment.

I think, for example, of our program for the District of Columbia. In addition to proposals already before the Congress, I will soon submit additional legislation outlining a special balanced program of physical and social development for the nation's capital as part of our Bicentennial celebration. In this and other ways, we can make that celebration both a fitting commemoration of our revolutionary origins and a bold further step to fulfill their promise.

I think, too, of our program to help small businessmen, of our proposals concerning communications, of our recommendations involving the construction of public buildings, and of our program for the arts and humanities—where the proposed new budget is 6 times the level of 3 years ago.

In all, some 90 pieces of major legislation which I have recommended to the Congress still await action. And that list is growing longer. It is now for the Congress to decide whether this agenda represents the beginning of new progress for America —or simply another false start.

The Need for Reason and Realism

I have covered many subjects in this message. Clearly, our challenges are many and complex. But that is the way things must be for responsible government in our diverse and complicated world.

We can choose, of course, to retreat from this world, pretending that our problems can be solved merely by trusting in a new philosophy, a single personality, or a simple formula. But such a retreat can only add to our difficulties and our disillusion.

If we are to be equal to the complexity of our times we must learn to move on many fronts and to keep many commitments. We must learn to reckon our success not by how much we start but by how much we finish. We must learn to be tenacious. We must learn to persevere.

If we are to master our moment, we must first be masters of ourselves. We must respond to the call which has been a central theme of this message—the call to reason and to realism.

To meet the challenge of complexity we must also learn to disperse and decentralize power—at home and abroad—allowing more people in more places to release their creative energies. We must remember that the greatest resource for good in this world is the power of the people themselves—not moving in lockstep to the commands of the few—but providing their own discipline and discovering their own destiny.

Above all, we must not lose our capacity to dream, to see, amid the realities of today, the possibilities for tomorrow. And then—if we believe in our dreams—we also must wake up and work for them.

RICHARD NIXON

THIRD YEAR: NEW NIXON ON ECONOMY, FOREIGN AFFAIRS

The third year of the Nixon Presidency was highlighted by a series of actions in conflict with positions Richard M. Nixon took earlier in his political life.

• The Administration started a diplomatic revolution in U.S. policy toward Communist China and the Soviet Union by scheduling presidential trips to Peking and Moscow in 1972—efforts by a President who made his early political reputation as a strong anti-Communist.

• Wage and price controls were imposed on an ailing economy by a Republican President who had objected to such controls and who had actively opposed the congressional authority granted him in 1970 to impose them.

• President Nixon Dec. 14 announced plans to devalue the U.S. dollar after earlier resisting moves that would increase the price of gold in relation to the dollar.

• A new international trade policy imposing a 10-percent surcharge on most imports hurt the nation's relations with Canada, Japan, Western Europe, Latin America and the underdeveloped countries of Asia and Africa. The thrust of Mr. Nixon's earlier actions had been to improve U.S. relations with foreign countries.

Public Reaction

After two decades of hostility and non-recognition of the People's Republic of China, the Nixon Administration's announcement in mid-1971 of a policy shift—supporting the admission of Communist China to the United Nations—generally was received favorably by Congress and the nation.

Mr. Nixon was beneficiary of two factors: general acceptance of the idea that world peace required the normalization of relations with the People's Republic of China and the fact that "pro-Communist" charges would not be hurled at Mr. Nixon the way they were at previous Democratic Administrations.

The Administration's surprise wage-price freeze, invoked in August, brought early opposition from organized labor. But this shifted to a general desire to conform when Phase Two took over in mid-November.

Dissent over the Vietnam war—which seemed on the rise in the spring of 1971—had waned by mid-year following further troop withdrawal announcements by Mr. Nixon. At year's end, 45,000 additional troops were scheduled for withdrawal from Vietnam, leaving 139,000 American soldiers there but practically bringing to an end the offensive combat involvement of U.S. ground troops.

The President's actions had succeeded in defusing much of the more vigorous public opposition to U.S. involvement in the war. But in Congress total U.S. withdrawal from Southeast Asia remained a major issue. For the first time, Congress in 1971 called for an end to the Indochina war. Yet, Mr. Nixon, when signing the bill containing the withdrawal amendment, told reporters the

measure was not binding and would not change his policies. A move was under way in Congress to restrict presidential war-making powers. It was likely to be an issue further dividing Congress and the Nixon Administration in 1972.

Mr. Nixon had conspicuous successes in international relations. His July announcement that he would visit Peking in early 1972 surprised the world. And, shortly after the announcement of the China trip, he announced a separate trip to Moscow.

His image suffered with other countries, though, after the Administration imposed a 10-percent import surcharge in a move to offset the U.S. balance-of-payments deficit. The deficit had reached $12.1-billion in the third quarter of 1971, the highest in history. The surcharge was removed on Dec. 20.

The New American Revolution

The President began his third year of the Presidency with a pledge to restructure government and turn power "back to the people." To do this he introduced "six great goals" of his Administration: welfare reform, revenue sharing, health insurance reform, environmental initiatives, government reorganization and full employment. All but the last needed new legislation. Mr. Nixon said achievement of all six goals would bring about a "new American revolution."

By the end of the year, none of the first five of the Nixon goals had been enacted. They were bogged down in what Mr. Nixon called a lagging Congress controlled by Democrats. His two major domestic proposals—welfare reform and revenue sharing—were locked in committee, partly because he asked that they be delayed.

Mr. Nixon during 1971 had difficulties with Congress on other issues as well: spending levels for domestic programs; his nominees to fill vacancies on the Supreme Court, although finally approved, and funding for the controversial supersonic transport plane which was turned down. Other trouble areas were anti-pollution efforts and foreign aid.

Congress was unenthusiastic about Mr. Nixon's government reorganization plan which would split seven Cabinet departments among four new ones. Hearings were begun but no action was taken.

The final goal of the "revolution"—reduction of unemployment—proved to be as elusive as the ones that required action by Congress. The November 1971 unemployment rate was 6 percent, with 4.6-million people out of work. In early 1970, unemployment was under 4 percent but had climbed to the 6-percent level by the end of the year. The rate remained near the 6-percent level for all of 1971.

Mr. Nixon vetoed three measures presented him by the 92nd Congress. Two of these—a $5.7-billion public works bill to give jobs to the unemployed and the $6.3-billion OEO extension containing a $2.1-billion child care program—were major pieces of legislation considered too costly by the Administration. The child care program would have provided extensive services for poor children in the areas of nutrition, health and day care.

Many members of Congress were alienated by what they called the President's method of "government by surprise." The President often announced policies to Congress at the same time he announced them to the nation—via television.

The Nixon Doctrine

In keeping with the Nixon Doctrine whereby the United States would avoid military involvement in remote parts of the world, but instead would give economic and military aid for self-determination, Mr. Nixon proposed increased military aid for Southeast Asia in his foreign aid request.

But this move met opposition in the Senate and the final version of the bill was $894-million less than that requested by the President.

Sen. J.W. Fulbright (D Ark.), chairman of the Senate Foreign Relations Committee, told the Senate, "The American people generally have been sold the idea that our policy is a total military withdrawal from Indochina.... But that is not the policy which we are being asked to support...." Fulbright said it was "difficult to escape the conclusion...that the President is still determined to control the future of Southeast Asia by the application of force."

Foreign Policy

China Policy. In three major steps announced in 1971, the President dramatically shifted U.S. policy toward Communist China:

● On June 10, the President ended a 21-year embargo on trade with Mainland China.

● On July 15, Mr. Nixon announced he would visit Peking, and the date of the visit later was set for Feb. 21-28, 1972.

● On Aug. 2, Secretary of State William P. Rogers announced that the United States would support the seating of Communist China in the United Nations.

In thus abandoning the long-standing policy of non-recognition of the Communist regime in Peking, the President cast himself in the role of a statesman seeking new roads to world peace. Reaction in Congress and in the nation generally was favorable to these moves.

In moving toward closer relations with Peking, however, the President aroused fears among conservatives that the United States would abandon its alliance with the Chinese Communists' bitter enemy, the Nationalist Chinese government on Taiwan.

In a worldwide context, the President's initiatives raised doubts about U.S. relations with its traditional allies as well as with the Soviet Union, which was suspicious of both U.S. and Chinese motives. To placate such uneasiness, the President announced that he would go to Moscow in May and also arranged to confer with the leaders of France, Britain and West Germany.

International Finance. In his meetings with the heads of state from other western nations, the Presi-

dent hoped to make progress toward ending another international concern—the disruption of the international finance system brought to a head by his new economic policy.

In announcing measures to stimulate the sagging U.S. economy Aug. 15, the President also took steps designed to protect the dollar by suspending its convertibility into gold owned by the U.S. government and by imposing a 10-percent surcharge on goods imported into the United States.

The ultimate objective of these measures was to force other nations to revalue their currencies to provide exchange rates more favorable to the U.S. economy.

While most currencies in effect were revalued, the world financial system remained in flux as the United States and other nations tried to negotiate a new set of exchange rates. Then, on Dec. 14, the President announced that the U.S. dollar would be devalued, the major step leading to a new exchange rate.

Foreign Aid. Foreign aid, an instrument of U.S. foreign policy since 1948, assumed an important role in Administration policy when the President in 1969 proclaimed the Nixon Doctrine of providing money and arms but not men to help other nations defend themselves.

In 1971, however, some Senators' doubts about the Nixon Doctrine were among a variety of conflicting ideas and positions that endangered the future of the foreign aid program. For the first time in the program's history, a foreign aid bill was defeated as the Senate rejected a measure authorizing fiscal 1972 funds.

The Senate revived the authorization legislation in a two-bill package in reduced form, and Senate and House conferees engaged in a bitter struggle to resolve differences over a Senate amendment setting a policy of complete withdrawal of troops from Vietnam within six months. The amendment finally was deleted.

Middle East, South Asia. No progress was made in 1971 in U.S. efforts to assure peace in the Middle East, and the Administration came under increasing congressional pressure to sell jet aircraft to Israel to offset reported increases in Soviet aid to Egypt.

After war broke out between India and Pakistan, members of Congress criticized the President for not making more vigorous efforts to settle differences over East Pakistan and for blaming India as the aggressor. The Administration countered that India had started the open fighting just as behind-the-scenes U.S. efforts to persuade Pakistan to grant East Pakistan autonomy were about to be successful.

Pentagon Papers. The Supreme Court ruled against Administration efforts to prevent further publication after several newspapers printed excerpts from a classified Pentagon history of U.S. involvement in Vietnam. While publication of the Pentagon Papers added some impetus to opposition to continuation of the war, the President's handling of the war was not directly affected as a result.

National Security

Indochina. Despite growing pressure from Congress, President Nixon held firm during 1971 and refused to set a specific date for the total withdrawal of U.S. troops from Indochina. Mr. Nixon continued phased withdrawals throughout the year, however, with his last announcement of the year scheduling a reduction to 139,000 men by Feb. 1, 1972. He told the nation that the United States was no longer involved in a ground combat role except as a defense against the Viet Cong or the North Vietnamese.

The President emphasized that he no longer expected any "striking breakthrough" at the deadlocked Paris Peace Talks and that, if no settlement were negotiated, the United States probably would keep troops in South Vietnam and continue to make U.S. air support available to the South Vietnamese as long as it was needed.

Three times the Senate passed amendments offered by Majority Leader Mike Mansfield (D Mont.) which set withdrawal deadlines for U.S. troops from Indochina. Although the House never fully endorsed any version of the Mansfield amendment, two weakened versions—minus the specific withdrawal deadline—were accepted by House members in order to clear various defense and foreign aid bills for the President's signature.

This marked a major breakthrough for the anti-war forces in the House and Senate. Inclusion of the weakened Mansfield amendment in a bill bound for the President's signature was the first legislative action by Congress urging a change of policy by the President in South Vietnam.

President Nixon signed the defense procurement bill—a measure which included the weakened Mansfield amendment. In signing the bill, the President told reporters he felt the amendment was "without binding force or effect and it does not reflect my judgment about the way in which the war should be brought to a conclusion. My signing of the bill that contains this section, therefore, will not change the policies I have pursued." He said he would not set a date even though the Mansfield amendment urged him to do so.

All-Volunteer Military. One of Mr. Nixon's 1968 campaign promises was his pledge to end the military draft, replacing it with an all-volunteer system. The Presidential Commission on an All-Volunteer Military, appointed by the President in 1969, reported in February 1970 that the draft could be abolished by mid-1971.

Mr. Nixon said he agreed with the basic intent of the commission report but could not accept the 1971 date for full implementation of the program. White House and Pentagon personnel expended extensive lobby efforts on Capitol Hill during the spring of 1971 to prevent moves in both the House and Senate to bring about an earlier end to the draft than the June 30, 1973, target date the President had set. The Administration was successful in thwarting all efforts to shorten the two-year draft extension requested by the Pentagon, although the House turned back a one-year extension amendment to the draft bill by just a two-vote margin.

Defense Spending. The President asked Congress for a $73.5-billion defense appropriations bill which would cover all Defense Department expenses during fiscal 1972 except for building programs. Congress cut $3-billion from the President's request with more than half the cuts coming from the weapons procurement budget.

NATO Troop Cut. Twice during the 1971 session of the 92nd Congress, the White House mounted lobby efforts to defeat attempts in the Senate to reduce the number of U.S. troops stationed in Europe.

After one week of debate, the Senate May 19 rejected a proposal to limit U.S. troops stationed in NATO countries to 150,000 men—a cut of about 50 percent. The White House gathered statements of opposition to the proposal from former Presidents Truman and Johnson as well as two dozen members of former Administrations.

Again in the fall, on an amendment to the defense appropriations bill, the Senate battled over a proposed cut of 50,000 men stationed in Europe. The White House cited on-going attempts to negotiate for a reduction with the Soviet Union, and the troop-reduction amendment was rejected by the Senate.

The Economy

After two and a half years of unsuccessful attempts to curb inflation, President Nixon Aug. 15 imposed wage and price controls on the economy and sought to reverse growing deficits in the U.S. balance of payments.

Under authority voted by Congress in 1970 (despite opposition from the White House) Mr. Nixon froze wages, prices and rents for 90 days and then set up mechanisms for continued limitations during the post-freeze "Phase Two."

Mr. Nixon Aug. 15 called for tax reductions to stimulate economic growth and reduce unemployment, a tax credit for business investment, a step-up in scheduled increases in personal tax exemptions and repeal of excise taxes on automobiles. He suspended the $35-an-ounce fixed price for gold, which had pegged the value of the dollar in international exchange for nearly 40 years, and imposed an indefinite 10-percent surcharge on imports. He established a Cost of Living Council to oversee the program.

In addition to new tax laws, he requested Congress to extend his authority to control wages, prices and rents and to add powers to regulate interest rates and dividends. Congress cleared such a bill Dec. 14.

The President established his Phase Two program by executive order under his existing authority. He established a Pay Board of five members each from the public, labor and management and a seven-member Price Commission to devise guidelines to take effect after the freeze ended.

The imposition of the freeze and subsequent actions of the Pay Board widened a rift between the Nixon Administration and organized labor. Labor objected chiefly to the Pay Board's action limiting wage increases scheduled by existing contracts.

Supreme Court

President Nixon won a major victory—with far-reaching implications—when the Senate in early December confirmed his nominations of Lewis F. Powell Jr. of Virginia and William H. Rehnquist of Arizona to the Supreme Court. This Senate action placed on the Court four men named by President Nixon: Chief Justice Warren E. Burger, Associate Justices Harry A. Blackmun, Powell and Rehnquist, and virtually assured a more conservative majority.

The nomination of Powell, a Virginian and former president of the American Bar Association, easily approved by the Senate; but Rehnquist, an Assistant Attorney General, was opposed by a group of liberal Senators and interest groups who criticized him as insensitive to the rights of the individual and minority-group members. After four days of debate his nomination was confirmed, 68-26.

During the 1970-1971 term, the Supreme Court announced several criminal decisions which appeared more to Mr. Nixon's liking than those of the Court under Chief Justice Earl Warren. On the other hand, on the question of school desegregation, the Court did not rule in accord with Administration positions, announcing unanimously April 20 that it upheld the use of busing to desegregate formerly segregated schools.

Civil Rights

Schools. After the Supreme Court decision in April sanctioned the use of busing and other extraordinary methods of pupil assignment to desegregate schools, the Administration appeared ready to carry out such a policy, proposing busing in desegregation plans for Austin, Texas, and Nashville, Tenn. By mid-summer, HEW had warned 64 school districts that they should move to increase the desegregation of their schools when school opened in the fall. Figures released by HEW in June showed that the South had outstripped the other parts of the nation in reducing racial isolation in its schools.

In Austin, the federal court in July rejected the extensive busing plan filed by HEW, and approved the school board's plan which called for less every-day busing.

The White House August 3 issued a statement by the President announcing that the Justice Department was appealing that decision—on the grounds that such part-time desegregation did not meet the constitutional standards for desegregation.

But the President specifically stated that the government's appeal was not to adopt the HEW plan which called for extensive busing.

Furthermore, Mr. Nixon restated his position on busing: "I am against busing as that term is commonly used in school desegregation cases. I have consistently opposed the busing of our nation's school children to achieve a racial balance, and I am opposed to the busing of children simply for the sake of busing."

Housing. In a long-awaited statement on equal opportunity in housing, President Nixon June 11 said he would enforce federal laws barring racial discrimination in the sale, rental or construction or housing—but that he would not approve a federal policy of forcing cities and neighborhoods to accept low-income housing. "We will not seek to impose economic integration upon an existing local jurisdiction," he said. But, he added, "we will not countenance any use of economic measures as a subterfuge for racial discrimination."

Employment. In the area of employment opportunities, the Administration continued to oppose a bill which would grant the Equal Employment Opportunity Commission (EEOC) the power to issue cease-and-desist orders against discriminatory employers and which would expand that agency's jurisdiction. The House went along with the Administration's position Sept. 16, rejecting the cease-and-desist measure for an Administration-backed substitute which authorized the EEOC to take discriminatory employers to court.

Agriculture

After a short but bitter floor fight, the Senate Dec. 2 confirmed Mr. Nixon's nomination of Earl L. Butz, a dean of Purdue University in Lafayette, Ind., to be Secretary of Agriculture. The roll-call vote was 51-44.

Opponents of the nomination charged that Butz was tied too closely to farming corporations and was unsympathetic to the needs of the family farmer. During his service at Purdue, Butz was a director of Ralston Purina, International Minerals and Stokely Van Camp.

In his State of the Union Message, Mr. Nixon asked Congress for authority to abolish the Agriculture Department as part of his reorganization plan. However, when he nominated Butz for the Cabinet post in November, he said he would retain the Agriculture Department.

Labor and Manpower

The Administration's efforts to reform and consolidate federal manpower programs met with no success during the first session of the 92nd Congress. The manpower revenue-sharing program was rejected by the House Education and Labor Committee, and the Senate Labor and Public Welfare Committee conducted one day of perfunctory hearings on the proposal but reported no legislation.

Although Mr. Nixon originally opposed a public service job program to ease unemployment, he eventually signed a Democratic-sponsored $2.25-billion authorization to provide public service jobs at the state and local levels. However, another Democratic move to provide $2-billion for hiring persons in public works projects, part of the $5.7-billion public works bill, was vetoed by the President.

Minimum Wage. Administration labor officials recommended a boost in the hourly minimum wage to $2 by 1974, but the House Education and Labor Committee reported a bill increasing the hourly standard to $2 by 1972. A Senate subcommittee held hearings on a measure to raise the minimum wage to $2.25. Floor action was expected when Congress returned in January.

Pension Funds. The Administration, in a Dec. 8 message by President Nixon, renewed its call to bring private pension funds under government regulation. The message came too late in the session for congressional hearings to be held, but action was certain in 1972. The Senate Labor and Public Welfare Committee conducted extensive studies of numerous pension plan operations, and committee members were eager for floor consideration of a pension bill.

Federal Election Reform

After much vacillation on the issue of political campaign spending reform, the Administration formed ranks behind the Federal Election Campaign Practices Act passed by the Senate in December. Mr. Nixon reportedly was "very pleased" with the bill. The House delayed action on the bill until early in 1972.

As approved by the Senate, the bill did not contain limitations on contributions and did not repeal the equal broadcast time requirement—two provisions opposed by Mr. Nixon. The Administration won the battle of the Democratic-backed "campaign checkoff" provision written into the tax bill.

Government Reorganization

The Administration's sweeping plan to restructure the executive branch of government floundered in Congress. Opposed by many committee chairmen and ranking committee members because it would detract from their jurisdiction, the reorganization proposal was never considered beyond the hearing stage.

One aspect of the plan, a proposal to create a Department of Community Development, seemed to arouse more congressional interest and may be acted upon in 1972. The new department would be created from parts of the existing Departments of Transportation and Housing and Urban Development.

Welfare

Congressional momentum to pass a welfare reform-Social Security bill during the first session of the 92nd Congress slowed after the President requested in his Aug. 15 economic policy speech that implementation of welfare reform be delayed one year.

The Senate Finance Committee began hearings on comprehensive welfare legislation July 27. A welfare bill (HR 1) passed the House June 22. The Finance Committee hearings were interrupted when the committee began hearings on a tax bill requested by President Nixon as part of his new economic policy.

The Family Assistance Plan in the welfare bill was controversial. The Administration supported the $2,400 federally guaranteed annual income to a family of four with no outside income that was in the House-passed welfare bill. Conservatives on the Senate Finance Committee said that $2,400 was too high. Liberals favored a higher guaranteed annual income.

The Senate Finance Committee has stated that it hopes to resume hearings on welfare legislation early in 1972.

Health

Health Insurance. President Nixon outlined his plan for a National Health Insurance Partnership in his health message. The President's plan proposed employment-related health insurance for most working people and a government-sponsored health insurance plan for low-income families with children.

The Health Subcommittee of the Senate Labor and Public Welfare Committee and the House Ways and Means Committee held extensive hearings on health insurance during the first session of the 92nd Congress. The Ways and Means Committee stated that it plans to go into executive session for consideration of a national health insurance bill in early 1972.

Three other national health insurance plans with strong support on the Ways and Means Committee were the Health Security Act introduced in the House by Rep. Martha W. Griffiths (D Mich.), the National Healthcare Act of 1971 introduced in the House by Rep. Omar Burleson (D Texas) and the Health Care Insurance Act of 1971 introduced in the House by Rep. Richard Fulton (D Tenn.).

Cancer Research. Congress Dec. 10 cleared for the President a bill (S 1828) expanding the cancer research efforts of the National Cancer Institute within the National Institutes of Health (NIH) and authorizing $1.59-billion over fiscal 1972-1974.

The cancer bill which cleared Congress was close to the version passed earlier by the House. The Senate version which called for an independent cancer research agency located at NIH originally was supported by the Administration. However, the Administration later told House and Senate conferees that either version would be acceptable.

In his 1971 State of the Union Message, President Nixon had asked for an additional $100-million appropriation for cancer research. In his February health message, he announced plans for an intensified cancer research program.

Anti-Poverty

President Nixon Dec. 9 vetoed a bill (S 2007) which provided a two-year extension of the Office of Economic Opportunity (OEO). The President vetoed the bill because of a section authorizing $2.1-billion for a comprehensive child development program.

OEO's legal and fiscal authority expired June 30, 1971, and President Nixon had requested a two-year extension for the agency in March. The child development section was added to the bill in the Senate. The House added a child development section despite strong Republican objections.

The Senate, in a 51-36 vote, was seven votes short of the two-thirds majority needed to override the President's veto.

Transportation

SST. In a major setback, the Administration, determined that the United States should continue development of a supersonic transport aircraft (SST), failed to convince Congress that the project was worth an additional $134-million for construction of two prototypes.

In March, Cabinet members, government agency heads, labor union officials and aerospace scientists and executives, as well as the President and his aides, told members of Congress—both publicly and privately—that the aircraft was essential to the economic interests of the nation. Opponents argued that the SST was an environmental threat and a potential economic disaster.

On March 18, the House, by a 13-vote margin on a recorded teller vote, decided to discontinue federal funding of the 300-passenger, 1,800 mile-an-hour plane; the Senate sealed the House decision on March 24, voting 51-46 against additional development funds.

But opponents of the supersonic transport received a jolt May 12 when the House turned an amendment to refund SST contractors around and approved $85.3-million to continue work on the controversial aircraft.

Congressional forces, working quietly behind the scenes, had lined up enough support in the House to win a 201-187 roll-call vote on an amendment added to a fiscal 1971 supplemental appropriations bill. They insisted that it would cost the government less to continue the SST project than to cancel it.

The Senate, however, refused to follow the House decision after the chairman of the board of the Boeing

Company said it would cost more—not less—to complete work on the two prototypes.

Revenue Sharing. Congress has yet to act on the President's transportation revenue-sharing program. Mr. Nixon had proposed that the program take effect on Jan. 1, 1972, and requested initial funding at an annual level of $2.566-billion.

Revenue for transportation under Mr. Nixon's plan would be drawn from 23 existing federal grant-in-aid programs, and then distributed to the states in the following amounts: $525-million (urban mass transit), $220-million (airports), $130-million (highway safety), $1.6-billion (federal aid for highways, except for the interstate system) and $66-million (highway beautification).

Transportation Strikes. During the May 17-18 rail strike that halted passenger and freight service throughout the nation, President Nixon once again urged Congress to consider his proposal to prevent future transportation disruptions.

Part of the Nixon plan would head off strikes by allowing a neutral panel to pick one of the "final offers" submitted by rail management and unions as the terms of a binding contract settlement.

But the unions contended it would encroach on their right to strike and that "final offer" is a "novel form of compulsory arbitration."

Education

Money. Once again there was a White House-Congress tug-of-war over federal funds for education. The House—fearing a third presidential veto of education funds in three years—refused to add $729-million to the bill, which would have brought its total to $5.4-billion. But the Senate approved a bill containing $5.6-billion, a total which it said was only $452-million more than requested but which HEW said was $904-million more than the President wanted. The threat of veto hung over the conferees, who reported out the final version of the bill, providing $5.1-billion. Congress cleared that measure June 30. The President signed the bill July 11.

Higher Education. Both the House and Senate rejected the major thrusts of Mr. Nixon's student aid proposals. Critics said that to direct aid primarily to students from the lowest income groups would deprive middle-income students of necessary aid—and that to shift the burden of funding of student loans to the private money market entirely would be to reduce drastically available funds for those loans.

The Administration then backed proposals adopted by the Senate—and rejected when proposed as amendments on the House floor. The Administration supported the nationwide basic student grant program approved by the Senate—and the cost-of-education approach to federal aid to colleges and universities. This payment would be based on the number of federally aided students attending the institution and would be used to meet the cost of educating those students.

The House continued the basic student grant program already in existence and authorized a new program of direct federal aid to colleges and universities for general operating expenses, based partially on the total amount of federal student aid its students received, but in great part on the number of students enrolled at the school.

The two versions of the bill had not gone to conference when Congress adjourned.

Environment

In a Feb. 8 message to Congress on the environment, President Nixon proposed setting authorizations for the federal share of water pollution programs administered by the Environmental Protection Agency (EPA) at $2-billion annually for fiscal years 1972 through 1974. Other proposals included imposing taxes on sulfur emission and lead gas additives, revisions of pesticide laws, noise controls, and other programs of research, land use controls and international cooperation.

In early June, the President sent Congress another message outlining his program for the production of "clean" energy. Among the recommendations were a federal commitment to continued funding of a liquid metal fast-breeder nuclear reactor, increased sale of oil and gas leases on the continental shelf and leases to develop oil shale reserves on federally owned lands in the West. Few of his requests required action by Congress.

The Senate in November unanimously passed a major water pollution bill which authorized $16.8-million over four years. The bill set the goal of making the nation's waterways virtually pollution-free by 1985, and established a new program of granting permits to control discharge of wastes. Shortly after passage of the bill, the Nixon Administration announced its opposition to the version of the water pollution bill passed by the Senate on the grounds that it gave too much authority to the federal government and not enough to the states. The White House called for the House Public Works Committee to reopen hearings on the measure, and hearings were held shortly before Congress adjourned.

Consumers

The President's first major consumer message of the 92nd Congress, delivered Feb. 24, called for federal authority to set new safety standards on all consumer products. This was a new recommendation. Many other programs in the message were holdovers from his recommendations to the 91st Congress, including limited class action suits, warranty standards and increased consumer protection authority for the Federal Trade Commission (FTC). The Senate passed a bill combining warranty standards with greater powers for the FTC, but the House did not vote on it.

A major consumer issue in Congress this year was no-fault automobile insurance. The Administration backs no-fault insurance in principle, but feels it should be enacted separately by state legislatures. The Senate Commerce Committee held extensive hearings on a package of bills setting up a national system of no-fault insurance for personal injury cases. Another bill aimed at reducing property loss in automobile crashes by making cars more damage-resistant or easier to repair passed the Senate despite Administration opposition.

BOLD MOVES ON ECONOMY BY NIXON ADMINISTRATION

President Nixon with decisive action switched the economic issue in 1971 from the foremost of his liabilities to a potential asset.

The President began the year in the wake of the 1970 congressional and state elections, in which the laggard economy blunted unprecedented campaign efforts by Mr. Nixon and his Vice President to make gains for their party. Mr. Nixon faced the chief economic problem he inherited when he took office—inflation—and another which was clearly identified with his Administration—unemployment.

In contrast, the President ended the year with a record of bold action and a dynamic policy in operation, designed to stimulate the economy to faster growth, hold down the trend of price increases and right the adverse balance of international payments which was draining away billions of dollars to foreign countries.

In a climax to months of strenuous activity to bring both the domestic and international situations under control, Mr. Nixon Dec. 18 announced devaluation of the dollar as part of a general realignment of currency values among the major industrial nations. The realignment virtually eliminated the chief advantage the other leading nations have had over the United States in foreign trade: overvaluation of the dollar and undervaluation of other currencies.

Congress opened the year in the same role it had played since Mr. Nixon took office—that of critic of his economic policies. Until Aug. 15 the majority Democrats, joined or supplemented on occasion by Republicans, peppered the President with economic advice.

On Aug. 15 the President froze wages and prices, called for a tax cut for individuals and businesses, imposed a 10-percent surtax on imports and cut the dollar loose from the $35-per-ounce gold price which had prevailed for almost 40 years. Congressional critics had been urging identical or similar action. The decisive effort to cope with the worsening economic problems gained the initiative for the President and some relief from criticism. This respite ended with the announcement of Phase Two—the post-freeze period of the new policy.

Phase Two brought promises that Congress would restrict the President's authority to control the economy and carefully oversee his stabilization program. But the major thrust at the President was the Senate effort to capitalize on his request for tax reduction by piggybacking the tax bill with a plan to finance the 1972—and subsequent—presidential election campaigns with public funds. Democrats wanted the campaign financing chiefly because they faced 1972 with a large deficit and limited fund-raising potential. Republicans, with full party coffers, generally opposed the plan.

Both efforts collapsed under presidential pressure. Congress extended the President's economic stabilization authority for a year—until April 30, 1973—before anyone knew whether the Phase Two program would work effec-

tively and fairly and well before the existing legislation expired. Mr. Nixon's power to control the economy was not significantly altered.

Under Mr. Nixon's threat to veto the tax bill if the campaign financing provision was included, Congress abandoned the effort for 1972 by making the plan effective in 1973. The President clearly won both battles.

As 1972 opened, there were no assurances that Mr. Nixon's new economic policy would succeed. The unemployment rate continued to hover around 6 percent of the labor force. There was no way to determine whether the leveling-off which began in July in the consumer price index (CPI) was permanent. Gross national product (GNP), the total output of the economy, expanded vigorously in the final quarter of the year, but growth was disappointing in the second and third quarters. The tax bill was not expected to show effects until well into 1972.

But there was no question that the President had taken the initiative on the economy much more forcefully than he ever had in his preceding two and one-half years in office. There was no doubt that, temporarily, at least, he had seized the economic issue from his opponents in a fashion that won broad support from the nation and left the Democratic Congress in some degree of disarray.

The economy was still the major domestic campaign issue Mr. Nixon faced in 1972. If his policies succeeded in holding down prices while reducing unemployment, increasing output and lessening the balance of payments deficit, his candidacy for a second term was certain to be formidable.

If unemployment refused to respond, or if control over inflation continued to elude him, Mr. Nixon's campaign for re-election faced serious problems on which the opposition was certain to capitalize.

Old Game Plan

The President began his third year in office with a new label for his fiscal policy and a new Secretary of the Treasury.

Mr. Nixon had sought to control inflation in 1969 with a combination of reduced federal expenditures, tight money and maintenance of existing relatively high tax levels. This policy, in a phrase borrowed from professional football—of which the President was an avid follower—was called the original "game plan."

Weakened by inflation, the economy under the influence of the 1969 policy slipped into recession late in the year. The stock market, which had begun to decline just as Mr. Nixon took office, continued on its downward path for a year and a half. But interest rates rose to historic high levels, and inflation continued unabated.

Congress cut taxes with the Tax Reform Act enacted in December 1969. A more liberal monetary policy was announced early in 1970, to be implemented by the Federal Reserve Board. It was designed to stimulate the

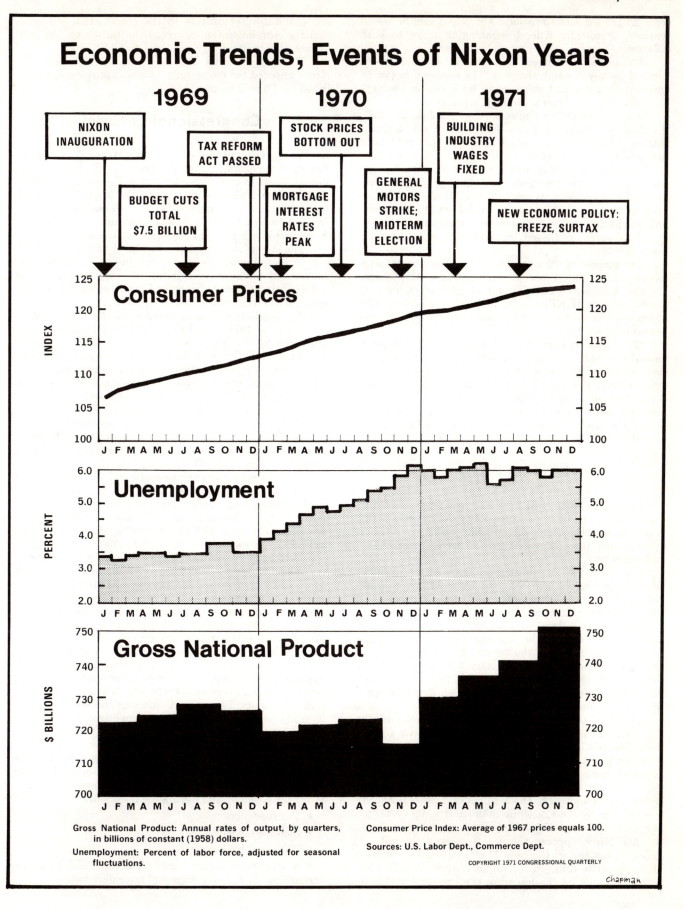

Economic Trends, Events of Nixon Years

1969   1970   1971

NIXON INAUGURATION

TAX REFORM ACT PASSED

STOCK PRICES BOTTOM OUT

BUILDING INDUSTRY WAGES FIXED

BUDGET CUTS TOTAL $7.5 BILLION

MORTGAGE INTEREST RATES PEAK

GENERAL MOTORS STRIKE; MIDTERM ELECTION

NEW ECONOMIC POLICY: FREEZE, SURTAX

Consumer Prices

INDEX

J F M A M J J A S O N D J F M A M J J A S O N D J F M A M J J A S O N D

Unemployment

PERCENT

J F M A M J J A S O N D J F M A M J J A S O N D J F M A M J J A S O N D

Gross National Product

$ BILLIONS

J F M A M J J A S O N D J F M A M J J A S O N D J F M A M J J A S O N D

Gross National Product: Annual rates of output, by quarters, in billions of constant (1958) dollars.

Unemployment: Percent of labor force, adjusted for seasonal fluctuations.

Consumer Price Index: Average of 1967 prices equals 100.

Sources: U.S. Labor Dept., Commerce Dept.

COPYRIGHT 1971 CONGRESSIONAL QUARTERLY

Chapman

economy toward a fast recovery. Mr. Nixon said he would continue to restrain federal spending in order to curb inflation.

But prices continued to rise and unemployment climbed steeply through the year. The economy began an unsteady recovery and was thrown back late in the year by a strike of the General Motors Corporation.

In his State of the Union message on Jan. 22, 1971, the President outlined a new approach, which was the guiding principle of the budget for fiscal year 1972 (sent to Congress one week later).

The new fiscal plan was a full-employment budget, which meant that the budget, with large deficits projected for both fiscal years 1971 and 1972, would have been in balance if the economy had been at full output and employment. The actual deficits represented the loss of federal revenues caused by economic performance below potential.

The purpose of the new plan was to stimulate a faster recovery from the recession. Accompanying the budget was the Administration's forecast of total economic output for the year (GNP)—$1.065-trillion—a projection with which most private economists disagreed and which later proved to be too high.

Mr. Nixon on Dec. 14, 1970, nominated a Democrat, former Gov. John Connally of Texas (1963-69) as Treasury Secretary, to succeed David M. Kennedy. The Senate confirmed Connally Feb. 8. Connally soon became the President's most influential economic adviser. He was regarded as the principal architect of the new economic policy. He also was considered to be a possible running mate for Mr. Nixon in 1972.

Incomes Policy

Mr. Nixon was urged with increasing frequency during the year to adopt an incomes policy. An incomes policy is a program of government influence on or intervention in wage and price decisions in the private economy to curb inflation.

Generally the Administration opposed an incomes policy as ineffective, and Mr. Nixon maintained an unremitting hostility toward wage and price controls well into his third year in office.

Yet the President took tentative steps toward an incomes policy early in the year when he intervened in the collective bargaining of the construction industry. Wage and price increases in the industry had been exceeding substantially those in other areas of the economy. Mr. Nixon tried unsuccessfully to get the industry to adopt a program of voluntary restraint.

On Feb. 23 he used his authority to suspend the Davis-Bacon Act, which required contractors on government-financed construction to pay prevailing (union) wage scales. A month later, on March 29, he invoked power to control wages and prices which Congress had given him the previous year and imposed a stabilization system on the industry. This was his first use of authority granted him by the Economic Stabilization Act of 1970, a new title added to the Defense Production Act.

Mr. Nixon opposed the new Act originally and said he would not use it. Congress May 5 passed an extension of the Act (HR 4246—PL 92-15) until April 30, 1972. Connally, testifying on the bill while the President was seeking voluntary stabilization in the construction industry, said the Administration accepted the legislation but still did not plan to use it.

The Act provided the authority under which Mr. Nixon imposed the freeze Aug. 15 and subsequently established his Phase Two program.

Congressional Criticism

Among the more persistent congressional critics of the President's economic policy was the Joint Economic Committee. In its March 29 report on the Economic Report of the President (which accompanied the budget submitted in January), the committee found "serious deficiencies" in the Administration's economic programs and judged the Administration's goals unlikely to be achieved.

The committee urged the President to adopt a clear-cut and comprehensive wage-price policy. It further recommended adoption of interim and long-term goals for inflation and unemployment and establishment of guidelines for the economy to meet the goals.

The committee recommended a speed-up in the effective dates, to 1971 from 1973, of individual tax reduction scheduled by the Tax Reform Act of 1969. A number of individual Senators and Representatives, in addition to committee members, endorsed this recommendation. Another proposal which gained congressional support was re-enactment of the tax credit for business investment, which had been repealed by the 1969 Act.

Both proposals were advanced as means of stimulating the economy to faster growth in order to reduce unemployment. Similar provisions were subsequently included in the President's tax bill.

Near midyear Congress passed a bill (S 31—PL 92-54) providing $2.25-billion for emergency employment in public service jobs at the state and local levels. President Nixon praised this bill, but he vetoed another congressional initiative—a $5.7-billion emergency public works bill (S 575) also designed to provide jobs.

Both bills reflected congressional concern over unemployment, which reached 6.2 percent of the work force in May, and mixed indications on the strength of the recovery from the recession.

Administration spokesmen singled out favorable indications as proof that the economy was progressing. They played down other indications which were less favorable. In March the Labor Department had discontinued its monthly press briefings on the unemployment rate, apparently in disapproval of interpretations of the figures by career-service economists who supervised their preparation. The Joint Economic Committee began a series of monthly hearings on the unemployment rates to take the place of the briefings.

On June 29 the President designated Connally as the Administration's chief economic spokesman. The Secretary announced immediately afterward that the President had ruled out four current proposals for stimulating the economy and controlling inflation:

- Tax reductions.
- Increased federal spending.
- Wage and price controls.
- A wage-price review board to monitor and influence, through public opinion, wage and price decisions.

Connally said the President was convinced that the economy was progressing and that further action was not necessary.

But the Administration was well aware that further action was needed, for various offices were already at work secretly devising the outlines and the justification for the new economic policy, which was to be revealed six weeks later. Connally had general responsibility for this effort.

Appearing on a television interview program, Connally on July 25 dropped a hint of what was afoot. He said international monetary problems, inflationary wage settlements and high interest rates might influence the President to impose wage and price controls.

On Aug. 4 a group of 14 Republican Senators publicly urged the President to adopt wage and price restraints to bring inflation under control. Twelve of the group said they planned to introduce a bill creating a wage-price board.

On July 28 the Administration had announced that the budget for the fiscal year just ended—fiscal 1971—had resulted in a deficit of $23.2-billion—nearly $5-billion more than had been estimated at the beginning of the year. It was the next-largest deficit since World War II, exceeded only by President Johnson's 1968 red-ink figure.

The nation's balance-of-payments deficit in the second quarter of the year was at annual rates of almost $23-billion on both the broad bases used to calculate the over-all position: net liquidity and official reserve transactions. These were record deficits, although they were subsequently exceeded by the third quarter figures.

Commerce Secretary Maurice H. Stans forecast on July 27 that the United States in 1971 faced the probability of a deficit in its export-import trade, which would be the nation's first in the 20th century.

Meanwhile the consumer price index had risen in May at an annual rate of 6 percent and in June at a rate of 7.2 percent. The Harris Survey reported that, in a sampling taken in June, only 26 percent of the persons questioned thought Mr. Nixon was doing a good job in economic matters while 70 percent gave him a negative rating.

Public Opinion

The Gallup Poll found in July that 49 percent of persons surveyed believed unemployment would be higher in six months while only 25 percent believed the rate would be lower. The Gallup organization found Republican support among business and professional persons at an all-time low—only 31 percent identified themselves with the Republican party while 34 percent said they supported the Democratic party. Surveying in August on the question of which party was best able to maintain prosperity, the Gallup Poll found that 46 percent of those questioned thought the Democratic party was better in this regard and only 23 percent had faith in the Republican party.

In a survey taken in late June, the Gallup organization found that 50 percent of the persons questioned favored wage and price controls.

What the indicators and public opinion surveys showed was that the old game plan was not stabilizing prices or fostering economic recovery fast enough to make an acceptable showing in 1972 and that the public did not approve of the results the Administration was getting.

New Economic Policy

President Nixon announced the new economic policy on Aug. 15, imposing the wage-price freeze and the surtax on imports without other warning to the public than hints dropped in late July and early August.

In addition to his primary orders and requests, Mr. Nixon:

• Ordered a 10-percent cut in foreign aid.

• Cut federal expenditures by ordering a year-long 5-percent reduction in federal employment, deferring for six months a federal pay raise scheduled for the beginning of 1972 and postponing the scheduled starting dates for his welfare reform and revenue-sharing programs, neither of which was likely to be enacted soon.

• Asked corporations to freeze dividends for 90 days.

The President appointed a Cost of Living Council, with Connally as chairman, to administer the stabilization program.

In his request to Congress for tax reduction, Mr. Nixon asked:

• An investment credit, but at 10 percent the first year and 5 percent after that, rather than at 7 percent, the rate of the previous credit and the rate Congress ultimately approved.

• Advancing to 1972 the increases in the personal exemption and standard deduction which were scheduled to go into effect for individuals in 1973.

• Repeal of the 7-percent excise on passenger automobiles.

In calling for tax reduction, the President's program coincided to a degree with recommendations of the Joint Economic Committee released only a few hours before his own Aug. 15 announcement. The committee recommended:

• Greater individual tax reduction than the President proposed.

• Increased (rather than decreased) federal spending.

The international part of the new policy accepted the two basic recommendations made by the Joint Economic Subcommittee on International Exchange and Payments in a report issued Aug. 7. These were to seek realignment of exchange rates of the currencies of the industrialized nations and to stop the interconvertibility of the dollar and gold.

Suspending convertibility of the dollar to gold had the effect of devaluing the overvalued dollar. The United States had long since severely limited the amount of its dwindling gold reserves which it would exchange for dollars held by foreign countries; it exchanged none for private individuals.

The high exchange rate of the dollar in relation to other currencies kept U.S. prices high and foreign prices low, both in American and foreign markets. Some of the strongest foreign currencies—the West German mark and the Japanese yen, for example—were substantially undervalued to maintain an advantage in foreign trade. Allowing the dollar to float in its value, relative to other currencies, reduced the U.S. disadvantage and the foreign advantage to a degree.

The program erected the surtax on imports as another means of reducing the advantage foreign traders had over their U.S. counterparts. The surtax evoked the most vehement protests from other nations, which charged that the tax was unfair, unnecessary and out of proportion to the actual disparities of the situation.

Connally explained at international meetings in London and Washington that other nations must help the United States turn its balance-of-payments deficit around by:

• Revaluing their currencies.

• Reducing or eliminating barriers to trade which discriminated against U.S. products.

• Bearing a greater share of the international defense burdens carried by the United States.

Generally, other countries took the position that realignment of currencies would not take place until the surtax was removed and then must include formal devaluation of the dollar as well as revaluation of other currencies. With realignment, most argued, the international monetary system should return to the fixed exchange rates generally prevailing before Mr. Nixon's action Aug. 15.

Phase Two

President Nixon addressed the nation Oct. 7 and outlined Phase Two of his stabilization program. He had previously—in a Sept. 9 address to Congress—said that the freeze would not extend beyond the original term of 90 days which he had ordered.

The President asked Congress to speed passage of his tax bill and to extend his economic stabilization authority for a year. He established a Pay Board and a Price Commission with authority to set guidelines for wage and price increases, issue orders and hear cases.

The Administration announced that, for stabilization purposes, the economy was to be divided into three sectors: the largest businesses and unions, which would be controlled most stringently and which would require prior approval for pay and price increases; less critical units, which would be required to report their wage and price actions, and the remainder, which would be controlled only through spot-checks and case investigations.

The control structure and distribution of authority showed that the Administration had not made the basic decisions on wages and prices but had left them to the Price Commission, composed of seven members representing the public, and the Pay Board, composed of five members each from labor, business and the public. The President won organized labor's participation in the Pay Board with a pledge that it would be autonomous—that the Cost of Living Council would not oversee either the board or the commission.

The Pay Board's general guideline of 5.5 percent per year for wage increases and its policy against retroactive payment of scheduled wage increases deferred by the freeze were adopted over labor's objections. The labor members considered terminating their relationship with the program but subsequently prevailed on Congress to provide for payment of the lost increases in most cases.

The Price Commission established an over-all annual guideline of 2.5 percent for price increases. The difference between the two guidelines was approximately equal to the long-term trend of increase in productivity. Phase Two began Nov. 14 in an aura of uncertainty heightened by the Pay Board's early approval of large wage increases greatly exceeding its guidelines.

Congress cleared the tax bill (PL 92—178) Dec. 9. The bill provided substantially more individual tax relief than the President had requested, offset in part by reduction of the benefits of the Administration's accelerated depreciation range system for business.

The requested extension of the Economic Stabilization Act (PL 92—210) was cleared by Congress Dec. 14. Some Democratic members of the House Banking and Currency Committee made efforts to postpone the extension Mr. Nixon requested until there had been time to study Phase Two in action and to establish in the law the elements of the stabilization structure and procedures. But there was not sufficient support on the committee or in the House. Similar Senate efforts failed. The Senate required confirmation of the chairmen of the Pay Board and Price Commission; this provision was incorporated in the final version of the bill.

Devaluation

President Nixon met Dec. 14 with President Georges Pompidou of France and subsequently, in a joint announcement, approved devaluation of the dollar as part of a general realignment of currencies. This concession by the United States broke an impasse in the international monetary arena which had prevailed since Aug. 15. It would have been virtually impossible politically for other countries to give up a major advantage in world trade by raising the value of their currencies if the United States had not agreed to devalue.

Moving with unforeseen speed, the major industrial nations, known as the Group of Ten, reached agreement on realignment at a Washington meeting Dec. 18. The dollar was to be devalued 8.57 percent by raising the price of gold to $38—from $35—per ounce. The West German mark and Japanese yen were to be raised the most through revaluation; the British pound, French franc and Canadian dollar were not revalued at all and the new values of other leading countries fell in between.

But the effect was that all were revalued in relation to the dollar. The currencies of West Germany and Japan, with which the United States had the greatest deficits in trade and international payments, effectively were revalued by 13 and 17 percent respectively.

Under the agreement the United States rescinded the import surcharge immediately. The monetary crisis which the new economic policy had deliberately precipitated was effectively resolved, and the way was cleared for negotiation leading toward attainment of the remaining U.S. international economic goals.

The International Monetary Fund placed the new currency values in effect on a temporary basis on Dec. 19. President Nixon, meeting in Bermuda Dec. 20 with Prime Minister Edward Heath of Great Britain, announced termination of the surcharge.

But only Congress could officially change the gold value of the dollar. Mr. Nixon asked Congress to grant him this authority early in 1972. Action was not expected until there were clear indications that other countries would begin dismantling trade barriers that discouraged American products.

1972 Outlook

Both the Administration and private economists forecast a good year in 1972—and a better year because of the Nixon program.

The Economic Report of the President and the Annual Report of the Council of Economic Advisers (CEA), sent to Congress Jan. 27, 1972, forecast the largest increase in GNP on record, further moderation of inflation and a modest decline in unemployment, as well as substantial progress against foreign trade problems and improvement in the balance of international payments.

The CEA forecast of a $98-billion GNP increase was corroborated by the consensus of private forecasts. The CEA report provided the following figures for GNP and other key measures:

(Calendar years, billions of dollars)

	1970 (actual)	1971 (preliminary)	1972 (forecast)
Gross national product	974.1	1,046.8	1,145
Personal income	803.6	857.0	924
Corporate profits (before taxes)	75.4	85.2	99

The GNP increase was approximately 9.5 percent over the 1971 total, compared with about 7.5 percent for the 1971 increase. About 6 percentage points of the increase, or about $60-billion, was expected to be in actual gain in output. The remainder represented price increases.

The broadest measure of inflation—the implicit price deflator of GNP—was expected to rise by about 3.25 percent in 1972, compared with a 4.6-percent increase in 1971. The expectation for the deflator was consistent with the administration's goal on inflation, which was that the rate would fall to the range of 2 to 3 percent by the end of 1972.

Consumer prices, which had slowed their rate of increase since the wage-price freeze was imposed Aug. 15, were expected to rise at a slightly higher rate than the deflator during 1972.

In constant (1958) prices, GNP was expected to rise about $44-billion during the year. This yielded the following figures for real GNP for the years 1970-1972:

(Billions of dollars)

	1970 (actual)	1971 (preliminary)	1972 (forecast)
GNP (1958 dollars)	720.0	739.5	784

Unemployment

No forecast, including that of the CEA, offered hope of reducing the unemployment rate to the accepted full-employment level of 4 percent of the labor force. The CEA predicted a vigorous rise in employment and a decline in the unemployment rate to about 5 percent by the end of 1972.

Many economists believed that an indirect relationship between prices and employment would again become apparent in 1972. According to traditional concepts, the rise in unemployment during 1970 and the high rate in 1971 should have been accompanied by a decline in the rate of price increases.

In 1972, many believed, a stronger growth rate would strengthen employment but make it less likely that the goal of the Nixon stabilization program—an annual rate of increase in the cost of living of 2 to 3 percent by the end of 1972—would be attained. A softer economy would, in this view, make the price goal more certain but hold unemployment at a higher rate than desired.

Politically, unemployment was of greater concern to the President. Improvement in consumer prices was evident, in comparison with the 5.5-percent increase in 1970. But, unless unemployment began to fall steadily, he was vulnerable to criticism of his stewardship over the economy.

At a closed-door briefing for Republican congressional leaders late in 1971, Mr. Nixon said he would put people to work raking leaves if necessary to drive the unemployment rate down. While an actual return to the sort of public works jobs associated with the New Deal was not anticipated, economists and others in the Administration were counting on an upsurge in output to shorten the unemployment rolls. Subsidized public employment, government programs and an increase in exports also were expected to create new jobs.

Mr. Nixon had other economic measures in mind. One of these was, in effect, a companion to revenue sharing with state and local governments, a proposal the President had been pushing for since 1969.

Mr. Nixon made a two-tiered program of revenue sharing one of the major goals of his Administration in 1971. It was to consist of general revenue sharing at an initial rate of $5-billion per year and special revenue sharing—a form of block grants totaling $11-billion the first year for six broad purposes. But Congress did not act on either proposal.

The Administration billed its program as a way to return a significant share of public funds to the state and local levels and, with it, a substantial share of decision-making responsibility. Viewed in another light, it also was a way to enable state and local governments to increase their spending without enacting new taxes or increasing their dependence on regressive taxes, such as the property tax.

At year's end the Administration was studying a new proposal to share federal revenues with local and state governments for education and perhaps other social purposes—also, like revenue sharing, without the usual strings attached to a federal aid program. Its major purpose was to relieve the burden on local and state taxpayers for the public services they were supporting. A secondary purpose was to stimulate expansion at the state and local levels.

To finance the program, the Administration had under consideration a new tax, in terms of American experience: a value-added tax. Widely used in Western Europe, a value-added tax is a national sales tax applied to the value added to goods at each stage of processing and handling. Though paid ultimately by the consumer, the tax is usually hidden in the price.

Whether Congress would approve such a levy, particularly in an election year, was problematical. The idea had provoked opposition previously, chiefly on grounds that the tax was regressive—that it cost the poor a higher percentage of income than those with higher incomes. But the prospect of property tax relief, however financed, raised a compelling campaign issue for 1972.

DRAMATIC SHIFT ACHIEVED IN RELATIONS WITH PEKING

"Any American policy toward Asia must come urgently to grips with the reality of China. This does not mean...rushing to grant recognition to Peking, to admit it to the United Nations and to ply it with offers of trade.... It does mean recognizing the present and potential danger from Communist China, and taking measures designed to meet that danger...this means a policy of firm restraint, of no reward, of a creative counterpressure...I would not recognize Red China now and I would not agree to admitting it to the UN...."

Richard M. Nixon, campaign, 1968

"A significant change has taken place among the members of the United Nations on the issue of admission of mainland China. We are now analyzing that situation...."

President Nixon, June 1, 1971

"The United States...will support action at the (United Nations) General Assembly this fall calling for seating the People's Republic of China. At the same time the United States will oppose any action to expel the Republic of China or otherwise deprive it of representation in the United Nations."

Secretary of State William P. Rogers, August 2, 1971

The Nixon Administration has been credited with bringing about the first stage of a momentous diplomatic revolution in United States' policy toward Communist China.

After two decades of hostility and nonrecognition of the People's Republic of China—the world's largest country with one-fourth of the earth's total population—the U.S. Government in mid-1971 announced a complete shift in policy:

• After 22 years of opposition, the United States would support the admission of Communist China to the United Nations.

• President Richard M. Nixon would personally go to China Feb. 21-28, 1972, becoming the first American President to visit the mainland and the first to deal face-to-face with the Chinese Communist government.

And, on Oct. 25 the People's Republic of China was admitted to the United Nations. The Republic of China (Taiwan) was expelled despite U.S. opposition and efforts at dual representation. *(United Nations action, p. 23)*

Although the shift in policy was a dramatic one, it was not sudden. The Administration's efforts seeking to expand contact with Mao Tse-tung's Communist government had been spread over two-and-a-half years beginning in early 1969 and could best be described as a series of slow and cautious moves toward rapprochement with Peking.

During that period the Nixon Administration had:

• Lifted a 21-year embargo on trade with China permitting free export of a wide variety of nonstrategic U.S. products and permitting commercial imports.

• Removed the $100 limit on purchases of Chinese goods which tourists were permitted to bring into the United States.

• Terminated all restrictions on the use of American passports for travel to China.

• Terminated in November 1969 the regular U.S. naval patrol in the Taiwan Strait.

• Announced the United States would reduce its military presence on the Asian mainland.

• Announced that it would remove all nuclear weapons which had been installed on Okinawa as a deterrent against Communist China.

• Suspended American air intelligence-gathering missions over mainland China.

The changes in U.S. policy toward Communist China reflected the view expressed by Mr. Nixon in his January 1969 inaugural address: the United States had passed the era of "confrontation" and was entering a period of "negotiation" with the Communist world.

And, two years later, in his second annual report on foreign policy, President Nixon forecast the U.S. acceptance of China's growing role in world affairs:

"It is a truism that an international order cannot be secure if one of the major powers remains largely outside it and hostile toward it. In this decade, therefore, there will be no more important challenge than that of drawing the People's Republic of China into a constructive relationship with the world community, and particularly with the rest of Asia....

"We are prepared to establish a dialogue with Peking. We cannot accept its ideological precepts, or the notion that Communist China must exercise hegemony over Asia. But neither do we wish to impose on China an international position that denies its legitimate national interests."

Remaining Problems

Despite efforts made in both Washington and Peking to begin a new chapter in Sino-American relations in mid-1971, it was evident that there remained serious complications. Among them:

• Settlement of the war in Indochina.

• American involvement in the Chinese Communist-Nationalist civil war through continued recognition of the Chiang Kai-shek government on Taiwan.

• Efforts to ease tensions with the Soviet Union, such as the strategic arms limitation (SALT) talks.

• The guarantee of Nationalist Chinese security under the 1954 mutual defense treaty and the Formosa Resolution of 1955 granting presidential authority to use U.S. armed forces in case of an attack on Taiwan.

• Maintenance of U.S. forces on Taiwan.

• The deep Sino-Soviet ideological rift and the frequent military clashes along their common border.

While the consequences of Mr. Nixon's initiatives to ease the rigid U.S. policy of isolating and ostracizing China could not be foreseen, his moves had definitely affected the domestic political arena. He had clearly staked out his claim as the peace candidate in the 1972 Presidential elections.

In 1966, Mr. Nixon was publicly warning that within five years the United States would be at war with China "if we reward aggression in Vietnam." His position had evolved by 1971 to the following, stated in an April 29th news conference:

"...the long-range goal of this administration is a normalization of our relationship with mainland China, the People's Republic of China, and the ending of its isolation from the other nations of the world."

It was thought ironical that Richard M. Nixon, who made his early reputation as a Communist-hunter, should be the very man credited with putting the United States back on speaking terms with 800 million Communist Chinese.

President Nixon actually became the beneficiary of two factors: general acceptance that world peace requires the normalization of relations with the People's Republic of China; and "pro-Communist" charges would not be hurled at Mr. Nixon the way they were at previous Democratic administrations.

President Nixon's efforts in the China-thaw were regarded as a remarkable achievement, whether viewed in the context of national security implications or domestic political impact.

Previous Administrations

Following the October 1949 Communist takeover of mainland China and the flight of the Nationalists to Formosa soon after, the Truman Administration assumed a wait-and-see posture toward Peking. But, with the outbreak of the Korean War and China's entry into the war in October 1950, U.S. policy and American opinion congealed into firm opposition of the mainland regime.

Thereafter, the U.S. Government focused on ostracizing Peking from the international community, containing Communist aggression and cementing the U.S. commitment to Taiwan. Anti-Communist sentiment reached a peak during the early 1950s.

The Eisenhower years (1953-1961) saw the continued hard-line position toward Peking.

Despite some expectations that the Administration of President John F. Kennedy would effect a major policy shift, the U.S. position remained basically unchanged during the Kennedy Administration. By the mid-1960s, however, there were indications that previous policy was being reappraised by the Johnson Administration in accordance with the President's overtures toward a general East-West detente. At the same time, however, the President and his advisers emphasized the need for vigilance against a continuing Communist Chinese military threat, with particular reference to the potential Chinese role in the Vietnam war and the country's potential nuclear capability.

Changed Climate

Immediately after the Nixon Administration took office, James C. Thomson Jr., a former East Asian specialist at the State Department, suggested that President Nixon was in a particularly favorable position to effect a change in U.S. policy. Democratic Presidents, Thomson wrote in the February 1969 *Atlantic,* "were acutely gun-shy on China policy; in the late forties and fifties Republicans had a political field day with the issue of the 'loss of China'.... A Republican President, and pre-eminently this Republican President, brings to the China problem some very special assets. Who, for instance, can pin the label of 'softness on Communism' on Richard M. Nixon when he makes overtures to Peking?"

Turning to the climate in Congress, Thomson observed, "Today much of the old so-called 'China Lobby' is either dead or retired. Equally important, the leadership of the new Congress lies with the relatively flexible Democrats, many of whom have been restive under the rigidity of (former Secretary of State) Rusk's China posture.... (They are joined by an) increasing number of moderate Republicans who have urged a review of China policy...."

Even before elected, Mr. Nixon, during his 1968 campaign for the Presidency, clearly outlined the need for a reversal in U.S. China policy.

"...We simply cannot afford to leave China forever outside the family of nations, there to nurture its fantasies, cherish its hates and threaten its neighbors. There is no place on this small planet for a billion of its potentially most able people to live in angry isolation...," he said.

Stressing what was to later become the Administration's Asian policy, Mr. Nixon said that "Only as the nations of non-Communist Asia become so strong—economically, politically and militarily—that they no longer furnish tempting targets for Chinese aggression, will the leaders in Peking be persuaded to turn their energies inward rather than outward. And that will be the time when the dialogue with mainland China will begin." He maintained that the world could not be safe until China changed and that the long-range goals of the United States would best be served by "pulling China back into the world community."

Speaking also in 1968 on China as a nuclear threat, Nixon said "At the end of this century, Communist China will have a billion people that will have unlimited atomic weapons and it can be exporting them all over the world, and it is essential that whoever is the next President of the United States develop policies now that will get Communist China to change so that we can open a dialogue with them."

On Jan. 27, 1969, Mr. Nixon stated in his first Presidential news conference, "Until some changes occur on their side...I see no immediate prospect of any change in our policy" toward Communist China.

Yet, by the end of the year, the Administration had made several cautious overtures toward increasing U.S. contacts with the Chinese People's Republic, despite the fact that at first Peking showed little interest in reciprocating.

Sino-Soviet-American Relations. A long-term relationship with Peking—drawing it into a constructive role in international affairs—appeared to be particularly necessary, not only for peace in Indochina but to give the Soviet leaders some pause for thought and reason for moderation in their own diplomacy. Mr. Nixon believed that China's continued isolation would be more dangerous to peace than their gradual involvement in world diplomacy.

One consequence of the deep Sino-Soviet idelogical rift and the frequent military clashes along their common border was that both Peking and the Soviet Union view improved U.S. relations with either as collusion. Peking for its part has repeatedly attacked the collusion of U.S. "imperialism" and Soviet "revisionism" in arms control efforts, has interpreted the U.S. position in the Sino-Soviet conflict as being pro-Soviet, and has expressed fears of a pre-emptive Soviet nuclear attack.

Summarizing the U.S. position in a major foreign policy speech in 1969, then Under Secretary of State Elliot Richardson acknowledged the danger of the situation:

"In the case of Communist China, long-run improvement in our relations is in our own national interest. We do not seek to exploit for our own advantage the hostility between the Soviet Union and the People's Republic. Ideological differences between the two Communist giants are not our affair. We could not fail to be deeply concerned, however, with an escalation of this quarrel into a massive breach of international peace and security. Our national security would in the long run be prejudiced by associating ourselves with either side against the other. Each is highly sensitive about American efforts to improve relations with the other. We intend, nevertheless, to pursue a long-term course of progressively developing better relations with both. We are not going to let Communist Chinese invective deter us from seeking agreements with the Soviet Union where those are in our interest. Conversely, we are not going to let Soviet apprehensions prevent us from attempting to bring Communist China out of its angry, alienated shell."

Nuclear Threat. In addition to the benefits to be derived from a Sino-Soviet-American detente, another need for improved relations with China was that country's eventual nuclear capability. China detonated its first nuclear device in October 1964.

Supporting the overtures to Peking, Sen. Stuart Symington (D Mo.) said in 1969 "Now that all peoples are beginning to realize the true implications of a nuclear exchange, it would appear that a change in our China policy is long overdue." The reaction of other Members of Congress to the growing Chinese nuclear capability has been to suggest involving Peking in international disarmament talks. Sen. Henry M. Jackson (D Wash.) made such a proposal as early as Nov. 5, 1969.

Vietnam. Would improved relations with China and a change in U.S.-China policy help hasten an end to the Vietnam war, or at least United States participation therein?

There was little doubt in the United States that American involvement in Vietnam was another factor which had had a significant impact on U.S.-Communist Chinese relations. As long as the war continued, a major source of tension between the two countries would remain.

From the American viewpoint, there was continued uncertainty and apprehension about Chinese Communist actions in Vietnam. From the Communist Chinese viewpoint, U.S. assurances that its aims were limited to ensur-

China Policy and the ABM

In Defense Secretary Melvin R. Laird's fiscal 1972 defense posture statement, one paragraph of the 191-page report was devoted to the Chinese missile threat.

Although China has clearly arrived in the nuclear age, emphasis on the country's threat to the United States as a nuclear power has been played down since early 1971.

In a Jan. 20, 1970, news conference, President Nixon focused on China as a threat requiring the deployment of a massive second phase of the anti-ballistic missile (ABM) system. Nixon argued that the second phase of the program was "absolutely essential against any minor power, a power, for example, like Communist China." Congress refused to authorize the expanded version of the ABM system later in 1970 and headlines warning of China's missile threat to the United States stopped appearing over stories quoting the ubiquitous, nameless "high Administration official."

In 1971 Dr. John S. Foster Jr., director of defense research and engineering, outlined for the Senate Armed Services Committee Chinese advances in weaponry:

"The Chinese have been testing since 1967 a thermonuclear device in the three-megaton class. The fourth such device was successfully detonated October 1970. They have continued to progress in propulsion and control is shown by their having launched a space satellite in April 1970 and another in March 1971."

Foster told the committee that China would probably have 10 to 25 intercontinental ballistic missiles (ICBM) in operation by mid-1977.

ing self-determination for the South Vietnamese were greeted with extreme suspicion, particularly on those occasions when U.S. combat activities were escalating.

Against this background, the Nixon Administration's policy of withdrawing U.S. troops from Vietnam may have had a positive effect on Peking's willingness to negotiate with the United States.

The Chinese also sent out signals suggesting they would back a new Geneva conference on Indochina and support the idea of a neutralized South Vietnam. And, American troops continued to leave Vietnam at a rate of several thousand a week. Thus, it appeared that improved relations between the United States and China would permit the United States to make a graceful exit from Vietnam.

Asian Policy. The Administration's intention of altering the U.S. role of "global policeman" also required a change in U.S. relations with Peking. The first detailed expression of this policy was contained in the Guam Doctrine enunciated by Mr. Nixon on the eve of his trip to Asia July 25, 1969. Henceforth, he said, the United States would seek to reduce its military presence on the Asian mainland, while providing Asian countries with the economic and military assistance they might need in assuming primary responsibility for their own defense.

The Chinese saw the Nixon Doctrine as contradictory in that while the United States proposed to reduce its commitments in the Pacific, it encouraged Japan and other countries to assume a larger military role. That, in turn could lead to greater anxiety on the part of China.

In an Aug. 5, 1971, interview with *New York Times* vice president and columnist James Reston, Premier Chou En-lai said that he found the Doctrine "indeed a contradiction." "There should be an effort at relaxation by all parties concerned," he said.

In order to implement the Guam Doctrine, the Administration would need to seek a mutual agreement with Peking on the renunciation of force. In light of a future reduced U.S. military posture in Asia, Peking may be more willing than it was previously to come to some sort of accommodation with the United States.

Some China experts in the U.S. government and the academic community are convinced that China, as it emerges from the chaos of the Cultural Revolution, is thinking politically beyond the Indochina war. Both Mr. Nixon and Secretary of State William P. Rogers are known to be tailoring the China policy to what they believe will be the realistic needs of Washington as well as Peking when the Indochina war has ended and new Asian security arrangements have to be worked out.

Trade. Peking is reported to be particularly interested in increasing trade with the United States. Yet, neither the Administration nor American business executives anticipate meaningful commerce with China in the foreseeable future despite the relaxation in 1971 of the two-decade embargo.

In theory, substantial trade could develop if Peking chose to shift some of its imports from Western Europe and Japan to the United States. Last year China imported some $2-billion worth of goods, 75 percent of which came from non-Communist countries. Peking exported an equal amount of goods.

The United States has had no trading experience since 1950 with Communist China. And, during that year, China bought only $50 million worth of American goods and sold $150 million worth of her products to this country.

A "China Trade Association," representing small manufacturers, was organized in Washington in March 1971.

The growth of trade between the two nations is apt to be limited by many factors:

• China is short of the things it could sell in quantity to the United States.

• Some raw materials it has in quantity the United States does not need.

• Doing business with the Chinese—as with any state-run economy—is difficult and time-consuming.

• Japan's closeness to China has given it a distinct competitive edge over Europeans wanting to trade there. The United States will likely encounter the same situation.

• Those in Europe who have traded with the Chinese have found them hard bargainers. The negotiations have taken a long time and profit margins have been low.

Speaking on the trade issue, scholar Alexander Eckstein urged unilateral steps toward the People's Republic of China. Eckstein, a professor of economics at the University of Michigan, told the Joint Economic Committee Dec. 9, 1970: "Seventeen years after the end of the Korean War it is about time to lift the embargoes pure and simple. It is an anachronism, a monument to bureaucratic rigidity and a symbol of a bankrupt China policy we have been pursuing for the last 20 years."

Nixon Administration and China

During its first year, the Nixon Administration took three cautious, but unilateral and unconditional, steps to improve U.S.-Communist Chinese relations:

• On July 21, 1969, the State Department announced a slight easing of travel and trade restrictions. (A total embargo had been in effect since President Truman invoked the 1917 Trading with the Enemy Act against Peking in 1950.) American tourists and residents abroad were allowed to bring into the United States $100 worth of Chinese Communist origin goods for noncommercial purposes. In addition, scholars, professors, journalists, university students, Members of Congress, scientists, physicians and Red Cross representatives were automatically entitled to have their passports validated for travel to mainland China.

• In November 1969, the Administration quietly ended the regular two-destroyer patrol (of the Seventh Fleet) in the Taiwan Strait. The U.S. Navy had maintained a presence in the Strait since June 1950.

• Dec. 19, 1969, the government announced that subsidiaries and affiliates of U.S. firms abroad would be permitted to sell nonstrategic goods to Communist China and buy Communist Chinese products for resale in foreign markets. Individuals would be able to bring products of Communist China origin into the United States for noncommercial purposes without limit on their value. The announcement followed negotiations early in the month on renewing the Warsaw sessions.

Warsaw Talks. The Warsaw talks between U.S. and Chinese representatives in Poland were the only official contacts between the two countries for 16 years. Despite the increasingly numerous and critical issues facing the two nations, the frequency of the ambassadorial talks had steadily decreased from 73 meetings between Aug. 1, 1955, and Dec. 12, 1957, to five meetings each in 1964 and 1965, three meetings in 1966, two in 1967, and one—the 134th—in 1968.

A meeting scheduled Feb. 21, 1969, was abruptly canceled by Peking—a little more than one month after Mr. Nixon took office. The meeting finally took place one year later, on Jan. 20, 1970, two years after the last previous session in Warsaw. The resumption of the talks and the announcement that another meeting would be held only one month later, on Feb. 20, was viewed by many observers as signalling possibly significant shifts in both Washington's and Peking's policies. But no one in the Nixon Administration publicly predicted what was likely to result from the discussions.

When the State Department announced March 15, 1969, that the annual extension of the general travel ban to Communist China, North Korea, North Vietnam and Cuba would be extended for only six months instead of the usual year, some observers speculated that a change of policy was in the offing; but the ban was extended another six months on Sept. 15, 1969.

Despite the Administration's policy of seeking to expand contacts with Peking, the President and Pentagon officials during Mr. Nixon's first year continued to emphasize Peking's aggressive intentions and pointed to the potential Chinese nuclear threat as a major justification

Nixon Administration Initiatives Aimed...

1969

Feb. 18. Secretary of State William P. Rogers implied that the U.S. was prepared to accept a Chinese recommendation that the two countries agree to principles of peaceful coexistence. He indicated that the Nixon Administration intended to extend previous offers for cultural and scientific exchanges. Rogers also said that a U.S. diplomat had been directed to propose the re-establishment of telecommunication links severed Nov. 18, 1968.

July 21. Eased restrictions on American travel to China and permitted tourists to buy Chinese goods up to $100 in value. Scholars, journalists, students, scientists and members of Congress would automatically have their passports validated for travel to Communist China.

July 25. The President—in what was to become known as the Nixon Doctrine—announced the United States would seek to reduce its military presence on the Asian mainland, while providing Asian countries with the economic and military assistance for "self-help."

Aug. 8. Rogers, during his Asian tour, expressed the desire of the U.S. to renew diplomatic talks with Communist China.

November. Suspension of patrol by the Navy's Seventh Fleet in Taiwan Strait.

Dec. 11. U.S. Ambassador to Poland, Walter J. Stoessel Jr., met with Chinese chargé d'affaires Lei Yang Chen in Warsaw, paving the way for resumption of U.S.-Chinese bilateral talks—begun in 1955—which had collapsed Jan. 8, 1968.

Dec. 15. U.S. announced that all nuclear weapons on Okinawa would be removed by the end of 1969. They reportedly had been installed as a nuclear deterrent against Communist China.

Dec. 19. Lifted the $100 limit on purchases of Chinese goods and permitted foreign subsidiaries of American companies to trade in nonstrategic goods with China.

1970

Jan. 2. Vice President Agnew, during his Asian tour, said the U.S. should seek "meaningful dialogue" with mainland China. He said he favored "initiatives to develop an atmosphere that will allow us to reduce the amount of military spending...."

Jan. 20. U.S.-Chinese ambassadorial talks resumed in Warsaw after a two-year lapse. A second meeting was held Feb. 20, and a third scheduled for May 20. The Chinese government canceled the May 20 talk due, they said, to the U.S. invasion of Cambodia. No future talks were held.

Feb. 18. Stated in the President's foreign policy report to Congress: "It is certainly to our interest... that we take what steps we can toward improved relations with Peking."

March 16. State Department continued relaxation of travel ban to Communist China.

April 29. The United States authorized the selective licensing of goods for export to the People's Republic.

July 28. U.S. Department of Commerce approved the sale by an Italian company to Communist China of 80 dump trucks containing General Motors engines and parts.

Aug. 26. Restrictions prohibiting American oil companies abroad from permitting foreign ships to use refueling facilities to and from mainland China were lifted.

Oct. 25. White House Press Secretary Ronald L. Ziegler indicated first softening of the U.S. position on UN membership for Communist China. Ziegler said: "The U.S. opposes the admission of the Peking regime into the UN at the expense of the expulsion of the Republic of China." The phrasing hinted at a U.S. "two-China" policy.

1971

Jan. 26. State Department revealed that the United States had been exchanging scientific informa-

for deploying the antiballistic missile system (ABM). *(Box p. 34)*

Administration statements about the People's Republic of China—most particularly those of Secretary of State William P. Rogers and Under Secretary Elliot Richardson, both of whom were leading advocates of increased contacts with Peking—seemed to have shed much of the cold-war vocabulary. Throughout 1969, both officials made it clear that the United States remained willing, and even eager, to renew the Warsaw discussions.

In an interview with *U.S. News and World Report* Jan. 17, 1970, Secretary Rogers said it was difficult to forecast what the Warsaw talks would accomplish. "We hope that we can open up some channels of communication," he said. "For example, we would hope that there might be reciprocal visits of journalists, educa-

tors and others. We hope that there might be more steps on trade matters...."

When the long-postponed 135th session was finally held Jan. 20, 1970, the topics remained confidential by mutual agreement. Caution was the watchword of U.S. officials. Peking was reported to be particularly interested in increasing trade with the United States. On the U.S. side, the Administration's unilateral actions in 1969 indicated receptiveness to a slight easing of the embargo.

The Taiwan Issue. The Taiwan issue during 1969 proved to be the major obstacle to a U.S.-Communist Chinese accommodation, even in the fields of trade and travel. Both Taipei and Peking insisted that Taiwan remain part of China; each firmly rejected any suggestion

...at Rapprochement with China: 1969-1971

tion with China since before 1949 and had continued to do so.

Feb. 17. The President, during a White House news conference, emphasized that the Laotian operation mounted by the U.S. presented "no threat" to Communist China and "should not be interpreted by Communist Chinese as being a threat against them."

Feb. 25. President Nixon referred, for the first time, to Communist China by its formal name, the People's Republic of China, in his foreign policy report to Congress.

March 15. State Department terminated all restrictions on the use of American passports for travel to China.

April 14. United States terminated 21-year-old embargo on trade with Communist China and announced that a long list of goods eligible for export to China would be released soon. The decision, announced by President Nixon, coincided with a Chinese invitation April 6 to a U.S. table tennis team to visit the mainland and with the team's friendly reception in Peking.

April 19. United Airlines applied to the Civil Aeronautics Board for permission to extend its routing system to include Peking, Shanghai and Canton.

April 21. President Nixon assured the U.S. Table Tennis Association that he "certainly will cooperate" with the association's invitation to the Chinese team to visit the U.S.

April 26. A special presidential commission headed by Henry Cabot Lodge, former chief U.S. delegate to the UN, recommended in a 100-page report that the U.S. try to obtain the admission of Communist China to the UN without the expulsion of Nationalist China. But, the report said, "under no circumstances" should Taiwan be expelled.

April 29. President Nixon expressed the hope that he could visit Communist China "sometime in some capacity."

May 7. U.S. Treasury Secretary John B. Connally announced a general license for the use of dollars in transactions with the People's Republic of China.

June 1. President Nixon announced that "a significant change has taken place among the members of the United Nations on the issue of admission of mainland China," and the U.S. was "analyzing that situation." The Administration, he said, would announce its position at the fall session of the UN.

June 10. A list of 47 categories of items considered exportable to China was released by the U.S.

July 9. President Nixon sent Assistant for National Security Affairs, Dr. Henry Kissinger, to Peking to talk with Premier Chou En-lai, announced July 15.

July 15. President Nixon announced that he will visit Communist China before May, 1972, "to seek normalization of relations between the two countries and also to exchange views on questions of concern to the two sides."

July 17. In view of President Nixon's efforts to improve relations with Peking, the nuclear weapons that were to be removed from Okinawa would not be placed closer to Communist China, U.S. government officials announced.

July 28. The U.S. government suspended American intelligence-gathering missions over Communist China by manned reconnaissance planes and unmanned drones.

Aug. 2. The U.S. ended 20 years of opposition to Communist China's presence in the United Nations by announcing it would "support action...calling for seating the People's Republic of China." The U.S. emphasized its continued resistance to any move to expel Nationalist China from the UN.

Aug. 17. U.S. representative to the UN George Bush, sumitted U.S. resolution supporting a "two-China" policy to the UN General Assembly agenda.

Oct. 20. Kissinger makes second trip to China.

Oct. 25. The UN General Assembly voted to seat Communist China and expel Taiwan.

Oct. 26. Kissinger returned from a six-day visit to China.

Nov. 30. Kissinger announces Mr. Nixon's China trip will take place Feb. 21-28, 1972.

---

of a "two-China" solution, since both claimed to be the sole legitimate representative of the Chinese people.

The United States was committed to defend Taiwan against armed attack by the Mutual Security Treaty of 1954 and the Formosa Resolution (H J Res 159—PL 84-4) passed by Congress Jan. 28, 1955.

The possibility of discussing a mutual Washington-Peking renunciation of force was raised Feb. 18, 1969, by Secretary Rogers, who said U.S. participants had been instructed to suggest at the Feb. 20 meeting (which Peking canceled) "consideration of an agreement on peaceful coexistence consistent with our treaty obligations in the area."

Some State Department advisers were wary of immediately bringing up the matter of peaceful coexistence or mutual renunciation of force, unless both sides

construed it to entail some kind of modus vivendi outside the Taiwan area.

The Nixon Administration during 1969 had ruled out any "two-China" policy. It continued to reaffirm the existing U.S. commitment to Taiwan's autonomy, but refrained from restating the previous U.S. position that the Nationalist government was the sole legitimate government of all China.

The gradual reduction of U.S. forces in the Taiwan area during the first year of the Nixon Administration led Fox Butterfield to conclude (Jan. 18, 1970, *New York Times* magazine) "Curiously, these changes have the cumulative effect of bringing the U.S. closer to meeting the Chinese Communists' demand that we withdraw from Taiwan and the (Formosa) Strait before any discussions of other issues, such as trade or visits by journalists."

But observers generally agreed in early 1970 that solution of the Taiwan issue was a long way off. Any easing of U.S.-Communist Chinese tension was likely to come about, they said, by very small steps in the areas of trade and cultural exchanges. Each government was in a transitional stage of developing policies toward the other.

1970

During 1970, the United States continued to relax trade and travel restrictions toward Peking.

Despite the official nonrecognition policy, the following tentative steps toward normalization between the two nations were undertaken in 1970 by the Nixon Administration:
- The U.S.-Chinese ambassadorial talks resumed in Warsaw after a two-year lapse.
- The selective licensing of goods for export to Communist China was authorized by the United States.
- The President noted that in 1970, 270 Americans had their passports validated for travel to the People's Republic of China. This brought the total number to nearly 1,000 though only three Americans had been permitted entry.

In his foreign policy speech in early 1971, Mr. Nixon said that these unilateral efforts would continue. Although Peking had made no new overtures to the United States and had given no indication of resuming the Warsaw ambassadorial talks, it had moderated its tone in foreign policy and had established diplomatic relations with Canada, Italy and Chile.

1971: Dramatic Shift

In his second annual State of the World report, President Nixon on Feb. 25, 1971, forecast U.S. acceptance of the growing role Communist China—the People's Republic of China—would play in the international arena.

The President repeated the U.S. commitment to the government of Nationalist China on Taiwan. But, he said, "The United States is prepared to see the People's Republic of China play a constructive role in the family of nations."

For the first time, the President referred to Communist China by its formal name, the People's Republic of China. Although his message to Congress and the nation did not include substantive changes in U.S.-China policy, it revealed a trend toward increased dialogue and contact with the Chinese people.

"The 22-year-old hostility between ourselves and the People's Republic of China is another unresolved problem, serious indeed in view of the fact that it determines our relationship with 750 million talented and energetic people," the President said.

He continued: "For the United States the development of a relationship with Peking embodies precisely the challenges of this decade: to deal with, and resolve, vestiges of the postwar period that continue to influence our relationship and to create a balanced international structure in which all nations will have a stake. We believe that such a structure should provide full scope for the influence to which China's achievements entitle it."

Presidential Visit

In April 1971, President Nixon raised the possibility of paying a visit to the long-forbidden land of Communist China.

At a meeting with the American Society of Newspaper Editors in Washington April 16, Mr. Nixon expressed the hope that he could visit China someday. A few days later on April 29, he returned to the theme at a news conference saying: "I hope and, as a matter of fact, I expect to visit mainland China sometime in some capacity...." Edgar Snow, an American writer who has had access to Chinese leaders for years, wrote in *Life* (April 30, 1971) that Chairman Mao told him in December 1970 that Mr. Nixon would be welcomed in China, whether as a tourist or as President of the United States.

Snow said that during his six-month stay in China in the fall and winter of 1970-71, he learned that "foreign diplomats in Peking were aware...that messages were being delivered from Washington to the Chinese government by certain go-betweens" to assure Chinese leaders that Nixon had a "new outlook" on Asia and wanted to end the impasse in Sino-American relations. It was believed there, Snow said, that Mr. Nixon had offered to send personal representatives to Peking.

It was during this period, the spring of 1971, that the Nixon Administration took what appeared to be a sudden shift in policy toward Communist China. The Administration:
- Terminated a 21-year-old embargo April 14 on trade with Communist China and announced that a long list of goods eligible for export to China would soon be released.
- Terminated all restrictions on the use of American passports for travel to China on March 15.

Nixon Announcement. On July 15 Mr. Nixon revealed to a nationwide television audience that his assistant for national security affairs, Henry A. Kissinger, had been diverted secretly from a round-the-world fact-finding mission to meet with Chinese Premier Chou En-lai in Peking July 9-11. Mr. Nixon said that he had been invited by Chou "to visit China at an appropriate date before May 1972," and he had accepted the invitation.

No American President has ever visited China. White House sources were quoted as saying the May 1972 deadline was the date before which the visit would have to occur to avoid becoming involved in the 1972 political campaign.

The President's planned visit changed the potential for the rapprochement sought by both Mr. Nixon and the government of the Chinese People's Republic almost instantaneously from a remote possibility to a practical prospect. The purpose of the trip, Mr. Nixon said, was "to seek normalization of relations between the two countries and also to exchange views on questions of concern to the two sides."

The President described the event as "a major development in our efforts to build a lasting peace in the world." It was clearly a breakthrough portending a likely end to 21 years of American nonrecognition of Mao Tse-tung's Communist government and two decades of hostility.

He stressed that his move would not be "at the expense of our old friends." This was interpreted as primarily reassurance for Nationalist China. But the Nationalist government was not assuaged. Premier C.K. Yen issued a statement of surprise and regret on July 16. Mr. Nixon assured Nationalist President Chiang Kai-shek, in a letter revealed July 20 in Taipei that the United States would honor its mutual security treaty commitment to the government on Taiwan.

The Issues. White House sources said U.S. recognition of Communist China was not likely before Mr. Nixon's trip, indicating that recognition was not a precondition posed by the Chinese. But recognition seemed the logical next step in the series of Administration initiatives which included rescission of travel restrictions and the April 14 termination of the 21-year U.S. embargo on trade.

The opening with China forecast a broadening of the focus of U.S. Asian policy from a settlement in Vietnam to a more general Far Eastern rapprochement.

Vietnam. Speculation arose immediately after the announcement of the President's trip that rapprochement with China would improve the chance of a negotiated peace in Vietnam. The White House tried to discourage this linking of China with Vietnam. Press Secretary Ronald L. Ziegler said that Mr. Nixon had declined to speculate on the Vietnam effect of the China journey and that such speculation would not be helpful.

Mr. Nixon's announcement reduced pressure on him to respond favorably to the North Vietnamese-National Liberation Front proposal, made in Paris July 1, to return all American prisoners of war by Dec. 31 if all U.S. troops were withdrawn by that date. But Chou, speaking in Peking July 19, said withdrawal of U.S. troops from Indochina must take precedence over other efforts to improve Chinese-American relations. In his Aug. 9 interview with columnist James Reston of *The New York Times*, Chou said: "(F)irst of all the question of Vietnam and Indochina should be solved, and not the question of Taiwan or other questions."

Members of Congress were divided as to whether the President would withdraw all U.S. combat troops from Vietnam before the trip and on Sept. 30 the Senate declared it U.S. policy that a withdrawal of U.S. troops from Indochina would be completed within six months. The Administration opposed the action. House conferees opposed the "six months" deadline and on Nov. 11 Congress cleared the amendment leaving it to the President to set a withdrawal date.

Soviet-U.S. Relations. Interpretations of the affect of the President's proposed trip on U.S.-Soviet relations differed, though they did not necessarily conflict.

In one view, the warming in U.S.-Chinese relations was a setback for the Soviet Union. It was an historic event in which the Russians had no part and dramatic evidence that Soviet efforts to improve its own relations with both the United States and China had failed to forestall rapprochement which excluded Moscow.

According to other opinion, the trip to Peking posed possible difficulties for U.S.-Soviet relations.

Reaction from Congress. President Nixon's announcement that he had accepted an invitation to visit Communist China won widespread approval from members of Congress in both major parties.

Democrats were nearly unanimous in praising the President's initiative toward closer relations with Peking. Some strongly anti-Communist Republican members warned against changes in the long-standing U.S. policy toward Communist China.

United Nations Issue

At the beginning of the 92nd Congress certain resolutions introduced reflected congressional interest in the idea that the 1971 session of the United Nations might open the way for the admission of the People's Republic of China and the simultaneous explusion of the Republic of China. Some members offered a "two China" approach as an alternative to the expulsion of Taiwan.

Presidential Action. President Nixon on July 9, 1970, had directed the 50-member Commission on the Observance of the Twenty-Fifth Anniversary of the United Nations to consult official and public opinion regarding United States participation in the UN.

The commission, headed by former U.S. Ambassador to the United Nations Henry Cabot Lodge and including prominent Americans from many professional fields, held public hearings in six cities before submitting its 100-page report.

On April 26, 1971, it urged that Communist China be admitted to the United Nations. The commission urged that the United States:

• Adopt the position that all firmly established governments should be included in the UN system inasmuch as the benefits to the United States for having such governments within the UN and subject to the international obligations laid down by the charter far outweigh the problems raised by ideological differences between various states; and that no member of the organization living up to its obligations under the charter be expelled;

• "Under no circumstances agree to the expulsion from the UN of the Republic of China on Taiwan but seek agreement as early as practicable whereby the People's Republic of China might accept the principles of the charter and be represented in the organization."

For two decades, the United States steadfastly had opposed the admission of the People's Republic to the General Assembly and to the China seat in the Security Council.

U.S. Acquiescence. The first indication that the United States would switch its stand opposing admission of Communist China to the United Nations came on June 4, 1971. The President at that time announced that "a significant change has taken place among the members of the United Nations on the issue of admission of mainland China," and the United States was "analyzing that situation."

Secretary of State William P. Rogers on Aug. 2, announced that the United States would abandon its firm policy of two decades and support the seating of the People's Republic of China in the United Nations at the fall 1971 UN General Assembly session.

But the Secretary made it clear that the United States would oppose any efforts to "expel the Republic of China or otherwise deprive it of representation in the United Nations."

Avoiding a position on whether the Nationalist Chinese government on Taiwan should retain its seat on the UN Security Council, Rogers said the United States would abide by the views of the majority of UN members on the question.

Chinese Response. Peking responded to the U.S. announcement by accusing Rogers of lying in order to push "the preposterous proposition of two Chinas." Rogers confirmed that he had no indication from either Peking or Taipei that they were willing to sit together in the United Nations. Premier Chou En-lai told James Reston, in an interview published in the *New York Times* August 10, that Peking would not join the UN unless Taiwan was excluded.

U.S. Resolutions. Just prior to the opening session Sept. 21 of the UN General Assembly's 26th session in New York, the United States announced Sept. 16 its intention to vote to seat the People's Republic of China in the UN Security Council.

But the Nixon Administration's efforts to prevent the ouster of Nationalist China from the UN encountered a setback Sept. 22 at a meeting of that organization's agenda committee.

The United States submitted two resolutions on the seating of a Chinese delegation in the UN. One text asked the General Assembly to agree that any move to oust Taiwan from its membership be considered an "important question" requiring the approval of two-thirds of the Assembly's members. The other text recommended that Peking be admitted as a Security Council member but noted that Taiwan had a continued right of representation in the General Assembly.

The UN Assembly's General Committee voted Sept. 22 against a U.S. proposal to have the U.S. resolution and a previously submitted Albanian resolution on the seating of a Chinese delegation discussed simultaneously by the General Assembly. The motion was defeated by a vote of 12-9.

The Committee voted 17-2 to put the Albanian resolution on the General Assembly's agenda as item 101. The U.S. resolutions, by a vote of 11-9, were to be placed on the agenda as item 105.

The Albanian resolution submitted July 15 called on the General Assembly to admit Communist China, seat it in the Security Council, and expel Nationalist China from all UN bodies. A similar resolution had been supported by the Assembly in 1970 by a vote of 51-49, but Peking's admission was blocked because the General Assembly had decided the question required a two-thirds majority.

The Albanian resolution was submitted well in advance of the Assembly's Sept. 21 opening date, reportedly to emphasize Peking's insistence on the expulsion of Nationalist China as a condition for its own membership.

Nixon Support. In an unscheduled news conference at the White House Sept. 16 President Nixon declared that the United States would support Peking's seating in the Security Council because such a move "reflects the realities of the situation."

Nixon said "in the event that the People's Republic is admitted to the United Nations, the seat in the Security Council would go to the People's Republic and that, of course, would mean the removal of the Republic of China from the Security Council seat." The President added: "We will vote against the expulsion of the Republic of China (from the UN) and we will work as effectively as we can to accomplish that goal."

On Oct. 4, Secretary of State Rogers warned the United Nations General Assembly that the expulsion of Taiwan might endanger the membership of other nations and weaken the United Nations as a whole. The struggle over Taiwan's continued membership in the UN became the first test of strength between Peking and Wash-

ington since Mr. Nixon opened the new dialogue between the two powers in mid-1971.

Kissinger Trip. Presidential assistant Henry A. Kissinger Oct. 20 made a second trip to Peking to make "concrete" plans for President Nixon's China visit.

UN Vote on China. After one week of intense UN debate on the China issue during which the United States was accused of exerting undue pressure for dual representation, the UN General Assembly Oct. 25 voted to admit Peking and to expel the delegates of Taiwan. The vote was 76-35 with 17 abstentions.

The United States, despite supporting the seating of Communist China, thus lost in its effort to keep Taiwan in the United Nations.

Prior to the vote, the U.S. resolution to declare the expulsion of Taiwan an important question requiring a two-thirds majority was defeated 59-55 with 15 abstentions. The United States had predicted victory.

The U.S. resolution for dual representation of Peking and Taiwan never came to a vote since the Albanian resolution was considered first and adopted. On the eve of the debate, the Peking government stated that it would accept nothing less than its substitution for Taiwan.

U.S. efforts to retain Taiwan's seat were said to have been badly hurt by the White House's dispatch of Kissinger to Peking in the middle of the China debate and his presence there at the actual time of the vote Oct. 25. Kissinger in fact remained in Peking two days longer than scheduled, returning the day after the UN vote.

Congressional Reaction. Most members of Congress expressed anger at the UN for the expulsion of Nationalist China and many favored slashing U.S. contributions to the peacekeeping organization. Most of the reaction centered around the $3.2-billion 1972 foreign aid bill being debated in the Senate at the time of the UN action. It contained $141-million for various UN agencies and was rejected Oct. 29 by a 21-47 roll-call vote.

Speaking for the Administration, Secretary of State William P. Rogers said the United States "will not support a reduction of funds for the United Nations in retaliation" for the vote. He emphasized that the United States would retain its ties with Nationalist China.

The White House had left all statements on the UN vote to Rogers in an apparent effort to keep the President's personal prestige separate from the voting setback and to avoid anything that might give offense in Peking and interfere with the President's 1972 China visit.

But, in what appeared to be a move to divert criticism from himself to the UN, Mr. Nixon, through Press Secretary Ronald L. Ziegler, denounced as "shocking" the "demonstration of undisguised glee shown by some delegates" after the Oct. 25 expulsion of Nationalist China from the UN. Ziegler said that Mr. Nixon supported the UN and wanted to see it succeed, but that action of some delegates "could lead to deterioration of support in Congress and the country" both for the United Nations and for the foreign aid program.

Change in Policy. On Nov. 30, Kissinger announced that Mr. Nixon would go to China Feb. 21-28, 1972. He also disclosed that the President believed the "ultimate relationship" between Taiwan and the mainland should be settled in negotiations between the Chinese themselves. This marked the first official public statement to that effect.

NIXON'S 1971 REQUESTS: ONLY 20 PERCENT APPROVED

The first session of the Democratic-controlled 92nd Congress approved one-fifth of President Nixon's legislative proposals. Missing from those passed were the "great goals" of the 1971 state-of-the-union message—welfare reform, environmental improvement, better health care, revenue sharing and government reorganization.

It was the third successive year that Congress failed to complete action on welfare reform and revenue sharing.

On the other hand, Congress handed the President victories on most of his drug and education proposals. A two-year draft extension, which the President had requested, also was approved—though almost three months after the draft law had expired.

As measured by Congressional Quarterly's annual boxscore, Nixon made 202 specific requests for legislation in 44 messages to Congress and public statements. Of those, 40—or about 20 percent—were enacted into law.

This reflected the detailed nature of Nixon's proposals as well as congressional inaction. Proceedings were not completed—or begun, in some cases—on many specific proposals on natural resources, taxes, small business, health or government operations.

Two major bills containing Nixon's proposals were in conference when the first session ended. They were the higher education opportunity bill (S 659) and the ocean dumping bill (HR 9727). Most of the President's other proposals awaited action during the second session.

The boxscore does not reflect issues unless they were publicly requested by the President or were the subject of messages to Congress. For instance, child care is not included in the boxscore, since Nixon did not make a request on the subject. But his veto of the legislation containing extensive child care provisions was an important event in the legislative year.

The boxscore also does not differentiate between major legislation and less significant proposals. (In District of Columbia affairs, however, one minor request of purely local interest was omitted.) The individual requests are itemized as they were presented.

Eight of the President's requests passed in 1971 were holdovers from 1970. Holdovers are included in this study only if they were repeated by Nixon in 1971. They are not included if he made the proposal in 1970 and did not repeat it in 1971.

Major Proposals

Following is a summary of the fate of Nixon's proposals during 1971.

Foreign Policy. The Senate ratified the treaty returning control of the island of Okinawa to Japan.

Congress approved a $5-million authorization to compensate the Micronesian people for World War II damages and established a five-member commission to settle their claims.

No White House Assessment

For the fourth straight year, the White House made no formal, post-session evaluation of how Congress treated the President's legislative requests. Aides of former President Johnson adopted the same stance in 1969, breaking a pattern set in 1961.

The President submitted bills to consolidate military and security assistance programs and to separate them from economic and humanitarian programs. The reorganization was incorporated in two bills: the International Security Assistance Act and the International Development and Humanitarian Assistance Act.

The Senate Foreign Relations Committee held hearings on the bills but did not report them; the Senate passed separate economic and military assistance authorization bills. The House postponed action on the reorganization and authorized all foreign assistance funds in one bill.

Nixon's plan would have established an International Development Corporation and an International Development Institute, which would have replaced the Agency for International Development.

The Senate authorized a total of $1.3-billion for the Asian Development Bank, the Inter-American Development Bank and the International Development Association. A $100-million Asian bank authorization had been killed by the Senate in 1970.

The foreign aid authorization bill, which Congress cleared Jan. 25, 1972, contained provisions authorizing the President to furnish aid to any nation or international organization to help control drug traffic.

Taxes and Economic Policy. Two of the President's major economic proposals—the 7-percent automobile excise tax repeal and the increase in personal income tax exemptions and deductions—sped through both houses. However, Congress reinstated the 7-percent business tax credit which was repealed in 1969 instead of approving the President's request for a credit of 10 percent the first year and 5 percent afterward.

Hearings were held in both houses on the President's $5-billion general revenue sharing plan. But, for the third year, Congress failed to approve that proposal. No bills were reported on the administration's plans for special revenue sharing for manpower, law enforcement, urban development, rural development, education and transportation.

The House Ways and Means Committee took no action on several administration-proposed tax measures.

National Security. The administration won its two-year military draft extension despite two threatened filibusters and a three-month lapse of the Selective Service Act.

How The Boxscore Works

The items tabulated in the Boxscore include only the specific legislative requests contained in the President's messages to Congress and other public statements.

Excluded from the Boxscore are proposals advocated by executive branch officials but not specifically by the President; measures endorsed by the President but not requested by him; nominations, and suggestions that Congress consider or study particular topics when legislative action is not requested.

Except for major proposals, presidential requests for District of Columbia legislation also are excluded from the Boxscore tabulation.

Routine appropriation requests, which provide funds for regular, continuing government operations, are excluded. Appropriation requests for specific programs, however, which the President indicated in special messages or other communications were important in his over-all legislative program, are included.

Because the Boxscore fundamentally is a tabular checklist of the President's program, presented in neither greater nor less detail than is found in presidential messages, the individual requests necessarily differ considerably from one another in their scope and importance.

Because Congress does not always vote "yes" or "no" on a proposal, CQ evaluates legislative action to determine whether compromises amount to approval or rejection of the President's requests.

Symbols in the Final Action column indicate whether Congress took favorable action on the proposal.

Complicating Senate passage were a number of amendments. They included a proposal by Sen. Mike Mansfield (D Mont.) for a nine-month deadline for troop withdrawal from Vietnam (which was accepted and later watered down in conference) and a proposal by Senators George McGovern (D S.D.) and Mark O. Hatfield (R Ore.) to force a troop pullout by Dec. 31, 1972 (which was defeated).

Mansfield's amendment deadlocked the conference committee for more than a month. The final compromise required that U.S. troop withdrawal be completed by an unspecified date, subject to the release of American prisoners of war. Congress cleared the bill Sept. 21.

Administration proposals for repeal of certain draft deferments and for a national draft lottery also were approved, but Congress exceeded the President's request for military authorization money by almost $1-billion.

Natural Resources. The Senate included most of the President's proposals in its four-year, $16.8-billion bill on water pollution, but the administration complained that the Senate version gave too much power to the federal government and not enough to the states. The House Public Works Committee was scheduled to report its version of the bill early in 1972.

Both houses included other administration proposals in their versions of an ocean dumping bill. There had been no conference report by the end of the session.

Public Works. The administration won approval of its bill to establish a bank to make loans to rural telephone companies and cooperatives. Congress also granted authority to the Farmers Home Administration to make direct loans to farmers.

Welfare and Urban Affairs. In an unexpected move, the Senate amended a Social Security death benefit bill to establish a work incentive program for welfare recipients. The House agreed to the amendment. It had already approved the program as a major provision of the administration's comprehensive welfare plan (HR 1), which was awaiting Senate action.

Congress provided a 10-percent across-the-board increase in old age, survivors and disability benefits instead of the 6-percent increase requested by Mr. Nixon.

The President won passage of the Alaskan Native Claims Act, which gave Eskimos, Aleuts and Indians 40 million acres of land and provided almost $1-billion to settle land claims.

General Government. The Senate passed the President's request for a Special Action Office for Drug Abuse Prevention to coordinate federal drug programs. Congress was cooperative on Mr. Nixon's program for drug abuse; in most cases, it approved the full amount of the administration's funding requests for drug abuse rehabilitation and law enforcement. (Health and Crime headings in boxscore.)

Congress approved the President's request for a non-profit Legal Services Corporation separate from the Office of Economic Opportunity (OEO). But Mr. Nixon vetoed the legislation containing that provision—a bill extending OEO programs. The President cited the comprehensive child-care provisions of the bill as the reason for his veto.

The Senate passed Nixon's measures on fair warranties and amendments to strengthen the Federal Trade Commission. The House held hearings on these proposals. By the end of the session, one house or the other had acted on almost all the President's consumer proposals.

While Congress extended the President's reorganization authority, his specific government reorganization plans—to establish cabinet-level Departments of Natural Resources, Human Resources, Community Development and Economic Development—got no farther than hearings in both houses.

Health and Education. The administration's proposals were included in the Higher Education Act of 1971 (S 659), which had not been reported from conference at the end of the session. Among other provisions, the bill continued existing programs of federal aid to colleges and college students and extended the program of educational opportunity grants for students in exceptional financial need.

The House included anti-busing amendments and the administration's desegregation aid program—$500-million in fiscal 1972 and $1-billion in fiscal 1973—in its version of the bill.

The Senate passed a $1.5-billion desegregation authorization bill as a separate measure in April.

Congress approved the President's proposal for a massive anti-cancer campaign but rejected a plan to

Source Key for President Nixon's 1971 Legislative Requests

The sources of President Nixon's 1971 legislative requests are indicated by symbols listed below. Page numbers refer to the text section of this book.

	Source, Message	Date	Page
A	University of Nebraska Speech	Jan. 14	110-A
B	White House Conference on Food, Nutrition and Health	Jan. 21	—
C	State of the Union	Jan. 22	2-A
D	Resubmission of Legislative Proposals	Jan. 26	6-A
E	Draft Reform	Jan. 28	21-A
F	Budget Message	Jan. 29	11-A
G	Federal Executive Service Message	Feb. 2	22-A
H	Labor Disputes in the Transportation Industry	Feb. 3	18-A
I	Revenue Sharing	Feb. 8	23-A
J	President's 1971 Environmental Program	Feb. 8	27-A
K	National Health Strategy	Feb. 22	33-A
L	Higher Education	Feb. 22	40-A
M	Consumer Protection	Feb. 24	41-A
N	State of the World Message	Feb. 25	45-A
O	Special Revenue Sharing for Law Enforcement	Mar. 2	55-A
P	Special Revenue Sharing for Manpower	Mar. 8	57-A
Q	Special Revenue Sharing for Urban Community Development	Mar. 5	60-A
R	Special Revenue Sharing for Rural Development	Mar. 10	64-A
S	Special Revenue Sharing for Transportation	Mar. 18	67-A
T	Reorganization of Government Volunteer Programs	Mar. 24	70-A
U	Executive Reorganization	Mar. 25	72-A
V	Cancer Control Month, 1971	Apr. 5	—
W	Special Revenue Sharing for Education	Apr. 6	79-A
X	Alaska Natives' Claims	Apr. 6	—
Y	District of Columbia	Apr. 7	81-A
Z	Marine Science Affairs	Apr. 7	—
AA	Summer Jobs for Disadvantaged Youth	Apr. 9	—
BB	District of Columbia Budget Message	Apr. 19	—
CC	Foreign Assistance Program	Apr. 21	82-A
DD	Wilderness Preservation	Apr. 28	89-A
EE	Salute to Agriculture	May 2	—
FF	Legal Services Corporation	May 5	88-A
GG	Cancer Cure Program	May 11	—
HH	Protection and Enhancement of the Cultural Environment	May 13	—
II	Railway Labor Dispute	May 17	
JJ	Energy Resources	June 4	90-A
KK	Drug Abuse Prevention and Control	June 17	94-A
LL	Declassification of World War II Documents	Aug. 3	—
MM	Nursing Homes	Aug. 6	—
NN	The Challenge of Peace	Aug. 15	—
OO	Grand Teton National Park Speech	Aug. 19	—
PP	President's Address to the Congress	Sept. 9	107-A
QQ	Minority Business Enterprise	Oct. 13	99-A
RR	Pension Plan Reform	Dec. 8	101-A

create an independent cancer research agency. The legislation located the program in an expanded National Cancer Institute in the National Institutes of Health and made the director an associate director of NIH. It gave the institute a measure of autonomy by providing that the cancer research budget would not be subject to NIH review.

Hearings were held on the administration's proposals for national health insurance, the family health insurance plan and health maintenance organizations, but no bills were reported.

Congress incorporated in the Health Manpower Act the administration's proposals for student scholarships, per-student grants to accredited schools and student loan forgiveness for certain medical school graduates.

The President received two of his three supplemental appropriations requests for drug programs. Congress approved $105-million for treatment and rehabilitation and $10-million for education and training. The President also requested an additional $25.6-million for the treasury department's drug control program; Congress approved $22.5-million.

Congress appropriated an additional $105-million for summer jobs for the Neighborhood Youth Corps instead of the $64.3-million the President had requested.

No hearings were held on the administration's pension plan bill, which was sent to Congress late in the session. The concept of the President's vesting rights proposal, however, had been covered in other hearings.

Agriculture and Labor. Congress approved a controversial $7.6-million additional agriculture appropriation to combat fire ants and other pests. Sen. Gaylord Nelson (D Wis.) offered an amendment to delete the appropriation on the grounds that the chemicals used to destroy the ants injured the environment. The Senate defeated his amendment on a 28-53 roll call.

The President in May requested emergency legislation stopping a national railroad strike and providing until July 1 to reach a settlement. Both houses of Congress rejected this proposal, providing a deadline of Oct. 1 instead and authorizing a 13.5-percent pay increase for railroad workers.

PRESIDENTIAL BOXSCORE FOR 1971

Following is a list of President Nixon's specific legislative requests to Congress in 1971 and a summary of the action taken on each, in tabular form. A letter in parentheses following each item indicates the Presidential statement or message which was the most definitive source of the request. A key to the sources appears on the preceding page. Each treaty ratification request made during the Nixon administration is followed by the date the treaty was sent to the Senate.

STATUS KEY

√ Favorable Action.
X Unfavorable Action.
No Action Taken.
H Hearings Held.
Congressional Inaction Constitutes Favorable Action.
***** Request Previously Submitted, But Denied or Not Acted Upon.

Foreign Policy

TRADE

	1 HOUSE COMMITTEE ACTION	2 HOUSE FLOOR ACTION	3 SENATE COMMITTEE ACTION	4 SENATE FLOOR ACTION	5 FINAL OUTCOME	6 PUBLIC LAW NUMBER
1. Authorize U.S. participation in system of generalized tariff preferences for developing countries. (CC)						

FOREIGN AID

	1	2	3	4	5	6
1.* Authorize a $5-million supplemental appropriation to compensate Micronesian people for World War II damages. (D)	√	√	√	√	√	39
2.* Establish a five-member commission to settle Micronesian claims from World War II. (D)	√	√	√	√	√	39
3.* Provide for additional immigration from Western hemisphere countries, with special provisions for Mexico and Canada. (D)						
4.* Authorize $100-million for the Special Fund of the Asian Development Bank. (D)	H		√	√		
5.* Authorize $900-million for the corresponding fund of the Inter-American Development Bank. (D)	H		√	√		
6.* Waive visa requirement for all business and pleasure visits of ninety days or less by nationals of countries designated by the secretary of state. (D)						
7. Authorize an annual contribution of $320-million for three years to the International Development Association to double its low interest lending capacity. (N)	H		√	√		
8. Enact the International Security Assistance Act to distinguish between security programs and development and humanitarian assistance programs and to provide a separate organizational structure for security. (CC)	X	X	√	√		
9. Enact the International Development and Humanitarian Assistance Act to distinguish between development and humanitarian assistance programs and security assistance programs and to provide a separate organizational structure for development and humanitarian assistance. (CC)	X	X	√	√		
10. Authorize $1,275-million to the International Development Institute for a three-year period. (CC)						
11. Authorize $100-million for the President's foreign assistance contingency fund in fiscal year 1972. (CC)	X	X	X	X	X	
12. Amend and approve the International Security Assistance Act of 1971 to permit assistance to presently proscribed nationals in their efforts to stop drug trafficking. (KK)		√	√	√	√	201
13. Amend and approve the International Humanitarian Assistance Act of 1971 to permit assistance to presently proscribed nationals in their efforts to stop drug trafficking. (KK)		√	√	√	√	201

TREATIES

	1	2	3	4	5	6

Consent to ratification of:

1. Hague Convention for the Suppression of Unlawful Seizure of Aircraft. 4/15/71 — 3: √, 4: √, 5: √, 6: —
2. Treaty resolving pending boundary differences and maintaining the Rio Grande and Colorado Rivers as the international boundary between the United States and Mexico. 4/21/71 — 3: √, 4: √, 5: √, 6: —
3. Protocol to the International Convention for the Northwest Atlantic Fisheries relating to amendments to the Convention. 5/11/71
4. Convention drafted by the Organization of American States to prevent and punish acts of terrorism taking the form of crimes against persons and related extortion that are of international significance. 5/11/71
5. Convention with Japan for avoidance of double taxation and fiscal evasion with respect to taxes on income. 5/11/71 — 3: √, 4: √, 5: √, 6: —
6. International Wheat Agreement consisting of Wheat Trade Convention and Food Aid Convention. 6/2/71 — 3: √, 4: √, 5: √, 6: —
7. Convention on Psychotropic Substances limiting to medical and scientific uses those manufactured drugs of a mind-altering nature which are liable to abuse but are not covered by existing treaties. 6/29/71
8. Treaty on the Prohibition of the Emplacement of Nuclear Weapons and Other Weapons of Mass Destruction on the Seabed and the Ocean Floor and in the Subsoil Thereof. 2/11/71
9. Locarno Agreement Establishing an International Classification for Industrial Designs. 8/3/71 — 3: √, 4: √, 5: √, 6: —
10. Agreement with Japan concerning the Ryukyu and Daito Islands, providing for the reversion of Okinawa to Japan and for the continuation of the Mutual Security Treaty, the Status of Forces Agreement of 1960 and the Treaty of Friendship, Commerce and Navigation of 1953. 9/21/71 — 3: √, 4: √, 5: √, 6: —
11. Protocol amending the Convention on Civil Aviation to enlarge from 27 to 30 the membership of the Council of the International Civil Aviation Organization. 10/1/71 — 3: √, 4: √, 5: √, 6: —
12. Vienna Convention on the Law of Treaties. 11/22/71

Taxes and Economic Policy

TAXES

	1	2	3	4	5	6

1.* Prohibit any use against the taxpayer of information obtained through his compliance with the federal wagering tax regulation. (D) — 4: √, 5: X
2.* Amend federal wagering tax to broaden coverage and increase level of taxation. (D)
3.* Increase airline passenger ticket tax 0.5 percent. (D)
4.* Add $2 to present $2 departure tax on all international flights. (D)
5.* Raise federal tax on diesel fuel to 6 cents per gallon. (D)
6.* Change annual use tax on trucks to a graduated tax schedule ranging from $3.50 to $9.50 per thousand pounds, to be applied to truck combinations weighing more than 26,000 pounds. (D)
7.* Authorize the Treasury Department to write off Federal Reserve Bank notes. (D)
8.* Remove the limitation of $200-million on such write-offs. (D)
9. Enact a $5-billion program of general revenue sharing to state and local governments (I) — 1: H, 2: H
10.* Impose a special tax to make the price of unleaded gasoline lower than the price of leaded gasoline. (J)
11. Provide $500-million for special revenue sharing for law enforcement. (O)
12. Provide $2-billion for special revenue sharing for manpower. (P) — 1: H, 2: H
13. Authorize $100-million program of planning and management assistance to states, areawide agencies and localities. (Q)
14. Provide $2-billion for special revenue sharing for urban community development. (Q) — 1: H, 2: H
15. Provide $1.1-billion for special revenue sharing for rural community development. (R) — 1: H, 2: H
16. Provide $2.6-billion for special revenue sharing for transportation. (S) — 1: H, 2: H
17. Provide $2.8-billion for special revenue sharing for education. (W) — 1: H, 2: H
18. Establish a 10-percent job development credit for one year, with a 5-percent credit after Aug. 15, 1972. (NN) — 1: X, 2: X, 3: X, 4: X, 5: X

	1	2	3	4	5	6
19. Repeal the 7-percent excise tax on automobiles. (NN)	✓	✓	✓	✓	✓	178
20. Speed up the personal income tax exemptions scheduled for Jan. 1, 1973 to Jan. 1, 1972. (NN)	✓	✓	✓	✓	✓	178
20. Amend revenue sharing proposals to postpone implementation for three months. (NN)						

SMALL BUSINESS

	1	2	3	4	5	6
1.* Allow private and corporate lenders an income tax deduction equal to 20 percent of the interest earned on Small Business Administration guaranteed loans to small businesses and minority enterprises. (D)						
2.* Provide managerial training to disadvantaged persons going into business for themselves. (D)			✓	✓		
3.* Authorize banks to become sole sponsors of minority enterprise small business investment companies (MESBICs). (D)			X	X		
4.* Authorize the Small Business Administration to pay interest subsidies on loans it guarantees, in cases of demonstrated need. (D)			✓	✓		
5.* Liberalize net operating loss carryover rules and stock option provisions for qualified small businesses. (D)						
6.* Allow tax deduction for contributions to nonprofit MESBICs.						
7. Appropriate an additional $40-million to the Office of Minority Business Enterprise. (QQ)	✓	✓	✓	✓	✓	184
8. Lower the level of private financing required to qualify for financing from the Small Business Administration on a three-for-one basis. (QQ)						
9. Provide increased equity to MESBICs in the form of preferred stock to be purchased by the Small Business Administration in place of part of the debt instrument purchased by that agency under current law.						
10. Lower the interest rate on Small Business Administration loans to MESBICs to three points below the normal rate set by the Treasury Department during the first five years of the loan. (QQ)						

National Security

	1	2	3	4	5	6
1.* Extend Defense Production Act for two years. (D)						
2.* Amend Defense Production Act by creating a new method of financing the production expansion provisions. (D)						
3.* Amend Defense Production Act by eliminating restriction on guaranteed transactions imposed the previous year. (D)						
4.* Amend Defense Production Act by authorizing the President to make adjustments in civilian pay and personnel administration to assure the effective functioning of government agencies in a civil defense emergency. (D)						
5. Authorize $1.5-billion to the military, most of which was for a pay raise for enlisted men with less than two years of service and one-fifth of which was for expansion in recruiting, medical scholarships, ROTC, improvement of housing and other programs. (E)	X	X	X	X	X	
6. Authorize test program of special pay incentives designed to attract more volunteers into training for Army combat skills. (E)	X	X	✓	✓	X	
7. Extend military draft induction authority for two years, to July 1, 1973. (E)	✓	✓	✓	✓	✓	129
8. Phase out undergraduate student deferments and divinity student exemptions. (E)	✓	✓	✓	✓	✓	129
9. Establish uniform national draft call by lottery sequence numbers each month. (E)	✓	✓	✓	✓	✓	129

Resources and Public Works

NATURAL RESOURCES

	1	2	3	4	5	6
1.* Create an Environmental Financing Authority to assist in securing loans for communities for water pollution control facilities. (F)	H	✓				
2. Authorize and appropriate $6-billion over three years to provide federal share of waste treatment facilities program. (J)	H		X	X		
3.* Revise existing money allocation formula from 30 percent to 40 percent for federal construction grants for community pollution control facilities, provided the state agrees to pay 25 percent through grants to localities. (J)	H		X	X		

	Item	1	2	3	4	5	6
4.	Amend existing law on federal construction grants to induce communities to provide for expansion and replacement of treatment facilities on a reasonably self-sufficient basis. (J)	H		√	√		
5.	Require municipalities receiving federal assistance for constructing treatment facilities to recover from industrial users the portion of project costs allocable to treatment of their wastes. (J))	H		√	√		
6.*	Extend federal-state water quality program to cover all navigable waters and their tributaries, ground waters and waters of contiguous zones. (J)	H		√	√		
7.*	Revise federal-state water quality standards to impose precise effluent limitations on both industrial and municipal sources. (J)	H		√	√		
8.	Establish federal water quality standards similar to those in the Clean Air Amendments of 1970 to regulate discharge of hazardous substances. (J)	H		√	√		
9.	Establish standards requiring best practicable technology to be used in new industrial facilities to ensure water quality. (J)	H		√	√		
10.	Authorize administrator of the Environmental Protection Agency to require prompt revision of water quality standards when necessary. (J)	H		√	√		
11.	Authorize administrator of EPA to issue abatement orders swiftly and to impose administrative fines of up to $25,000 per day and up to $50,000 per day for repeated violations. (J)	H		√	√		
12.*	Authorize administrator of EPA to seek immediate injunctive relief in emergency situations in which severe water pollution constitutes an imminent danger to health, or threatens irreversible damage to water quality. (J)	H		X	X		
13.	Replace enforcement conference and hearing mechanism with a provision for swifter public hearings as a prelude to issuance of abatement orders or requiring revision of standards. (J)	H		√	√		
14.	Authorize legal actions against violations of standards by private citizens, in order to bolster state and federal enforcement efforts. (J)	H		√	√		
15.	Empower administrator of EPA to require reports by any person responsible for discharging effluents covered by water quality standards. (J)	H		√	√		
16.*	Triple federal grants to state pollution control enforcement agencies over four-year period—from $10-million to $30-million. (J)	H		X	X		
17.	Control use of pesticides in appropriate circumstances through registration procedure providing for designation of pesticides for "general use," "restricted use," or "use by permit only." (J)	X	X				
18.	Streamline procedure for cancellation of a pesticide registration. (J)	√	√				
19.	Authorize administrator of EPA to stop sale or use of, and to seize, pesticides being distributed or held in violation of federal law. (J)	X	X				
20.	Empower administrator of EPA to restrict the use or distribution of any substance which he found hazardous to human health or the environment. (J)	X	X				
21.	Authorize administrator of PEA to stop sale or use of any substance in violation of the legislation and to seek immediate injunctive relief when use or distribution of a substance presented an imminent hazard to health or the environment. (J)	X	X				
22.	Authorize administrator of EPA to prescribe minimum standard tests to be performed on toxic substances. (J)			H			
23.	Establish a national policy banning unregulated ocean dumping of all materials and placing strict limits on ocean disposal of any materials harmful to the environment. (J)	√	√	√	√		
24.	Require permit from the administrator of EPA for dumping any material into oceans, estuaries or Great Lakes. (J)	√	√	√	√		
25.	Authorize administrator of EPA to ban dumping of wastes dangerous to the marine ecosystem. (J)	√	√	√	√		
26.	Authorize administrator of EPA to set noise standards on transportation, construction and other equipment and require labeling of noise characteristics of certain products. (J)	H		H			
27.	Establish a national land use policy to encourage states, in cooperation with local governments, to plan for and regulate major developments affecting growth and the use of critical land areas. (J)	H		H			
28.	Require establishment within each state or region a single agency with responsibility for assuring consideration of environmental matters in certification of specific power plant sites and transmission line routes. (J)	H					
29.	Enact Mined Area Protection Act to establish federal requirements and guidelines for state programs to regulate environmental consequences of surface and underground mining. (J)						

	1	2	3	4	5	6
30.* Enact Ports and Waterways Safety Act increasing authority of Coast Guard to protect against oil spills. (Z)	✓	✓				
31. Appropriate an additional $12-million to the Soil Conservation Service for more manpower for soil conservation. (EE)	✓	✓	✓	✓	✓	35

PUBLIC WORKS

1. Permit federal insurance of home improvement loans for restoration of historic residential properties to a maximum of $15,000 per dwelling unit. (J)

PARKS AND RECREATION AREAS

1. Amend the Internal Revenue Code to expand the use of charitable land transfers for conservation purposes. (J)
2. Reform state grant program to make allocation of federal grants for purchase and development of recreation lands consistent with population distribution. (J)

	1	2	3	4	5	6
3. Add 14 areas to the National Wilderness System. (DD)	H		✓	✓		

4. Establish Gateway National Recreation Area in New York and New Jersey. (OO)

Welfare and Urban Affairs

TRANSPORTATION

	1	2	3	4	5	6
1.* Empower secretary of transportation to prescribe and enforce standards and regulations for a coordinated safety program in American waters. (D)	✓	✓	✓	✓	✓	75
2.* Require certain vessels on inland and coastal waterways to carry equipment for direct bridge-to-bridge contact. (D)	✓	✓	✓	✓	✓	63

VETERANS

1.* Increase the Veterans Administration budget by $14-million to permit immediate initiation of drug rehabilitation programs. (KK)

INDIANS

	1	2	3	4	5	6
1.* Provide cash payment of $500-million to Alaskan natives and grant them a 2-percent share, up to a maximum of $500-million in oil revenues generated on public lands in Alaska. (X)	✓	✓	✓	✓	✓	203
2.* Provide full title to 40-million acres of land to Alaskan natives. (X)	✓	✓	✓	✓	✓	203
3.* Require that the corporation managing these assets for the Alaskan natives be entirely native-controlled. (X)	✓	✓	✓	✓	✓	203

GENERAL WELFARE

	1	2	3	4	5	6
1.* Enact the family assistance program of the Welfare Reform Act to provide guaranteed welfare payments for poor families with children, including the working poor. (B)	✓	✓	H			
2. Enact higher (6 percent) Social Security benefits. (B)	X	X	X	X	X	
3.* Increase minimum disability compensation under the Longshoremen's and Harbor Workers' Compensation Act and liberalize certain other provisions. (D)						
4. Provide automatic Social Security adjustments for increases in the cost of living, and increase widows' pensions. (F)	✓	✓	H			
5. Provide additional training opportunities under the Welfare Reform Act for employable welfare recipients and incentives for them to accept suitable employment or job training. (F)	✓	✓	✓	✓	✓	223

6. Amend welfare reform proposals to postpone implementation for one year. (NN)

General Government

CRIME

1. Authorize judicial officers, under prescribed conditions, to require that suspects give significant non-testimonial evidence, such as blood samples or fingerprints. (D)

	1	2	3	4	5	6
2. Provide $2-million to research and develop equipment and techniques for detection of illegal drugs and drug traffic. (KK)			✓	✓	✓	77

	1	2	3	4	5	6

3. Permit chemists to submit written findings of analyses in drug cases. (KK)
4. Provide $1-million for Bureau of Narcotics and Dangerous Drugs for training foreign narcotics enforcement officers. (KK) — √ (3) √ (4) √ (5) 77 (6)

DISTRICT OF COLUMBIA

(Major Requests Only)

1.* Create a Federal City Bicentennial Corporation to prepare plans for revitalizing the heart of Washington, D.C., and to generate maximum private and commercial investment. (D)
2.* Authorize District of Columbia government to issue its own local bonds and to limit borrowing according to a permanent flexible formula based on district revenues. (D)
3. Extend for six months the authority of the Commission on the Organization of the Government of the District of Columbia and authorize it to prepare a second report on expanded self-government for the district. (Y) — √ (1) √ (2) √ (3) √ (4) √ (5) 25 (6)
4. Enact supplemental appropriation request for fiscal year 1971 to permit the district to maintain its share of support for the Blue Plains water pollution control plant. (Y)
5. Establish a development bank for the District of Columbia. (Y)

Consumer Protection

1.* Enact a Consumer Fraud Prevention Act to make unfair and deceptive practices unlawful and to permit individual or class action consumer suits for violation of the Act. (M) — H (3)
2. Establish a product safety program within the Department of Health, Education and Welfare and grant the Secretary authority to fix minimum safety standards for products and ban products that fail to meet standards. (M) — H (1) H (2)
3. Amend the Federal Trade Commission Act to increase effectiveness of the Federal Trade Commission. (M) — H (1) √ (3) √ (4)
4.* Enact Consumer Products Test Methods Act to provide incentives for increasing the amount of accurate and relevant information provided consumers about complex consumer products. (M)
5.* Enact a Fair Warranty Disclosure Act for clearer warranties, and prohibit use of deceptive warranties. (M) — H (1) √ (3) √ (4)
6.* Enact Drug Identification Act to require identification coding of prescription drug tablets and capsules. (M)
7. Authorize Federal Trade Commission to seek preliminary injunctions in Federal courts against unfair or deceptive business practices. (M) — H (1) √ (3) √ (4)
8. Adjust penalty schedule for violation of FTC cease-and-desist orders from maximum of $5,000 per violation to maximum of $10,000 per violation. (M) — H (1) √ (3) √ (4)
9. Enact Wholesome Fish and Fishery Products Act to provide for inspection of domestic and imported fish and fishery products during their harvesting, processing and transport. (Z) — √ (3) √ (4)

Government Operations

1.* Extend General Services Administration authority to police federal property to all buildings leased or occupied by federal agencies. (D)
2.* Prohibit obstruction of passages into or out of government offices, use of loud, abusive or threatening language, all disorderly conduct aimed at disruption of government business and all physical violence within a government facility. (D)
3. Permit Farmers Home Administration to substitute insured for direct loans to farmers up to a level of $275-million for fiscal year 1972. (D) — √ (1) √ (2) √ (3) √ (4) √ (5) 133 (6)
4. Create mixed-ownership bank to make loans ranging from 4 percent up to market interest rates to telephone companies and cooperatives which rely almost exclusively on the Rural Electrification Administration for their financing. (D)
5.* Permit the President to merge related federal assistance programs. (D) — √ (1) √ (2) √ (3) √ (4) √ (5) 12 (6)
6.* Authorize Federal agencies to pool certain related funds and adopt common administrative procedures to be carried out by a lead agency. (D)
7.* Authorize Atomic Energy Commission to collect license fees from any other government agency engaged in generating electric power on the same basis as charges to other electric utility systems for licensing nuclear power plants. (D)

	1	2	3	4	5	6
8.* Clarify President's authority to designate the chairman of the Federal Power Commission. (D)						
9.* Remove the Cost Accounting Standards Board from the authority of Congress. (D)						
10.* Authorize GSA to sell from government stockpiles quantities of 16 commodities exceeding national security needs. (D)						
11.* Prohibit use of interstate facilities to transport unsolicited salacious advertising or to deliver harmful and offensive matter to minors. (D)	✓	✓				
12.* Enable Veterans Administration to make advance payments to veterans as soon as they submit evidence they have registered in an educational institution. (D)	H					
13.* Remove statutory price limitation on sale of Veterans Administration loans. (D)	✓	✓	✓	✓	✓	66
14.* Limit Veterans Administration's burial payment to the difference between $250 and non-VA burial payments. (D)	✓	✓				
15.* Terminate veterans' disability compensation for cured tuberculosis. (D)						
16.* Require private health insurance companies to reimburse the federal government for costs incurred by veterans in Veterans Administration hospitals with non-service-connected ailments. (D)						
17. Extend President's reorganization authority. (F)	✓	✓	✓	✓	✓	179
18. Merge seven existing departments and several independent agencies into Departments of Natural Resources. (F)	H		H			
19. Human Resources (F);	H		H			
20. Community Development (F); and	H		H			
21. Economic Development. (F)	H		H			
22. Establish a new personnel system for upper-level officials of the executive branch, the Federal Executive Service. (G)			H			
23. Help state and local governments maintain transferred Federal historic sites by allowing their use for revenue-raising purposes. (J)						
24. Simplify relocation of Federal installations occupying properties that could better be used for other purposes. (J)			H			
25. Consolidate five current programs for construction of medical education facilities into a single grant authority. (K)	✓	✓	✓	✓	✓	157
26. Eliminate Medicaid coverage for most welfare families. (K)	H		H			
27. Finance outpatient services under Medicare by increasing Social Security wage base. (K)	✓	✓	H			
28. Approve Reorganization Plan No. 1 of 1971 to establish an agency, to be known as ACTION, combining the Peace Corps, VISTA and other service agencies. (T)		✓		✓	✓	—
29. Strengthen authority of the Secretary of each of the four new Departments to be created by reorganizing seven existing Departments (18-21, above).	H		H			
30. Authorize Federal guarantee of revenue bonds of the Washington Metropolitan Area Transit Authority. (Y)						
31. Create a separate, nonprofit Legal Services Corporation with funding transferred from legal services activities in the Office of Economic Opportunity. (FF) †	✓	✓	✓	✓	X	
32. Appropriate an additional $50-million for a breeder reactor demonstration plant. (JJ)	X	X	X	X	X	
33. Appropriate an additional $27-million in fiscal year 1972 for the Atomic Energy Commission's liquid fast breeder reactor program. (JJ)	X	X	X	X	X	
34. Appropriate an additional $2-million for controlled nuclear fusion research in fiscal year 1972. (JJ)	X	X	X	X	X	
35. Appropriate an additional $3-million for nuclear reactor safety and supporting technology. (JJ)	X	X	X	X	X	
36. Establish a central authority—the Special Action Office for Drug Abuse Prevention—with over-all responsibility for all major Federal drug abuse prevention, education, treatment, rehabilitation, training and research programs in all Federal agencies.				✓	✓	
37. Appropriate an additional $636,000 for fiscal year 1972 for the General Services Administration to declassify World War II documents. (LL)						

Health and Education

EDUCATION

	1	2	3	4	5	6
1.* Create a National Institute of Education in the Department of Health, Education and Welfare for research and development. (D)	✓	✓	✓	✓		
2.* Provide emergency financial assistance to desegregating school districts. (D)		✓	✓	✓		

†*President Nixon vetoed the Office of Economic Opportunity extension bill (S 2007), which contained this provision, on Dec. 9, 1971. The Senate refused to override Dec. 10, 1971.*

	1	2	3	4	5	6
3. Direct more Federal education funds to students from lower-income working families. (F)	✓	✓	✓	✓		
4. Forgive repayment of student loans for doctors, dentists, nurses and certain other professionals practicing in scarcity areas, particularly those specializing in primary care skills in short supply. (K)	✓	✓	✓	✓	✓	157
5. Provide more Federal aid to schools of medicine, dentistry and osteopathy, including $60-million in new money, in the form of per-student grants. (K)	✓	✓	✓	✓	✓	157
6. Increase funding for scholarship grant programs for lower-income students entering medical and dental schools.	✓	✓	✓	✓	✓	157
7. Enact the Higher Education Opportunity Act of 1971. (L)	✓	✓	✓	✓		
8. Establish the National Foundation for Higher Education to broaden opportunity through renewal, reform and innovation in higher education. (L)	H		✓	✓		

HEALTH

	1	2	3	4	5	6
1. Appropriate an additional $100-million to launch anti-cancer campaign. (C)	✓	✓	✓	✓	✓	218
2. Require public and private health insurance plans to allow beneficiaries to use their plans to purchase membership in health maintenance organizations when available. (K)			H			
3. Establish a $23-million health maintenance organization (HMO) program of planning grants to aid potential private and public sponsors. (K)			H			
4. Establish program of Federal loan guarantees to enable private HMO sponsors to raise $300-million in private loans during the first year of the program. (K)			H			
5. Appropriate an additional $10-million to implement the Emergency Health Personnel Act to mobilize the National Health Service Corps. (K)			H			
6. Expand allied health personnel training programs to $29-million, with $15-million devoted to training physicians' assistants. (K)	X	X	X	X	X	
7. Enact National Health Insurance Standards Act requiring employers to provide basic health coverage for their employees. (K)	H		H			
8. Establish a family health insurance plan to meet needs of poor families not covered by the proposed National Health Insurance Standards Act—those headed by unemployed, intermittently employed or self-employed persons. (K)	H		H			
9. Appropriate an additional $5-million for fiscal year 1971 and an additional $8-million over amounts included in the 1972 budget to implement new Occupational Safety and Health Act. (K)			X	X	X	
10. Establish a cancer-cure program in the National Institutes of Health, with independent budgetary status and under a director directly responsible to the President. (GG)	X	X	✓	✓	X	
11. Appropriate an additional $105-million to be used solely for treatment and rehabilitation of drug-addicted individuals. (KK)	✓	✓	✓	✓	✓	49
12. Appropriate an additional $10-million to increase and improve education and training in the field of dangerous drugs. (KK)	✓	✓	✓	✓	✓	49
13. Amend the Narcotic Addict Rehabilitation Act of 1966 to broaden authority for methadone maintenance programs. (KK)	✓	✓				
14. Pass supplemental appropriation of $25.6-million for the Treasury Department for drug abuse control. (KK)			X	X	X	
15. Authorize Federal assumption of 100 percent of necessary costs of state inspection terms for nursing homes under the Medicaid program. (MM)						
16. Provide funds to enlarge Federal nursing home program by creating 150 additional positions. (MM)						

Agriculture and Labor

LABOR

	1	2	3	4	5	6
1. Enact Emergency Public Interest Protection Act to give President authority to deal with national emergency disputes in transportation industries. (H)	H		H			
2. Appropriate an additional $64.3-million to provide an additional 100,000 Neighborhood Youth Corps summer employment opportunities for high school student and to finance the recreation support program in the largest cities. (AA)						
3. Extend railway labor negotiations, with a deadline of July 1, 1971. (II)	X	X		X	X	
4. Pass the (Rural) Job Development Act of 1971. (NN)	X	X		X	X	
5. Make contributions to retirement savings programs individual deductible up to $1,500 per year or 20 percent of income. (RR)						

6. Raise annual limit for deductible contributions by the self-employed to $7,500 or 15 percent of income. (RR)
7. Establish formula for vesting pension rights—preserving pension rights of employees even though they leave their jobs before retirement. (RR)

AGRICULTURE

1. Appropriate an additional $7.6-million to the Agricultural Research Service and to the state agricultural experiment stations. (EE)
2. Appropriate an additional $2-million to the Department of Agriculture for research and development of herbicides to destroy growth of narcotic-producing plants without adverse ecological effects. (KK)

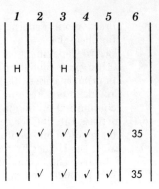

	1	2	3	4	5	6
7.	H		H			
1.	√	√	√	√	√	35
2.		√	√	√	√	35

Nixon's Score: Lowest of Any President Since 1954

Congress' approval of 20 percent of President Nixon's 202 legislative requests in 1971 was the lowest figure handed to any administration since Congressional Quarterly began its existing method of compiling the presidential boxscore in 1954.

This figure represents a sharp drop from Nixon's 46-percent record of the previous year. The decline reflected the detailed nature of Nixon's proposals as well as congressional inaction on several major requests, including welfare reform, revenue sharing and governmental reorganization.

President Lyndon B. Johnson in 1965 enjoyed the highest score—69 percent—recorded since 1954. That year the first session of the 89th Congress cleared the bulk of his "Great Society" legislation, including Medicare, aid to education bills and the Voting Rights Act.

Forty-eight percent of President John F. Kennedy's recommendations were enacted in 1961. But by 1963,

the Kennedy score dropped to 27 percent, the second lowest approved by Congress since 1954.

In 1954, the Republican 83rd Congress gave President Dwight D. Eisenhower victories in 65 percent of his requests. But only 31 percent of his proposals were approved by the Democratic 86th Congress in 1960, his last year in office.

Legislative scores for President Nixon in the first session of the 92nd Congress (1971, Democratic), 91st Congress (1969-70, Democratic); for President Johnson in the 90th Congress (1967-68, Democratic), and 89th Congress (1965-66, Democratic); for Presidents Kennedy and Johnson in the 88th Congress (1963-64, Democratic); for President Kennedy in the 87th Congress (1961-62, Democratic); for President Eisenhower in the 86th Congress (1959-60, Democratic), 85th Congress (1957-58, Democratic), 84th Congress (1955-56, Democratic) and second session of the 83rd Congress (1954, Republican):

Year	President	Congress	Session	Number of Requests	Number of Messages	Number Approved	Percentage Approved
1971	Nixon	92nd	first	202	44	40	20
1970	Nixon	91st	second	210	41	97	46
1969	Nixon	91st	first	171	40	55	32
1968	Johnson	90th	second	414	52	231	56
1967	Johnson	90th	first	431	56	205	48
1966	Johnson	89th	second	371	55	207	56
1965	Johnson	89th	first	469	63	323	69
1964	Johnson	88th	second	217	27	125	58
1963	Kennedy	88th	first	401	33	109	27
1962	Kennedy	87th	second	298	44	133	45
1961	Kennedy	87th	first	355	66	172	48
1960	Eisenhower	86th	second	183	16	156	31
1959	Eisenhower	86th	first	228	18	93	41
1958	Eisenhower	85th	second	234	29	110	47
1957	Eisenhower	85th	first	206	20	76	37
1956	Eisenhower	84th	second	225	25	103	46
1955	Eisenhower	84th	first	207	30	96	46
1954	Eisenhower	83rd	second	232	31	150	65

CONGRESS AND THE PRESIDENT: SUPPORT LEVEL STEADY

President Nixon in 1971 won 75 percent of the 139 recorded congressional votes that presented clear-cut tests of support for his views.

The figure represented a decrease of 2 percentage points from his 77 percent support score in 1970 but bettered his 74 percent mark in 1969. For the entire 91st Congress (1969-70), the President was backed by the Democratic-controlled House and Senate on 209 of 275 roll calls, for a 76 percent score.

Of the 139 record votes in 1970, President Nixon won 104. He was successful on 47 of 57 in the House (82 percent) and 57 of 82 in the Senate (70 percent).

Ground Rules. Congressional Quarterly's 1970 presidential support study was based on those votes on which there was a clear indication of the President's preference, revealed before each vote in his own messages and public statements. *(List p. 55, rules p. 57)*

Support Breakdowns

Party Differences. There was a clear difference in presidential support between Democrats and Republicans. The average Republican backed the President in 1971 on 64 percent of the votes in the Senate and 72 percent in the House. Democrats, on the other hand, supported the President an average of 40 percent of the time in the Senate and 47 percent in the House.

Also consistent with past years, southerners were the single regional bloc most likely to go along with the President's legislative wishes. Among Democrats, the average southerner supported the President a majority of the time (51 percent in the Senate, 59 percent in the House). And among Republicans, southerners also had the highest regional averages of presidential support (68 percent in the Senate, 76 percent in the House).

The group voting in opposition to the President most often was composed of Democrats from the Midwest. They went along with Mr. Nixon an average of only 31 percent of the time in the Senate, 39 percent in the House.

Individual Scores. Among individual supporters in the Senate, the most frequent Nixon backers were Delaware Republicans J. Caleb Boggs and William V. Roth Jr. and Michigan Republican Robert P. Griffin, the party whip. All three backed the President on 85 percent of the test votes.

The leading Nixon supporter among Democrats in the Senate was John C. Stennis (Miss.), who went along with the President 68 percent of the time. The eight top Nixon supporters among Senate Democrats were all southerners; they included the chairmen of committees for Armed Services (Stennis), Judiciary (James O. Eastland of Mississippi), Appropriations (Allen J. Ellender of Louisiana) and Agriculture (Herman E. Talmadge of Georgia).

The four most frequent Nixon opponents in the Senate were all midwestern Democrats—Gaylord Nelson and

William Proxmire (Wis.), Harold E. Hughes (Iowa) and Walter F. Mondale (Minn.). Hughes led the opponents with a 66 percent opposition score.

Among Senate Republicans, the President was most often opposed by Mark O. Hatfield (Ore.). Hatfield voted against the President on 55 percent of the tests, marking the only time in the history of the Nixon Administration that any Republican Senator failed to go along with the President a majority of the time, as measured by the CQ study. Hatfield also was the most frequent Republican opponent in 1969. Clifford P. Case (N.J.), the 1970 leader, finished third in 1971 behind Hatfield and Richard S. Schweiker (Pa.).

The two most loyal Nixon supporters in the House were Republicans Charlotte T. Reid (Ill.) and John Ware (Pa.). Each backed Mr. Nixon on 93 percent of the test votes. Among House Democrats, Goodloe E. Byron (Md.) backed Nixon most frequently, 84 percent of the time. Technically the leader in both houses was Rep. William P. Curlin Jr. (D Ky.), but Curlin was not sworn in until December and participated in only two of the test votes.

Democrats from New York and California dominated the list of Nixon opponents in the House. Herman Badillo (N.Y.) led with 77 percent, followed by Bella S. Abzug (N.Y.) at 75. Tied for third at 74 were Philip Burton (Calif.), Ronald V. Dellums (Calif.) and William F. Ryan (N.Y.). The two most frequent Nixon opponents among House Republicans were Donald W. Riegle Jr. (Mich.) and Ogden R. Reid (N.Y.) with 54 percent opposition. Riegle and Reid were two of the five House Republicans who opposed the President a majority of the time. The others were Charles A. Mosher (Ohio), H. R. Gross (Iowa), and Gilbert Gude (Md.).

A member's support and opposition scores do not necessarily add up to 100 percent because votes for which he was absent are excluded from the study. Absences also lower regional and party averages.

Key Nixon Wins and Losses

Foreign policy issues dominated the crucial test votes on President Nixon's policies during 1971.

The President succeeded in fighting off the Mansfield amendment setting a withdrawal deadline for American troops in Indochina, even though the amendment passed the Senate three times. He also was victorious in persuading the Senate not to adopt another Mansfield amendment withdrawing half the American troops from Europe at the end of 1971.

Foreign aid provided a setback for the President when the Senate unexpectedly killed the entire program by a 41-27 vote Oct. 29, but the package was later divided into two parts and was well on the way to enactment as the session ended.

A more lasting defeat for the President was the decision by Congress to cancel federal support for the supersonic transport plane (SST). The key SST vote came in March, as the House bucked the President and its own leaders to ground the plane by successive votes of 217-204 and 216-203. A later attempt at revival failed.

Mr. Nixon was more successful in the economic field; after he announced his new economic policy in August he had little trouble persuading Congress to give him the tools he wanted for the job.

Congress passed by overwhelming votes a bill to extend the President's wage-price control authority through April 1973 and another bill reducing personal and corporate income taxes by more than $15-billion over a three-year period.

The President had better luck with nominations than in previous years. His choices of William H. Rehnquist and Lewis F. Powell Jr. for the Supreme Court passed the Senate easily, Powell by 89-1 and Rehnquist by 68-26. A closer vote came on the President's nomination of Earl Lauer Butz as Secretary of Agriculture. Butz drew 44 votes in opposition to him but was confirmed by a seven-vote margin in December.

Congress voted twice on bills vetoed by the President. One was a $5.7-billion public works acceleration and regional development bill, the other a child development and day care bill. He was upheld both times.

Average Scores

Composites of Republican and Democratic scores for presidential support and opposition in 1971 and the 91st Congress (1969-70):

	1971		**91st CONGRESS**	
	Dems.	**Reps.**	**Dems.**	**Reps.**
SUPPORT				
Senate	40%	64%	46%	63%
House	47	72	51	62
OPPOSITION				
Senate	44%	20%	36%	22%
House	41	19	33	24

Breakdown by Regions

Regional presidential support scores for 1971:

	East	**West**	**South**	**Midwest**
DEMOCRATS				
Senate	37%	38%	51%	31%
House	40	42	59	39
REPUBLICANS				
Senate	65%	61%	68%	62%
House	68	73	76	72

Regional presidential opposition scores for 1971:

	East	**West**	**South**	**Midwest**
DEMOCRATS				
Senate	47%	43%	36%	53%
House	50	46	26	51
REPUBLICANS				
Senate	25%	18%	18%	15%
House	23	13	17	19

High Scorers—Support

Highest individual scores in Nixon support—those who voted with the President most often in 1971:

SENATE

Democrats		**Republicans**	
Stennis (Miss.)	68%	Boggs (Del.)	85%
Byrd (Va.)	66	Roth (Del.)	85
Eastland (Miss.)	62	Griffin (Mich.)	85
Ervin (N.C.)	62	Gurney (Fla.)	84
Bentsen (Texas)	61	Dole (Kan.)	80
Ellender (La.)	60	Buckley (N.Y.)	80
Allen (Ala.)	59	Fannin (Ariz.)	79
Talmadge (Ga.)	57	Hruska (Neb.)	79
Cannon (Nev.)	56	Scott (Pa.)	78
Byrd (W.Va.)	55	Beall (Md.)	78

HOUSE

Democrats		**Republicans**	
Curlin (Ky.)	100%*	Reid (Ill.)	93%
Byron (Md.)	84	Ware (Pa.)	93
Fountain (N.C.)	82	Teague (Calif.)	91
Hull (Mo.)	77	Hillis (Ind.)	91
Mahon (Texas)	77	Cederberg (Mich.)	91
Downing (Va.)	77	Betts (Ohio)	91
Satterfield (Va.)	77	Mailliard (Calif.)	89
Daniel (Va.)	77	Shriver (Kan.)	89
Flowers (Ala.)	75	Keith (Mass.)	89
Henderson (N.C.)	75	Ford (Mich.)	89
Zablocki (Wis.)	75	Chamberlain (Mich.)	89
		Nelsen (Minn.)	89

*Not eligible for all roll calls in 1971 (only eligible for two Nixon issues).
#Resigned Oct. 7, 1971.

High Scorers—Opposition

Highest individual scores in Nixon opposition—those who voted against the President most often in 1971:

SENATE

Democrats		**Republicans**	
Hughes (Iowa)	66%	Hatfield (Ore.)	55%
Mondale (Minn.)	63	Schweiker (Pa.)	49
Nelson (Wis.)	63	Case (N.J.)	48
Proxmire (Wis.)	62	Brooke (Mass.)	45
Cranston (Calif.)	60	Mathias (Md.)	40
Williams (N.J.)	60	Percy (Ill.)	30
Fulbright (Ark.)	59	Javits (N.Y.)	30

HOUSE

Democrats		**Republicans**	
Badillo (N.Y.)	77%	Riegle (Mich.)	54%
Abzug (N.Y.)	75	Reid (N.Y.)	54
Burton (Calif.)	74	Mosher (Ohio)	53
Dellums (Calif.)	74	Gross (Iowa)	51
Ryan (N.Y.)	74	Gude (Md.)	51
Begich (Alaska)	72	Heckler (Mass.)	49
Edwards (Calif.)	72	Fulton (Pa.)	49*
Mitchell (Md.)	72	Conte (Mass.)	47
Drinan (Mass.)	72	Halpern (N.Y.)	46
Rosenthal (N.Y.)	72	Whalen (Ohio)	46
Kastenmeier (Wis.)	72		

*Died Oct. 6, 1971

House Presidential Support Votes

Numbers refer to CQ House and Senate vote numbers in 1971 CQ *Almanac*. An "N" means a nay vote supported the President; a "Y" means a yea vote supported him.

13. Labor Department Supplemental Appropriations, fiscal 1971. Nixon-Y. Passed 355-0.

14. Department of Transportation Appropriations, fiscal 1971. Amendment deleting SST funds. Nixon-N. Adopted 217-204.

15. Department of Transportation Appropriations, fiscal 1971. Confirmation of amendment deleting SST funds. Nixon-N. Adopted 216-203.

16. Lower Voting Age. Passage of constitutional amendment. Nixon-Y. Adopted 401-19.

21. Draft Extension. Amendment repealing President's authority to induct draftees. Nixon-N. Rejected 62-331.

22. Draft Extension. Amendment limiting extension to one year. Nixon-N. Rejected 198-200.

24. Draft Extension. Amendment forbidding assignment of draftees to Indochina after 1971. Nixon-N. Rejected 122-260.

25. Draft Extension. Amendment forbidding use of draftees in undeclared war. Nixon-N. Rejected 96-278.

26. Draft Extension. Amendment limiting extension to 18 months. Nixon-N. Rejected 170-200.

43. Executive Reorganization. Passage. Nixon-Y. Passed 301-20.

51. Second Supplemental Appropriation Bill, fiscal 1971. Amendment restoring SST construction funds. Recorded teller vote. Nixon-Y. Adopted 201-195.

52. Second Supplemental Appropriation Bill, fiscal 1971. Amendment restoring SST construction funds. Roll call. Nixon-Y. Adopted 201-197.

57. National Advisory Committee on the Oceans and Atmosphere. Passage. Nixon-Y. Passed 293-10.

65. Merger of Peace Corps, Vista and other volunteer organizations. Veto resolution. Nixon-N. Defeated 131-224.

67. Emergency Public Service Employment Act. Amendment substituting manpower revenue-sharing plan. Nixon-Y. Rejected 182-204.

83. Defense Procurement Authorization. Amendment limiting anti-ballistic missile funding. Nixon-N. Rejected 129-267.

84. Defense Procurement Authorization. Amendment striking funds for B-1 bomber. Nixon-N. Rejected 97-307.

85. Defense Procurement Authorization. Amendment limiting reduction of research and development funds. Nixon-N. Rejected 135-258.

86. Defense Procurement Authorization. Amendment placing ceiling on authorization. Nixon-N. Rejected 118-278.

89. Defense Procurement Authorization. Amendment cutting off Indochina funds after 1971. Nixon-N. Rejected 81-327.

90. Defense Procurement Authorization. Amendment cutting off Indochina funds after 1971 but allowing President to seek extension from Congress. Nixon-N. Rejected 158-255.

91. Defense Procurement Authorization. Amendment cutting off Indochina funds after June 1, 1972, assuming release of American POW's. Nixon-N. Rejected 147-237.

99. Welfare-Social Security. Amendment deleting Family Assistance Plan. Nixon-N. Rejected 187-234.

100. Welfare-Social Security. Passage. Nixon-Y. Passed 288-132.

104. State, Justice, Commerce Appropriations, fiscal 1972. Amendment adding funds for support of International Labor Organization. Nixon-Y. Rejected 147-227.

107. Military Draft. Motion tabling motion in support of amendment calling for withdrawal of troops from Indochina within nine months. Nixon-Y. Adopted 219-175.

113. Emergency Public Service Employment Act. Adoption of conference report. Nixon-Y. Adopted 343-14.

117. Prohibit mail delivery of obscene mail to minors and others. Passage. Nixon-Y. Passed 356-25.

141. Public Works-Appalachian Regional Development Extension. Passage. Nixon-Y. Passed 376-27.

144. Department of Transportation Appropriations, fiscal 1972. Motion to agree to amendment paying aircraft companies for termination costs of SST. Nixon-Y. Adopted 307-99.

152. Emergency Loan Guarantee for Lockheed Aircraft Corp. and other failing businesses. Passage. Nixon-Y. Passed 192-189.

160. Military Draft. Adoption of rule barring points of order against conference report. Nixon-Y. Adopted 250-150.

161. Military Draft. Motion to recommit conference report. Nixon-N. Rejected 131-273.

162. Military Draft. Adoption of conference report. Nixon-Y. Adopted 298-108.

165. Emergency Supplemental Labor Appropriations. Passage. Nixon-Y. Passed 321-76.

173. Equal Employment Opportunities Enforcement Act. Amendment providing the Equal Employment Opportunities Commission with power to bring suit against discriminatory employers but not to issue cease-and-desist orders. Nixon-Y. Adopted 200-195.

174. Equal Employment Opportunities Enforcement Act. Confirmation of above amendment. Nixon-Y. Adopted 202-197.

176. Equal Employment Opportunities Enforcement Act. Passage of bill as amended above. Nixon-Y. Passed 285-106.

179. Economic Opportunity Amendments of 1971. Amendment increasing number of communities eligible for child development funds. Nixon-N. Adopted 226-158.

180. Economic Opportunity Amendments of 1971. Amendment coordinating child development fees with those charged in other federal day-care programs. Nixon-Y. Rejected 187-189.

181. Economic Opportunity Amendments of 1971. Amendment establishing comprehensive child development program. Nixon-N. Adopted 203-181.

184. Economic Opportunity Amendments of 1971. Confirmation of vote No. 181. Nixon-N. Adopted 186-183.

185. Economic Opportunity Amendments of 1971. Motion to recommit the bill with instructions to include amendments considered in vote No. 180. Nixon-Y. Adopted 191-180.

187. Federal Pay Raise. Motion postponing action on resolution vetoing plan to delay salary increases. Nixon-N. Rejected 175-198.

188. Federal Pay Raise. Resolution vetoing plan to delay salary increases. Nixon-N. Rejected 174-207.

200. Establish Consumer Protection Agency. Passage. Nixon-Y. Passed 345-44.

205. Defense Procurement Authorization. Motion effectively blocking direct vote on Vietnam troop withdrawal amendment. Nixon-Y. Adopted 215-193.

214. Higher Education Act of 1971. Amendment establishing national basic grant program. Nixon-Y. Rejected 117-257.

227. Higher Education Act of 1971. Amendment deleting authorization of general federal aid for institutions of higher education. Nixon-Y. Rejected 84-310.

239. Higher Education Act of 1971. Amendment barring use of funds for busing to overcome racial imbalance in schools. Nixon-Y. Adopted 233-124.

240. Higher Education Act of 1971. Amendment authorizing federal study of the needs of desegregating school districts. Nixon-N. Rejected 92-269.

241. Higher Education Act of 1971. Amendment adding to the bill the Emergency School Aid Act of 1971. Nixon-Y. Adopted 211-159.

269. Defense Appropriations, fiscal 1972. Amendment cutting off funds for U.S. military operations in Indochina on July 1, 1972. Nixon-N. Rejected 163-238.

286. D.C. Appropriations, fiscal 1972. Amendment adding cost of a rapid transit system. (Recorded teller vote.) Nixon-Y. Adopted 196-183.

288. D.C. Appropriations, fiscal 1972. Amendment adding cost of a rapid transit system. (Roll-call vote). Nixon-Y. Adopted 195-174.

306. Revenue Act of 1971. Adoption of conference report reducing personal and corporate taxes. Nixon-Y. Adopted 321-75.

312. Economic Stabilization Extension. Passage of bill extending President's wage-price control authority. Nixon-Y. Passed 326-33.

Senate Presidential Support Votes

13. Extend Appalachian Redevelopment. Passage. Nixon-N. Passed 77-3.

23. Department of Transportation Appropriations, fiscal 1971. Amendment restoring SST funds. Nixon-Y. Rejected 46-51.

34. Emergency School Aid and Quality Integrated Education Act. Motion tabling amendment providing desegregation aid. Nixon-Y. Motion rejected 35-43.

35. Emergency School Aid and Quality Integrated Education Act. Amendment providing desegregation aid. Nixon-N. Rejected 35-51.

38. Emergency School Aid and Quality Integrated Education Act. Amendment declaring it national policy to deal uniformly with segregation wherever it occurs. Nixon-N. Adopted 44-34.

40. Emergency School Aid and Quality Integrated Education Act. Amendment deleting language allowing use of federal funds in non-public schools. Nixon-N. Rejected 15-62.

41. Emergency School Aid and Quality Integrated Education Act. Amendment barring federal aid to non-public schools which discriminate on the basis of religion. Nixon-N. Rejected 14-65.

42. Emergency School Aid and Quality Integrated Education Act. Amendment restoring freedom-of-choice school attendance plans. Nixon-N. Rejected 32-51.

43. Emergency School Aid and Quality Integrated Education Act. Amendment barring federal action to require busing to affect racial composition of schools. Nixon-N. Rejected 35-46.

44. Emergency School Aid and Quality Integrated Education Act. Amendment barring federal action to interfere with the neighborhood school system. Nixon-N. Rejected 33-48.

45. Emergency School Aid and Quality Integrated Education Act. Passage. Nixon-Y. Passed 74-8.

48. Military Draft. Amendment calling for a withdrawal of 150,000 American troops from Europe by 1974 unless multilateral negotiations are held. Nixon-N. Rejected 26-63.

49. Military Draft. Amendment calling for withdrawal of 150,000 American troops from Europe by the end of 1971 unless NATO nations agreed to compensate the U.S. for balance-of-payments losses resulting from their upkeep. Nixon-N. Rejected 13-81.

50. Military Draft. Amendment calling for negotiations to achieve multilateral reductions of forces in Europe. Nixon-N. Rejected 24-73.

51. Military Draft. Amendment limiting the U.S. troop level in Europe to 150,000 after 1971 unless the President could justify the need for more. Nixon-N. Rejected 29-68.

52. Military Draft. Amendment reducing American troop levels in Europe to 250,000 after 1971. Nixon-N. Rejected 15-81.

53. Military Draft. Amendment reducing American troop levels in Europe to 150,000 after 1971. Nixon-N. Rejected 36-61.

54. Second Supplemental Appropriations Bill, fiscal 1971. Amendment deleting funds for the SST. Nixon-N. Adopted 58-37.

61. Military Draft. Amendment barring the assignment of draftees to combat outside the United States after 1971 unless authorized by Congress. Nixon-N. Rejected 7-61.

62. Military Draft. Amendment barring the assignment of draftees to combat in Southeast Asia after 1971, unless they volunteer. Nixon-N. Rejected 21-52.

63. Military Draft. Amendment barring bonuses for enlisting or re-enlisting in the armed forces. Nixon-N. Rejected 25-49.

64. Military Draft. Amendment limiting the extension to 18 months. Nixon-N. Rejected 8-67.

Ground Rules for CQ Presidential Support-Opposition

• **Presidential Issues**—CQ analyzes all messages, press conference remarks and other public statements of the President to determine what he personally, as distinct from other Administration spokesmen, does or does not want in the way of legislative action.

• **Borderline Cases**—By the time an issue reaches a vote, it may differ from the original form on which the President expressed himself. In such cases, CQ analyzes the measure to determine whether, on balance, the features favored by the President outweigh those he opposed or vice versa. Only then is the vote classified.

• **Some Votes Excluded**—Occasionally, important measures are so extensively amended on the floor that it is impossible to characterize final passage as a victory or defeat for the President.

• **Motions**—Roll calls on motions to recommit, to reconsider or to table often are key tests that govern the legislative outcome. Such votes are necessarily included in the Nixon support tabulations.

• **Rules**—In the House, debate on most significant bills is governed by rules that restrict time and may bar floor amendments. These rules must be adopted by the House before the bills in question may be considered. Members may vote for the rule, in order to permit debate, although they intend to vote against

the bill. Generally, however, a vote against a rule is a vote against the bill, and vice versa, since rejection of the rule prevents consideration of the bill. CQ assumes that if the President favored a bill, he favored the rule unless it was a closed rule that would prevent amendments he wanted.

• **Appropriations**—Generally, roll calls on passage of appropriation bills are not included in this tabulation, since it is rarely possible to determine the President's position on the over-all revisions Congress almost invariably makes in the sums allowed. Votes to cut or increase specific funds requested in the President's Budget, however, are included.

• **Failures to Vote**—In tabulating the Support or Opposition scores of Members on the selected Nixon issue roll calls, CQ counts only "yea" and "nay" votes on the ground that only these affect the outcome. Most failures to vote reflect absences because of illness or official business.

• **Weighting**—All Nixon-issue roll calls have equal statistical weight in the analysis.

• **Changed Position**—Presidential Support is determined by the position of the President at the time of a vote even though that position may be different from an earlier position, or may have been reversed after the vote was taken.

---

65. Military Draft. Amendment increasing funds for military pay increases. Nixon-N. Rejected 31-42.

66. Reorganization Plan merging Peace Corps, Vista and other volunteer agencies. Veto resolution preventing the merger. Nixon-N. Veto resolution defeated 29-54.

67. Military Draft. Amendment ending the draft after June 30, 1971, but maintaining the Selective Service System. Nixon-N. Rejected 23-67.

68. Military Draft. Amendment limiting draft extension to one year. Nixon-N. Rejected 43-49.

72. Military Draft. Amendment increasing funds for military pay increases, primarily in lower ranks. Nixon-N. Adopted 51-27.

82. Military Draft. Amendment cutting off funds for U.S. military activities in Indochina after June 1, 1972, if prisoners of war had been released sixty days before that date. Nixon-N. Rejected 44-52.

83. Military Draft. Amendment cutting off funds for U.S. military activities in Indochina after 1971, with a 60-day extension if POWs had not been released by that date. Nixon-N. Rejected 42-55.

84. Military Draft. Amendment limiting draft extension to 20 months. Nixon-N. Rejected 35-48.

90. Military Draft. Amendment barring use of the draft except in declared wars. Nixon-N. Rejected 12-58.

93. Military Draft. Amendment substituting increased hostile fire pay for a combat enlistment bonus. Nixon-N. Rejected 27-47.

100. Military Draft. Amendment setting no withdrawal deadline for American troops in Indochina but

declaring an early termination date to be U.S. policy and providing for withdrawal within nine months of the release of prisoners of war. Nixon-N. Adopted 57-42.

101. Military Draft. Amendment using the language of vote No. 100 to modify an earlier, stronger version of the amendment. Nixon-N. Adopted 61-38.

107. Military Draft. Amendment exempting from future induction all men holding deferments when draft law expires in 1973. Nixon-N. Rejected 29-61.

112. Emergency Public Service Employment Act. Adoption of conference report. Nixon-Y. Adopted 75-11.

120. Public Works Acceleration and Regional Development Extension. Vote on whether to override the President's veto. Nixon-N. Veto sustained 57-36.

141. Public Works-Economic Development and Appalachian Regional Development Extension. Passage. Nixon-Y. Passed 88-2.

164. Emergency Loan Guarantees. Emergency Loan Guarantee for Lockheed Aircraft Corp. and other failing businesses. Passage. Nixon-Y. Passed 49-48.

188. Emergency Supplemental Labor Appropriations, fiscal 1972. Passage of bill creating public service jobs. Nixon-Y. Passed 68-10.

193. Economic Opportunity Amendments of 1971. Amendment deleting language prohibiting the transfer of Office of Economic Opportunity Programs to other government agencies without congressional approval. Nixon-Y. Rejected 26-31.

194. Economic Opportunity Amendment of 1971. Amendment redefining the concept of the "economically disadvantaged" child. Nixon-Y. Rejected 20-44.

195. Economic Opportunity Amendments of 1971. Amendment deleting provisions earmarking authorizations for specific OEO programs. Nixon-Y. Rejected 17-47.

196. Economic Opportunity Amendments of 1971. Amendment providing that Child Development Councils would be advisory rather than policy-making bodies. Nixon-Y. Rejected 17-41.

197. Economic Opportunity Amendments of 1971. Motion recommitting the bill with instructions to delete certain child development programs. Nixon-Y. Rejected 17-46.

198. Economic Opportunity Amendments of 1971. Amendment prohibiting the National Legal Services Corporation from using funds to provide legal assistance for criminal proceedings. Nixon-Y. Rejected 28-34.

201. Military Draft. Motion to table conference report on the bill. Nixon-N. Rejected 36-47.

202. International Convention Relating to Intervention on the High Seas in Cases of Oil Pollution Casualties. Ratification. Nixon-Y. Ratified 75-0.

203. International Convention for the Prevention of Pollution of the Sea by Oil. Ratification of convention as amended. Nixon-Y. Ratified 75-0.

204. Military Draft. Motion to invoke cloture on the conference report. Nixon-Y. Agreed to 61-30.

205. Military Draft. Adoption of the conference report. Nixon-Y. Agreed to 55-30.

214. Defense Procurement Authorization. Amendment deleting funds for deployment of anti-ballistic missile system. Nixon-N. Rejected 21-64.

216. Defense Procurement Authorization. Amendment declaring it U.S. policy that U.S. troops would be withdrawn from Indochina within six months of enactment if U.S. prisoners of war had been released. Nixon-N. Adopted 57-38.

217. Defense Procurement Authorization. Amendment allowing the President to decide the advisability of importing chromium ore from Rhodesia. Nixon-Y. Adopted 45-43.

223. Defense Procurement Authorization. Amendment providing money for new pay increases for military personnel. Nixon-Y. Adopted 65-4.

224. Defense Procurement Authorization. Amendment limiting funds for U.S. programs in Laos during 1972, except air operations. Nixon-N. Adopted 67-11.

225. Defense Procurement Authorization. Amendment calling for an end to air attacks on Indochina unless the President determined they were necessary to protect U.S. troop withdrawals. Nixon-N. Rejected 19-64.

229. Defense Procurement Authorization. Amendment giving the President discretion in removing import restrictions on chromium ore from Rhodesia. Nixon-Y. Rejected 38-44.

230. Defense Procurement Authorization. Motion to table amendment providing salary increases for federal employees in 1972. Nixon-Y. Rejected 34-54.

231. Defense Procurement Authorization. Amendment providing salary adjustments for federal employees in 1972. Nixon-N. Adopted 60-27.

232. Defense Procurement Authorization. Passage. Nixon-Y. Passed 82-4.

233. Federal Pay Raise. Resolution vetoing the President's plan deferring federal pay raises. Nixon-N. Rejected 32-51.

238. Inter-American Development Bank Authorization. Passage. Nixon-Y. Adopted 49-31.

239. International Development Association Authorization. Passage. Nixon-Y. Adopted 49-34.

244. Foreign Aid Authorization. Amendment deleting provision prohibiting use of funds in Indochina for any purpose other than withdrawal or protection of American troops. Nixon-Y. Adopted 47-44.

245. Foreign Aid Authorization. Motion to table motion to reconsider vote No. 244. Nixon-Y. Rejected 44-45.

246. Foreign Aid Authorization. Motion to reconsider vote No. 244. Nixon-N. Rejected 44-48.

247. Foreign Aid Authorization. Amendment increasing military aid to Cambodia. Nixon-Y. Rejected 35-52.

250. Foreign Aid Authorization. Amendment deleting provision ending foreign assistance to Greece unless the President determined it was necessary for national security. Nixon-Y. Adopted 49-31.

251. Foreign Aid Authorization. Amendment limiting assistance to Cambodia. Nixon-N. Rejected 26-53.

263. Automobile Repair Costs. Amendment deleting provisions authorizing the Transportation Department to set federal standards for reducing property damage caused by accidents. Nixon-Y. Rejected 29-64.

270. Agreement Between the United States and Japan Concerning the Ryukyu Islands and the Daito Islands, returning control of Okinawa to Japan. Nixon-Y. Adopted 84-6.

295. Revenue Act of 1971. Amendment requiring the President to issue reports explaining the impoundment of any federal funds by the executive branch. Nixon-N. Adopted 48-18.

311. Revenue Act of 1971. Amendment deleting a provision transferring some excise tax revenues from general accounts to the Highway Trust Fund. Nixon-Y. Rejected 43-46.

354. Revenue Act of 1971. Amendment providing presidential campaign funds from federal income tax revenue. Nixon-N. Adopted 52-47.

361. Defense Appropriations, fiscal 1972. Amendment prohibiting the use of funds after June 15, 1972, for the support of U.S. troops in Europe in excess of 250,000. Nixon-N. Rejected 39-54.

396. Economic Stabilization Act Extension. Passage. Nixon-Y. Passed 86-4.

397. Nomination of Earl L. Butz as Secretary of Agriculture. Nixon-Y. Confirmed 51-44.

408. Nomination of Lewis F. Powell Jr. as Justice of the U.S. Supreme Court. Nixon-Y. Confirmed 89-1.

412. National Cancer Act of 1971. Adoption of conference report expanding National Cancer Institute. Nixon-Y. Adopted 85-0.

417. Nomination of William H. Rehnquist as Justice of the U.S. Supreme Court. Nixon-Y. Confirmed 68-26.

418. Economic Opportunity Amendments of 1971. Vote on whether to override the President's veto. Nixon-N. Veto sustained 51-36.

Presidential Support and Opposition: Senate

1. Support Score, 1971. Percentage of 82 Nixon-issue roll calls in 1971 on which Senator voted "yea" or "nay" *in agreement* with the President's position. Failures to vote lower both Support and Opposition scores.

2. Opposition Score, 1971. Percentage of 82 Nixon-issue roll calls in 1971 on which Senator votes "yea" or "nay" *in disagreement* with the President's position. Failures to vote lower both Support and Opposition scores.

3. Support Score, 91st Congress. Percentage of 163 Nixon-issue roll calls in 1969 and 1970 on which Senator voted "yea" or "nay" *in agreement* with the President's position. Failures to vote lower both Support and Opposition scores.

4. Opposition Score, 91st Congress. Percentage of 163 Nixon-issue roll calls in 1969 and 1970 on which Senator voted "yea" or "nay" *in disagreement* with the President's position. Failures to vote lower both Support and Opposition scores.

	1	2	3	4
ALABAMA				
Allen	59	38	53	40
Sparkman	52	18	52	21
ALASKA				
Gravel	17	56	37	29
Stevens	60	24	62	18
ARIZONA				
Fannin	79	13	58	23
Goldwater	55	10	33	13
ARKANSAS				
Fulbright	27	59	32	44
McClellan	49	45	57	31
CALIFORNIA				
Cranston	35	60	47	38
Tunney	38	51	—	—
COLORADO				
Allott	73	6	77	13
Dominick	61	12	61	13
CONNECTICUT				
Ribicoff	30	57	44	39
Weicker	67	20	—	—
DELAWARE				
Boggs	85	10	77	20
Roth	85	15	—	—
FLORIDA				
Chiles	45	44	—	—
Gurney	84	16	64	26
GEORGIA				
Gambrell	48	40	—	—
Talmadge	57	41	56	34
HAWAII				
Inouye	30	43	42	34
Fong	72	11	60	23
IDAHO				
Church	33	50	42	42
Jordan	57	20	72	23
ILLINOIS				
Stevenson	40	52	31*	63*
Percy	50	30	63	18
INDIANA				
Bayh	22	46	36	34
Hartke	20	39	34	41
IOWA				
Hughes	29	66	42	41
Miller	52	17	72	21
KANSAS				
Dole	80	13	79	18
Pearson	62	28	73	18
KENTUCKY				
Cook	61	27	60	27
Cooper	66	22	60	25
LOUISIANA				
Ellender	60	32	55	34
Long	54	26	51	28
MAINE				
Muskie	21	40	45	43
Smith	76	13	70	28
MARYLAND				
Beall	78	17	—	—
Mathias	44	40	53	25
MASSACHUSETTS				
Kennedy	30	50	38	42
Brooke	43	45	56	33
MICHIGAN				
Hart	32	56	43	44
Griffin	85	9	77	13
MINNESOTA				
Humphrey	37	44	—	—
Mondale	32	63	45	43
MISSISSIPPI				
Eastland	62	21	44	30
Stennis	68	26	57	33
MISSOURI				
Eagleton	41	49	45	42
Symington	40	54	41	34
MONTANA				
Mansfield	28	55	45	42
Metcalf	27	50	43	40
NEBRASKA				
Curtis	70	15	74	23
Hruska	79	12	73	18
NEVADA				
Bible	52	33	56	33
Cannon	56	30	41	35
NEW HAMPSHIRE				
McIntyre	40	44	56	36
Cotton	68	18	75	17
NEW JERSEY				
Williams	34	60	43	39
Case	49	48	57	39
NEW MEXICO				
Anderson	44	35	47	20
Montoya	43	46	31	39
NEW YORK				
Buckley[1]	80	15	—	—
Javits	48	30	52	33
NORTH CAROLINA				
Ervin	62	32	55	40
Jordan	38	52	50	36
NORTH DAKOTA				
Burdick	35	54	47	39
Young	65	22	74	25
OHIO				
Saxbe	63	12	50	21
Taft	74	7	—	—
OKLAHOMA				
Harris	20	30	50	41
Bellmon	63	12	71	,16
OREGON				
Hatfield	33	55	48	37
Packwood	62	20	63	20
PENNSYLVANIA				
Schweiker	49	49	63	36
Scott	78	2	73	20
RHODE ISLAND				
Pastore	43	48	52	37
Pell	34	48	47	37
SOUTH CAROLINA				
Hollings	43	29	50	34
Thurmond	73	21	67	23
SOUTH DAKOTA				
McGovern	13	41	42	48
Mundt	0	0	23	5
TENNESSEE				
Baker	67	18	69	18
Brock	65	16	—	—
TEXAS				
Bentsen	61	37	—	—
Tower	68	12	57	12
UTAH				
Moss	26	45	39	35
Bennett	57	15	72	15
VERMONT				
Aiken	62	29	64	25
Stafford[2]	56†	28†	—	—
VIRGINIA				
Byrd, Jr.[3]	66	30	60	36
Spong	45	48	55	40
WASHINGTON				
Jackson	40	23	55	34
Magnuson	41	40	47	37
WEST VIRGINIA				
Byrd	55	35	52	39
Randolph	46	43	58	37
WISCONSIN				
Nelson	28	63	40	50
Proxmire	38	62	51	49
WYOMING				
McGee	60	21	56	26
Hansen	66	17	75	20

- KEY -

† Not eligible for all roll calls in 1971.

* Not eligible for all roll calls in 91st Congress.

—Not a member of the 91st Congress.

Democrats   *Republicans*

1. Buckley elected as Conservative
2. Sen. Winston L. Prouty (R Vt.) died Sept. 10, 1971. His scores for 1971 were 61 percent support and 11 percent opposition. Sen. Robert T. Stafford was sworn in Sept. 17, 1971, to replace Prouty. (See House chart)
3. Byrd elected as independent

- KEY -

† Not eligible for all roll calls in 1971.

* Not eligible for all roll calls in 91st Congress.

—Not a member of the 91st Congress.

● Speaker Albert votes only on recorded teller votes.

	1	2	3	4
ALABAMA				
1 Edwards	75	14	62	28
2 Dickinson	74	19	55	32
3 Andrews[1]	67	26	53	36
4 Nichols	65	19	43	41
5 Flowers	75	16	45	44
6 Buchanan	86	11	68	28
7 Bevill	65	25	48	41
8 Jones	60	28	57	33
ALASKA				
AL Begich	28	72	—	—
ARIZONA				
1 Rhodes	86	7	71	17
2 Udall	23	63	63	29
3 Steiger	63	23	58	33
ARKANSAS				
1 Alexander	44	32	60	29
2 Mills	58	25	57	28
3 Hammerschmidt	77	19	69	29
4 Pryor	35	54	62	29
CALIFORNIA				
1 Clausen	82	12	67*	23*
2 Johnson	65	28	59	29
3 Moss	25	56	38	34
4 Leggett	40	49	42	36
5 Burton	21	74	54	36
6 Mailliard	89	7	68*	15*
7 Dellums	14	74	—	—
8 Miller	70	9	52	24
9 Edwards	26	72	39	38
10 Gubser	67	2	65	21
11 McCloskey	46	40	71	17
12 Talcott	79	16	70	20
13 Teague	91	5	61*	17*
14 Waldie	25	63	46	39
15 McFall	72	19	65	30
16 Sisk	56	33	55	27
17 Anderson	44	53	54	41
18 Mathias	67	11	61	16
19 Holifield	68	23	53	31
20 Smith	61	19	67*	26*
21 Hawkins	30	53	32	30
22 Corman	42	42	54	29
23 Clawson	63	14	54	31
24 Rousselot	53	28	45*	29*
25 Wiggins	77	5	70	17
26 Rees	30	56	46	33
27 Goldwater	65	14	53*	17*
28 Bell	79	12	55	14
29 Danielson	49	49	—	—
30 Roybal	26	63	45	40
31 Wilson	37	28	41	29
32 Hosmer	88	4	72	13
33 Pettis	88	11	57	26
34 Hanna	47	26	50*	23*
35 Schmitz	58	42	39*	61*
36 Wilson	77	7	77	4
37 Van Deerlin	44	42	59	30
38 Veysey	79	5	—	—
COLORADO				
1 McKevitt	75	14	—	—
2 Brotzman	82	18	72	24
3 Evans	39	53	58	32
4 Aspinall	70	21	47	24
CONNECTICUT				
1 Cotter	46	46	—	—
2 Steele	58	28	69*	8*
3 Giaimo	51	33	47	33

	1	2	3	4
4 McKinney	67	28	—	—
5 Monagan	56	42	60	28
6 Grasso	33	40	—	—
DELAWARE				
AL DuPont	79	21	—	—
FLORIDA				
1 Sikes	61	18	49	31
2 Fuqua	61	26	52	39
3 Bennett	53	47	55	45
4 Chappell	63	23	46	44
5 Frey	74	11	59	28
6 Gibbons	46	49	53	37
7 Haley	65	35	46	44
8 Young	81	16	—	—
9 Rogers	67	33	54	43
10 Burke	72	23	51	38
11 Pepper	61	32	47	25
12 Fascell	47	47	47	27
GEORGIA				
1 Hagan	70	19	46	46
2 Mathis	67	28	—	—
3 Brinkley	74	26	56	44
4 Blackburn	65	23	57	28
5 Thompson	82	16	63	29
6 Flynt	42	21	41	34
7 Davis	67	16	46	32
8 Stuckey	40	19	48	40
9 Landrum	42	25	46	27
10 Stephens	63	21	46	23
HAWAII				
1 Matsunaga	39	58	61	34
2 Mink	23	68	59	41
IDAHO				
1 McClure	54	5	54	36
2 Hansen	84	4	66	19
ILLINOIS				
1 Metcalfe	26	37	—	—
2 Mikva	23	66	43	43
3 Murphy, M.	42	42	64	30
4 Derwinski	49	12	59	30
5 Kluczynski	60	26	47	25
6 Collins	23	58	31*	15*
7 Annunzio	56	32	65	28
8 Rostenkowski	49	35	53	22
9 Yates	30	70	54	39
10 Collier	82	11	55*	27*
11 Pucinski	46	51	50	35
12 McClory	77	16	66	16
13 Crane	60	33	51*	36*
14 Erlenborn	86	7	68	15
15 Reid[2]	93†	2†	74	22
16 Anderson	88	7	68	11
17 Arends	82	5	77	13
18 Michel	75	16	70	17
19 Railsback	58	25	62	15
20 Findley	68	19	69	15
21 Gray	56	33	46	29
22 Springer	82	11	76	18
23 Shipley	53	37	53	38
24 Price	72	21	63	32
INDIANA				
1 Madden	33	61	54	39
2 Landgrebe	70	26	53	37
3 Brademas	37	60	55	37
4 Roush	32	63	—	—
5 Hillis	91	5	—	—
6 Bray	84	7	57	25
7 Myers	82	16	63*	31*
8 Zion	81	11	62	32
9 Hamilton	42	54	68	27
10 Dennis	68	25	64	28
11 Jacobs	30	67	54	40
IOWA				
1 Schwengel	65	33	77	22
2 Culver	25	63	58	35
3 Gross	47	51	41	58
4 Kyl	81	14	54	34
5 Smith	44	51	59	29
6 Mayne	74	18	77	21
7 Scherle	61	28	51	39

	1	2	3	4
KANSAS				
1 Sebelius	77	12	63	23
2 Roy	35	61	—	—
3 Winn	79	11	62	25
4 Shriver	89	11	78	20
5 Skubitz	77	9	66	27
KENTUCKY				
1 Stubblefield	60	33	53	39
2 Natcher	63	37	61	39
3 Mazzoli	44	54	—	—
4 Snyder	54	42	46	36
5 Carter	82	12	65	27
6 Curlin[3]	100†	0†	—	—
7 Perkins	56	44	67	32
LOUISIANA				
1 Hebert	56	9	36	15
2 Boggs	60	26	71	25
3 Caffery	70	25	41	38
4 Waggonner	74	18	55	37
5 Passman	63	19	48	32
6 Rarick	56	37	31	53
7 Edwards	0	0	33	20
8 Long	11	4	32	34
MAINE				
1 Kyros	37	61	64	30
2 Hathaway	32	65	63	33
MARYLAND				
1 Mills[4]	81†	16†	—	—
2 Long	28	68	46	45
3 Garmatz	58	28	61	32
4 Sarbanes	28	67	—	—
5 Hogan	77	18	68	29
6 Byron	84	16	—	—
7 Mitchell	23	72	—	—
8 Gude	47	51	66	29
MASSACHUSETTS				
1 Conte	49	47	71	26
2 Boland	51	47	65	29
3 Drinan	28	72	—	—
4 Donohue	18	44	64	32
5 Morse	53	44	59	25
6 Harrington	33	67	46*	44*
7 Macdonald	35	53	48	44

	1	2	3	4
8 O'Neill	46	51	61	31
9 Hicks	54	39	—	—
10 Heckler	39	49	63	29
11 Burke	40	60	67	33
12 Keith	89	4	71	19
MICHIGAN				
1 Conyers	19	61	21	39
2 Esch	51	35	66	20
3 Brown	79	18	65	21
4 Hutchinson	68	32	64	32
5 Ford	89	7	84	12
6 Chamberlain	89	7	74	22
7 Riegle	32	54	57	31
8 Harvey	72	26	68	19
9 Vander Jagt	61	21	69	15
10 Cederberg	91	5	70	10
11 Ruppe	47	23	64*	17*
12 O'Hara	32	60	59	35
13 Diggs	12	32	31	31
14 Nedzi	35	61	49	37
15 Ford	25	61	49	38
16 Dingell	46	51	52	32
17 Griffiths	44	32	53	24
18 Broomfield	72	26	65	23
19 McDonald	51	44	63	21
MINNESOTA				
1 Quie	72	26	74	20
2 Nelsen	89	5	73	16
3 Frenzel	56	30	—	—
4 Karth	35	58	55	35
5 Fraser	28	68	54	38
6 Zwach	60	33	61	32
7 Bergland	39	61	—	—
8 Blatnik	25	54	43	29
MISSISSIPPI				
1 Abernethy	74	19	51	42
2 Whitten	68	26	49	42
3 Griffin	68	21	45	42
4 Montgomery	70	18	43	34
5 Colmer	63	21	48	30
MISSOURI				
1 Clay	12	51	29	30
2 Symington	37	58	52	33

Presidential Support And Opposition: House

1. Support Score, 1971. Percentage of 57 Nixon-issue roll calls in 1971 on which Representative voted "yea" or "nay" *in agreement* with the President's position. Failures to vote lower both Support and Opposition scores.

2. Opposition Score, 1971. Percentage of 57 Nixon-issue roll calls in 1971 on which Representative voted "yea" or "nay" *in disagreement* with the President's position. Failures to vote lower both Support and Opposition scores.

1. Rep. George W. Andrews (D Ala.) died Dec. 26, 1971.

2. Rep. Charlotte T. Reid (R Ill.) resigned Oct. 7, 1971.

3. Rep. John C. Watts (D Ky.) died Sept. 24, 1971. His scores for 1971 were 74 percent support and 11 percent opposition. Rep. William P. Curlin was sworn in Dec. 6, 1971, to replace Watts.

4. Rep. William O. Mills (R Md.) sworn in May 27, 1971, to replace Rep. Rogers C. B. Morton (R), resigned. Morton was not eligible for any presidential issue roll calls in 1971.

Democrats　　　　　　　　　　　*Republicans*

	1	2	3	4
3 Sullivan	37	42	48	30
4 Randall	61	26	46	51
5 Bolling	53	46	44	26
6 Hull	77	21	47*	35*
7 Hall	58	32	46	34
8 Ichord	72	16	43	45
9 Hungate	33	58	46	46
10 Burlison	47	53	51	41
MONTANA				
1 Shoup	72	14	—	—
2 Melcher	37	54	60*	35*
NEBRASKA				
1 Thone	74	26	—	—
2 McCollister	79	21	—	—
3 Martin	72	14	51	29
NEVADA				
AL Baring	65	18	30	31
NEW HAMPSHIRE				
1 Wyman	84	12	64	31
2 Cleveland	74	25	67	33
NEW JERSEY				
1 Hunt	72	19	62	30
2 Sandman	84	9	68	24
3 Howard	25	67	56	35
4 Thompson	28	63	50	32
5 Frelinghuysen	77	5	77	15
6 Forsythe	72	28	92*	8*
7 Widnall	68	16	72	17
8 Roe	44	51	55*	37*
9 Helstoski	28	58	52	39
10 Rodino	33	51	61	33
11 Minish	39	56	64	36
12 Dwyer	53	32	64	21
13 Gallagher	54	30	42	32
14 Daniels	56	40	57	29
15 Patten	49	49	68	29
NEW MEXICO				
1 Lujan	53	16	49	21
2 Runnels	32	21	—	—
NEW YORK				
1 Pike	54	46	63	36
2 Grover	81	14	62	25
3 Wolff	39	53	46	43

	1	2	3	4
4 Wydler	70	19	67	24
5 Lent	72	19	—	—
6 Halpern	26	46	51	28
7 Addabbo	39	58	52	40
8 Rosenthal	28	72	46	43
9 Delaney	68	25	42	40
10 Celler	25	53	42	27
11 Brasco	33	58	50	37
12 Chisholm	21	70	25	41
13 Podell	35	58	48	36
14 Rooney	58	35	55	34
15 Carey	30	61	38	26
16 Murphy	60	16	54	26
17 Koch	28	58	54	40
18 Rangel	18	63	—	—
19 Abzug	25	75	—	—
20 Ryan	26	74	46	44
21 Badillo	14	77	—	—
22 Scheuer	30	65	39	39
23 Bingham	26	70	46	41
24 Biaggi	40	49	52	40
25 Peyser	77	16	—	—
26 Reid	44	54	57	33
27 Dow	23	70	—	—
28 Fish	68	23	65	23
29 Stratton	67	25	55	27
30 King	79†	14†	52	25
31 McEwen	72	14	63	21
32 Pirnie	75	7	67	21
33 Robison	65	32	67	18
34 Terry	77	16	—	—
35 Hanley	54	42	57	33
36 Horton	65	30	60	28
37 Conable	82	7	73	17
38 Hastings	72	16	53	21
39 Kemp	81	14	—	—
40 Smith	84	9	77	14
41 Dulski	42	49	58	35
NORTH CAROLINA				
1 Jones	67	28	47	46
2 Fountain	82	16	55	45
3 Henderson	75	23	51	40
4 Galifianakis	53	37	65	34
5 Mizell	88	11	66	29

	1	2	3	4
6 Preyer	61	39	67	29
7 Lennon	70	16	46	36
8 Ruth	82	18	67	29
9 Jones	74	11	67*	29*
10 Broyhill	74	18	63	33
11 Taylor	61	23	54	38
NORTH DAKOTA				
1 Andrews	74	23	60	21
2 Link	37	61	—	—
OHIO				
1 Keating	88	12	—	—
2 Clancy	84	12	51	35
3 Whalen	53	46	65	30
4 McCulloch	19	4	64	19
5 Latta	74	19	59	27
6 Harsha	70	21	58	35
7 Brown	86	5	69	23
8 Betts	91	5	70	24
9 Ashley	49	25	59	30
10 Miller	70	30	62	38
11 Stanton	74	18	77	17
12 Devine	75	16	51	33
13 Mosher	47	53	66	27
14 Seiberling	25	68	—	—
15 Wylie	75	19	67	29
16 Bow	81	7	75	15
17 Ashbrook	63	23	43	41
18 Hays	54	40	40	32
19 Carney	46	44	62*	23*
20 Stanton	42	51	—	—
21 Stokes	21	58	39	46
22 Vanik	35	63	58	40
23 Minshall	63	19	57	27
24 Powell	81	16	—	—
OKLAHOMA				
1 Belcher	82	5	68	24
2 Edmondson	58	26	51	29
3 Albert	63•	37•	68	27
4 Steed	61	28	58	31
5 Jarman	60	16	59	30
6 Camp	70	19	52	25
OREGON				
1 Wyatt	65	14	65	20
2 Ullman	40	51	59	29
3 Green	37	53	56	25
4 Dellenback	77	21	73	21
PENNSYLVANIA				
1 Barrett	33	39	53	33
2 Nix	40	56	59	38
3 Byrne	44	42	54	37
4 Eilberg	30	60	54	38
5 Green	25	54	54	39
6 Yatron	33	56	57	38
7 Williams	86	14	68	25
8 Biester	56	42	67	32
9 Ware	93	5	100*	0*
10 McDade	67	32	72	23
11 Flood	70	28	60	35
12 Whalley	81	5	54	22
13 Coughlin	61	37	67	26
14 Moorhead	40	51	53	36
15 Rooney	49	46	61	31
16 Eshleman	58	16	69	26
17 Schneebeli	72	21	68	23
18 Heinz[5]	63†	13†	—	—
19 Goodling	70	26	63	32
20 Gaydos	39	54	49	41
21 Dent	14	32	44	26
22 Saylor	54	21	46	32
23 Johnson	70	11	66	22
24 Vigorito	60	40	71	29
25 Clark	49	11	49	34
26 Morgan	67	21	57	37
27 Fulton[6]	51†	49†	62	33
RHODE ISLAND				
1 St Germain	40	56	51	36
2 Tiernan	33	53	58	34
SOUTH CAROLINA				
1 Davis[7]	65†	29†	—	—
2 Spence	72	19	—	—
3 Dorn	65	19	52	38
4 Mann	72	21	53	29

	1	2	3	4
5 Gettys	53	28	49	33
6 McMillan	65	16	40	31
SOUTH DAKOTA				
1 Denholm	18	65	—	—
2 Abourezk	23	70	—	—
TENNESSEE				
1 Quillen	81	7	61*	31*
2 Duncan	74	26	63	38
3 Baker	74	11	—	—
4 Evins	40	18	50*	25*
5 Fulton	33	53	42	22
6 Anderson	25	42	45	20
7 Blanton	54	18	52	32
8 Jones	51	21	38*	39*
9 Kuykendall	77	7	67	14
TEXAS				
1 Patman	49	25	42	29
2 Dowdy	44	16	38	37
3 Collins	68	30	58	31
4 Roberts	70	11	47	40
5 Cabell	68	23	44	33
6 Teague	61	16	38	33
7 Archer	75	23	—	—
8 Eckhardt	35	58	51	34
9 Brooks	54	37	46	25
10 Pickle	61	28	63	33
11 Poage	46	30	47	37
12 Wright	67	19	54	28
13 Purcell	58	18	39	31
14 Young	65	28	54	29
15 de la Garza	46	42	51	30
16 White	74	21	60	32
17 Burleson	72	25	54	38
18 Price	77	14	57	32
19 Mahon	77	23	66	27
20 Gonzalez	60	39	62	38
21 Fisher	70	21	41	40
22 Casey	72	23	59*	32*
23 Kazen	65	35	58	40
UTAH				
1 McKay	63	37	—	—
2 Lloyd	82	9	70	16
VERMONT				
AL Stafford[8]	59†	26†	74	19
VIRGINIA				
1 Downing	77	21	63	31
2 Whitehurst	86	14	60	31
3 Satterfield	77	21	54	42
4 Abbitt	72	16	43	29
5 Daniel	77	23	56*	44*
6 Poff	74	11	72	21
7 Robinson	82	16	—	—
8 Scott	75	23	54	42
9 Wampler	77	19	65	29
10 Broyhill	70	19	61	31
WASHINGTON				
1 Pelly	81	4	66*	12*
2 Meeds	47	44	59	29
3 Hansen	58	30	50	29
4 McCormack	46	47	—	—
5 Foley	53	39	62	32
6 Hicks	53	46	57	37
7 Adams	46	46	61	34
WEST VIRGINIA				
1 Mollohan	63	19	51	28
2 Staggers	60	25	56	33
3 Slack	54	37	59	37
4 Hechler	32	68	55	45
5 Kee	58	23	58	32
WISCONSIN				
1 Aspin	35	58	—	—
2 Kastenmeier	26	72	51	46
3 Thomson	79	19	72	23
4 Zablocki	75	25	59	38
5 Reuss	33	63	54	40
6 Steiger	74	21	66	21
7 Obey	33	67	54*	44*
8 Byrnes	74	14	79	14
9 Davis	84	7	78	19
10 O'Konski	75	25	42	31
WYOMING				
AL Roncalio	28	68	—	—

Presidential Support And Opposition: House

3. Support Score, 91st Congress. Percentage of 112 Nixon-issue roll calls in 1969 and 1970 on which Representative voted "yea" or "nay" *in agreement* with the President's position. Failures to vote lower both Support and Opposition scores.

4. Opposition Score, 91st Congress. Percentage of 112 Nixon-issue roll calls in 1969 and 1970 on which Representative voted "yea" or "nay" *in disagreement* with the President's position. Failures to vote lower both Support and Opposition scores.

5. *Rep. Robert J. Corbett (R Pa.) died April 25, 1971. His scores for 1971 were 27 percent support and 18 percent opposition. Rep. H. John Heinz III was sworn in Nov. 4, 1971, to replace Corbett.*

6. *Rep. James G. Fulton (R Pa.) died Oct. 6, 1971.*

7. *Rep. Mendel J. Davis (D S.C.) sworn in April 29, 1971, to replace Rep. L. Mendel Rivers (D), deceased. Rep. Rivers was not eligible for any presidential issue roll calls in 1971.*

8. *Rep. Robert T. Stafford (R Vt.) resigned Sept. 17, 1971, to accept appointment to the Senate. (See Senate chart.)*

APPROPRIATIONS IN 1st SESSION, 92nd CONGRESS

Compiled by Congressional Quarterly as of Dec. 18, 1971

HS —Hearings Scheduled   IC—In Conference
HU—Hearings Underway   C—Committee
HC—Hearings Completed   F—Floor

BILL	Nixon Request 1972 Fiscal Year	HOUSE	SENATE	CONFERENCE and FINAL
Agriculture-Environmental (HR 9270)	$12,102,813,850*	C-$12,080,596,050 F-$12,423,896,050 (June 23)	C-$13,090,266,050 F-$13,621,677,050 (July 15)	$13,276,900,050 (July 30, PL 92-35) $11,493,783,000**
Defense (HR 11731)	$73,543,829,000*	C-$71,048,013,000 F-$71,048,013,000 (Nov. 17)	C-$70,242,513,000 F-$70,849,113,000 (Nov. 23)	$70,518,463,000 (Dec. 18, PL 92-204) $69,898,293,000**
District of Columbia (HR 11932)	$1,045,281,700*	C-$901,476,700 F-$973,962,700 (Dec. 2)	C-$873,040,700 F-$882,040,700 (Dec. 3)	$932,512,700 (Dec. 18, PL 92-202) $337,012,000**
Foreign Assistance (HR 12067)	$4,342,635,000	C-$2,845,461,000 F-$3,003,461,000 (Dec. 8)	HC (July 16)	
HUD, NASA, Veterans (HR 9382)	$17,451,357,000*	C-$18,108,203,000 F-$18,115,203,000 (June 30)	C-$18,677,518,000 F-$18,698,518,000 (July 20)	$18,339,738,000 (Aug. 10, PL 92-78) $18,150,247,000**
Interior Department (HR 9417)	$2,385,231,035*	C-$2,350,145,035 F-$2,350,145,035 (June 29)	C-$2,417,839,035 F-$2,417,964,035 (July 16)	$2,415,809,035 (Aug. 10, PL 92-76) $2,285,848,000**
Labor-HEW (HR 10061)	$20,223,638,000*	C-$20,364,746,000 F-$20,461,247,000 (July 27)	C-$21,032,725,000 F-$21,118,317,000 (July 30)	$20,804,662,000 (Aug. 10, PL 92-80) $21,038,060,000**
Legislative Branch (HR 8825)	$535,349,607*	C-$449,739,605 F-$449,899,605 (June 4)	C-$532,582,749 F-$532,582,749 (June 21)	$529,309,749 (July 9, PL 92-51) $452,471,000**
Military Construction (HR 11418)	$2,313,375,000*	C-$2,012,446,000 F-$2,012,446,000 (Oct. 27)	C-$2,002,312,000 F-$2,002,312,000 (Nov. 1)	$2,037,097,000 (Nov. 18, PL 92-160) $2,229,875,000**
Office of Education (HR 7016)	$4,753,186,000*	C-$4,769,508,000 F-$4,800,088,000 (April 7)	C-$5,604,918,000 F-$5,615,918,000 (June 10)	$5,146,311,000 (July 9, PL 92-48) $4,887,661,000**
AEC Public Works (HR 10090)	$4,647,445,000*	C-$4,576,148,000 F-$4,607,673,000 (July 29)	C-$4,746,377,000 F-$4,748,422,000 (July 31)	$4,706,625,000 (Oct. 5, PL 92-134) $5,309,708,000**
State-Justice-Commerce (HR 9272)	$4,216,802,000*	C-$4,036,898,000 F-$3,684,183,000 (June 24)	C-$4,091,973,337 F-$4,338,627,000 (July 19)	$4,307,660,000 (Aug. 10, PL 92-77) $3,895,655,000**
Transportation Department (HR 9667)	$2,860,327,997*	C-$7,753,562,997 F-$7,983,464,000 (July 14)	C-$8,209,013,000 F-$8,210,013,000 (July 22)	$8,156,105,000 (Aug. 10, PL 92-74) $7,838,377,000**
Treasury, Executive Branch (HR 9271)	$4,809,216,000*	C-$4,487,289,000 F-$4,487,676,190 (June 28)	C-$4,740,702,690 F-$4,752,789,690 (June 29)	$4,528,986,690 (July 9, PL 92-49) $3,974,252,000**
Supplemental, 1972 (HR 11955)	$3,254,924,371*	C-$756,282,654 F-$786,282,654 (Dec. 2)	C-$3,833,828,371 F-$3,998,045,371 (Dec. 3)	$3,406,385,371 (Dec. 15, PL 92-184) $1,800,291,000**
Supplemental, Urgent, 1971 (H J Res 567)	$1,042,294,000	C-$1,037,872,000 F-$1,037,872,000 (April 23)	C-$1,037,872,000 F-$1,037,872,000 (April 23)	$1,037,872,000 (April 30, PL 92-11)
Supplemental, Second, 1971 (HR 8190)	$7,779,740,077	C-$6,781,152,545 F-$6,889,152,545 (May 12)	C-$7,098,398,093 F-$7,184,898,973 (May 19)	$7,028,195,973 (May 25, PL 92-18)

*Total includes amendments submitted after original budget request.
**Outlays as reported by the Joint Committee on Reduction of Federal Expenditures.

$229.2-BILLION BUDGET: A RECORD HIGH, AND A DEFICIT

President Nixon sent to Congress Jan. 29 a record $229.2-billion budget with an $11.6-billion deficit for the federal government's fiscal year 1972.

Mr. Nixon called it a "full-employment" budget, adopting an economists' term. It meant that expenditures would actually be in balance with revenues if the economy were at full employment (instead of at the existing rate of 6-percent unemployment) and producing the full revenues that the existing tax structure was capable of.

In his budget message, the President described the full-employment budget as "a tool to promote orderly economic expansion." He compared it to a self-fulfilling prophecy: "By operating as if we were at full employment, we will help to bring about that full employment."

Mr. Nixon's budget also estimated that for fiscal year 1971 the government would have an expansionary deficit of $18.6-billion. The summary figures:

(In $billions)	1970 (actual)	1971 (estimated)	1972 (estimated)
Receipts	193.7	194.2	217.6
Outlays	196.6	212.8	229.2
Deficit	-2.8	-18.6	-11.6
Surplus (if at full employment)	2.6	1.4	0.1
Budget authority requested	213.0	236.3	249.0

Note: The actual deficit in fiscal year 1971 was $23-billion. The deficit for fiscal year 1972 was re-estimated at $38.8-billion by the Administration in the budget for fiscal year 1973, which was sent to Congress in January 1972.

References

Text of President's budget message, p. 11-A; President's State of the Union message, p. 2-A; analysis of revenue sharing, p. 23-A.

Table of budget authority and outlays by function, p. 66-67; table of budget authority and outlays by agency, p. 68; table comparing past budgets, this page; box on budget terminology, p. 70.

The budget for fiscal year 1972 was based on optimistic economic assumptions and raised ambitious goals for the federal government and the nation.

The President presented his budget as an engine of economic policy, designed to create conditions for recovery from recession to prosperity without inflation. It was to operate in harness with an expansionary monetary policy and with wage and price restraint in the private sector.

It was a budget which Mr. Nixon characterized as continuing the transition begun in fiscal 1971 from wartime to peacetime. For the second straight year, funds budgeted to meet human needs were to exceed those budgeted for defense, although defense funds were increased on grounds that an increase was necessary to progress toward peace. High priorities included improvement of both the natural and the man-made environment.

Mr. Nixon presented the economic underpinning of the budget in the Economic Report of the President, which he sent to Congress Feb. 1. Chief among the assumptions underlying the budget was a total output of the economy (gross national product) of $1.065-trillion in calendar year 1971. This was approximately $20-billion higher than the consensus of estimates by economists outside the government and about $18-billion more than the economy actually achieved. *(Box on economic report, p. 64; economic summary, p. 26)*

Priorities

Mr. Nixon listed five priorities in addition to the economic recovery to be stimulated by the full-employment budget:

Federal Budget 1954-1972

(in $ billions)

Fiscal Year	Receipts	Outlays	Surplus/ Deficit
1954	69,719	70,890	—1,170
1955	65,469	68,509	—3,041
1956	74,547	70,460	+4,087
1957	79,990	76,741	+3,249
1958	79,636	82,575	—2,939
1959	79,249	92,104	—12,855
1960	92,492	92,223	+269
1961	94,389	97,795	—3,406
1962	99,676	106,813	—7,137
1963	106,560	111,311	—4,751
1964	112,662	118,584	—5,922
1965	116,833	118,430	—1,596
1966	130,856	134,652	—3,796
1967	149,552	158,254	—8,702
1968	153,671	178,833	—25,161
1969	187,784	184,548	+3,236
1970	193,743	196,588	—2,845
1971 est	194,193	212,755	—18,562
1972 est	217,593	229,232	—11,639

Note: Figures for years before fiscal year 1969 adjusted to conform to unified budget concept adopted in fiscal 1969.

Economic Report: Nixon Promised Recovery In 1971

President Nixon sent to Congress Feb. 1 his Economic Report holding out promise of vigorous recovery in 1971 from the recession of late 1969 and early 1970.

The year 1970, the President began his report, "was the year in which we paid for the excesses of 1966, 1967 and 1968, when federal spending went $40-billion beyond full-employment revenues."

"But we are nearing the end of these payments," he continued, "and 1971 will be a better year, leading to a good year in 1972—and to a new steadiness of expansion in the years beyond."

In the accompanying Annual Report of the Council of Economic Advisers (CEA), 1971 was pictured as an outstanding year. Gross national product, the total output of the economy, was forecast at an $88-billion gain, to $1.065-trillion, over 1970, measured in current (inflated) prices.

Chairman Paul W. McCracken of the CEA, defending the council's figures, said the council had not prepared a passive forecast. To the contrary, he said, it was a goal and an exposition of the actions and conditions necessary to achieve it. (Economic reports cover calendar years; budgets cover fiscal years.)

Review of 1970

In 1970, the rate of inflation was slowed, Mr. Nixon said. He said the rate of price increases was reduced, productivity rose and per-unit costs of labor increased less than in 1969. The federal government reduced its level of defense spending, he added.

"These two simultaneous transitions, from a wartime to a peacetime economy and from a higher to a lower rate of inflation," the President said, "would inevitably be accompanied by some decline in output and rise in unemployment."

Gross national product (GNP), measured in constant (1958) prices, declined from $724.7-billion in 1969 to $720.0-billion in 1970. Unemployment, which was 3.5 percent of the labor force in December 1969, rose to 6.1 percent in December 1970.

"The performance of the economy disappointed many expectations and intentions, including those of this council," the report of the conomic advisers said of 1970. But, it continued, "The policies of 1969 and 1970 set a ceiling to the mounting inflation and turned the inflation down; they set a floor to declining output and turned it upward." Emphasis shifted early in 1970 from the counter-inflation policy of 1969 to expansionary fiscal and monetary policies.

Outlook for 1971

Mr. Nixon said powerful forces were present in the economy which made expansion probable. But they were not strong enough by themselves to assure a sufficient increase in output. Expansionary fiscal and monetary policies also were necessary, he said.

The full-employment budget for fiscal year 1972 would stimulate substantial expansion, he said. Monetary policy would be called upon to meet the remainder of the need.

The CEA outlined two possible courses of action and rejected both. "Confining the economic expansion to a pace which would keep unemployment about where it now is...would permit a significant decline in the rate of inflation during 1971 and 1972....Trying to restore what has been commonly regarded as 'full employment'—a 4-percent unemployment rate—within the present planning period that extends to the end of fiscal year 1972 would entail risks on the inflation side."

The council chose a path between those courses—reduction of unemployment "to the 4.5-percent zone" by the second quarter of 1972 and reduction of the rate of inflation so that it approached the range of 3 percent at the same time.

This path required expansionary policies sufficient to raise GNP to $1.065-trillion in 1971. The council noted that others were forecasting GNP at $1.045-trillion to $1.050-trillion for the year. But it found the higher level feasible and "consistent with the targets for unemployment and inflation."

Achievement of the GNP goal would require a 9-percent increase in 1971 over 1970. Morever, it would require a 12-percent gain from the fourth quarter of 1970 to the fourth quarter of 1971. Opinion differed, McCracken said, as to whether monetary growth greater than an annual rate of 6 percent would be necessary; growth in the money supply was about 6 percent in 1970.

The report anticipated price inflation would absorb slightly less than half the GNP growth in current prices. That left a real growth rate of about 4.5-percent which would yield a GNP gain in constant prices of about $45-billion—to about $765-billion for 1971. According to McCracken, unemployment should average slightly above 5 percent for the year.

Walter W. Heller, former chairman of the council (1961-64), testifying Feb. 1 before the Joint Economic Committee, found the Nixon Administration's forecasts unconvincing. He said the GNP forecast was $20-billion higher than the "standard" private projection and $17-billion higher than his own. The economy, he said, was running about 5 percent below its full-employment potential, with a loss of $50-billion a year in output. The Administration's policies, he predicted, would take until 1973 for the economy to achieve full employment.

Saul H. Hymans of the University of Michigan, writing in *Economic Activity 3*, published by the Brookings Institution, compared the forecasts of three econometric models for 1971 and found they agreed on a constant-price GNP increase of about 3 percent for the year. They also agreed on a lower over-all rate of inflation of 3.5 to 4 percent. The forecasts of real GNP gains ranged from $20-billion to $26-billion. The unemployment forecast ranged from 5.1 percent to 6.1 percent.

• Revenue sharing with state and local governments at an initial annual rate of $16-billion.

• Meeting human needs through improved health, welfare, education, civil rights and crime-prevention programs.

• Moving toward world peace through greater military strength, negotiation and realistic foreign aid programs.

• Improving the physical environment by abating pollution and through more effective housing and community development programs.

• Restoring confidence in government through reorganization and reform.

Revenue Sharing. Mr. Nixon's plan, as announced in his State of the Union message, had two parts: $5-billion for general revenue sharing with state and local governments with virtually no strings attached; and $11.1-billion in federal aids for six broad purposes packaged together by consolidating some 130 existing aid programs (totaling $10.4-billion, or about one-third of such aids, in fiscal 1971) and adding $700-million in new funds.

On a full-year basis, the breakdown by purpose was:

Urban community development	$2-billion
Rural community development	1-billion
Education	3-billion
Manpower training	2-billion
Law enforcement	.5-billion
Transportation	2.6-billion

General revenue sharing was scheduled in the budget to go into effect Oct. 1, if Congress approved the necessary legislation (substantial congressional opposition faced Mr. Nixon's plan). The consolidated grant program was scheduled to take effect Jan. 1, 1972. The budget included outlays of $9.5-billion for the partial-year cost of the programs.

The grant program, referred to as special revenue sharing, would eliminate requirements of existing programs that state and local funds match federal funds on a one-to-one basis or various other bases. Officials estimated this would free some $4.25-billion in state and local funds currently tied to specific federal programs to maintain eligibility for federal aids.

Shifting Priorities. The reordering of priorities begun with the budget for fiscal 1971, according to Mr. Nixon's message, was to be continued in 1972.

In fiscal 1972, he said, defense spending would fall from 36 percent of the total budget to 34 percent. Total defense spending was budgeted at $77.5-billion. Human resources programs would remain at approximately 42 percent of total spending, with outlays of $96.1-billion.

Comparisons

With outlays totaling $229.2-billion, the new budget proposed spending $16.4-billion more than the estimated total for fiscal year 1971. It asked for an increase of $12.7-billion in new budget authority, for a total of $249-billion.

Mr. Nixon's budget for fiscal 1971, when submitted, projected a surplus of $1.3-billion. The economy in early 1970, when that budget was sent to Congress, was responding to the stringent anti-inflation program which Mr. Nixon and the Federal Reserve Board were following. Unemployment climbed throughout the year, reaching 6 percent of the labor force in December (the unemployment rate had been 3.5 percent in December 1969). Gross national product—the total output of the economy in goods and services—was actually less in 1970 than the previous year, when measured in constant (uninflated) dollars, despite the fact that in current inflated dollars GNP attained an annual rate of $1-trillion late in the year. Inflation continued through the year, though at a moderately declining rate.

The President announced a revision of his budget May 19 and forecast a deficit of $1.3-billion for the fiscal year. The change, he said, was largely due to a shortfall in revenues, due to the slowing down of the economy.

The deficit estimated for fiscal 1971 in the new budget was $18.6-billion, which was expected to have a substantial expansionary effect on the sluggish economy. Yet the fiscal 1971 budget was estimated to be in surplus on a full-employment basis, and the 1972 budget, with a projected deficit of $11.6-billion, was estimated to be approximately in balance on that basis.

The budget forecast a substantial economic recovery in calendar year 1971 from the recession which dominated 1970. Gross national product was estimated at $1.065-trillion, compared with the $977-billion preliminary calculation for calendar 1970. On that basis, the forecast for fiscal 1972 was for a year of expansion.

At $217.6-billion, revenues were to be up $23.4-billion from the estimated total in fiscal 1971. In contrast, revenues gained only about $500-million from fiscal 1970 to 1971—far less than the loss to inflation.

Individual income tax receipts were estimated at $93.7-billion, up $5.4-billion from fiscal 1971. Corporation income taxes were up $6.6-billion, to $36.7-billion. Both corporate and individual income tax receipts in fiscal 1971 were below fiscal 1970 levels. The other major component of the revenue increase was Social Security taxes, scheduled for an increase of $8.6-billion to a total of $57.6-billion. The increase reflected both greater employment and greater contributions per employee through the Social Security tax. Mr. Nixon proposed to send Congress legislation adjusting the tax and the wage base subject to it. Legislation increasing both Social Security benefits and the wage base died at the end of the 91st Congress.

Revenues if the economy were operating at full employment were estimated at $214.2-billion for fiscal 1971 and $229.3-billion in fiscal 1972.

1972 Trends

Public Debt. The federal debt was expected to rise by $22.4-billion in fiscal 1972, to a total of $429.4-billion. The comparable 1971 figure was $24.4-billion. Debt held by the public was to increase by only $10.6-billion, the remainder being held by trust funds, such as the Social Security fund.

'Federal Funds' Budget. All budget figures were calculated under the unified budget concept first used in fiscal year 1969. The unified budget combines receipts and disbursements of the trust funds with other federal transactions. These were not included in the Administrative budget in use before fiscal 1969.

If trust fund transactions were eliminated, the remaining federal funds budget—approximating the Ad-

FISCAL 1972 BUDGET PROPOSED $229.2-BILLION IN...

(in millions of dollars)†

	BUDGET AUTHORITY‡			EXPENDITURES		
	1970	1971 est.	1972 est.	1970	1971 est.	1972 est.
NATIONAL DEFENSE						
Military Defense	$ 74,083	$ 71,335	$ 77,585	$ 77,070	$ 73,296	$ 74,898
Loan Authority and Net Lending, Military Defense #	0	0	0	—1	—*	—*
Civil Defense	70	73	78	80	74	77
Military Assistance	330	1,290	1,080	731	1,130	1,025
Atomic Energy	2,220	2,308	2,251	2,453	2,275	2,318
Defense-related Activities	104	110	115	80	—53	93
Loan Authority and Net Lending, Defense-related Activities #	—*	—*	—*	—1	—1	—1
Deductions for Offsetting Receipts	—118	—278	—898	—118	—278	—898
TOTAL	$ 76,689	$ 74,838	$ 80,211	$ 80,294	$ 76,443	$ 77,512
INTERNATIONAL AFFAIRS AND FINANCE						
Conduct of Foreign Affairs	$ 398	$ 441	$ 451	$ 398	$ 421	$ 453
Economic and Financial Assistance	2,261	2,796	3,128	1,939	1,939	2,225
Loan Authority and Net Lending, Economic and Financial Assistance #	0	0	225	292	251	410
Foreign Information and Exchange	222	231	245	235	240	243
Food for Peace	920	702	1,320	937	1,014	962
Deductions for Offsetting Receipts	—232	—279	—261	—232	—279	—261
TOTAL	$ 3,568	$ 3,892	$ 5,108	$ 3,570	$ 3,587	$ 4,032
SPACE RESEARCH AND TECHNOLOGY	$ 3,752	$ 3,310	$ 3,283	$ 3,755	$ 3,381	$ 3,164
Deductions for Offsetting Receipts	—6	—13	—13	—6	—13	—13
TOTAL	$ 3,746	$ 3,297	$ 3,270	$ 3,749	$ 3,368	$ 3,151
AGRICULTURE AND RURAL DEVELOPMENT						
Farm Income Stabilization	$ 5,166	$ 3,445	$ 4,419	$ 4,655	$ 4,065	$ 4,488
Loan Authority and Net Lending, Farm Income Stabilization #	80	75	82	—63	10	—261
Financing Rural Housing and Public Facilities	137	210	138	183	186	205
Loan Authority and Net Lending, Financing Rural Housing and Public Facilities #	289	292	593	395	—126	227
Agricultural Land and Water Resources	359	368	321	344	353	334
Loan Authority and Net Lending, Agricultural Land and Water Resources #	0	0	0	*	*	0
Research and Other Services	735	823	852	730	816	855
Deductions for Offsetting Receipts	—41	—42	—43	—41	—42	—43
TOTAL	$ 6,726	$ 5,171	$ 6,362	$ 6,201	$ 5,262	$ 5,804
NATURAL RESOURCES						
Water Resources and Power	$ 2,812	$ 6,428	$ 4,296	$ 2,242	$ 3,020	$ 3,851
Loan Authority and Net Lending, Water Resources and Power #	3	7	9	3	4	14
Land Management	822	897	874	754	864	830
Mineral Resources	110	138	72	94	173	68
Recreational Resources	430	662	788	370	536	615
Other Natural Resources Programs	123	134	145	122	133	143
Deductions for Offsetting Receipts	—1,105	—2,093	—1,276	—1,105	—2,093	—1,276
TOTAL	$ 3,195	$ 6,172	$ 4,908	$ 2,480	$ 2,635	$ 4,244
COMMERCE AND TRANSPORTATION						
Air Transportation	$ 2,161	$ 1,601	$ 1,708	$ 1,223	$ 1,620	$ 1,835
Water Transportation	836	1,117	1,165	911	1,073	1,130
Loan Authority and Net Lending, Water Transportation #	—7	—6	—6	—9	—7	—7
Ground Transportation	5,859	8,844	6,025	4,629	5,110	5,275
Loan Authority and Net Lending, Ground Transportation #	100	100	0	3	35	35
Postal Service	1,758	12,735	1,472	1,510	2,353	1,333
Advancement of Business	620	579	638	359	372	283
Loan Authority and Net Lending, Advancement of Business #	175	380	508	128	163	253
Area and Regional Development	719	803	742	537	672	755
Loan Authority and Net Lending, Area and Regional Development #	61	63	69	53	74	46
Regulation of Business	129	136	143	121	132	141
Loan Authority and Net Lending, Regulation of Business #	—1	44	—*	—1	44	—*
Deductions for Offsetting Receipts	—154	—200	—142	—154	—200	—142
TOTAL	$ 12,256	$ 26,195	$ 12,320	$ 9,310	$ 11,442	$ 10,937
COMMUNITY DEVELOPMENT AND HOUSING						
Concentrated Community Development	$ 1,367	$ 1,469	$ 778	$ 825	$ 1,175	$ 1,246
Loan Authority and Net Lending, Concentrated Community Developments #	6	0	0	—10	—7	—11
Community Environment	1,096	1,302	805	1,111	1,126	1,396
Loan Authority and Net Lending, Community Environment #	0	0	0	—6	47	1
Community Facilities	184	404	1,063	142	188	383
Loan Authority and Net Lending, Community Facilities #	2	—2	0	39	40	33
Community Planning and Administration	110	138	202	69	133	153
Loan Authority and Net Lending, Community Planning and Administration #	0	0	0	*	—2	—2

EXPENDITURES, $249 BILLION IN SPENDING AUTHORITY

(in millions of dollars)†

	BUDGET AUTHORITY‡			EXPENDITURES		
	1970	**1971 est.**	**1972 est.**	**1970**	**1971 est.**	**1972 est.**
Low and Moderate Income Housing Aids	554	895	1,421	493	883	1,441
Loan Authority and Net Lending, Low and Moderate Income Housing Aids #	2,795	45	40	787	750	507
Maintenance of Housing Mortgage Market	22	99	101	—443	—433	—375
Loan Authority and Net Lending, Maintenance of Housing Mortgage Market #	3,000	75	60	—44	10	—276
Deductions for Offsetting Receipts	—*	—53	—*	—*	—53	—*
TOTAL	$ 9,137	$ 4,372	$ 4,470	$ 2,964	$ 3,858	$ 4,495
EDUCATION AND MANPOWER						
Elementary and Secondary Education	$ 2,970	$ 3,857	$ 4,258	$ 2,968	$ 3,245	$ 3,562
Loan Authority and Net Lending, Elementary and Secondary Education #	1	*	—*	—*	—*	—*
Higher Education	966	1,055	1,597	1,141	1,267	1,246
Loan Authority and Net Lending, Higher Education #	12	—19	403	240	191	56
Vocational Education	378	527	480	289	423	501
Manpower Training and Employment Services	1,973	2,064	2,321	1,602	2,017	2,156
Science Education and Basic Research	440	506	622	464	502	546
Other Education Aids	389	399	430	429	419	463
Loan Authority and Net Lending, Other Education Aids #	5	0	0	0	0	0
Other Manpower Aids	187	253	310	169	248	308
Deductions for Offsetting Receipts	—14	—12	—29	—14	—12	—29
TOTAL	$ 7,307	$ 8,628	$ 10,391	$ 7,288	$ 8,300	$ 8,808
HEALTH						
Development of Health Resources	$ 2,014	$ 2,337	$ 2,418	$ 2,091	$ 2,223	$ 2,369
Loan Authority and Net Lending, Development of Health Resources #	5	10	—*	6	5	11
Providing or Financing Medical Services	10,587	13,937	17,147	10,344	12,037	12,945
Prevention and Control of Health Problems	611	730	837	561	664	703
Deductions for Offsetting Receipts	—6	—2	—18	—6	—2	—18
TOTAL	$ 13,212	$ 17,013	$ 20,384	$ 12,996	$ 14,927	$ 16,010
INCOME SECURITY						
Retirement and Social Insurance	$ 45,894	$ 48,763	$ 55,014	$ 37,275	$ 46,003	$ 49,030
Public Assistance	5,438	7,905	9,902	5,182	7,856	9,785
Loan Authority and Net Lending, Public Assistance #	4	4	5	3	3	5
Social and Individual Services	1,474	1,819	1,989	1,331	1,684	1,937
Deductions for Offsetting Receipts	—1	—1	—18	—1	—1	—18
TOTAL	$ 52,808	$ 58,490	$ 66,892	$ 43,790	$ 55,546	$ 60,740
VETERANS BENEFITS AND SERVICES						
Income Security	$ 5,995	$ 6,544	$ 6,924	$ 5,916	$ 6,440	$ 6,853
Loan Authority and Net Lending, Income Security #	105	111	120	105	111	120
Education, Training and Rehabilitation	1,044	1,696	1,932	1,015	1,715	1,981
Loan Authority and Net Lending, Education, Training and Rehabilitation #	0	0	0	*	0	0
Housing	—68	159	133	—45	—24	17
Loan Authority and Net Lending, Housing #	73	—153	—127	99	—123	—350
Hospital and Medical Care	1,837	2,055	2,214	1,802	2,056	2,230
Other Veterans Benefits and Services	270	284	303	260	288	301
Deductions for Offsetting Receipts	—476	—493	—508	—476	—493	—508
TOTAL	$ 8,780	$ 10,204	$ 10,991	$ 8,676	$ 9,969	$ 10,644
INTEREST	$ 19,424	$ 20,924	$ 21,273	$ 19,424	$ 20,924	$ 21,273
Deductions for Offsetting Receipts	—1,110	—1,491	—1,586	—1,110	—1,491	—1,586
TOTAL	$ 18,314	$ 19,433	$ 19,687	$ 18,314	$ 19,433	$ 19,687
GENERAL GOVERNMENT	$ 3,788	$ 4,934	$ 5,783	$ 3,483	$ 4,496	$ 5,339
Loan Authority and Net Lending, General Government #	88	50	58	112	138	137
Deductions for Offsetting Receipts	—259	—254	—506	—259	—254	—506
TOTAL	$ 3,617	$ 4,730	$ 5,335	$ 3,336	$ 4,380	$ 4,970
REVENUE SHARING	0	0	$ 4,106	0	0	$ 4,019
CIVILIAN PAY INCREASES	0	$ 525	$ 1,050	0	$ 500	$ 1,000
CONTINGENCIES	0	$ 500	$ 1,250	0	$ 300	$ 950
UNDISTRIBUTED INTRAGOVERNMENTAL PAYMENTS	$ —6,380	$ —7,197	$ —7,771	$ —6,380	$ —7,197	$ —7,771
GRAND TOTAL	$212,973	$236,263	$248,965	$196,587	$212,754	$229,232

† Figures may not add to totals due to rounding.
‡ Primarily appropriations.
SOURCE: OFFICE OF MANAGEMENT AND BUDGET

* Less than $500 thousand.
 # Figures in the first three columns are Loan Authority; figures in the remaining columns are Net Lending.

Budget Authority and Outlays by Agency

(in millions of dollars)

Department or other unit	Budget authority			Outlays		
	1970 actual	1971 estimate	1972 estimate	1970 actual	1971 estimate	1972 estimate
Legislative Branch	359	430	519	343	396	430
The Judiciary	126	148	169	128	143	167
Executive Office of the President	38	49	56	36	50	55
Funds appropriated to the President	4,980	5,680	5,248	4,774	4,924	4,676
Agriculture	8,929	8,357	10,493	8,307	8,702	9,510
Commerce	1,056	1,235	1,428	1,079	1,203	1,281
Defense—Military [1]	74,153	71,408	77,663	77,150	73,370	74,975
Defense—Civil	1,202	1,338	1,452	1,210	1,426	1,508
Health, Education & Welfare	58,313	66,660	78,790	52,249	61,940	68,719
Housing & Urban Development	5,384	3,432	3,629	2,603	3,333	3,888
Interior	1,119	509	1,532	823	357	1,434
Justice	861	1,238	1,540	640	1,071	1,412
Labor	5,167	6,418	7,115	4,356	7,521	7,224
State	456	517	530	448	482	525
Transportation	8,685	11,169	8,448	6,417	7,367	7,805
Treasury	19,546	20,909	21,205	19,509	20,893	21,180
Atomic Energy Commission	2,220	2,308	2,251	2,453	2,275	2,318
Environmental Protection Agency	1,004	1,286	2,451	350	679	1,364
General Services Administration	394	441	—188	446	335	—275
National Aeronautics & Space Administration	3,746	3,297	3,270	3,749	3,368	3,151
Postal Service	1,758	12,735	1,472	1,510	2,353	1,333
Veterans Administration	8,750	10,171	10,954	8,653	9,948	10,622
Other independent agencies	11,106	12,698	10,303	5,733	7,015	7,734
Allowances for:						
Added amount—revenue sharing	—	—	4,106	—	—	4,019
Pay increases (excluding DOD)	—	525	1,050	—	500	1,000
Contingencies	—	500	1,250	—	300	950
Undistributed intragovernmental transactions:						
Employer share, employee retirement	—2,444	—2,486	—2,461	—2,444	—2,486	—2,461
Interest from trust funds	—3,936	—4,711	—5,310	—3,936	—4,711	—5,310
Total budget authority and outlays	212,973	236,263	248,965	196,588	212,755	229,232

1 Includes allowance for all-volunteer force and civilian and military pay increases for Department of Defense.

ministrative budget—was in deficit by $23.1-billion in fiscal 1972. For 1971 the figure was $25.5-billion; for fiscal 1970 it was $13.1-billion.

Expenditure Ceiling. Congress adopted an expenditure ceiling for fiscal 1971, as it had for the two previous fiscal years. The legislation made allowances for increases due to Congressional action and to uncontrollable expenditures, resulting from fixed or unavoidable commitments of the federal government (such as interest on the public debt or benefits under Social Security).

The new budget estimated the current ceiling at $214.5-billion, an increase of $13.7-billion over the original figure of $200.8-billion. With fiscal 1971 outlays estimated at $212.8-billion, the budget estimated there was a cushion remaining of $1.7-billion.

Program Cutbacks. As in the 1971 budget, the President proposed elimination or reduction of obsolete, inefficient and low-priority programs. The budget estimated a saving of $3.7-billion in full-year effect and $2.7-billion in fiscal 1972 if the Administration's proposed economies in this area were carried out. A similar listing of proposed program reductions and terminations in the fiscal 1971 budget, totaling $2.1-billion, was only partially approved by the 91st Congress.

Federal Payroll. The budget estimated that federal employment would decline from 5,632,200 in June 1971 to 5,440,300 in June 1972, a reduction of 191,900. Fulltime permanent government employees were expected to increase by 15,300 to a total of 2,589,300. Other civilian employees would decline to 306,600, a reduction of 13,700.

A reduction of 193,900 in military personnel (not including Coast Guard) accounted for most of the overall reduction in federal employment. The 1972 military total was expected to be 2,504,800. The Coast Guard was expected to increase by 400, to 39,600.

The total civilian payroll, including employee benefits, was estimated at $32.3-billion in fiscal 1972. This was an increase of about $800-million over 1971. The military payroll was expected to decline $1.6-billion, to a new total of $18.3-billion. The total federal payroll for fiscal 1972 was estimated at $50.6-billion, excluding members of Congress and military reserve personnel.

Five-Year Outlook

Mr. Nixon established a precedent with his 1971 budget by including a five-year forecast of resources available to the government and private sectors of the economy. According to that forecast, federal revenues would exceed currently known demands by only $22-billion in fiscal 1975, unless additions were made to the tax structure.

The President included an expanded five-year forecast in the 1972 budget. According to the estimates, his initiatives and Congressional action during the intervening year plus the effect of inflation had reduced the potential surplus in 1975 to $12-billion.

A forecast for fiscal 1976 estimated revenues at $315-billion and anticipated outlays at $285-billion, leaving a potential $30-billion surplus to cover the net cost of all new initiatives in the five-year period. The forecast was based on an assumed 4.3-percent annual economic growth rate. Gross national product would exceed $1.5-trillion in 1976, according to the estimate. All figures were in constant dollars (eliminating the effect of inflation).

National Security, Space

Atomic Energy. Outlays for the Atomic Energy Commission were put at $2.3-billion, a slight increase over fiscal 1971 but a reduction from $2.5-billion in 1970. The only major increase was for weapons developments— $19-million.

Defense. The budget contained outlays of $77.5-billion for defense activities, an increase from the $76.4-billion estimated for fiscal 1971, but less than the $80.2-billion spent in fiscal 1970. Included in the over-all figure of $77.5-billion, representing 34 percent of the federal budget, were all military expenditures plus certain defense-related activities such as the Atomic Energy Commission, Selective Service, stockpiling of strategic materials and emergency preparedness activities.

The Department of Defense requested $76-billion, an increase from the fiscal 1971 estimate of $74.5-billion, but a reduction from the $77.8-billion spent in fiscal 1970. The $76-billion Defense Department request, although larger than the 1971 estimate, represented the lowest percentage of the total Federal budget since 1950—32 percent as compared to 33.9 percent in fiscal 1971.

International Affairs. Outlays for foreign aid and other international programs were estimated at $4-billion compared to $3.6-billion in fiscal 1971. Outlays for international development assistance were estimated at $1.5-billion, an increase of $140-million over fiscal 1971. Military supporting assistance was estimated at $1.7-billion, approximately the same as for fiscal 1971.

Space. The budget outlay request for fiscal 1972 for space research and technology was $3.1-billion, about $200-million less than for fiscal 1971. Outlays for the space program hit a peak of $5.9-billion in 1966 and had been declining ever since.

Veterans. Budget requests for the Veterans Administration were $10.6-billion, which was an increase from fiscal 1971 estimates of $9.9-billion. Outlays in 1970 were $8.6-billion. Increasing numbers of veterans from Vietnam and legislation yielding greater benefits were cited as causes for the increase.

Community Development

Housing and Community Development. The budget contained requests totaling $4.5-billion in outlays for community development and housing in fiscal 1972, up from an estimated $3.9-billion in the current fiscal year. About $1.3-billion of the 1972 outlays was requested for urban renewal projects.

Budget authority requested for the Department of Housing and Urban Development was $3.6-billion, an increase of $197.2-million over the fiscal 1971 estimate and $286.1-million over the fiscal 1971 appropriation. Major program estimates included $115.1-million for community development planning and management, $600-million for urban renewal (six months), $45-million for research and technology, $40-million for neighborhood facilities and $200-million for open space land acquisition, particularly small parks in urban and other areas. No funds were estimated for model cities, basic water and sewer facilities and for the last half of fiscal 1972 for urban renewal and the rehabilitation loan fund, all of which were to be replaced by a revenue-sharing program.

Economic Development

Commerce, Transportation, Postal Service. The budget set outlays for commerce, transportation and the new U.S. Postal Service at $10.9-billion compared with $11.4-billion in fiscal 1971. The decrease was attributed primarily to an anticipated postal rate increase. Total new obligational authority in fiscal 1972 amounted to $12.3-billion for the combined programs compared with $26.2-billion in fiscal 1971. The decrease reflected a $11.3-billion reduction in budget authority for postal operations, due to the conversion of the Post Office Department to the independent U.S. Postal Service at about the beginning of the fiscal year.

Outlays in fiscal 1972 by department or agency: Commerce Department, $1.28-billion; Transportation Department, $7.8-billion; U.S. Postal Service, $1.3-billion.

Human Resources

Education. The budget contained requests totaling $13.5-billion in outlays for aid-to-education programs

Budget Terminology

The federal budget is a plan of expected receipts and expenditures, a statement of priorities, an accounting of how funds have been and will be spent and a request for authority to spend public money.

The 1972 budget covered the government's fiscal year beginning July 1, 1971, and ending June 30, 1972.

The federal expenditures reported are most frequently outlays: amounts spent, obligated, or committed during the year. They include net lending—the difference between disbursements and repayments under government loan programs. Examples are funds spent to buy equipment or property, to meet the government's liability under a contract, or to pay the salary of an employee.

The Administration's request to Congress, presented in the form of the budget, is for authority to obligate or lend funds: New Obligational Authority (abbreviated NOA) and Loan Authority (LA).

This Budget Authority determines the scope of operations of the government. Congress confers Budget Authority on a federal agency in general in the form of appropriations.

Appropriations may be for a single year, a specified period of years, or an indefinite number of years, according to the restrictions Congress wishes to place on spending for particular purposes.

Congress also restricts itself in the appropriation process by requiring that an appropriation be preceded by an authorization to appropriate a certain or an indefinite amount of money for a certain purpose. These authorizations, which in practice are often larger than the actual appropriations, are self-imposed limits on Congress, distinct from Budget Authority.

Budget Authority, either NOA or LA, often differs from actual outlays. This is because, in practice, funds actually spent or obligated during a year are drawn partly from the Budget Authority conferred in the year in question and partly from Budget Authority conferred in previous years.

Similarly, part of the Budget Authority granted for the current year will not be spent or obligated until succeeding years. Delays, first in appropriating and then in making expenditures under federal programs, produce the lag. Consequently a change in Budget Authority is not necessarily reflected immediately in a change of the same amount and direction in outlays.

in fiscal 1972. More than one-third of this amount—$4.7-billion—was for programs administered by the Office of Education in the Department of Health, Education and Welfare (HEW).

Total estimated outlays for education in fiscal 1972 were $900-million more than for fiscal 1971. Of this increase, more than $250-million was for Office of Education programs and more than $260-million for GI education benefits.

Labor and Manpower. The Labor Department request included $4.9-billion for manpower training programs, excluding vocational education, which accounted for $384-million of the Office of Education's budget.

The budget recommended total outlays of $3.7-billion in fiscal 1972 for manpower programs (excluding vocational education).

Total projected expenditures were $444-million more than the estimated outlays for fiscal 1971—an 11.8 percent increase over 1971 and 62 percent over 1970.

To support the new outlays, the budget said that $4-billion in new obligational authority would be sought for 1972. This compared with a similar request of $3.4-billion for fiscal 1971.

Health. The budget proposed an increase of $1.1-billion for health programs in fiscal 1972—from a fiscal 1971 outlay of $14.9-billion to $16-billion for fiscal 1972.

The total included a $100-million budget authority increase for cancer research, of which the fiscal 1972 outlay was expected to be $30-million. Other major increases included an $89-million outlay for training health manpower (from $488-million to $577-million) and a $33-million outlay for family planning services (from $25-million to $58-million).

Federal outlays for construction of health facilities under the Hill-Burton program were reduced by $11-million from the fiscal 1971 total of $291-million.

Income Security and Welfare. The budget proposed a $60.7-billion outlay for income security programs in fiscal 1972—an increase of $5.2-billion over the fiscal 1971 total of $55.5-billion. Of the fiscal 1972 total, $49-billion or 81 percent was for retirement and social insurance. The estimated $3.2-billion fiscal 1972 rise in this category was attributed by Health, Education and Welfare (HEW) officials to an increase in the number of beneficiaries, the 15-percent increase in benefits which became effective January 1970 and an Administration proposal for an additional 6-percent increase, effective January 1971.

The budget proposed a $6.7-billion outlay for public assistance payments in fiscal 1972—a $1.1-billion increase over the $5.6-billion fiscal 1971 total. The budget also included a request for $502-million to begin the President's proposed welfare reform program, the Family Assistance Plan. HEW officials said benefit payments under the program would not begin until July 1, 1972 (fiscal 1973).

Natural Resources

Agriculture. The budget set outlays for agriculture and rural development programs at $5.8-billion, compared to $5.3-billion for the previous year. The biggest single outlay—about $3.6-billion—was for price support programs. Rural housing loan requests increased by about $600-million over fiscal 1971 to a total of almost $1.6-billion.

Natural Resources. The budget contained fiscal 1972 outlays of $4.2-billion for natural resources programs administered by the Interior Department, the Environmental Protection Agency, the Army Corps of Engineers and related agencies. Included was $2-billion for waste treatment grants, for which new authorizing legislation would be required.

Three Cabinet Posts, Two Justices Appointed in 1971

President Nixon made three Cabinet changes in 1971. John B. Connally was named Secretary of the Treasury, Earl L. Butz was appointed Secretary of Agriculture and Rogers C. B. Morton was confirmed as Secretary of the Interior.

In addition, eight former Representatives were confirmed to positions as ambassadors, judges and various positions on independent agencies.

The Senate confirmed President Nixon's two Supreme Court nominees, Lewis F. Powell Jr. and William H. Rehnquist. Rehnquist, the more controversial of the two, was the subject of lengthy Senate debate while Powell was easily confirmed.

Rehnquist. The fourth Justice nominated by President Nixon to be confirmed to the Supreme Court, William H. Rehnquist, was also the youngest Justice on the Court. During Senate debate on the Rehnquist nomination, a cloture vote to cut off debate failed 54-42. His nomination was confirmed Dec. 10 by a vote of 68-26.

Powell. The Senate confirmed Lewis F. Powell Jr. Dec. 6 as an Associate Justice of the Supreme Court. He filled the seat left vacant by the late Justice Hugo L. Black. The only Democrat of the Nixon Court nominees, Powell was the first Justice from Virginia since 1841. He was confirmed by a vote of 89-1.

Connally. On Feb. 8, the Senate by voice vote confirmed the nomination of John B. Connally, 53, to be Secretary of the Treasury. Connally, a Democrat, had served for three terms as Governor of Texas (1962-1968) and as Secretary of the Navy during the first year (1961-1962) of the Kennedy administration. He had long and varied experience in law and business, particularly in the oil and gas industries, but limited background in banking and finance.

Connally replaced David M. Kennedy, who resigned as secretary to become ambassador-at-large. Connally first gained national prominence on Nov. 22, 1963, when he was seriously wounded during the assassination of President Kennedy.

Connally had been active in Texas Democratic politics and a campaign strategist and fund-raiser for Representative, then Sen. Lyndon B. Johnson (D Texas; House 1937-49; Senate 1949-61) for more than two decades when in 1962 he resigned after a year as Secretary of the Navy to run successfully for the Texas Governorship.

The Governor of a generally conservative state, Connally at times openly opposed initiatives of the national Democratic party and White House during the Johnson Presidency. He did not support Great Society legislative proposals for a war on poverty and Medicare

program. He led lobbying efforts aimed at the state's Congressional delegation to defeat a Johnson proposal that Congress repeal Section 14 (b) of the Taft-Hartley Act, which allows states to enact "right-to-work" laws.

Despite his early doubts about the poverty program, by 1966 Gov. Connally was expressing pride in Job Corps, Head Start and neighborhood youth corps projects in the state.

In his final report to the legislature, the Governor cited significant increases in spending for all levels of education and the attraction of new industry to the state as major accomplishments of his tenure.

The state's sales tax doubled during his six years in the statehouse.

Connally as Governor, spoke of the need for a program resembling Mr. Nixon's "revenue sharing," advocating a rebate of some of the Federal income tax to the states.

Asked on a nationally televised news interview program in 1966 if he felt the distinctions between the two parties were blurring, Connally replied, "What I try to do is gauge an issue and judge an issue on its merits.... I am not here to represent the Democrats and to fight the Republicans....Some of my positions on issues appeal to Republicans; there is no question about that."

In 1968, when he left office, Connally told reporters that his net worth was "slightly over $1 million."

At the time of his designation, he was senior partner in the Houston law firm of Vinson, Elkins, Searls & Connally.

In addition to corporate directorships, Connally was a director of the First City National Bank of Houston and the U.S. Trust Company of New York. He has resigned both bank posts.

In the first week of January, Connally met in New York with the chief executives of 10 New York banks. At the end of the session, the host, Hoyt Ammidon, chairman of U.S. Trust Company, is reported by *American Banker* to have said he "clearly won the confidence" of the bankers.

For a decade preceding his appointment as Secretary of the Navy in 1961, Connally was attorney and administrative executive for oilmen Sid W. Richardson and Perry R. Bass and a director and vice president of Richardson Oil Inc. When Richardson died in 1959, Connally was named coexecutor of his estate.

At his confirmation hearings for the Navy post, Connally told the Senate Armed Services Committee he had personal oil and gas holdings, but at that time they amounted to income of only $325 a month.

During Senate Finance Committee consideration of Connally's nomination, a major point of controversy involved acceptance of $750,000 in fees over a 10-year period for services rendered as co-executor of the $105-million Richardson estate. During part of the period

Connally was being paid the fees, he was Governor of Texas.

The innuendo was that there was a conflict of interest and possible illegalities in his financial dealings while he was Governor of Texas.

Texas law prohibits the Governor from receiving any "salary, reward or compensation or the promise thereof from any service rendered or performed during" his tenure in office.

An article in *The New York Times* Feb. 1 questioned whether Connally had been rendering some service for the Richardson Foundation while accepting fees during his three terms as Governor. The article claimed that it was a matter of public record (by a story printed in the *Texas Observer*) that Connally had denied not only rendering any service for the Foundation but also accepting any fees while he was Governor.

Appearing before the Senate Finance Committee Feb. 2, in an additional hearing which he had requested, Connally discounted the *Texas Observer* as a reliable source of information and said there was nothing improper about receiving fees for work he had done "years ago." He said he had not denied or concealed his connection with the Richardson estate. The same day the committee voted, 13-0, to approve his nomination.

Butz. President Nixon nominated Earl L. Butz Nov. 11 to replace Clifford M. Hardin as Secretary of Agriculture. Butz had served as Assistant Secretary of Agriculture for marketing and foreign affairs from 1954-57 under Secretary Ezra Taft Benson. Butz's nomination encountered stiff Senate opposition from both farm-belt Republicans and liberal Democrats. His opponents accused him of maintaining too close ties with corporate farming or "agribusiness," and of favoring the interests of large agricultural corporations over those of the family farmer. Critics noted that Butz was a director of four corporate food-producing chains, that he had expressed opposition to expanded government aid to small farmers, and that he was part of the administration of Benson, very unpopular with midwestern farmers because of its "adapt or die" attitude toward small farmers.

The Senate Agriculture Committee voted 8-6 to report the nomination favorably to the Senate. The Senate confirmed the nomination Dec. 2 by a 51-44 vote.

Morton. Rogers C. B. Morton, former Representative from Maryland and Republican National Chairman, was unanimously confirmed by voice vote as Secretary of the Interior on Jan. 28. He replaced Walter J. Hickel, who was removed from his Interior Department post by the President in November 1970.

Morton built a reputation as a conservationist while still a member of the House. He sought federal protection of local park areas marked for commercial development in Maryland. However, national conservation groups opposed his nomination claiming Morton's voting record on conservation issues had been poor. At the time of his nomination, Morton said he would support development of wilderness areas in the populous East.

Adair. President Nixon announced March 30 the nomination of E. Ross Adair to be Ambassador to Ethiopia. Adair, a Representative from Indiana (1951-71), was defeated in the 1970 election. He was confirmed to his new position on May 11.

Kennedy. David M. Kennedy, former Secretary of the Treasury, was confirmed by the Senate Feb. 8 to become ambassador-at-large. He had served as Treasury Secretary since the beginning of the Nixon administration.

Bush. George Bush, former Texas Representative, was nominated by President Nixon Jan. 25 to be Ambassador to the United Nations. He served in Congress from 1967 until he was defeated in a race for the Senate in 1970.

Bedell. President Nixon nominated Catherine May Bedell on May 27 to become a member and chairman of the U.S. Tariff Commission. She succeeded Chester L. Mize, who resigned while his nomination was still pending in the Senate. The White House said Mize told the President he was resigning for "personal reasons." Mrs. Bedell served as a Representative from Washington from 1959-71. Her nomination was confirmed June 24.

Kleppe. Thomas S. Kleppe, former Representative from North Dakota, was confirmed as Administrator of the Small Business Administration Feb. 10. Kleppe replaced Hilary Sandoval Jr., who resigned Jan. 1 because of poor health.

Judicial Nominations

The Senate in 1971 confirmed President Nixon's nominations to 61 federal circuit and district judgeships. At the end of January 1972, there were 17 vacancies in the federal courts. There were 5 in the circuit courts and 12 in the district courts.

Total Nominations

In the first session of the 92nd Congress, the Senate received 50,499 nominations and confirmed 48,855. President Nixon withdrew six nominations which had been submitted to the Senate.

Regulatory Agencies

President Nixon made 16 appointments in 1971 to the federal regulatory agencies. He had made 13 appointments to the agencies in 1970.

By the end of his first term in early 1973, President Nixon would have, through his appointments, nominal control over 9 of 11 independent agencies and commissions that exercise regulatory powers over a broad range of public interests.

Only the Federal Reserve System Board of Governors and the Federal Trade Commission would retain through 1972 a majority membership, appointed by previous Presidents.

Federal Communications Commission. Charlotte T. Reid, former Representative from Illinois, was confirmed as a member of the Federal Communications Commission on July 29. She replaced Thomas J. Houser, whose term expired June 30. Mrs. Reid was the first woman to be nominated to the FCC since 1948.

Securities and Exchange Commission. On March 25 the Senate by voice vote confirmed William J. Casey as chairman of the Securities and Exchange Commission. His confirmation came after two sets of Senate hearings in which his alleged involvement in law suits concerning securities law violations was probed in depth.

The Senate Banking Committee held a hearing Feb. 10 and voted to approve the nomination, deciding to delay floor action until the committee could examine the transcript of a plagiarism trial in which Casey had been involved in 1959.

Subsequent press reports disclosed that Casey had been involved in two other suits, which he had not mentioned to the committee. The committee voted March 2 to reopen hearings on the nomination. Casey appeared before the committee March 9 and conceded that his earlier testimony to the committee had been incomplete, and in some instances, erroneous. He testified for several hours about the two newly disclosed lawsuits.

In one he had been sued, as a director of an electronics company, by a stockholder for allegedly helping to sell unregistered stock on the basis of false information. The case was settled out of court. In the second, still pending, Casey—as director of another corporation—had been sued by stockholders for evading state law in acquiring another company. The committee March 9 voted again to approve the nomination.

Confirmations of the President's Major 1971 Nominations

Listed below are the names of 158 persons named to major federal posts by President Nixon and confirmed by the Senate in 1971. Information is given in the following order: name of office, salary, appointee, voting residence, occupation before appointment, date and place of birth, party affiliation (if known) and date of Senate confirmation. Ambassadorial confirmations are listed only if the appointment was of more than routine interest.

Executive Office of the President

Office of Emergency Preparedness
Assistant Director, $36,000—**Elmer F. Bennett**; Sumner, Md.; special assistant for oil and energy and general counsel of OEP; Sept. 17, 1917, in Longmont, Colo.; Nov. 12.

Office of Economic Opportunity
Director, $42,500—**Frank Charles Carlucci III**; Wilkes-Barre, Pa.; assistant director of operations (OEO); Oct. 18, 1930, in Scranton, Pa.; March 24.

Director, $42,500—**Phillip V. Sanchez**; Fresno County, Calif.; assistant director (operations) for OEO; July 28, 1929, in Pinedale, Calif.; Rep.; Nov. 17.

Assistant Director (Operations), $38,000—**Phillip Victor Sanchez**; Fresno County, Calif.; Fresno County administrator; July 28, 1929, in Pinedale, Calif.; Rep.; May 3.

Assistant Director, $38,000—**Roy E. Batchelor**; Chattanooga, Tenn.; regional director of the southeastern region of OEO; July 8, 1924, in Haleyville, Ala.; Rep.; Dec. 3.

Office of Science and Technology
Deputy Director, $38,000—Dr. **John Dickson Baldeschwieler**; Portola Valley, Calif.; professor of chemistry at Stanford University (on leave of absence); Nov. 14, 1933, in Elizabeth, N.J.; Rep.; Aug. 4.

Council of Economic Advisers
Member; $38,000—**Ezra Solomon**; Stanford, Calif.; Dean Witter Professor of Finance, Stanford University; March 20, 1920, in Rangoon, Burma; June 17.

Departments

State Department
Assistant Secretary (Administration), $38,000—**Joseph F. Donelan Jr.**; New York City; Deputy Assistant Secretary of State (budget and finance); Feb. 16, 1918, in New York City; June 9.

Ambassadors
(Salaries for ambassadors depend upon seniority and station, and range between $36,000 and $42,500 per year. Only those appointments which are of more than routine interest are listed.)

At Large, **David M. Kennedy**; Northfield, Ill.; Secretary of the Treasury, 1969-71; July 21, 1905, in Randolph, Utah; Rep.; Feb. 8.

Ethiopia, **E. Ross Adair**; Washington, D.C.; member, U.S. House of Representatives (R Ind. 1951-1971); Dec. 14, 1907, in Albion, Ind.; Rep.; May 11.

United Nations, **George Bush**; Houston, Texas; member, U.S. House of Representatives (R Texas 1967-1971); June 12, 1924, in Milton, Mass.; Rep.; Feb. 10.

Western Samoa, **Kenneth Franzheim**; Houston, Texas; independent oil operator and investor; Sept. 12, 1925, in New York City; Rep.; Feb. 10.

Agency for International Development
Assistant Administrator (administration), $38,000—**James F. Campbell**; Bethesda, Md.; chairman of the board of directors and managing director for an affiliate of the Standard Oil Co. of New Jersey; May 14, 1912, in Lonaconing, Md.; Rep.; Aug. 6.

Assistant Administrator (Latin America), $38,000—**Herman Kleine**; Bethesda, Md.; deputy U.S. coordinator for the Alliance for Progress; March 6, 1920, in New York City; Sept. 29.

Treasury Department
Secretary, $60,000—**John B. Connally**; Houston, Texas; senior partner in Houston law firm of Vinson, Elkins, Searls & Connally; former Governor of Texas; Feb. 27, 1917, in Floresville, Texas; Dem.; Feb. 8.

Treasurer of the United States, $36,000—**Romana Acosta Banuelos**; Gardena, Calif.; head of Ramona's Mexican Food Products Inc.; March 25, 1925, in Miami, Ariz.; Rep.; Dec. 6.

Internal Revenue Service
Commissioner of Internal Revenue, $40,000—**Johnnie M. Walters**; Greenville, S.C.; Assistant Attorney General (tax) at Justice Department; Dec. 20, 1919, in Hartsville, S.C., Rep.; Aug. 4.

Defense Department
Assistant Secretary (Intelligence), $38,000—Dr. **Albert C. Hall**; Arnold, Md.; vice president of Martin Marietta Corp.; June 27, 1914, in Port Arthur, Texas; Rep.; Nov. 2.

Assistant Secretary (health and environment), $38,000—Dr. **Richard S. Wilbur**; Lake Forest, Ill.; deputy executive vice president of the American Medical Association; April 8, 1924, in Boston, Mass.; Rep.; July 16.

Army
Secretary, $42,500—**Robert F. Froehlke**; Stevens Point, Wis.; Assistant Secretary of Defense (administration); Oct. 15, 1922, in Neenah, Wis.; Rep.; June 30.

Assistant Secretary (manpower and reserve affairs), $38,000—**Hadlai Austin Hull**; Wayzata, Minn.; senior vice president of finance, Dayton Hudson Corp.; May 30, 1914, in New London, Conn.; Rep.; May 14.

Assistant Secretary (installations and logistics), $38,000—**Dudley C. Mecum**; Potomac, Md.; vice president with Peat, Marwick, Mitchell and Co.; Dec. 21, 1934, in Chicago, Ill.; Rep.; Oct. 7.

Navy
Assistant Secretary (installations and logistics), $38,000—**Charles L. Ill**; Potomac, Md.; special assistant to the Secretary of the Navy; Jan. 7, 1926, in Newark, N.J.; July 16.

Assistant Secretary (manpower and reserve affairs), $38,000 —**James E. Johnson**; Sacramento, Calif.; commissioner and vice chairman, U.S. Civil Service Commission; March 26, 1926, in Madison, Ill.; Rep.; May 14.

Justice Department

Assistant Attorney General (tax), $38,000—**Scott P. Crampton**; Lorton, Va.; partner in the law firm of Worth & Crampton; Sept. 1, 1913, in Cleveland, Ohio; Rep.; Nov. 12.

Assistant Attorney General (civil rights), $38,000—**David Luke Norman**; Washington, D.C.; Deputy Asstant Attorney General (civil rights) at Justice Department; Oct. 21, 1924, in Stromsburg, Neb.; Aug. 3.

Law Enforcement Assistance Administration

Administrator, $40,000—**Jerris Leonard**; Milwaukee, Wis.; Assistant Attorney General (civil rights); Jan. 17, 1931, in Chicago, Ill.; Rep.; April 21.

Interior Department

Secretary, $60,000—**Rogers C. B. Morton;** Easton, Md.; U.S. House of Representatives (R Md. 1963-Jan. 29, 1971); Sept. 19, 1914, in Louisville, Ky.; Rep.; Jan. 28.

Under Secretary, $40,000—**William T. Pecora**; Newark, N.J.; director of Geological Survey, Interior Department; Feb. 1, 1913, in Belleville, N.J.; May 3.

Assistant Secretary (management and budget), $38,000—**Richard Stockwell Bodman**; San Francisco, Calif.; Assistant Secretary (administration) at Interior Department; April 9, 1938, in Detroit, Mich.; Rep.; July 14.

Assistant Secretary (program policy), $38,000—**John W. Larson**; Ross, Calif.; partner in the law firm of Brobeck, Phleger and Harrison; June 24, 1935, in Detroit, Mich.; Rep.; July 27.

Assistant Secretary (fish and wildlife), $38,000—**Nathaniel Pryor Reed**; Hobe Sound, Fla.; chairman of Florida Department of Air and Water Pollution Control; July 22, 1933, in New York City; Rep.; May 11.

Agriculture Department

Secretary, $60,000—**Earl Lauer Butz**; Lafayette, Ind.; dean of continuing education and vice president of the research foundation at Purdue University; July 3, 1909, in Albion, Ind.; Rep.; Dec. 2.

Transportation Department

Assistant Secretary (safety and consumer affairs), $38,000—**Benjamin Oliver Davis Jr.**; Arlington, Va.; director of civil aviation security at Transportation Department; Dec. 18, 1912, in Washington, D.C.; July 29.

Assistant Secretary (environment and urban systems), $38,000—**Herbert F. DeSimone**; North Providence, R.I.; attorney general for Rhode Island; Sept. 5, 1929, in Providence, R.I.; Rep.; March 16.

General Counsel, $38,000—**John W. Barnum**; New York City; partner in the law firm of Cravath, Swain, and Moore; Aug. 25, 1928, in New York City; Rep.; June 30.

Administrator, National Highway Traffic Safety Administration, $40,000—**Douglas W. Toms**; Olympia, Wash.; director of Department of Motor Vehicles, State of Washington; Sept. 17, 1930, in Cheboygan, Mich.; Rep.; July 16.

Commerce Department

Under Secretary, $40,000—**James T. Lynn**; Cleveland, Ohio; general counsel, Department of Commerce; Feb. 27, 1927, in Cleveland, Ohio; Rep.; April 26.

Assistant Secretary (science and technology), $38,000—**James H. Wakelin Jr.**; Washington, D.C.; advisory board member, Teledyne Ryan Aeronautical Company; May 6, 1911, in Holyoke, Mass.; Rep.; Feb. 19.

General Counsel, $38,000—**William N. Letson**; Warren, Ohio; partner in the law firm of Letson, Letson, Griffith & Kightlinger; March 24, 1930, in New York City; Rep.; April 26.

Labor Department

Assistant Secretary (policy evaluation and research), $38,000 —**Richard J. Grunewald**; New Haven, Conn.; vice president for administration for the Winchester Group of the Olin Corporation; March 4, 1920, in Amsterdam, N.Y.; Rep.; Oct. 21.

Assistant Secretary (occupational safety and health), $38,000—**George C. Guenther**; Wyomissing, Pa.; director of Bureau of Labor Standards; Aug. 27, 1931, in Reading, Pa.; Rep.; April 14.

Solicitor of Labor, $38,000—**Richard Schubert**; Easton, Pa.; assistant manager of labor relations with Bethlehem Steel; Nov. 2, 1936, in Trenton, N.J.; Rep.; Oct. 21.

Administrator, Wage and Hour Division, $36,000—**Horace E. Menasco**; Pasco, Wash.; Deputy Assistant Secretary (employment standards), Labor Department; March 3, 1925, in Cushing, Okla.; Rep.; April 14.

Department of Health, Education and Welfare

Assistant Secretary (health and scientific affairs), $38,000—**Merlin K. DuVal Jr.**; Tucson, Ariz.; Dean of College of Medicine, University of Arizona; Oct. 12, 1922, in Montclair, N.J.; Ind.; June 18.

Assistant Secretary (legislation), $38,000—**Stephen Kurzman**; Washington, D.C.; lawyer; March 25, 1932, in New York City; Rep.; March 25.

Assistant Secretary (planning and evaluation), $38,000—**Laurence E. Lynn Jr.**; Washington, D.C.; associate professor of business economics, Stanford University; June 10, 1937, in Long Beach, Calif.; June 24.

Assistant Secretary (public affairs), $38,000—**Robert O. Beatty**; Boise, Idaho; director of communications, Boise Cascade Corporation; Nov. 12, 1924, in Chicago, Ill.; Rep.; March 25.

Department of Housing and Urban Development

Assistant Secretary (housing management), $38,000—**Norman Vickers Watson**; Washington, D.C.; deputy director of Metro Dade County, Department of Housing and Urban Development; Jan. 14, 1935, in Columbus, Ga.; Rep.; May 12.

Independent Agencies

Atomic Energy Commission

Member (chairman) for the term expiring June 30, 1975, $42,500—**James R. Schlesinger**; Arlington, Va.; assistant director of the Office of Management and Budget; Feb. 15, 1929, in New York City; Rep.; Aug. 6.

Member for the term expiring June 30, 1976, $40,000—**William Offutt Doub**; Baltimore, Md.; chairman, Maryland Public Service Commission; Sept. 3, 1931, in Cumberland, Md.; Rep.; Aug. 6.

Civil Service Commission

Commissioner for the term expiring March 1, 1977, $38,000—**Jayne Baker Spain**; Cincinnati, Ohio; board of directors, Litton Industries; March, 1928, in Cincinnati, Ohio; Rep.; June 8.

Corporation for Public Broadcasting

Member of the board of directors for the term expiring March 26, 1972, paid per diem—**Zelma George**; Cleveland, Ohio; executive director, Cleveland Job Corps for Women; Dec. 8, 1904, in Hearne, Texas; Rep.; July 29.

Equal Employment Opportunity Commission

Member for the term expiring July 1, 1976, $38,000—**Raymond Telles**; El Paso, Texas; consultant to private industry in Texas and Oklahoma; Sept. 15, 1915, in El Paso, Texas; Dem.; Sept. 30.

Member for the term expiring July 1, 1975, $38,000—**Ethel Bent Walsh**; Washington, D.C.; director, Office of Advisory Councils of the Small Business Administration; Dec. 29, 1923, in Bridgeport, Conn.; Rep.; May 3.

Environmental Protection Agency

Deputy Administrator, $40,000—**Robert W. Fri**; Bethesda, Md.; principal, McKinsey and Co., Inc.; Nov. 16, 1935, in Kansas City, Kan.; Rep.; June 11.

Assistant Administrator (categorical programs), $38,000—**David D. Dominick**; Cody, Wyo.; commissioner of Federal Water Quality Administration; Jan. 24, 1937, in Philadelphia, Pa.; Rep.; June 11.

Assistant Administrator (planning and management), $38,000—**Thomas Edmund Carroll**; Chevy Chase, Md.; executive vice president, Evans Broadcasting Corp.; April 21, 1928, in Columbus, Ohio; Rep.; Feb. 10.

Assistant Administrator (regional programs), $38,000—**Donald MacMurphy Mosiman**; Indianapolis, Ind.; financial consultant, Perine Leisure International Inc.; July 16, 1929, in Indianapolis, Ind.; Rep.; Feb. 10.

Assistant Administrator (research and monitoring), $38,000—**Stanley M. Greenfield**; Woodland Hills, Calif.; manager of environmental studies program, Rand Corporation; April 16, 1927, in New York City; Dem.; Feb. 10.

Assistant Administrator (standards and compliance) and general counsel, $38,000—**John R. Quarles Jr.**; Reston, Va.; assistant to the Secretary of the Interior; April 26, 1935, in Boston, Mass.; Rep.; Feb. 10.

Federal Communications Commission

Member for the term expiring July 1, 1971, $38,000—**Thomas J. Houser**, Arlington Heights, Ill.; deputy director of Peace Corps; June 28, 1929, in Chicago, Ill.; Rep.; Feb. 26.

Member for the term expiring July 1, 1978, $38,000—**Charlotte T. Reid**; Aurora, Ill.; member U.S. House of Representatives (R 1963-1971); Sept. 27, 1913, in Kankakee, Ill.; Rep.; July 29.

Member for the term expiring July 1, 1976, $38,000—**Robert Wells**, Garden City, Kan.; reappointment; March 7, 1919, in Garden City, Kan.; Rep.; Feb. 26.

Federal Home Loan Bank Board

Member for the term expiring June 30, 1975, $38,000—**Carl O. Kamp**; Potomac, Md.; reappointment; Dec. 20, 1914, in St. Louis, Mo.; Rep.; June 30.

Federal Maritime Commission

Commissioner for the term expiring June 30, 1976, $38,000—**Clarence Morse**; California; retired civil service employee; Feb. 7, 1904; Rep.; Oct. 7.

Federal Metal and Nonmetallic Mine Safety Board of Review

Member for the term expiring Sept. 15, 1972, $50 per diem including travel time—**Peter J. Bensoni**; Duluth, Minn.; assistant director and safety and health coordinator for District 33 of the United Steelworkers of America; Jan. 29, 1915, in Hurley, Wis.; July 15.

Member for the term expiring Sept. 15, 1975, $50 per diem including travel time—Dr. **Howard L. Hartman**; Nashville, Tenn.; dean of the school of engineering at Vanderbilt University; Aug. 7, 1924, in Indianapolis, Ind.; July 15.

Member for the term expiring Sept. 15, 1976, $50 per diem including travel time—**W. W. Little**; Douglas, Ariz.; reappointment; Nov. 7, 1911, in Birmingham, Ala.; Oct. 21.

Member for the term expiring Sept. 15, 1973, $50 per diem including travel time—**Robert W. McVay**; Jefferson City, Mo.; staff representative for District 34 of United Steelworkers of America; Jan. 27, 1910, in Fort Smith, Sebastian County, Ark.; July 15.

Member for the term expiring Sept. 15, 1974, $50 per diem including travel time—**Charles E. Schwab**; New York City; senior vice president of Anaconda Corp.; Aug. 4, 1915, in Shadesville, Ohio; July 15.

Federal Power Commission

Member for the term expiring June 22, 1976, $38,000—**Rush Moody**; Midland, Texas; partner in the law firm of Stubbeman, McRae, Sealy, Laughlin & Browder; 1930, in Alpine, Texas; Dem.; Oct. 8.

Member for the term expiring June 22, 1972, $38,000—**Pinkney Calvin Walker**; Columbia, Mo.; dean of School of Business and Public Administration, University of Missouri; Nov. 2, 1917, in Graham, Texas; Rep.; May 20.

Federal Railroad Administration

Administrator, $40,000—**Thomas S. Kleppe**; Kensington, Md.; member, U.S. House of Representatives (R N.D. 1967-71); 6, 1929, in Cleveland, Ohio; Sept. 30.

Interstate Commerce Commission

Commissioner for the term expiring Dec. 31, 1977, $38,000—**Virginia Mae Brown**; Washington, D.C.; reappointment; Nov. 13, 1923, in Pliny, W.Va.; Dem.; June 30.

Commissioner for the term expiring Dec. 31, 1977, $38,000—**Dale Wayne Hardin**; Alexandria, Va.; reappointment; Sept. 9, 1922, in Peoria, Ill.; Rep.; June 30.

Commissioner for the term expiring Dec. 31, 1972, $38,000—**Lawrence Walrath**, Ponte Vedra Beach, Fla.; reappointment; Aug. 16, 1909, in Meadville, Pa.; Dem.; June 30.

National Aeronautics and Space Administration

Administrator, $42,500—Dr. **James C. Fletcher**; McLean, Va.; president, University of Utah; June 5, 1919, in Millburn, N.J.; March 11.

National Labor Relations Board

General Counsel for the term expiring Aug. 15, 1975, $38,000—**Peter G. Nash**; Potomac, Md.; solicitor, U.S. Department of Labor; Jan. 4, 1937, in Newark, N.Y.; Rep.; Aug. 5.

National Mediation Board

Member for the term expiring July 1, 1974, $38,000—**Peter C. Benedict**; Alexandria, Va.; minority counsel to the Subcommittee on Labor of the Senate Labor and Public Welfare Committee; May 28, 1926, in Rutland, Vt.; Rep.; Aug. 4.

National Oceanic and Atmospheric Administration

Administrator, $40,000—Dr. **Robert M. White**; Bethesda, Md.; administrator, Environmental Science Services Administration (Commerce Department); Feb. 13, 1923, in Boston, Mass.; Ind.; Feb. 19.

Deputy Administrator, $38,000—**Howard W. Pollock**; Anchorage, Alaska; member, U.S. House of Representatives (R Alaska, 1967-1971); April 11, 1920, in Chicago, Ill.; Rep.; Feb. 19.

Associate Administrator, $36,000—Dr. **John W. Townsend Jr.**; Severna Park, Md.; deputy administrator, Environmental Science Services Administration (Commerce Department); March 19, 1924, in Washington, D.C.; Dem.; Feb. 19.

Railroad Retirement Board

Member for the term expiring Aug. 28, 1973, $38,000—**Wythe D. Quarles Jr.**; Alexandria, Va.; vice chairman of National Railway Labor Conference; Feb. 13, 1916, in Richmond, Va.; June 18.

Renegotiation Board

Member (chairman), $36,000—**Richard T. Burress**; Mohican Hills, Md.; deputy counsel to the President; Dec. 2, 1922, in Omaha, Neb.; Rep.; Oct. 21.

Securities and Exchange Commission

Chairman for the term expiring June 5, 1974, $40,000—**William J. Casey**; Roslyn Harbor, N.Y.; partner in the law firm of Hall, Casey, Dicklen & Howley; March 13, 1913, in Elmhurst, N.Y.; Rep.; March 25.

Member for the term expiring June 5, 1976, $38,000—**A. Sidney Herlong Jr.**; Leesburg, Fla.; reappointment; Feb. 14, 1909, in Manistee, Ala.; Dem.; June 17.

Member for the term expiring June 1972, $40,000—**Philip A. Loomis Jr.**; Pasadena, Calif.; general counsel of Securities and Exchange Commission; June 11, 1915, in Colorado Springs, Colo.; Rep.; Sept. 23.

Small Business Administration

Administrator, $40,000—**Thomas S. Kleppe**; Kensington, Md.; member, U.S. House of Representatives (R N.D. 1967-71); July 1, 1919, in Kintyre, N.D.; Rep.; Feb. 10.

U.S. Tariff Commission

Member (chairman) for the term expiring June 16, 1974, $38,000—**Catherine May Bedell**; Yakima, Wash.; member, U.S. House of Representatives (R Wash. 1959-1971); May 18, 1914, in Yakima, Wash.; Rep.; June 24.

Member (vice chairman) for the term expiring June 16, 1977, $36,000—**Joseph O. Parker**; Alexandria, Va.; lawyer; Dec. 11, 1908, in Pratt, Kan.; June 24.

Judiciary

Judges' party affiliations, available in the past from the Justice Department, were compiled from entries in *Who's Who in American Politics* and from the Senators of the states involved.

U.S. Supreme Court

Associate Justice, $60,000—**Lewis F. Powell Jr.**; Richmond, Va.; partner in the law firm of Hunton, Gay, Powell and Gibson; Sept. 19, 1907, in Suffolk, Va.; Dem.; Dec. 6.

Associate Justice, $60,000—**William H. Rehnquist**; Phoenix, Ariz.; Assistant Attorney General (office of legal counsel); Oct. 1, 1924, in Milwaukee, Wis.; Rep.; Dec. 10.

U.S. Circuit Courts of Appeal

Judge for the Second Circuit, $42,500—**Walter R. Mansfield**; New York City; U.S. district judge, Southern District of New York; July 1, 1911, in Boston, Mass.; Rep.; May 20.

Judge for the Second Circuit, $42,500—**William Hughes Mulligan**; Bronxville, N.Y.; dean and professor, Fordham University Law School; March 5, 1918, in Bronx, N.Y.; Rep.; May 20.

Judge for the Second Circuit, $42,500—**James L. Oakes**, Brattleboro, Vt.; U.S. district judge, District of Vermont; Feb. 21, 1924, in Springfield, Ill.; Rep.; May 20.

Judge for the Second Circuit, $42,500—**William H. Timbers**; Darien, Conn.; U.S. District Judge, District of Connecticut; Sept. 5, 1915, in Yonkers, N.Y.; Rep.; July 29.

Judge for the Third Circuit, $42,500—**James Hunter III**; Haddonfield, N.J.; partner in the law firm of Archer, Breiner, Hunter & Read; Dec. 26, 1916, in Westville, N.J.; Rep.; Sept. 21.

Judge for the Third Circuit, $42,500—**James Rosen**; West New York, N.J.; judge of the Superior Court of New Jersey; Oct. 23, 1909, in Brooklyn, N.Y.; Rep.; Sept. 21.

Judge for the Fourth Circuit, $42,500—**John A. Field Jr.**; Charleston, W.Va.; U.S. District Judge, Southern District of West Virginia; Rep.; Sept. 21.

Judge for the Fourth Circuit, $42,500—**Donald Stuart Russell**; Spartanburg, S.C.; U.S. district judge, District of South Carolina; Feb. 22, 1906, in Lafayette Springs, Miss.; Dem.; April 21.

Judge for the Seventh Circuit, $42,500—**Robert A. Sprecher**; Evanston, Ill.; partner in the law firm of Crowley, Sprecher, Barrett & Karaba; May 30, 1917, in Chicago, Ill.; Rep.; April 21.

Judge for the Eighth Circuit, $42,500—**Roy L. Stephenson**; Des Moines, Iowa; U.S. district judge, Southern District of Iowa; March 14, 1917, in Spirit Lake, Iowa; Rep.; June 18.

Judge for the Ninth Circuit, $42,500—**Herbert Y. C. Choy**; Honolulu, Hawaii; partner in the law firm of Fong, Miho, Choy & Robinson; Jan. 6, 1916, in Makaweli, Kauai, Hawaii; Rep.; April 21.

Judge for the Ninth Circuit, $42,500—**Alfred T. Goodwin**; Portland, Ore.; U.S. district judge, district of Oregon; June 29, 1923, in Bellingham, Wash.; Rep.; Nov. 23.

Judge for the Tenth Circuit, $42,500—**James E. Barrett**; Cheyenne, Wyo.; attorney general, State of Wyoming; April 8, 1922, in Lusk, Wyo.; Rep.; April 21.

Judge for the Tenth Circuit, $42,500—**William E. Doyle**; Denver, Colo.; U.S. district judge, District of Colorado; Feb. 5, 1911, in Denver, Colo.; Dem.; April 21.

U.S. Court of Customs

Judge, $40,000—**Nils A. Boe**; Sioux Falls, S.D.; director, Office of Intergovernmental Affairs (also former Governor of South Dakota from 1965-69); Sept. 10, 1913, in Baltic, S.D.; Rep.; Aug. 6.

Judge for the Southern District of Iowa, $40,000—**William C. Stuart**; Chariton, Iowa; judge on the Iowa supreme court; April 28, 1920, in Knoxville, Iowa; Rep.; Oct. 28.

U.S. Tax Court

Judge for the term expiring Nov. 4, 1986, $40,000—**William A. Goffe**; Sulphur, Okla.; lawyer; Aug. 30, 1929, in Sulphur, Okla.; lawyer; Aug. 30, 1929, in Sulphur, Okla.; Rep.; Oct. 28.

U.S. Court of Military Appeals

Judge for the term expiring May 1, 1986, $42,500—**Robert M. Duncan**; Columbus, Ohio; judge on the Ohio supreme court, Aug. 24, 1927, in Urbana, Ohio; Rep.; Oct. 6.

U.S. District Courts

Judge for the Southern District of Alabama, $40,000—**William Brevard Hand**; Mobile, Ala.; partner in the law firm of Hand, Arendall, Bedsole, Creaves & Johnson; Jan. 18, 1924, in Mobile, Ala.; Rep.; Sept. 21.

Judge for the Middle District of Alabama, $40,000—**Robert E. Varner**; Montgomery, Ala.; partner in the law firm of Jones, Murray, Stewart & Varner; June 11, 1921, in Montgomery, Ala.; Rep.; April 21.

Judge for the Central District of California, $40,000—**William M. Byrne Jr.**; Los Angeles, Calif.; executive director, Presidential Commission on Campus Unrest; Sept. 3, 1930, in Los Angeles, Calif.; Dem.; May 20.

Judge for the Central District of California, $40,000—**Malcolm M. Lucas**; Los Alamitos, Calif.; judge of Superior Court, County of Los Angeles; April 19, 1927, in Berkeley, Calif.; Rep.; July 29.

Judge for the Central District of California, $40,000—**Lawrence T. Lydick**; California; partner in the law firm of Adams, Duque and Hazeltine; June 22, 1916, in San Diego, Calif.; Rep.; July 29.

Judge for the Southern District of California, $40,000—**Leland C. Nielsen**; La Jolla, Calif.; judge, Superior Court in San Diego, Calif.; June 14, 1919, in Vasper, Kan.; Rep.; May 20.

Judge for the Northern District of California, $40,000—**Charles B. Renfrew**; San Francisco, Calif.; partner in the law firm of Pillsbury, Madison and Sutro; Oct. 31, 1928, in Detroit, Mich.; Dem.; Dec. 2.

Judge for the Northern District of California, $40,000—**Spencer M. Williams**; Sacramento, Calif.; of counsel for firms of Evans, Jackson & Kennedy, and Rankin, Oneal, Center, Luckhardt, Bonney, Marlain & Lund; Feb. 24, 1922, in Reading, Mass.; Rep.; July 29.

Judge for the District of Colorado, $40,000—**Sherman G. Finesilver**; Denver, Colo.; judge, Denver District Court; Oct. 1, 1927, in Denver, Colo.; Rep.; Sept. 21.

Judge for the District of Columbia District, $40,000—**Thomas A. Flannery**; Springfield, Md.; U.S. Attorney for the District of Columbia (Justice Department); May 10, 1918, in Washington, D.C.; Rep.; Dec. 1.

Judge for the District of Columbia District, $40,000—**Charles R. Richey**; Potomac, Md.; general counsel, Maryland Public Service Commission; Oct. 16, 1923, in Middleburg, Ohio; Rep.; April 29.

Judge for the Southern District of Georgia, $40,000—**Anthony A. Alaimo**; Sea Island, Ga.; partner in the law firm of Alaimo, Taylor & Bishop; March 29, 1920, in Termini, Sicily, Italy; Rep.; Dec. 2.

Judge for the Northern District of Georgia, $40,000—**Richard C. Freeman**, Atlanta, Ga.; partner in the law firm of Haas, Holland, Freeman, Levison & Gilbert; Dec. 14, 1926, in Atlanta, Ga.; Rep.; April 21.

Judge for the Northern District of Illinois, $40,000—**Richard W. McLaren**; Winnetka, Ill.; Assistant Attorney General (antitrust); April 21, 1918, in Chicago, Ill.; Rep.; Dec. 2.

Judge for the Northern District of Illinois, $40,000—**Thomas R. McMillen**; Winnetka, Ill.; judge, Circuit Court of Cook County; June 8, 1916, in Decatur, Ill.; Rep.; April 21.

Judge for the Northern District of Illinois, $40,000—**Philip W. Tone**; Park Ridge, Ill.; lawyer with the law firm of Jenner and Block; April 9, 1923, in Chicago, Ill.; Rep.; Dec. 2.

Judge for the Southern District of Iowa, $40,000—**William C. Stuart**; Chariton, Iowa; judge on the Iowa supreme court; April 28, 1920, in Knoxville, Iowa; Rep.; Oct. 28.

Judge for the District of Kansas, $40,000—**Earl E. O'Connor**; Topeka, Kansas; judge on the Kansas supreme court; Oct. 6, 1922, in Paola, Kan.; Rep.; Oct. 28.

Judge for the Western District of Kentucky, $40,000—**Charles M. Allen**; Louisville, Ky.; judge on the Jefferson County Circuit Court (Fourth Division); Nov. 22, 1916, in Louisville, Ky.; Rep.; Nov. 23.

Judge for the Eastern District of Louisiana, $40,000—**Jack M. Gordon**; Metairie, La.; partner in the law firm of Phelps, Dunbar, Marks, Clavarie & Sims; Feb. 13, 1931, in Lake Charles, La.; Rep.; June 18.

Judge for the Eastern District of Louisiana, $40,000—**R. Blake West**; New Orleans, La.; partner in the law firm of Phelps, Dunbar, Marks, Claverie & Sims; May 10, 1928, in New Orleans, La.; Rep.; June 18.

Judge for the District of Maryland, $40,000—**C. Stanley Blair**; Darlington, Md.; private law practice (also candidate for Governor of Maryland in 1970); Dec. 20, 1927, in Kinsville, Md.; Rep.; July 29.

Judge for the District of Maryland, $40,000—**Herbert F. Murray**; Baltimore, Md.; partner in the law firm of Smith, Somerville & Case; Dec. 29, 1923, in Waltham, Mass.; Rep.; July 29.

Judge for the District of Maryland, $40,000—**Joseph H. Young**; Baltimore, Md.; partner in the law firm of Piper & Marbury; July 18, 1922, in Hagerstown, Md.; Rep.; July 29.

Judge for the District of Massachusetts, $40,000—**Levin H. Campbell**; Cambridge, Mass.; associate justice, Superior Court for the Commonwealth of Massachusetts; Jan. 2, 1927, in Summit, N.J.; Rep.; Nov. 23.

Judge for the Eastern District of Michigan, $40,000—**Robert E. DeMascio**; Detroit, Mich.; judge in the Recorder's Court in Detroit, Mich.; Jan. 11, 1923, in Coraopolis, Pa.; Rep.; July 22.

Judge for the District of Nebraska, $40,000—**Robert V. Denney**; Fairbury, Neb.; member, U.S. House of Representatives (R Neb. 1967-1971); April 11, 1916, in Council Bluffs, Iowa; Rep.; March 4.

Judge for the District of Nebraska, $40,000—**Richard A. Dier**; Omaha, Neb.; U.S. Attorney (Justice Department) in Omaha; Feb. 27, 1914, in Exeter, Neb.; Rep.; Dec. 6.

Judge for the Southern District of New York, $40,000—**Charles L. Brieant Jr.**; Ossining, N.Y.; assistant counsel for the New York State Joint Legislative Committee on Fire Insurance Rates; March 13, 1923, in Ossining, N.Y.; Rep.; July 29.

Judge for the Eastern District of New York, $40,000—**Mark A. Costantino**; Staten Island, N.Y.; acting justice of the Supreme Court of the Second Judicial District, Richmond and King Counties, N.Y.; April 9, 1920, in Staten Island, N.Y.; Rep.; May 20.

Judge for the Southern District of New York, $40,000—**Murray I. Gurfein**; New York City; partner in the law firm of Goldstein, Gurfein, Shames and Hyde; Nov. 17, 1907, in New York City; Rep.; May 20.

Judge for the Eastern District of New York, $40,000—**Edward R. Neaher**; Garden City, N.Y.; U.S. Attorney for the Eastern District of New York; May 2, 1912, in Brooklyn, N.Y.; Rep.; July 22.

Judge for the Southern District of New York, $40,000—**Lawrence W. Pierce**; East Chatham, N.Y.; professor of criminal justice in Graduate School of Criminal Justice, State University of New York; Dec. 31, 1924, in Philadelphia, Pa.; Rep.; May 20.

Judge for the District of North Dakota, $40,000—**Paul Benson**; Grand Forks, N.D.; partner in the law firm of Shaft, Benson, Shaft & McConn; June 1, 1918, in Verona, N.D.; Rep.; July 29.

Judge for the Northern District of Ohio, $40,000—**Leroy J. Contie Jr.**; Canton, Ohio; judge, Common Pleas Court in Stark County, Ohio; April 2, 1920, in Canton, Ohio; Rep.; Dec. 1.

Judge for the Southern District of Ohio, $40,000—**Carl B. Rubin**; Cincinnati, Ohio; partner in the law firm of Tyler, Kane and Rubin; March 27, 1920, in Cincinnati, Ohio; Rep.; May 20.

Judge for the Eastern District of Pennsylvania, $40,000—**Raymond J. Broderick**; Philadelphia, Pa.; lieutenant governor of Pennsylvania; May 29, 1914, in Philadelphia, Pa.; Rep.; April 21.

Judge for the Eastern District of Pennsylvania, $40,000—**Clarence C. Newcomer**; Lancaster, Pa.; partner in the law firm of Newcomer, Roda and Morgan; Jan. 18, 1923, in Mount Joy, Pa.; Rep.; Nov. 23.

Judgeships as Patronage

The prestige of a federal judgeship is high, and appointment to the judiciary is considered by most attorneys and politicians to be the apex of a legal and public career.

Federal judgeships are lifetime appointments and pay $42,500 in the circuit court and $40,000 in the district court annually. There is no mandatory retirement age, but judges may retire at full salary at age 65 after 15 years or at 70 after 10 years on the bench.

The following list gives the number of confirmed federal circuit and district court judges appointed by President Nixon during his first three years in office and by his five immediate predecessors.

	Democrats	Republicans
Roosevelt	188	6
Truman	116	9
Eisenhower	9	165
Kennedy	111†	11
Johnson	159	9
Nixon (1969)	2	24
Nixon (1970)	1	62*
Nixon (1971)	6‡	55‡

† One New York Liberal also was appointed.
* One judge was appointed from the New Progressive Party of Puerto Rico.
‡ Judges' party affiliations, available in the past from the Justice Department, were compiled from entries in Who's Who in American Politics and from the Senators of the states involved.

Judge for the Western District of Pennsylvania, $40,000—**Ralph F. Scalera**; Beaver, Pa.; partner in the law firm of Wallover, Scalera, Reed and Steff; June 28, 1930, in Midland, Pa.; Rep.; Nov. 23.

Judge for the District of South Carolina, $40,000—**Solomon Blatt Jr.**; Barnwell, S.C.; partner in the law firm of Blatt, Fales, Peeples, Bedingfield & Loadholt; Sept. 20, 1921, in Sumter, S.C.; Dem.; May 26.

Judge for the District of South Carolina, $40,000—**Robert F. Chapman**; Spartanburg, S.C.; associate and senior member of the law firm of Butler, Chapman, Parler & Morgan; April 24, 1926, in Inman, S.C.; Rep.; May 26.

Judge for the District of Utah, $40,000—**Aldon J. Anderson**; Salt Lake City, Utah; instructor parttime at Latter Day Saints Business College and the University of Utah; Jan. 3, 1917, in Salt Lake City, Utah; Rep.; July 22.

Judge for the District of Vermont, $40,000—**James S. Holden**; North Bennington, Vt.; chief justice of Supreme Court of Vermont; Jan. 29, 1914, in Bennington, Vt.; Rep.; Nov. 23.

Judge for the Eastern District of Virginia, $40,000—**Albert V. Bryan Jr.**; Alexandria, Va.; judge in the 16th Judicial Circuit of Virginia; Nov. 8, 1926, in Alexandria, Va.; Rep.; July 29.

Judge for the Western District of Washington, $40,000—**Walter T. McGovern**; Seattle, Wash.; associate justice, Supreme Court of State of Washington; May 24, 1922, in Seattle, Wash.; Rep.; April 21.

Judge for the Western District of Washington, $40,000—**Morell E. Sharp**; Bellevue, Wash.; associate justice, Supreme Court of Washington; Sept. 12, 1920, in Portland, Ore.; Rep.; Dec. 2.

Judge for the Southern District of West Virginia, $40,000—**Kenneth K. Hall**; Charleston, W.Va.; administrative hearing examiner, Bureau of Hearing and Appeals in the Social Security Administration; Feb. 24, 1918, in Greenview, W.Va.; Dem.; Dec. 1.

Membership of Federal Regulatory Agencies 1971

Atomic Energy Commission

(Five members appointed for five-year terms; no statutory limitation on political party membership)

Member	Party	Term Expires	Nominated By Nixon	Confirmed By Senate
*James R. Schlesinger (C)	R	6/30/75	7/21/71	8/6/71
*William Offutt Doub	R	6/30/76	7/21/71	8/6/71
Wilfred E. Johnson	R	6/30/72		
James T. Ramey	D	6/30/73		
*Clarence E. Larson	R	6/30/74	6/30/69	8/8/69

Civil Aeronautics Board

(Five members appointed for six-year terms; not more than three members from one political party)

Member	Party	Term Expires	Nominated By Nixon	Confirmed By Senate
*Robert D. Timm	R	12/31/76	12/14/70	12/16/70
**Whitney Gillilland	R	12/31/77	12/13/71†	
Robert T. Murphy	D	12/31/72		
Joseph G. Minetti	D	12/31/73		
*Secor D. Browne (C)	R	12/31/74	9/12/69	10/3/69

Federal Communications Commission

(Seven members appointed for seven-year terms; not more than four members from one political party)

Member	Party	Term Expires	Nominated By Nixon	Confirmed By Senate
*Charlotte T. Reid	R	6/30/78	7/6/71	7/29/71
*Richard E. Wiley	R	6/30/77	recess appointment	
Robert T. Bartley	D	6/30/72		
Nicholas Johnson	D	6/30/73		
Robert E. Lee	R	6/30/74		
H. Rex Lee	D	6/30/75		
*Dean Burch (C)	R	6/30/76	9/17/69	10/30/69

Federal Maritime Commission

(Five members appointed for five-year term; not more than three members from one political party)

Member	Party	Term Expires	Nominated By Nixon	Confirmed By Senate
*Clarence Morse	R	6/30/76	8/7/71	10/7/71
Helen D. Bentley (C)	R	6/30/75	5/5/70	6/3/70
Ashton C. Barrett	D	6/30/72		
George H. Hearn	D	6/30/73		
**James V. Day	R	6/30/74	9/17/69	10/23/69

Federal Power Commission

(Five members appointed for five-year terms; not more than three members from one political party)

Member	Party	Term Expires	Nominated By Nixon	Confirmed By Senate
*Rush Moody Jr.	D	6/22/76	7/20/71	10/8/71
*John N. Nassikas (C)	R	6/22/75	3/23/70	4/30/70
*Pinkney Calvin Walker	R	6/22/72	2/17/71	5/20/71
John A. Carver Jr.	D	6/22/73		
**Albert B. Brooke Jr.	R	6/22/74	6/23/69	10/23/69

Federal Reserve System, Board of Governors

(Seven members appointed for fourteen-year terms; no statutory limitation on political party membership, but not more than one member may be appointed from each Federal Reserve District. No member may be appointed to serve more than one full term.)

Member	Party	Term Expires	Nominated By Nixon	Confirmed By Senate
*Eugene Sheehan	R	1/31/82	recess appointment	
*Arthur F. Burns (C)	R	1/31/84	10/22/69	12/18/69
Sherman J. Maisel	NA	1/31/72		
J. Dewey Daane	NA	1/31/74		
George W. Mitchell	D	1/31/76		
J. L. Robertson	NA	1/31/78		
Andrew F. Brimmer	D	1/31/80		

Federal Trade Commission

(Five members appointed for seven-year terms; not more than three members from one political party)

Member	Party	Term Expires	Nominated By Nixon	Confirmed By Senate
*David S. Dennison Jr.	R	9/25/77	9/22/70	10/13/70
Mary G. Jones	R	9/25/73		
Paul Rand Dixon	D	9/25/74		
A. Everette MacIntyre	D	9/25/75		
*Miles W. Kirkpatrick (C)	R	9/25/76	8/12/70	8/24/70

Interstate Commerce Commission

(Eleven members appointed for seven-year terms; not more than six members from one political party)

Member	Party	Term Expires	Nominated By Nixon	Confirmed By Senate
*Virginia Mae Brown	D	12/31/77	4/14/71	6/30/71
**Dale W. Hardin	R	12/31/77	4/14/71	6/30/71
*William Donald Brewer	R	12/31/76	5/18/70	7/14/70
Rupert L. Murphy	D	12/31/71		
John W. Bush	D	12/31/71		
Willard Deason	D	12/31/72		
*Lawrence Walrath	D	12/31/72	4/14/71	6/30/71
*Donald L. Jackson	R	12/31/73	2/20/69	3/13/69
George M. Stafford (C)	R	12/31/73		
*Robert C. Gresham	R	12/31/74	9/25/69	11/19/69
Kenneth H. Tuggle	R	12/31/75		

National Labor Relations Board

(Five members appointed for five-year terms; no statutory limitation on political party membership)

Member	Party	Term Expires	Nominated By Nixon	Confirmed By Senate
*Ralph E. Kennedy	R	8/27/75	9/21/70	12/2/70
John H. Fanning	D	12/16/72		
Howard Jenkins Jr.	R	8/27/73		
Edward B. Miller (C)	R	12/16/74	2/20/70	5/21/70
Vacancy				

National Mediation Board

(Three members appointed for three-year terms; not more than two members from one political party)

Member	Party	Term Expires	Nominated By Nixon	Confirmed By Senate
*Peter C. Benedict	R	7/1/74	7/21/71	8/4/71
David H. Stowe	D	7/1/73	9/22/70	12/2/70
*George S. Ives (C)	R	7/1/72	8/29/69	9/17/69

Securities and Exchange Commission

(Five members appointed for five-year terms; not more than three members from one political party)

Member	Party	Term Expires	Nominated By Nixon	Confirmed By Senate
*William J. Casey (C)	R	6/5/74	2/4/71	3/25/71
**Hugh F. Owens	D	6/5/75	5/13/70	5/20/70
*A. Sydney Herlong Jr.	D	6/5/76	6/3/71	6/17/71
*Philip A. Loomis Jr.	R	6/5/72	9/10/71	9/23/71
*James J. Needham	R	6/5/73	5/27/69	6/18/69

(C) chairman.
* Nixon appointment.
**Reappointed by Nixon; first appointed in a previous Administration.
†Renominated but not yet confirmed; still serving.

PRESIDENTIAL MESSAGES
AND STATEMENTS

CQ

Nixon Presents 'Six Great Goals' To Congress:
Stresses Welfare Reform and Stabilization of the Economy

Following is the text, as made available by the White House, of President Nixon's Jan. 22 State of the Union address to Congress.

Mr. Speaker, Mr. President, my colleagues in the Congress, our distinguished guests and my fellow Americans:

This 92nd Congress has a chance to be recorded as the greatest Congress in America's history.

In these troubled years just past, America has been going through a long nightmare of war and division, of crime and inflation. Even more deeply, we have gone through a long, dark night of the American spirit. But now that night is ending. Now we must let our spirits soar again. Now we are ready for the lift of a driving dream.

The people of this nation are eager to get on with the quest for new greatness. They see challenges, and they are prepared to meet those challenges. It is for us here to open the doors that will set free again the real greatness of this nation—the genius of the American people.

How shall we meet this challenge? How can we truly open the doors, and set free the full genius of our people?

The way in which the 92nd Congress answers these questions will determine its place in history. More importantly, it can determine this nation's place in history as we enter the third century of our independence.

Tonight, I shall present to the Congress six great goals. I shall ask not simply for more new programs in the old framework, but to change the framework itself—to reform the entire structure of American government so we can make it again fully responsive to the needs and the wishes of the American people.

If we act boldly—if we seize this moment and achieve these goals—we can close the gap between promise and performance in American government, and bring together the resources of the nation and the spirit of the people.

In discussing these great goals, I am dealing tonight only with matters on the domestic side of the nation's agenda. I shall make a separate report to the Congress and the nation next month on developments in our foreign policy.

The first of these six great goals is already before the Congress.

I urge that the unfinished business of the 91st Congress be made the first priority of the 92nd.

Over the next two weeks, I will call upon Congress to take action on more than 35 pieces of proposed legislation on which action was not completed last year.

Welfare Reform

The most important is welfare reform.

The present welfare system has become a monstrous, consuming outrage—an outrage against the community, against the taxpayer, and particularly against the children it is supposed to help.

We may honestly disagree on what to do about it. But we can all agree that we must meet the challenge not by pouring more money into the old system, but by abolishing it and adopting a new one.

Let us place a floor under the income of every family with children in America—and without those demeaning, soul-stifling affronts to human dignity that so blight the lives of welfare children today. But let us also establish an effective work incentive and an effective work requirement.

Let us provide the means by which more can help themselves. Let us generously help those who are not able to help themselves. But let us stop helping those who are able to help themselves but refuse to do so.

The Economy

The second great goal is to achieve what Americans have not enjoyed since 1957—full prosperity in peacetime.

The tide of inflation has turned. The rise in the cost of living, which had been gathering dangerous momentum in the late Sixties, was reduced last year. Inflation will be further reduced this year.

But as we have moved from runaway inflation toward reasonable price stability, and at the same time have been moving from a wartime economy to a peacetime economy, we have paid a price in increased unemployment.

We should take no comfort from the fact that the level of unemployment in this transition from a wartime to a peacetime economy is lower than in any peacetime year of the 1960s.

This is not good enough for the man who is unemployed in the Seventies. We must do better for workers in peacetime and we will do better.

To achieve this, I will submit an expansionary budget this year—one that will help stimulate the economy and thereby open up new job opportunities for millions of Americans.

It will be a full employment budget, a budget designed to be in balance if the economy were operating at its peak potential. By spending as if we were at full employment, we will help to bring about full employment.

I ask the Congress to accept these expansionary policies—to accept the concept of the full employment budget.

At the same time, I ask the Congress to cooperate in resisting expenditures that go beyond the limits of the full employment budget. For as we wage a campaign to bring about a widely shared prosperity, we must not re-ignite the fires of inflation and so undermine that prosperity.

With the stimulus and the discipline of a full employment budget; with the commitment of the independent Federal Reserve System to provide fully for the monetary needs of a growing economy; and with a much greater effort by labor and management to make their wage and price decisions in the light of the national interest and their own long-run best interests—then for the worker, the farmer, the consumer, and for Americans everywhere we shall gain the goal of a new prosperity: more jobs, more income and more profits, without inflation and without war.

This is a great goal, and one that we can achieve together.

The Environment

The third great goal is to continue the effort so dramatically begun this past year: to restore and enhance our natural environment.

Building on the foundation laid in the 37-point program I submitted to Congress last year, I will propose a strong new set of initiatives to clean up our air and water, to combat noise, and to preserve and restore our surroundings.

I will propose programs to make better use of our land, and to encourage a balanced national growth—growth that will revitalize our rural heartland and enhance the quality of life throughout America.

And not only to meet today's needs but to anticipate those of tomorrow, I will put forward the most extensive program ever proposed by a President to expand the nation's parks, recreation areas and open spaces in a way that truly brings parks to the people. For only if we leave a legacy of parks will the next generation have parks to enjoy.

Health Care

As a fourth great goal, I will offer a far-reaching set of proposals for improving America's health care and making it available more fairly to more people.

I will propose:

- A program to insure that no American family will be prevented from obtaining basic medical care by inability to pay.

- A major increase in and redirection of aid to medical schools, to greatly increase the number of doctors and other health personnel.

- Incentives to improve the delivery of health services, to get more medical care resources into those areas that have not been adequately served, to make greater use of medical assistants and to slow the alarming rise in the costs of medical care.

- New programs to encourage better preventive medicine, by attacking the causes of disease and injury, and by providing incentives to doctors to keep people well rather than just to treat them when they are sick.

I will also ask appropriation of an extra $100 million to launch an intensive campaign to find a cure for cancer, and I will ask later for whatever additional funds can effectively be used. The time has come when the same kind of concentrated effort that split the atom and took man to the moon should be turned toward conquering this dread disease. Let us make a total national commitment to achieve this goal.

America has long been the wealthiest nation in the world. Now it is time we became the healthiest nation in the world.

Revenue Sharing

The fifth great goal is to strengthen and renew our State and local governments.

As we approach our 200th anniversary in 1976, we remember that this nation launched itself as a loose confederation of separate States, without a workable central government. At that time, the mark of its leaders' vision was that they quickly saw the need to balance the separate powers of the States with a government of central powers.

And so they gave us a Constitution of balanced powers, of unity with diversity—and so clear was their vision that it survives as the oldest written Constitution still in force in the world today.

For almost two centuries since—and dramatically in the 1930s—at those great turning points when the question has been between the States and the Federal Government, it has been resolved in favor of a stronger central government.

During this time the nation grew and prospered. But one thing history tells us is that no great movement goes in the same direction forever. Nations change, they adapt, or they slowly die.

The time has come to reverse the flow of power and resources from the States and communities to Washington, and start power and resources flowing back from Washington to the States and communities and, more important, to the people, all across America.

The time has come for a new partnership between the Federal Government and the States and localities—a partnership in which we entrust the States and localities with a larger share of the nation's responsibilities, and in which we share our revenues with them so they can meet those responsibilities.

To achieve this goal, I propose to the Congress tonight that we enact a plan of revenue sharing historic in scope and bold in concept.

All across America today, States and cities are confronted with a financial crisis. Some already have been cutting back on essential services—for example, just recently San Diego and Cleveland cut back on trash collections. Most are caught between the prospects of bankruptcy on the one hand and adding to an already crushing tax burden on the other.

As one indication of the rising costs of local government, I discovered the other day that my home town of Whittier, California—with a population of only 67,000—has a budget for 1971 bigger than the entire Federal budget in 1791.

Now the time has come to take a new direction, and once again to introduce a new and more creative balance in our approach to government.

So let us put the money where the needs are. And let us put the power to spend it where the people are.

I propose that the Congress make a $16 billion investment in renewing State and local government—with $5 billion of this in new and unrestricted funds, to be used as the States and localities see fit, and with the other $11 billion provided by allocating $1 billion of new funds and converting one-third of the money going to the present narrow-purpose aid programs into Federal revenue sharing funds for six broad purposes—urban development, rural development, education, transportation, job training and law enforcement—but with the States and localities making their own local decisions on how it should be spent.

For the next fiscal year, this would increase total Federal aid to the States and localities by more than 25 percent over the present level.

The revenue sharing proposals I send to the Congress will include the safeguards against discrimination that accompany all other Federal funds allocated to the States. Neither the President nor the Congress nor the conscience of the nation can permit money which comes from all the people to be used in a way which discriminates against some of the people.

The Federal Government will still have a large and vital role to play in achieving our national purposes. Established functions that are clearly and essentially Federal in nature will still be performed by the Federal Government. New functions that need to be sponsored or performed by the Federal Government—such as those I have urged tonight in welfare and health—will be added to the Federal agenda. Whenever it makes the best sense for us to act as a whole nation, the Federal Government will lead the way. But where State or local governments can better do what needs to be done, let us see that they have the resources to do it.

Under this plan, the Federal Government will provide the States and localities with more money and less interference—and by cutting down the interference the same amount of money will go a lot further.

Let us share our resources:

- To rescue the States and localities from the brink of financial crisis.

- And to give homeowners and wage earners a chance to escape from ever-higher property taxes and sales taxes.

Let us share our resources for two other reasons as well.

The first of these reasons has to do with government itself, and the second with the individual.

Let's face it. Most Americans today are simply fed up with government at all levels. They will not—and should not—continue to tolerate the gap between promise and performance.

The fact is that we have made the Federal Government so strong it grows muscle-bound and the States and localities so weak they approach impotence.

If we put more power in more places, we can make government more creative in more places. For that way we multiply the number of people with the ability to make things happen—and we can open the way to a new burst of creative energy throughout America.

The final reason I urge this historic shift is much more personal, for each and every one of us.

As everything seems to have grown bigger, and more complex; as the forces that shape our lives seem to have grown more distant and more impersonal a great feeling of frustration has crept across the land.

Whether it is the working man who feels neglected, the black man who feels oppressed or the mother concerned about her children, there has been a growing feeling that "things are in the saddle, and ride mankind."

Millions of frustrated young Americans today are crying out —asking not what will government do for me, but what can I do, how can I contribute, how can I matter?

Let us answer them. To them and to all Americans, let us say: "We hear you and we will give you a chance. We are going to give you a new chance to have more to say about the decisions that affect your future—to participate in government—because we are going to provide more centers of power where what you do can make a difference that you can see and feel in your own life and the life of your whole community."

The further away government is from people, the stronger government becomes and the weaker people become. And a nation with a strong government and a weak people is an empty shell.

I reject the patronizing idea that government in Washington, D.C., is inevitably more wise, more honest and more efficient than government at the local or State level. The honesty and efficiency of government depends on people. Government at all levels has good people and bad people. And the way to get more good people into government is to give them more opportunity to do good things.

The idea that a bureaucratic elite in Washington knows best what is best for people everywhere and that you cannot trust local government is really a contention that you cannot trust people to govern themselves. This notion is completely foreign to the American experience. Local government is the government closest to the people and most responsive to the individual person; it is people's government in a far more intimate way than the government in Washington can ever be.

People came to America because they wanted to determine their own future rather than to live in a country where others determined their future for them.

What this change means is that once again we are placing our trust in people.

I have faith in people. I trust the judgment of people. Let us give the people a chance, a bigger voice in deciding for themselves those questions that so greatly affect their lives.

Federal Government Reorganization

The sixth great goal is a complete reform of the Federal Government itself.

Based on a long and intensive study with the aid of the best advice obtainable, I have concluded that a sweeping reorganization of the Executive Branch is needed if the government is to keep up with the times and with the needs of the people.

I propose that we reduce the present twelve Cabinet Departments to eight.

I propose that the Departments of State, Treasury, Defense and Justice remain, but that all the other departments be consolidated into four: Human Resources, Community Development, Natural Resources, and Economic Development.

Let us look at what these would be:

• First, a department dealing with the concerns of people— as individuals, as members of a family—a department focused on human needs.

• Second, a department concerned with the community—rural communities and urban—and with all that it takes to make a community function as a community.

• Third, a department concerned with our physical environment, and with the preservation and balanced use of those great natural resources on which our nation depends.

• And fourth, a department concerned with our prosperity— with our jobs, our businesses, and those many activities that keep our economy running smoothly and well.

Under this plan, rather than dividing up our departments by narrow subjects, we would organize them around the great pur-poses of government. Rather than scattering responsibility by adding new levels of bureaucracy, we would focus and concentrate the responsibility for getting problems solved.

With these four departments, when we have a problem we will know where to go—and the department will have the authority and the resources to do something about it.

Over the years we have added departments and created agencies, each to serve a new constituency or to handle a particular task—and these have grown and multiplied in what has become a hopeless confusion of form and function.

The time has come to match our structure to our purposes— to look with a fresh eye, and to organize the government by conscious, comprehensive design to meet the new needs of a new era.

One hundred years ago, Abraham Lincoln stood on a battlefield and spoke of a government of the people, by the people and for the people. Too often since then, we have become a nation of the Government, by the Government, and for the Government.

By enacting these reforms, we can renew that principle that Lincoln stated so simply and so well.

By giving everyone's voice a chance to be heard, we will have government that truly is of the people.

By creating more centers of meaningful power, more places where decisions that really count can be made, by giving more people a chance to do something, we can have government that truly is by the people.

And by setting up a completely modern, functional system of government at the national level, we in Washington will at last be able to provide government that truly is for the people.

I realize that what I am asking is that not only the Executive Branch in Washington but even this Congress will have to change by giving up some of its power.

Change is hard. But without change there can be no progress. And for each of us the question must be, not "Will change cause me inconvenience?" but "Will change bring the country progress?"

Giving up power is hard. But I would urge all of you, as leaders of this country, to remember that the truly revered leaders in world history are those who gave power to people, not those who took it away.

As we consider these reforms we will be acting, not for the next two years or the next ten years, but for the next hundred years.

So let us approach these six great goals with a sense, not only of this moment in history, but also of history itself.

Let us act with the willingness to work together and the vision and the boldness and the courage of those great Americans who met in Philadelphia almost 190 years ago to create a Constitution.

Let us leave a heritage as they did—not just for our children but for millions yet unborn—of a nation where every American will have a chance not only to live in peace and to enjoy prosperity and opportunity, but to participate in a system of government where he knows not only his votes but his ideas count—a system of government which will provide the means for America to reach heights of achievement undreamed of before.

Those men who met in Philadelphia left a great heritage because they had a vision—not only of what the nation was, but of what it could become.

As I think of that vision, I recall that America was founded as the land of the open door—as a haven for the oppressed, a land of opportunity, a place of refuge and of hope.

When the first settlers opened the door of America three and a half centuries ago, they came to escape persecution and to find opportunity—and they left wide the door of welcome for others to follow.

When the thirteen colonies declared their independence almost two centuries ago, they opened the door to a new vision of liberty and of human fulfillment—not just for an elite, but for all.

To the generations that followed, America's was the open door that beckoned millions from the old world to the new in search of a better life, a freer life, a fuller life, in which by their own decisions they could shape their own destinies.

For the black American, the Indian, the Mexican-American, and for those others in our land who have not had an equal chance, the nation at last has begun to confront the need to press open the door of full and equal opportunity, and of human dignity.

New Era

For all Americans, with these changes I have proposed tonight we can open the door to a new era of opportunity. We can open the door to full and effective participation in the decisions that affect their lives. We can open the door to a new partnership among governments at all levels, and between those governments and the people themselves. And by so doing, we can open wide the doors of human fulfillment for millions of people here in America.

In the next few weeks I will spell out in greater detail the way I propose that we achieve these six great goals. I ask this Congress to be responsive. If it is, then the 92nd Congress, at the end of its term, will be able to look back on a record more splendid than any in our history.

This can be the Congress that helped us end the longest war in the nation's history, and end it in a way that will give us at last a genuine chance for a full generation of peace.

This can be the Congress that helped achieve an expanding economy, with full employment and without inflation—and without the deadly stimulus of war.

This can be the Congress that reformed a welfare system that has robbed recipients of their dignity while it robbed States and cities of their resources.

This can be the Congress that pressed forward the rescue of our environment, and established for the next generation an enduring legacy of parks for the people.

This can be the Congress that launched a new era in American medicine, in which the quality of medical care was enhanced while the costs were made less burdensome.

But above all, what this Congress can be remembered for is opening the way to a New American Revolution—a peaceful revolution in which power was turned back to the people—in which government at all levels was refreshed and renewed, and made truly responsive. This can be a revolution as profound, as far-reaching, as exciting, as that first revolution almost 200 years ago—and it can mean that just five years from now America will enter its third century as a young nation new in spirit, with all the vigor and freshness with which it began its first century.

My colleagues in the Congress—these are great goals, and they can make the sessions of this Congress a great moment for America. So let us pledge together to go forward together—by achieving these goals to give America the foundation today for a new greatness tomorrow and in all the years to come—and in so doing to make this the greatest Congress in the history of this great and good nation.

RICHARD NIXON

NIXON'S STATEMENT ON CONGRESS

Following is the text, as made available by the White House, of President Nixon's Jan. 5 statement criticizing the 91st Congress.

The Ninety-First Congress of the United States has now passed into history. Much useful and valuable, even historic legislation, was enacted—responsive in whole or part to the initiatives and recommendations of the Administration. Yet, regrettably, this Congress will be remembered and remarked upon in history, not so much for what it did, but for what it failed to do.

With the rising national demand for governmental reform and innovation in the arena of social policy, with a multiplicity of Administration initiatives before it, the Ninety-First Congress had the opportunity to write one of the most productive and memorable chapters in the history of American Government. That opportunity was lost. The nation was the loser.

In the final month and weeks of 1970, especially in the Senate of the United States, the nation was presented with the spectacle of a legislative body that had seemingly lost the capacity to decide and the will to act. When the path was finally cleared, vital days had been lost, and major failures insured.

In probably no month in recent memory did the reputation of the whole Congress suffer more in the eyes of the American people, than in the month of December, 1970. In these times when the need to build confidence in government is so transparent, that was good neither for the Congress nor the country. Let us hope that it never takes place again.

Even a partial listing of the vital legislation rejected, or left un-enacted, by the departing Ninety-First Congress provides a yardstick of just how far this Congress fell short of the mark of becoming the Great Congress—that might have been. Left un-enacted were—

• Our proposal to consolidate the complex and complicated grant-in-aid system, jerry-built over the years of the Federal Government.

• The historic proposal, endorsed by both party platforms in 1968, to share federal revenues on an annual basis with the revenue-starved states, counties and cities.

• The Family Assistance Plan, the most far-reaching social reform in four decades, to overhaul America's chaotic and costly welfare system by providing a floor of dignity under every family and the incentives for Americans to begin to move off welfare rolls.

Rejection of these reforms is nothing short of tragic at a time when the burden of welfare bears down with increasing severity upon states and municipalities confronted, all, with a mounting fiscal crisis.

But there were other excellent proposals, excellent ideas, that died of neglect in the Ninety-First Congress:

• The emergency school aid proposal to assist those school districts bearing the special burdens of the rapid desegregation now underway.

• The proposal for establishment of a National Institute of Education.

• The Higher Education Opportunity Act itself, a long overdue reform.

• Pay increases for enlisted men in the armed services, a first step toward realization of our goal of zero draft calls, and an army composed entirely of volunteers.

• Added reforms to make selective service more equitable and just for young Americans.

• Half a dozen separate measures dealing with control of pollution and threats to the environment.

• Four separate bills designed to help protect the consumer from victimization.

• Vitally needed Administration legislation for helping the nation deal with national emergency strikes, a recurring and dangerous phenomenon.

• The proposed increase in Social Security benefits that died in the very last days of this Congress.

• The proposed cost-of-living escalator in Social Security to provide permanent protection to old age recipients from the rages of inflation.

• Trade legislation, giving the Administration authority over textile quotas, providing incentive programs for American exports and repealing the American Selling Price.

• Electoral college reform.

• National bail reform legislation.

• Wagering tax amendments.

• Authority to tax airline tickets to pay for protection against highjackings.

• Additional legislation to deal with the distribution of pornographic and obscene materials.

• Proposals to assist those who are perhaps America's most needy minority, the American Indian.

• The proposal for establishment of a Federal City Bicentennial Development Corporation.

These are but some of the measures. All of them were worthwhile; none of them was enacted.

Congress' failure to enact them, however, in no way diminishes the desirability of the Administration's commitment. When the Ninety-Second Congress convenes, these and others will be presented for action, as the first order of Administration business.

Further, the Congress may wish to consider revision of the "turn-of-the-century," work schedules and procedures that now obtain on Capital Hill. While there are many excuses for Congressional inaction—there are no good reasons.

Hopefully, the Ninety-Second Congress will pick up where Ninety-First Congress did not; hopefully, it will become the Great Congress that the Ninety-First Congress did not become.

To the members of the Ninety-Second Congress I say: Let us open the New Year in a new spirit. Let us mutually commit ourselves to work, and work hard, for the record of achievement which we all can share. Let us thereby build the kind of society we all desire for our children and grandchildren. To that end, I pledge the full cooperation of this Administration.

MESSAGE ON LEGISLATION

Following is the text, as made available by the White House, of President Nixon's Jan. 26 message to Congress asking for passage of certain legislation.

TO THE CONGRESS OF THE UNITED STATES:

This first special message to the Ninety-second Congress concerns itself not with the new, but with the familiar. As indicated in my State of the Union Message, this first request is that unfinished business of the Ninety-first Congress be made the first business of the Ninety-second.

With this message, I am proposing to the Ninety-second Congress more than three dozen items of legislation which were previously submitted to the Ninety-first Congress. Some were acted on favorably by either the Senate or the House of Representatives. Some are being resubmitted in their original form. Others have been modified to meet legitimate concerns expressed by members of the Congress. Most will be in the hands of Congress today. All are bills which I consider to be in the national interest.

Although lengthy, this list does not contain all the measures proposed over the past two years which will be resubmitted to the Congress in this session.

There are other measures—measures to deal with strikes creating national emergencies, Social Security amendments, bail reform, aid for higher education, reform of the draft and steps to move toward an all-volunteer armed force, and other initiatives —which the Congress must also consider. I will deal with these separately.

In my message on the State of the Union, I outlined six great goals—goals which, by their accomplishment, could make this the greatest Congress in America's history as a nation.

These included one especially urgent item of unfinished business which I proposed to the 91st Congress: welfare reform. In fairness to the taxpayers, to the communities, and also to the children, we can afford to delay no longer in discarding the present system and replacing it with a new one.

In due course, I will be making more detailed proposals to the Congress for achieving the other goals that I outlined. Meanwhile, I believe that the items of unfinished business I propose today merit the prompt and careful consideration of the Congress.

I believe they are good measures. I believe they are wise proposals. I believe they are necessary legislation. I urge the Congress to act favorably upon them.

Economic Justice

Two proposals being resubmitted would promote economic justice. One would provide broader opportunities for Americans entering into new small businesses—especially black Americans and members of other minorities who need, but cannot acquire, the seed capital to go into business for themselves. The other would provide improved benefits for certain American workers.

Aid to Small Business

Ten months ago, several proposals were sent to the Congress to promote the prospects for success of small businesses in the United States. They included:

• Allowing private and corporate lenders an income tax deduction equal to twenty percent of the interest earned on Small Business Administration guaranteed loans, which would act as an incentive for loans to small businesses and minority enterprises;

• Providing managerial training to disadvantaged persons going into business for themselves;

• Authorizing banks to become sole sponsors of Minority Enterprise Small Business Investment Companies (MESBICs);

• Authorizing SBA to pay interest subsidies on loans it guarantees, in cases of demonstrated need;

• Liberalizing the net operating loss carryover rules and stock option provisions for qualified small businesses;

• Allowing tax deduction for contributions to nonprofit MESBICs.

Many of these amendments passed the Senate in the 91st Congress. I urge this Congress to give them a favorable response.

Longshoremen's Disability Compensation

The existing minimum disability compensation for longshoremen and harbor workers was established in 1956—the maximum a decade ago. I am renewing the administration's proposal that these benefits be increased to a level more in line with the increased wages and living costs since the present levels were set. Other liberalizing provisions of the Longshoremen's and Harbor Workers' Compensation Act are being resubmitted as part of this proposal.

Under this legislation the recovery of damages by employees from their employers, including shipowners, would be limited to those specified under the Act. We seek to eliminate situations in which longshoremen are permitted to recover damages in suits against shipowners, which usually require the longshore employer to indemnify the shipowner for the damages paid.

America's Overdue Debts

There are three groups of peoples, two of them among the earliest inhabitants of the Western Hemisphere, to whom this nation has outstanding obligations that ought to be met.

American Indians and Alaska Natives

The first two of these are the American Indians and the Alaska Natives. After full consultation with Indian leaders is complete, the unenacted legislation outlined in my Message of last July 8 will be reviewed and promptly submitted again. An Alaska Native Claims bill will also be submitted which I believe will equitably resolve the Native claims in that State. These legislative proposals would take America in a new more hopeful direction in dealing with the problems of a terribly neglected minority of our people.

The Micronesians

Under the Executive Agreement of April 18, 1969 between Japan and the United States, inhabitants of the Trust Territory of the Pacific Islands are to be compensated for damages suffered during World War II. The agreement stipulates that each government will make ex gratia contributions of $5 million for the welfare of the People of Micronesia.

I am renewing the administration's request that the Congress authorize appropriations of $5 million to meet that commitment, and also that the Congress establish a five-member commission to settle the claims of individual Micronesians resulting from World War II and to determine the validity of additional claims for property damage arising after the war.

Congressional action on these matters would render overdue justice to the people of Micronesia.

Pure Food and Drugs

Two pieces of "preventive" legislation are being resubmitted dealing with the health of the American people. The first has to do with the wholesomeness of fish and fish products which form so significant a segment of the American diet; the second with preventing illness and death from accidental misuse of prescription drugs.

Fish Inspection

Fish and fish products, a major source of protein in the American diet, are highly perishable foods. Improperly handled, they become a medium for bacterial growth. The Wholesome Fish and Fishery Products Act, which is being resubmitted, would establish a broad surveillance and inspection system to assure the wholesomeness and quality of both domestic and imported fishery products.

Recent reports of mercury residues in both inland and deep sea fish provide urgent and concurring arguments for immediate passage of this legislation.

Drug Identification

Every year some Americans, in times of medical emergency, are poisoned by drugs of unidentified composition. Some of these men, women, and children die from these poisonings; others suffer lasting physical harm. While these occurrences are not commonplace, their number can and should be reduced to an absolute minimum. To achieve that objective—to permit the rapid identification of prescription drugs in emergency situations—this administration again proposes the coding of all drugs. Such coding will also facilitate recalls of drugs when necessary to protect public health.

Some manufacturers already use coding systems for immediate identification and inventory control. A universal system of coding of drugs would benefit the entire drug industry—and perhaps save the lives of scores of Americans and their children in years ahead.

Toward a More Secure and Decent Society

Within this broad category, I again urge action on five previously submitted measures. One of them would provide new and needed protection for the orderly processes of government in the event of disruptive activities conducted in or near Federal offices. Passed by the Senate, this measure should be viewed favorably by the House. It is needed to protect government workers as they carry out their duties. The wagering tax and the administration's proposal to give law enforcement officers the right to gather non-testimonial evidence are reforms which would provide us with new weapons in the war against crime. The final proposals, dealing with obscenity and pornography, I believe to be essential at a time when the tide of offensive materials seems yet to be rising.

Protection of Public Buildings

If the Federal Government is to discharge its duties, the employees of government must cease being victimized by raucous and disorderly demonstrations in the offices where they work. Such disruptions have occurred too frequently in recent years.

To help end this harassment, I propose that the General Services Administration's authority to police Federal property be extended to all buildings leased or occupied by Federal agencies.

Further, I ask Congress to prohibit specifically:

• The obstruction of passage into or out of a government office;

• The use of loud, abusive, or threatening language, or any disorderly conduct that has as its goal the disruption of government business; and,

• Any act of physical violence within a GSA facility.

These are similar to the safeguards which the Congress provided for its own employees in the U.S. Capitol Buildings and Grounds Security Act of 1967.

Under this proposal the maximum penalties for violation of the rules promulgated by GSA would be raised from a $50 fine or thirty days in jail to a $500 fine or six months in prison.

Passage of this legislation would help divert future protests back into the legitimate democratic channels where they belong.

Federal Wagering Tax

The Federal wagering tax can be a useful tool in our increasingly successful effort against organized crime. Some of its provisions, however, were ruled unconstitutional in 1968 as violative of the Fifth Amendment right against self-incrimination. Both to retain this needed weapon and to bring the law into accord with the rulings of the Supreme Court, I again propose a prohibition on any use—against the taxpayer—of information obtained through his compliance with this statute. At the same time, the new amendments would broaden the coverage of the wagering tax and increase the level of taxation.

Non-Testimonial Identification

Currently, law enforcement officers are often handicapped in obtaining significant non-testimonial evidence—such as blood samples or fingerprints—in a way to qualify it for use as legal evidence. Under this proposal, a judicial officer could, under prescribed conditions, issue an order *requiring* that a suspect give such kinds of evidence. This is a constitutionally sound step that would advance the cause of criminal justice without infringing upon any of the legitimate rights of suspects and defendants.

Obscenity and Pornography

The overwhelming majority of Americans is rightly appalled at the burgeoning growth of the pornography industry here in the United States. Though Court rulings have restricted some government countermeasures, in other instances they have left us the freedom to act. They have both recognized the right to protect minors from the products of this obnoxious enterprise, and reaffirmed the right to restrict pandering through advertising. I propose anew that Congress pass measures, with stiff penalties, prohibiting the use of interstate facilities to transport unsolicited salacious advertising, or to deliver any harmful and offensive matter to youngsters. It would be difficult to overstate the strength of my support for these two pieces of legislation.

Education: Reform and Opportunity

Under this broad category, I have included three measures submitted to the Ninety-first Congress, all of which I believe have great merit and would serve great needs. The first is for a National Institute of Education, the need for which is becoming increasingly apparent; the second is a measure to provide financial assistance to those school districts carrying the strain of desegregation; the third is to encourage and assist the men coming home from Vietnam to make better use of the educational opportunity the country affords them. Higher education proposals will be resubmitted later to the new Congress.

National Institute of Education

A National Institute of Education—to bring to education the intensity and quality of research now developed in the fields of space and health—is truly a national need. Year by year, the American people grow more disenchanted with the returns on their education tax dollars. The schools of the nation are in growing need of new counsel and new ideas. Here is the opportunity to find the answers, by bringing to bear on the problems the wisdom, the knowledge and the experience of the most able men and women in the field. This Institute was a key part of my education proposals of last year. Today I again urge the Congress to act favorably upon this request.

Emergency School Aid

Last year, both to encourage and to expedite desegregation of the public schools in the United States, I asked the Congress for a two-year Emergency School Aid Act. Although great progress has been made, the need for such aid remains. Therefore, today I reissue this request. The changes needed to desegregate our schools—either under court order or through voluntary action—place a heavy strain upon local school systems, and the Federal Government should assist the school systems in this effort. The measure I propose today is similar to the one which passed the House of Representatives in the closing days of the Ninety-first Congress. I urge the Congress to complete action at an early date.

Vietnam Veterans Education Allowance

It is this administration's hope that more veterans coming home from Vietnam will take advantage of the educational opportunities the nation affords them. The bill I now again recommend will help achieve that objective.

Under the GI Bill, the monthly allowances received by veterans begin only after they have enrolled and completed at least a month of their education or training. This deferral of payment often deters veterans from taking training or additional schooling because they lack the initial funds to meet tuition and living expenses.

This legislation would enable the Veterans Administration to make advance payments to veterans as soon as they submit evidence they have registered. This will provide them with funds when their need for funds is most pressing.

The Federal City

Two proposals being resubmitted deal with the nation's capital. The first envisions a corporation to carry out the revitalization of the heart of Washington. The second would give the District Government a new measure of freedom and control over its own capital outlay programs, reducing District dependency on the Federal Government.

Federal City Bicentennial Development Corporation

The American Bicentennial—midway through the present decade—presents a powerful incentive and a realistic deadline for realization of Pierre L'Enfant's vision for the Federal City. The proposal being resubmitted would create a public corporation to prepare plans for carrying forward the revitalization of the heart of Washington, and for generating the maximum private and commercial investment for the fulfillment of that dream. I urge the Congress not to allow any more time to be lost in completing this promising enterprise.

D.C. Capital Program Financing Act

Currently, when the District of Columbia Government is confronted with the need to borrow for major new building and construction, it must turn to the United States Treasury; and it can borrow only up to a temporary formula limit set by the Congress.

I now renew this administration's proposal that the Congress grant the District of Columbia Government the authority to issue its own local bonds, and that the future limit on borrowing be set according to a permanent flexible formula based on District revenues. Removing the District's capital spending requirements from the Federal budget would mean savings to the Treasury. Further, it would give Washington responsibilities and rights commensurate with those of other great American cities.

Transportation

Under this heading, two proposals are being resubmitted. They relate to waterways safety, the need for which has become increasingly apparent as more and more great vessels ply the navigable waters of the United States. Decreasing accidents at sea is an important part of our over-all program to provide greater safety to the traveling public. In addition, these bills enhance our efforts to prevent the damaging pollution of the Nation's waterways which often results from collisions at sea.

Ports and Waterways Safety Act

As commerce grows, and as world trade expands, more and more great ships use American waters. Many carry hazardous cargoes—potential dangers to America's ports, harbors, waterfront areas, the waters themselves and the resources they contain. There would, I believe, be a substantial benefit in the creation of a coordinated safety program. And I again ask that the Secretary of Transportation be empowered to prescribe standards and regulations, and to act upon them, to give the protection the nation increasingly needs.

Vessel-to-Vessel Radio Phones

With the increasing number of vessels operating on inland and coastal waterways, the danger of accidents and collisions has become more serious. To help prevent unnecessary loss of life and property in future years, I am again proposing to the Congress legislation requiring that certain vessels transiting these waterways carry equipment for direct bridge-to-bridge contact. While most vessels today carry radio equipment, there is not always a compatible and open communication channel between two ships—and hence, they often cannot communicate even the most basic navigational information. Many vessels are already adequately equipped to meet the new requirements; the cost to the remaining shipowners would not be great.

Rural America

Two measures again being proposed concern Americans living in the countryside or on farms. One would establish a mixed-ownership bank to make loans to telephone borrowers, along the lines of the Farm Credit Administration; the other would reduce Federal expenditures by replacing direct loans to some farmers with government guaranteed loans.

The Telephone Bank

I propose creation of a mixed-ownership bank to make loans—at from 4 percent to market interest rates—to telephone companies and cooperatives which now rely almost exclusively on the Rural Electrification Administration for their financing.

The bank would be partially capitalized through Treasury purchase of stock at a rate of up to $30 million annually until the Treasury holdings reached $300 million.

When total capital stock plus paid-in surplus reached $400 million, the bank would begin to retire the Federal investment. Further, the bank would be empowered to sell stock to its borrowers, and to borrow from private investors up to eight times the paid-in capital and retained earnings of the bank. This could bring about bank loans during Fiscal Year 1972 of $94.5 million to telephone borrowers—and the 1972 budget assumes timely enactment of this legislation.

Insured Farm Operating Loans

This proposal would permit the Farmers Home Administration to substitute insured for direct loans to farmers up to a level of $275 million for the coming fiscal year.

This could reduce Treasury outlays by $275 million, while leaving a Federal guarantee for the loans. It is consistent with our belief in maximum use of the private sector in achieving public purposes, and its enactment is assumed in our 1972 Budget.

Government and Administrative Reform

A number of proposals being resubmitted deal with the smoother, more efficient and more responsive operation of the Federal Government. They argue for themselves on their own considerable merits.

Grant Consolidation

First, I urge the Congress to enact legislation permitting the President to merge related Federal assistance programs, subject to Congressional review and concurrence. This authority, similar to presidential power to reorganize the Executive Branch, would be a vital part of our total effort to simplify the Federal system and make the delivery of goods and services at the regional, State and local level more effective. The consolidation

I am renewing the administration's request that the Congress authorize appropriations of $5 million to meet that commitment, and also that the Congress establish a five-member commission to settle the claims of individual Micronesians resulting from World War II and to determine the validity of additional claims for property damage arising after the war.

Congressional action on these matters would render overdue justice to the people of Micronesia.

Pure Food and Drugs

Two pieces of "preventive" legislation are being resubmitted dealing with the health of the American people. The first has to do with the wholesomeness of fish and fish products which form so significant a segment of the American diet; the second with preventing illness and death from accidental misuse of prescription drugs.

Fish Inspection

Fish and fish products, a major source of protein in the American diet, are highly perishable foods. Improperly handled, they become a medium for bacterial growth. The Wholesome Fish and Fishery Products Act, which is being resubmitted, would establish a broad surveillance and inspection system to assure the wholesomeness and quality of both domestic and imported fishery products.

Recent reports of mercury residues in both inland and deep sea fish provide urgent and concurring arguments for immediate passage of this legislation.

Drug Identification

Every year some Americans, in times of medical emergency, are poisoned by drugs of unidentified composition. Some of these men, women, and children die from these poisonings; others suffer lasting physical harm. While these occurrences are not commonplace, their number can and should be reduced to an absolute minimum. To achieve that objective—to permit the rapid identification of prescription drugs in emergency situations—this administration again proposes the coding of all drugs. Such coding will also facilitate recalls of drugs when necessary to protect public health.

Some manufacturers already use coding systems for immediate identification and inventory control. A universal system of coding of drugs would benefit the entire drug industry—and perhaps save the lives of scores of Americans and their children in years ahead.

Toward a More Secure and Decent Society

Within this broad category, I again urge action on five previously submitted measures. One of them would provide new and needed protection for the orderly processes of government in the event of disruptive activities conducted in or near Federal offices. Passed by the Senate, this measure should be viewed favorably by the House. It is needed to protect government workers as they carry out their duties. The wagering tax and the administration's proposal to give law enforcement officers the right to gather non-testimonial evidence are reforms which would provide us with new weapons in the war against crime. The final proposals, dealing with obscenity and pornography, I believe to be essential at a time when the tide of offensive materials seems yet to be rising.

Protection of Public Buildings

If the Federal Government is to discharge its duties, the employees of government must cease being victimized by raucous and disorderly demonstrations in the offices where they work. Such disruptions have occurred too frequently in recent years.

To help end this harassment, I propose that the General Services Administration's authority to police Federal property be extended to all buildings leased or occupied by Federal agencies.

Further, I ask Congress to prohibit specifically:

• The obstruction of passage into or out of a government office;

• The use of loud, abusive, or threatening language, or any disorderly conduct that has as its goal the disruption of government business; and,

• Any act of physical violence within a GSA facility.

These are similar to the safeguards which the Congress provided for its own employees in the U.S. Capitol Buildings and Grounds Security Act of 1967.

Under this proposal the maximum penalties for violation of the rules promulgated by GSA would be raised from a $50 fine or thirty days in jail to a $500 fine or six months in prison.

Passage of this legislation would help divert future protests back into the legitimate democratic channels where they belong.

Federal Wagering Tax

The Federal wagering tax can be a useful tool in our increasingly successful effort against organized crime. Some of its provisions, however, were ruled unconstitutional in 1968 as violative of the Fifth Amendment right against self-incrimination. Both to retain this needed weapon and to bring the law into accord with the rulings of the Supreme Court, I again propose a prohibition on any use—against the taxpayer—of information obtained through his compliance with this statute. At the same time, the new amendments would broaden the coverage of the wagering tax and increase the level of taxation.

Non-Testimonial Identification

Currently, law enforcement officers are often handicapped in obtaining significant non-testimonial evidence—such as blood samples or fingerprints—in a way to qualify it for use as legal evidence. Under this proposal, a judicial officer could, under prescribed conditions, issue an order *requiring* that a suspect give such kinds of evidence. This is a constitutionally sound step that would advance the cause of criminal justice without infringing upon any of the legitimate rights of suspects and defendants.

Obscenity and Pornography

The overwhelming majority of Americans is rightly appalled at the burgeoning growth of the pornography industry here in the United States. Though Court rulings have restricted some government countermeasures, in other instances they have left us the freedom to act. They have both recognized the right to protect minors from the products of this obnoxious enterprise, and reaffirmed the right to restrict pandering through advertising. I propose anew that Congress pass measures, with stiff penalties, prohibiting the use of interstate facilities to transport unsolicited salacious advertising, or to deliver any harmful and offensive matter to youngsters. It would be difficult to overstate the strength of my support for these two pieces of legislation.

Education: Reform and Opportunity

Under this broad category, I have included three measures submitted to the Ninety-first Congress, all of which I believe have great merit and would serve great needs. The first is for a National Institute of Education, the need for which is becoming increasingly apparent; the second is a measure to provide financial assistance to those school districts carrying the strain of desegregation; the third is to encourage and assist the men coming home from Vietnam to make better use of the educational opportunity the country affords them. Higher education proposals will be resubmitted later to the new Congress.

National Institute of Education

A National Institute of Education—to bring to education the intensity and quality of research now developed in the fields of space and health—is truly a national need. Year by year, the American people grow more disenchanted with the returns on their education tax dollars. The schools of the nation are in growing need of new counsel and new ideas. Here is the opportunity to find the answers, by bringing to bear on the problems the wisdom, the knowledge and the experience of the most able men and women in the field. This Institute was a key part of my education proposals of last year. Today I again urge the Congress to act favorably upon this request.

of programs will make possible broader and more flexible use of funds and facilitate program administration at all levels of government. Originally submitted almost two years ago, this request for authority is thoroughly in keeping with the administration's unprecedented revenue sharing proposals contained in my State of the Union Message. The time has come to move on this bill.

Joint Funding

Often when States, communities or even individuals apply for Federal grants, the funds must be drawn from more than a single agency. To answer these requests more quickly, more simply and more efficiently, I recommend that the Congress authorize Federal agencies to pool certain related funds—and to adopt common administrative procedures, to be carried out by a lead agency. The House passed this joint funding measure last year. I again urge both Houses to act favorably upon it early in the Ninety-second Congress.

AEC Amendments

This proposal would authorize the Atomic Energy Commission to collect license fees from any other government agency engaged in generating electric power on the same basis it now charges other electric utility systems for licensing nuclear powerplants. The cost of a license for a nuclear powerplant is part of the cost of doing business. Thus, it is appropriate that Federal power agencies should be placed on the same footing.

Clarifying Certain Presidential Authority

Under Reorganization Plan No. 9 of 1950, the President was given authority to designate the Chairman of the Federal Power Commission. However, because the basic statute has not been amended to accord precisely with that plan, the President's authority is not crystal clear. This resulted, some time ago, in certain ambiguities when one of my predecessors sought to designate a new FPC Chairman.

The Ninety-first Congress was urged to clarify this situation, and I now request that the Ninety-second Congress enact the necessary clarifying legislation.

Natural Gas Act Amendment

The Federal Power Commission has asked the Congress for broader authority to gather and publish information on the natural gas industry. This would benefit the industry, its consumers and investors, government agencies and the Congress itself, as well as enable the FPC to exercise more effectively its own regulatory powers. The proposal is comparable to existing provisions of the Federal Power Act concerning the electric power industry—and in no way would it expand the regulatory responsibilities of the FPC. I urge the Congress to act favorably upon this request.

Cost Accounting Standards Board

Last year, in extending the Defense Production Act, the Congress established a Cost Accounting Standards Board—and then placed that Board under the authority of the Legislative Branch.

This Board is responsible for establishing cost accounting standards, rules and regulations for use by defense contractors and subcontractors. Since these standards necessarily affect the negotiation and administration of government contracts, and since government contracts are the responsibility of the Executive Branch under the Constitution, placing this board under the Legislative Branch violates the fundamental principle of the separation of powers.

On August 17, 1970, we asked Congress to remedy this situation. With this message I am reissuing that request.

Defense Production Act Amendments

Under the Defense Production Act, the nation's industrial capacity is expanded and critical materials are produced and allocated in times of national emergency. I now renew the administration's proposal that this Act be extended for another two years and needed changes be made. These include:

• A new method of financing the production expansion provisions.

• Elimination of the unnecessary and undesirable restriction on guaranteed transactions imposed last year.

• Authority for the President to make adjustments in civilian pay and personnel administration to assure the effective functioning of government agencies in a civil defense emergency.

Stockpile Disposals

Proposed legislation will be resubmitted which would authorize GSA to sell off from the government's stockpiles quantities of sixteen commodities which we now hold in excess of our needs for national security. The sales would bring substantial returns to the Treasury. In the near future, new legislation will be submitted to the Congress for authority to dispose of other commodities—authority which I urge the Congress to grant as consistent with both sound government and a sound economic policy.

Lost Currency Write-Off

Millions of dollars in U.S. currency and silver certificates issued since 1929 have been lost or destroyed, or are held permanently in collections—and will never be presented for redemption. I now renew the administration's proposal that the Department of the Treasury be authorized to write off these Federal Reserve bank notes and national bank notes, and to remove the limitation of $200 million on such write-offs. In anticipation of favorable Congressional action, the Fiscal Year 1972 budget reflects these write-offs as a receipt of $228 million.

Reform of Veterans' Programs

Three separate reforms can be made in veterans' programs which would lift an unwarranted burden from the general taxpayer without in any way diminishing the legitimate rights or privileges of veterans. I am again asking the Congress to enact them, along with a proposal to facilitate sale of direct loans by the Veterans Administration.

Burial Allowance

The first deals with the veterans burial allowance which runs to $250. This allowance was established before the existence of other Federal programs—such as social security and railroad retirement—which often provide similar or greater burial benefits to the same eligible veterans. The legislation proposed would eliminate duplication by limiting the Veterans Administration's burial payment to the difference between $250 and the non-VA burial payment.

Tuberculosis Disability Compensation

Secondly, some veterans are still receiving disability compensation for tuberculosis long after the disease has reached a stage of complete arrest. The Congress has enacted legislation prohibiting future awards of compensation for arrested tuberculosis, recognizing that such awards no longer reflect medical reality. However, those on the rolls before that law was enacted continue to receive monthly payments, although their disease has been cured. This preferential treatment of a relatively few veterans should be terminated.

Medical Insurance

My third proposal deals with the cost of caring in VA hospitals for veterans who have non-service connected ailments and who have private health insurance.

Generally, veterans who are over 65 or have war-time service, and who state that they cannot afford hospitalization, are entitled to VA care on a bed-available basis.

In many cases, the private insurance could pay part or all of the cost of hospitalization. But the insurance contracts often bar reimbursement to a veteran hospitalized in a VA hospital. This represents both an unwarranted windfall to the insurance company, and an unnecessary burden on the Federal Treasury.

Veterans should not be barred from receiving care in a VA hospital. But there is no reason why insurance companies should not reimburse the Federal Government in the same manner in which they pay a non-Federal private hospital. The proposed legislation will correct this discriminatory situation.

Sale of VA Direct Loans

Under present law, the Veterans Administration can sell direct loans from its portfolio only if the price received is at least 98 percent of par. Recent market conditions have resulted in prices below that level and this proposal would remove the statutory price limitation, allowing the Veterans Administration, when necessary, to sell loans if "reasonable prices" prevail.

User Taxes

Two of my proposals deal with a more equitable allocation of user costs of transportation services. Under one proposal, the cost of providing security against aircraft hijackers would be borne by the passengers themselves and not by the general public. Under the other, the large trucks which use our national highway system would be made to bear a more appropriate share of the cost of highway construction.

Airline User Taxes

The number of airline hijackings that seemed to be taking place almost daily months ago has been reduced. Partly, this is due to the civil air and ground security program, particularly the sky marshals, established by the Federal Government. This program should be continued and strengthened—but its cost should be borne, not by the entire tax-paying public, but by the airline users themselves. For that reason I urge approval of legislation the administration is resubmitting to provide for an increase of one-half of one percent in the eight percent airline passenger ticket tax, and for an additional charge of $2 to be added to the present $3 departure tax on all international flights. Those who use our airlines are the principal beneficiaries of this new security service, and it is appropriate, therefore, that they should bear the cost.

Highway User Taxes

Believing that the burden of highway taxes should be more equitably distributed between larger trucks and smaller vehicles and automobiles, I again ask that the Federal tax on diesel fuel be raised from four cents per gallon to six cents, and that the present $3 per thousand pounds annual use tax on trucks weighing over 26,000 pounds, be changed to a graduated tax schedule ranging from $3.50 to $9.50 per thousand pounds. This new tax would be applied only to those truck combinations weighing in excess of 26,000 pounds.

Immigration and Foreign Assistance

Finally, I urge passage of several measures which are being resubmitted dealing with the immigration policies of the United States, and with American contributions to international banks to assist the economic development of friendly nations.

Reform in the Immigration Law

To improve our immigration laws and to enlarge upon our national tradition as an open nation and an open society, legislation is being resubmitted which would, among other reforms, provide:
• A higher percentage of immigrant visas for professionals, needed workers and refugees.
• Additional visas for the Western hemisphere, with special provisions for our nearest neighbors, Mexico and Canada.
Further, to encourage travel and tourism in the United States, the requirement for a visa would be waived for all business and pleasure visits of ninety days or less by nationals of countries designated by the Secretary of State.

Contributions to Asian Development Bank and Inter-American Development Bank

In recent years, the benefits of increased multilateral aid to developing countries have become more and more manifest. Multilateral aid enables a pooling of the assistance of the donor nations; it reduces political frictions inherent in some bilateral programs; it strengthens international institutions; it is preferred by many recipient nations.

Thus, I again urge the Congress to authorize $100 million in United States contributions to the Special Fund of the Asian Development Bank, and $900 million to the corresponding fund of the Inter-American Development Bank. The former will enable the nations of free Asia to assume greater responsibility for the successes of their own development. The latter, along with the $100 million first installment authorized by the last Congress, will make possible significant advances in the economic development of the hemisphere, in which we ourselves have so vital a stake, and also give substance to the partnership of the Americas.

To the veterans of the Ninety-first Congress, the measures proposed once again in this message will of course be familiar. In the case of many of them, the work begun by the Ninety-first Congress should aid prompt consideration by the Ninety-second. Each is worthy, and by moving promptly and favorably on these matters of unfinished business this Congress will make an auspicious beginning on what could become a record of splendid achievement.

RICHARD NIXON

RAIL STRIKE MESSAGE

Following is the text, as made available by the White House, of President Nixon's May 17 statement on the railroad strike.

TO THE CONGRESS OF THE UNITED STATES:

After extended efforts at settlement the Nation is once more confronted by an emergency arising from an unresolved labor dispute in the railroad industry. The dispute involves disagreement over wages, hours and working conditions between the Brotherhood of Railway Signalmen representing approximately 10,000 employees and the National Railway Labor Conference representing the Nation's railroads. Throughout the course of negotiations, the parties have had the assistance of the Federal Government in their efforts to resolve their differences. Now, all existing governmental procedures for resolving this dispute have been exhausted and the union has called a nationwide work stoppage this morning, May 17, 1971.

A nationwide stoppage of rail service would cause great hardship to all Americans and strike a serious blow at the Nation's economy. It is essential that our railroads continue to operate. I had hoped for a voluntary negotiated settlement of this dispute; however, this was not forthcoming. I am, therefore, recommending that Congress enact legislation which would extend the present negotiations until July 1, 1971. Such a recommendation is not only consistent with the national interest in continued rail service but preserves the processes of free collective bargaining. I have asked the Secretary of Labor to follow closely the situation as it develops, to continue assisting the parties and, if no settlement has been reached, to report to me and the Congress by June 21, 1971.

It is indeed regrettable that Congress must act once again to forestall another in a long line of crises occurring in the railroad industry. This situation reemphasizes the chaotic nature of collective bargaining in the transportation industry as it functions under existing legislation. The time has long since passed for active consideration and action by the Congress on the proposals which I have twice presented to it to resolve emergencies such as this in an equitable and conclusive manner and, thus, to preclude the necessity of Congressional action on each individual dispute. It is inexcusable that the Nation should continue to pay the price of archaic procedures for the resolution of labor-management disputes in the transportation industry.

However, pending such action, I must urge that Congress act immediately on the proposal we are now presenting so that a crippling stoppage can be averted and the Nation can continue to have rail service.

RICHARD NIXON

PRESIDENT NIXON'S MESSAGE ON FISCAL 1972 BUDGET

Following is the complete text, as made available by the White House, of President Nixon's Jan. 29 budget message to Congress.

TO THE CONGRESS OF THE UNITED STATES:

In the 1971 budget, America's priorities were quietly but dramatically reordered: For the first time in 20 years, we spent more to meet human needs than we spent on defense.

In 1972, we must increase our spending for defense in order to carry out the Nation's strategy for peace. Even with this increase, defense spending will drop from 36% of total spending in 1971 to 34% in 1972. Outlays for human resources programs, continuing to rise as a share of the total, will be 42% of total spending in 1972.

The 1972 budget has a historic identity of its own.

- *It provides a new balance of responsibility and power in America* by proposing the sharing of Federal revenues with States and communities on a grand scale—and in a way that will both alleviate the paralyzing fiscal crisis of State and local governments and enable citizens to have more of a say in the decisions that directly affect their lives.
- *It introduces a new fairness in American life,* with the development of national strategies to improve the health care of our citizens and to assure, with work incentives and requirements, an income floor for every family in this Nation.
- *It adopts the idea of a "full employment budget,"* in which spending does not exceed the revenues the economy could generate under the existing tax system at a time of full employment. In this way, the budget is used as a tool to promote orderly economic expansion, but the impact of the resulting actual deficit is in sharp contrast to the inflationary pressure created by the deficits of the late

sixties, which were the result of excessive spending that went far beyond full employment revenues. *The full employment budget idea is in the nature of a self-fulfilling prophecy: By operating as if we were at full employment, we will help to bring about that full employment.*

The 1972 budget reaffirms the determination of the Federal Government to take an activist role in bringing about the kind of prosperity that has rarely existed in the American economy—a prosperity without war and without runaway inflation. In the 1972 budget, the Government accepts responsibility for creating the climate that will lead to steady economic growth with improving productivity and job stability.

Of course, our objective of prosperity without inflation cannot be achieved by budget policy alone. It also requires:

—the monetary policy adopted by the independent Federal Reserve System to provide fully for the growing needs of the economy; and
—increased restraint in wage and price decisions by labor and business—in their own and the Nation's interest and as a matter of common sense.

Only by working together can the budget, monetary policy, and common sense in the private sector make orderly expansion the order of the day.

The full employment 1972 budget—expansionary but not inflationary—does its full share to provide a defense strong enough to protect our national security, higher standards of income and care for the poor and the sick, a reorganized and responsive Federal structure, and the basis for a sound prosperity in a full generation of peace.

TOWARD A GROWING NONINFLATIONARY ECONOMY

Economic setting.—When I took office 2 years ago, rampant inflation was the Nation's principal economic problem.

This inflation was a direct result of the economic policies of the period 1966 to 1968, when we were mired in war in Vietnam, and when Federal spending rose sharply. Federal outlays were allowed to exceed full-employment revenues by $6 billion in 1966, $10 billion in 1967, and $25 billion in 1968. Expansive monetary policy in the summer of 1968 helped upset the hoped-for stabilizing impact of an income tax surcharge. The effect of these actions was to turn the thermostat up in an economy that was already hot enough.

My administration acted promptly to move us out of that war and cool the superheated economy.

We controlled Federal spending in 1969 and achieved a budget surplus. Spending was restrained again in 1970. Independently, the Federal Reserve System maintained a monetary policy of restraint which increased in severity throughout calendar year 1969 and continued into early 1970.

The forces of inflation have been durable and persistent—and they remain strong. But their momentum was slowed in calendar year 1969 and early 1970. Excessive demand was eliminated as a source of inflationary pressure during this period. The turnaround of this inflationary trend permitted us to enter the second phase of our plan: to follow more expansive economic policies without losing ground in the battle against inflation.

Budget policy.—Last July, I set forth the budget policy of this administration:

"At times the economic situation permits—even calls for—a budget deficit. There is one basic guideline for the budget, however, which we should never violate: except in emergency conditions, expenditures must never be allowed to outrun the revenues that the tax system would produce at reasonably full employment. When the Federal government's spending actions over an extended period push outlays sharply higher, increased tax rates or inflation inevitably follow."

THE BUDGET DOLLAR
Fiscal Year 1972 Estimate

Where it comes from . . .

Corporation Income Taxes 16¢
Individual Income Taxes 41¢
Social Insurance Taxes and Contributions 25¢
Excise Taxes 8¢
Borrowing 5¢
Other 5¢

Where it goes . . .

Human Resources 42¢
National Defense 34¢
Physical Resources 11¢
Other 5¢
Interest 8¢*

*Excludes Interest Paid to Trust Funds

Full Employment Budget —Surplus or Deficit

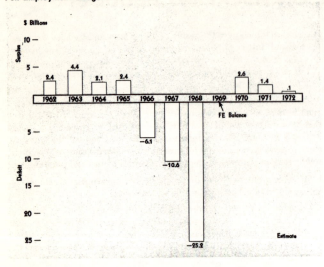

The principle of holding outlays to revenues at full employment serves three necessary purposes:

- It imposes the discipline of an upper limit on spending, a discipline that is essential because the upward pressures on outlays are relentless.
- It permits Federal tax and spending programs to be planned and conducted in an orderly manner consistent with steady growth in the economy's productive capacity.
- It helps achieve economic stability by automatically imposing restraint during periods of boom and providing stimulus during periods of slack.

The budget policy of this administration is to keep firm control over Federal spending. The outlay total of $229.2 billion in 1972 is the sum of spending for programs that were scrutinized carefully to make certain that they would be managed effectively and efficiently,

SUMMARY OF THE 1972 BUDGET

The budget that I propose for 1972 is consistent with the fiscal policy I announced 6 months ago.

THE BUDGET AT A GLANCE

[Fiscal years. In billions]

Description	1970 actual	1971 estimate	1972 estimate
Budget receipts	$193.7	$194.2	$217.6
Budget outlays	196.6	212.8	229.2
Actual deficit (−)	−2.8	−18.6	−11.6
Full-employment surplus	2.6	1.4	0.1
Budget authority	213.0	236.3	249.0

	1969 actual			
Outstanding debt, end of year:				
Gross Federal debt	$367.1	$382.6	$407.0	$429.4
Debt held by the public	279.5	284.9	302.5	313.1
Outstanding Federal and federally assisted credit, end of year:				
Direct loans [1]	46.5	51.1	53.8	56.5
Guaranteed and insured loans [2]	104.0	106.4	119.4	140.3
Direct loans by Government-sponsored agencies	27.0	37.6	45.4	53.2

[1] Including loans in expenditure account.
[2] Excluding loans held by Government or Government-sponsored agencies.

and that they are essential to carry out present laws or to achieve desirable changes in our national priorities.

If this careful scrutiny were not maintained—if we weaken in our resolve to control spending—we would risk permitting outlays to build up a momentum that will carry them beyond full employment receipts in the longer run, and we would risk losing the ability to restrain spending in times when a deficit is undesirable.

Budget receipts in 1972 are estimated to be $217.6 billion, $23.4 billion more than in 1971, but still below the $229.3 billion of revenue that would be produced if the economy were operating at full employment throughout the year.

The estimates reflect a reduction in revenues of $2.7 billion due to the new tax depreciation rules announced on January 11. These rules are part of our plan to expand the economy and help the Nation achieve full employment without inflation.

Budget outlays in 1972 are expected to be $229.2 billion, an increase of $16.4 billion over the previous year.

The increase in outlays will help move the economy toward higher employment and production. At the same time, outlays are being held to full employment receipts.

I am requesting *budget authority*—the right to make commitments to spend—of $249.0 billion in 1972. Over $170 billion of this total will require new action on the part of the Congress.

REVENUE SHARING: RETURNING POWER TO PEOPLE

During the 1960's, more governmental initiative and power shifted to Washington and away from elected officials in State and local governments. Towards the end of the decade it became apparent that, despite new programs and massive Federal expenditures, government at all levels was not working well.

When this administration took office, I directed that an intensive review of our governmental system be made. We found that State and local governments were breaking down under an incredible fiscal burden. We also found that the red tape involved in the narrow categorical grant system made it almost impossible for the Federal Government to be effective and responsive to the needs of individuals in different localities.

The financial squeeze on State and local governments is acute, and shows no sign of becoming less painful. These governments rely mainly on receipts from consumer and property taxes, which have not grown nearly as fast as the demand for State and local government services. As a result, combined State and local debt has increased by over 600% since 1948.

The Federal Government helped meet some of this demand by increasing its financial aid, largely through grant programs, which now accounts for 18% of State and local revenues.

The results of grant programs have been impressive in some cases. But the grant structure has become a haphazard collection of hundreds of separate programs, each with its own policies, its own requirements and procedures, and its own funding.

Such a complicated method of providing Federal assistance is not only inefficient, but it:

—*restricts the freedom* of State and local governments to spend funds in accordance with their priorities;
—*is unresponsive* to the needs of specific local situations because the funds are distributed and regulated by guidelines that do not—perhaps cannot—sufficiently take account of differences among local communities; and
—*separates resources and responsibility*, because State and local governments have the responsibility for providing services, but, all too often, they do not have the money to provide those services. The Federal Government dominates the field of income taxation, and its redtape restricts the discretion of State and local governments over the services they provide.

Clearly, not enough authority over the use of resources for federally assisted programs is now lodged at the State and local level. More of the power—and the responsibility—for using federally collected funds must be given to elected officials in these governments.

The need for remedying this situation is urgent. The time for reform is now.

Local freedom of action.—I propose a revenue sharing plan to give State and local governments the money they need to deliver the services that can best be performed by government closest to the people.

This is how the new "freedom of action" plan will work:

In the first full year of the plan, $16 billion will be directed to the States and localities, in a way that will enable them to decide as never before how that money will be spent.

Of this amount, $5 billion will be in the form of *general revenue sharing*, without restrictions. This will all be "new" money, without matching requirements and with the decision on how it is to be used exclusively a State and local matter.

The remaining $11 billion will be in the form of *special revenue sharing*, with the discretion on how it will be used within each of six broad subject areas strictly a State and local matter. These areas are:

—Urban community development,

—Rural community development,

—Education,

—Manpower training,

—Law enforcement, and

—Transportation.

The hobbling restrictions now on much of the Federal aid in these areas would be removed, along with matching requirements that presently force localities to spend their own matching money on low-priority projects for fear of "losing" available Federal aid.

To emphasize the importance of the special revenue sharing funds, the change from the present tightly restrictive categorical grants to special revenue sharing in the six broad areas will be accompanied by an *increase* of $709 million in the amounts budgeted for 1972 for Federal aid to States and localities. But even more important is the fact that these governments would have far greater freedom of action in deciding how money is to be spent within each of the six areas. For example, although the Federal Government would designate the total amount of special revenue sharing for education, the State or local area would decide how much is to be spent on new textbooks, new schools, equipment, or other matters of priority to it in the field of education.

In this way, both general and special revenue sharing will redirect the control of State and local decisions on $16.1 billion to the States and localities affected most by those decisions. This is about half of Federal Government aid, excluding public assistance grants, to States and communities—a historic and massive reversal of the flow of power in America.

BUDGET AUTHORITY PROPOSED FOR REVENUE SHARING PLAN, FIRST FULL YEAR

Description	Billions
General revenue sharing	$5.0
Special revenue sharing:	
Urban community development	2.0
Rural community development	1.0
Education	3.0
Manpower training	2.0
Law enforcement	0.5
Transportation	2.6
Total	16.1

We must make provision at the outset of this freedom of action plan for both growing State and local needs and growing State and local capacity to manage their affairs.

The new funds for general revenue sharing will grow in years to come because they will be tied to the Federal personal income tax base. As that tax base expands, more unrestricted money will flow to States and localities.

To help State and local governments develop greater capacity to plan and manage their own affairs, I will send to the Congress a planning-management assistance plan, which will provide $100 million to help these governments make their own long-range plans and enhance their capability for the efficient use of their growing revenues.

In essence, this is what revenue sharing will do:

—*for the individual taxpayer*, it will provide a stronger voice in how his tax money is spent locally, new confidence in government that comes from more "citizen control," and the hope that, in some States and localities, taxes may be reduced, or that the rising cost of government can be met without raising taxes;

—*for State and local governments*, it will not only help meet the current financial crisis, but will also wipe out rigidities and delays in Federal aid and permit them to build their capacity to respond to local needs;

—*for our federal system*, it will provide new strength by assigning services to the level of government best equipped to perform them; and

—*for all our people*, it will provide a means of encouraging local diversity and experimentation within the framework of our great national purposes.

Of course, these revenue sharing proposals will not be the vehicle for any retreat from the Federal Government's responsibility to ensure equal treatment and opportunity for all. The proposals I send to the Congress will include the safeguards against discrimination that now accompany all other Federal funds allocated to the States.

This massive revenue sharing proposal is central to my philosophy of giving people the opportunity to become more involved in the decisions that affect their lives. The magnitude of the problem calls for this kind of bold move; by acting decisively and without delay, we will strengthen our federal system and respond better to the needs of our people.

Welfare reform.—One of the first steps in our review of the federal system was to sort out those activities that are appropriate for the Federal Government from those that are best performed at the State and local level or in the private sector. We decided early on one primary Federal responsibility—providing, with a combination of work incentives and work requirements, an income floor for every American family.

We knew beforehand that the existing welfare system was in desperate need of reform. We also knew that the existing system imposes a crushing and growing financial burden on States.

My welfare reform proposals, described later in this message, are an integral part of our effort to give people the ability to make their own decisions, to build the capacity of State and local government, and to encourage more orderly national growth.

By building a floor under the income of every family everywhere in America with Federal funds, we provide each dependent family a new dignity, we help State and local governments finance what is now their fastest growing expenditure, and we remove one magnet that has already drawn too many persons to our congested cities.

Federal Aid to State and Local Governments

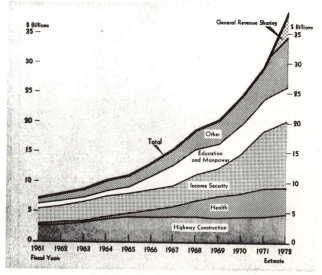

In government operations, form should follow function. Just as revenue sharing decentralizes power to meet one need, welfare reform sets a basic national standard to meet a different need. The decision to centralize or decentralize should be based on which method best serves the larger purposes of 206 million Americans.

Revenue sharing and welfare reform are of a piece: the level of government best equipped to respond should respond in a way that raises standards and contributes to the sum of personal freedom and human dignity.

RESTORING CONFIDENCE IN GOVERNMENT

In seeking ways to reform the federal system, I have paid particular attention to the ability of the executive branch of the Federal Government to produce the results intended by the Congress and the President.

In 1971, the Federal Government will employ almost 2,900,000 civilians, operate thousands of separate programs, and spend $212.8 billion. Through its tax laws, credit activities, grant programs, and in other ways, the Government affects millions of people and influences the disposition of many more billions of dollars than it controls directly.

Toward the end of the sixties, there was mounting evidence that our Government was so complex, clumsy, and unresponsive, that it was becoming unable to meet the needs and priorities of the people or to use efficiently the funds entrusted to it.

This must not be permitted in America.

We have already taken actions to improve the organization and management of the Federal Government and, thereby, make it more efficient and responsive.

But we must do more. The Federal Government is not organized properly to deal with the Nation's most significant problems in the domestic area. Programs that should be joined together to achieve common goals are fragmented among different departments and agencies, impairing the capacity of government to respond effectively to urgent national needs. Modernization of that structure will restore vigor to our federal system, permitting a constructive partnership among Federal, State, and local governments.

In the next few months, I shall propose sweeping legislation to help achieve these goals by merging seven existing departments and several independent agencies into four departments:

—a Department of Natural Resources,
—a Department of Human Resources,
—a Department of Community Development, and
—a Department of Economic Development.

These new departments will match the domestic programs of the Federal Government with the objectives each is intended to fulfill:

—the balanced and constructive use and conservation of the land and other natural resources of the Nation;
—the development and well-being of individuals and families;
—the quality of urban and rural communities as places for people to work and live; and
—the maintenance and strengthening of the American economy.

To continue the modernization of the Federal Government, I will also ask an extension of the President's reorganization authority. We must seek to expand current efforts to shift operating responsibility for Federal programs out of Washington and closer to the people these programs are designed to serve.

To fulfill its responsibilities, the Federal Government must attract, develop, and retain capable career executives. We must have a more effective manpower planning and utilization system. I shall propose legislation to establish a Federal Executive Service which will permit:

—more effective career executive search;
—flexibility in the allocation and assignment of available talent; and
—strengthened executive development programs and policies.

By improving the organization and management of government, we will make it more responsive to the needs of the people and the new priorities of the Nation.

REFORMING THE BUDGET PROCESS

Reform of the budget process is long overdue. Fifty years have passed since the Federal budget system currently in use was adopted. The system was a major step forward in 1921. Because of congressional inaction, it has become a travesty a half-century later.

Enactment of appropriations 6 months or more after the start of the fiscal year they are supposed to cover is evidence of a major weakness. I have sent two budgets to the Congress. In each, I have had to formulate budget proposals for the year ahead without knowing what the Congress would provide in its action on the prior year's budget, which was transmitted 11 months earlier. Even now, as this message is being written, action on last year's appropriations request for one department has not been completed.

I have, therefore, had to act on parts of the budget without knowing the totals that would result. This is an intolerable situation, but one that the Congress seems to accept as the normal way of doing business. It completes action on appropriation bills over a 10- to 12-month period without any goal or determination of the total expenditures that will result after the last bill is passed.

Excess in the number and detail of appropriations often diverts attention to minutiae. It also impairs the ability of agency heads to manage their agencies responsibly and economically.

The budget is our principal instrument for coordinated management of Federal programs and finances. Close cooperation between the executive and legislative branches is needed now to make the budget an efficient and effective instrument for this purpose. Therefore we must seek a more rational, orderly budget process. The people deserve one, and our Government, the largest fiscal unit in the free world, requires it.

Furthermore, Federal credit programs which the Congress has placed outside the budget—guaranteed and insured loans, or loans by federally sponsored enterprises—escape regular review by either the executive or the legislative branch. The evaluation of these extra-budgetary programs has not been fully consistent with budget items. Their effects on fiscal policy have not been rigorously included in the overall budget process. And their effects on overall debt management are not coordinated well with the overall public debt policy. For these reasons, I will propose legislation to enable these credit programs to be reviewed and coordinated along with other Federal programs.

TOWARD A FULL GENERATION OF PEACE

Our goal is a full generation of peace in which all nations can focus their energies on improving the lives of their citizens.

To achieve this, we must continue to work in close cooperation with our allies, move from confrontation to negotiation with those with whom we differ, and—together with our allies—maintain enough military strength to deter aggression. Sufficient and effective programs of military and economic assistance to help our friends help themselves are an integral part of our program.

National security.—This Nation's strategy for peace will—as it must—be based upon a position of military strength. The purpose of this strength is to prevent war; and, to this end, we will negotiate with those whose vital interests and policies conflict with our own.

We are pursuing negotiations on strategic arms limitations, on Vietnam, on Berlin, and on the Middle East. These negotiations are difficult and often slow, but we have the stamina and commitment necessary to proceed with patience and purpose.

As we carry on negotiations, we couple them with other efforts to achieve the same goal. The Vietnamization program is an example, and we are making good progress. By this spring, our authorized troop strength will have been cut approximately in half since the time I took office, and we will continue to bring American troops home.

Supporting these efforts, the military forces of this Nation and its allies will provide the armed might necessary to deter aggression or to deal with it effectively where necessary. We expect our allies to do more in their own behalf, and, in the spirit of the Nixon doctrine, many are taking steps in that direction. But we must also do our share. The kind of partnership we seek to forge works both ways. We have a vital interest in peace and stability abroad and we plan to maintain the capabilities necessary to protect that interest.

Our withdrawals from Vietnam and the change in our general purpose force planning and strategy permit a smaller force structure than in the past. At the same time, the preoccupation with Vietnam has limited our ability to meet some of our military needs elsewhere, particularly in NATO. We must be certain that our military forces are combat-ready and properly equipped to fulfill their role in our strategy for peace. In addition, we face formidable Soviet nuclear and conventional forces, including increased naval forces, and a further rise in the costs of our military equipment and personnel.

For these reasons, I am recommending an increase of $6 billion in budget authority for military and military assistance programs. This Nation has the will and the resources to meet its vital national security needs. At a time when we are urging our allies to do more and when our potential adversaries may seek military advantage, I cannot in good conscience recommend less.

We often think of military strength primarily in terms of equipment and massive organizations. While these are important, attracting and holding able citizens in the Armed Forces is the key to an effective and efficient military force. The service of Americans in uniform is worthy of respect, and I am dedicated to the goal of making all such service voluntary. This budget, and subsequent legislation which I will recommend to the Congress, will make significant progress toward ending reliance on the draft.

Foreign assistance.—Our present foreign assistance programs were established for a world that has long since changed. I will propose legislation to adapt them to the conditions of the 1970's.

We must clearly distinguish the varied purposes of foreign aid—the security of the United States and friendly nations, the long-term development of lower income countries, and humanitarian needs—and make possible a realistic assessment of our progress toward each. In 1972, our assistance programs will:

—promote a strong partnership among nations and a vigorous leadership role for multilateral development institutions;

—recognize that other nations have a growing ability and responsibility to determine their own development priorities;

—continue security assistance at a higher level than in recent years in order to help friendly nations meet the responsibility for their own defense; and

—improve coordination of our humanitarian assistance efforts.

These changes will carry out a major theme of U.S. foreign policy—less direct U.S. involvement in the affairs of other nations, less potential for friction and resentment, and a stable world order more conducive to lasting peace.

MEETING HUMAN NEEDS

The proposals that I submit today are a major step forward in the reform of our Nation's efforts to meet the needs of its 206 million citizens. They will introduce a new fairness into American life by providing:

—a basic income floor under every family with children in this Nation;

—health care to help make needed services possible for all of our people when and where such services are required;

—better systems of support for education and manpower training; and

—continued progress in assuring the civil rights of all citizens, and in controlling crime.

Income strategy.—Last year was one of great promise for the long-term income security of American families. Some of that promise reached fruition in the reform of unemployment insurance and food stamp programs:

• Unemployment insurance was extended to 4.8 million additional Americans, including farmworkers and hospital workers, and special extended benefits were established to be triggered automatically by adverse economic conditions.

• Food stamp benefits were improved by establishing national eligibility standards, requiring family allotments large enough to

purchase an adequate diet, providing free food stamps to the poorest recipients, and automatically raising benefits with increases in the cost of living.

However, much of that promise was left unrealized. As I have pointed out, in 1972 I will redouble my efforts to make essential and fundamental reforms in income maintenance programs. First, and foremost, I will seek:

• *Basic welfare reform.*—Last year I proposed that our archaic and demeaning welfare system be reformed. A landmark plan that would have accomplished this was approved by the House but did not come to a vote in the Senate.

The urgency of the need for welfare reform grows with every passing day. I have already stressed the need for early enactment of the Welfare Reform Act of 1971 by the 92d Congress.

This plan would remove the principal evils of the existing system by:

—setting national eligibility standards;

—balancing strong training and work requirements with equally strong training and work incentives;

—giving financial relief to the States; and

—establishing a Federal floor under benefit payments for *all* needy families with children, including those with working fathers, for the first time.

• *Social security improvements.*—I will propose a significant reform of the social security system, providing *automatic* adjustments for increases in the cost of living. Such an adjustment now calls for a 6% benefit, effective retroactively to January 1, 1971, to cover the cost of living increase since January 1, 1970. I will also propose increases in widows' pensions.

Beyond these basic reforms, I will seek to harmonize related income maintenance programs with the principles of our income strategy. This will include:

—reform of services provided to welfare recipients to encourage greater accountability and effectiveness in the use of funds, and to establish national standards for foster care, with new incentives for the adoption of handicapped children; and

—proposals to put railroad retirement funds on a financially sound basis.

Improving health care.—During the current session, I will send a message to the Congress that will set out a national health strategy for the seventies and propose significant changes in the Federal role in the Nation's system of health care.

This strategy will seek to expand preventive care, to train more doctors and other health personnel, and to achieve greater equity and efficiency in the delivery of health services. It will include a new health insurance program for all low-income families with children.

The budget reflects in a preliminary way the emphasis that this administration will place on health in 1971, with:

—an increase of $100 million to accelerate greatly the search for a means of preventing and curing cancer;

—a vigorous effort to find a cure for sickle cell anemia;

—a $95 million increase in Federal support for schools that train our Nation's health manpower; and

—a rational policy of using Federal resources to help bring the rapid increase in medical care costs under control.

The budget also provides for:

—a substantial improvement in the quality of medical care provided to veterans with service-connected injuries;

—expansion of services for mothers and children, Indians and Alaska natives, and women who cannot afford family planning services;

—expanded programs to combat drug abuse and alcoholism;

—emphasis on assuring purity of foods and drugs; and

—encouraging greater use of less costly services and facilities in delivering medical care.

Community safety and crime prevention.—My commitment to the reform and revitalization of our system of criminal justice is supported by this budget. The budget proposes a 32% increase in outlays to improve law enforcement, to make our judicial system fairer and more efficient, and to raise the effectiveness of correction and rehabilitation. In this way, we will:

—step up the war on organized crime and the gambling operations that finance it;

—destroy major criminal systems that import and distribute narcotics and dangerous drugs;

—strengthen local law enforcement through the special revenue sharing fund for this purpose;

—continue the antihijacking campaign to protect the Nation's air travelers;

—expand our correctional improvement programs to develop more innovative correctional institutions, and improve probation, parole, and other community-based services; and

—develop, in cooperation with State and local governments, ways to provide more accurate information on law enforcement activities.

Outlays for Crime Reduction

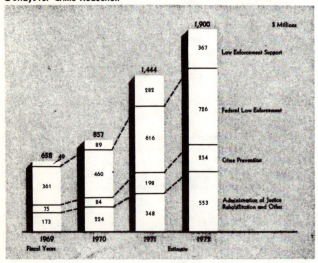

Guaranteeing civil rights.—The ideals of our Nation require that the civil rights of *all* citizens be respected, regardless of race, sex, religion, or national origin.

My budget for 1972 proposes to strengthen our efforts to eliminate discrimination in private as well as Federal employment, in activities supported by Federal assistance to State and local governments and other recipients, in education, in housing, and in other aspects of society.

We will take these specific steps to improve the lives of all our people:

—increase by more than 50% our efforts to prevent employment discrimination by Federal contractors and other private employers;

—increase nearly threefold the Federal assistance to school districts that are desegregating;

—reorganize the field operations of the Equal Employment Opportunity Commission to make more effective efforts to halt discrimination in private employment;

—focus the activities of the Civil Service Commission to assure equal Federal employment opportunities for all our citizens, with special emphasis on opportunity for Spanish-surnamed Americans;

—serve 46 localities with conciliation assistance through the Community Relations Service;

—expand administration of the fair housing and equal opportunity

laws to increase residential housing choices for all Americans; and

—increase by 15% funds to agencies to assure nondiscrimination by recipients in their use of Federal assistance.

Education and manpower training.—The education and manpower training programs proposed in this budget reflect my determination to find better ways to carry out Federal programs. Special revenue sharing is proposed for both of these vital areas. I will also submit major reform proposals to:

—reform Federal aid programs for higher education to increase their effectiveness;

—direct more funds to students from lower income working families;

—establish a National Institute of Education for research and development; and

—provide additional training opportunities and strong incentives under the Welfare Reform Act of 1971 for employable welfare recipients to undertake suitable employment or job training.

Research and development on social problems.—The Office of Economic Opportunity will emphasize its leadership role in research, development, and evaluation in social programs.

IMPROVING OUR ENVIRONMENT

The improvement and prudent use of our physical resources is vital to our Nation's prosperity and to the goal of helping all Americans enjoy a clean environment, adequate housing, and a better standard of living. In 1972, outlays to achieve these objectives will increase by $2.4 billion to $26.1 billion. The actions that I am proposing will:

—expand my administration's vigorous efforts to protect and enhance the quality of our environment and recreation resources;

—revitalize housing and community development programs; and

—increase Federal research and development efforts.

Environmental quality.—The primary responsibility for protecting and enhancing the environment lies with State and local governments, industry, and the public, but the Federal Government must—and will—provide vigorous leadership.

During the past year, this administration moved forcefully to exercise that leadership:

• Major Federal pollution control and abatement activities were consolidated in a new Environmental Protection Agency;

• The Council on Environmental Quality was given a major role within the Executive Office of the President to advise on environmental problems and on national policies to deal with them;

• New legislation to strengthen national efforts for reducing pollution was proposed to the Congress; and

• Funds for major environmental quality programs were increased significantly.

Pollution control and abatement programs will get even greater attention in the 1972 budget. Outlays will be increased by $764 million. Budget authority will rise even more, by $1.3 billion. The higher amounts will provide for:

—doubling grants for municipal waste treatment facilities;

—curbing pollution from Federal facilities;

—expanding EPA pollution control operations, including implementation of new air quality and solid waste legislation; and

—developing new pollution abatement techniques.

Legislation is again proposed to create the Environmental Financing Authority, which will assist communities that have difficulty in borrowing at reasonable rates to meet their share of the cost of water pollution control facilities.

I shall shortly propose, in a special message to the Congress, a series of further measures to control pollution and improve the quality of our environment.

Recreation.—Greater opportunity for leisure is valued highly in America and, as a result, the demand for recreation facilities is growing. The 1972 budget proposes a substantial increase in grants to help State and local governments provide some of these facilities.

I am recommending that the Land and Water Conservation Fund be fully funded to provide:

—grants of $280 million to help States and localities meet local recreation needs; and

—appropriations of $100 million for Federal acquisition to preserve nationally significant natural and historic areas.

I propose that the urban open space program be more than doubled, to $200 million, to provide more recreational areas in and near our cities.

Cultural activities.—I have again recommended that we double the appropriation for the National Foundation on the Arts and the Humanities, so that we can bring the benefits of these great cultural efforts to an increasing number of people throughout the country.

Major Environmental Quality Programs

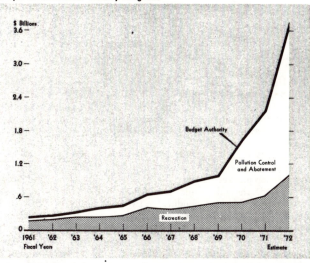

Housing.—The housing industry has already begun to lead our economic expansion. Fiscal and monetary actions taken in the past year have resulted in a significant easing of mortgage interest rates. Federal policy must help this industry meet the pent-up demand for housing.

The effectiveness of our housing programs will not be improved by merely continuing to increase Federal subsidies. The programs must be simplified and fitted into a rational framework. Inconsistencies must be removed, along with the obsolete rigidities in statutes that at times prevent programs from operating at all.

The administration will again propose legislation to carry out these badly needed reforms, which I urge the Congress to enact.

Community development.—I will also propose reform of the community development programs of the Department of Housing and Urban Development, and of certain economic development programs of the Departments of Agriculture and Commerce. Narrowly defined categorical grant programs in this field have frequently conflicted with local priorities and unnecessarily generated red tape.

With special urban and rural revenue sharing programs, we will permit localities to plan and carry out community development in accordance with their own needs.

Initial funding of the new urban program will begin at a level of $1 billion for the second half of 1972, upon enactment of the necessary legislation. An additional $2 billion appropriation is anticipated for 1973, when the program will be in effect for a full year. Rural development revenue sharing will be $1 billion in the first full year.

Science and technology.—Science and technology can make major contributions to the public by developing creative solutions to a wide range of national problems that will help us all enjoy a better life. I am proposing in this budget a substantial expansion in outlays for federally supported research and development.

While a large portion of this increase is needed to strengthen our defense capabilities I am also recommending substantial increases in civilian areas to:

—make greater use of our scientific and engineering capabilities and resources to cope with major national problems such as pollution, crime, health, transportation, and other environmental and social problems;

—strengthen research essential to the advancement of our technology and economic productivity; and

—increase our investment in fundamental science which leads to the long-term progress of our society.

As an example of the concern of this administration for the use of science and technology in the public service, I am recommending that the budget for the National Science Foundation be increased from $506 million in 1971 to $622 million in 1972. A significant portion of these added funds will be directed to research on pressing national problems.

THE LONGER VIEW

Federal budget decisions must be made with an awareness of their influence on the economy and on resource allocation in the future as well as the present.

Too often in the past, consideration of objectives and priorities focused only on Federal spending. Only immediate issues, rather than longer term goals, were considered. And this fact was ignored: when we increase the priority of some programs, the relative priority assigned to others must be reduced. In short, the sum of the resources allocated to the various functions—such as health, education, defense—cannot exceed the total resources that we command.

Looking to the future, we find that resources likely to be available to the Nation grow more rapidly than the expenditures required by existing commitments. But our freedom to use these resources will shrink as we approach each future year and make financial or program commitments in the interim. Thus, the allocation of each year's resources is largely a reflection of our past priorities.

As we make choices this year, we will be determining the use of our available resources and expenditures in future years.

The resource allocation questions that the Nation will answer—either explicitly or by default—are:

• Shall we increase the available margin by ending some existing commitments?

• Who should use the margin—the Federal Government, State and local governments, or private citizens?

• To what objectives should the available margin be applied?

In answering these questions, the Nation will be setting its priorities for the future.

My preferences are clear. *One great objective of my administration is to increase the role of private citizens and State and local governments in allocating our national resources in accordance with individual and local needs. Another great objective is to set minimum standards to make certain that every American family in every locality is treated with a fairness that reflects the national conscience.*

Ours is not a regimented economy, nor will it be. Yet, we cannot ignore the influence of the budget on the economy and on the use of our national resources in the present and in the future. To do so is to take the chance that government spending will preempt resources that should be left to be used by private citizens or State and local governments.

In the last few decades, the Federal Government, disturbingly, has taken over the determination of how too many of the Nation's resources will be allocated. In spite of the Federal Government's domination, resources have not been appropriately allocated to overall national needs. Instead, they have been allocated by a process in which small additions were usually made in existing programs, and a few new categorical grant programs were created each year. These new grants were generally aimed at alleviating some narrow problem—without reference to the Nation's real need in that general problem area.

I have in this budget proposed the outlines of a new process for allocating funds according to national priorities.

Instead of continuing "more of the same" to more than a hundred narrow categorical grant programs, I have proposed replacing them with six *special* revenue sharing programs designed to deal with major national problems. These are problems that have different characteristics in different parts of the country. With these special revenue sharing funds, State and local governments can set their priorities within the national objective, design a solution fitted to their particular needs, and solve their problems locally.

The *general* revenue sharing program provides unrestricted funds to State and local governments to achieve our Nation's top domestic priority—the creation of a system of government that is effective and responsive to the needs of all of the American people. General revenue sharing will allow State and local governments to overcome their immediate fiscal crises and to come to grips with those problems that concern their citizens most.

The revenue sharing programs which I have proposed result from shared goals, provide federally shared revenues, and involve shared Federal-State-local responsibility for solving America's most important problems. Our system of government must be one of shared goals—shared revenues—shared responsibilities.

CONCLUSION

The 1972 budget befits a strong, free, compassionate, and enlightened Nation.

- It reverses the trend of the past decade toward Federal domination of the Nation's decisions, and begins to make government more responsive to the will of the people.

- It recognizes that a strong defense is vital to all our objectives, most of all to the attainment of peace.

- It provides the resources needed to meet the Nation's commitments at home, with a new standard of fairness to the poor and sick.

- It accepts the principle that budget policy, together with monetary policy and the active cooperation of the private sector, must be used to help achieve full employment in peacetime with relative price stability.

This budget expresses our fiscal program for the New American Revolution—a peaceful revolution in which power will be turned back to the people—in which government at all levels will be refreshed, renewed, and made truly responsive. This can be a revolution as profound, as far-reaching, as exciting, as that first revolution almost 200 years ago.

JANUARY 29, 1971.   RICHARD NIXON.

TEXT ON LABOR DISPUTE MESSAGE

Following is the text, as made available by the White House, of President Nixon's Feb. 3 message to Congress on proposed legislation to deal with labor disputes.

TO THE CONGRESS OF THE UNITED STATES:

Early in 1970, I proposed to the Congress a new approach for dealing with national emergency labor disputes in the transportation industry. The proposal was based upon my belief that existing law did not provide adequate remedies for settling such disputes, and thus failed to protect the national interest.

Today, I am again recommending that proposal, the Emergency Public Interest Protection Act. Events since the bill's first introduction have made its enactment even more urgent. I am hopeful that the Congress will give the proposal its prompt and favorable consideration—before there is another crisis in the transportation industry.

The bill I propose would give the President vital new authority to deal with national emergency disputes in the railroad, airline, maritime, longshore, and tucking industries.

First, the bill would abolish the emergency strike provisions of the Railway Labor Act—which now govern railroad and airline disputes—and make all transportation industries subject to the national emergency provisions of the Taft-Hartley Act.

Second, the bill would amend the Taft-Hartley Act to give the President three new options in the case of a national emergency dispute in a transportation industry, when that dispute is not settled within the eighty-day "cooling-off period" authorized by Taft-Hartley. Under those circumstances, if a strike or lockout should threaten or occur, and national health or safety continued to be endangered, the President could select any one of the following courses of action:

- He could extend the cooling-off period for as long as thirty days. This might be most useful if the President believed the dispute to be very close to settlement.

- He could empanel a special board to determine if partial operation of the industry were feasible and, if so, to set out the boundaries for such an operation. This alternative would allow a partial strike or lockout without endangering the national health or safety. It could not extend beyond 180 days.

- He could invoke a "final offer selection" alternative. Under this procedure, the final offers of each party would be submitted to a neutral panel. This panel would select, without alteration, the most reasonable of these offers as the final and binding contract to settle the dispute. Unlike arbitration, which too often merely splits the difference between the parties, and thereby encourages them to persist in unreasonable positions, this procedure would reward reasonableness and thereby facilitate negotiation and settlement.

Third, the bill would establish a National Special Industries Commission to conduct a two-year study of labor relations in industries which are particularly vulnerable to national emergency disputes.

Fourth, the bill would amend the Railway Labor Act to conform the management of labor relations under that Act to the practices prevalent in most other industries, including the encouragement of voluntary settlement of grievances by overhauling the existing grievance procedures.

The urgency of this matter should require no new emphasis by anyone; the critical nature of it should be clear to all. But if emphasis is necessary, we need only remember that barely two months ago the nation was brought to the brink of a crippling railroad shutdown, the strike being averted only by legislation passed after a walkout had actually begun. That legislation, we should also remember, settled little; it merely postponed the strike deadline. A few weeks from now another railroad strike over the same issues which precipitated the last one is a distinct possibility.

I believe we must face up to this problem, and face up to it now, before events overtake us and while reasoned consideration is still possible.

Time and again, as the nation has suffered major disruptions from a transportation shutdown, voices have been raised on all sides declaring emphatically that this must not happen again—that better laws are needed to protect the public intrest, and that the time to enact those laws is before, not after, the next crippling emergency. But with the same regularity, as each emergency in turn has passed the voices have subsided—until the next time. So nothing has been done, and emergency has followed emergency, at incalculable cost to millions of innocent bystanders and to the nation itself.

The legislation I propose today would establish a framework for settling emergency transportation disputes in a reasonable and orderly fashion, fair to the parties and without the shattering impact on the public of a transportation shutdown. I urge that this time we not wait for the next emergency, but rather join together in acting upon it now.

RICHARD NIXON

TEXT OF PRESIDENT NIXON'S ECONOMIC MESSAGE

Following is the text, as made available by the White House, of President Nixon's Feb. 1 message accompanying his annual Economic Report to Congress.

TO THE CONGRESS OF THE UNITED STATES:

1970 was the year in which we paid for the excesses of 1966, 1967, and 1968, when Federal spending went $40 billion beyond full employment revenues. But we are nearing the end of these payments, and 1971 will be a better year, leading to a good year in 1972—and to a new steadiness of expansion in the years beyond.

We are facing the greatest economic test of the postwar era. It is a test of our ability to root out inflation without consigning our free economy to the stagnation of unemployment. We will pass that test. But it is a real test and we shall pass it only by doing all we are capable of doing.

The key to economic policy in 1971 is orderly expansion. While continuing to reduce the rate of inflation, total spending and total output should rise as rapidly as possible to lift the economy to full employment and full production. Fiscal policy must play its full and responsible role, and the economy's course in the year ahead will also reflect the extent to which the monetary and credit needs of economic expansion are met. With the stimulus and discipline from the budget that I have put forward, and with the Federal Reserve System providing fully for the monetary needs of the economy, we can look forward confidently to vigorous and orderly expansion during 1971.

At the same time we must be relentless in our efforts toward the greater stability of costs and prices that is the foundation for an enduring and full prosperity. Much has already been accomplished. Prices in the market place have been rising less rapidly, and some that usually change early have actually declined, responding to changing pressures in the market.

In some cases the response of costs and prices has been slow, as the result of insulation from market forces. Often these market problems have been created by the Government itself. Accordingly, the Government has a responsibility to prevent misuses and imbalances of market power which impede orderly operation of our free economic system. This Administration intends to carry out that responsibility fully and fairly.

To get the economy rising at the right rate, neither too rapidly nor too slowly, is never an easy task. Economic policy does not operate with the precision needed to keep the economy exactly on a narrow path. But fortunately absolute precision is not required. What is required is that we operate within a range where both unemployment and inflation are moving unmistakably downward toward our goal. The full resources of Government, with the understanding and cooperation of the citizens, can accomplish that.

The Dual Transition of 1970

Faced with one of the largest inflations in American history we have sought first to stop its rate from speeding up and then to get the rate down. This has been done. The annual rate of increase of the consumer price index, which was 6.0 percent from June 1969 to June 1970, dropped to 4.6 percent in the last half of 1970. Wholesale prices, which usually move before the prices consumers pay, have slowed down even more, from a 5.3 percent rate in the first half of 1969 to a 2.1 percent rate in the second half of 1970. Because productivity began to rise, after earlier sluggishness, labor costs per unit of output rose much less in 1970 than they did in 1969, and this contributed to slower price increases.

While the Nation was making the transition to a less inflationary economy it was also making the transition to a lower level of defense spending. Men released from the Armed Forces have been out of touch with the civilian labor market and need time to readjust. Workers laid off from defense production are likely to be concentrated in particular areas, which are often not the areas where nondefense activity is expanding. Their curtailed purchasing power further tends to lower employment of others in their area. During 1970, the number of persons in military and civilian employment for defense was reduced by about 1 million. Most of these people have found work, and others will soon do so. But during the transition many were unemployed, and their number added to the total unemployment rate.

These two simultaneous transitions, from a wartime to a peacetime economy and from a higher to a lower rate of inflation, would inevitably be accompanied by some decline in output and rise in unemployment. The aim of our policy was to keep the decline in output and the rise in unemployment as small as possible.

Fiscal and monetary policy both became more expansive early in 1970, in order to get output rising again while the cost of living slowed its rise. This result was achieved. Total output declined only 1 percent from its high reached in the third quarter of 1969 to the first quarter of 1970; it leveled out in the second quarter and rose in the third. Fourth-quarter output was held down by the auto strike; without it, another increase would have been shown.

The timely shift of policy limited the decline of output; it also helped counter the increase in unemployment caused by the dual transition. The average unemployment rate for the year was 4.9 percent. At the end of the year, partly as a result of the auto strike, the unemployment rate was about 6 percent. About half of the unemployed had been without work for less than 6 weeks. Most of the unemployed who had lost their most recent job were receiving unemployment compensation.

The Road to Orderly Expansion

Our first task now must be to assure more rapid expansion and so to reduce the unemployment rate. We are now in a position to do that, while the progress against inflation continues. The restraint of 1969 and the slowdown of 1970 have set in motion strenuous efforts at cost reduction. These actions, as the pace of the economy quickens, will bear fruit in better productivity and costs. Prices have begun to rise less rapidly. There are the first faint signs of a retardation in wage increases in some sectors. Much of the anti-inflationary effect of the 1970 slowdown still has to be felt. And if the expansion is properly controlled in 1971 the conditions for further slackening of the inflation rate will remain. The expectation of continued rapid inflation has been weakened by the firm policies of the past 2 years and we must strengthen this growing confidence in the future value of money.

Forces now present in the economy, partly resulting from policies of 1970, make economic expansion in 1971 probable.

• The greater supply and lower cost of mortgage money has stimulated a 40-percent increase in the rate at which construction of new houses is started.

• Improved financial conditions are leading to a strong increase of State and local spending.

• Interest rates have dropped; the prime rate is down sharply from its peak of 8 ½ percent.

• Consumers' after-tax incomes have increased and their saving has been high.

• In the early part of 1971 the economy will get a boost as the production lost during last year's auto strike is made up.

• Exports have been strong, and in 1970 were 14 percent above those of a year earlier.

These are powerful upward pressures, but existing and foreseeable expansionary forces in the economy are not strong enough to assure than output will rise as much as is desired and feasible. These forces must, therefore, be supplemented by expansive fiscal and monetary policies.

The full employment budget that I have submitted will do its full share in stimulating a solid expansion. Outlays will rise by $16 ½ billion, or about 7 ½ percent, between the current fiscal year and the next—appropriate for orderly expansion, but far short of the inflationary 15 percent average annual increases from 1965 to 1968. In addition, receipts have been reduced $2.7 billion by the depreciation reform which I have initiated to stimulate investment, jobs, and growth.

In fiscal 1971, the Federal Government will spend $212.8 billion, which is equivalent to the revenues the economy would be generating at full capacity. The actual deficit is expected to be $18 ½ billion. In fiscal 1972, also, the planned expenditures are equivalent to the revenues we would get at full employment. How big the actual deficit will be next year, in fiscal 1972, will depend on economic conditions. If the economy follows the expected path of a vigorous, noninflationary expansion, the deficit will decline to $11 ½ billion. This combination of deficits is appropriate to the situation through which the economy has been passing. The budget moved into deficit during calendar 1970 as the economy lagged below its potential. Accepting this deficit helped to keep the decline in the economy moderate. It was a policy of not subjecting individuals and businesses to higher tax rates, and of not cutting back Federal spending, when the economy is weak because such actions would have weakened economic conditions further.

To say that deficits are appropriate in certain conditions is not to say that deficits are always appropriate or that the size of the deficit is ever a matter of indifference. Such a policy of free-for-all deficit financing would be an invitation to inflation and to wasteful spending.

As I stated last June, we need to abide by a principle of budget policy which permits flexibility in the budget and yet limits the inevitable tendency to wasteful and inflationary action. The useful and realistic principle of the full employment budget is that, except in emergencies, *expenditures should not exceed the revenues that the tax system would yield when the economy is operating at full employment.* The budget for fiscal 1972 follows this principle.

Balancing the budget at full employment does not deny or conceal the deficit that will exist this year and almost certainly next year. It does, however, avoid large deficits when they would be inflationary, like the swing to a big deficit in fiscal 1968. It means that even when the economy is low we must not allow our expenditures to outrun the revenue-producing capacity of the tax system, piling up the prospect of dangerous deficits in the future when the economy is operating at a high level. Moreover, to say that expenditures must not exceed the full employment revenues draws a clear line beyond which we must not raise the budget unless we are willing to pay more taxes. This is an irreplaceable test of the justification for spending. It keeps fiscal discipline at the center of budget decisions.

Fiscal policy should do its share in promoting economic expansion, and our proposed budget would do that. But fiscal policy cannot undertake the responsibility of doing by itself everything needed for economic expansion in the near future. To try to do that would drive taxes and expenditures off the course that is needed for longer run. The task of economic stabilization must be accomplished by a concert of economic policies. The combined use of these policies, starting near the beginning of 1969, finally checked the accelerating inflation that had kept the economy overheated for years. A turn of fiscal and monetary policies in a more expansive direction at the beginning of 1970 limited the economic decline and initiated an upturn. Concerted policies of expansion are needed now to lift the economy fast enough to make rapid progress toward full employment, and these needs will be fully met.

Price Stability and Full Prosperity

In a fundamental sense, as I have always emphasized, the control of inflation and the achievement of full employment are mutually supporting, not conflicting, goals. Nothing would contribute more to the new expansion than confidence that the threat of inflation is fading. As part of my program of expansion I propose to justify that confidence.

The basic conditions to bring about a simultaneous reduction of unemployment and inflation are coming into being. We are going to continue to slow down the rate of inflation in the middle of an orderly expansion. And we are going to do it by relying upon free markets and strengthening them, not by suppressing them. Free prices and wages are the heart of our economic system; we should not stop them from working even to cure an inflationary fever. I do not intend to impose wage and price controls which would substitute new, growing and more vexatious problems for the problems of inflation. Neither do I intend to rely upon an elaborate facade that seems to be wage and price control but is not. Instead, I intend to use all the effective and legitimate powers of Government to unleash and strengthen those forces of the free market that hold prices down. This is a policy of action, but not a policy of action for action's sake.

The process of reducing inflation is a process of learning. Business and labor must learn a pattern of behavior different from the one they have learned and practiced during the inflationary boom. Labor contracts and price lists cannot embody the expectation that prices will continue rising at the peak rates of recent years. Business cannot expect to pass all cost increases along in higher prices. The ritual of periodic increases in prices has no place in an economy moving toward greater stability.

These lessons are being learned. Most of all they are being taught by the facts of economic life today. Consumers are already imposing stern discipline in markets where sellers have not begun to adapt their pricing to the new, less-inflationary conditions of the economy.

But there are cases where these lessons are not being learned and actions have been taken or are under review. In those cases the Government will act to correct the conditions which give rise to excessive price and wage increases.

Actions were taken to augment the supply of lumber, and to deal with domestic copper prices that were out of line with world markets. To restrain increases in the price of crude oil, this Administration took steps to permit greater production on Federal offshore leases and to increase oil imports. Faced with inflationary price increases for some steel products, I have ordered a review of the conditions which permit or cause such increases, and threaten jobs in steel-using industries.

We have been particularly concerned with increases in the costs of construction. It is now more critical than ever to check inflationary wage and price increases in an industry where unemployment is high. The 1972 Budget provides for a large increase in construction expenditures. This should support increased employment in construction, but will do so only if the larger appropriations are not eaten up by higher wages and other costs. I have asked the leaders of labor unions and contractors in the industry to propose a plan for bringing the behavior of construction wages, costs, and prices into line with the requirements of national economic policy. A workable voluntary plan will avert the need for Government action.

Those of us who value the free market system most cannot disregard the cases where it is being kept from working well. In some of these cases it is Government which limits the free market's effectiveness and Government has the means to make it work better. We must constantly review our economic institutions to see where the competitive market mechanism that has served us so well can replace restrictive arrangements originally introduced in response to conditions that no longer exist. We must also devise efficient solutions to problems that have become more urgent recently, such as those of pollution and adequate health care. Where inadequate market arrangements are delaying our advance toward full employment with price stability, we have a responsibility now to correct them.

In our market-oriented policy, our domestic goals and our international goals are interrelated. Success in our struggle against inflation will help to safeguard our international economic strength, and allow our highly productive enterprises and workers to compete in world markets. The liberal policy with respect to international trade to which this Administration is committed will help keep price increases in check here while giving our farms, factories, and banks a profitable market abroad. At the same time we have to make sure that the burden of adjustment to changing conditions in world markets does not fall entirely on a few exposed industries.

With the cooperation of the private sector, an expansionary public economic policy will achieve a goal we have not seen in the American economy in many years: full prosperity without war, full prosperity without inflation.

In the record of progress toward that new prosperity, I am convinced that economic historians of the future will regard 1970 as a necessarily difficult year of turnaround—but a year that set the stage for strong and orderly expansion.

RICHARD NIXON

MESSAGE ON DRAFT REFORM

Following is the text, as made available by the White House, of President Nixon's Jan. 28 message to Congress on draft reform and an all-volunteer military service.

TO THE CONGRESS OF THE UNITED STATES:

On April 23, 1970, in a message to the 91st Congress, I proposed that the nation embrace a new approach to meeting our military manpower requirements—an approach that recognized both the necessity for maintaining a strong national defense and the desirability of ending the draft.

In that message I put forth two sets of proposals.

The first set of proposals dealt with the fundamental question of how this nation should raise the armed force necessary to defend the lives and rights of its people and to fulfill its existing commitments abroad.

After carefully weighing both the requirements of national security and the desirability of reducing infringements on individual liberties, I urged that we should begin moving toward an end of the draft and its replacement with an all-volunteer armed force, with an eye to achieving this goal as soon as we can do so without endangering our national security.

The second set of proposals dealt with reforming the draft system itself, while this continues to be needed in the immediate future to maintain our armed strength as we move toward an all-volunteer force.

Now, more than nine months later, I am even more strongly convinced of the rightness of these proposals. Now, as then, the objective of this administration is to reduce draft calls to zero, subject to the overriding considerations of national security—and as long as we need the draft, to make it as fair and equitable as we can.

Over the past nine months the Secretary of Defense and the Director of Selective Service have initiated a comprehensive series of steps designed to help us achieve that goal. Average draft calls are now substantially lower than they were when this administration assumed office, and we have significantly improved the consistency and fairness of the draft system. We shall continue these actions at an accelerated pace.

However, to continue the progress that now is possible toward both goals—toward ending the draft, and in the meantime making it more nearly fair—legislative as well as Executive action will be needed.

Ending the Draft

Since my April 1970 message, a 7.9 percent across-the-board increase in the rate of basic pay has been enacted that will raise the pay of members of the Armed Forces by almost $1.2 billion a year. Building on this base, I am submitting a number of legislative proposals (some of which were previously submitted to the 91st Congress) which, together with Executive actions I shall take, would move us substantially closer to the goal of an all-volunteer force.

• I propose that we invest an additional $1.5 billion in making military service more attractive to present and potential members, with most of this to be used to provide a pay raise for enlisted men with less than two years of service, effective May 1, 1971. If approved by the Congress, this action would result in a total additional investment of $2.7 billion for military manpower, and would substantially reduce the present inequity in the pay of men and women serving in the Armed Forces. The proposed pay raise would increase rates of basic pay at the entry level *50 percent* over present levels. Also, I am proposing increases in the quarters allowance for personnel in the lower enlisted grades.

• I am proposing a test program of special pay incentives designed to attract more volunteers into training for Army combat skills.

• Existing law provides that as general adjustments are made in civilian pay, corresponding increases will be made in military pay. In addition, I am directing the Secretary of Defense to recommend for the 1973 fiscal year such further additions to military compensation as may be necessary to make the financial rewards of military life fully competitive with those in the civilian sector.

• The Department of Defense, through Project Volunteer, has been actively engaged in expanding programs designed to increase enlistments and retentions in the services. A fair level of pay, while necessary, is only one factor in increasing the relative attractiveness of a military career. I will propose that approximately one-fifth of the additional $1.5 billion be devoted to expanding our efforts in the areas of recruiting, medical scholarships, ROTC, improvement of housing, and other programs to enhance the quality of military life.

• During the past year, the Department of Defense has reviewed the policies and practices of the military services and has taken actions to emphasize recognition of the individual needs and capabilities of all military personnel. These efforts will be continued and strengthened.

Extension of Induction Authority

No one knows precisely when we can end conscription. It depends on many things—including the level of military forces that will be required for our national security, the degree to which the combination of military pay increases and enhanced benefits will attract and hold enough volunteers to maintain the forces we need, and the attitude of young people toward military service.

Current induction authority expires on July 1, 1971. While I am confident that our plan will achieve its objective of reducing draft calls to zero, even the most optimistic observers agree that we would not be able to end the draft in the next year or so without seriously weakening our military forces and impairing our ability to forestall threats to the peace. Considerations of national security thus make it imperative that we continue induction authority at this time.

Normally, the Congress has extended induction authority for four year intervals. I propose that this Congress extend induction authority for two years, to July 1, 1973. We shall make every endeavor to reduce draft calls to zero by that time, carefully and continually reexamining our position as we proceed toward that goal.

Reform of the Draft

As long as we must continue to rely on the draft to meet a portion of our military manpower requirements, we must make the draft as equitable as possible. To that end I am proposing legislation to modify the present draft law, including the resubmission of recommendations I sent to the Congress last year. This proposed legislation would:

• Permit the phasing out of undergraduate student deferments, and also exemptions for divinity students.

• Establish a uniform national call, by lottery sequence numbers each month, to ensure that men throughout the country with the same lottery numbers have relatively equal liability to induction by their local boards.

In addition, the legislation I am proposing includes a number of other amendments which will improve the administration of existing law.

For the immediate future we will need the draft, and moreover, even when the draft has been ended, we will have to maintain some form of a standby system that could be re-activated in case of emergency. Therefore, I urge favorable Congressional action on these proposals to reform the draft and make it as nearly fair as we can for the time it is needed.

While the reforms proposed in our existing draft system are essential, however, it must be remembered that they are improvements in a system that will be used only as long as the draft is necessary.

This Congress has both the power and the opportunity to take an historic action. As I stated in last year's message, with an end to the draft we will demonstrate to the world the responsiveness of our system of government—and we will also demonstrate our continuing commitment to the principle of ensuring for the individual the greatest possible measure of freedom.

I urge the 92nd Congress to seize this opportunity, and to make the bold decisions necessary to achieve this goal.

RICHARD NIXON

EXECUTIVE MANAGEMENT TEXT

Following is the text, as made available by the White House, of President Nixon's Feb. 2 message to Congress on reorganizing executive branch management.

In my State of the Union message, one of the six great goals that I proposed to the Congress was a renewal of the Federal Government itself through a sweeping reorganization of the executive branch. The structural changes I outlined would enable us to bring greater coherence to the management of Federal programs, and to raise them to a new level of effectiveness. But even the best of structures requires the effective utilization of highly qualified people. The need for the best people and for making the best use of their talents, becomes more vital as we improve the structure and organization of the Federal Government.

It is on our Federal executives—both career and non-career —that the task of translating broad public policy into operational reality rests most heavily. These men and women are among the most valuable resources that we have as a government. We must not use them wastefully. We must not let their talents and their dedication be squandered. And we must constantly seek better ways of attracting into the executive ranks of the Federal service new people with the capacity and the drive to help us meet our national needs.

The time has come, therefore, to take a critical look at the existing Federal system for selecting, training, assigning and rewarding executive manpower, and to see whether it cannot be improved. We have carried out such an examination, and have concluded that it can be significantly improved by incorporating principles of modern personnel management.

For some time now, the Government's executive manpower systems have shown increasing evidence of weakness. The present arrangements have grown up over the years without any comprehensive plan. Disparate systems for the authorization, appointment and assignment of Government executives have prevented adequate planning and provision for constantly changing requirements. The resulting complexities and rigidities have reached a point at which it is now futile to try to patch the present structure further. Too often, the present system serves only to frustrate the conscientious agency head and the dedicated career executive alike.

At my request, the Civil Service Commission has completed a painstaking and systematic analysis of the existing manpower management programs for executives. The Commission has informed me that reforms are essential, reforms that cannot be made within existing law. I agree. Accordingly, I recommend legislative action to establish an entirely new personnel system for upper-level officials of the executive branch, to be called the Federal Executive Service.

This Service would apply to those persons—now about 7,000 in all—serving in executive branch positions presently established at grades GS-16, 17 and 18, or within the same pay range under several other salary systems. It is designed to meet the special needs of managing the Federal establishment, and at the same time to preserve and strengthen merit principles.

In order to accomplish these purposes, the legislation I am proposing would:

• Abolish the present so-called supergrade system and establish the Federal Executive Service, to include both career and non-career officials. Preserving the present ratio, it would establish a minimum of 75 percent career appointments and a maximum of 25 percent non-career appointments.

• Establish a general salary range (from about $28,000 to the equivalent of level V, now $36,000), within which the agency head can set the salary of each individual member, provided that he maintains an average salary for all members of the Federal Executive Service employed by his agency as established annually by the Civil Service Commission after collaboration with the Office of Management and Budget.

• Require the appointment of Qualification Boards to pass on the eligibility, under merit standards, of all persons selected for future entry into the Federal Executive Service as career members. Holders of present supergrade positions and persons chosen for non-career appointment to the Federal Executive Service would be exempt from this requirement.

• Provide that new entrants into the career system be employed under renewable three-year agreements, and give present holders of career type supergrade executive positions the choice of entering the new Service under the renewable three-year agreements or retaining their present positions and salaries.

• In the case of a career Federal executive whose employment agreement expires without being extended (whether because renewal was not offered by the agency, or because the executive chose not to accept the renewal offered), the legislation would provide for either severance pay, retirement, or reversion to the top grade of the Classification Act (GS-15) without reduction in pay from his previous level for a period of two years.

• Provide for the Civil Service Commission, after collaboration with the Office of Management and Budget, to establish annually maximum numbers and average salary for members of the Federal Executive Service in each agency, taking into account program priorities, level of work, work load, and budget allowances for the agency concerned.

To assure proper, periodic Congressional review of the operation of the Federal Executive Service the proposed legislation would also require the Civil Service Commission to make an annual report to the Congress on April 1, detailing the number of Federal Executive Service members it proposes to allow each agency for the coming year and the average salary level it proposes to set for each agency. At the same time, the Commission would report any variances it had allowed during the previous year under its statutory authority to meet emergency needs or provide for needs occasioned by changes in existing programs. If the Congress did not make any changes within the 90-day period, the Commission's proposed authorizations would take effect.

By establishing eminent Qualifications Boards, composed of highly respected professionals, to review the qualifications of all persons proposed for entry into career positions, this legislation would ensure the continued high quality of Federal career executives and enhance the prestige associated with executive service in the Federal Government.

By differentiating clearly, for appointment and retention purposes, between executives who make the Federal service their career and those appointed for brief periods, it would preserve the integrity of the career service.

By providing for renewable, fixed-term agreements for career executives, it would give agency heads the flexibility needed to use their high-level personnel most effectively in meeting the changing demands made on the Federal Government.

By giving him access to positions of high responsibility without jeopardizing his career rights, it would enlarge the horizons of the individual career executive. One of the many faults of the present system is that it results too often in bunching non-career officials at the top, with career officials relegated to lower positions. This new proposal would strengthen executive development programs and reduce the present obstacles to executive mobility.

By providing for an annual assessment of executive manpower requirements in relation to program activity in each agency, it would make it possible to respond promptly to changing needs and to eliminate wasteful overstaffing of low-priority programs.

In addition, it would give the Congress annually a comprehensive overview of Federal executive manpower programs and policies, an indispensable measure for ensuring the exercise of Congressional responsibilities in monitoring the use of this manpower resource in partnership with the executive branch.

The Federal Executive Service proposal has been designed to ensure against an increase in the partisan political component of the executive group. It is to this end that I am recommending retention of the approximate present ratio of career to non-career executives—a ratio that has proved an effective one during several administrations of both political parties. I feel that it is imperative that we strengthen the career service and make Government careers more rewarding to individuals of high ability. This proposal will materially serve that end.

The proposed new Federal Executive Service would result in simplification of the existing fragmented system. But its most important result would be to improve the capacity of the executive branch to meet the challenges of our democratic system. Freed from unnecessary obstacles and from much red tape, the career executives of the Federal Government would be better able to realize their potential, both personally and in terms of program accomplishment. At the same time those responsible for agency performance would be given sufficient authority over the selection and use of their most able manpower to meet their agencies' goals more fully and more efficiently.

The demands upon Government today are great and pressing. I am convinced that the Government has attracted, and will continue to attract, men and women of the highest caliber. But too often we have enmeshed them in a web of rigid and intricate personnel policies which have frustrated their efforts and arrested their professional growth.

We need both dedication and high performance from our Federal executives. Mere competence is not enough. Mere continuity is self-defeating. We must create an environment in the Government service in which excellence and ingenuity can flourish—and in which these qualities are both encouraged and rewarded.

It is to this end that I urge prompt and favorable consideration of this landmark legislation.

RICHARD NIXON

REVENUE SHARING

Following is the text, as made available by the White House, of President Nixon's Feb. 4 message to Congress on revenue sharing.

TO THE CONGRESS OF THE UNITED STATES:

One of the best things about the American Constitution, George Washington suggested shortly after it was written, was that it left so much room for change. For this meant that future generations would have a chance to continue the work which began in Philadelphia.

Future generations took full advantage of that opportunity. For nearly two turbulent centuries, they continually reshaped their government to meet changing public needs. As a result, our political institutions have grown and developed with a changing, growing nation.

Today, the winds of change are blowing more vigorously than ever across our country and the responsiveness of government is being tested once again. Whether our institutions will rise again to this challenge now depends on the readiness of our generation to "think anew and act anew," on our ability to find better ways of governing.

Better Ways of Governing

Across America today, growing numbers of men and women are fed up with government as usual. For government as usual too often means government which has failed to keep pace with the times.

Government talks more and taxes more, but too often it fails to deliver. It grows bigger and costlier, but our problems only seem to get worse. A gap has opened in this country between the worlds of promise and performance—and the gap is becoming a gulf that separates hope from accomplishment. The result has been a rising frustration in America, and a mounting fear that our institutions will never again be equal to our needs.

We must fight that fear by attacking its causes. We must restore the confidence of the people in the capacities of their government. I believe the way to begin this work is by taking bold measures to strengthen State and local governments—by providing them with new sources of revenue and a new sense of responsibility.

Potential of State and Local Government

Part of the genius of our American system is that we have not just one unit of government but many, not just one Chief Executive and Congress in Washington, but many chief executives and legislators in statehouses and courthouses and city halls across our land. I know these men and women well. I know that they enter office with high hopes and with sweeping aspirations. I know they have the potential to be full and effective partners in our quest for public progress.

But once they have taken office, our leaders at the State and local level often encounter bitter disappointment. For then they discover that while the need for leadership is pressing, and their potential for leadership is great, the power to provide effective leadership is often inadequate to their responsibilities. Their dollars are not sufficient to fulfill either their dreams or their most immediate and pressing needs.

And the situation is getting worse.

A Growing Fiscal Crisis

Consider how State and local expenditures have been growing. In the last quarter century, State and local expenses have increased twelvefold, from a mere $11 billion in 1946 to an estimated $132 billion in 1970. In that same time, our Gross National Product, our personal spending, and even spending by the Federal government have not climbed at even one third that rate.

How have the States and localities met these growing demands? They have not met them. State and local revenues have not kept pace with rising expenditures, and today they are falling even further behind. Some authorities estimate that normal revenue growth will fall $10 billion short of outlays in the next year alone.

The Heavy Burden of State and Local Taxes

The failure of State and local revenues to keep pace with demands is the inherent result of the way in which our tax system has developed. Ever since the 16th Amendment in 1913 made it possible for the Federal government to tax personal income, this source of revenue has been largely pre-empted and monopolized by Washington. Nine out of every ten personal income tax dollars are collected at the Federal level.

Income tax revenues are quick to reflect economic growth. Often, in fact, they grow much faster than the economy. As a result, budget increases at the Federal level can more readily be financed out of the "natural growth" in revenues, without raising tax rates and without levying new taxes.

State and local governments are not so fortunate. Nearly three-fourths of their tax revenues come from property and sales taxes, which are slow to reflect economic expansion. It is estimated, in fact, that the natural growth in revenues from these sources lags some 40 to 50 percent behind the growth rate for State and local expenditures. This means that budget expansion at these levels must be financed primarily through new taxes and through frequent increases in existing tax rates.

As a result, the weight of State and local taxes has constantly been getting heavier. On a per capita basis, they have climbed almost 50 percent in the last fourteen years. Property tax receipts are six times as great as they were a quarter century ago. In the past dozen years alone, States have been forced to institute new taxes or raise old ones on 450 separate occasions. Consumer and service taxes have sprung up in bewildering variety in many cities.

These rising State and local levies are becoming an almost intolerable burden to many of our taxpayers. Moreover, they often fall hardest on those least able to pay. Poor and middle income consumers, for example, must pay the same sales taxes as the wealthy. The elderly—who often own their own homes—must pay the same property taxes as younger people who are earning a regular income. As further pressures are placed on State and local taxes, the impact is felt in every part of our society. The hard-pressed taxpayer—quite understandably—is calling for relief.

The result is a bitter dilemma for State and local leaders. On the one hand, they must cut services or raise taxes to avoid bankruptcy. On the other hand, the problems they face and the public they serve demand expanded programs and lower costs. Competition between taxing jurisdictions for industry and for residents adds further pressure to keep services up and taxes down.

While political pressures push State and local leaders in one direction, financial pressures drive them in another. The result has been a rapid and demoralizing turnover in State and local officeholders. The voters keep searching for men and women who will make more effective leaders. What the State and localities really need are the resources to make leaders more effective.

The Best of Both Worlds

The growing fiscal crisis in our States and communities is the result in large measure of a fiscal mismatch; needs grow fastest at one level while revenues grow fastest at another. This fiscal mismatch is accompanied, in turn, by an "efficiency mismatch"; taxes are collected most efficiently by the highly centralized Federal tax system while public funds are often spent most efficiently when decisions are made by State and local authorities.

What is needed, then, is a program under which we can enjoy the best of both worlds, a program which will apply fast growing Federal revenues to fast growing State and local requirements, a program that will combine the efficiencies of a centralized tax system with the efficiencies of decentralized expenditure. What is needed, in short, is a program for sharing Federal tax revenues with State and local governments.

A Word about Present Grants-In-Aid

There is a sense in which the Federal Government already shares its revenues with governments at the lower levels. In fact, Federal aid to the States and localities has grown from less than one billion dollars in 1946 to over 30 billion dollars this year. Unfortunately, most of this assistance comes in the form of highly restricted programs of categorical grants-in-aid. These programs have not provided an effective answer to State and local problems; to the contrary, they provide strong additional evidence that a new program of unrestricted aid is badly needed.

The major difficulty is that States and localities are not free to spend these funds on their own needs as they see them. The money is spent instead for the things Washington wants and in the way Washington orders. Because the categories for which the money is given are often extremely narrow, it is difficult to adjust spending to local requirements. And because these categories are extremely resistant to change, large sums are often spent on outdated projects. Pressing needs often go unmet, therefore, while countless dollars are wasted on low priority expenditures.

This system of categorical grants has grown up over the years in a piecemeal fashion, with little concern for how each new program would fit in with existing old ones. The result has been a great deal of overlap and very little coordination. A dozen or more manpower programs, for example, may exist side by side in the same urban neighborhood—each one separately funded and separately managed.

All of these problems are compounded by the frequent requirement that Federal dollars must be matched by State and local money. This requirement often has a major distorting effect on State and local budgets. It guarantees that many Federal errors will be reproduced at the State and local level. And it leaves hard pressed governments at the lower levels with less money to finance their own priorities.

The administrative burdens associated with Federal grants can also be prohibitive. The application process alone can involve volumes of paperwork and delays of many months. There are so many of these programs that they have to be listed in large catalogs and there are so many catalogs that a special catalog of catalogs had to be published. The guidelines which are attached to these grants are so complicated that the government has had to issue special guidelines on how the guidelines should be interpreted. The result of all this has been described by the Advisory Commission on Intergovernmental Relations as "managerial apoplexy" on the State and local level.

Meanwhile, the individual human being, that single person who ultimately is what government is all about, has gotten lost in the shuffle.

State and local governments need Federal help, but what they need most is not more help of the sort they have often been receiving. They need more money to spend, but they also need greater freedom in spending it.

A New Approach

In the dark days just after the Battle of Britain, Winston Churchill said to the American people: "Give us the tools and we will finish the job."

I now propose that we give our States and our cities, our towns and our counties the tools—so that they can get on with the job.

I propose that the Federal Government make a $16 billion investment in State and local government through two far-reaching revenue sharing programs: a $5 billion program of of General Revenue Sharing which I am describing in this message to the Congress, and an $11 billion program of Special Revenue Sharing grants which will be spelled out in a series of subsequent messages.

General Revenue Sharing: How It Works

The General Revenue Sharing program I offer is similar in many respects to the program I sent to the Congress almost eighteen months ago. But there are also some major differences.

For one thing, this year's program is much bigger. Expenditures during the first full year of operation would be ten times larger than under the old plan. Secondly, a greater proportion—roughly half—of the shared funds would go to local governments under the new proposal. In addition, the 1971 legislation contains a new feature designed to encourage States and localities to work out their own tailor-made formulas for distributing revenues at the State and local level.

The specific details of this program have been worked out in close consultation with city, county and State officials from all parts of the country and in discussions with members of the Congress. Its major provisions are as follows:

1. Determining the Size of the Overall Program.

The Congress would provide a permanent appropriation for General Revenue Sharing. The size of this appropriation each year would be a designated percentage of the nation's taxable personal income—the base on which individual Federal income taxes are levied. This arrangement would relieve the States and localities of the uncertainty which comes when a new level of support must be debated every year.

Since the fund would grow in a steady and predictable manner with our growing tax base, this arrangement would make it easier for State and local governments to plan intelligently for the future.

The specific appropriation level I am recommending is 1.3 percent of taxable personal income; this would mean a General Revenue Sharing program of approximately $5 billion during the first full year of operation, a sum which would rise automatically to almost $10 billion by 1980. All of this would be "new" money—taken from the increases in our revenues which result from a growing economy. It would not require new taxes nor would it be transferred from existing programs.

2. Dividing Total Revenues Among the States.

Two factors would be used in determining how much money should go to each state: the size of its population and the degree to which it has already mobilized its own tax resources. By using a distribution formula which takes their tax effort into account, this program would encourage the States to bear a fair share of responsibility. A State which makes a strong effort to meet its own needs would receive more help from the Federal Government.

One other incentive has also been built into the new legislation: those States which negotiate with their local governments a mutually acceptable formula for passing money on to the local level, would receive more money than those States that rely on the Federal formula. This provision would encourage a State and its localities to work out a distribution plan which fits their particular requirements. States which develop such plans would receive a full 100 percent of the money allocated to them under the formula described above. Other States would receive only 90 percent of their allocation, with the remaining ten percent being carried over and added to the following year's overall allocation.

3. Distributing Revenues Within the States.

Those States which do not adopt their own plan for subdividing shared revenues would follow a formula prescribed in the Federal legislation. This formula would assign to the State

government and to all units of local government combined a share of the new money equal to that portion of State and local revenues currently raised at each level. On the average, this "pass through" requirement would mean that about one-half of the revenue sharing funds would go to the States and half would go to the localities. Governmental units of all sizes would be eligible for aid—but only if they were set up for general purposes. This would exclude special purpose units such as sewer districts, school districts, and transit authorities. Each general purpose unit would then receive its proportionate share of revenues based on how much money it raises locally.

4. Other Procedures and Requirements.

General Revenue Sharing monies would come without program or project restrictions. The funds would be paid out at least quarterly through the Treasury Department; no massive new Federal agencies would be established. Each State would be required to pass on to local units their proper share of the Federal funds and to observe appropriate reporting and accounting procedures.

In my State of the Union message I emphasized that these revenue-sharing proposals would "include the safeguards against discrimination that accompany all other Federal funds allocated to the States." The legislation I am recommending provides these safeguards. It stipulates that: "No person in the United States shall on the ground of race, color or national origin be excluded from participation in, be denied the benefits of, or be subjected to discrimination under any program or activity funded in whole or in part with general revenue sharing funds."

The Secretary of the Treasury would be empowered to enforce this provision. If he found a violation and was unable to gain voluntary compliance, he could then call on the Attorney General to seek appropriate relief in the Federal Courts, or he could institute administrative proceedings under Title VI of the Civil Rights Act of 1964—leading to a cutoff of Federal funds. The Federal Government has a well defined moral and constitutional obligation to ensure fairness for every citizen whenever Federal tax dollars are spent. Under this legislation, the Federal Government would continue to meet that responsibility.

Enhancing Accountability

Ironically, the central advantage of revenue sharing—the fact that it combines the advantages of Federal taxation with the advantages of State and local decision-making—is the very point at which the plan is frequently criticized. When one level of government spends money that is raised at another level, it has been argued, it will spend that money less responsibly; when those who appropriate tax revenues are no longer the same people who levy the taxes, they will no longer be as sensitive to taxpayer pressures. The best way to hold government accountable to the people, some suggest, is to be certain that taxing authority and spending authority coincide.

If we look at the practice of government in modern America, however, we find that this is simply not the case. In fact, giving States and localities the power to spend certain Federal tax monies will increase the influence of each citizen on how those monies are used. It will make government more responsive to taxpayer pressures. It will enhance accountability.

In the first place, there is no reason to think that the local taxpayer will be less motivated to exert pressure concerning the way shared revenues are spent. For one thing, the local taxpayer is usually a Federal taxpayer as well; he would know that it was his tax money that was being spent.

Even if local taxpayers were only concerned about local taxes, however, they would still have a direct stake in the spending of Federal revenues. For the way Federal money is used determines how much local money is needed. Each wise expenditure of Federal dollars would mean an equivalent release of local money for other purposes—including relief from the need to raise high local taxes even higher. And every wasted

Federal dollar would represent a wasted opportunity for easing the pressure on local revenues.

Most voters seldom trace precisely which programs are supported by which levies. What they do ask is that each level of government use all its money—wherever it comes from—as wisely as possible.

The average taxpayer, then, will be no less disposed to hold public officials to account under revenue sharing. What is more, he will be able to hold them to account far more effectively.

The reason for this is that "accountability" really depends, in the end, on accessibility—on how easily a given official can be held responsible for his spending decisions. The crucial question is not where the money comes from but whether the official who spends it can be made to answer to those who are affected by the choices he makes. Can they get their views through to him? Is the prospect of their future support a significant incentive for him? Can they remove him from office if they are unhappy with his performance?

These questions are far more likely to receive an affirmative answer in a smaller jurisdiction than in a larger one.

For one thing, as the number of issues is limited, each issue becomes more important. Transportation policy, for example, is a crucial matter for millions of Americans—yet a national election is unlikely to turn on that issue when the great questions of war and peace are at stake.

In addition, each constituent has a greater influence on policy as the number of constituents declines. An angry group of commuters, for example, will have far less impact in a Senatorial or Congressional election than in an election for alderman or county executive. And it is also true that the alderman or county executive will often be able to change the local policy in question far more easily than a single Congressman or Senator can change policy at the Federal level.

Consider what happens with most Federal programs today. The Congress levies taxes and authorizes expenditures, but the crucial operating decisions are often made by anonymous bureaucrats who are directly accountable neither to elected officials nor to the public at large. When programs prove unresponsive to public needs, the fact that the same level of government both raises and spends the revenues is little comfort.

At the local level, however, the situation is often reversed. City councils, school boards and other local authorities are constantly spending revenues which are raised by State governments—in this sense, revenue sharing has been with us for some time. But the separation of taxing and spending authority does not diminish the ability of local voters to hold local officials responsible for their stewardship of all public funds.

In short, revenue sharing will not shield State and local officials from taxpayer pressures. It will work in just the opposite direction. Under revenue sharing, it will be harder for State and local officials to excuse their errors by pointing to empty treasuries or to pass the buck by blaming Federal bureaucrats for misdirected spending. Only leaders who have the responsibility to decide and the means to implement their decisions can really be held accountable when they fail.

Other Advantages

The nation will realize a number of additional advantages if revenue sharing is put into effect. The need for heavier property and sales taxes will be reduced. New job opportunities will be created at the State and local level. Competition between domestic programs and defense needs will be reduced as the State and local share of domestic spending increases. As the States and localities are renewed and revitalized, we can expect that even more energy and talent will be attracted into government at this level. The best way to develop greater responsibility at the State and local level is to give greater responsibility to State and local government.

In the final analysis, the purpose of General Revenue Sharing is to set our States and localities free—free to set new priorities, free to meet unmet needs, free to make their own mistakes, yes, but also free to score splendid successes which otherwise would never be realized.

For State and local officials bring many unique strengths to the challenges of public leadership. Because they live day in and day out with the results of their decisions, they can often measure costs and benefits with greater sensitivity and weigh them against one another with greater precision. Because they are closer to the people they serve, State and local officials will often have a fuller sense of appreciation of local perspectives and values. Moreover, officials at these lower levels are often more likely to remember what Washington too often forgets: that the purpose of government is not budgets and programs and guidelines, but people.

This reform will also help produce better government at the Federal level.

There is too much to be done in America today for the Federal Government to try to do it all. When we divide up decision-making, then each decision can be made at the place where it has the best chance of being decided in the best way. When we give more people the power to decide, then each decision will receive greater time and attention. This also means that Federal officials will have a greater opportunity to focus on those matters which ought to be handled at the Federal level.

Laboratories For Modern Government

Strengthening the States and localities will make our system more diversified and more flexible. Once again these units will be able to serve—as they so often did in the 19th century and during the Progressive Era—as laboratories for modern government. Here ideas can be tested more easily than they can on a national scale. Here the results can be assessed, the failures repaired, the successes proven and publicized. Revitalized State and local governments will be able to tap a variety of energies and express a variety of values. Learning from one another and even competing with one another, they will help us develop better ways of governing.

The ability of every individual to feel a sense of participation in government will also increase as State and local power increases. As more decisions are made at the scene of the action, more of our citizens can have a piece of the action. As we multiply the centers of effective power in this country, we will also multiply the opportunity for every individual to make his own mark on the events of his time.

Finally, let us remember this central point: the purpose of revenue sharing is not to prevent action but rather to promote action. It is not a means of fighting power but a means of focusing power. Our ultimate goal must always be to locate power at that place—public or private—Federal or local—where it can be used most responsibly and most responsively, with the greatest efficiency and with the greatest effectiveness.

'The Cardinal Question'

Throughout our history, at one critical turning point after another, the question on which the nation's future turned was the relationship between the States and the central government. Woodrow Wilson properly described it as "the cardinal question of our constitutional system."

In most cases—in the 1780's and in the 1860's and in the 1930's, for example—that question was resolved in favor of a stronger government at the Federal level. But as President Wilson went on to say, this question is one which "cannot...be settled by the opinion of any one generation, because it is a question of growth, and every successive stage of our political economic development gives it a new aspect, makes it a new question."

Because America has now reached another new stage of development, we are asking that "cardinal question" again in the 1970's. As in the past, this is a matter beyond party and beyond faction. It is a matter that summons all of us to join together in a common quest, considering not our separate interests but our shared concerns and values.

To a remarkable degree, Americans are answering Wilson's cardinal question in our time by calling on the Federal Government to invest a portion of its tax revenues in stronger State and local governments. A true national consensus is emerging in support of revenue sharing. Most other nations with Federal systems already have it. Most Mayors and Governors have endorsed it. So have the campaign platforms of both major political parties. This is a truly bipartisan effort.

Revenue sharing is an idea whose time has clearly come. It provides this Congress with an opportunity to be recorded as one that met its moment, and answered the call of history. So let us join together, and, by putting this idea into action, help revitalize our Federal system and renew our nation.

RICHARD NIXON

TEXT OF ENVIRONMENT MESSAGE

Following is the text, as made available by the White House, of President Nixon's Feb. 8 message to Congress on the environment.

TO THE CONGRESS OF THE UNITED STATES:

Last August I sent to the Congress the first annual report on the state of the nation's environment. In my message of transmittal, I declared that the report "describes the principal problems we face now and can expect to face in the future, and it provides us with perceptive guidelines for meeting them....They point the directions in which we must move as rapidly as circumstances permit."

The comprehensive and wide-ranging action program I propose today builds upon the 37-point program I submitted to the Congress a year ago. It builds upon the progress made in the past year, and draws upon the experience gained in the past year. It gives us the means to ensure that, as a nation, we maintain the initiative so vigorously begun in our shared campaign to save and enhance our surroundings. This program includes:

- Measures to strengthen pollution control programs
  1. Charges on sulfur oxides and a tax on lead in gasoline to supplement regulatory controls on air pollution
  2. More effective control of water pollution through a $12 billion national program and strengthened standard-setting and enforcement authorities
  3. Comprehensive improvement in pesticide control authority
  4. A Federal procurement program to encourage recycling of paper
- Measures to control emerging problems
  1. Regulation of toxic substances
  2. Regulation of noise pollution
  3. Controls on ocean dumping
- Measures to promote environmental quality in land use decisions
  1. A national land use policy
  2. A new and greatly expanded open space and recreation program, bringing parks to the people in urban areas
  3. Preservation of historic buildings through tax policy and and other incentives
  4. Substantial expansion of the wilderness areas preservation system
  5. Advance public agency approval of power plant sites and transmission line routes
  6. Regulation of environmental effects of surface and underground mining
- Further institutional improvement
  1. Establishment of an Environmental Institute to conduct studies and recommend policy alternatives
- Toward a better world environment
  1. Expanded international cooperation

2. A World Heritage Trust to preserve parks and areas of unique cultural value throughout the world

1970 - A Year of Progress

The course of events in 1970 has intensified awareness of and concern about environmental problems. The news of more widespread mercury pollution, late summer smog alerts over much of the East Coast, repeated episodes of ocean dumping and oil spills, and unresolved controversy about important land use questions have dramatized with disturbing regularity the reality and extent of these problems. No part of the United States has been free from them, and all levels of government—Federal, State and local—have joined in the search for solutions. Indeed, there is a growing trend in other countries to view the severity and complexity of environmental problems much as we do.

There can be no doubt about our growing national commitment to find solutions. Last November voters approved several billion dollars in State and local bond issues for environmental purposes, and Federal funds for these purposes are at an all time high.

The program I am proposing today will require some adjustments by governments at all levels, by our industrial and business community, and by the public in order to meet this national commitment. But as we strive to expand our national effort, we must also keep in mind the greater cost of *not* pressing ahead. The battle for a better environment can be won, and we are winning it. With the program I am outlining in this message we can obtain new victories and prevent problems from reaching the crisis stage.

During 1970, two new organizations were established to provide Federal leadership for the Nation's campaign to improve the environment. The Council on Environmental Quality in the Executive Office of the President has provided essential policy analysis and advice on a broad range of environmental problems, developing many of our environmental initiatives and furnishing guidance in carrying out the National Environmental Policy Act, which requires all Federal agencies to devote specific attention to the environmental impact of their actions and proposals. Federal pollution control programs have been consolidated in the new Environmental Protection Agency. This new agency is already taking strong action to combat pollution in air and water and on land.

I have requested in my 1972 budget $2.45 billion for the programs of the Environmental Protection Agency—nearly double the funds appropriated for these programs in 1971. These funds will provide for the expansion of air and water pollution, solid waste, radiation and pesticide control programs and for carrying out new programs.

In my special message on the Environment last February, I set forth a comprehensive program to improve existing laws on air and water pollution, to encourage recycling of materials and to provide greater recreational opportunities for our people. We have been able to institute some of these measures by executive branch action. While unfortunately there was no action on my water quality proposals, we moved ahead to make effective use of existing authorities through the Refuse Act water quality permit program announced in December. New air pollution control legislation, which I signed on the last day of 1970, embodies all of my recommendations and reflects strong bipartisan teamwork between the administration and the Congress—teamwork which will be needed again this year to permit action on the urgent environmental problems discussed in this message.

We must have action to meet the needs of today if we would have the kind of environment the nation demands for tomorrow.

I. STRENGTHENING POLLUTION CONTROL PROGRAMS

The Clean Air Amendments of 1970 have greatly strengthened the Federal-State air quality program. We shall vigorously administer the new program, but propose to supplement it with measures designed to provide a strong economic stimulus to achieve the pollution reduction sought by the program.

Air Pollution

Sulfur Oxides Emissions Charge. Sulfur oxides are among the most damaging air pollutants. High levels of sulfur oxides have been linked to increased incidence of diseases such as bronchitis and lung cancer. In terms of damage to human health, vegetation and property, sulfur oxide emissions cost society billions of dollars annually.

Last year in my State of the Union message I urged that the price of goods "should be made to include the cost of producing and disposing of them without damage to the environment." A charge on sulfur emitted into the atmosphere would be a major step in applying the principle that the costs of pollution should be included in the price of the product. A staff study underway indicates the feasibility of such a charge system.

Accordingly, I have asked the Chairman of the Council on Environmental Quality and the Secretary of the Treasury to develop a Clean Air Emissions Charge on emissions of sulfur oxides. Legislation will be submitted to the Congress upon completion of the studies currently underway.

The funds generated by this charge would enable the Federal Government to expand programs to improve the quality of the environment. Special emphasis would be given to developing and demonstrating technology to reduce sulfur oxides emissions and programs to develop adequate clean energy supplies. My 1972 budget provides increased funds for these activities. They will continue to be emphasized in subsequent years.

These two measures—the sulfur oxides emissions charge and expanded environmental programs—provide both the incentive for improving the quality of our environment and the means of doing so.

Leaded Gasoline. Leaded gasolines interfere with effective emission control. Moreover, the lead particles are, themselves, a source of potentially harmful lead concentrations in the environment. The new air quality legislation provides authority, which I requested, to regulate fuel additives, and I have recently initiated a policy of using unleaded or low-lead gasoline in Federal vehicles whenever possible. But further incentives are needed. In 1970, I recommended a tax on lead used in gasoline to bring about a gradual transition to the use of unleaded gasoline. This transition is essential if the automobile emission control standards scheduled to come into effect for the 1975 model automobiles are to be met at reasonable cost.

I shall again propose a special tax to make the price of unleaded gasoline lower than the price of leaded gasoline. Legislation will be submitted to the Congress upon completion of studies currently under way.

Water Quality

We have the technology now to deal with most forms of water pollution. We must make sure that it is used.

In my February 1970 special message to the Congress on the Environment, I discussed our most important needs in the effort to control water pollution: adequate funds to ensure construction of municipal waste treatment facilities needed to meet water quality standards; more explicit standards, applicable to all navigable waters; more effective Federal enforcement authority to back up State efforts; and funds to help States build the necessary capability to participate in this joint endeavor.

Municipal Wastes. Adequate treatment of the large volume of commercial, industrial and domestic wastes that are discharged through municipal systems requires a great expenditure of funds for construction of necessary facilities. A thorough study by the Environmental Protection Agency completed in December 1970 revealed that $12 billion will be required by 1974 to correct the national waste treatment backlog. The urgency of this need, and the severe financial problems that face many communities, require that construction of waste treatment facilities be jointly funded by Federal, State, and local governments. We must also assure that adequate Federal funds are available to reimburse States that advanced the Federal share of project costs.

I propose that $6 billion in Federal funds be authorized and appropriated over the next three years to provide the full Federal share of a $12 billion program of waste treatment facilities.

Some municipalities need help in overcoming the difficulties they face in selling bonds on reasonable terms to finance their share of construction costs. The availability of funds to finance a community's pollution control facilities should depend not on its credit rating or the vagaries of the municipal bond market, but on its waste disposal needs.

I again propose the creation of an Environmental Financing Authority so that every municipality has an opportunity to sell its waste treatment plant construction bonds.

A number of administrative reforms which I announced last year to ensure that Federal construction grant funds are well invested have been initiated. To further this objective:

• I again propose that the present, rigid allocation formula be revised, so that special emphasis can be given to those areas where facilities are most needed and where the greatest improvements in water quality would result.

• I propose that provisions be added to the present law to induce communities to provide for expansion and replacement of treatment facilities on a reasonably self-sufficient basis.

• I propose that municipalities receiving Federal assistance in constructing treatment facilities be required to recover from industrial users the portion of project costs allocable to treatment of their wastes.

Standards and Enforcement. While no action was taken in the 91st Congress on my proposals to strengthen water pollution standard setting and enforcement, I initiated a program under the Refuse Act of 1899 to require permits for all industrial discharges into navigable waters, making maximum use of present authorities to secure compliance with water quality standards. However, the reforms I proposed in our water quality laws last year are still urgently needed.

Water quality standards now are often imprecise and unrelated to specific water quality needs. Even more important, they provide a poor basis for enforcement: without a precise effluent standard, it is often difficult to prove violations in court. Also, Federal-State water quality standards presently do not apply to many important waters.

• I again propose that the Federal-State water quality program be extended to cover all navigable waters and their tributaries, ground waters and waters of the contiguous zone.

• I again propose that Federal-State water quality standards be revised to impose precise effluent limitations on both industrial and municipal sources.

• I also propose Federal standards to regulate the discharge of hazardous substances similar to those which I proposed and the Congress adopted in the Clean Air Amendments of 1970.

• I propose that standards require that the best practicable technology be used in new industrial facilities to ensure that water quality is preserved or enhanced.

• I propose that the Administrator of the Environmental Protection Agency be empowered to require prompt revision of standards when necessary.

We should strengthen and streamline Federal enforcement authority, to permit swift action against municipal as well as industrial and other violators of water quality standards. Existing authority under the Refuse Act generally does not apply to municipalities.

• I propose that the Administrator of EPA be authorized to issue abatement orders swiftly and to impose administrative fines of up to $25,000 per day for violation of water quality standards.

• I propose that violations of standards and abatement orders be made subject to court-imposed fines of up to $25,000 per day and up to $50,000 per day for repeated violations.

• I again propose that the Administrator be authorized to seek immediate injunctive relief in emergency situations in which severe water pollution constitutes an imminent danger to health, or threatens irreversible damage to water quality.

• I propose that the cumbersome and time-consuming enforcement conference and hearing mechanism in the current law be replaced by a provision for swift public hearings as a prelude to issuance of abatement orders or requiring a revision of standards.

• I propose an authorization for legal actions against violations of standards by private citizens, as in the new air quality legislation, in order to bolster State and Federal enforcement efforts.

• I propose that the Administrator be empowered to require reports by any person responsible for discharging effluents covered by water quality standards.

• I again propose that Federal grants to State pollution control enforcement agencies be tripled over the next four years—from $10 million to $30 million—to assist these agencies in meeting their expanded pollution control responsibilities.

Control of Oil Spills. Last May I outlined to the Congress a number of measures that should be taken to reduce the risks of pollution from oil spills. Recent events have underlined the urgency of action on these proposals. At the outset of this present Congress I resubmitted the Ports and Waterways Safety Act and the legislation requiring the use of bridge-to-bridge radiotelephones for safety of navigation. Such legislation would have decreased the chances of the oil spill which occurred as a result of a tanker collision in San Francisco Bay.

• I have provided $25 million in next year's budget for development of better techniques to prevent and clean up oil spills and to provide more effective surveillance. I am asking the Council on Environmental Quality in conjunction with the Department of Transportation and the Environmental Protection Agency to review what further measures can be developed to deal with the problem.

• I also am renewing my request that the Senate give its advice and consent on the two new international conventions on oil spills and the pending amendments to the 1954 Oil Spills Convention for the Prevention of Pollution of the Sea by Oil.

The Intergovernmental Maritime Consultative Organization (IMCO) is presently preparing a convention to establish an International Compensation Fund to supplement the 1969 Civil Liability Convention. Our ratification of the 1969 convention will be withheld until this supplementary convention can also be brought into force because both conventions are part of a comprehensive plan to provide compensation for damages caused by oil spills. In addition, we have taken the initiative in NATO's Committee on the Challenges of Modern Society and achieved wide international support for terminating all intentional discharges of oil and oily wastes from ships into the oceans by 1975, if possible, and no later than the end of this decade. We will continue to work on this matter to establish through IMCO an international convention on this subject.

Pesticides

Pesticides have provided important benefits by protecting man from disease and increasing his ability to produce food and fiber. However, the use and misuse of pesticides has become one of the major concerns of all who are interested in a better environment. The decline in numbers of several of our bird species is a signal of the potential hazards of pesticides to the environment. We are continuing a major research effort to develop nonchemical methods of pest control, but we must continue to rely on pesticides for the foreseeable future. The challenge is to institute the necessary mechanisms to prevent pesticides from harming human health and the environment.

Currently, Federal controls over pesticides consist of the registration and labeling requirements in the Federal Insecticide, Fungicide, and Rodenticide Act. The administrative processes contained in the law are inordinately cumbersome and time-consuming, and there is no authority to deal with the actual use of pesticides. The labels approved under the Act specify the uses to which a pesticide may be put, but there is no way to ensure that the label will be read or obeyed. A comprehensive strengthening of our pesticide control laws is needed.

• I propose that the use of pesticides be subject to control in appropriate circumstances, through a registration procedure which provides for designation of a pesticide for "general use," "restricted use," or "use by permit only." Pesticides designated for restricted use would be applied only by an approved pest control applicator. Pesticides designated for "use by permit only" would be made available only with the approval of an approved pest control consultant. This will help to ensure that pesticides which are safe when properly used will not be misused or applied in excessive quantities.

• I propose that the Administrator of the Environmental Protection Agency be authorized to permit the experimental use of pesticides under strict controls, when he needs additional information concerning a pesticide before deciding whether it should be registered.

• I propose that the procedures for cancellation of a registration be streamlined to permit more expeditious action.

• I propose that the Administrator be authorized to stop the sale or use of, and to seize, pesticides being distributed or held in violation of Federal law.

Recycling of Wastes

The Nation's solid waste problem is both costly and damaging to the environment. Paper, which accounts for about one-half of all municipal solid waste, can be reprocessed to produce a high quality product. Yet the percentage the Nation recycles has been declining steadily.

To reverse this trend, the General Services Administration, working with the Council on Environmental Quality, has reviewed the Federal Government's purchasing policies. It found a substantial number of prohibitions against using paper with recycled content. Such prohibitions are no longer reasonable in light of the need to encourage recycling.

As a result of this review, the GSA has already changed its specifications to require a minimum of 3 to 50 percent recycled content, depending on the product, in over $35 million per year of paper purchases. GSA is currently revising other specifications to require recycled content in an additional $25 million of annual paper purchases. In total, this will amount to more than one-half of GSA's total paper products purchases. All remaining specifications will be reviewed to require recycled content in as many other paper products as possible. The regulations will be reviewed continually to increase the percentage of recycled paper required in each.

I have directed that the Chairman of the Council on Environmental Quality suggest to the Governors that they review State purchasing policies and where possible revise them to require recycled paper. To assist them, I have directed the Administrator of GSA to set up a technical liaison to provide States with the federally revised specifications as well as other important information on this new Federal program, which represents a significant first step toward a much broader use of Federal procurement policies to encourage recycling.

II. CONTROLLING EMERGING PROBLEMS

Environmental control efforts too often have been limited to cleaning up problems that have accumulated in the past. We must concentrate more on preventing the creation of new environmental problems and on dealing with emerging problems. We must, for example, prevent the harmful dumping of wastes into the ocean and the buildup of toxic materials throughout our environment. We must roll back increasingly annoying and hazardous levels of noise in our environment, particularly in the urban environment. Our goal in dealing with emerging environmental problems must be to ward them off before they become acute, not merely to undo the damage after it is done.

Toxic Substances

As we have become increasingly dependent on many chemicals and metals, we have become acutely aware of the potential toxicity of the materials entering our environment. Each year hundreds of new chemicals are commercially marketed and some of these chemicals may pose serious potential threats. Many existing chemicals and metals, such as PCB's (polychlorinated biphenyls) and mercury, also represent a hazard.

It is essential that we take steps to prevent chemical substances from becoming environmental hazards. Unless we develop better methods to assure adequate testing of chemicals, we will be inviting the environmental crises of the future.

• I propose that the Administrator of EPA be empowered to restrict the use or distribution of any substance which he finds is a hazard to human health or the environment.

• I propose that the Administrator be authorized to stop the sale or use of any substance that violates the provisions of the legislation and to seek immediate injunctive relief when use or distribution of a substance presents an imminent hazard to health or the environment.

• I propose that the Administrator be authorized to prescribe minimum standard tests to be performed on substances.

This legislation, coupled with the proposal on pesticides and other existing laws, will provide greater protection to humans and wildlife from introduction of toxic substances into the environment. What I propose is not to ban beneficial uses of chemicals, but rather to control the use of those that may be harmful.

Ocean Dumping

Last year, at my direction, the Council on Environmental Quality extensively examined the problem of ocean dumping. Its study indicated that ocean dumping is not a critical problem now, but it predicted that as municipalities and industries increasingly turned to the oceans as a convenient dumping ground, a vast new influx of wastes would occur. Once this happened, it would be difficult and costly to shift to land-based disposal.

Wastes dumped in the oceans have a number of harmful effects. Many are toxic to marine life, reduce populations of fish and other economic resources, jeopardize marine ecosystems, and impair aesthetic values. In most cases, feasible, economic, and more beneficial methods of disposal are available. Our national policy should be to ban unregulated ocean dumping of all wastes and to place strict limits on ocean disposal of harmful materials. Legislation is needed to assure that our oceans do not suffer the fate of so many of our inland waters, and to provide the authority needed to protect our coastal waters, beaches, and estuaries.

• I recommend a national policy banning unregulated ocean dumping of all materials and placing strict limits on ocean disposal of any materials harmful to the environment.

• I recommend legislation that will require a permit from the Administrator of the Environmental Protection Agency for any materials to be dumped into the oceans, estuaries, or Great Lakes and that will authorize the Administrator to ban dumping of wastes which are dangerous to the marine ecosystem.

The legislation would permit the Administrator to begin phasing out ocean dumping of harmful materials. It would provide the controls necessary to prevent further degradation of the oceans.

This would go far toward remedying this problem off our own shores. However, protection of the total marine environment from such pollution can only be assured if other nations adopt similar measures and enforce them.

I am instructing the Secretary of State, in coordination with the Council on Environmental Quality, to develop and pursue international initiatives directed toward this objective.

Noise

The American people have rightly become increasingly annoyed by the growing level of noise that assails them. Airplanes, trucks, construction equipment, and many other sources of noise interrupt sleep, disturb communication, create stress, and can produce deafness and other adverse health effects. The urban environment in particular is being degraded by steadily rising noise levels. The Federal Government has set and enforces standards for noise from aircraft, but it is now time that our efforts to deal with many other sources of noise be strengthened and expanded.

The primary responsibility for dealing with levels of noise in the general environment rests upon local governments. However, the products which produce the noise are usually marketed nationally, and it is by regulating the noise-generating characteristics of such products that the Federal Government can best assist the State and local governments in achieving a quieter environment.

I propose comprehensive noise pollution control legislation that will authorize the Administrator of EPA to set noise standards on transportation, construction and other equipment and require labeling of noise characteristics of certain products.

Before establishing standards, the Administrator would be required to publish a report on the effects of noise on man, the major sources, and the control techniques available. The legislation would provide a method for measurably reducing major noise sources, while preserving to State and local governments the authority to deal with their particular noise problems.

III. PROMOTING ENVIRONMENTAL QUALITY IN OUR LAND USE DECISIONS

The use of our land not only affects the natural environment but shapes the pattern of our daily lives. Unfortunately, the sensible use of our land is often thwarted by the inability of the many competing and overlapping local units of government to control land use decisions which have regional significance.

While most land use decisions will continue to be made at the local level, we must draw upon the basic authority of State government to deal with land use issues which spill over local jurisdictional boundaries. The States are uniquely qualified to effect the institutional reform that is so badly needed, for they are closer to the local problems than is the Federal Government and yet removed enough from local tax and other pressures to represent the broader regional interests of the public. Federal programs which influence major land use decisions can thereby fit into a coherent pattern. In addition, we must begin to restructure economic incentives bearing upon land use to encourage wise and orderly decisions for preservation and development of the land.

I am calling upon the Congress to adopt a national land use policy. In addition, I am proposing other major initiatives on land use to bring "parks to the people," to expand our wilderness system, to restore and preserve historic and older buildings, to provide an orderly system for power plant siting, and to prevent environmental degradation from mining.

A National Land Use Policy

We must reform the institutional framework in which land use decisions are made.

I propose legislation to establish a National Land Use Policy which will encourage the States, in cooperation with local government, to plan for and regulate major developments affecting growth and the use of critical land areas. This should be done by establishing methods for protecting lands of critical environmental concern, methods for controlling large-scale development, and improving use of lands around key facilities and new communities.

One hundred million dollars in new funds would be authorized to assist the States in this effort—$20 million in each of the next five years—with priority given to the States of the coastal zone. Accordingly this proposal will replace and expand my proposal submitted to the last Congress for coastal zone management, while still giving priority attention to this area of the country which is especially sensitive to development pressures. Steps will be taken to assure that federally-assisted programs are consistent with the approved State land use programs.

Public Lands Management. The Federal public lands comprise approximately one-third of the Nation's land area. This vast domain contains land with spectacular scenery, mineral and timber resources, major wildlife habitat, ecological significance, and tremendous recreational importance. In a sense, it is the "breathing space" of the Nation.

The public lands belong to all Americans. They are part of the heritage and the birthright of every citizen. It is important, therefore, that these lands be managed wisely, that their environmental values be carefully safeguarded, and that we deal with these lands as trustees for the future. They have an important place in national land use considerations.

The Public Land Law Review Commission recently completed a study and report on Federal public land policy. This

Administration will work closely with the Congress in evaluating the Commission's recommendations and in developing legislative and administrative programs to improve public land management.

The largest single block of Federal public land lies in the State of Alaska. Recent major oil discoveries suggest that the State is on the threshold of a major economic development. Such development can bring great benefits both to the State and to the Nation. It could also—if unplanned and unguided —despoil the last and greatest American wilderness.

We should act now, in close cooperation with the State of Alaska, to develop a comprehensive land use plan for the Federal lands in Alaska, giving priority to those north of the Yukon River. Such a plan should take account of the needs and aspirations of the native peoples, the importance of balanced economic development, and the special need for maintaining and protecting the unique natural heritage of Alaska. This can be accomplished through a system of parks, wilderness, recreation, and wildlife areas and through wise management of the Federal lands generally. I am asking the Secretary of the Interior to take the lead in this task, calling upon other Federal agencies as appropriate.

Preserving Our Natural Environment. The demand for open space, recreation, wilderness and other natural areas continues to accelerate. In the face of rapid urban development, the acquisition and development of open space, recreation lands and natural areas accessible to urban centers is often thwarted by escalating land values and development pressures. I am submitting to the Congress several bills that will be part of a comprehensive effort to preserve our natural environment and to provide more open spaces and parks in urban areas where today they are often so scarce. In addition, I will be taking steps within the executive branch to assure that all agencies are using fully their existing legislative authority to these ends.

'Legacy of Parks.' Merely acquiring land for open space and recreation is not enough. We must bring parks to where the people are so that everyone has access to nearby recreational areas. In my budget for 1972, I have proposed a new "Legacy of Parks" program which will help States and local governments provide parks and recreation areas, not just for today's Americans but for tomorrow's as well. Only if we set aside and develop such recreation areas now can we ensure that they will be available for future generations.

As part of this legacy, I have requested a $200 million appropriation to begin a new program for the acquisition and development of additional park lands in urban areas. To be administered by the Department of Housing and Urban Development, this would include provision for facilities such as swimming pools to add to the use and enjoyment of these parks.

Also, I have recommended in my 1972 budget that the appropriation for the Land and Water Conservation Fund be increased to $380 million, permitting the continued acquisition of Federal parks and recreation areas as well as an expanded State grant program. However, because of the way in which these State grant funds were allocated over the past five years, a relatively small percentage has been used for the purchase and development of recreational facilities in and near urban areas. The allocation formula should be changed to ensure that more parks will be developed in and near our urban areas.

I am submitting legislation to reform the State grant program so that Federal grants for the purchase and development of recreation lands bear a closer relationship to the population distribution.

I am also proposing amendments to the Internal Revenue Code which should greatly expand the use of charitable land transfers for conservation purposes and thereby enlarge the role of private citizens in preserving the best of America's landscape.

Additional public parks will be created as a result of my program for examining the need for retention of real property owned by the Government. The Property Review Board, which I established last year, is continuing its review of individual properties as well as its evaluation of the Government's overall Federal real property program. Properties identified as suitable for park use and determined to be surplus can be conveyed to States and political subdivisions for park purposes without cost. The State or other political subdivision must prepare an acceptable park use plan and must agree to use the property as a park in perpetuity. More than 40 properties with high potential for park use have already been identified.

Five such properties are now available for conversion to public park use. One, Border Field, California, will be developed as a recreation area with the assistance of the Department of the Interior. The other four will be conveyed to States or local units of government as soon as adequate guarantees can be obtained for their proper maintenance and operation. These four are: (1) part of the former Naval Training Devices Center on Long Island Sound, New York; (2) land at a Clinical Research Center in Fort Worth, Texas; (3) about ten miles of sand dunes and beach along the Atlantic Coast and Sandy Hook Bay, a part of Fort Hancock, New Jersey; and (4) a portion of Fort Lawton, Washington, a wooded, hilly area near the heart of Seattle. In addition, efforts are underway to open a significant stretch of Pacific Ocean Beach Front and Coastal Bluffs at Camp Pendleton, California.

Many parcels of federal real property are currently underutilized because of the budgetary and procedural difficulties that are involved in transferring a Federal operation from the current site to a more suitable location.

I am again proposing legislation to simplify relocation of federal installations that occupy properties that could better be used for other purposes.

This will allow conversion of many additional Federal real properties to a more beneficial public use. Lands now used for Federal operations but more suited to park and recreational uses will be given priority consideration for relocation procedures. The program will be self-financing and will provide new opportunities for improving utilization of Federal lands.

Wilderness Areas. While there is clearly a need for greater efforts to provide neighborhood parks and other public recreation areas, there must still be places where nature thrives and man enters only as a visitor. These wilderness areas are an important part of a comprehensive open space system. We must continue to expand our wilderness preservation system, in order to save for all time those magnificent areas of America where nature still predominates. Accordingly, in August last year I expressed my intention to improve our performance in the study and presentation of recommendations for new wilderness areas.

I will soon be recommending to the Congress a number of specific proposals for a major enlargement of our wilderness preservation system by the addition of a wide spectrum of natural areas spread across the entire continent.

National Parks

While placing much greater emphasis on parks in urban areas and the designation of new wilderness areas, we must continue to expand our national park system. We are currently obligating substantial sums to acquire the privately owned lands in units of the National Park System which have already been authorized by the Congress.

Last year, joint efforts of the administration and the Congress resulted in authorization of ten areas in the National Park System, including such outstanding sites as Voyageurs National Park in Minnesota, Apostle Islands National Lakeshore in Wisconsin, Sleeping Bear Dunes National Lakeshore in Michigan, Gulf Islands National Seashore in Mississippi and Florida, and the Chesapeake and Ohio Canal National Historical Park in the District of Columbia, Maryland and West Virginia.

However, the job of filling out the National Park System is not complete. Other unique areas must still be preserved. Despite all our wealth and scientific knowledge, we cannot re-create these unspoiled areas once they are lost to the onrush of development. I am directing the Secretary of the Interior to review the outstanding opportunities for setting aside nationally significant natural and historic areas, and to develop priorities for their possible addition to the National Park System.

Power Plant Siting. The power shortage last summer and continuing disputes across the country over the siting of power plants and the routing of transmission lines highlight the need for longer-range planning by the producers of electric power to project their future needs and identify environmental concerns well in advance of contruction deadlines. The growing number of confrontations also suggest the need for the establishment of public agencies to assure public discussion of plans, proper resolution of environmental issues, and timely construction of facilities. Last fall, the Office of Science and Technology sponsored a study entitled "Electric Power and the Environment," which identified many of these issues. Only through involving the environmental protection agencies early in the planning of future power facilities can we avoid disputes which delay construction timetables. I believe that these two goals of adequacy of power supply and environmental protection are compatible if the proper framework is available.

I propose a power plant siting law to provide for establishment within each State or region of a single agency with responsibility for assuring that environmental concerns are properly considered in the certification of specific power plant sites and transmission line routes.

Under this law, utilities would be required to identify needed power supply facilities ten years prior to construction of the required facilities. They would be required to identify the power plant sites and general transmission routes under consideration fives years before construction and apply for certification for specific sites, facilities, and routes two years in advance of construction. Public hearings at which all interested parties could be heard without delaying construction timetables would be required.

Mined Area Protection. Surface and underground mining have scarred millions of acres of land and have caused environmental damages such as air and water pollution. Burning coal fires, subsidence, acid mine drainage which pollutes our streams and rivers and the destruction of aesthetic and recreational values frequently but unnecessarily accompany mining activities. These problems will worsen as the demand for fossil fuels and other raw materials continues to grow, unless such mining is subject to regulation requiring both preventive and restorative measures.

I propose a Mined Area Protection Act to establish Federal requirements and guidelines for State programs to regulate the environmental consequences of surface and underground mining. In any State which does not enact the necessary regulations or enforce them properly, the Federal Government would be authorized to do so.

Preserving Our Architectural and Historic Heritage

Too often we think of environment only as our natural surroundings. But for most of us, the urban environment is the one in which we spend our daily lives. America's cities, from Boston and Washington to Charleston, New Orleans, San Antonio, Denver, and San Francisco, reflect in the architecture of their buildings a uniqueness and character that is too rapidly disappearing under the bulldozer. Unfortunately, present Federal income tax policies provide much stronger incentives for demolition of older buildings than for their rehabilitation.

Particularly acute is the continued loss of many buildings of historic value. Since 1933 an estimated one-quarter of the buildings recorded by the Historic American Building Survey have been destroyed. Most lending institutions are unwilling to loan funds for the restoration and rehabilitation of historic buildings because of the age and often the location of such buildings. Finally, there are many historic buildings under Federal ownership for which inadequate provision has been made for restoration and preservation.

I shall propose tax measures designed to overcome these present distortions and particularly to encourage the restoration of historic buildings.

I shall propose new legislation to permit Federal insurance of home improvement loans for historic residential properties to a maximum of $15,000 per dwelling unit.

I am recommending legislation to permit State and local governments more easily to maintain transferred Federal historic sites by allowing their use for revenue purposes and I am taking action to ensure that no Federally owned property is demolished until its historic significance has first been reviewed.

IV. TOWARD A BETTER WORLD ENVIRONMENT

Environmental problems have a unique global dimension, for they afflict every nation, irrespective of its political institutions, economic system, or state of development. The United States stands ready to work and cooperate with all nations, individually or through international institutions, in the great task of building a better environment for man. A number of the proposals which I am submitting to Congress today have important international aspects, as in the case of ocean dumping. I hope that other nations will see the merit of the environmental goals which we have set for ourselves and will choose to share them with us.

At the same time, we need to develop more effective environmental efforts through appropriate regional and global organizations. The United States is participating closely in the initiatives of the Organization for Economic Cooperation and Development (OECD), with its emphasis on the complex economic aspects of environmental controls, and of the Economic Commission for Europe (ECE), a U.N. regional organization which is the major forum for East-West cooperation on environmental problems.

Following a United States initiative in 1969, the North Atlantic Treaty Organization has added a new dimension to its cooperative activities through its Committee on the Challenges of Modern Society. CCMS has served to stimulate national and international action on many problems common to a modern technological society. For example, an important agreement was reached in Brussels recently to eliminate intentional discharges of oil and oily wastes by ships into the oceans by 1975 if possible or, at the latest, by the end of the decade. CCMS is functioning as an effective forum for reaching agreements on the development of pollution-free and safe automobiles. Work on mitigating the effects of floods and earthquakes is in progress. These innovative and specific actions are good examples of how efforts of many nations can be focused and coordinated in addressing serious environmental problems facing all nations.

The United Nations, whose specialized agencies have long done valuable work on many aspects of the environment, is sponsoring a landmark Conference on the Human Environment to be held in Stockholm in June 1972. This will, for the first time, bring together all member nations of the world community to discuss those environmental issues of most pressing common concern and to agree on a world-wide strategy and the basis for a cooperative program to reverse the fearful trend toward environmental degradation. I have pledged full support for this Conference, and the United States is actively participating in the preparatory work.

Direct bilateral consultations in this field are also most useful in jointly meeting the challenges of environmental problems. Thus, the United States and Canada have been working closely together preparing plans for action directed to the urgent task of cleaning up the Great Lakes, that priceless resource our two nations share. Over the past few months, ministerial level discussions with Japan have laid the basis for an expanded program of cooperation and technological exchange from which both nations will benefit.

It is my intention that we will develop a firm and effective fabric of cooperation among the nations of the world on these environmental issues.

World Heritage Trust

As the United States approaches the centennial celebration in 1972 of the establishment of Yellowstone National Park, it would be appropriate to mark this historic event by a new international initiative in the general field of parks. Yellowstone is the first national park to have been created in the modern world, and the national park concept has represented a major contribution to world culture. Similar systems have now been established throughout the world. The United Nation lists over 1,200 parks in 93 nations.

The national park concept is based upon the recognition that certain areas of natural, historical, or cultural significance have such unique and outstanding characteristics that they must be treated as belonging to the nation as a whole, as part of the nation's heritage.

It would be fitting by 1972 for the nations of the world to agree to the principle that there are certain areas of such unique worldwide value that they should be treated as part of the heritage of all mankind and accorded special recognition as part of a World Heritage Trust. Such an arrangement would impose no limitations on the sovereignty of those nations which choose to participate, but would extend special international recognition to the areas which qualify and would make available technical and other assistance where appropriate to assist in their protection and management. I believe that such an initiative can add a new dimension to international cooperation.

I am directing the Secretary of the Interior, in coordination with the Council on Environmental Quality, and under the foreign policy guidance of the Secretary of State, to develop initiatives for presentation in appropriate international forums to further the objective of a World Heritage Trust.

Confronted with the pressures of population and development, and with the world's tremendously increased capacity for environmental modification, we must act together now to save for future generations the most outstanding natural areas as well as places of unique historical, archeological, architectural, and cultural value to mankind.

V. FURTHER INSTITUTIONAL IMPROVEMENT

The solutions to environmental and ecological problems are often complex and costly. If we are to develop sound policies and programs in the future and receive early warning on problems, we need to refine our analytical techniques and use the best intellectual talent that is available.

After thorough discussions with a number of private foundations, the Federal Government through the National Science Foundation and the Council on Environmental Quality will support the establishment of an Environmental Institute. I hope that this nonprofit institute will be supported not only by the Federal Government but also by private foundations. The Institute would conduct policy studies and analyses drawing upon the capabilities of our universities and experts in other sectors. It would provide new and alternative strategies for dealing with the whole spectrum of environmental problems.

VI. TOWARD A BETTER LIFE

Adoption of the proposals in this message will help us to clean up the problems of the past, to reduce the amount of waste which is disposed, and to deal creatively with problems of the future before they become critical. But action by government alone can never achieve the high quality environment we are seeking.

We must better understand how economic forces induce some forms of environmental degradation, and how we can create and change economic incentives to improve rather than degrade environmental quality. Economic incentives, such as the sulfur oxides charge and the lead tax, can create a strong impetus to reduce pollution levels. We must experiment with other economic incentives as a supplement to our regulatory efforts. Our goal must be to harness the powerful mechanisms of the marketplace, with its automatic incentives and restraints, to encourage improvement in the quality of life.

We must also recognize that the technological, regulatory, and economic measures we adopt to solve our environmental problems cannot succeed unless we enlist the active participation of the American people. Far beyond any legislative or administrative programs that may be suggested, the direct involvement of our citizens will be the critical test of whether we can indeed have the kind of environment we want for ourselves and for our children.

All across the country, our people are concerned about the environment—the quality of the air, of the water, of the open spaces that their children need. The question I hear everywhere is "What can *I* do?"

Fortunately, there is a great deal that each of us can do. The businessman in his everyday decisions can take into account the effects on the environment of his alternatives and act in an environmentally responsible way. The housewife can make choices in the marketplace that will help discourage pollution. Young people can undertake projects in their schools and through other organizations to help build a better environment for their communities. Parents can work with the schools to help develop sound environmental teaching throughout our education system. Every community in the nation can encourage and promote concerned and responsible citizen involvement in environmental issues, an involvement which should be broadly representative of the life-styles and leadership of the community. Each of us can resolve to help keep his own neighborhood clean and attractive and to avoid careless, needless littering and polluting of his surroundings. These are examples of effective citizen participation; there are many others.

The building of a better environment will require in the long term a citizenry that is both deeply concerned and fully informed. Thus, I believe that our educational system, at all levels, has a critical role to play.

As our nation comes to grips with our environmental problems, we will find that difficult choices have to be made, that substantial costs have to be met, and that sacrifices have to be made. Environmental quality cannot be achieved cheaply or easily. But, I believe the American people are ready to do what is necessary.

This nation has met great challenges before. I believe we shall meet this challenge. I call upon all Americans to dedicate themselves during the decade of the seventies to the goal of restoring the environment and reclaiming the earth for ourselves and our posterity. And I invite all peoples everywhere to join us in this great endeavor. Together, we hold this good earth in trust. We must—and together we can—prove ourselves worthy of that trust.

RICHARD NIXON

HEALTH INSURANCE

Following is the text, as made available by the White House, of President Nixon's Feb. 18 message to Congress on health insurance.

TO THE CONGRESS OF THE UNITED STATES:

In the last twelve months alone, America's medical bill went up eleven percent, from $63 to $70 billion. In the last *ten* years, it has climbed 170 percent, from the $26 billion level in 1960. Then we were spending 5.3 percent of our Gross National Product on health; today we devote almost 7% of our GNP to health expenditures.

This growing investment in health has been led by the Federal Government. In 1960, Washington spent $3.5 billion on medical needs—13 percent of the total. This year it will spend $21 billion—or about 30 percent of the nation's spending in this area.

But what are we getting for all this money?

For most Americans, the result of our expanded investment has been more medical care and care of higher quality. A profusion of impressive new techniques, powerful new drugs, and splendid new facilities has developed over the past decade. During that same time, there has been a six percent drop in the number of days each year that Americans are disabled. Clearly there is much that is right with American medicine.

But there is also much that is wrong.

One of the biggest problems is that fully 60 percent of the growth in medical expenditures in the last ten years has gone not for additional services but merely to meet price inflation. Since 1960, medical costs have gone up twice as fast as the cost of living. Hospital costs have risen five times as fast as other prices. For growing numbers of Americans, the cost of care is becoming prohibitive. And even those who can afford most care may find themselves impoverished by a catastrophic medical expenditure.

The shortcomings of our health care system are manifested in other ways as well. For some Americans—especially those who live in remote rural areas or in the inner city—care is simply not available. The quality of medicine varies widely with geography and income. Primary care physicians and outpatient facilities are in short supply in many areas and most of our people have trouble obtaining medical attention on short notice. Because we pay so little attention to preventing disease and treating it early, too many people get sick and need intensive treatment.

Our record, then, is not as good as it should be. Costs have skyrocketed but values have not kept pace. We are investing more of our nation's resources in the health of our people but we are not getting a full return on our investment.

Building a National Health Strategy

Things do not have to be this way. We can change these conditions—indeed, we must change them if we are to fulfill our promise as a nation. Good health care should be readily available to all of our citizens.

It will not be easy for our nation to achieve this goal. It will be impossible to achieve it without a new sense of purpose and a new spirit of discipline. That is why I am calling today not only for new programs and not merely for more money but for something more—for a *new* approach which is equal to the complexity of our challenges. I am calling today for a new National Health Strategy that will marshall a variety of forces in a coordinated assault on a variety of problems.

This new strategy should be built on four basic principles.

Assuring Equal Access. Although the Federal Government should be viewed as only one of several partners in this reforming effort, it does bear a special responsibility to help all citizens achieve equal access to our health care system. Just as our National Government has moved to provide equal opportunity in areas such as education, employment and voting, so we must now work to expand the opportunity for all citizens to obtain a decent standard of medical care. We must do all we can to remove any racial, economic, social or geographic barriers which now prevent any of our citizens from obtaining adequate health protection. For without good health, no man can fully utilize his other opportunities.

Balancing Supply and Demand. It does little good, however, to increase the demand for care unless we also increase the supply. Helping more people pay for more care does little good unless more care is available. This axiom was ignored when Medicaid and Medicare were created—and the nation paid a high price for that error. The expectations of many beneficiaries were not met and a severe inflation in medical costs was compounded.

Rising demand should not be a source of anxiety in our country. It is, after all, a sign of our success in achieving equal opportunity, a measure of our effectiveness in reducing the barriers to care. But since the Federal Government is helping to remove those barriers, it also has a responsibility for what happens after they are reduced. We must see to it that our approach to health problems is a balanced approach. We must be sure that our health care system is ready and able to welcome its new clients.

Organizing for Efficiency. As we move toward these goals, we must recognize that we *cannot* simply *buy* our way to better medicine. We have already been trying that too long. We have been persuaded, too often, that the plan that *costs* the most will *help* the most and too often we have been disappointed.

We cannot be accused of having underfinanced our medical system—not by a long shot. We have, however, spent this money poorly—reenforcing inequities and rewarding inefficiencies and placing the burden of greater new demands on the same old system which could not meet the old ones.

The toughest question we face then is not how much we should spend but how we should spend it. It must be our goal not merely to finance a more expensive medical system but to organize a more efficient one.

There are two particularly useful ways of doing this:

• *Emphasizing Health Maintenance.* In most cases our present medical system operates episodically—people come to it in moments of distress—when they require its most expensive services. Yet both the system and those it serves would be better off if less expensive services could be delivered on a more regular basis.

If more of our resources were invested in preventing sickness and accidents, fewer would have to be spent on costly cures. If we gave more attention to treating illness in its early stages, then we would be less troubled by acute disease. In short, we should build a true "health" system—and not a "sickness" system alone. We should work to maintain health and not merely to restore it.

• *Preserving Cost Consciousness.* As we determine just who should bear the various costs of health care, we should remember that only as people are aware of those costs will they be motivated to reduce them. When consumers pay virtually nothing for services and when, at the same time, those who provide services know that all their costs will also be met, then neither the consumer nor the provider has an incentive to use the system efficiently. When that happens, unnecessary demand can multiply, scarce resources can be squandered and the shortage of services can become even more acute.

Those who are hurt the most by such developments are often those whose medical needs are most pressing. While costs should never be a barrier to providing needed care, it is important that we preserve some element of cost consciousness within our medical system.

Building on Strengths. We should also avoid holding the whole of our health care system responsible for failures in some of its parts. There is a natural temptation in dealing with any complex problem to say: "Let us wipe the slate clean and start from scratch." But to do this—to dismantle our entire health insurance system, for example—would be to ignore those important parts of the system which have provided useful service. While it would be wrong to ignore any weaknesses in our present system, it would be equally wrong to sacrifice its strengths.

One of those strengths is the diversity of our system—and the range of choice it therefore provides to doctors and patients alike. I believe the public will always be better served by a pluralistic system than by a monolithic one, by a system which creates many effective centers of responsibility—both public and private—rather than one that concentrates authority in a single governmental source.

This does not mean that we must allow each part of the system to go its own independent way, with no sense of common purpose. We must encourage greater cooperation and build better coordination—but not by fostering uniformity and eliminating choice. One effective way of influencing the system is by structuring incentives which reward people for helping to achieve national goals without forcing their decisions or dictating the way they are carried out. The American people have always shown a unique capacity to move toward common goals in varied ways. Our efforts to reform health care in America will be more effective if they build on this strength.

These, then, are certain cardinal principles on which our National Health Strategy should be built. To implement this strategy, I now propose for the consideration of the Congress the following six point program. It begins with measures designed to increase and improve the supply of medical care and concludes with a program which will help people pay for the care they require.

Reorganizing the Delivery of Service

In recent years, a new method for delivering health services has achieved growing respect. This new approach has two essential attributes. It brings together a comprehensive range of medical services in a single organization so that a patient is assured of convenient access to all of them. And it provides needed services for a fixed contract fee which is paid in advance by all subscribers.

Such an organization can have a variety of forms and names and sponsors. One of the strengths of this new concept, in fact, is its great flexibility. The general term which has been applied to all of these units is "HMO"—Health Maintenance Organization.

The most important advantage of Health Maintenance Organizations is that they increase the value of the services a consumer receives for each health dollar. This happens, first, because such organizations provide a strong financial incentive for better preventive care and for greater efficiency.

Under traditional systems, doctors and hospitals are paid, in effect, on a piece work basis. The more illnesses they treat —and the more service they render—the more their income rises. This does not mean, of course, that they do any less than their very best to make people well. But it does mean that there is no economic incentive for them to concentrate on keeping people healthy.

A fixed-price contract for comprehensive care reverses this illogical incentive. Under this arrangement, income grows not with the number of days a person is sick but with the number of days he is well. HMO's therefore have a strong financial interest in preventing illness, or, failing that, in treating it in its early stages, promoting a thorough recovery and preventing any reoccurence. Like doctors in ancient China, they are paid to keep their clients healthy. For them, economic interests work to reenforce their professional interests.

At the same time, HMO's are motivated to function more efficiently. When providers are paid retroactively for each of their services, inefficiencies can often be subsidized. Sometimes, in fact, inefficiency is rewarded—as when a patient who does not need to be hospitalized is treated in a hospital so that he can collect on his insurance. On the other hand, if an HMO is wasteful of time or talent or facilities, it cannot pass those extra costs on to the consumer or to an insurance company. Its budget for the year is determined in advance by the number of its subscribers. From that point on it is penalized for going over its budget and rewarded for staying under it.

In an HMO, in other words, cost consciousness is fostered. Such an organization cannot afford to waste resources—that costs more money in the short run. But neither can it afford to economize in ways which hurt patients—for that increases long-run expenses.

The HMO also organizes medical resources in a way that is more convenient for patients and more responsive to their needs. There was a time when every housewife had to go to a variety of shops and markets and pushcarts to buy her family's groceries. Then along came the supermarket—making her shopping chores much easier and also giving her a wider range of choice and lower prices. The HMO provides similar advantages in the medical field. Rather than forcing the consumer to thread his way through a complex maze of separate services and specialists, it makes a full range of resources available through a single organization—often at a single stop—and makes it more likely that the right combination of resources will be utilized.

Because a team can often work more efficiently than isolated individuals, each doctor's energies go further in a Health Maintenance Organization—twice as far according to some studies.

At the same time, each patient retains the freedom to choose his own personal doctor. In addition, services can more easily be made available at night and on weekends in an HMO. Because many doctors often use the same facilities and equipment and can share the expense of medical assistants and business personnel, overhead costs can be sharply curtailed. Physicians benefit from the stimulation that comes from working with fellow professionals who can share their problems. appreciate their accomplishments and readily offer their counsel and assistance. HMO's offer doctors other advantages as well, including a more regular work schedule, better opportunities for continuing education, lesser financial risks upon first entering practice, and generally lower rates for malpractice insurance.

Some seven million Americans are now enrolled in HMO's —and the number is growing. Studies show that they are receiving high quality care at a significantly lower cost—as much as one-fourth to one-third lower than traditional care in some areas. They go to hospitals less often and they spend less time there when they go. Days spent in the hospital each year for those who belong to HMO's are only three-fourths of the national average.

Patients and practitioners alike are enthusiastic about this organizational concept. So is this Administration. That is why we proposed legislation last March to enable Medicare recipients to join such programs. That is why I am now making the following additional recommendations:

• We should require public and private health insurance plans to allow beneficiaries to use their plan to purchase membership in a Health Maintenance Organization when one is available. When, for example, a union and an employer negotiate a contract which includes health insurance for all workers, each worker should have the right to apply the actuarial value of his coverage toward the purchase of a fixed-price, health maintenance program. Similarly, both Medicare and the new Family Health Insurance Plan for the poor which I will set out later in this message should provide an HMO option.

• To help new HMO's get started—an expensive and complicated task—we should establish a new $23 million program of planning grants to aid potential sponsors—in both the private and public sector.

• At the same time, we should provide additional support to help sponsors raise the necessary capital, construct needed facilities, and sustain initial operating deficits until they achieve an enrollment which allows them to pay their own way. For this purpose, I propose a program of Federal loan guarantees which will enable private sponsors to raise some $300 million in private loans during the first year of the program.

• Other barriers to the development of HMO's include archaic laws in 22 States which prohibit or limit the group practice of medicine and laws in most States which prevent doctors from delegating certain responsibilities (like giving injections) to their assistants. To help remove such barriers, I am instructing the Secretary of Health, Education and Welfare to develop a model statute which the States themselves can adopt to correct these anomalies. In addition, the Federal Government will facilitate the development of HMO's in all States by entering into contracts with them to provide service to Medicare recipients and other Federal beneficiaries who elect such programs. Under the supremacy clause of the Constitution, these contracts will operate to preempt any inconsistent State statutes.

Our program to promote the use of HMO's is only one of the efforts we will be making to encourage a more efficient organization of our health care system. We will take other steps in this direction, including stronger efforts to capitalize on new technological developments.

In recent years medical scientists, engineers, industrialists, and management experts have developed many new techniques for improving the efficiency and effectiveness of health care. These advances include automated devices for measuring and recording body functions such as blood flow and the electrical activity of the heart, for performing laboratory tests and making the results readily available to the doctor, and for reducing the time required to obtain a patient's medical history. Methods have also been devised for using computers in diagnosing diseases, for monitoring and diagnosing patients from remote locations, for keeping medical records and generally for restructuring the layout and administration of hospitals and other care centers. The results of early tests for such techniques have been most promising. If new developments can be widely implemented, they can help us deliver more effective, more efficient care at lower prices.

The hospital and outpatient clinic of tomorrow may well bear little resemblance to today's facility. We must make every effort to see that its full promise is realized. I am therefore directing the Secretary of Health, Education, and Welfare to focus research in the field of health care services on new techniques for improving the productivity of our medical system. The Department will establish pilot experiments and demonstration projects in this area, disseminate the results of this work, and encourage the health industry and the medical profession to bring such techniques into full and effective use in the health care centers of the nation.

Meeting the Special Needs of Scarcity Areas

Americans who live in remote rural areas or in urban poverty neighborhoods often have special difficulty obtaining adequate medical care. On the average, there is now one doctor for every 630 persons in America. But in over one-third of our counties the number of doctors per capita is less than one-third that high. In over 130 counties, comprising over eight percent of our land area, there are no private doctors at all—and the number of such counties is growing.

A similar problem exists in our center cities. In some areas of New York for example, there is one private doctor for every 200 persons but in other areas the ratio is one to 12,000. Chicago's inner city neighborhoods have some 1700 fewer physicians today than they had ten years ago.

How can we attract more doctors—and better facilities—into these scarcity areas? I propose the follow actions:
• We should encourage Health Maintenance Organizations to locate in scarcity areas. To this end, I propose a $22 million program of direct Federal grants and loans to help offset the special risks and special costs which such projects would entail.
• When necessary, the Federal Government should supplement these efforts by supporting out-patient clinics in areas which still are underserved. These units can build on the experience of the Neighborhood Health Centers experiment which has now been operating for several years. These facilities would serve as a base on which full HMO's—operating under other public or private direction—could later be established.

I have also asked the Administrator of Veterans Affairs and the Secretary of Health, Education, and Welfare to develop ways in which the Veterans Administration medical system can be used to supplement local medical resources in scarcity areas.
• A series of new area Health Education Centers should also be established in places which are medically underserved—as the Carnegie Commission on Higher Education has recommended. These centers would be satellites of existing medical and other health science schools; typically, they could be built around a community hospital, a clinic or an HMO which is already in existence. Each would provide a valuable teaching center for new health professionals, a focal point for the continuing education of experienced personnel, and a base for providing sophisticated medical services which would not otherwise be available in these areas. I am requesting that up to $40 million be made available for this program in Fiscal Year 1972.
• We should also find ways of compensating—and even rewarding—doctors and nurses who move to scarcity areas, despite disadvantages such as lower income and poorer facilities.

As one important step in this direction, I am proposing that our expanding loan programs for medical students include a new forgiveness provision for graduates who practice in a scarcity area, especially those who specialize in primary care skills that are in short supply.

In addition, I will request $10 million to implement the Emergency Health Personnel Act. Such funds will enable us to mobilize a new National Health Service Corps, made up largely of dedicated and public-spirited young health professionals who will serve in areas which are now plagued by critical manpower shortages.

Meeting the Personnel Needs of our Growing Medical System

Our proposals for encouraging HMO's and for serving scarcity areas will help us use medical manpower more effectively. But it is also important that we produce more health professionals and that we educate more of them to perform critically needed services. I am recommending a number of measures to accomplish these purposes.
• First, we must use new methods for helping to finance medical education. In the past year, over half of the nation's medical schools have declared that they are in "financial distress" and have applied for special Federal assistance to meet operating deficits.

More money is needed—but it is also important that this money be spent in new ways. Rather than treating the symptoms of distress in a piecemeal and erratic fashion, we must rationalize our system of financial aid for medical education so that the schools can make intelligent plans for regaining a sound financial position.

I am recommending, therefore, that much of our present aid to schools of medicine, dentistry and osteopathy—along with $60 million in new money—be provided in the form of so-called "capitation grants," the size of which would be determined by the number of students the school graduates. I recommend that the capitation grant level be set at $6,000 per graduate.

A capitation grant system would mean that a school would know in advance how much Federal money it could count on. It would allow an institution to make its own long-range plans as to how it would use these monies. It would mean that we could eventually phase out our emergency assistance programs.

By rewarding output—rather than subsidizing input—this new aid system would encourage schools to educate more students and to educate them more efficiently. Unlike formulas which are geared to the annual number of enrollees, capitation grants would provide a strong incentive for schools to shorten their curriculum from four years to three—in line with another sound recommendation of the Carnegie Commission on Higher Education. For then, the same sized school would qualify for as much as one-third more money each year, since each of its graduating classes would be one-third larger.

This capitation grant program should be supplemented by a program of special project grants to help achieve special goals. These grants would support efforts such as improving planning and management, shortening curriculums, expanding enrollments, team training of physicians and allied health personnel, and starting HMO's for local populations.

In addition, I believe that Federal support dollars for the construction of medical education facilities can be used more effectively. I recommend that the five current programs in this area be consolidated into a single, more flexible grant authority and that a new program of guaranteed loans and other financial aids be made available to generate over $500 million in private construction loans in the coming Fiscal Year—five times the level of our current construction grant program.

Altogether, these efforts to encourage and facilitate the expansion of our medical schools should produce a 50 percent increase in medical school graduates by 1975. We must set that as our goal and we must see that it is accomplished.
• The Federal Government should also establish special support programs to help low income students enter medical and dental schools. I propose that our scholarship grant program for these students be almost doubled—from $15 to $29

million. At the same time, this Administration would modify its proposed student loan programs better to meet the needs of medical students. To help alleviate the concern of low income students that such a loan might become an impossible burden if they fail to graduate from medical school, we will request authority to forgive loans where such action is appropriate.

• One of the most promising ways to expand the supply of medical care and to reduce its costs is through a greater use of allied health personnel, especially those who work as physicians' and dentists' assistants, nurse pediatric practitioners, and nurse midwives. Such persons are trained to perform tasks which must otherwise be performed by doctors themselves, even though they do not require the skills of a doctor. Such assistance frees a physician to focus his skills where they are most needed and often allows him to treat many additional patients.

I recommend that our allied health personnel training programs be expanded by 50% over 1971 levels, to $29 million, and that $15 million of this amount be devoted to training physicians' assistants. We will also encourage medical schools to train future doctors in the proper use of such assistants and we will take the steps I described earlier to eliminate barriers to their use in the laws of certain States.

In addition, this administration will expand nationwide the current MEDIHC program—an experimental effort to encourage servicemen and women with medical training to enter civilian medical professions when they leave military duty. Of the more than 30,000 such persons who leave military service each year, two-thirds express an interest in staying in the health field but only about one-third finally do so. Our goal is to increase the number who enter civilian health employment by 2,500 per year for the next five years. At the same time, the Veterans Administration will expand the number of health trainees in VA facilities from 49,000 in 1970 to over 53,000 in 1972.

A Special Problem: Malpractice Suits and Malpractice Insurance

One reason consumers must pay more for health care and health insurance these days is the fact that most doctors are paying much more for the insurance they must buy to protect themselves against claims of malpractice. For the past five years, malpractice insurance rates have gone up an average of 10 percent a year—a fact which reflects both the growing number of malpractice claims and the growing size of settlements. Many doctors are having trouble obtaining any malpractice insurance.

The climate of fear which is created by the growing menace of malpractice suits also affects the quality of medical treatment. Often it forces doctors to practice inefficient, defensive medicine —ordering unnecessary tests and treatments solely for the sake of appearance. It discourages the use of physicians' assistants, inhibits that free discussion of cases which can contribute so much to better care, and makes it harder to establish a relationship of trust between doctors and patients.

The consequences of the malpractice problem are profound. It must be confronted soon and it must be confronted effectively —but that will be no simple matter. For one thing, we need to know far more than we presently do about this complex problem.

I am therefore directing—as a first step in dealing with this danger—that the Secretary of Health, Education and Welfare promptly appoint and convene a Commission on Medical Malpractice to undertake an intensive program of research and analysis in this area. The Commission memberships should represent the health professions and health institutions, the legal profession, the insurance industry, and the general public. Its report—which should include specific recommendations for dealing with this problem—should be submitted by March 1, 1972.

New Measures Needed to Prevent Illnesses and Accidents

We often invest our medical resources as if an ounce of cure were worth a pound of prevention. We spend vast sums to treat illnesses and accidents that could be avoided for a fraction of those expenditures. We focus our attention on making people well rather than keeping people well, and—as a result—both our health and our pocketbooks are poorer. A new National Health Strategy should assign a much higher priority to the work of prevention.

As we have already seen, Health Maintenance Organizations can do a great deal to help in this effort. In addition to encouraging their growth, I am also recommending a number of further measures through which we can take the offensive against the long-range causes of illnesses and accidents.

• To begin with, we must reaffirm—and expand—the Federal commitment to biomedical research. Our approach to research support should be balanced—with strong efforts in a variety of fields. Two critical areas, however, deserve special attention.

The first of these is cancer. In the next year alone, 650,000 new cases of cancer will be diagnosed in this country and 340,000 of our people will die of this disease. Incredible as it may seem, one out of every four Americans who are now alive will someday develop cancer unless we can reduce the present rates of incidence.

In the last seven years we spent more than 30 billion dollars on space research and technology and about one-twenty-fifth of that amount to find a cure for cancer. The time has now come to put more of our resources into cancer research and—learning an important lesson from our space program—to organize those resources as effectively as possible.

When we began our space program we were fairly confident that our goals could be reached if only we made a great enough effort. The challenge was technological; it did not require new theoretical breakthroughs. Unfortunately, this is not the case in most biomedical research at the present time; scientific breakthroughs are still required and they often cannot be forced—no matter how much money and energy is expended.

We should not forget this caution. At the same time, we should recognize that of all our research endeavors, cancer research may now be in the best position to benefit from a great infusion of resources. For there are moments in biomedical research when problems begin to break open and results begin to pour in, opening many new lines of inquiry and many new opportunities for breakthrough.

We believe that cancer research has reached such a point. This Administration is therefore requesting an additional $100 million for cancer research in its new budget. And—as I said in my State of the Union Message—"I will ask later for whatever additional funds can effectively be used" in this effort.

Because this project will require the coordination of scientists in many fields—drawing on many projects now in existence but cutting across established organizational lines—I am directing the Secretary of Health, Education and Welfare to establish a new Cancer Conquest Program in the Office of the Director of the National Institutes of Health. This program will operate under its own Director who will be appointed by the Secretary and supported by a new management group. To advise that group in establishing priorities and allocating funds —and to advise other officials, including me, concerning this effort—I will also establish a new Advisory Committee on the Conquest of Cancer.

A second targeted disease for concentrated research should be sickle cell anemia—a most serious childhood disease which almost always occurs in the black population. It is estimated that one out of every 500 black babies actually developes sickle cell disease.

It is a sad and shameful fact that the causes of this disease have been largely neglected throughout our history. We cannot rewrite this record of neglect, but we can reverse it. To this end, this Administration is increasing its budget for research and treatment of sickle cell disease fivefold, to a new total of $6 million.

• A second major area of emphasis should be that of health education.

In the final analysis, each individual bears the major responsibility for his own health. Unfortunately, too many of us fail to meet that responsibility. Too many Americans eat too much, drink too much, work too hard, and exercise too little. Too many are careless drivers.

These are personal questions, to be sure, but they are also public questions. For the whole society has a stake in the health of the individual. Ultimately, everyone shares in the cost of his illnesses or accidents. Through tax payments and through insurance premiums, the careful subsidize the careless, the nonsmokers subsidize those who smoke, the physically fit subsidize the rundown and the overweight, the knowledgeable subsidize the ignorant and vulnerable.

It is in the interest of our entire country, therefore, to educate and encourage each of our citizens to develop sensible health practices. Yet we have given remarkably little attention to the health education of our people. Most of our current efforts in this area are fragmented and haphazard—a public service advertisement one week, a newspaper article another, a short lecture now and then from the doctor. There is no national instrument, no central force to stimulate and coordinate a comprehensive health education program.

I have therefore been working to create such an instrument. It will be called the National Health Education Foundation. It will be a private, non-profit group which will receive no Federal money. Its membership will include representatives of business, labor, the medical profession, the insurance industry, health and welfare organizations, and various governmental units. Leaders from these fields have already agreed to proceed with such an organization and are well on the way toward reaching an initial goal of $1 million in pledges for its budget.

This independent project will be complemented by other Federal efforts to promote health education. For example, expenditures to provide family planning assistance have been increased, rising four-fold since 1969. And I am asking that the great potential of our nation's day care centers to provide health education be better utilized.

• We should also expand Federal programs to help prevent accidents—the leading cause of death between the ages of one and 37 and the fourth leading cause of death for persons of all ages.

Our highway death toll—50,000 fatalities last year—is a tragedy and an outrage of unspeakable proportions. It is all the more shameful since half these deaths involved drivers or pedestrians under the influence of alcohol. We have therefore increased funding for the Department of Transportation's auto accident and alcohol program from $8 million in Fiscal Year 1971 to $35 million in Fiscal Year 1972. I am also requesting that the budget for alcoholism programs be doubled, from $7 million to $14 million. This will permit an expansion of our research efforts into better ways of treating this disease.

I am also requesting a supplemental appropriation of $5 million this year and an addition of $8 million over amounts already in the 1972 budget to implement aggressively the new Occupational Safety and Health Act I signed last December. We must begin immediately to cut down on the 14,000 deaths and more than two million disabling injuries which result each year from occupational illnesses and accidents.

The conditions which affect health are almost unlimited. A man's income, his daily diet, the place he lives, the quality of his air and water—all of these factors have a greater impact on his physical well-being than does the family doctor. When we talk about our health program, therefore, we should not forget our efforts to protect the nation's food and drug supply, to control narcotics, to restore and renew the environment, to build better housing and transportation systems, to end hunger in America, and—above all—to place a floor under the income of every family with children. In a sense this special message

on health is one of many health messages which this Administration is sending to the Congress.

A National Health Insurance Partnership

In my State of the Union message, I pledged to present a program "to ensure that no American family will be prevented from obtaining basic medical care by inability to pay." I am announcing that program today. It is a comprehensive national health insurance program, one in which the public and the private sectors would join in a new partnership to provide adequate health insurance for the American people.

In the last twenty years, the segment of our population owning health insurance has grown from 50 percent to 87 percent and the portion of medical bills paid for by insurance has gone from 35 percent to 60 percent. But despite this impressive growth, there are still serious gaps in present health insurance coverage. Four such gaps deserve particular attention.

First—too many health insurance policies focus on hospital and surgical costs and leave critical outpatient services uncovered. While some 80 percent of our people have some hospitalization insurance, for example, only about half are covered for outpatient and laboratory services and less than half are insured for treatment in the physician's office or the home. Because demand goes where the dollars are, the result is an unnecessary—and expensive—overutilization of acute care facilities. The average hospital stay today is a full day longer than it was eight years ago. Studies show that over one-fourth of hospital beds in some areas are occupied by patients who do not really need them and could have received equivalent or better care outside the hospital.

A second problem is the failure of most private insurance policies to protect against the catastrophic costs of major illnesses and accidents. Only 40 percent of our people have catastrophic cost insurance of any sort and most of that insurance has upper limits of $10,000 or $15,000. This means that insurance often runs out while expenses are still mounting. For many of our families, the anguish of a serious illness is thus compounded by acute financial anxiety. Even the joy of recovery can often be clouded by the burden of debt—and even by the threat of bankruptcy.

A third problem with much of our insurance at the present time is that it cannot be applied to membership in a Health Maintenance Organization—and thus effectively precludes such membership. No employee will pay to join such a plan, no matter how attractice it might seem to him, when deductions from his paycheck—along with contributions from his employer—are being used to purchase another health insurance policy.

The fourth deficiency we must correct in present insurance coverage is its failure to help the poor gain sufficient access to our medical system. Just one index of this failure is the fact that fifty percent of poor children are not even immunized against common childhood diseases. The disability rate for families below the poverty line is at least 50 percent higher than for families with incomes above $10,000.

Those who need care most often get care least. And even when the poor do get service, it is often second rate. A vicious cycle is thus reinforced—poverty breeds illness and illness breeds greater poverty. This situation will be corrected only when the poor have sufficient purchasing power to enter the medical marketplace on equal terms with those who are most affluent.

Our National Health Insurance Partnership is designed to correct these inadequacies—not by destroying our present insurance system but by improving it. Rather than giving up on a system which has been developing impressively, we should work to bring about further growth which will fill in the gaps we have identified. To this end, I am recommending the following combination of public and private efforts.

• I am proposing that a National Health Insurance Standards Act be adopted which will require employers to provide basic health insurance coverage for their employees.

In the past, we have taken similar actions to assure workers a minimum wage, to provide them with disability and retirement benefits, and to set occupational health and safety standards. Now we should go one step further and guarantee that all workers will receive adequate health insurance protection.

The minimum program we would require under this law would pay for hospital services, for physicians' services—both in the hospital and outside of it, for full maternity care, well-baby care (including immunizations), laboratory services and certain other medical expenses. To protect against catastrophic costs, benefits would have to include not less than $50,000 in coverage for each family member during the life of the policy contract. The minimum package would include certain deductible and coinsurance features. As an alternative to paying separate fees for separate services, workers could use this program to purchase membership in a Health Maintenance Organization.

The Federal Government would pay nothing for this program; the costs would be shared by employers and employees, much as they are today under most collective bargaining agreements. A ceiling on how much employees could be asked to contribute would be set at 35 percent during the first two and one-half years of operation and 25 percent thereafter. To give each employer time to plan for this additional cost of doing business—a cost which would be shared, of course, by all of his competitors—this program would not go into effect until July 1, 1973. This schedule would also allow time for expanding and reorganizing our health system to handle the new requirements.

As the number of enrollees rises under this plan, the costs per enrolee can be expected to fall. The fact that employees and unions will have an even higher stake in the system will add additional pressures to keep quality up and costs down. And since the range within which benefits can vary will be somewhat narrower than it has been, competition between insurance companies will be more likely to focus on the overall price at which the contract is offered. This means that insurance companies will themselves have a greater motivation to keep medical costs from soaring.

I am still considering what further legislative steps may be desirable for regulating private health insurance, including the introduction of sufficient disincentive measures to reinforce the objective of creating cost consciousness on the part of consumers and providers. I will make such recommendations to the Congress at a later time.

• I am also proposing that a new Family Health Insurance Plan be established to meet the special needs of poor families who would not be covered by the proposed National Health Insurance Standards Act headed by unemployed, intermittently employed or self-employed persons.

The Medicaid program was designed to help these people, but—for many reasons—it has not accomplished its goals. Because it is not a truly national program, its benefits vary widely from State to State. Sixteen States now get 80 percent of all Medicaid money and two States, California and New York, get 30 percent of Federal funds though they have only 20 percent of the poverty population. Two States have no Medicaid program at all.

In addition, Medicaid suffers from other defects that now plague our failing welfare system. It largely excludes the working poor—which means that all benefits can suddenly be cut off when family income rises ever so slightly—from just under the eligibility barrier to just over it. Coverage is provided when husbands desert their families, but is often eliminated when they come back home and work. The program thus provides an incentive for poor families to stay on the welfare rolls.

Some of these problems would be corrected by my proposal to require employers to offer adequate insurance coverage to their employees. No longer, for example, would a workingman receive poorer insurance coverage than a welfare client—a condition which exists today in many States. But we also need an additional program for much of the welfare population.

Accordingly, I propose that the part of Medicaid which covers most welfare families be eliminated. The new Family Health Insurance Plan that takes its place would be fully financed and administered by the Federal Government. It would provide health insurance to all poor families with children headed by self-employed or unemployed persons whose income is below a certain level. For a family of four persons, the eligibility ceiling would be $5,000.

For the poorest of eligible families, this program would make no charges and would pay for basic medical costs. As family income increased beyond a certain level ($3,000 in the case of a four-person family) the family itself would begin to assume a greater share of the costs—through a graduated schedule of premium charges, deductibles, and coinsurance payments. This provision would induce some cost consciousness as income rises. But unlike Medicaid—with its abrupt cutoff of benefits when family income reaches a certain point—this arrangement would provide an incentive for families to improve their economic position.

The Family Health Insurance Plan would also go into effect on July 1, 1973. In its first full year of operation, it would cost approximately $1.2 billion in additional Federal funds—assuming that all eligible families participate. Since States would no longer bear any share of this cost, they would be relieved of a considerable burden. In order to encourage States to use part of these savings to supplement Federal benefits, the Federal Government would agree to bear the costs of administering a consolidated Federal-State benefit package. The Federal Government would also contract with local committees—to review local practices and to ensure that adequate care is being provided in exchange for Federal payments. Private insurers, unions and employees would be invited to use these same committees to review the utilization of their benefits if they wished to do so.

This, then, is how the National Health Insurance Partnership would work: The Family Health Insurance Plan would meet the needs of most welfare families—though Medicaid would continue for the aged poor, the blind and the disabled. The National Health Insurance Standards Act would help the working population. Members of the Armed Forces and civilian Federal employees would continue to have their own insurance programs and our older citizens would continue to have Medicare.

Our program would also require the establishment in each State of special insurance pools which would offer insurance at reasonable group rates to people who did not qualify for other programs: the self-employed, for example, and poor risk individuals who often cannot get insurance.

I also urge the Congress to take further steps to improve Medicare. For one thing, beneficiaries should be allowed to use the program to join Health Maintenance Organizations. In addition, we should consolidate the financing of Part A of Medicare—which pays for hospital care—and Part B—which pays for outpatient services, provided the elderly person himself pays a monthly fee to qualify for this protection. I propose that this charge—which is scheduled to rise to $5.60 per month in July of this year—be paid for instead by increasing the Social Security wage base. Removing this admission cost will save our older citizens some $1.3 billion annually and will give them greater access to preventive and ambulatory services.

Why is a National Health Insurance Partnership Better Than Nationalized Health Insurance?

I believe that our government and our people, business and labor, the insurance industry and the health profession can work together in a national partnership to achieve our health objectives. I do not believe that the achievement of these objectives requires the nationalization of our health industry.

To begin with, there simply is no need to eliminate an entire segment of our private economy and at the same time add a multi-billion dollar responsibility to the Federal budget. Such a step should not be taken unless all other steps have failed.

More than that, such action would be dangerous. It would deny people the right to choose how they will pay for their health care. It would remove competition from the insurance system—and with it an incentive to experiment and innovate.

Under a nationalized system, only the Federal Government would lose when inefficiency crept in or when prices escalated; neither the consumer himself, nor his employer, nor his union, nor his insurance company would have any further stake in controlling prices. The only way that utilization could be effectively regulated and costs effectively restrained, therefore, would be if the Federal Government made a forceful, tenacious effort to do so. This would mean—as proponents of a nationalized insurance program have admitted—that Federal personnel would inevitably be approving the budgets of local hospitals, setting fee schedules for local doctors, and taking other steps which could easily lead to the complete Federal domination of all of American medicine. That is an enormous risk—and there is no need for us to take it. There is a better way—a more practical, more effective, less expensive, and less dangerous way—to reform and renew our nation's health system.

Confronting A Deepening Crisis

"It is health which is real wealth," said Ghandi, "and not pieces of gold and silver." That statement applies not only to the lives of men but also the life of nations. And nations, like men, are judged in the end by the things they hold most valuable.

Not only is health more important than economic wealth, it is also its foundation. It has been estimated, for example, that ten percent of our country's economic growth in the past half century has come because a declining death rate has produced an expanded labor force.

Our entire society, then, has a direct stake in the health of every member. In carrying out its responsibilities in this field, a nation serves its own best interests, even as it demonstrates the breadth of its spirit and the depth of its compassion.

Yet we cannot truly carry out these responsiblities unless the ultimate focus of our concern is the personal health of the individual human being. We dare not get so caught up in our systems and our strategies that we lose sight of his needs or compromise his interests. We can build an effective National Health Strategy only if we remember the central truth that the only way to serve our people well is to better serve each person.

Nineteen months ago I said that America's medical system faced a "massive crisis." Since that statement was made, that crisis has deepened. All of us must now join together in a common effort to meet this crisis—each doing his own part to mobilize more effectively the enormous potential of our health care system.

RICHARD NIXON

TEXT OF EDUCATION MESSAGE

Following is the text, as made available by the White House, of President Nixon's Feb. 22 message to Congress on higher education.

TO THE CONGRESS OF THE UNITED STATES:

Nearly a year ago, in my first special message on higher education, I asked the Congress to join me in expanding higher education opportunities across the nation. First, I proposed to reform and increase aid to students. Second, I proposed a National Foundation for Higher Education designed to reform and strengthen post secondary education.

Neither house of Congress acted on these proposals. Now the time for action is growing short. Existing legislative authority

for the basic Federal higher education programs expires at the end of the current fiscal year.

1971 can be a year of national debate on the goals and potentials of our system of higher education. It can be a time of opportunity to discover new concepts of mission and purpose, which are responsive to the diverse needs of the people of our country. I therefore again urge the Congress to join with me in expanding opportunities in two major ways:

● To help equalize individual opportunities for higher education, I am proposing the Higher Education Opportunity Act of 1971.

● To broaden opportunities through renewal, reform and innovation in higher education, I am proposing a separate act establishing the National Foundation for Higher Education.

Equalizing Individual Opportunities for Higher Education

At the present time, a young person whose family earns more than $15,000 a year is almost five times more likely to attend college than a young person whose family earns less than $3,000.

At the present time, Federal student assistance programs do not always reach those who need them most.

At the present time, there are just not enough funds to go around to all deserving students. Needy students often do not have access to grants. Higher-income students are frequently unable to borrow for their education, even when loans are guaranteed by the Federal Government.

I repeat the commitment which I made in my message of last year: that no qualified student who wants to go to college should be barred by lack of money. The program which I am again submitting this year would benefit approximately one million more students than are currently receiving aid. It would assure that Federal funds go first, and in the largest amounts, to the neediest students, in order to place them on an equal footing with students from higher-income families. Abundant resources for loans would also be available to students from higher-income families. The budget I submitted in January provides funds for these reforms and stands behind the commitments of this administration. Failure to pass this program would not only deny these benefits to many students, but also would limit their opportunity to make major choices about their lives.

A major element of my higher education proposal to the last Congress is the creation of a National Student Loan Association. For too long, the volume of funds available to students for federally insured loans has been arbitrarily restricted by the lack of a secondary market in which lenders could sell paper in order to replenish their supply of loan capital.

Establishment of the National Student Loan Association would relieve this squeeze on liquidity by making available an additional $1 billion for student loan funds. The Association would be authorized to buy student loans made by qualified lenders—universities as well as commercial lending institutions. This secondary market would enable universities and commercial lenders to make loans to students in far greater quantity than they have in the past.

It is important to be clear on what this reform would mean. It would mean that higher education would be open to all the people of this country as never before. It would mean that students still in high school would know that their efforts to qualify for college need not be compromised by doubts about whether they can afford college. It would mean that their choice of a college would be based on their educational goals rather than upon their family's financial circumstances.

Renewal, Reform and Innovation

If we are to make higher education finally accessible to all who are qualified, then our colleges must be prepared both for the diversity of their goals and the seriousness of their intent. While colleges and universities have made exceptional efforts to serve unprecedented numbers of students over the last decade, they must find additional ways to respond to a new set of challenges:

• All too often we have fallen prey to the myth that there is only one way to learn—by sitting in class, reading books, and listening to teachers. Those who learn best in other ways are rejected by the system.

• While the diversity of individuals seeking higher education has expanded in nearly every social dimension—age, class, ethnic background—higher education institutions have become increasingly uniform and less diverse.

• Increasingly, many colleges, and particularly universities, have become large, complex institutions which have lost their way. The servants of many masters and the managers of many enterprises, they are less and less able to perform their essential tasks well.

• At the present time, thousands of individuals of all ages and circumstances are excluded from higher education for no other reason that that the system is designed primarily for 18-22 year olds who can afford to go away to college.

• At the present time, institutional and social barriers discourage students from having sustained experiences before or during their college years which would help hem get more out of college and plan for their future lives.

The relationship between the Federal Government and the universities has contributed little to meeting these needs because it has not been a genuine partnership. In many cases the Federal Government has hired universities to do work which has borne little natural relationship to the central functions of the institution. Too often, the Federal Government has been part of the problem rather than part of the solution.

Certain Federal agencies promote excellence, innovation, and reform in particular areas. The National Science Foundation has played a magnificent role in the public interest for science, and the National Institutes of Health have played a similar role for health.

The National Foundation for Higher Education would fulfill a new role in the Federal Government. It would have as its mandate a review of the overall needs of the American people for post-secondary education. It would have as its operating premises, the principles of selectivity and flexibility. Its constituency would include people as well as institutions—and not only the usual secondary student entering college, but also others—such as the person who wants to combine higher education with active work experience, or the one who has left school and wants to return.

The Foundation can do much to develop new approaches to higher education:

• New ways of "going to college." I am impressed with the need for new and innovative means of providing higher education to individuals of all ages and circumstances (Britain and Japan, for example, have already taken significant steps in the use of television for this purpose).

• New patterns of attending college. A theme of several recent reports is that students are isolated too long in school, and that breaking the educational "lockstep" would enable them to be better and more serious students (as were the GI's after World War II). If so, student bodies would reflect a greater mix of ages and experience, and colleges would be places for integrating rather than separating the generations.

• New approaches to diversify institutional missions. Colleges and universities increasingly have aspired to become complex and "well rounded" institutions providing a wide spectrum of general and specialized education. The Foundation could help institutions to strengthen their individuality and to focus on particular missions by encouraging and supporting excellence in specific areas—be it a field of research, professional training, minority education, or whatever.

Special Help for Black Institutions

Colleges and universities founded for black Americans are an indispensable national resource. Despite great handicaps they educate substantial numbers of black Americans, thereby helping to bring about a more rapid transition to an integrated society.

Black institutions are faced with an historic inadequacy of resources. To help these institutions compete for students and faculty with other colleges and universities, the combined help of government at all levels, other institutions of higher learning, and the private sector must be summoned.

This administration has taken a series of actions to assist these institutions:

• The proposed reform of student aid programs, with its concentration of funds on the neediest students, would significantly aid students at black institutions.

• The National Foundation for Higher Education will direct special efforts toward meeting the needs of black colleges.

• Additional funds for black colleges have been requested for fiscal year 1972 in programs administered by the U.S. Office of Education, the National Science Foundation, and the Department of Agriculture.

Conclusion

These are but some of the new approaches to higher education which need to be pursued. A theme common to all of them is a new kind of engagement between all the citizens of our society and our system of higher education. All of us can make a contribution to bringing about such an engagement by taking part in a thoughtful national discussion about our priorities for higher education. Students and faculties can make a contribution by reexamining their goals and the means they choose to achieve them. The Federal Government can do its part by supporting access to higher education for all of our people and by providing the resources needed to help develop new forms of higher education which would be responsive to all of their needs.

RICHARD NIXON

TEXT OF CONSUMER MESSAGE

Following is the text, as made available by the White House, of President Nixon's Feb. 24 message to Congress requesting consumer legislation.

TO THE CONGRESS OF THE UNITED STATES:

The history of American prosperity is the history of the American free enterprise system. The system has provided an economic foundation of awesome proportions, and the vast material strength of the nation is built on that foundation. For the average American, this strength is reflected in a standard of living that would have staggered the imagination only a short while ago. This constantly rising standard of living benefits both the consumer and the producer.

In today's marketplace, however, the consumer often finds himself confronted with what seems an impenetrable complexity in many of our consumer goods, in the advertising claims that surround them, the merchandising methods that purvey them and the means available to conceal their quality. The result is a degree of confusion that often confounds the unwary, and too easily can be made to favor the unscrupulous. I believe new safeguards are needed, both to protect the consumer and to reward the responsible businessman.

I indicated my deep concern for this matter in my special message to the Congress of October 30, 1969. At that time I urged the Congress to enact a legislative program aimed at establishing a "Buyer's Bill of Rights." This proposal found little success in the 91st Congress. But putting the remedies aside has not sufficed to put the problems aside. These remain. They must be dealt with.

Accordingly, I am again submitting proposals designed to provide such a Buyer's Bill of Rights by:

• Creating by Executive Order a new Office of Consumer Affairs in the Executive Office of the President which will be responsible for analyzing and coordinating all Federal activities in the field of consumer protection.

• Recognizing the need for effective representation of consumer interests in the regulatory process and making recommendations to accomplish this after full public discussion of the findings of the Advisory Council on Executive Organization.

• Establishing within the Department of Health, Education, and Welfare a product safety program. The Secretary of Health, Education, and Welfare would have authority to fix minimum safety standards for products and to ban from the marketplace those products that fail to meet those standards.

• Proposing a Consumer Fraud Prevention Act which would make unlawful a broad but clearly-defined range of practices which are unfair and deceptive to consumers and would be enforced by the Department of Justice and the Federal Trade Commission. This act, where appropriate, would also enable consumers either as individuals or as a class to go into court to recover damages for violations of the act.

• Proposing amendments to the Federal Trade Commission Act which will increase the effectiveness of the Federal Trade Commission.

• Calling upon interested private citizens to undertake a thorough study of the adequacy of existing procedures for the resolution of disputes arising out of consumer transactions.

• Proposing a Fair Warranty Disclosure Act which will provide for clearer warranties, and prohibit the use of deceptive warranties.

• Proposing a Consumer Products Test Methods Act to provide incentives for increasing the amount of accurate and relevant information provided consumers about complex consumer products.

• Resubmitting the Drug Identification Act which would require identification coding of all drug tablets and capsules.

• Encouraging the establishment of a National Business Council to assist the business community in meeting its responsibilities to the consumer; and by

• Other reforms, including exploration of a Consumer Fraud Clearinghouse in the Federal Trade Commission, increased emphasis on consumer education and new programs in the field of food and drug safety.

New Office of Consumer Affairs

The President's Committee on Consumer Interests has made important gains on behalf of the American consumer in the past two years.

It has brought a new and innovative approach to the problem of keeping the consumer informed and capable of handling the complex choices presented to him in today's commercial world. One such measure involves the dissemination of information which the United States Government, as the nation's largest single consumer, collects on the products it uses. In my message of October 30, 1969, I announced that I was directing my Special Assistant for Consumer Affairs to develop a program for providing the buying public with this information.

On the strength of her recommendations, on October 26, 1970, I signed Executive Order 11566 which establishes a means for making available to the public much of the product information which the Federal Government acquires in making its own purchases. A Consumer Product Information Coordinating Center has been established in the General Services Administration with continuing policy guidance from my Special Assistant for Consumer Affairs to make these data available to the public through Federal information centers and other sources throughout the country.

In addition, the Committee on Consumer Interests has made significant strides in developing Federal, State and local cooperation in consumer programs, encouraging establishment of strong State and local consumer offices, and advising on the enactment of effective consumer laws and programs.

Nevertheless, further cooperation among Federal, State and local governments is essential if we are truly to insure that the consumer is properly served. Therefore, I am asking my Special Assistant for Consumer Affairs to intensify her efforts on behalf of the consumers at the State and local level. I am also directing her to conduct regional meetings with State officials concerned with consumer issues, with consumer groups, and with individual consumers to discuss common problems and possible solutions.

But I believe the greatest overall accomplishment of this office has been to give the consumer new assurance of this administration's concern for his and her welfare in the marketplace. In manifesting this concern during the past two years, the responsibility of the President's Committee on Consumer Interests has grown, as has its impact on consumer problems. I have therefore signed today a new Executive Order creating a new Office of Consumer Affairs in the Executive Office of the President. I am appointing my Special Assistant for Consumer Affairs to be Director of this new office. This change reflects the increasingly broad scope of responsibilities assigned to the Special Assistant for Consumer Affairs and will increase the effectiveness of the Office. The Office will advise me on matters of consumer interests, and will also assume primary responsibility for coordinating all Federal activity in the consumer field.

Finally, while I am deeply concerned with obtaining justice for all consumers, I have a special concern to see justice for those who, in a sense, need it most and are least able to get it. Therefore, I am directing my Special Assistant for Consumer Affairs to focus particular attention in the new Office on the coordination of consumer programs aimed at assisting those with limited income, the elderly, the disadvantaged, and minority group members.

A Consumer Advocate

In my message of October 30, 1969, I pointed out that effective representation of the consumer requires that an appropriate arm of the government be given the tools to serve as an advocate before the Federal agencies. I proposed then that this function be performed by a Consumer Protection Division created for the purpose and located within the Department of Justice. That proposal was not acted on.

Since that time my Advisory Council on Executive Organization has completed its Report on Selected Independent Regulatory Agencies. This report makes sweeping recommendations on the reorganization of those agencies for the purpose of helping them better serve the interests of the consumer.

One specific recommendation involves the creation of a new Federal Trade Practices Agency dealing exclusively with matters of consumer protection. This Agency would result from a general restructuring of the Federal Trade Commission. The report specifically suggests that a consumer advocate might be placed within the Federal Trade Practices Agency.

I believe that this is a better approach than the creation of still another independent agency which would only add to the proliferation of agencies without dealing with the problems of effectiveness to which the Advisory Council report addresses itself.

As I indicated at the release of the Advisory Council's report, I am delaying legislative proposals on these issues pending full public discussion of the findings and recommendations of the Council. I urge that those who comment on the Advisory Council recommendations also focus on the manner in which the consumer interest can best be represented in Federal agency proceedings. I further urge the Congress to view the problems of consumer advocacy and agency structure as part of the general problem of making the Federal Government sufficiently responsive to the consumer interest.

After April 20, when comments have been received, I will make the recommendations I consider necessary to provide effective representation of consumer interests in the regulatory process. If the Congress feels it must proceed on the matter of consumer advocacy prior to receiving my recommendations, then I strongly urge and would support, as an interim measure, the placement of the advocacy function within the Federal Trade Commission.

A Product Safety Act

Technology, linked with the American free enterprise system, has brought great advantages and great advances to our way of life. It has also brought certain hazards.

The increasing complexity and sophistication of many of our consumer goods are sometimes accompanied by the increasing possibility of product failure, malfunction, or inadvertent misuse resulting in physical danger to the consumer.

Therefore, I propose legislation providing broad Federal authority for comprehensive regulation of hazardous consumer products.

This product safety legislation will encompass five major responsibilities which would be assigned to a new consumer product safety organization within the Department of Health, Education, and Welfare. Through this organization the Secretary of Health, Education, and Welfare will:

• Gather data on injuries from consumer products;

• Make preliminary determinations of the need for particular standards;

• Develop proposed safety standards with reliance on recognized private standards setting organizations;

• Promulgate standards after a hearing and testimony on the benefits and burdens of the proposed legislation; and

• Monitor industry compliance and enforce mandatory standards.

The mechanisms which will be included in this bill provide for full participation on the part of private organizations and groups in the development of standards.

National Attack on Consumer Fraud

Consumer fraud and deception jeopardize the health and welfare of our people. They cheat consumers of millions of dollars annually. They are often directed against those who can least afford the loss, and are least able to defend themselves—the elderly, the handicapped, and the poor.

At the same time, the honest businessman is damaged by fraud and deceptive practices every bit as much as the consumer—and perhaps more. He is subjected to the unfair money. He is subjected to the opprobrium of those who have suffered at the hands of unscrupulous businessmen, and he loses the goodwill of the public. For it is a fact, however unfortunate, that in the area of business especially, the many are commonly judged by the actions of the few.

Efforts to eliminate these unethical business practices have not been successful enough. It is commonly profitable for unscrupulous businessmen to operate in defiance of the enforcement authorities, to accept whatever penalties and punishments are incurred, and to continue to operate in spite of these. The penalty is just part of the overhead. I want these practices brought to an end.

With this message I am committing this administration to a full and forceful effort to see that they are brought to an end.

Consumer Fraud Prevention Act. I am again submitting and I urge prompt attention to a bill to make unlawful a broad but clearly defined range of practices which are deceptive to consumers. The legislation would provide that the Department of Justice be given new powers to enforce prohibitions against those who would victimize consumers by fraudulent and deceptive practices.

It would give consumers who have been victimized by such practices the right to bring cases in the Federal courts to recover damages, upon the successful termination of a government suit under the Consumer Fraud Prevention Act.

I am also recommending civil penalties of up to $10,000 for each offense in violation of this act.

The Department of Justice has created a new Consumer Protection Section within the Antitrust Division, which has centralized the Department's enforcement in the courts of existing statutes designed to protect the consumer interest. Thus the Department of Justice is prepared to enforce promptly the proposed Consumer Fraud Prevention Act.

Federal Trade Commission. While there is a need for new legislation to insure the rights of the consumer, there is also a need to make more effective use of the legislation we already have, and of the institutions charged with enforcing this legislation.

A principal function of the Federal Trade Commission has historically been to serve as the consumer's main line of resistance to commercial abuse. In the past year the Commission, under new leadership, has been substantially strengthened. A major organizational restructuring has produced within the Commission a Bureau of Consumer Protection, a Bureau of Competition, and a Bureau of Economics. An Office of Policy Planning and Evaluation has been created to establish a more effective ordering of priorities for the Commission's enforcement efforts.

In order to make FTC procedures more responsive to the needs of consumers, responsibilities of the eleven Commission field offices have been extended to include trying cases before hearing examiners in the field, negotiating settlements, conducting investigations, and referring complaints to the Commission. Six Consumer Protection Coordinating Committees have been established in selected metropolitan areas.

I am submitting today legislation which would provide the FTC with the authority to seek preliminary injunctions in Federal courts against what it deems to be unfair or deceptive business practices. The present inability to obtain injunctions commonly results in the passage of extended periods of time before relief can be obtained. During this time the practices in question continue, and their effects multiply.

The proposed bill would expand the jurisdiction of the Commission to include those activities "affecting" interstate commerce, as well as those activities which are "in" interstate commerce.

Finally, I recommend that the penalty schedule for violation of a Commission cease-and-desist order be adjusted from a maximum of $5,000 per violation to a maximum of $10,000 per violation.

Guarantees and Warranties. A constant source of misunderstanding between consumer and businessman is the question of warranties. Guarantees and warranties are often found to be unclear or deceptive.

In 1970, I submitted a proposal for legislation to meet this problem. I am submitting new legislation for this purpose.

This proposal would increase the authority of the Federal Trade Commission to require that guarantees and warranties on consumer goods convey adequate information in simple and readily understood terms.

It would further seek to prevent deceptive warranties; and it would prohibit improper use of a written warranty or guarantee to avoid implied warranty obligations arising under State law.

Consumer Fraud Clearinghouse. My Special Assistant for Consumer Affairs is examining the feasibility of a consumer fraud clearinghouse—a prompt exchange of information between appropriate Federal, State and local law enforcement officials which can be especially helpful in identifying those who perpetrate fraudulent, unfair and deceptive practices upon the consumer and deprive the honest businessman of his legitimate opportunities in the marketplace.

Upon her recommendation, I am asking the FTC to explore with State and local consumer law enforcement officials an effective mechanism for such an exchange.

Consumer Education

Legislative remedies and improved enforcement procedures are powerful weapons in the fight for consumer justice. But as important as these are, they are only as effective as an aware and an informed public make them. Consumer education is an integral part of consumer protection. It is vital if the consumer is to be able to make wise judgments in the marketplace. To enable him or her to do this will require a true education process beginning in childhood and continuing on.

The Office of the Special Assistant for Consumer Affairs has established guidelines for consumer education suggested for use at the elementary and high school level. Those guidelines have been sent to every school system in the country, and their reception has been encouraging. I believe they mark an effective step toward developing an informed consumer. The Office has also begun the development of suggested guidelines for adult and continuing education with particular emphasis on special socio-economic groups and senior citizens.

Now, in order to expand and lend assistance to Consumer Education activities across the nation, I am asking the Secretary of Health, Education, and Welfare, in coordination with my Special Assistant for Consumer Affairs, to work with the nation's education system to (1) promote the establishment of consumer education as a national educational concern; (2) provide technical assistance in the development of programs; (3) encourage teacher training in consumer education; and (4) solicit the use of all school and public libraries as consumer information centers.

Iam also asking the Secretary of Health, Education, and Welfare, in coordination with my Special Assistant for Consumer Affairs, to develop and design programs for the most effective dissemination of consumer information, and particularly to explore the use of the mass media, including the Corporation for Public Broadcasting.

Additional Proposals

Consumer Remedies. As we move to shape new consumer legislation, I believe we must also review all consumer remedies. Although this is primarily a matter of State and local responsibility, I believe that the problem is also of national concern. Accordingly, I am asking the Chairman of the Administrative Conference of the United States to join with other interested citizens representing a broad spectrum of society to undertake a thorough study of the adequacy of existing procedures for resolving disputes arising out of consumer transactions.

The study would (1) focus particularly on the means of handling small claims and explore methods for making small claims courts more responsive to the needs of consumers; (2) examine existing and potential voluntary settlement procedures, including arbitration, and potential means of creating incentives to voluntary, fair settlements of consumer disputes; (3) address the difficult and troublesome questions presented by mass litigation; (4) examine problems and solutions at the State as well as the Federal level; and (5) draw on the experience of other nations in improving consumer remedies.

The purpose of this study will be to gather those facts needed to determine the means of gaining the greatest benefit to consumers with the least cost to production processes and to the country. I urge Federal, State, local and private bodies to cooperate in this effort. I also ask that recommendations to the President, the Congress, the courts and the general public be made within the shortest practicable time.

Food and Drug Programs

Events in the past year have reconfirmed the need for urgent action to insure thorough and effective quality control through the Food and Drug Administration over the food Americans consume and the drugs they take.

In my message of October 30, 1969, I called for stronger efforts in the field of food and drug safety.

At that time I announced that the Secretary of Health, Education, and Welfare had initiated a thorough study of the Food and Drug Administration. As a result of that study, a number of management reforms have contributed to a more effective functioning of the FDA.

Food. During the past two years consumer concern about the quality of certain foods in this nation has become acute. I have instructed the Food and Drug Administration to develop new and better methods for inspecting foods—domestic and imported—to insure that they are entirely free from all natural or artificial contamination. In addition, a major study is under way reviewing the safety of all food additives. Finally, because too many Americans have no understanding of the most basic nutritional principles, the Food and Drug Administration has developed programs of nutritional guidelines and nutritional labeling. Different approaches to labeling are presently being tested for method and effectiveness.

Drugs. In the past year the Food and Drug Administration has been engaged in an extensive program to insure the effectiveness of the drugs Americans use. Decisions have been made on some 3,000 drugs marketed between 1938 and 1962 and representing 80% of the most commonly prescribed drugs.

In addition, the Food and Drug Administration will expand its research efforts aimed at insuring that all drugs available on the market are capable of producing the therapeutic effects claimed for them.

I have resubmitted legislation requiring the identification coding of drug tablets and capsules to prevent those poisonings which result from the use of drug products of unknown or mistaken composition.

A Consumer Product Test Methods Act. Consumers are properly concerned with the reliability of the information furnished them about the goods they buy, and I believe they have a right to such information.

Accordingly, I again propose legislation aimed at stimulating product testing in the private sector. Under this legislation, the Secretary of Commerce, through the National Bureau of Standards, in consultation with my Special Assistant for Consumer Affairs, would identify products that should be tested. Competent Federal agencies would identify product characteristics that should be tested and would approve and develop, where necessary, testing methods to assess those characteristics. Suppliers of goods would be permitted to advertise their compliance with government approved testing standards. In addition, interested private organizations may receive accreditation indicating their competence to perform the approved tests, and the use of an accredited organization in testing a product may be advertised.

National Business Council for Consumer Affairs. Most businessmen recognize and accept their responsibility to the consumer, and in many cases they have voluntarily undertaken efforts to assure more fully that these responsibilities are met throughout the business community.

To emphasize and encourage such voluntary activity, a National Business Council for Consumer Affairs will be organized by the Secretary of Commerce. It will work closely with my Special Assistant for Consumer Affairs, the Federal Trade Commission, the Justice Department and others as appropriate in the further development of effective policies to benefit American consumers.

The Council will be a vehicle through which Government can work with business leaders to establish programs for accomplishing the goal I stated in my 1969 message on consumer protection of fostering "a marketplace which is fair both to those who sell and those who buy." And it will encourage everyone who does business to do an even better job of establishing competitive prices for high quality goods and services.

Conclusion

In submitting the foregoing proposals, I want to emphasize that the purpose of this program is not to provide the consumer with something to which he is not presently entitled; it is rather to assure that he receives what he is, in every way, fully entitled to. The continued success of our free enterprise system depends in large measure upon the mutual trust and goodwill of those who consume and those who produce or provide.

Today, in America, there is a general sense of trust and goodwill toward the world of business. Those who violate that trust and abuse that goodwill do damage to the free enterprise system. Thus, it is not only to protect the consumer, but also to protect that system and the honest men who have created and who maintain it that I urge the prompt passage of this legislative program.

RICHARD NIXON

FOREIGN POLICY REPORT

Following is the text of the introduction and conclusion and excerpts from other portions of "United States Foreign Policy for the 1970s: Building for Peace," President Nixon's second annual report on foreign policy. The message was presented to Congress Feb. 25.

Introduction

"No goal could be greater than to make the next generation the first in this century in which America was at peace with every nation in the world."
Address on the State of the Union
January 22, 1970

In the first year of this Administration we outlined a new American role. In 1970, we implemented policies which embody our new purpose.

This year, as any year, saw crises. We dealth with them without new war and while winding down the war we inherited. But our fundamental goal is deeper. It is to get at the roots of crises and to build a durable structure of international relationships.

This second annual report to the Congress and the Nation, therefore, like the first, is more than a recital of events. It reviews the premises and philosophy of our foreign policy and discusses events in the context of purposes. It explains why we have done as we have, and sets forth our hopes and concerns for the years to come.

A Period of Transition. This Administration must lead the nation through a fundamental transition in foreign policy.

As I explained in last year's report, we are at the end of an era. The postwar order of international relations—the configuration of power that emerged from the Second World War—is gone. With it are gone the conditions which have determined the assumptions and practice of United States foreign policy since 1945.

No single sudden upheaval marked the end of the postwar era in the way that the World Wars of this century shattered the prewar orders of international relations. But the cumulative change since 1945 is profound nonetheless:

• Western Europe and Japan, nations physically or psychologically debilitated by the war, have regained their economic vitality, social cohesion, and political self-assurance. Their new vigor transforms our relationship into a more balanced and dynamic coalition of independent states.

• New nations have found identity and self-confidence and are acting autonomously on the world stage. They are able to shoulder more responsibility for their own security and well-being.

• In the last twenty years, the nature of the Communist challenge has been transformed. The Stalinist bloc has fragmented into competing centers of doctrine and power. One of the deepest conflicts in the world today is between Communist China and the Soviet Union. The most prevalent Communist threats now are not massive military invasions, but a more subtle mix of military, psychological and political pressures. These developments complicate the patterns of diplomacy, presenting both new problems and new prospects.

• At the same time, the Soviet Union has expanded its military power on a global scale and has moved from an inferior status in strategic weapons to one comparable to the United States. This shift in the military equation has changed both defense doctrines and the context of diplomacy.

• Around the globe, East and West, the rigid bipolar world of the 1940's and 1950's has given way to the fluidity of a new era of multilateral diplomacy. Fifty-one nations joined the United Nations at its founding in 1945; today 127 are members. It is an increasingly heterogeneous and complex world, and the dangers of local conflict are magnified. But so, too, are the opportunities for creative diplomacy.

• Increasingly we see new issues that transcend geographic and ideological borders and confront the world community of nations. Many flow from the nature of modern technology. They reflect a shrinking globe and expanding interdependence. They include the challenges of exploring new frontiers of space and sea and the dangers of polluting the planet. These global issues call for a new dimension of international cooperation.

The New American Role. How is America to conduct itself in a world so different? How should we define the form and content of American participation in the 1970's?

In the era of American predominance we resorted to American prescriptions as well as resources. In the new era, our friends are revitalized and increasingly self-reliant while the American domestic consensus has been strained by 25 years of global responsibilities. Failure to draw upon the growth of others would have stifled them and exhausted ourselves. Partnership that was always theoretically desirable is now physically and psychologically imperative.

In the era of overwhelming U.S. military strength, we and our allies could rely on the doctrine of massive retaliation. In the new era growing Soviet power has altered the military equation. Failure to adapt to this change could lead to confrontations which pose an agonizing choice between paralysis and holocaust. Strength that served the cause of peace during a period of relative superiority needs new definitions to keep the peace during a period of relative equality.

In the era of Communist solidarity we pursued an undifferentiated negotiating approach toward Communist countries. In the new era we see a multipolar Communism marked by a variety of attitudes toward the rest of the world. Failure to respond to this diversity would have ignored new opportunities for improving relations. Negotiation with different Communist countries on specific issues carries more promise.

Finally, in the new era unprecedented challenges beckon nations to set aside doctrine and focus on a common agenda. A new global partnership could promote habits of working for the world's interests instead of narrow national interests.

We in this generation have before us an historic opportunity to turn the transformations of the last 25 years into new avenues for peace, and to realize the creative possibilities of a pluralistic world. We must begin with the vision of the world we seek, to infuse our actions with a sense of direction. We need a vision so that crises do not consume our energies, and tactics do not dominate our policies.

America has always had a belief in a purpose larger than itself. Two centuries ago our mission was to be a unique exemplar of free government. Two decades ago it was to take up worldwide burdens of securing the common defense, economic recovery, and political stability.

Today we must work with other nations to build an enduring structure of peace. We seek a new and stable framework of international relationships:

• Which reflects the contributions and reconciles the aspirations of nations.

• Which is cemented by the shared goal of coexistence and the shared practice of accommodation.

• Which liberates countries and continents to realize their destinies free from the threat of war.

• Which promotes social justice and human dignity.

Our participation remains crucial. Because of the abundance of our resources and the stretch of our technology, America's impact on the world remains enormous, whether by our action or by our inaction. Our awareness of the world is too keen, and our concern for peace too deep, for us to remove the measure of stability which we have provided for the past 25 years.

But we need the resources and concepts of others so that they will build this structure with us. For it will not endure unless other nations sense that it is also of their making. Their growth in the past decades enables other nations to do more, and peace in the coming decades will require all nations to do some.

With others we will strive for something that America and the world have not experienced in this century, a full generation of peace.

The first step, of course, is to still the sound of war. We are moving toward that goal. Beyond that, we are focusing on something that men alive today can achieve for themselves and their children, on a span of peace we can realize here and now. This will be our ultimate test.

Thus the core of our new foreign policy is a partnership that reflects the basic theme of the international structure we seek. Its necessary adjuncts are strength to secure our interests and negotiation to reconcile them with the interests of others. Its fullest extension encompasses adversaries as well as friends.

It will take many years to shape the new American role. The transition from the past is underway but far from completed. During this period the task of maintaining a balance abroad and at home will test the capacity of American leadership and the understanding of the American people.

Adjustments in our policies surely will be required, but our experience in 1970 confirmed the basic soundness of our approach.

We have set a new direction. We are on course.

The Nixon Doctrine

This Administration began with the conviction that a global structure of peace requires a strong but redefined American role. In other countries there was growing strength and autonomy. In our own there was nascent isolationism in reaction to overextension. In the light of these changed conditions, we could not continue on the old path....

Perception of the growing imbalance between the scope of America's role and the potential of America's partners thus prompted the Nixon Doctrine. It is the key to understanding what we have done during the past two years, why we have done it, and where we are going.

The Doctrine seeks to reflect these realities:

• That a major American role remains indispensable.

• That other nations can and should assume greater responsibilities, for their sake as well as ours.

• That the change in the strategic relationship calls for new doctrines.

• That the emerging polycentrism of the Communist world presents different challenges and new opportunities.

Toward New Forms of Partnership. The tangible expression of the new partnership is in greater material contributions by other countries. But we must first consider its primary purpose —to help make peace that belongs to all....

The Nixon Doctrine, then, should not be thought of primarily as the sharing of burdens or the lightening of our load.

It has a more positive meaning for other nations and for ourselves.

In effect we are encouraging countries to participate fully in the creation of plans and the designing of programs. They must define the nature of their own security and determine the path of their own progress. For only in this manner will they think of their fate as truly their own....

It was in this context that at Guam in the summer of 1969, and in my November 3, 1969, address to the Nation, I laid out the elements of new partnership.

"First, the United States will keep all of its treaty commitments." We will respect the commitments we inherited—both because of their intrinsic merit, and because of the impact of sudden shifts on regional or world stability. To desert those who have come to depend on us would cause disruption and invite aggression. It is in everyone's interest, however, including those with whom we have ties, to view undertakings as a dynamic process. Maintaining the integrity of commitments requires relating their tangible expression, such as troop deployments or financial contributions, to changing conditions.

The concrete results vary. In South Korea fewer U.S. troops are required, but Korean forces must receive more modern equipment. In NATO a continuing level of U.S. forces and greater European contributions are in order. The best way of maintaining stable relationships with our allies is jointly to reach common conclusions and jointly to act on them....

"Second, we shall provide a shield if a nuclear power threatens the freedom of a nation allied with us or of a nation whose survival we consider vital to our security...."

"Third, in cases involving other types of aggression we shall furnish military and economic assistance when requested in accordinace with our treaty commitments. But we shall look to the nation directly threatened to assume the primary responsibility of providing the manpower for its defense...."

The Process of Implementation. Policy becomes clearer only in the process of translation into programs and actions.

In this process the Nixon Doctrine seeks to reflect the need for continuity as well as the mandate for change. There are two concurrent challenges:

• To carry out our new policy so as to maintain confidence abroad;

• To define our new policy to the American people and to elicit their support....

For the American people have grown somewhat weary of 25 years of international burdens. This weariness was coming in any event, but the anguish of the Vietnam war hastened it, or at least our awareness of it. Many Americans, frustrated by the conflict in Southeast Asia, have been tempted to draw the wrong conclusions. There are lessons to be learned from our Vietnam experience—about unconventional warfare and the role of outside countries the nature of commitments, the balance of responsibilities, the need for public understanding and support. But there is also a lesson not to be drawn: that the only antidote for undifferentiated involvement is indiscriminate retreat....

While cutting back overseas forces prudently, we must resist the automatic reduction of the American presence everywhere without regard to consequences. While trimming our defense budget where possible and adjusting defenses to modern realities, we must resist ritualistic voting against defense spending. Mere scaling down is not an end in itself. We need to determine the proper role for our forces abroad; the level of assistance for allied forces; and the shape of our respective budgets.

The Nixon Doctrine will enable us to remain committed in ways that we can sustain. The solidity of domestic support in turn will reverberate overseas with continued confidence in American performance....

In 1970 there were also examples of policies which belied oversimplified interpretations of the Nixon Doctrine as a formula for heedless withdrawal:

• The Cambodian sanctuary operations were not inconsistent with the plan for American disengagement. Rather they furthered the strategic purposes of insuring the Vietnamization and withdrawal programs.

• Maintaining the present level of U.S. forces in Europe does not contradict the principle of self-help and burden sharing in Asia. Rather it is the best means of eliciting greater partnership in the European theater, while recognizing the reality of the security problem.

• The discreet projection of American presence in the Mediterranean during the Jordanian crisis did not increase the chances of outside intervention. Rather it served as a reminder that outside intervention carried great risks.

The Nixon Doctrine applies most directly to our dealings with allies and friends. But it animates all areas of our new foreign policy:

• In our economic posture. We look towards increased U.S. economic and military assistance in certain areas to help our friends make full use of their resources and move on to greater self-reliance. International trade and monetary policies will demand mutual accommodations and adjustment.

• In our defense posture. We will provide the nuclear shield of the Nixon Doctrine. Our general purpose forces are more and more keyed to our partners' capabilities, to provide truly flexible response when our commitments are involved. And our security assistance program will provide indispensable support to our friends, especially where there are reductions in U.S. manpower.

• In our negotiating posture. When we conduct bilateral negotiations with the USSR, as in SALT, partnership involves close consultations with our allies both to protect their interests and solicit their views. In turn partnership requires our allies in their negotiations to pursue their course within a framework of common objectives. And there are areas of multilateral negotiations in which partnership is most immediately involved.

• In our global posture. Nonpolitical world problems call for cooperation that transcends national rivalries. Here, more comprehensively than in traditional realms, there is a need for shared approaches and shared participation.

The Necessity for Dialogue. The Nixon Doctrine, then, is a means to fulfill our world responsibilities on a sustained basis by evoking both the contributions of our friends and the support of our own people. Its very nature calls for continuing dialogue abroad and at home.

We recognize that the Doctrine, like any philosophic attitude, is not a detailed design. In this case ambiguity is increased since it is given full meaning through a process that involves other countries. When other nations ask how the Doctrine applies to them in technical detail, the question itself recalls the pattern of the previous period when America generally provided technical prescriptions. The response to the question, to be meaningful, partly depends on them, for the Doctrine's full elaboration requires their participation. To attempt to define the new diplomacy completely by ourselves would repeat the now presumptuous instinct of the previous era and violate the very spirit of our new approach....

Western Europe is uniting, and will soon be in a position to forge an identity of its own, distinct from America within the Atlantic world. As nations and peoples we in the West now share both the horizons and the burdens of the most advanced modern societies. This challenges us to develop a partnership engaging the collective energies and wisdom of our fifteen sovereign states.

The expansion of Soviet military power has put NATO's postwar reliance on U.S. strategic nuclear strength into a new perspective. America's guarantee of nuclear defense remains crucial, but it can no longer be the sole basis of Allied deterrence. The constant evolution of strategic conditions—in arms control as well as in weaponry—is of vital concern to our allies as well as to us. This requires us to adapt our Alliance strategy to new conditions and share its burdens....

For years, however, it was believed uncritically that a unified Western Europe would automatically lift burdens from the shoulders of the United States. The truth is not so simple. European unity will also pose problems for American policy, which it would be idle to ignore....

The common interest requires the prosperity of both. This means freer and expanded trade and restraint in protecting special interests. We must negotiate a reduction in our trade restrictions. We must work toward a more equitable worldwide trading system which is based upon most-favored-nation treatment among all industrial nations and in which all of them accord the same tariff preferences to the entire developing world. In short, we must define our self-interest in the widest terms and fix our sights on our fundamental rather than tactical purposes....

U.S. Forces in Europe. The United States faced pressures to withdraw our forces from Western Europe for budgetary reasons, and pressures to keep them there for purely symbolic reasons. All these arguments evaded the crucial question: What defense function do and should our forces in Europe perform?

I decided, despite these pressures, that given a similar approach by our allies, the United States would maintain and improve its forces in Europe and not reduce them without reciprocal action by our adversaries. This decision, which I announced at the December NATO meeting, flowed directly from the analysis we had conducted in the NSC system and reinforced in NATO consultation. It had become clear to me that without undiminished American participation in European defense, neither the Alliance's strategy, nor America's commitment, nor Western cohesion would be credible....

The Major Issues. We must translate our consensus on objectives into specific policies.

Allied efforts toward mutual force reductions in Europe will continue in the coming year. Reducing the military confrontation in Europe is in the common interest of East and West. Our mutual objective should be to create a more stable military balance at lower levels and lower costs.

The problem of defining a fair agreement in precise terms is extremely complex. As in the preparations for SALT, I instructed our Government to develop the analytical building blocks of an agreement and evaluate them in differing combinations, as our contribution to the Alliance's collective deliberations. Our technical analysis is described in the Arms Control chapter of this report.

The USSR has frequently proposed a general Conference on European Security. But such a conference, in the Soviet formulation, would not address the main security issues—the German question, Berlin, mutual force reductions—but only very general themes. We and our allies are prepared to negotiate with the East in any forum. But we see little value in a conference whose agenda would be unlikely to yield progress on concrete issues, but would only deflect our energies to drafting statements and declarations the interpretation of which would inevitably be a continuing source of disagreements. Once a political basis for improving relations is created through specific negotiations already in process, a general conference might build on it to discuss other intra-European issues and forms of cooperation.

Any lasting relaxation of tension in Europe must include progress in resolving the issues related to the division of Germany....

Issues for the Future. Within our evolving Atlantic community, we must deepen and extend our unity:

• To complete the transition from American predominance to a more nearly equal partnership, sharing the responsibilities of leadership.

• To reaffirm our commitment to cooperative economic and political relations across the Atlantic as a Western European entity emerges.

• To intensify our collective attack on the problems of modern society and expand it into a worldwide collaboration.

In the security field, following through on the conclusions of our joint review of Alliance defense, we must:

• Insure that our common strategy is backed up by the force levels and qualitative improvements required to make it credible.

• Share the common defense burden equitably.

For a wider partnership and true security in Europe, continuing our quest for reconciliation between East and West, we must:

• Continue our close Allied consultation as SALT and other East-West negotiations progress.

• Harmonize our individual approaches to insure that they are complementary, and preserve the cohesion and stability which make detente possible.

• Seek to engage our adversaries in negotiations addressing the concrete issues that keep Europe divided.

I have repeatedly emphasized that the Nixon Doctrine is a philosophy of invigorated partnership, not a synonym for American withdrawal. Our relationship with Western Europe proves it.

For more than a century and a half, our most consistent peacetime foreign relations were hemispheric relations. We have shared with our sister republics the experience of gaining and preserving our independence from the Old World. It was only natural that the nations of the New World should see their destinies as intertwined and continue to pay special attention to their ties with each other. Geography and history have bound us together and nurtured a sense of community, now formalized in the treaties and institutions of the inter-American system.

The purposes and practices of our association have changed over time, but its benefits have endured. It has helped to maintain the independence of the hemisphere from outside domination, to facilitate political and economic progress, and to enhance the region's influence in the world community.

Forces of Change. It is nevertheless understandable that tensions should develop. There is great ferment in Latin America and the Caribbean. Modernization brings extensive and frequently unsettling change, accompanied by growing nationalism. Some in the region view the United States—with its disproportionate size and wealth—more as a hindrance and threat than as a source of support.

Thus, when this Administration came into office, we had to reassess our approach. If the inter-American system was to realize the aspirations of its peoples, we would have to shape our role by the realities of the 1970's and tune our view to the perceptions of others....

Issues for the Future. We have only begun. Implementing our new approach will require difficult adjustments, for ourselves and for our partners. Together we must:

• Respect and protect the independence of all members;

• Provide for the peaceful resolution of disputes;

• Make a better life for our peoples; and

• Embrace our diversity in a framework of partnership.

In such an association will the nations of this hemisphere share a stake. There will be unity not so much in common domestic structures as in mutual support for independence and mutual respect for diversity.

Our self-interest requires our creative contributions to the development of such a community, but three sets of problems constrain us:

The need to balance Western Hemisphere interests against other domestic and foreign policy considerations. To reflect this concern in the councils of government, I again urge Congress to establish an office of Under Secretary of State for Western Hemisphere Affairs.

To promote Latin American trade I will:

• Soon submit legislation to implement generalized tariff preferences.

• Assure special attention in trade policies for commodities of particular interest to the region.

• Continue to press for elimination or reduction of non-tariff barriers, especially those which harm the exports of Latin America and other developing areas.

To maintain an equitable share in our new bilateral assistance programs for hemisphere development, I will establish guidelines for the resources to be provided to the region through the new development institutions.

To free the use of bilateral aid we will seek final agreement among industrial countries in 1971 to untie the bulk of development assistance.

The present limitations of inter-American machinery. The United States will seek further reform of inter-American instrumentalities. Two factors limit their current effectiveness—outdated methods and some members' concern for stronger institutions could become devices for U.S. domination. The system will be increasingly tested by the pervasive change and instabilities in the region. Together with our partners, we must resist efforts to weaken our regional system. Together we must provide it with financial support, reshape its institutions, and participate in a spirit of mutual respect.

The forces of nationalism and extremism. The United States must accommodate diversity and seek to maintain the fabric of hemispheric unity. We cannot afford to withdraw out of frustration or allow ourselves to become isolated. We shall be prepared to negotiate pragmatically to prevent or resolve bilateral disputes. And we shall avoid actions which foster or reinforce anti-U.S. nationalism.

The experience of 1970 confirmed the judgment of October, 1969: "Partnership—mutuality—these do not flow naturally. We have to work at them." But the year also signalled that a more balanced relationship is taking root. In a turbulent age, the mandate for our hemispheric policy is to act compassionately, to work cooperatively, and to strengthen the bonds of a maturing partnership.

Indochina

Vietnam

"There are many nations involved in the fighting in Indochina. Tonight, all those nations, except one, announce their readiness to agree to a cease-fire. The time has come for the Government of North Vietnam to join its neighbors in a proposal to quit making war and to start making peace."

Address to the Nation
October 7, 1970

"The allied sweeps into the North Vietnamese and Vietcong base areas along the Cambodia-South Vietnamese border:
• *Will save American and allied lives in the future;*
• *Will assure that the withdrawal of American troops from South Vietnam can proceed on schedule;*
• *Will enable our program of Vietnamization to continue on its current timetable;*
• *Should enhance the prospects for a just peace."*

Report to the Nation
June 30, 1970

These passages concern the two most important events of our Indochina policy during 1970. The first refers to our initiative for a cease-fire-in-place throughout Indochina, the centerpiece of the comprehensive peace proposals that I set forth on October 7. These proposals could end the war rapidly for all participants through negotiations.

The second describes the purposes of the allied operations last spring against enemy bases in Cambodia which helped to assure the progress of Vietnamization and our withdrawal program. These operations were crucial to our effort to reduce our involvement in the war in the absence of negotiations.

The Cambodian operations have borne immediate fruit while our Indochina peace proposals have not yet done so. These two events thus symbolize what has been true in Vietnam since this Administration took office: The South Vietnamese have made great progress in assuming the burdens of the war, a process which is in their hands and ours, but we have made little progress toward a negotiated peace, a process which requires Hanoi's participation.

After two years of the mandate by the American electorate, we can look back with satisfaction on the great distance we have travelled. This is my tenth major report on Indochina to the American people. The overall trend is consistent and unmistakable.... Some urged that we escalate in an attempt to impose a military solution on the battlefield. We ruled out this approach because of the nature of the conflict and the enemy, the costs of such a policy, the risks of a wider war, and the deeply held convictions of many of our people. Increased military pressure could not alone win a struggle that was in part guerrilla war as well as conventional invasion, and included political as well as military aspects. It would have entailed a greatly increased toll in lives, treasure and diplomatic objectives. It would have heightened the prospects of direct intervention by Hanoi's allies. It would have split apart our own society.

Others urged that we liquidate our presence immediately, cut our losses, and leave the South Vietnamese on their own. I have repeatedly explained why I considered this a disastrous path: For the South Vietnamese people, who would have lost their collective political choice and countless individual lives. For other non-Communist countries, especially in Asia, among whom not a single leader recommended such a policy. For the global credibility of the U.S. word. For those Americans who had made such heavy sacrifices. And for the integrity of American society in the post-Vietnam era.

Thus we rejected both of these routes. Yet we knew that we could not continue previous policies which offered no hope for either peace or reduced American involvement.

We chose instead what we considered the most responsible course left to us. We sought above all a rapid negotiated solution to the conflict by progressively defining the terms of a settlement that would accommodate the legitimate interests of both sides. And in the absence of a settlement we sought, through Vietnamization, to shift American responsibilities to the South Vietnamese.

In charting this course we recognized the following realities:

• The way we treated the most painful vestige of the previous era was crucial for a successful transition to a new foreign policy for a new era.

• The other side which had fought for two decades would agree to a negotiated settlement only if the terms were generous, and the battlefield looked less promising than the conference table.

• Progressive turnover of the burden to the Vietnamese themselves, however uncertain, was the only policy available once we had rejected the status quo, escalation and capitulation.

• The support of the American people during the remainder of the conflict required a diminishing U.S. involvement.

• The health of the American society after the conflict called for a solution that would not mock the sacrifices that had been made.

There has been one guiding principle, one irreducible objective, for both our negotiations and Vietnamization. I stated it on May 14, 1969 and consistently since: "We seek the opportunity for the South Vietnamese people to determine their own political future without outside interference...."

Problems For The Future. There are sobering problems still remaining in Vietnam:

• Enemy Capabilities and Intentions. Despite heavy losses, the North Vietnamese have the manpower, the logistical network and the dedication to continue fighting if they wish. Although their main force units have been greatly reduced, they still pose a considerable threat, especially in Military Regions I and II in South Vietnam. Hanoi could instead use its buildup of forces in South Laos and Northeastern Cambodia to step up its pressures against the Cambodian government or to increase its hold on Cambodian territory. In any event, Communist terrorist activities, assassinations, and kidnappings continue to exact a tragic toll from the Vietnamese people.

• The Vietnamization Process. Vietnamization made very encouraging advances during 1970. The fundamental question remains: can the South Vietnamese fully stand on their own against a determined enemy? We—and more importantly the South Vietnamese—are confident that they can. Substantial problems remain, however: improving the leadership of South Vietnamese forces at all levels; enhancing their ability to take on support as well as combat functions; providing assistance to Cambodia and bettering Vietnamese-Cambodian understanding; rooting out the Viet Cong infrastructure in the countryside; assuring political stability in the cities; managing the strains on the Vietnamese economy as we continue to Vietnamize other aspects of the conflict; and moving against corruption which not only poisons the moral atmosphere but also carries potential political impact. This is a formidable agenda, but South Vietnamese accomplishments to date demonstrate their capacity to deal with it.

• The Negotiating Stalemate. Our intensive efforts in 1970 failed to yield progress in the Paris negotiations. We frankly expected that our elaboration of political principles, the appointment of Ambassador Bruce, and the October 7 peace initiative would produce some movement from the other side. We will not give up on negotiations, though the past year indicated that it will be extremely difficult to overcome the enemy's mix of doctrine, calculations and suspicion. There is the additional fact that as our forces decline, the role we can play on many aspects of a settlement is also bound to decline.

The substantial record of achievement in the first two years of this Administration cannot obscure one fundamental fact—the fighting continues.

Laos and Cambodia

"The war in Indochina has been proved to be of one piece; it cannot be cured by treating only one of its areas of outbreak."

Address by the President
October 7, 1970

The Prospects. We do not underestimate the difficulties ahead for Laos and Cambodia. Hanoi has intensified the war on these fronts and its focus is likely to remain there in the coming months.

The Lao government has already demonstrated determination to preserve its independence in the face of overt aggression, diplomatically if possible, militarily if necessary. The Cambodians also have the essential ingredients for success—national unity, maximum self-help and the support of friends. The country's small, unprepared army is gaining both in size and ability, and the spirit of its people continues to inspire all observers. We can expect major testing of Cambodia over the coming months, but we believe that time is on its side.

Our future policy in Laos and Cambodia will follow the lines we have established. We face some very serious problems:

• At the conference table. Even if Hanoi were to negotiate genuinely about Vietnam, difficult issues remain concerning its neighbors: the removal of North Vietnamese and Viet Cong troops, the securing of South Vietnam's borders, and the reestablishment of the Geneva Agreements.

• On the battlefield. Enemy intentions and capabilities in Indochina will pose some hard choices about the deployment of allied troops as we pursue our own withdrawals. While North Vietnamese activities have subsided in South Vietnam, some of their 60,000 troops massed in southern Laos could move into South Vietnam, or into Cambodia or against northern Laos. In Cambodia we can expect sustained enemy thrusts against the government.

• In the United States. We will have the continuing responsibility of explaining the purpose and extent of our activities in Laos and Cambodia. North Vietnamese actions could require high levels of American assistance and air operations in order to further Vietnamization and our withdrawals.

I will continue to do what is necessary to protect American men as they leave Vietnam. Throughout I will keep the American people and the Congress fully informed.

A negotiated settlement for all Indochina remains our highest priority. But if the other side leaves us no choice, we will follow the alternate route to peace—phasing out our involvement while giving the region's friendly countries the time and the means to defend themselves.

East Asia And The Pacific

"Today, as we look to the future of the Pacific, we recognize that whether peace survives in the last third of the century will depend more on what happens in the Pacific than in any other area of the world."

Remarks Upon the Arrival of
Prime Minister Sato of Japan,
November 19, 1969

The home of almost half the population of the earth, second to none in the richness of its human talents and energy, possessing vast material resources, and encompassing the central land mass of the earth, Asia and the Pacific region lie at the heart of the task of creating a stable structure of world peace. Since the Second World War, it is only in this region that developments have impelled America to send her sons to war. Asia and the Pacific includes territories of the seven most populous and the three wealthiest powers, with all that implies for the vital nature of their interests. A Pacific power ourselves, our security and economic interests are inextricably involved with the future of Asia....

In the next decade our Asia policy will be dealing simultaneously with three phases of Asian development. In some countries, there will still be an absolute—though we hope diminishing—need for us to play a central role in helping them meet their security and economic requirements. In others, we will complete the process of adjusting our relationship to the concepts of the Nixon Doctrine. And with all countries, we will be striving to establish a new and stable structure reflecting the renewed vigor of the smaller Asian states, the expanding role of Japan, and the changing interests of the Soviet Union and the Peoples Republic of China. In the past twenty years the American people have sacrificed much, in both blood and treasure, to help set the stage where such a structure can be created in the Pacific region. It is now in sight.

The major elements of the emerging structure are clear. The nations of Asia acting in concert will play the key role. So will the individual policies of Japan, China, the Soviet Union, and the United States. But the relationship of these elements to each other is not yet clear. They will depend largely upon decisions still to be made. I would like to discuss the more salient problems involved, and their implications for American policy....

Active regionalism, then, is one of the new realities of Asia. Its vigor is one of the guarantees of the influence of Asia's smaller states in the future political structure of the region. The strength which combination gives enables them to move toward such a structure with confidence in their stability and security.

Japan

Japan's economic growth is unprecedented. It has made her the third greatest economic power on earth. However, Japanese living standards still rank below those of many other developed countries, and there is a strong feeling in Japan that these standards must be raised—and raised rapidly....

Fortunately, they are not. Both the Japanese and the American Governments regard each other with profound goodwill and mutual respect. Both are determined to show the greatest possible understanding of the interests of the other. The maintenance of that spirit of cooperation and goodwill is not only the goal of our policy toward Japan. It is also the best assurance that the policy will succeed....

The friendly competitive relationship, which properly characterizes this greatest transoceanic commerce in the history of mankind, is not without difficulties. An example is the protracted negotiations over the question of Japan's textile exports to the U.S., but I am confident we can find a solution which will be in our mutural interest....

China

We are prepared to establish a dialogue with Peking. We cannot accept its ideological precepts, or the notion that Communist China must exercise hegemony over Asia. But neither do we wish to impose on China an international position that denies its legitimate national interests.

The evolution of our dialogue with Peking cannot be at the expense of international order or our own commitments. Our attitude is public and clear. We will continue to honor our treaty commitments to the security of our Asian allies. An honorable relationship with Peking cannot be constructed at their expense.

Among these allies is the Republic of China. We have been associated with that government since its inception in 1911 and with particular intimacy when we were World War II allies. These were among the considerations behind the American decision to assist the Government of the Republic of China on Taiwan, with its defense and economic needs....

In that connection, I wish to make it clear that the United States is prepared to see the Peoples Republic of China play a constructive role in the family of nations. The question of its place in the United Nations is not, however, merely a question of whether it should participate. It is also a question of whether Peking should be permitted to dictate to the world the terms of its participation. For a number of years attempts have been made to deprive the Republic of China of its place as a member of the United Nations and its Specialized Agencies. We have opposed these attempts. We will continue to oppose them....

South Asia

American policy toward the great subcontinent of South Asia parallels that toward the East Asia and Pacific region. Our aim is a structure of peace and stability within which the people of this region can develop its great potential and their independent vision of the future. Our policy is to help these nations deal with their own problems, and to bring our activity into a stable balance with that of the other major powers with interests in the area.

In the pursuit of that goal in South Asia, however, both the nature of our interests and the condition of the region permit a sharper focus of our efforts. South Asia's fundamental problems are two: to meet the challenges of economic and political development and to turn the relationship between India and Pakistan from hostility to cooperation....

We have a deep interest in ensuring that the subcontinent does not become a focus of great power conflict. Over the past decade the major countries of South Asia have profoundly changed their relationships with the rest of the world. Pakistan has gradually moved from its position of close association with us to a complex triangular relationship, balancing her contacts with the three great powers with interests in South Asia—China, the USSR, and ourselves. India continues to follow a policy of non-alignment but of a cast significantly changed since the Chinese attack of 1962. These policy changes, by definition, affect the intimacy of our relationship with the countries of South Asia. We have no desire to try to press upon them a closer relationship than their own interests lead them to desire. Our current posture in South Asia, therefore, accords with the restraint implied in the Nixon Doctrine....

We will try to keep our activities in the area in balance with those of the other major powers concerned. The policy of the Soviet Union appears to be aimed at creating a compatible area of stability on its southern borders, and of countering Chinese Communist influence. The Peoples Republic of China, for its part, has made a major effort to build a strong relationship with Pakistan. We will do nothing to harm legitimate Soviet and Chinese interests in the area. We are equally clear, however, that no outside power has a claim to a predominant influence, and that each can serve its own interests and the interests of South Asia best by conducting its activities in the region accordingly.

Africa

"Our stake in the Continent will not rest on today's crisis, on political maneuvering for passing advantage, or on the strategic priority we assign it. Our goal is to help sustain the process by which Africa will gradually realize economic progress to match its aspirations."

U.S. Foreign Policy For the 1970's
Report to the Congress
February 18, 1970

Africa is a continental experiment in nation building. The excitement and enthusiasm of national birth have phased into the more sober period of growth....

Within the framework of African efforts, however, there are three primary needs of the continent to which we can contribute. Africa seeks peace, economic development, and justice; and she seeks our assistance in reaching those goals. It is in our interest to respond as generously as our resources permit....

The Middle East

Vietnam is our most anguishing problem. It is not, however, the most dangerous. That grim distinction must go to the situation in the Middle East with its vastly greater potential for drawing Soviet policy and our own into a collision that could prove uncontrollable.

There are three distinct and serious aspects of the Middle East problem, each by itself difficult enough to resolve. They cannot, however, be treated in isolation. They have become enmeshed, and each tends to exacerbate and make more intractable the others. The Middle East crisis must be recognized as the product of these three dimensions:

• The Arab-Israeli conflict, which for more than twenty years has festered when it has not burned. It is the core problem of the Middle East crisis, and its intensity today is undiminished.

• Intra-Arab differences which focus primarily on whether a negotiated settlement of the Israeli conflict is acceptable or whether force is the only solution. There are also differences over how Arab nations should be governed, which have led more than once to civil conflict. And there are rivalries growing out of disagreement about the relation of Arab states to each other in the quest for unity in the Arab world.

• The conflict between the interests of the Soviet Union and the United States, each of which is now more deeply than ever engaged in the Arab-Israeli conflict. Events surrounding the hostilities in Jordan in September showed how fragile are the barriers to direct great power confrontation in the Middle East....

Issues for the Future. The search for peace—especially an Arab-Israeli settlement—and the quest for a stable U.S.-Soviet relationship that will help preserve the independence and integrity of each nation in this area will remain our top priorities. Our aim is to see an epoch begin in which strong independent nations in this area—in association with each other as they choose—relate freely and constructively with the world outside. The U.S. is prepared to consider new and fresh ways to assist in the development of the region to the benefit of both Arabs and Israelis once a real peace agreement is achieved.

In pursuing those goals, the United States will face these principal issues in the months ahead:

First, if the United States is to play a major role—as we have promised to do—in helping to bring about an Arab-Israeli settlement and provide supplementary guarantees, what should be the nature and extent of our diplomatic involvement? As I pointed

out at the United Nations last October, the primary responsibility for peace rests on the nations of the Middle East. What is the proper relation between the efforts of the international community to encourage a settlement and the responsibility of the negotiating parties themselves?

Second, our bilateral relations with Arab nations are in flux. With some, formal diplomatic relations have been suspended. In others, attitudes toward the U.S. and the West are undergoing reassessment. The changing relationships in the Persian Gulf necessarily raise new issues for American policy. How do we best encourage and assist the constructive forces in the area to build a regional system of stable relationships?

Finally, there is a range of broader worldwide issues that form the background to Middle East politics. Limiting the external supply of arms to the area is one such issue. The U.S.-Soviet military relationship in the Mediterranean area is another. Beyond this, what is our policy toward the broadening commercial association which the European Common Market is establishing with nations in the area? How can we help assure the access of Western Europe and Japan to the supply of oil, and also help assure that the producing states receive fair revenues for their oil?

On some of these issues, our work is already well advanced. With others we are coming to grips for the first time. Our purpose is to resolve them in a way that helps us and every nation involved in the Middle East, including above all the states of the area, to build and strengthen the relationships—at every level—that will hold together the structure of peace.

International Economic Policy

Material well-being is not the only goal of men and nations. But it is one of the bases of a decent life. The tragedy of our time is that there is not enough of it. For many members of the human race it is a matter of survival; for most nations, economic advancement and prosperity are the means of liberating men and societies from the weight of deprivation and allowing them to realize their full dignity and destiny.

Economic advancement will never approach its full potential if pursued solely within national boundaries. The interdependence of national economies in the 1970's gives all people a major stake in the effective functioning of the world economy. Economic relations have thus become centrally important in international affairs. An American policy which retreated from cooperation, or which moved toward increasing the barriers to fair and equitable economic intercourse among nations, would threaten the foundations of the partnerships which are our central foreign policy objective.

The United States remains the largest single national factor in the world economy. We thus have a strong interest in minimizing the impediments to international economic transactions for domestic economic reasons as well as for the foreign policy reasons which are highlighted in this report.

Issues for the Future. There is a full and challenging agenda of international economic problems before us. Our success in dealing with this agenda will have a major impact on our overall foreign policy. Our goals will be to:

• Found our global economic relations on a strong domestic base. International economic policy begins at home.

• Improve the management of our international economic relations. We will look to the new Council on International Economic Policy to integrate our governmental efforts and blend our domestic and foreign economic policies.

• Improve the means by which national economies can adjust to each other in a world of increased economic interdependence. We must work with others to solidify and further improve the world monetary system.

• Help promote the development of lower income countries. We will seek Congressional approval of our new foreign assistance program and apply its principles of partnership with recipients and other donors alike.

• Defend and encourage liberal trade policies abroad and at home. Fresh policies and enlightened partnership with our friends will be required to stem protectionism, solve the problems that feed it, and regain momentum toward a world of freer commerce.

The Soviet Union

In my Inaugural Address, and again at the United Nations last October, I urged the Soviet leaders to join with us in building a new and constructive relationship....

An assessment of U.S.-Soviet relations at this point in my Administration has to be mixed. There have been some encouraging developments and we welcome them. We are engaged in a serious dialogue in SALT. We have both signed the treaty to prohibit nuclear weapons from the seabeds. We have both ratified the treaty on non-proliferation of nuclear weapons. We have entered negotiations on the issue of Berlin. We have taken the first step toward practical cooperation in outer space.

On the other hand, certain Soviet actions in the Middle East, Berlin, and Cuba are not encouraging. Taken against a background of intensive and unrestrained anti-American propaganda, these actions inevitably suggest that intransigence remains a cardinal feature of the Soviet system.

Yet these events may have provided a basis for future progress in our relations. Properly understood, they illustrate the altogether incommensurate risks inherent in a policy of confrontation, and the marginal benefits achievable by it.

Against this background it is an appropriate moment to take stock of our relations, and to weigh the decisions necessary for further progress.

The Soviet leaders will be reviewing their own policies and programs in connection with the 24th Congress of their Party. This report sets forth my own assessment of our relations with the USSR, and the principles by which we propose to govern our relations in the future. I have outlined the factors that make for common interests and suggested an agenda of outstanding opportunities:

• A more stable military relationship for the next decade.
• A peaceful settlement of the Middle East conflict.
• An agreed framework for security in Europe....

Strategic Policy And Forces

Strategic forces, both offensive and defensive, are the backbone of our security.

• They are the primary deterrent to strategic attacks against us or our allies.

• They face an aggressor contemplating less than all-out attacks, with an unacceptable risk of escalation.

• They are essential to the maintenance of a stable political environment within which the threat of aggression or coercion against the U.S. and its allies is minimized.

Our strategic forces must be numerous enough, efficient enough, and deployed in such a way that an aggressor will always know that the sure result of a nuclear attack against us is unacceptable damage from our retaliation. That makes it imperative that our strategic power not be inferior to that of any other state. Thus I am committed to my pledge to keep our strategic forces strong. I am equally committed to seeking a stable strategic relationship with the Soviet Union through negotiations. There is no inconsistency between those goals; they are in fact complementary....

The Doctrine of Strategic Sufficiency. Our policy remains, as I explained last year, to maintain strategic sufficiency. The concept of sufficiency is not based solely on debatable calculations and assumptions regarding possible scenarios of how a war might occur and be conducted. It is in part a political concept, and it involves judgments whether the existing and foreseeable military environment endangers our legitimate interests and aspirations.

Specifically, sufficiency has two meanings. In its narrow military sense, it means enough force to inflict a level of damage on a potential aggressor sufficient to deter him from attacking. Sole reliance on a "launch-on warning" strategy, sometimes suggested by those who would give less weight to the protection of our forces, would force us to live at the edge of a precipice and deny us the flexibility we wish to preserve.

In its broader political sense, sufficiency means the maintenance of forces adequate to prevent us and our allies from being coerced. Thus the relationship between our strategic forces and those of the Soviet Union must be such that our ability and resolve to protect our vital security interests will not be underestimated. I must not be—and my successors must not be—limited to the indiscriminate mass destruction of enemy civilians as the sole possible response to challenges. This is especially so when that response involves the likelihood of triggering nuclear attacks on our own population. It would be inconsistent with the political meaning of sufficiency to base our force planning solely on some finite—and theoretical—capacity to inflict casualties presumed to be unacceptable to the other side....

The mix of forces. For several years we have maintained three types of strategic forces—land-based ICBMs, bombers, and submarine-launched missiles. Each is capable of inflicting a high level of damage in response to a nuclear first strike. Taken together they have an unquestioned capability of inflicting an unacceptable level of damage. This concept takes advantage of the unique characteristics of each delivery system. It provides insurance against surprise enemy technological breakthroughs or unforeseen operational failures and complicates the task of planning attacks on us. It complicates even more the longer range planning of the levels and composition of the opposing forces. It the effectiveness and survivability of one element were eroded, the Soviet Union could choose to concentrate its resources on eroding the effectiveness and survivability of the others. This would confront us with serious new decisions and we will therefore continue to review our forces in the light of changing threats and technology to ensure that we have the best possible mix to meet the requirements of sufficiency....

General Purpose Forces

The change in the strategic situation in recent years profoundly enhances the importance of our general purpose forces. The Soviet Union's build-up alters the character of the strategic threat. China also is developing strategic forces, though her current capabilities are still quite limited.

With this shift in strategic realities, our potential adversaries may be tempted by the use or the threat of force below what they consider the level of general nuclear war. General purpose forces, therefore, now play a larger role in deterring attacks than at any time since the nuclear era began....

Agenda for the Future. While maintaining a realistic deterrent, we will further adjust our general purpose forces in response to changing circumstances. Our attention, for example, will be focused on:

• Manpower. Our ultimate goal is to meet our military manpower requirements, without resort to the draft. In the meantime, we are working on reform of the selective service system. We have adopted a new method of selection to ensure a more equitable spreading of the burden of military service, and reduce to a minimum the uncertainties associated with the draft. Draft calls have been substantially reduced. As Vietamization progresses, and our program of upgrading the rewards of the career service takes effect, we hope to make further reductions.

• NATO. We and our NATO Allies have agreed to improve the quality of alliance forces. In 1971, we will move to concrete programs for improving NATO's conventional capabilities, and insuring modern and sufficient strategic and theater nuclear forces.

• Asia. We will, with our allies, determine how best to help them improve their defensive capabilities. This will enable us to deal with the allocation of resources between U.S. forces and increased assistance in the area.

• Defense Review. We have defined new strategic doctrines for our nuclear forces and for our general purpose forces. But we must continue to refine our assessments of the implications of our strategies for our force composition. This will be a continuing task of this Administration.

We will also be taking measures to increase the efficiency and effectiveness of our defense establishment. The Secretary of Defense is reviewing the proposals of the Blue Ribbon Defense Panel on the organization and management of the Department of Defense. He has implemented many of them, and is preparing his recommendations to me on others. These matters will be covered fully in the Secretary's Defense Report to the Congress.

Security Assistance

This year I will present to the Congress the design of a new International Security Assistance Program. It will be reorganized to gear it more effectively to the purposes of the Nixon Doctrine:

• It will clearly separate out our security assistance from other forms of assistance to enhance the integrity and effectiveness of each.

• It will pull together all types of security assistance into one coherent program. This will make it possible to coordinate them more efficiently and to exercise stronger policy guidance and program direction.

• It will place increasing emphasis on fostering the self-reliance of those with whom we are engaged in a cooperative effort. We will encourage them, and give them the technical assistance needed, to determine their own requirements and to make the hard decisions on resource allocation which a meaningful security posture demands.

This is a program for the 1970's, building on partnership in the security sphere and responding to new conditions and the lessons of recent history. We look to the day when our friends and allies are free from threats to their security and able to concentrate their energies and resources—and our assistance—on the constructive tasks of economic and social development.

Arms Control

The World has no more urgent interest than reducing the danger of war, and above all, nuclear war. This creates responsibilities for all nations, but particularly for the nuclear superpowers....

Strategic Arms Limitation Talks (SALT). The most important area in which progress is yet to be made is the limitation of strategic arms. Perhaps for the first time, the evolving strategic balance allows a Soviet-American agreement which yields no unilateral advantages. The fact we have begun to discuss strategic arms with the USSR is in itself important. Agreement in such a vital area could create a new commitment to stability and influence attitudes toward other issues....

Mutual and Balanced Force Reductions in Europe. Our preliminary conclusions suggest that the pattern of the SALT negotiations might be valid as an approach to discussions of mutual force reductions in Europe. Rather than exchanging concrete proposals at the outset we could first explore major substantive issues and their relation to specific problems. Within this common framework we could move to more detailed discussion of individual issues. This building block approach could resolve the complex technical issues and lead to an agreement.

The United Nations

International cooperation has always been both a human dream and a human necessity. This is more true in our time than it has ever been before.

The dream is important. Mankind aspires to lasting peace, and since its founding twenty-five years ago, the United Nations has symbolized this profound wish. But while the realization of the dream remains elusive, the necessity of international cooperation for other purposes has become imperative. For the march of technology has pressed upon the world an increasing number of exigent problems which can only be solved by collaboration among governments. As a result, the United Nations' role in facilitating international cooperation has taken on a new importance....

The Need for Restraint. Because the stresses of the Cold War have limited the ability of the Security Council to play an energetic role in alleviating political crises and preserving the peace, much of the political agenda at the UN has flowed toward the General Assembly. But the operations of the Assembly have shortcomings related to the strains of a rapid growth in membership and demands for actions beyond the capacities of the United Nations....

The UN does in fact mirror much of the world's social turmoil, national conflicts, and ideological differences. It has to its credit substantial accomplishments in peacekeeping, in social and economic betterment, and in drafting principles of international law. It will be strengthened to the extent that its members forswear unrealistic rhetoric and concentrate on using the UN constructively to settle rather than publicize disputes. The UN must not become the forum where differences are exacerbated by intemperate advocacy.

Global Challenges. The United Nations was, and is, a child of the mid-Twentieth Century. It stemmed from the perception that modern problems required a new pattern of interchange to supplement the older processes of diplomacy. Human institutions evolve in response to felt needs, and some of our most serious international needs have only recently become evident. For mankind now shares a number of new and urgent problems, which stem from the contrast between man's progress in the technological arts and his shortcomings in achieving a stable organization for international cooperation. The world has grown small, and we live increasingly in what has been described as a "global village".

The world now has community problems such as the population explosion, the uses of the oceans and seabeds, maintenance of a healthy natural environment, control of drug abuse, deterrence of airplane hijackings, and cooperation in the use of outer space....

The Future. In the 1970s, the United Nations faces both a challenge and an opportunity. For the member states there is a challenge to prove themselves capable of using the UN framework to meet the common needs of the international community. For the UN itself, there is an opportunity to mold itself into the efficient instrument for international cooperation which the times require.

The United States will try to meet the challenge, and to help the UN seize its opportunity.

Global Challenges—The New Dimension

In Foreign Affairs

"Across this planet let us attack the ills that threaten peace. "In the untapped oceans of water and space, let us harvest in peace."

Address to the United Nations
General Assembly
October 23, 1970

It was a poet who expressed the profound political truth that the world has become a frail spaceship and that the people of the earth are its passengers. The technology which inspired that concept has also brought with it a degree of global interdependence which differs from the past, not only in degree but in kind.

For our progress mocks us. The more we have succeeded in controlling our environment, the more our environment needs to be controlled. The more means we have devised to improve the qualify of human life, the more that quality of life needs protection from the means we have devised.

Along with its vast contribution to our well-being, technology has given us the common capability to pollute the earth's oceans and air. It has increased the incentives for nations to assert, and attempt to enforce, territorial claims to the oceans so immoderate as to endanger the ancient right of freedom of the seas. It has brought the ability to tap—or to ravage—the resources of the sea and the ocean floor, to the vast benefit—or to the huge harm—of mankind.

These are examples of problems in which every country had a deep national interest, but which, as a practical matter, are simply not subject to satisfactory resolution by national means. They are matters on which the nations of the world must subsume their narrower interests in a broad and generous concept of the world interest. For without such an approach, we will not find the solutions which both the world interest and the national interests require. Without such an approach, we cannot fully harness the capacity of technology to meet these global challenges.

Thus there has come into being a new dimension in the foreign policy of the United States, not as a matter of choice and deliberate action on our part but as a reflection of the demanding realities of the world in which we live. Foreign policy has, of course, always aimed at serving the nation's security and well-being. What is new is the fact that we now face an increasing range of problems which are central to our national well-being, but which are, be definition, global problems, or problems which can only be dealt with effectively on a global scale.

In addressing these problems a narrow calculation of national interests is inadequate. For viewed from that perspective, the nations of the world do sometimes have conflicting interests of a real and substantial nature. Of greater import, however, is our shared and transcendent interest in the livability of our common home, the earth. To these problems, and the opportunities they present, that interest must be our guide and the guide of others. The nurturing of that interest has now become a prime task of American leadership.

During the past year, this new dimension of our international activity has been evident at the United Nations, in a number of its associated organizations, in various regional activities, and through frequent bilateral contacts with many nations around the world. It is encouraging that the international community is showing an increasing willingness to grapple with these problems. But the fact remains that the time available for finding a solution to many of them is perilously short. I want to review our attitude toward some of the more salient issues, and the steps that are being taken by the international community to meet those issues.

The Environment. No nation can keep its pollution to itself. Wastes discharged into the air and water in fact befoul a common resource. Restraint on the part of individual states, however laudable and necessary, is inadequate to the problem, for, in the absence of international action competitive economic pressures will severely limit national abilities to require the costly measures needed to protect the environment. A broad international approach is therefore necessary....

The Oceans. The oceans cover two-thirds of the earth. Man's use of this common asset is now undergoing a transformation. New techniques exist or are being developed which will lead to a vastly increased exploitation of the mineral and living resources of the oceans, including the mineral riches of the world's seabeds.

It is, frankly, not yet clear whether this fact will prove a boon to mankind. There is at present, no authority, international or otherwise, which can ensure the orderly and rational exploitation of these resources. That fact, plus the vast potential wealth at stake, gives cause for deep concern. There is a clear world interest in this matter, and there is a clear danger that, unless it is asserted in time, it may be lost in the confusion of unbridled commercial and national ambitions....

Population Control. One of the greatest threats to the well-being of mankind is the burden of excessive population growth. If things continue as they are, this planet, which at the beginning of the century supported about 1.6 billion lives, and which now supports—often inadequately—some 3.7 billion lives, will be called upon to sustain about 7.5 billion human beings by the end of this century. Already, there are many areas of the world where population growth makes improvements in standards of living intolerably slow, if not impossible. And this is most often true where living standards are lowest. The world is already experiencing a population explosion of unprecedented dimensions. We are, in short, in a rush toward a Malthusian nightmare. That surely is not our destiny....

International Cooperation Against Crime. The need for international cooperation to solve certain types of criminal problems has become increasingly clear in recent years. The explosion in international travel and intercourse has had the unintended effect of greatly reducing the ability of national societies alone to control such old criminal activity as the illegal narcotics traffic, and such new criminal forms as hijacking and terrorists attacks on diplomats.

Assisting the Victims of Disaster. Natural and man-made disasters continue to afflict mankind, and to call forth from the peoples of the world a generous and noble response. This compulsion to help when tragedy befalls others is evidence of the sense of common humanity which binds us together and which, in times of stress and great need, transcends the political and other issues which divide mankind....

Modern technology has greatly affected both the world's desire and ability to provide disaster assistance. Modern communications are such that disasters of scale are known around the world almost immediately, and in a form which powerfully arouses the instinct to help. And modern transportation is such that aid can be effectively brought to bear in a very short period of time.

Protection of Endangered Species. It is hardly tolerable that mankind should permit, much less cause, the extinction of fish and wildlife species. Yet, for a number of species, that is the stark prospect. For two reasons, international cooperation is required to prevent it. First, these creatures move without respect to national boundaries and cannot, therefore, be completely protected through national action. Second, the economic demand in other countries for wildlife species, both living animals and their products, has often nullified the protective efforts of individual nations of origin....

Science and Technology. Science and technology are central to the problems of national defense, to the vigor of our own and the world economy, and to the improvement of the quality of life on this planet. They are basic tools in the effort to narrow the gap between the richer and the poorer nations.

Basic research is the source of the knowledge from which scientific and technological benefits flow to mankind. Research is one of mankind's great adventures. Its rules are as unequivocal and uncompromising as the laws of nature. Research is a unique and universally understood medium of discourse among those who practice it....

Space is already a matter of broad international cooperation. We have some 250 agreements with 74 countries covering space cooperations.

And space has already been put to the service of man in the new global communications systems and in weather monitoring systems. But this is only a beginning. Space is the only area of which it can literally be said that the potential for cooperation is infinite....

A New Step in Nuclear Energy Cooperation. In the field of peaceful nuclear energy, over the years there has developed a broad network of international relationships. This began with research cooperation between governments and now includes exchanges of information, fuel supply contracts and support of the International Atomic Energy Agency as well as sales of United States products and services....

An International Center for Systems Analysis. Our National Academy for Sciences is also actively working with the Soviet Union and other countries to establish a Center for the application of systems analysis techniques to the complex problems of advanced societies. This international, non-governmental institution, would initially bring together scholars from some eight nations of East and West to apply the most sophisticated analytical tools available to the major problems of contemporary civilization.

Better Use of Technology in Foreign Assistance Activities. No more severe task faces the developed world than facilitating the economic and social progress of the less developed nations. The role of science and technology can be crucial to success, and we need to organize our effort in this field more effectively.

My proposals to the Congress to reorganize our foreign assistance programs will, therefore, reflect the higher priority we intend to give to cooperation with the developing countries in the transfer and application of technology. It will include legislation to permit the establishment of machinery specifically designed to work with recipient countries on their own needs for research, and technological training and development.

The problems—and the opportunities—created by science and technology dominate an increasing share of our international activity. The problems we can no longer ignore, and can solve only through international cooperation. The opportunities we are determined not to miss, and can realize only through international cooperation. Taken together, these challenges constitute the new dimension of our foreign policy and of international life. The greatest importance attaches to our performance in this new dimension, for upon it rests much of the hope for a better future.

The National Security Council System

Upon my inauguration, I reestablished the National Security Council as the principal forum for consideration of foreign policy issues and created a system of supporting committees to serve it. Chaired by the President and comprising the Vice President, the Secretaries of State and Defense, the Director of the Office of Emergency Preparedness and others at my invitation, the Council provides a focus at the highest level of our government for full and frank discussions of national security issues. Of course, I also consult the Secretaries of State and Defense and other senior advisors individually to obtain their views on national security issues.

Too often in the past our foreign policy machinery was the captive of events. Day-to-day tactical considerations occupied our time and determined our actions. Policy emerged from a narrow rather than conceptual perspective.

The Process. Creativity, systematic planning, and thorough analysis are given special emphasis. It is every concerned agency's obligation to contribute information and analysis and to present and argue its position. Only in this way can I be certain that the full range of views and reasonable options has been explored.

The system helps us to bring together all the knowledge available and to bring to bear the best analytical thought of which we are capable:

• Analysis and decision must rest on the broadest possible factual base. There must be a common appreciation of the facts and of their relevance.

• Coherent policy needs a conceptual framework. Where do we want to go in the long run? What are our purposes? Our analysis must bring out all reasonable interpretations of the facts, and treat the facts in the framework of our longer-range trends and objectives.

• I have made sure that my choice is not limited to ratifying or rejecting bureaucratic compromises which submerge differences to accommodate varying interests within the govern-

ment. I insist that the facts, issues, and conceptual framework for decision be presented together with alternative courses of action, their pros and cons, and costs and consequences....

Conclusion

Our new course of partnership in the world can only be steered with the sustained understanding of the American people.

With our allies and friends, first of all, we are deepening a partnership that provides the dignity and the stimulus of an increased role.

To those who have been our adversaries, we offer a partnership on the paramount world interest—to rid the earth of the scourge of war.

For all nations we visualize a partnership that will make this planet a better place to live.

And for the American people, we seek a partnership of purpose.

Just as America will listen more to others abroad, so must Americans listen more to each other at home. We have a responsiblity to debate the means of achieving our foreign policy goals. But these turbulent years have taught us not so much that we must know the right answers, but that we should ask the right questions. We, therefore, have an even greater responsibility to discuss the goals themselves and, together, understand the new character of America's involvement in the world.

This partnership at home must include the advice and support of the Congress. Charged with constitutional responsibilities in foreign policy, the Congress can give perspective to the national debate and serve as a bridge between the Executive and the people.

Our new direction abroad and our new approach at home are parts of a whole. Both rest on the belief that decisions are made better when they are made by those most directly concerned. At home as well as abroad, we seek to distribute responsiblities more widely, so that new partnerships flourish in which all contribute their ideas as well as their energies.

The essence of any kind of partnership is mutual respect.

We will build that mutual respect with our friends, without dominating them or abandoning them.

We will strive for that mutual respect with our adversaries, without compromising our principles or weakening our resolve.

And we will dedicate ourselves to that mutual respect among our own people, without stifling dissent or losing our capacity for decisive action.

In America this calls for tolerance that leads to understanding, not for sentimentality that clouds perceptions. It means as well that compassion is a more profound guide than righteousness. Leaders and the public alike must pursue their goals with a sense of interdependence.

Such qualities will enable us to bring Americans together and, in so doing, help to bring the world together.

REVENUE FOR CRIME-FIGHTING

Following is the text, as made available by the White House, of President Nixon's March 2 message to Congress urging the sharing of revenues for purposes of fighting crime.

TO THE CONGRESS OF THE UNITED STATES:

Many of our State and local governments today are in serious financial difficulty. This has not diminished the growing demands on their financial resources, however: their needs continue, their populations increase and their social problems multiply. All these circumstances point to the need for outside assistance, and the Federal Government has tried to provide such assistance. But in doing so, it has frequently added to, rather than reduced, State burdens.

In the past decade, the Federal Government has turned increasingly to a complex system of grants for providing financial assistance to State and local governments. Today Federal aid programs account for one-fifth of State and local revenues. In theory this income should reduce the pressure on State and local budgets and it should free financial resources at those levels for use at those levels. In practice the reverse is commonly the case.

To qualify for Federal grants, States and local government units are frequently required to match Federal funding, often seriously restricting flexibility in the use of State and local resources. Recipients are placed in the position of having to accept Federal money with its concomitant restrictions on State funds, or receive no Federal money at all. Thus, we may find States and local governing units pursuing projects which may be of low priority to them simply because money for these projects is available, but the matching requirements for such grants may have to be met at the expense of programs of higher priority to the community.

In other cases, State and local agencies are required to maintain their financial commitment to a project in order to qualify for Federal grants to that project. The result, again, is diminished flexibility in the use of financial resources at the State and local levels.

Equally burdensome are project-by-project requirements for prior Federal approval of grants. These requirements often delay the availability of much needed funds, generate Federal, as well as State and local, bureaucratic delay, and inject needless confusion into the Federal, State and local relationship. Rigidity in adhering to exact requirements is rewarded, and new or imaginative ideas are frequently lost because they fail to fit exact bureaucratic guidelines.

Finally, Federal grants have proliferated to such a degree that simply discovering their availability is a bureaucratic chore all in itself. The processes of application frequently contribute to the difficulty, and delay the process, of obtaining grants to a degree which further aggravates the problem the money is designed to assuage. And, because the Federal Government, with all the best intentions, cannot really know the needs of the States and local governing units as well as the people who govern at those levels, these grants frequently cannot be aimed with real precision at the needs which exist at those levels.

Certain of these difficulties are most prevalent in the narrowly-defined "categorical grants," and therefore I have long supported the concept of block grants which permit State and local governing units to receive financial assistance on the basis of what *they* know is necessary. This eliminates many of the problems of the categorical grants. The block grant does, however, retain other shortcomings: requirements for matching of effort, maintenance of effort, and prior approval by the Federal Government. I believe the time has come to further reform our system of providing financial assistance, and to streamline, where we can, the system of grant aid by adopting a system of Special Revenue Sharing which provides the benefits of Federal assistance without the burdens of assistance built into the present grant programs.

The purposes of 130 of our narrowly based categorical grant programs now in existence can be reduced to six broad areas of national concern. In a series of special messages, of which this is the first, I will propose that funds be made available to States and localities to assist them in meeting their problems in the areas of law enforcement, manpower training, urban development, transportation, rural development and education, by converting these grants to Special Revenue Sharing. Funds for assistance in these areas, as I proposed in my State of the Union message, will include more than $10 billion of the money allocated for the narrow-purpose grants plus $1 billion of new funds. Special Revenue Sharing would require no matching funds, no maintenance of effort, no prior project approval and, within the six broad areas, recipients would have the authority to spend these funds on programs which are of the highest priority to them.

I am proposing today legislation for the first of these six Special Revenue Sharing programs. This legislation is directed to matters of primary concern in our national life: the control of crime and the improvement of this nation's system of criminal justice. Much has been accomplished in combatting these problems, but much remains to be accomplished.

Part of the marked progress of the past two years can be attributed to the Law Enforcement Assistance Administration (LEAA). The LEAA was created by the Omnibus Crime Control and Safe Streets Act of 1968 to aid State and local law enforcement agencies in funding programs for police, courts, corrections, control of organized crime, civil disorders, and other related crime problems. This is a national problem—but the basic responsibilities for solving this problem rest at the State and local level and the LEAA provides for Federal assistance to these levels of government.

This program is based on the assumption that those who bear responsibility at the State and local level are best qualified to identify their enforcement problems, and to set the priorities and develop the means to solve these problems. It is designed particularly to encourage and provide for experimentation and innovation in the search for more effective solutions to the crime problem. With LEAA assistance each State has developed, in partnership with local governments, a comprehensive statewide approach to improving law enforcement and reducing crime. Each State is receiving funds under this program, and is moving to execute its plans.

The program is effective. In the District of Columbia, LEAA assistance has played a role in achieving encouraging reductions in various categories of crime. With LEAA assistance, Oakland, California, has launched a unique effort against street crime using citizen-police cooperation. A feature of this effort has been more than thirty bilingual "citizen forums" in high-crime areas.

LEAA has launched the first major Federal research and development program in criminal justice. It has initiated the first nationwide computerized information system—Project SEARCH, which will help provide instant interstate information on offenders. It has funded the first national survey of crime victims, and the first national jail survey. In the six New England States a joint program is under way to collect and analyze intelligence information and plan a coordinated effort against organized crime in that area. This was funded by LEAA. LEAA assistance to the States for corrections has increased from $3 million in fiscal 1969 to over $68 million in fiscal 1970. This final year the total exceeds $100 million. In another area LEAA has initiated the first major Federal program to enable law enforcement and criminal justice personnel to continue their educations. More than nine hundred colleges are involved in this program.

I think it is clear that LEAA has assumed a vital and effective role in this area of Federal, State and local concern. But, I believe it can and must be made more effective. Therefore, I am proposing amendments to the Law Enforcement Assistance legislation which I believe would strengthen and increase its effectiveness in the war on crime by increasing both the resources of State and local enforcement and judicial agencies, as well as their freedom to use the resources at their disposal.

Matching Funds

I propose that the requirement for matching funds be eliminated from LEAA grants being converted to Special Revenue Sharing.

Maintenance of Effort

I propose that requirements for maintenance of effort be eliminated as a condition for receiving Special Revenue Sharing payments.

Prior Project Approval

I am recommending that State planning agencies continue to prepare comprehensive statewide law enforcement plans. These will continue to be submitted to LEAA for review and evaluation, to assist LEAA in its role of counseling State and local government agencies. I am proposing, however, that requirements for prior approval of these plans by LEAA be eliminated. Prior approval would not be required to receive Special Revenue Sharing funds.

Coverage

Special Revenue Sharing would replace the present LEAA action grants and their payment would be automatic. Special Revenue Sharing for law enforcement for the first full year would be $500 million. Fifteen percent of this would be in grants which can be awarded at the discretion of LEAA, and the remainder in grants awarded automatically on the basis of population.

Civil Rights

I urge that the protection from discrimination now provided minorities under Title VI of the Civil Rights Act of 1964 be expressly extended to Special Revenue Sharing.

Conclusion

The changes provided in the LEAA legislation are not extensive. But I believe they will have a profound effect. They are designed to improve a good program which already has many of the elements we seek to obtain in other programs. Special Revenue Sharing will permit the needed improvements. And by further freeing State and local governments, both from the restrictions of onerous Federal control, and from the administrative and fiscal restrictions which accompany or result from much of our Federal assistance, we can release the creative capacities of each level of government in these areas of national concern.

RICHARD NIXON

TEXT OF MANPOWER MESSAGE

Following is the text, as made available by the White House, of President Nixon's March 4 message to Congress asking revenue for manpower programs.

TO THE CONGRESS OF THE UNITED STATES:

Like the 1770s, which produced an American Revolution, the 1970s can be a decade of revolutionary change. We have an opportunity to build on the strengths of the federal system, and by so doing to forge a strong new partnership in which each level of government does what it does best, and in which each function of government is lodged at that level at which it can best be performed.

One of the keys to this reform is Revenue Sharing—General and Special, $16 billion in all.

Four weeks ago I asked the Congress to enact a $5 billion General Revenue Sharing program. It was essentially a proposal to take some of the tax dollars the Federal Government raises and use them as a transfusion for our hard-pressed States, counties and cities—to be spent as the people in each jurisdiction agree with their own elected officials makes the best sense.

Two days ago in my message on Law Enforcement Assistance, I presented to the Congress the first of six proposals that will account for a total of $11 billion in Special Revenue Sharing programs. Unlike General Revenue Sharing, which is new money without project restrictions, Special Revenue Sharing consists of $10 billion now going into present Federal grant programs, plus $1 billion in new funds, rescued from a thicket of narrow categories and earmarked for spending in six broad areas of national concern.

Today I am proposing legislation in the second major area of Special Revenue Sharing—Manpower. The Manpower Revenue Sharing Act of 1971 would:

• Provide $2 billion during the first full year of its operation—$4 for every $3 now being spent—to help move men and women into productive employment.
• Unify into one the many programs under which Federal manpower money is now channeled to State and local governments.
• Free city, county, and State budgets from matching and maintenance-of-effort encumbrances, and officials of those governments from intricate administrative procedures.
• Vest the power to shape local manpower assistance efforts in governments close to the people they assist.

Manpower Assistance: In Whose Hands?

Labor, like other economic resources, is allocated by the market under our system. But as the American economy has grown increasingly complex and technological, we have seen that the job market has imperfections—frictions, lags, slack in the gears—whose costs in unemployment, underemployment and inadequate incomes must be reduced. A degree of cautious intervention in the market process over the long term is clearly a human imperative and a matter of national interest—as the Congress recognized nine years ago this month with a substantial commitment of Federal money and attention under the Manpower Development and Training Act of 1962. That Act, and the Economic Opportunity Act of 1964, currently include more than a dozen categorical grant programs in the manpower field, funded in Fiscal 1971 at $1.5 billion.

While these efforts proceed from the best of intentions, they are overcentralized, bureaucratic, remote from the people they mean to serve, overguidelined, and far less effective than they might be in helping the unskilled and the disadvantaged. The reason: by and large, their direction does not belong in Federal hands.

Designing a manpower program that can best deliver its intended services starts with the recognition, one, that the "job market" is really thousands of interacting but separate markets spread all over the economic and geographic map of the United States, and two, that the "labor force" is actually 87 million individual men and women with a wide diversity of training needs. Under the circumstances it makes little sense for Washington to dominate decisions on manpower assistance—not when 50 States and thousands of local government units, each in touch with its own territory and close to its own people, stand ready to apply their know-how if Washington will only help pay the bills.

Penalizing Diversity and Subsidizing Bureaucracy

I recognize that there are many Federal purposes for which categorical grants are still the best available approach. My Special Revenue Sharing proposals are targeted specifically at those program areas in which I believe the case for local decision is overriding.

Manpower is an area in which the need to adapt to diverse and changing local conditions is especially compelling, and in which the advantages of local control are correspondingly great.

When nationwide categorical programs are applied to diverse job markets, some cities and States may find their needs met nicely—but many others, inevitably, will come off second best. They will, in effect, be penalized for differing from the models according to which Federal programs are designed. They find themselves forced into funding projects of low local priority ahead of those of higher priorities simply because Federal program inflexibilities mean funding the available ones or none at all. Those who suffer as a result are not governmental units in the abstract but real people with bills to pay and families to feed. The injury is compounded when local funds, scarce at best, must be set aside to match—in effect, to buy into—the Federal money, if the money is not to be lost.

In one respect only do all States and cities fare equally under a system of narrow categorical grants: officials of all must, as a matter of survival, learn their way through a bureaucratic jungle.

For example:

• Merely to describe one State's Federal manpower programs in 1970 required a jargon-heavy tome 1185 pages long.

• Last fall a businessmen's group attempting to list all the public manpower programs in New York City gave up after 44 entries, commenting that "attempting to unravel the intricate mass of detailed data on the individual programs has been an exhausting undertaking."

• Harried vocational school administrators must cope with a 930-page Labor Department manual and hundreds of pages more of Federal standards and conditions, to meet the requirements of a single program—MDTA institutional training.

In light of all this, Americans' discontent with government is no mystery. The Federal money put to low-priority uses, the captive local matching money, the waste of time by local officials in threading their way through Byzantine administrative tangles—all are unfair: to a Nation that deserves a healthy employment market, to people out of work who deserve effective job assistance, and to taxpayers who deserve a hundred cents worth of public benefits on every dollar government takes from them.

To Make Good On A Good Idea

The active Federal commitment to manpower training and development was a good idea in 1962, when Congress in enacting MDTA expressed concern that "the problem of assuring sufficient employment opportunities will be compounded by the extraordinarily rapid growth of the labor force in the next decade." It is an even better idea today, with the labor force already enlarged by 19 percent in the nine years since, and with technological change still rapid. But one of the great lessons of the dramatic Federal Government growth in the 1960s is that even a good idea like this can fall short of its promise if the way in which it is carried out runs against the grain of the Federal system. By converting the Nation's manpower programs from categorical grants to Special Revenue Shring, we can play to the strengths of the Federal partnership, teaming Federal dollars with State and local decision-making. This is the purpose of the Manpower Revenue Sharing Act of 1971 which I am proposing today.

Where The Money Goes

I have proposed that $2 billion be provided for the first full year of the Manpower Revenue Sharing Act, which would replace the Manpower Development and Training Act and manpower provisions of the Economic Opportunity Act on January 1, 1972. This represents an increase of almost one-third over current levels of funding for the affected categorical grants. Since the need for job training and other manpower assistance expands as the Nation grows, the Act would set no ceiling on future appropriations.

Of this amount provided, 85 percent would be distributed to the States and to cities and counties with a population of 100,000 or more. Since jobs and workers cross city and county lines, bonus funds within the formula distribution would be awarded to consortia of local governments which embrace entire major labor market areas. Governments which can agree to act in concert in smaller urban areas would also qualify for funds. The remaining 15 percent would be made available to the Secretary of Labor to fund special activities.

The shared revenues would be allocated by statutory formula. Each State or local area's share would be determined by its proportionate number of workers, unemployed persons and low income adults.

What Are Manpower Programs?

Manpower programs develop job skills. They help the unemployed and underemployed, particularly welfare recipients and other disadvantaged persons, make the transition to better jobs, better pay and higher skill levels.

An effective program focuses on individual needs and available jobs. It embraces a wide range of manpower activities, providing combinations of services to move people toward their employment goals. Authorized manpower activities include:

• Recruitment, counseling, testing, placement, and follow-up services.

• Classroom instruction in both remedial education and occupational skills.

• Training on the job with both public and private employers, aided by manpower subsidies.

• Job opportunities, including work experience and short-term employment for special age groups and the temporary unemployed, and transitional public service employment at all levels of government.

• Ancillary services like child care assistance, relocation assistance, and minor health services.

Decisions on the mix and specifics of State and local activities under this broad umbrella would be up to each government. However, payments and allowances for individuals would be limited to two consecutive years, in recognition of the fact that these manpower programs are designed not to provide long-term public support but rather to assist job seekers in making the transition to permanent or better jobs.

New Flexibility And Accountability

In keeping with the principles of Special Revenue Sharing, State and local governments would be given wide discretion in determing how the funds provided should be used.

This manpower program, unlike its predecessors, would have no exhaustive volumes of Federal standards to be met. There would be no towering piles of Federal program applications to complete and no frustrating delays at the Federal level. State and local money now tied down by matching requirements and maintenance of effort would be freed for spending elsewhere as community priorities might dictate.

Giving State and local officials full power to spend Federal manpower funds would sharply increase the citizen's ability to influence how the funds are spent. It would make government more responsive to legitimate demands for quality services.

To enhance public accountability for manpower programs, State and local governments would be required to publish a statement of program objectives and projected uses of funds each year, prior to receiving their shared revenues. These statements would include information on the area's economic and labor market conditions; targeted client groups; proposed activities; wages, allowances and other benefits; manpower agencies involved; and the positions and salaries of the program's administrators. In addition, the statements would review the previous year's programs.

Both State and local governments would be required to publish comments about each other's program statements. In particular they would be responsible for coordinating and making full use of all other State and local manpower activities available. After full public exposure and discussion they would be required to publish their final program statements for the coming year.

To increase the information available to the public, the Labor Department would publish evaluations of program effectiveness.

The people would have the hard facts needed to hold their public officials directly and readily accountable for the manner in which manpower programs are administered.

Programs And Purposes

Manpower Revenue Sharing is a partnership. Washington puts up the purse and sets out the broad purposes of authorized spending, while program decisions are turned over to the state-houses, county governments and city halls. My proposal neither mandates nor terminates any programs. It provides that the continuation, expansion or modification of each program would be determined, as it ought to be, by the test of performance alone—and determined by the State or community which the program serves. Programs that have proved themselves in practice could be continued with the use of the Federal funds provided. Indeed many current categorical programs probably would continue and expand in response to local needs once arbitrary Federal restrictions were removed. On the other hand, programs whose past claims of effectiveness are not justified by the record deserve to be replaced by others more responsive to community needs. Vesting the program authority in governments close to the people will make it harder for programs to coast along on their momentum from year to year, and easier to tailor manpower assistance to on-the-scene realities.

The Federal Role

The special activities financed by the 15 percent of manpower funds retained for use by the Secretary of Labor would include support and assistance for State and local programs through staff training and technical aid, through research, and through experimental and demonstration programs to develop new manpower techniques.

The Department of Labor would also maintain a comprehensive system of labor market information and computerized job banks to facilitate exchange of information among different areas. It would monitor State and local programs for fiscal accountability and compile comparative data on all programs to help the Congress and the public assess their effectiveness.

In addition, the Labor Department would have funds to help support certain programs which operate most effectively across State and local boundaries.

This Act, like my other revenue sharing proposals, would include rigorous safeguards against all discrimination. The legislation I am recommending today stipulates that revenue shared and other funds expended by the Secretary of Labor under this Act would be considered Federal financial assistance within the meaning of Title VI of the Civil Rights Act of 1964.

Manpower Policy and Public Service Employment

One of the most innovative features of my proposed Manpower Training Act of 1969 was an automatic "trigger" which provided more manpower funds when the national unemployment rate rose to 4.5 percent or more for three consecutive months.

The Manpower Revenue Sharing Act contains a similar feature. Triggered funds would be distributed by the Secretary of Labor to areas of high unemployment to provide additional training and employment opportunities.

Under such conditions many State and local governments might choose to use these funds to create temporary public service jobs to offset the rise in unemployment.

This is an acceptable and appropriate use of triggered funds—and of regular shared revenues for manpower programs.

Transitional and short-term public employment can be a useful component of the Nation's manpower policies. But public employment not linked to real jobs or not devoted to equipping the individual to compete in the labor market is only a palliative, not a solution for manpower problems.

Thus, this Act would also provide permanent authority for public service job creation as part of an overall manpower program—but with the proviso that such jobs must constitute transitional opportunities. Within a two-year period participants must be enabled to move into the public employer's regular payroll, or helped to obtain other public or private employment.

Public jobs created through manpower funds would thus be used to develop skills and abilities, with participants moving through such positions into permanent opportunities.

Federal funds already support almost 2 million jobs in State and local government. When enacted, General Revenue Sharing may support tens of thousands more.

Furthermore, last week the administration requested Congressional approval for the creation of at least 200,000 new public jobs for welfare recipients. A part of my welfare reform proposals, these new jobs would lead to non-subsidized employment for welfare recipients for whom other jobs are not available.

Fitting Programs to People

This new reliance on local flexibility and local initiative should benefit citizens and communities across the country. For example:

• This Act would allow city governments to bring jobless ghetto residents onto city payrolls in education, health safety and anti-pollution work while preparing them to move into permanent jobs.

• This Act would allow State governments to reach out to isolated rural poor people with training and job programs shaped to their special needs.

• This Act would allow county governments to provide skill training and transitional employment to welfare recipients to move them toward self-support and new dignity.

It would, in short, allow each State or community to fit its programs to its people.

Looking Ahead

In August 1969 I submitted the Manpower Training Act of 1969. It was one of three key proposals to begin reversing the tide of power which for a generation has flowed from the States and communities to Washington.

For over a year the Ninety-First Congress considered the proposed new manpower legislation, adding many new and creative ideas to our original proposals. Legislation was approved by both houses of Congress which entrusted important new manpower responsibilties to State and local governments. Unfortunately, the final bill also contained serious flaws, and I was forced to withhold my approval from it last December. With this message I am fulfilling my pledge then to submit new manpower legislation in 1971.

This bill builds upon the foundation that was laid during the last Congress.

It responds to Governors' and Mayors' appeals for increased responsibility and increased flexibility.

It makes manpower programs more readily accountable to the clients they serve and the taxpayers who support them.

It recognizes that transitional public service employment is an integral part of manpower policy—and places no ceiling on its extent within the manpower program.

It triggers extra Federal funds to counteract periods of rising unemployment.

In summary, this proposal is designed to give more effective help to those who need it, and to give Americans full return for their tax dollars spent on manpower assistance in the years ahead—full return in the form of unemployment brought down and kept down, and in the form of new income and achievement opportunities for millions of deserving men and women.

And its effects could reach far beyond the field of manpower: As it gives State and local governments the resources and authority to deal with their problems in a single area, it can build the confidence and competence of those governments in all areas. As it cuts away the layers of bureaucracy that have separated the people from one specific exercise of their governing power, it can help restore the people's faith in the democratic process generally. Teamed with my other Special and General Revenue Sharing proposals, it can help to launch the United States on a new era of revolutionary change for the better.

RICHARD NIXON

TEXT OF URBAN AID MESSAGE

Following is the text, as made available by the White House, of President Nixon's March 5 message to Congress asking revenues for cities.

TO THE CONGRESS OF THE UNITED STATES:

As the size of Federal programs for renewing our cities has grown in recent years, so has the evidence of their basic defects. Plagued by delay and duplication, by waste and rigidity, by inconsistency and irrationality, Federal grant-in-aid programs for urban development have simply not achieved the purposes for which they were established. Sometimes, they have even worked to complicate and extend the very problems they were designed to remedy.

The time has come for us to stop merely giving more money to these programs and to begin giving more thought to them. That is why I am proposing today two new instruments for renewing and rebuilding our cities. One is a new plan of Special Revenue Sharing for Urban Community Development. The other is a new program of Planning and Management Assistance for State and local governments which will benefit both urban and rural areas.

Growing Needs and Growing Expenditures

The Federal Government's first significant involvement in community development came with the passage of the Housing Act of 1949, which established as a national goal the realization of "a decent home and a suitable living environment for every American family...." We were already a nation of cities when that legislation was passed. In the two decades since that time we have become even more highly urbanized.

In 1950, some 56 percent of our population lived in metropolitan areas; today the comparable figure is almost 69 percent. The recent Census shows that three-fourths of our population growth in the last ten years came in metropolitan areas, especially in the suburbs which grew by more than 25 percent.

This concentration of population growth in already crowded areas is not a trend that we wish to perpetuate. This administration would prefer a more balanced growth pattern—and we are taking a number of steps to encourage more development and settlement in the less densely populated areas of our country. But this does not mean that we will avoid or slight the challenge of the cities and the suburbs. This is a highly metropolitan nation. It must have an effective strategy for meeting metropolitan problems.

As those problems have mounted in recent years we have often responded by creating more programs and by spending more money. Since 1949, we have committed more than $10 billion to those urban development programs which I would consolidate into this Special Revenue Sharing Program. We will commit almost three times as much money to these programs this year as we did six years ago. While a number of good things have been accomplished with this money, the returns have still fallen far short of even the most reasonable expectations.

On every hand we see the results of this failure: a sorely inadequate supply of housing and community facilities, vast wastelands of vacant and decaying buildings, acre upon acre of valuable urban renewal land lying empty and fallow, and an estimated 24 million Americans still living in substandard housing. Many of our central cities—once symbols of vitality and opportunity—have now become places of disillusion and decay.

As many suburban neighborhoods have grown older, they, too, have begun to deteriorate and to take on the problems of the central cities. Even some of the newest suburban "subdivisions," planned and developed in a shortsighted, haphazard manner, are not prepared to provide essential public services to their growing populations. They are already on their way to becoming the slums of tomorrow.

It is a sad and ironic fact that even as America has become a more highly urbanized nation, its cities have become less attractive and their governments less able to deal with their problems. Federal assistance has failed to reverse these trends and frequently has compounded them.

Problems with the Present System

Just what is it that is wrong with our present system of Federal aid? There are two basic problems. First, Federal assistance is excessively fragmented—it is channeled through many separate and independent grant programs. Second, spending under each of these programs is excessively controlled at the Federal level.

Fragmentation. The present system of categorical grants-in-aid has grown up over the years by bits and by pieces. As each new goal or concern was articulated, new categorical programs were set up. Conventional urban renewal was begun in 1949 to help acquire and clear land in deteriorating areas and plan for its development. Other specialized urban renewal programs followed which focused on the demolition of unsafe structures, on making interim repairs in neighborhoods which were scheduled for renewal, and on helping localities enforce their own housing codes. In 1968 a new Neighborhood Development Program was established for funding urban renewal projects on a year-by-year basis rather than through commitments extending many years into the future.

Other programs were also created over the years for a variety of other purposes, including the rehabilitation of private buildings and the construction of water and sewer facilities and other public works. The tangle of separate Federal programs became so frustrating that when a new Model Cities program was added in 1966, it was expressly designed to provide general, flexible support for coordinated development programs, though only in a limited number of targeted areas.

The proliferation of separate grant programs has created a difficult situation for local governments that wish to utilize Federal development money. For each community must now make a series of separate applications to a series of Federal officials for a series of separate grants, each of which must be spent for a stipulated purpose—and for nothing else. Ideally, all of these grants should fit into a single comprehensive development program, tailored to each community's particular needs. But it is extremely difficult for any community to create an overall strategy for development when each element in that strategy must be negotiated separately by officials who cannot be sure about the outcome of all the other negotiations.

To make things even worse, some of these Federal programs require local communities to work through semi-autonomous local officials—often bypassing the elected local leaders. Thus, even if one leader, a mayor, for example, does manage to create a comprehensive development plan for the money he controls, he is often unable to include in his plan that Federal assistance which goes directly to an urban renewal agency or a local sanitary district. Often, mayors are unable even to calculate the overall level of Federal development aid that is coming into their communities.

These categorical programs, in other words, are separated not only on the giving end in Washington, but also on the receiving end in the local community. And there is no one, anywhere, who can plan so that all the various parts will fit into a comprehensive whole.

The fragmentation which afflicts the planning process continues after the grants are made. Each program is surrounded by its own wall of regulations and restrictions and coordination between programs is often very difficult. Sometimes programs work at cross-purposes and sometimes they needlessly duplicate one another. For example, the Federal Government, working through two different agencies, has been known to fund two different local authorities to build two sewer systems to serve the same neighborhood.

The inflexibility of the present system often means that money cannot be used where the need for money is greatest. If a city suddenly finds that it must put in new street lights, it cannot use funds that are earmarked for demolition or rehabilitation. Geographic restrictions are also a problem. Money for an urban renewal project which has been approved for one carefully defined neighborhood, for example, cannot be used at a closely related site just across the street, if that street happens to be the boundary of the renewal area.

The result of these fragmented and inflexible grant programs has been a highly irrational pattern of development in many urban communities. Rather than focusing and concentrating resources in a coordinated assault on a common problem, the categorical grant system works to divide and scatter those resources and severely to diminish their impact.

Federal Control. The first major problem, fragmentation, concerns what happens *among* various grant programs. The second major problem concerns what happens *within* each program as a result of excessive Federal control.

Almost all of our present development grant programs require a local community to file an extensive application with Federal authorities who, if they approve the plan, will then pay out available money on a project-by-project basis. Because competition between localities for limited Federal dollars is most intense, local officials are highly motivated to meet both the formal requirements and the informal preferences of Federal officials as they file their applications. And since Federal monitoring often continues after the funds are approved, local decisions inevitably continue to reflect Federal viewpoints.

But what is gained by these requirements? There is simply no good reason why a Federal official should have to approve in advance a local community's decision about the shape a new building will have or where a new street will run or on what corner it will put a new gas station. Yet that is precisely the kind of matter that now must be reviewed at the Federal level. In one case, in fact, the Federal reviewer actually turned down a grant application because the architect had included an eight-sided building in his design and the Federal regulations did not specifically allow for funding octagonal buildings.

Decisions about the development of a local community should reflect local preferences and meet local needs. No group of remote Federal officials—however talented and sincere—can effectively tailor each local program to the wide variety of local conditions which exists in this highly diversified land. The only way that can be done is by bringing more tailors into the act, tailors who are elected to make sure that the suit fits the customer.

While little is gained by inordinate Federal involvement, a great deal can be lost. Excessive Federal influence can work to limit the variety and diversity of development programs—which means that the opportunity to experiment with new techniques and to learn from a wide range of experiences is also limited. Because little decisions tend to drive out bigger ones, the present arrangements give the Federal Government less opportunity to focus on the questions it can answer best. And even under the best of circumstances, excessive Federal control results in massive inefficiency and intolerable delays.

I looked recently at some of the applications that communities have submitted for certain urban development funds. One of them was two and a half feet high. I am told that Federal participation in any given urban renewal project now involves almost 300 separate procedural steps. No wonder it now takes an average of three years for an urban renewal plan to be developed and accepted and an average of ten years before a project is completed.

One result of such delays is a particularly troubling urban problem which is known as "planner's blight." It often sets in between the time a Federal renewal project is announced and the time it is actually started. During this interval, a neighborhood frequently stagnates. Since they have been marked for eventual destruction, streets and parks and buildings are allowed to fall into disrepair. Residents and businesses move away and no one moves in to replace them. As the quality of life declines in one area, surrounding neighborhoods—which have not been marked for renewal—can also be adversely affected. Thus a program which was set up to cure a problem, can actually work to make that problem worse, particularly for the poorer residents of the neighborhood who are often unable to receive relocation assistance until the project actually begins.

"Planner's blight" is one dramatic result of Federal red tape. But there are many other costs as well. Instead of focusing their time and their resources and their talents on meeting local needs, city officials must concentrate on pleasing Washington. They must learn to play a terrible game called "grantsmanship," in which the winners are those who understand the rules and intricacies of the Federal bureaucracy rather than those who understand the problem that needs to be solved. Many local governments now feel they must hire experts who have specialized in grantsmanship to carry on their dealings with Washington. Additional distortions in local efforts occur when local resources are diverted from higher priority programs in order to provide the matching funds whch are needed to qualify for many Federal grants.

Deprived of the freedom and the tools to undertake broad programs of renewal and development in their jurisdictions, local officials grow more and more frustrated. And so do local voters who too often find that the official who is most accessible to them can escape from their complaints by saying, "We had to do it this way to qualify for Federal money."

Two Traps to Avoid

Clearly we can do better than this—indeed, we must do better if our cities are to be revived. But our search for a better answer will never be successful unless we avoid two temptations which have trapped us in the past.

The first is the temptation to try to force progress with money. If only we appropriate more funds, we are often told, then everything will be all right. How long will it take us to learn the danger of such thinking? More money will never compensate for ineffective programs. The question we must ask is not "how much?" but "how?"—and the answer to that question lies not in the quantity of our resources, but in the quality of our thinking.

The second trap we must avoid is that of confusing national interest with Federal control. We have too easily assumed that because the Federal Government has a stake in meeting a certain problem and because it wants to play a role in attacking that problem, it therefore must direct all the details of the attack. The genius of the Federal system is that it offers a way of combining local energy and local adaptability with national resources and national goals. We should take full advantage of that capacity as we address the urban challenge.

How the New Program Would Operate

The $5 billion program for General Revenue Sharing which I proposed to the Congress on February 4th was designed to give greater resources to hard-pressed States and localities. But a lack of resources is only one of the deficiencies from which State and local governments now suffer. They also lack the opportunity to exercise sufficient responsibility in meeting social needs. As a further step in revitalizing State and local governments, I am therefore recommending a series of six Special Revenue Sharing programs under which the National Government would set certain general goals while programmatic decisions would be made at the State and local level. I have already sent two such proposals to the Congress—in the fields of law enforcement and manpower training.

My third Special Revenue Sharing proposal is for urban community development. I recommend that four categorical grant programs now administered by the Department of Housing and Urban Development be consolidated into a single fund. The size of this fund in the first full year of operation would be $2 billion. Cities would be able to spend their money as they see fit, provided only that they used it for community development purposes.

The four elements which would be combined to form this new fund would be the current programs for urban renewal, Model Cities, water and sewer grants, and loans for the rehabilitation of existing structures. The urban renewal program, in turn, now contains several sub-categories which money will become part of the new fund, including so-called "conventional" urban renewal, the Neighborhood Development Program, assistance for concentrated local code enforcement, interim assistance for blighted neighborhoods, demolition grants and rehabilitation grants. I am proposing that this new program begin on January 1, 1972. In its second year of operation, I would add to this fund by including the money which the Office of Economic Opportunity now spends on some of the elements of its Community Action Programs.

Distributing the Funds

How would the money be distributed? Because these funds are designed to achieve the specific purpose of urban development, most of this money would be sent to the metropolitan areas of our nation where the vast majority of Americans live and work. Eighty percent of the Special Revenue Sharing fund would be assigned for use in Standard Metropolitan Statistical Areas. The Office of Management and Budget defines a Standard Metropolitan Statistical Area as an area which contains a central city or cities with an aggregate population of 50,000 or more and those surrounding counties which have a metropolitan character and are socially and economically integrated with the central city. There are 247 such areas in the United States at the present time.

The money assigned to Standard Metropolitan Statistical Areas—eighty percent of the total fund—would be allocated among the SMSA's according to a strict formula which would be written into the law so that each SMSA would be assured in advance of its fair share. The central cities and other cities in each SMSA with a population of more than 50,000 would, in turn, automatically receive a stable annual share of the SMSA's funds—again, according to the same objective formula.

In each Standard Metropolitan Statistical Area, some balance would remain after the major communities had received their formula share. In the initial years, this balance would be used by the Department of Housing and Urban Development to compensate any major city in that metropolitan area which received less from the formula allocation than it received annually from the old categorical grant programs over the past few years. Thus, all of these cities would be "held harmless" against reductions in the total urban development support they receive from Washington. None would be hurt—and many would receive more assistance than they do at present.

This administration also recognizes the needs of the growing and changing suburban and smaller communities—with populations under 50,000—within metropolitan areas. After the formula allocation and "hold harmless" commitments have been honored within each Standard Metropolitan Statistical Area, the remaining balance would be available to assist such smaller units, as well as counties, and to encourage areawide developmental cooperation.

The formula according to which the funds would be distributed among the Standard Metropolitan Statistical Areas and among the cities within them would be "problem oriented"—so that the money would be channeled into the cities which need it most. The formula would take into account the number of people who live in an area or a city, the degree of overcrowding there, the condition of its housing units, and the proportion of its families whose income is below the poverty level.

The remaining twenty percent of the Special Revenue Sharing fund for Urban Community Development—the part that did not go by formula to the Standard Metropolitan Statistical Areas—would be available to the Secretary of Housing and Urban Development to distribute. Much of this money would be used during the transitional period to help hold communities harmless against reductions in the overall level of their urban development support. These funds would also be used to encourage state involvement in urban community development, to perform research, to demonstrate new techniques and to aid localities with special needs and with special opportunities to implement national growth policy.

Spending the Funds

How would cities use this money? For community development purposes—which could include investments in both physical and human resources. All of the activities which are eligible for support under the present urban development categorical grants would be eligible for support from the new Special Revenue Sharing fund which would take their place. Cities could thus use their allocations to acquire, clear and renew blighted areas, to construct public works such as water and sewer facilities, to build streets and malls, to enforce housing codes in deteriorating areas, to rehabilitate residential properties, to fund demolition projects, and to help relocate those who have been displaced from their homes or businesses by any activities which drew on these urban community development special revenue sharing funds. They could also fund a range of human resource activities including those now funded by Model Cities and Community Action programs.

Just which of these activities would be supported and what proportion of available funds would be channeled into each activity are decisions that would be made locally. No Federal approval would be required. Cities would simply be asked to indicate how they plan to use their funds and to report periodically on how the money was expended. This requirement is included merely to insure that funds would be used for eligible activities.

As is the case with all other revenue sharing programs, there could be no discrimination in the use of these funds. The rights of all persons to equitable treatment would be protected. Any monies expended under this program would be considered as Federal financial assistance within the meaning of Title VI of the Civil Rights Act of 1964.

The Transition Process

The Department of Housing and Urban Development has already taken a number of steps designed to achieve more coordination among grant programs and greater decentralization of decisionmaking within the present structure of categorical grants. For example, the Department has been encouraging cities to create total community development strategies and has been working to fit categorical aids into such strategies wherever possible. It has also delegated substantial authority to its own regional and area offices. Such efforts are helping to lay a foundation for Special Revenue Sharing and all of them will continue.

One of the most important existing stepping stones to revenue sharing is the Model Cities program which was designed to provide a local community with flexible funding and sufficient freedom so that it can coordinate a wide variety of development programs in a given target area. The Model Cities idea grew out of a mounting frustration with traditional categorical grants. Ideally, it embodies—on a limited basis—the principles we are trying to extend to all development aid through Special Revenue Sharing.

Even in the Model Cities program, however, the ideal has not yet been fully realized. The program is still limited in scope and it still suffers from certain restrictions—the need to negotiate projects with Washington, for example, and the fact that some programs are still limited to certain neighborhoods. The

Department of Housing and Urban Development has worked to minimize these limitations and it will continue to do so. At the same time, I hope that the Congress will enact this Special Revenue Sharing program and thus complete the work which began when the Model Cities program was set up five years ago.

I would emphasize that there will be no lessening of Federal support for urban development activities between now and January 1, 1972, the proposed starting date for the new program. Our problems will not take "time out" and neither can our efforts to deal with them. Where long-range commitments have been made to fund urban renewal projects, those commitments will be honored. Amendatories—supplementary pledges which cover cost increases in urban renewal projects—will also continue to be funded. We will, however, discourage applications for new conventional urban renewal projects—since they would tie up future funds today which would mean cash through Special Revenue Sharing in future years. Instead, we will prepare for Special Revenue Sharing by placing greater emphasis in all programs on annual incremental funding—of the sort that is now used in Neighborhood Development Programs.

Similarly, all other affected programs will continue to be funded until the new program comes into effect. This includes our Model Cities and Community Action commitments. As soon as the starting date for Special Revenue Sharing is established by the Congress, this administration will work out transition arrangements, so that there will be neither a funding gap nor a period of double funding.

What This Program Will— and Will Not—Do

Special Revenue Sharing for Urban Community Development offers a precise and direct solution to the problems which now afflict our system of urban aid. Unlike fragmented and rigid categorical grants, this new plan would allow local leaders to marshal Federal and local dollars according to a simple, comprehensive plan which could be rationally formulated and then intelligently adjusted as conditions change. And—unlike the present system of Federal approval for local project grants—Special Revenue Sharing would give the responsibility for making local decisions back to local officials who can make them best. It is this feature which distinguishes Special Revenue Sharing from the so-called "block grant" which also consolidates categorical grants into a single fund but which retains the Federal approval process and the concomitant disadvantages of excessive Federal control.

Instead of spending their time trying to please Federal officials in Washington—so that money will continue to flow—local leaders would be able to concentrate on pleasing the people who live in their city—so that the money would do more good. A great deal of red tape would be eliminated at both the local and the Federal level—and with it a great deal of waste and delay.

The merger of several categorical programs into a single development fund would enhance the authority and capacity of local officials. It would also serve as a means to dramatize the overall share of national resources which are allocated to this process. The concern of Federal officials and the Congress would no longer be with the details of local projects but with the general place of urban development among our national priorities.

For a variety of reasons, local governments would find that they are better off financially under Special Revenue Sharing than they were before. In the first place, the new plan would provide cities with a level of urban development funding which is at least comparable to that which they have now. In addition, it would contain some extra money which would allow many communities to improve their position. In future years, the overall program could reasonably be expected to grow.

General Revenue Sharing, of course, would provide still more new dollars for these local governments. In addition, cities would get back their discretionary power over the money they were previously spending on matching funds. Because they would not have to prepare and follow up on immense applica-

tions and detailed reports for Washington, local governments would save a considerable administrative expense. And, to the degree that they used their new freedom to make wiser spending decisions, they would find that their new Special Revenue Sharing dollars would go further than did their old grants-in-aid.

One point that should be very clearly understood is that *no* program currently funded by categorical grants need be discontinued under the new arrangement. Every community would have the capacity to maintain—and many would have the capacity to expand—any of these current programs. The suggestion that Model Cities programs, for example, would be terminated is extremely misleading. That would happen only if a locality made a deliberate decision that it wanted to terminate the program, something it is free to do right now. Since existing Model Cities programs require local governments to take the initiative in applying for participation, there is little reason to think that many cities would be motivated to dismantle their Model Cities projects under Special Revenue Sharing—unless they were fairly certain they could use the development money more effectively somewhere else.

Similarly, there is little reason to fear that the problems of impoverished areas would somehow be neglected under this plan. The political leverage of those who live in poverty areas has increasingly been focused on local governments in recent years— and it often has greater impact in such places than when it is diluted at the national level.

Strengthening the Federal System

This Special Revenue Sharing program is built upon a fundamental faith in the inherent capacity of local governments to govern well—if they are given sufficient resources and sufficient responsibility.

Some will argue against such a program by contending that a number of State and local officials will prove to be unresponsive or irresponsible. But this is no reason to reject revenue sharing. Whenever one is dealing with thousands of local officials, there is always a danger that some will prove to be less worthy of one's confidence than others. That is always the risk of moving toward greater freedom—it necessarily becomes more difficult for any one authority to guarantee how the many will behave.

The question is not whether revenue sharing is a foolproof way to avoid bad decisions. No system can do that. The question is whether—on balance—revenue sharing is more likely or less likely to produce *good* decisions than our present system of grants-in-aid.

The question is not whether there are risks in this program. Of course there are. The question is whether the rewards outweigh those risks.

I have already presented a number of reasons why I believe the potential rewards of revenue sharing are considerable. It should also be emphasized, however, that the risks are really very small. The Model Cities program has both demonstrated and enhanced the growing capacity of local leaders to deal skillfully with developmental questions. Moreover, those who talk about the risks of revenue sharing often forget that revenue sharing will *itself* do a great deal to strengthen and improve State and local government. That is why I so strongly believe that those who are most concerned about the shortcomings of State and local governments ought to be most enthusiastic about a strong Federal revenue sharing program.

In many fields today, State and local officials are often forced to function as wards of the Federal Government. Often, they are treated as children who are given a meager allowance, told precisely how to spend it, and then scolded for not being self-reliant enough to handle more responsibility. If we want State and local government to survive, then we must break into this vicious cycle.

The best way to develop greater responsibility at the State and local level is to give greater responsibility to State and local leaders. Only then can we reward and strengthen the many leaders who are effective and help the public to identify and to replace the few who are not. If we want to get more good people into government, then we must give them more opportunity to do good things. To do otherwise, to continue with programs that assign to appointed Federal bureaucrats decisions that should be made by elected local leaders, will only serve to compound the danger of governmental atrophy at the State and local level.

A New Planning and Management Program

To strengthen State and local capacities even further, I am presenting a second proposal today, one that would do a great deal to help *all* of our revenue sharing proposals work even better. I am asking the Congress to authorize a new program of Planning and Management Assistance to States, to areawide agencies and to localities. Under this program, $100 million would be available for these purposes.

The new program would involve more money, and would provide recipient governments with broader and more flexible support for building up their capacity to govern effectively. It would be focused primarily on the chief executives of State and local general purpose governments—on governors, mayors and county executives—to enhance their ability to make well informed policy decisions, to lay intelligent long range plans, to allocate their budgetary resources wisely, and to coordinate complex development activities in many fields. It will place new emphasis on the creation of a comprehensive management process, one that ties together planning and action, not just in the community development field, but in fields such as transportation, education, law enforcement and all other fields of local and areawide governmental endeavor. Local officials would have a great deal of discretion in determining just how this planning and management assistance would be utilized.

Special Revenue Sharing itself can do a great deal to liberate local governments so that their planning and their programs can become more imaginative and more effective. A new program of planning and management assistance would help States and local officials take full advantage of this opportunity. It is a significant companion proposal to *all* of our revenue sharing initiatives.

Conclusion

For a variety of reasons, then, we can be confident that the States and localities will prove equal to their revenue sharing responsibilities. But as we consider these programs, we should also remember one more thing. To choose the revenue sharing mechanism is not to choose any *one* level of government over another level of government. In supporting revenue sharing we are not deciding against the Federal Government, but for the Federal system.

That system is one which has served our country well for nearly two centuries, allowing us to combine national unity and regional diversity, to balance our common ideals with our highly varied ways of pursuing them, to solve the ancient philosophical challenge of reconciling the many and the one.

But the Federal system does not work automatically. Like democracy itself, it lives only because those who work within it are committed to its success. It is now for us to decide whether the Federal system will decay or flourish in our time.

RICHARD NIXON

RURAL DEVELOPMENT TEXT

Following is the text, as made available by the White House, of President Nixon's March 10 message to Congress asking funds for rural community development.

TO THE CONGRESS OF THE UNITED STATES:

I am today proposing a new program of Rural Community Development through revenue sharing—the fourth of my six Special Revenue Sharing proposals. I have spoken of revenue sharing as a new partnership between the Federal Government and the State and local governments within our federal system. The proposal I am advancing today would use that essential government partnership to strengthen an equally essential social and economic partnership between rural America, where the farms that feed us and the great open spaces that renew our spirit are found, and urban America, where the majority of our people and the greater share of our wealth are concentrated. Rural Americans deserve a full share in the nation's prosperity and growth, just as urban Americans deserve cities that are livable and alive. Both objectives are attainable—and rural development revenue sharing, linked to urban development revenue sharing by the comprehensive planning proposal also put forward in this message, could be a giant step toward them.

Rural America in Transition

Rural America begins with farm America. Agriculture was America's first industry, and it remains one of the keystones of our national economy today. It has made Americans the best-fed people in history, and now exports the produce of one-fourth of its acreage to help feed the world. American farmers have led all sectors of the economy in annual increases in productivity for most of the years in this century. This Nation's farms are among our most efficient producers, and they are of central importance to a strong future for rural America.

Yet, there is sharp irony in this success. Ever more fruitful, American agriculture has required fewer people every year to produce food and fibers for our people, and to supply the expanding export market for our commodities abroad.

Hence the departure of people from the farms began to swell as farming grew more mechanized, efficient, and large-scale. Americans living on farms numbered more than 30,000,000 in 1940; today that figure is only about 10,000,000. Once the farm people had left their homes—often the homes of generations in their families—the opportunities often did not exist in rural America to keep them close to those roots. While some jobs began to open up in agricultural service, supply, and processing enterprises, usually known as "agri-business," the number of openings was not nearly enough to match the number of people cast adrift by technological progress.

Migration began toward where people thought opportunities existed—the cities. Not only were there more jobs in the cities, but they paid more. For most decades in this century, the gap between median income in the cities and that in non-metropolitan areas has been wide. Even though income gains outside the metropolis have been almost half again as great as those in the cities during the last decade, median family income in non-metropolitan areas is still 22 percent below that in metropolitan areas.

While the people who have been leaving rural America by the millions have often improved their own and their families' situations by leaving, the trend they represent has had several disturbing effects.

First, in rural America itself, the loss in human resources has compounded the problems of diversifying the economy and fostering a vigorous and progressive community life. Those who have chosen to stay have found it harder and harder to pay for and provide services such as good schools, health facilities, transportation systems, and other infra-structure attractive enough to keep people in rural America, or to lure jobs and opportunity to rural America. Many of the small towns which dot the countryside have to struggle for existence; they often have difficulty attracting good school-teachers or physicians; many fight stagnation while most of the economy is expanding; they cannot give the older, the disadvantaged, the less educated people needed assistance and care.

The Urban Stake in Rural Development

At the same time the urban effects of migration have been profound. While the explosive growth in the proportion of

Americans living in cities has not been fed solely by the influx of people from rural America—immigration from other countries has also been massive—the millions who have moved from the South and the Midwest to the North and the West have been a major factor in making a nation that was 75 percent rural a century ago, 73 percent urban today.

Many of these people pouring into the cities in search of opportunity have experienced difficulties in adapting to urban life and have required supportive services. Some made the transition successfully—but others have remained tax users rather than taxpayers.

Furthermore, the very size and density of many of our cities has produced new problems: whereas in the most rural areas it is hard to achieve economies of scale in public activities, the most heavily urban areas have grown far past the size range in which a community can function most economically. It often costs far more per capita to provide essential services, such as police protection, sanitation collection, and public transportation in our dense urban areas than in less congested smaller and medium-sized cities. Many of our cities have, in short, become inefficient and less and less governable. At times, this has led to near-paralysis of public services in our largest cities. Current trends indicate that unless there is a marked shift in public and private attitudes, the increase of population in and around our great metropolitan centers will continue, and the problems of urban management will be further aggravated.

In addition, by even conservative estimates, there will be some 75 million additional Americans by the end of the twentieth century. Whether this growth is beneficial or burdensome depends on our foresight in planning and preparing for it—a process that must begin now and must take a broader view than merely feeding the expansion of the megalopolis.

As never before, the Nation is beginning to see that urban America has a vital stake in the well-being and progress of rural America. This is one Nation, and for the good of all Americans we need one national policy of balanced growth.

Federal Resources for Rural Development

For the sake of balanced growth, therefore, but even more for the sake of the farmer and all his neighbors in rural America —first-class citizens who deserve to live in first-class communities —I am proposing that the Federal Government re-think America's rural development needs and rededicate itself to providing the resources and the creative leadership those needs demand.

It takes many different kinds of activities to create rural development—to create opportunity. One must start with the individual—his education, his skill training, and his health. Next the individual needs to be linked to resources and markets through transportation. Public sector infrastructure such as water and sewers is needed to encourage industry to locate in new areas. The environment is also becoming an increasingly important factor in industrial locations.

Essentially what I am proposing is to unite the funding for a number of programs operating directly in rural areas and smaller cities into a Rural Community Development Revenue Sharing Program, to add $179 million to that fund, and then to bolster this effort with new initiatives in critically related areas, such as health and welfare reform.

The following chart shows the programs which I propose to combine into the Rural Development Revenue Sharing Program:

Programs Combined Under Rural Development Revenue Sharing

- General
  New Money $179 Million
  Title V Regional Commissions
  Appalachian Regional Commission
  Economic Development Administration
  Resource Conservation and Development Program
- Education
  Cooperative Agricultural Extension Service
- Water and Sewer
  Rural Water and Waste Disposal Grants
- Environment
  Rural Environmental Assistance Program
  Forestry Assistance Grants
  Great Plains Agricultural Conservation Program
  Water Bank Program
  Tree Planting Grants

Altogether, the eleven programs listed above are spending $921 million in Fiscal 1971.

But much more is needed to extend to rural Americans the full share of national prosperity and the full participation in the rich benefits of our society, which they rightly deserve. Much more would be done if the Congress acts to set in motion the broad strategy for accelerated rural development which I have placed before it in recent weeks.

Rural communities throughout the nation would share in the $5 billion of General Revenue Sharing which I have proposed. Rural communities would receive direct assistance in building their human resources, their social services, and their economic base through my Special Revenue Sharing proposals for manpower, education, transportation and law enforcement. My proposals for improving our system of health care include Area Health Education Centers to be located in rural areas and financial incentives for doctors and providing medical care in scarcity areas. My welfare reform proposals would have immediate and dramatic effects on rural poverty: in the first year nearly $1 billion in new cash benefits would go into rural areas to add to the incomes of the millions of rural Americans who are poor or underemployed.

To unify and consolidate the rural development effort in each State—I am today proposing that the Federal Government establish a $1.1 billion fund to be shared among all the States for fully discretionary spending to meet their rural needs and accelerate their rural development. This would be accomplished by combining programs which I listed above into a new program of Special Revenue Sharing for Rural Community Development, and by increasing their present annual funding of $921 million by $179 million during the first year.

How Revenue Sharing Works

Beginning January 1, 1972, these funds would be paid out to the States and to Puerto Rico, the Virgin Islands, and Guam, in regular installments on a formula basis, according to an index of need based on three factors: the State's rural population, the State's rural per capita income compared to the national average of per capita incomes, and the State's change in rural population compared to the change in population of all States. All 53 recipients would share equally in 1 percent of the funds. Every State would receive at least as much from Special Revenue Sharing for Rural Community Development, as it now receives from the eleven existing rural assistance programs combined.

This proposal recognizes that patterns of development potential vary widely within the different States and seldom conform neatly to intra-State governmental jurisdictions. It therefore imposes no Federally dictated distribution of shared revenues within the States. Neither would it require matching or maintenance of effort spending by a State in return for the shared rural development funds. Indeed the shared funds could if necessary be used to match other Federal grants-in-aid for rural assistance. But there would be a firm requirement that all rural community development funds be spent for the direct benefit of rural people. The funds could be spent for any of the purposes now authorized under the existing aid programs, including the option of direct grant assistance to private firms which locate in rural communities.

Rural areas would be defined in this Act as counties with a population density less than 100 people per square mile, and all other counties, regardless of population density, which are not included in one of the 247 Standard Metropolitan Statistical Areas (SMSAs) which the U.S. Census Bureau defines around cities of 50,000 or more.

I will also propose $100 million in additional non-formula funds for the Urban Community Development Special Revenue Sharing program, to assist those smaller cities of population between 20,000 and 50,000 which have been receiving grant assistance from the Department of Housing and Urban Development but which would not now be eligible for a formula share of Urban Community Development Revenue Sharing. The Secretary of Housing and Urban Development would administer this fund on a discretionary basis. Such communities would thus be eligible for funds from both the urban and rural revenue sharing programs—as they should be, since many communities of this size have not only urban problems and needs but also strong rural development potential as economic and social opportunity centers for nearby rural counties. The same overlap would be true as well of some of the smaller and less densely populated Standard Metropolitan Statistical Areas which have less than 100 people per square mile, and thus qualify for both formula grants under Urban Community Development Special Revenue Sharing, and use of funds from the Rural Community Development Special Revenue Sharing.

The Act would apply the requirements of Title VI of the Civil Rights Act of 1964 to prohibit discriminatory use of the Federal money.

Building on Success

Conversion of the existing categorical aid programs for agriculture and development into Special Revenue Sharing for Rural Community Development is a logical evolution in line with the history of these efforts and consistent with their basic purposes.

Over a number of years the Department of Agriculture has been moving to make its assistance to farmers and rural residents more effective and flexible by a steady process of decentralization. Placing these programs fully in the hands of the States is just one more step in sharpening their ability to deliver the services they were designed to provide. Whether the transfer will be beneficial and the transition smooth is a question to which the example of the Cooperative Extension Service may provide a partial answer. The States are ready to take charge of the Extension Service, which they already largely administer and which all States now fund above the present Federal contribution.

In the case of EDA, the Appalachian Regional Commission and the Title V Commissions, revenue sharing in superseding them would actually incorporate the coordinated development approach that has made them successful, at the same time it removed some of the Federal "fences" that may have restricted their activities unduly in the past. The grass roots planning process which has proved itself under the Appalachian Regional Commission is carried over into the statewide development plan I am now proposing for all States under rural and urban development revenue sharing. Close account would be taken of the human factor and of the continuity of on-going development efforts as the program transition is effected. Counties that have launched projects under the Appalachian Regional Commission, for example, would continue to receive adequate funding to make good on the money already obligated for such projects.

With revenue sharing, therefore, as with all change, there would be adjustments to make but great benefits to be gained. Every single activity now carried on under the Commissions and categorical programs could be continued in any State whose own people decide it is worth continuing. The farm, forest, and conservation programs that have succeeded in the past could go right on doing so—and freed of Federal restrictions, they could probably reach out farther and keep better pace with changing needs and technologies. In each instance the people of the State would make the decision.

Streamlining the Rural Assistance Effort

What Special Revenue Sharing for Rural Community Development would do is to remove many of the negative and inhibiting side effects which now plague rural assistance as a result of categorical narrowness, lack of coordination, and excessive Federal involvement. By combining these programs we could produce a new whole significantly greater than the sum of the present parts. It is worthwhile here to discuss some of the problems that would be eliminated—principally inflexibility, priority distortion and flawed accountability.

Inflexibility. As well-intentioned as past rural development efforts have been, strict Federal eligibility rules have often stood in the way of fair sharing of all the Federal resources for rural development, or have made it difficult for States and localities to do what they must to attract industry and services. For instance, many parts of the Midwest, which experienced some of the heaviest rural outmigration in the Nation during the 1960s, still do not qualify for Economic Development Administration grants.

In other cases Federal standards have acted to bar aid from those communities in a region where it could do the most good. Experts in rural development feel that the most leverage is achieved by reinforcing healthy development trends, rather than fighting them—that is, by concentrating aid in these smaller and medium sized cities of a rural area which have shown strength and effort in attracting industry. Every area of rural America has such centers of potential growth. Using government assistance to strengthen their development trends could make the difference in attracting new job-producing industry and expanding employment opportunities for rural people living in the surrounding counties. It could also help these communities attract doctors, teachers and others whose services are so needed in or near rural areas. Yet current Federal program restrictions, by and large, do not permit aid to be used this way, because of a "worst-first" criterion which often puts funds into areas that lack the development potential to help either themselves or others near them—rather than using funds to open up new opportunities regionally so that benefits flow out to low-potential areas nearby.

Distortion of State Budgets. Narrow Federal project definitions can force States and localities to spend scarce revenues on "matching shares," urgent community priorities aside, or risk the loss of Federal funds. Once begun, a Federal project may demand additional local spending, beyond the matching money, for support facilities to tie the project into community usefulness.

Flawed Accountability. The quasi-governmental agencies which often exercise a determining influence on the conduct of these programs tend to obscure and fragment responsibility for decisions made and therefore to subvert the democratic accountability of elected officials. Regional commissions, comprised of a Federal Co-chairman and Governors from member States, take part in many program and planning decisions which really affect only one Governor's State. Too often the Federal officials responsible for rural assistance are geographically distant, and the local, State or multi-State institutions that have a say are politically insulated or remote.

The Statewide Development Plan

Special Revenue Sharing for Rural Community Development would be administered initially by the Secretary of Agriculture; eventually both this program and the urban community development program would come under the direction of the Department of Community Development whose formation I have proposed. In addition to paying out each year's rural development funds to the States and territories, the Secretary of Agriculture would stay abreast of rural development aspects of the statewide development plans which each Governor would file with him annually.

The statewide planning process which would help States and localities coordinate activities carried on under both urban and rural community development revenue sharing will be established in legislation that I will submit shortly. It would require annual preparation of a comprehensive statewide development plan outlining spending intentions for programs in metropolitan, suburban, smaller city, and rural areas alike. The $100 million Planning and Management Assistance program which I proposed in my message to the Congress on Urban Community Development Revenue Sharing would provide funds which States and local jurisdictions could use in this planning process.

The Governor of each State would be given the responsibility for drawing up the statewide development plan. Formation of the plan would be based on a consultative process which considers plans submitted by State-established, multi-jurisdictional planning districts covering all areas of the State. Planning bodies of these districts would be composed of local elected officials. One member from each of the district planning bodies would sit on a panel which would assist the Governor in the planning process. The Secretaries of Housing and Urban Development and Agriculture could accept an alternative consultative process proposed by the State.

The completed plan would be filed with the Secretaries of Agriculture and of Housing and Urban Development—not for their approval, but as a declaration of intent; a Governor could amend his plan by letter during the course of a year.

The process of developing the statewide plan would focus official concern and public attention upon the inter-relationship of urban and rural community development within the State. The plan could identify potential growth areas, potential new community development sites, and environmentally important areas. It should seek to integrate all important community development factors, including land use.

All the money a State receives under Special Revenue Sharing for Rural Community Development would have to be spent for the benefit of persons in rural areas as outlined in the statewide plan. A State could of course also supplement its own rural development activities with money received under General Revenue Sharing and under other Special Revenue Sharing programs within program definitions. The Secretary of Agriculture would conduct an annual post-audit of State rural development activities, with payment of the next year's rural revenue sharing funds conditional upon State compliance with rural development spending plans for the year past.

The Logic of Rural Development Revenue Sharing

To review briefly:

The major challenge facing rural America is to diversify its economy and to provide full opportunity for its people to enjoy the benefits of American life. Meeting this challenge will enhance the quality of life for those who remain to operate the nation's family farms and for all their neighbors in the small towns and countryside of America. As a secondary effect—like upstream watershed management for downstream flood control—meeting the rural challenge will also help to relieve the over-burdened urban structure by stemming rural outmigration and attracting a share of future growth to rural communities.

The key to a rural development strategy is my proposal for $1.1 billion in Special Revenue Sharing for Rural Community Development—money which all States and territories could share and which they could spend in their rural areas as they deem wisest. Other proposed Federal assistance for rural America includes part of the $5 billion General Revenue Sharing program and part of five Special Revenue Sharing programs, as well as the benefits of a reformed welfare system and an improved health care system.

At the core of rural development revenue sharing would be eight agricultural grant programs and three broad development assistance programs now in being. Consolidating them, the revenue sharing approach would build on decentralizing trends in the agricultural programs and on the multi-State, State, and multi-county development planning experience accumulated under EDA and the regional commissions. It would do away with narrow aid categories, spending restrictions, duplication, and red tape now surrounding these programs. It would make the money now devoted to them go further and would provide more money.

Existing programs and development projects could continue or not at the discretion of each State, and the right of choice would rest close to the rural people at whom the aid is directed. A statewide planning requirement with a broadly representative input would promote coordinated development of a sort not now approached and would insure that all areas of the State have a voice in the planning process; but in no case could rural development revenue sharing money be diverted from rural needs.

Urban-Rural Partnership

More money, plus more freedom to spend it, plus better planning in doing so, add up to better living for rural Americans and brighter futures for rural communities. Mutual benefits of the urban-rural partnership would be manifest as cities enjoyed the fruits of a healthy agricultural economy and the relief of more evenly distributed population growth, while rural areas felt the effect of new social and economic advantages. Rural and urban communities would no longer siphon off one another's strengths and resources nor shunt problems and burdens from one to the other. They would progress together in a dynamic balance, as partners in the best sense.

RICHARD NIXON

TRANSPORTATION FUNDS

Following is the text, as made available by the White House, of President Nixon's March 18 message to Congress asking revenue sharing for transportation purposes.

TO THE CONGRESS OF THE UNITED STATES:

When the early settlers first encountered the American wilderness, a man's mobility was dependent upon his strong legs and the sharp axe with which he cleared his path. But even in those pioneering times, Americans quickly came to realize that good roads and docks and bridges were community concerns.

Over the years, government has become increasingly involved in improving the Nation's transportation systems, from the building of post roads and canals in the early periods of our history, to the construction of airports and superhighways in recent years. The question we face today, therefore, is not whether government should participate in transportation matters, but how government should participate—and which levels of government should undertake which responsibilities. These are the central questions I am addressing in this message as I outline a new Special Revenue Sharing Program for Transportation.

Growing Transportation Systems and Growing Problems

As the demand for mobility has mushroomed and as new means of transportation have been invented in recent years, the size of our transportation system has reached staggering proportions. It has been less than 70 years, for example, since the Wright brothers flew at Kitty Hawk. In that time, our aviation system has grown to the point that last year it served over 173 million commercial passengers and handled more than 4 billion ton miles of air freight. An open field with a windsock was a sufficient airport for most communities only a few decades ago. Today many airports are cities in themselves and air traffic is controlled by highly sophisticated electronic systems.

At the turn of the century there were only 8,000 automobiles in America. By 1920 nearly 8 million cars traveled our highways and today we have more than 100 million registered vehicles which travel over one trillion miles annually. The people of our Nation are driving more than twice as many automobiles as they did just 20 years ago.

These two technological developments—the airplane and the automobile—give dramatic evidence of both the successes and the failures of American transportation. The automobile and the airplane are mechanized masterpieces. The highways and airports which they use are often glowing displays of America's engineering genius. But behind the mystique of jet travel and the convenience of the family car lie serious problems that have been growing more acute in recent years.

The airplane means fast travel over great distances, to be sure. But it also can mean harmful noise and air pollution, congested terminals, misplaced luggage and airports that are difficult to reach. Highways that speed motorists between cities can become long and narrow parking lots where cars are stalled for hours within urban areas. It often takes longer to move by "horseless carriage" across our major cities today as it did by horsedrawn carriage a century ago. Efforts to improve this situation by building new highways often have the effect of destroying neighborhoods and disrupting lives. It is estimated, moreover, that automobiles are responsible for almost half of our air pollution—a growing problem that is slowly choking our central cities.

And there is another serious problem, as well. For with our heavy investment in automobiles and air transportation has come a sharp decline in rail passenger service and in public mass transit systems.

The first electric streetcar lines and the first subway appeared at about the same time as the automobile and, like the automobile, they grew in popularity during the first quarter of this century. In 1905, local urban transit systems carried 5 billion passengers. By 1926, ridership had more than trebled, but that was the peak of mass transit's popularity—except for a brief period during World War II. After 1945, public transit ridership, revenue and service declined steadily. In 1950, there were still some 1,400 urban transit companies operating 87,000 vehicles and carrying 17.25 billion passengers. By 1970, however, there were 327 fewer companies and 25,000 fewer vehicles carrying only 7.3 billion passengers.

Public transportation has been caught up in a vicious cycle of increasing costs, rising fares, shrinking profits, decreasing quality, and declining ridership. Ironically, this decline in mass transit has come at the same time that the need for fast, convenient, economical public transportation has become greater than ever before. This Nation has the technology to provide such transportation. If we can move three men a quarter million miles to the moon, then surely we can also find ways to move millions of men and women over short distances in our cities. This is another of the great transportation challenges of our time.

How Have These Problems Been Met?

All of these problems—pollution, congestion, inefficiency, and the lack of sufficient mass transit services—have been recognized for years. And for years the Federal Government has been working to alleviate them. In the past two years, this administration has recommended a number of new programs to improve American transportation. As a result, we now have an accelerated program to develop urban mass transit systems, new authorizations for the expansion and improvement of airports and airways, and a quasi-public corporation to operate a national rail passenger system.

It is clear, however, that more money and more regulations alone will not solve our transportation problems. Nor will they make the Federal Government more responsive to local needs and local aspirations. It is equally clear that the established relationships among Federal, State and local governments are unsuitable for achieving the goals we pursue.

What are those goals? They can be usefully described under the general heading of "balanced transportation."

Achieving Balanced Transportation

A balanced transportation system is essentially one that provides adequate transportation not just for some of the people in a community but for all the people in a community. A balanced system also recognizes that an individual can have different transportation needs at different times. Such a system treats speed as only one of the factors in the transportation equation and does not ignore the importance of other qualities such as comfort, safety, and reliability.

Despite our technological capacity, we do not enjoy a fully balanced transportation system in modern America, particularly in our larger cities. We have relied too much in our cities on cars and on highways; we have given too little attention to other modes of travel. Approximately 94 percent of all travel in urbanized areas is by automobile, yet only about 25 percent of our people—especially the old, the very young, the poor and the handicapped—do not drive a car. They have been poorly served by our transportation strategy.

Distortions Caused by Matching Requirements

One of the most disturbing elements in the present transportation picture is the fact that such inequities have often been reinforced and even precipitated by the Federal Government. One reason is that Federal dollars have been relatively easy to obtain for highway building but more difficult to obtain for other transportation purposes. The Federal Government now pays 90 percent of the costs for a new interstate expressway, for example, but only 67 percent of the costs for a new mass transit system and only 50 percent of the costs of building an airport. It is little wonder that State and local planners are encouraged to cover the landscape with ribbons of concrete. Such distortions of local priorities are among the major problems that this administration is seeking to correct.

Excessive Federal Control

But local priorities are not only distorted by Federal requirements concerning matching funds. Local determinations of what is needed most must constantly yield to Federal judgments about what a local community should do with the money it receives from Washington.

The Federal Government has a great influence on the particular mixture of transportation spending in any locale, for it carefully allocates so much of its money for one kind of transportation and so much for another. Each program is funded separately—and even at the State and local level, different agencies frequently administer monies which are designated for different purposes. As a result, it is extremely difficult to achieve sound intermodal planning of comprehensive transportation systems. There is no single place where sufficient resources and authority are available for making wise choices between various transportation alternatives. Nor can anyone effectively coordinate investments in any one mode of transportation with efforts in other transportation fields. We err, in short, by treating the transportation challenge as a series of separate problems rather than as a single problem with many interrelated parts.

The hard fact is that the best mixture of transportation modes is not something that remote officials in Washington can determine in advance for all cities, of all sizes and descriptions, in all parts of the country. Nor do the Federal officials who grant money for specific projects understand local needs well enough to justify their strong influence over how local projects should be planned and run.

As I have contended in a number of messages to the Congress in the past two years, our society has become too complex and too diversified to profit from such highly centralized control. This is not to deny that improving our transportation systems is a national concern. It is a national concern and that is why it should continue to be funded in part from Federal tax resources. But the specific manner in which any city or metropolitan area goes about achieving this goal is not something that can be most effectively determined at the Federal level. In fact, transportation needs are among the social and economic factors that vary most widely from one place to another. That is why many of our Federal transportation programs can profit so much from conversion to the Special Revenue Sharing approach.

Community organizations, concerned individuals and local units of government should not have to shout all the way to Washington for attention. Community standards and community transportation goals are changing and some of those who only five years ago welcomed the prospect of a new highway or airport are now protesting in front of bulldozers. Transportation planning and appropriations mechanisms must be flexible enough to meet the challenge of changing community values. This flexibility can best be achieved by concentrating more decisionmaking power in the States and the localities.

The purpose of Special Revenue Sharing is to focus Federal resources on major public problems and at the same time maximize flexibility of choice at the State and local level. The Special Revenue Sharing approach provides an ideal means for addressing national problems that have local solutions.

A Special Revenue Sharing Program for Transportation

The proposal I am submitting today would establish a new Special Revenue Sharing Program for Transportation. In simplest terms, this program means returning Federal tax dollars to States and to local communities for investment in transportation—without the usual Federal controls and restraints. It signals a philosophical return to the days when the man who best understood the local terrain was the man who blazed the trail.

Funding

I propose that the Special Revenue Sharing Program for Transportation become effective on January 1, 1972, and that it be funded initially at an annual level of $2.566 billion. All funds that would be included in this new program would come from twenty-three existing Federal grant-in-aid programs which are now grouped under five major headings: Urban Mass Transit Grants, Airport Grants, Highway Safety Grants, Federal Aid for Highways (but not the Interstate System), and Highway Beautification Grants. The size of these programs in my proposed budget for Fiscal Year 1972 is as follows:

	Millions of Dollars
Urban Mass Transit Grants	$ 525
Airport Grants	220
Highway Safety Grants	130
Federal Aid for Highways (Except for the Interstate System)	1,625
Highway Beautification Grants	66
	$2,566

The money for these programs presently comes from three different funding sources: general tax revenues, the Highway Trust Fund and the Airport and Airway Trust Fund. The two trust funds were established so that money could be collected directly from those who use highways or airports—through special taxes on gasoline and on air tickets—and then used to improve the related transportation mode.

This principle would continue to be observed under Special Revenue Sharing. In the first year of operation, Special Revenue Sharing money would be drawn from the two trust funds and from general revenues in the same proportion as under the existing categorical grant system, though it could be spent as the localities see fit. After that, however, the portion of the Special Revenue Sharing Program for Transportation derived from the trust funds in any year would equal the portion of the program

that was used for highways and for aviation-related purposes in the preceding year. Thus the money in the trust funds would still go to achieve the general purposes for which the funds were established. General funds would pay for all other transportation activities.

The National System of Interstate and Defense Highways would not be included in this Special Revenue Sharing Program. This 42,500-mile system is now 74 percent finished and is scheduled for completion in 1978. The Interstate highways that have been built under this program have helped to open America to new dimensions of intercity travel. The system has advanced the cause of highway safety while at the same time permitting unparalleled individual mobility. In my judgment, it would not be in the national interest to alter the basic funding mechanism for the construction of this system at this time.

Although all Special Revenue Sharing funds would be assigned to governmental units, the recipient government could, in turn, channel the funds to private enterprises which meet public transportation needs. This would include the many urban bus systems that are privately owned and operated.

No State or local matching funds would be required under this program. The Federal Government would not rigidly apportion funds among a variety of narrow transportation programs nor would it approve specific local projects. Thus the Special Revenue Sharing Program for Transportation would stimulate State and local governments to take the initiative in meeting transportation needs, to experiment with new and more creative projects, to listen to local opinion and to mobilize local energies which are often stifled under present arrangements.

I would emphasize in addition that each State would receive at least as much money from the new Special Revenue Sharing Program for Transportation as it has been receiving under the current categorical grant programs. Each State would thus be "held harmless" against any reduction in the overall level of support it receives from programs which become a part of this Special Revenue Sharing fund.

Two Fund Elements

The Special Revenue Sharing Program for Transportation would consist of two elements, one for General Transportation activities and one for Mass Transit Capital Investment.

General Transportation Element

The General Transportation element would total $2.041 billion for the first full year of revenue sharing. This money could be spent for the planning, construction, acquisition, improvement, operation and maintenance of a broad spectrum of transportation systems and services, including highway, aviation and mass transit.

The money in this General Transportation element would be distributed in the following manner: Ten percent would be allocated among the States and localities at the discretion of the Secretary of Transportation. This money would be used to encourage planning, to fund research development and demonstration projects, and to finance other activities related to the development and implementation of national transportation objectives.

The remaining 90 percent of this General Transportation element would be allocated to the States according to the following four-part formula: 25 percent of this remainder would be distributed according to the ratio of each State's total population to the total population of the United States; 35 percent would go to States according to the ratio of their population in urban places (over 2,500 in population) to the Nation's total population in urban places; 20 percent would be given out according to the ratio of the geographic area of each State to the total area of the United States; and the remaining 20 percent would be allocated according to the ratio of each State's star and rural post route mileage to the total of that mileage in the country.

This formula, which resembles formulas which are used under current categorical grants, would provide the best means for distributing Special Revenue Sharing funds in a similar pattern as under the present system. In addition to the guarantee that it would be held harmless against any reduction in support, each State would be guaranteed a minimum allocation of one-half of one percent of this General Transportation element.

As I have noted above, a percentage of the General Transportation element would be distributed among the States according to their share of the Nation's population that lives in urban areas. Each State would be required to pass along its share of this money directly to its communities of more than 2,500 persons to spend as their local governments think best. If we are to restore confidence in local government then we must give public officials at the local level a reasonable opportunity to make sound plans and courageous investment decisions. This means that they must be able to rely upon a certain amount of funding. Our "pass-through" formula is designed to provide this needed assurance.

Mass Transit Capital Investment Element

The second part of the new Special Revenue Sharing fund is the Mass Transit Capital Investment element—which would total $525 million for the first full year. This money would be distributed to each State according to its share of the Nation's population that lives in Standard Metropolitan Statistical Areas (SMSA). An SMSA is defined as an area which contains a central city or cities with an aggregate population of 50,000 or more and those surrounding counties which have a metropolitan character and are socially and economically integrated with the central city. There are 247 such areas in the United States.

Eighty percent of the funds in this Mass Transit Capital Investment element would be distributed according to each State's share of the Nation's population that lives in SMSAs of over one million persons. The remaining 20 percent would be allocated according to each State's share of the Nation's population that lives in SMSAs of less than one million persons. Every State would be guaranteed a minimum allocation of $250,000.

In the Mass Transit Capital Investment element as in the General Transportation fund element, I propose that a portion of the funds be passed through the States directly to urban areas. Of the 80 percent distributed to States on the basis of SMSAs of more than one million in population, I propose that half go directly to the local governments within these SMSAs to spend for mass transit purposes as they see fit. The other half of this money would also have to be spent within these same larger SMSAs, but it would be spent at the State's discretion. Currently, there are 33 SMSAs with more than a million persons in the United States and these are the areas that would automatically receive "pass-through" funds for Mass Transit Capital Investment.

In 1969, I submitted to the Congress a proposal for establishing an Urban Mass Transportation Assistance program. The passage of that legislation helped to create a significant momentum for the rejuvenation of public transit systems. I feel very strongly that this momentum must not be lost and that is why I propose that a part of this new Special Revenue Sharing Program for Transportation be devoted to this purpose.

I believe that this Mass Transit Capital Investment element would assure continued support and enthusiasm for mass transit initiatives. It would also provide fast relief for many systems which now suffer from inadequate equipment, allowing them to undertake the essential work of modernization without further delay.

Combining Old and New Strengths

Special Revenue Sharing would strengthen our transportation efforts in many significant ways without sacrificing the strengths of our present programs. Any transportation project that is working well today could be continued, and in all probability expanded, under the new arrangements. While narrow grant categories would be eliminated, none of the programs which they now support need be discontinued if the State or locality believes they are worthwhile.

In recent years, governments at all levels—and private groups and individuals as well—have become more sensitive to problems such as transportation safety and the environmental impact of transportation. Our whole society can be proud, for example, of the fact that there were no fatalities from commercial airline accidents in the United States last year. We can be grateful, too, that despite increasing traffic on our highways, automobile fatalities in 1970 decreased significantly for the first time since 1958.

We have also become more alert to the effects which transportation has on the beauty of the landscape and the quality of the environment. Our traditional economic concerns have been complemented by our growing esthetic concerns and the result has been a strong effort at all levels of society to improve the quality of American life.

There is no reason why growing sensitivity on matters such as safety and environmental quality should not continue to grow under this new Special Revenue Sharing program. State and local governments, after all, have often been particularly responsive to citizen pressure in these areas and they have frequently acted as bold pioneers in meeting these concerns. I am confident that as more responsibility is given to governments closer to the people, the true and abiding interests of the people will be even better reflected in public policy decisions.

I would emphasize again, as I have in presenting each of my revenue sharing programs, that there could be no discrimination in the use of any of these monies. All of the funds included in this Special Revenue Sharing Program for Transportation would be subject to the provisions of Title VI of the Civil Rights Act of 1964.

The Importance of Planning

No transportation system—on the national, regional, or local level—can serve the public with maximum effectiveness unless there is a great deal of cooperative planning between various modes of conveyance and between various levels of government. A multitude of government jurisdictions, public authorities and private companies must learn to work closely together if our needs are to be met in a comprehensive manner. The legislation I present to the Congress will therefore require that transportation plans be developed in coordination with the development plans prepared under my proposed Special Revenue Sharing Programs for Urban and Rural Community Development.

Recognizing Diversity

Just as each unique individual has unique transportation problems, so do cities, States and other governmental jurisdictions. The single most important fact about our Special Revenue Sharing Program for Transportation is that it recognizes this diversity. It combines the resources of the Federal Government with the flexibility of State and local governments. It provides the best way to meet the problems which diversity implies by utilizing the energies which diversity produces.

RICHARD NIXON

TEXT OF MESSAGE ON VOLUNTEERS

Following is the text, as made available by the White House, of President Nixon's March 24 message to Congress on volunteer service.

TO THE CONGRESS OF THE UNITED STATES:

America is a nation unique in the political history of the world. More than any other nation, it is the sum of the energies and efforts of all of its people. The American tradition of voluntary involvement—of freely committing one's time and talents in the search for civic improvement and social progress—gives an extra dimension to the meaning of democracy. In the past decade, the Federal Government has built on this tradition by developing channels for joining the spirit of voluntary citizen service in America with public needs, both domestically and abroad. Many of these efforts have had marked success. But the circumstances in which these efforts were conceived have changed.

National and international needs have altered. The opportunities for voluntary service must be adapted and improved to meet these new needs.

Recognizing that private channels of voluntary action are a vital source of strength in our national life, I have supported the establishment and development of the National Center for Voluntary Action. The National Center is a private, non-profit partner in the effort to generate and encourage volunteer service. The Center works to promote the establishment of local Voluntary Action Centers, as well as to assist in the expansion of voluntary action organizations already in existence. It stimulates voluntary action by providing information on successful voluntary efforts, and it assists in directing those who wish to volunteer services to areas and endeavors in which their services are needed.

The National Center for Voluntary Action is functioning now to fill a vital need in the private voluntary sector. Now we must turn our attention to bringing government volunteer programs into line with new national priorities and new opportunities for meeting those priorities. We must take full advantage of the lessons of the past decade, and we must build on the experience of that period if we are to realize the full potential of voluntary citizen service. This is no longer a matter of choice. We cannot afford to misuse or ignore the considerable talents and energies of our people. In the coming years, the continued progress of our society is going to depend increasingly upon the willingness of more Americans to participate in voluntary service and upon our ability to channel their service effectively.

One matter of consequence to the problems of properly channeling volunteer services and expanding government's role in the development of volunteer resources is the proliferation of government volunteer programs. It was perhaps inevitable that these programs would be generated almost at random across the spectrum of government concern for human needs. This occurred in a period when the Federal Government was still attempting to define its relationship with, and its purposes in, the area of voluntary service. Now the role of government has been confirmed and its responsibilities and obligations are clear. Meeting these responsibilities and obligations will be a long, difficult, and challenging adventure. But it is an adventure we can look to with excitement and with the knowledge that the only sure source of failure can be a failure of the will of the American people. I do not believe it will fail.

The foundation for a greatly expanded government contribution to volunteer service already exists. Now we must consolidate that foundation in order to build on it. To accomplish this, I propose a reorganization of the present volunteer service system. Accordingly, I herewith transmit to the Congress Reorganization Plan No. 1 of 1971, prepared in accordance with chapter 9 of title 5 of the United States Code. Reorganization would bring together within a single agency a number of voluntary action programs presently scattered throughout the executive branch of the Federal Government. The new agency would be called Action.

Composition

Under the reorganization plan Action would administer the functions of the following programs:

• Volunteers in Service to America: VISTA volunteers work in domestic poverty areas to help the poor break the poverty cycle.

• Auxiliary and Special Volunteer Programs in the Office of Economic Opportunity: At present the National Student Volun-

teer Program is administered under this authority. This program stimulates student voluntary action programs which deal with the problems of the poor.

• Foster Grandparents: This program provides opportunities for the elderly poor to assist needy children.

• Retired Senior Volunteer Program: RSVP provides opportunities for retired persons to perform voluntary services in their communities.

• Service Corps of Retired Executives: SCORE provides opportunities for retired businessmen to assist in the development of small businesses.

• Active Corps of Executives: ACE provides opportunities for working businessmen to assist in the development of small businesses.

After investigation I have found and hereby declare that each reorganization included in the accompanying reorganization plan is necessary to accomplish one or more of the purposes set forth in section 901 (a) of title 5 of the United States Code. In particular, the plan is responsive to section 901 (a) (1), "to promote the better execution of the laws, the more effective management of the executive branch and of its agencies and functions and the expeditious administration of the public business" and section 901 (a) (3), "to increase the efficiency of the operations of the Government to the fullest extent practicable."

The reorganizations provided for in the plan make necessary the appointment and compensation of new officers as specified in section 1 of the plan. The rates of compensation fixed for these officers would be comparable to those fixed for officers in the executive branch who have similar responsibilities.

The reorganization plan should result in more efficient operation of the Government. It is not practical, however, to itemize or aggregate the exact expenditure reductions which would result from this action.

Upon the establishment of Action, I would delegate to it the principal authority for the Peace Corps now vested in me as President and delegated to the Secretary of State. In addition, the function of the Office of Voluntary Action now operating in the Department of Housing and Urban Development would be transferred to the new agency by executive action.

Finally, I will submit legislation which would include the transfer of the functions of the Teacher Corps from the Department of Health, Education, and Welfare to the new agency. This legislation would expand authority to develop new uses of volunteer talents, it would provide a citizens' advisory board to work with the director of the new agency, and it would provide authority to match private contributions.

Goals

Although reorganization is only a step, it is the essential first step toward the goal of a system of volunteer service which uses to the fullest advantages the power of all the American people to serve the purposes of the American nation.

In pursuing this goal, the new agency would, first, expand the testing and development of innovations in voluntary actions. Health services, housing, the environment, educational development, manpower, and community planning are just a few of the areas in which we would act to accomplish more through voluntary service, and I intend to ask for additional funds and additional authority for Action to explore new approaches to these and other problems.

In the future, we are going to have to find new ways for more people to fulfill themselves and to lead satisfying and productive lives. The problems are of concern even now, but they must be put in perspective quickly because they will soon be upon us. I believe at least some of the answers will be found in volunteer service. Action would work to find those answers and apply them.

Second, there are many Americans who want to contribute to our national life through voluntary citizen service but who cannot serve full time. Their contributions must not be wasted. Volunteers in full-time service would work with part time volunteers and the new agency would develop and provide opportunities for more people to give part time service.

Third, Action would bring together in one place programs which appeal predominantly to younger Americans with those that appeal to older Americans, and would work to bring the energy, the innovative spirit, the experience, and the skills of each to bear on specific problems. The generations in America share America's problems—they must share in the search for solutions so that we all may share in the benefits of our solutions.

Fourth, Action would develop programs for combining foreign service with domestic service to accommodate volunteers interested in such an opportunity. I believe that young people in particular would be interested in the chance for this experience and would greatly benefit from it. I know there would be great value, for example, in permitting those who have served the needs of the poor abroad to turn their skills and experience to helping the poor at home and vice versa. In addition, if volunteers are to reap the full benefit of serving, and if they are to be able to provide others the full benefit of their service, then we must open the doors to a fuller exchange of ideas and experiences between overseas and domestic volunteer efforts. These exchanges would considerably enhance the value of the experience gained in these endeavors by broadening the areas in which that experience is applied.

Fifth, at the present time valuable professional skills offered in voluntary service are too frequently limited by narrow categorical programs when their broader application is urgently needed. For example, the contributions of businessmen made through SCORE and ACE are provided only through the Small Business Administration. We know that the skills of business can be used in many areas where they are not used presently. Action would open new channels for service and would permit a more extensive utilization of business and other vocational and professional abilities.

Finally, by centralizing administrative functions of the volunteer services, the new agency would provide a more effective system of recruitment, training and placement of full time volunteers than the present circumstances permit. It would provide a single source of information and assistance for those who seek to volunteer full time service. And it would permit more effective management of services than is currently possible in the administration of volunteer programs as well as the more efficient use of resources.

Principles

In restructuring our system of volunteer services, we can accomplish the goals which I have set forth. But we must do more than this. We must restructure our thinking about volunteer services. We must determine how to use our volunteer resources to accomplish more than they accomplish now. We need an increased effort to stimulate broader volunteer service, to involve more volunteers, and to involve them not simply as foot-soldiers in massive enterprises directed from the top but in those often small and local efforts that show immediate results, that give immediate satisfaction—those efforts that return to citizens a sense of having a hand in the business of building America. Part of our rethinking of this matter must look to the past so that we may properly meet the needs of the present and prepare for the possibilities of the future.

Volunteer service in poverty areas is a case in point. We already have considerable experience in dealing with the problems of poverty through the use of volunteers. Now we must build upon this experience and find new ways to use more effectively the volunteers presently serving in poverty areas, as well as in all other areas, and to stimulate new programs so that additional numbers of volunteers can assist in the solution of community and national problems.

In line with this effort to build on what we have learned, Action would function with particular concern for these basic principles:

• It would encourage local initiative, and would support local programs to solve local problems.

• Where appropriate, the new agency would assign volunteers to assist, and work under the technical supervision of other Federal agencies, State and local agencies or organizations, and private sponsors.

• The services of local part time volunteers would be sought and supported in the effort to accomplish specific jobs. They would be assisted, when necessary, by full-time volunteers.

• Universities and colleges, State, city and private organizations must be engaged in the effort to broaden opportunities for volunteer service and under the new agency they would be assisted in these efforts.

• Finally, to meet the increasing need for skilled volunteers Action would give increased emphasis to recruiting and applying the skills of trained craftsmen and professional workers.

Funding

To insure that the new agency has the financial resources to begin working toward the goals I have outlined, I will seek for this agency an additional $20 million above the budget requests I have already submitted for the component agencies. These funds would be directed primarily to finding new ways to use volunteer services.

Conclusion

The early nineteenth century observer of America, Alexis de Tocqueville, was intrigued by the propensity of Americans to join together in promoting common purposes. "As soon as several of the inhabitants of the United States have taken up an opinion or a feeling which they wish to promote in the world, they look out for mutual assistance, and as soon as they have found one another out, they combine. From that moment they are no longer isolated men, but a power seen from afar...."

Though we have seen the success of Government volunteer efforts in the past ten years, I believe voluntary citizen service is still little more than a power seen from afar. In relation to its potential, this power is virtually undeveloped. We must develop it.

There are those today, as there always will be, who find infinite fault with life in this Nation and who conveniently forget that they share responsibility for the quality of life we lead. But our needs are too great for this attitude to be accepted. America belongs to all of its people. We are all responsible for the direction this Nation will take in the century ahead, for the quality of life we will lead and our children will lead. We are all responsible, whether we choose to be or not, for the survival and the success of the American experience and the American dream.

So there is little room for the luxury of making complaints without making commitments.

America must enlist the ideals, the energy, the experience, and the skills of its people on a larger scale than it ever has in the past. We must insure that these efforts be used to maximum advantage. We must insure that the desire to serve be linked with the opportunity to serve. We must match the vision of youth with the wisdom of experience. We must apply the understanding gained from foreign service to domestic needs, and we must extend what we learn in domestic service to other nations. And in all these endeavors, I believe, we can bring the power seen from afar to focus clearly on the problems and the promise of our time.

RICHARD NIXON

GOVERNMENT REORGANIZATION

Following is the text, as made available by the White House, of President Nixon's March 25 message to Congress on reorganization of the executive branch.

TO THE CONGRESS OF THE UNITED STATES:

When I suggested in my State of the Union Message that "most Americans today are simply fed up with government at all levels," there was some surprise that such a sweeping indictment of government would come from within the government itself. Yet it is precisely there, within the government itself, that frustration with government is often most deeply experienced.

A President and his associates often feel that frustration as they try to fulfill their promises to the people. Legislators feel that frustration as they work to carry out the hopes of their constituents. And dedicated civil servants feel that frustration as they strive to achieve in action the goals which have been established in law.

Good Men and Bad Mechanisms

The problem with government is not, by and large, the people in government. It is a popular thing, to be sure, for the public to blame elected officials and for elected officials to blame appointed officials when government fails to perform. There are times when such criticism is clearly justified. But after a quarter century of observing government from a variety of vantage points, I have concluded that the people who work in government are more often the victims than the villains when government breaks down. Their spirit has usually been willing. It is the structure that has been weak.

Good people cannot do good things with bad mechanisms. But bad mechanisms can frustrate even the noblest aims. That is why so many public servants—of both political parties, of high rank and low, in both the legislative and executive branches— are often disenchanted with government these days. That is also why so many voters feel that the results of elections make remarkably little difference in their lives.

Just as inadequate organization can frustrate good men and women, so it can dissipate good money. At the Federal level alone we have spent some $1.1 trillion on domestic programs over the last 25 years, but we have not realized a fair return on this investment. The more we spend, the more it seems we need to spend and while our tax bills are getting bigger our problems are getting worse.

No, the major cause of the ineffectiveness of government is not a matter of men or of money. It is principally a matter of machinery. It will do us little good to change personnel or to provide more resources unless we are willing to undertake a critical review of government's overall design.

Most people do not pay much attention to mechanical questions. What happens under the hood of their automobile, for example, is something they leave to the specialists at the garage. What they do care about, however, is how well the automobile performs. Similarly, most people are willing to leave the mechanical questions of government organization to those who have specialized in that subject—and to their elected leaders. But they do care very deeply about how well the government performs.

At this moment in our history, most Americans have concluded that government is not performing well. It promises much, but it does not deliver what it promises. The great danger, in my judgment, is that this momentary disillusionment with government will turn into a more profound and lasting loss of faith.

We must fight that danger. We must restore the confidence of the people in the capacities of their government. In my view, that obligation now requires us to give more profound and more critical attention to the question of government organization than any single group of American leaders has done since the Constitutional Convention adjourned in Philadelphia in September of 1787. As we strive to bring about a new American Revolution, we must recognize that central truth which those who led the original American Revolution so clearly understood: often it is how the government is put together that determines how well the government can do its job.

This is not a partisan matter, for there is no Republican way and no Democratic way to reorganize the government. This is not a matter for dogmatic dispute, for there is no single, ideal blueprint which will immediately bring good order to Federal

affairs. Nor is this a matter to be dealt with once and then forgotten. For it is important that our political institutions remain constantly responsive to changing times and changing problems.

Renewed Interest in Comprehensive Reform

The last two years have been a time of renewed interest in the question of how government is organized. The Congress has instituted a number of reforms in its own procedures and is considering others. Judicial reform—at all levels of government— has also become a matter of intense concern. The relationship between various levels of government has attracted increased attention—and so, of course, has the subject of executive reform.

This administration, with the counsel and the cooperation of the Congress, has taken a number of steps to reorganize the executive branch of the Federal Government. We have set up a new Domestic Council and a new Office of Management and Budget in the Executive Office of the President. We have created a new Environmental Protection Agency and a new United States Postal Service. We have worked to rationalize the internal structure of Federal departments and agencies.

All of these and other changes have been important, but none has been comprehensive. And now we face a fundamental choice. We can continue to tinker with the machinery and to make constructive changes here and there—each of them bringing some marginal improvement in the government's capacities. Or we can step back, take a careful look, and then make a concerted and sustained effort to reorganize the executive branch according to a coherent, comprehensive view of what the Federal Government of this Nation ought to look like in the last third of the twentieth century.

The impulse for comprehensive reorganization has been felt before in recent decades. In fact, the recommendations I am making today stem from a long series of studies which have been made under several administrations over many years. From the report of the President's Committee on Administrative Management (the Brownlow Committee) in 1937, down through the findings of the Commission on Organization of the Executive Branch of the Government (the Hoover Commission) in 1949, the President's Task Force on Government Organization in 1964, and my own Advisory Council on Executive Organization during the last two years, the principles which I am advancing today have been endorsed by a great number of distinguished students of government and management from many backgrounds and from both political parties.

I hope the Congress will now join me in concluding, with these authorities, that we should travel the course of comprehensive reform. For only if we travel that course, and travel it successfully, will we be able to answer affirmatively in our time the fundamental question posed by Alexander Hamilton as the Constitution was being debated in 1788: "whether societies of men are really capable or not of establishing good government from reflection and choice...."

The Fragmentation of Federal Responsibility

As we reflect on organizational problems in the Federal Government today, one seems to stand out above all others; the fact that the capacity to do things—the power to achieve goals and to solve problems—is exceedingly fragmented and broadly scattered throughout the Federal establishment. In addressing almost any of the great challenges of our time the Federal Government finds itself speaking through a wide variety of offices and bureaus, departments and agencies. Often these units trip over one another as they move to meet a common problem. Sometimes they step on one another's toes. Frequently, they behave like a series of fragmented fiefdoms—unable to focus Federal resources or energies in a way which produces any concentrated impact.

Consider these facts:

Nine different Federal departments and twenty independent agencies are now involved in education matters. Seven departments and eight independent agencies are involved in health. In many major cities, there are at least twenty or thirty separate manpower programs, funded by a variety of Federal offices. Three departments help develop our water resources and four agencies in two departments are involved in the management of public lands. Federal recreation areas are administered by six different agencies in three departments of the government. Seven agencies provide assistance for water and sewer systems. Six departments of the government collect similar economic information—often from the same sources—and at least seven departments are concerned with international trade. While we cannot eliminate all of this diffusion we can do a great deal to bring similar functions under common commands.

It is important that we move boldly to consolidate the major activities of the Government. The programmatic jumble has already reached the point where it is virtually impossible to obtain an accurate count of just how many Federal grant programs exist. Some estimates go as high as 1,500. Despite impressive attempts by individual legislators and by the Office of Economic Opportunity, there is still no agreement on a comprehensive list. Again and again I hear of local officials who are unable to determine how many Federal programs serve their areas or how much Federal money is coming into their communities. One reason is that the assistance comes from such a wide variety of Federal sources.

The Consequences of Scattered Responsibility

What are the consequences of this scattering of Federal responsibility? There are many.

In the first place, the diffusion of responsibility makes it extremely difficult to launch a coordinated attack on complex problems. It is as if the various units of an attacking army were operating under a variety of highly independent commands. When one part of the answer to a problem lies in one department and other parts lie in other departments, it is often impossible to bring the various parts together in a unified campaign to achieve a common goal.

Even our basic analysis of public needs often suffers from a piecemeal approach. Problems are defined so that they will fit within established jurisdictions and bureaucratic conventions. And the results of government action are typically measured by the degree of activity within each program rather than by the overall impact of related activities on the outside world.

The role of a given department in the policy making process can be fundamentally compromised by the way its mission is defined. The narrower the mission, the more likely it is that the department will see itself as an advocate within the administration for a special point of view. When any department or agency begins to represent a parochial interest, then its advice and support inevitably become less useful to the man who must serve all of the people as their President.

Even when departments make a concerted effort to broaden their perspectives, they often find it impossible to develop a comprehensive strategy for meeting public needs. Not even the best planners can set intelligent spending priorities, for example, unless they have an opportunity to consider the full array of alternative expenditures. But if one part of the problem is studied in one department and another part of the problem is studied elsewhere, who decides which element is more important? If one office considers one set of solutions and a separate agency investigates another set of solutions, who can compare the results? Too often, no official below the very highest levels of the Government has access to enough information to make such comparisons wisely. The result is that the Government often fails to make a rational distribution of its resources among a number of program alternatives.

Divided responsibility can also mean that some problems slip between the cracks and disappear from the Government's view. Everybody's business becomes nobody's business and embarrassing gaps appear which no agency attempts to fill. At other times, various Federal authorities act as rivals, competing with one another for the same piece of "turf."

Sometimes one agency will actually duplicate the work of another; for instance, the same locality may receive two or more grants for the same project. On other occasions, Federal offices will actually find themselves working at cross purposes with one another; one agency will try to preserve a swamp, for example, while another is seeking to drain it. In an effort to minimize such problems, government officials must spend enormous amounts of time and energy negotiating with one another that should be directed toward meeting people's needs. And even when they are able to work out their differences, officials often reach compromise solutions which merely represent the lowest common denominator of their original positions. Bold and original ideas are thus sacrificed in the quest for intra-governmental harmony.

Scattered responsibility also contributes to the overcentralization of public decision making. Because competing offices are often in different chains of command, it is frequently impossible for them to resolve their differences except by referring them to higher authorities, a process which can mean interminable delays. In an attempt to provide a means for resolving such differences and for providing needed coordination, an entire new layer of bureaucracy has emerged at the interagency level. Last year, the Office of Management and Budget counted some 850 interagency committees. Even so, there are still many occasions when only the White House itself can resolve such interjurisdictional disputes. Too many questions thus surface at the Presidential level that should be resolved at levels of Government closer to the scene of the action.

Inefficient organization at the Federal level also undermines the effectiveness of State and local governments. Mayors and Governors waste countless hours and dollars touching base with a variety of Federal offices—each with its own separate procedures and its own separate policies. Some local officials are so perplexed by the vast array of Federal programs in a given problem area that they miss out on the very ones that would be most helpful to them. Many State and local governments find they must hire expensive specialists to guide them through the jungles of the Federal bureaucracy.

If it is confusing for lower levels of government to deal with this maze of Federal offices, that challenge can be even more bewildering for individual citizens. Whether it is a doctor seeking aid for a new health center, a businessman trying to get advice about selling in foreign markets, or a welfare recipient going from one office to another in order to take full advantage of Federal services, the people whom the Government is supposed to be serving are often forced to weave their way through a perplexing obstacle course as a condition of receiving help.

The Hobbling of Elected Leadership

Perhaps the most significant consequence of scattered responsibility in the executive branch is the hobbling effect it has on elected leadership—and, therefore, on the basic principles of democratic government. In our political system, when the people identify a problem they elect to public office men and women who promise to solve that problem. If these leaders succeed, they can be reelected; if they fail, they can be replaced. Elections are the people's tool for keeping government responsive to their needs.

This entire system rests on the assumption, however, that elected leaders can make the government respond to the people's mandate. Too often, this assumption is wrong. When lines of responsibility are as tangled and as ambiguous as they are in many policy areas, it is extremely difficult for either the Congress or the President to see that their intentions are carried out.

If the President or the Congress wants to launch a program or change a program or even find out how a program is working, it often becomes necessary to consult with a half dozen or more authorities, each of whom can blame the others when something goes wrong. It is often impossible to delegate to any one official the full responsibility for carrying out a specific mandate, since the machinery for doing that job is divided among various agencies. As a result, there is frequently no single official—even at the Cabinet level—whom the President or the Congress can hold accountable for Government's success or failure in meeting a given need.

No wonder bureaucracy has sometimes been described as "the rule of no one." No wonder the public complains about programs which simply seem to drift. When elected officials cannot hold appointees accountable for the performance of government, then the voters' influence on government's behavior is also weakened.

How Did Things Get This Way?

The American people clearly pay a very high price for the incapacities of governmental structures—one that is measured in disappointment, frustration and wasted tax dollars. But how did things get this way?

What happened, essentially, was that the organization of Government—like the grant-in-aid programs which I have discussed in my special messages to the Congress concerning revenue sharing—grew up in a haphazard, piecemeal fashion over the years. Whenever Government took on an important new assignment or identified an important new constituency, the chances were pretty good that a new organizational entity would be established to deal with it. Unfortunately, as each new office was set up, little or no attention was given to the question of how it would fit in with the old ones. Thus office was piled upon office in response to developing needs; when new needs arose and still newer units were created, the older structures simply remained in place.

Of the twelve executive departments now in existence, only five can trace their origins to the beginnings of our country. The Departments of State and Treasury were set up in 1789; so was the War Department—the predecessor of the Department of Defense. The positions of Attorney General and Postmaster General were also established in 1789, though it was not until later that the departments they head were set up in their present form. One of these five units, the Post Office Department, will soon become an independent corporation. But, under my proposals, the other four "original" departments would remain intact. It is the seven newer departments of the Government which would be affected by the changes I recommend.

These seven departments were set up to meet the changing needs of a growing nation, needs which have continued to change over the years. The Department of the Interior, for example, was established in 1849 to deal with newly opened western lands and especially with the Indians who inhabited them. The Department of Agriculture was also added in the nineteenth century, at a time when the overwhelming majority of our people were directly affected by the tremendous expansion of agricultural enterprise. In the early years of the twentieth century, in a time of rapid and unsettling industrial growth, the Department of Commerce and Labor was set up. The Labor Department was split off from it in 1913, in response to feelings that labor was suffering from an imbalance of power and needed additional influence. The three newest departments of the Government—Health, Education, and Welfare, Housing and Urban Development, and Transportation—were all created after World War II. Each represented a first step toward bringing together some of the new Federal offices and agencies which had proliferated so rapidly in recent decades.

Organizing Around Goals

As we look at the present organization of the Federal Government, we find that many of the existing units deal with methods and subjects rather than with purposes and goals. If we have a question about labor we go to the Labor Department and if we have a business problem we go to the Commerce De-partment. If we are interested in housing we go to one department and if we are interested in highways we go to another.

The problem is that as our society has become more complex, we often find ourselves using a variety of means to achieve a single set of goals. We are interested, for example, in economic development—which requires new markets, more productive workers and better transportation systems. But which department do we go to for that? And what if we want to build a new city, with sufficient public facilities, adequate housing, and decent recreation areas—which department do we petition then?

We sometimes seem to have forgotten that government is not in business to deal with subjects on a chart but to achieve real objectives for real human beings. These objectives will never be fully achieved unless we change our old ways of thinking. It is not enough merely to reshuffle departments for the sake of reshuffling them. We must rebuild the executive branch according to a new understanding of how government can best be organized to perform effectively.

The key to that new understanding is the concept that the executive branch of the government should be organized around basic goals. Instead of grouping activities by narrow subjects or by limited constituencies, we should organize them around the great purposes of government in modern society. For only when a department is set up to achieve a given set of purposes, can we effectively hold that department accountable for achieving them. Only when the responsibility for realizing basic objectives is clearly focused in a specific governmental unit, can be reasonably hope that those objectives will be realized.

When government is organized by goals, then we can fairly expect that it will pay more attention to results and less attention to procedures. Then the success of government will at last be clearly linked to the things that happen in society rather than the things that happen in government.

Under the proposals which I am submitting, those in the Federal Government who deal with common or closely related problems would work together in the same organizational framework. Each department would be given a mission broad enough so that it could set comprehensive policy directions and resolve internally the policy conflicts which are most likely to arise. The responsibilities of each department would be defined in a way that minimizes parochialism and enables the President and the Congress to hold specific officials responsible for the achievement of specific goals.

These same organizational principles would also be applied to the internal organization of each department. Similar functions would be grouped together within each new entity, making it still easier to delegate authority to lower levels and further enhancing the accountability of subordinate officials. In addition, the proposals I submit today include a number of improvements in the management of Federal programs, so that we can take full advantage of the opportunities afforded us by organizational restructuring.

The administration is today transmitting to the Congress four bills which, if enacted, would replace seven of the present executive departments and several other agencies with four new departments: the Department of Natural Resources, the Department of Community Development, the Department of Human Resources and the Department of Economic Affairs. A special report and summary—which explain my recommendations in greater detail—have also been prepared for each of the proposed new departments.

The Department of Natural Resources

One of the most notable developments in public consciousness in recent years has been a growing concern for protecting the environment and a growing awareness of its highly interdependent nature. The science of ecology—the study of the inter-relationships between living organisms and their environments—has experienced a sudden rise in popularity. All of us have become far more sensitive to the way in which each element of our natural habitat affects all other elements.

Unfortunately, this understanding is not yet reflected in the way our Government is organized. Various parts of the interdependent environment are still under the purview of highly independent Federal offices. As a result, Federal land policies, water programs, mineral policies, forestry practices, recreation activities and energy programs cannot be easily coordinated, even though the manner in which each is carried out has a great influence on all the others.

Again and again we encounter intragovernmental conflicts in the environmental area. One department's watershed project, for instance, threatens to slow the flow of water to another department's reclamation project downstream. One agency wants to develop an electric power project on a certain river while other agencies are working to keep the same area wild. Different departments follow different policies for timber production and conservation, for grazing, for fire prevention and for recreational activities on the Federal lands they control, though the lands are often contiguous.

We cannot afford to continue in this manner. The challenges in the natural resource field have become too pressing. Some forecasts say that we will double our usage of energy in the next 10 years, of water in the next 18 years, and of metals in the next 22 years. In fact, it is predicted that the United States will use more energy and more critical resources in the remaining years of this century than in all of our history up until now. Government must perform at its very best if it is to help the Nation meet these challenges.

I propose that a new Department of Natural Resources be created that would bring together the many natural resource responsibilities now scattered throughout the Federal Government. This Department would work to conserve, manage and utilize our resources in a way that would protect the quality of the environment and achieve a true harmony between man and nature. The major activities of the new Department would be organized under its five subdivisions: Land and Recreation Resources, Water Resources, Energy and Minerals Resources, Oceanic, Atmospheric and Earth Sciences, and Indian and Territorial Affairs.

The new Department of Natural Resources would absorb the present Department of the Interior. Other major programs which would be joined to it would include: The Forest Service and the soil and water conservation programs from the Department of Agriculture, planning and funding for the civil functions of the Army Corps of Engineers and for the civilian power functions of the Atomic Energy Commission, the interagency Water Resources Council, the oil and gas pipeline safety functions of the Department of Transportation, and the National Oceanic and Atmospheric Administration from the Department of Commerce. Because of their historical association with the Department of the Interior, the programs of the Bureau of Indian Affairs would be administered by the new Department until such time as an acceptable alternative arrangement could be worked out with Indian leaders and other concerned parties.

The Department of Community Development

A restless and highly mobile people, Americans are constantly creating new communities and renewing old ones throughout our land. In an era of rapid change, this process—which once took generations—can now be repeated in just a few years.

At the same time, the process of community development is becoming even more complex, particularly as the problems of urban and rural communities begin to merge. The elements of community life are many and the mark of a cohesive community is the harmonious way in which they interrelate. That is why we hear so much these days about the importance of community planning. And that is why it is essential that Federal aid for community development be designed to meet a wide range of related needs in a highly coordinated manner.

Often this does not happen under the present system. The reason is that the basic community development programs of

the Federal Government are presently divided among at least eight separate authorities—including four executive departments and four independent agencies.

A community that seeks development assistance thus finds that it has to search out aid from a variety of Federal agencies. Each agency has its own forms and regulations and timetables—and its own brand of red tape. Each has its own field organizations, often with independent and overlapping boundaries for regions and districts. Sometimes a local community must consult with Federal offices in three or four different States.

The result is that local leaders often find it virtually impossible to relate Federal assistance programs to their own local development strategies. The mayor of one small town has observed that by the time he finishes dealing with eight Federal planning agencies, he has little time to do anything else.

Occasionally, it must be admitted, a community can reap unexpected benefits from this diffusion of Federal responsibility. The story is told of one small city that applied to six different agencies for help in building a sewage treatment plant and received affirmative responses from all six. If all the grants had been completed, the community would have cleared a handsome profit—but at the Federal taxpayer's expense.

To help correct such problems, I propose that the major community development functions of the Federal Government be pulled together into a new Department of Community Development. It would be the overriding purpose of this Department to help build a wholesome and safe community environment for every American. This process would require a comprehensive series of programs which are equal to the demands of growing population and which provide for balanced growth in urban and rural areas. The new Department would operate through three major administrations: a Housing Administration, a Community Transportation Administration and an Urban and Rural Development Administration. A fourth unit, the Federal Insurance Administration, would be set up administratively by the Secretary.

The new Department of Community Development would absorb the present Department of Housing and Urban Development. Other components would include certain elements of the Economic Development Administration and the Regional Commission programs from the Department of Commerce, the independent Appalachian Regional Commission, various Department of Agriculture programs including water and waste disposal grants and loans, the Rural Electrification Administration, and rural housing programs. The Community Action and Special Impact Programs of the Office of Economic Opportunity would be included, as would the Public Library construction grant program from the Department of Health, Education, and Welfare and certain disaster assistance functions now handled by the Office of Emergency Preparedness and the Small Business Administration. Most Federal highway programs and the Urban Mass Transportation Administration would be transferred from the present Department of Transportation.

I would note that while the Department of Transportation is a relatively new entity, it, too, is now organized around methods and not around purposes. A large part of the Department of Transportation would be moved into the new Department of Economic Affairs—but those functions which particularly support community development would be placed in the Department which is designed to meet that goal.

The Department of Human Resources

The price of obsolete organization is evidenced with special force in those Government programs which are directly designed to serve individuals and families. In part this is because there has been so much new legislation in the human resource field in recent decades; the old machinery is simply overstrained by its new challenges. But whatever the reasons, human resource programs comprise one area in which the Government is singularly ill-equipped to deliver adequate results.

I have already commented on the broad dispersion of Federal health and education activities. Similar examples abound. Income support programs, including those which administer food stamps, welfare payments, retirement benefits and other forms of assistance, are scattered among three departments and a number of other agencies. The Department of Agriculture, the Department of Health, Education, and Welfare, and the Office of Economic Opportunity all handle food and nutrition matters. Child care programs, migrant programs, manpower programs, and consumer programs often suffer from similarly divided attention.

In one city, two vocational training centers were built three blocks apart at about the same time and for the same purpose, with money from two different Federal agencies. And for every case of overattention, there are many more of neglect. Consider the plight of a poor person who must go to one office for welfare assistance, to another for food stamps, to another for financial counseling, to still another for legal aid, to a fifth office for employment assistance, to a sixth place for job training, and to a number of additional offices for various kinds of medical help. The social worker who might guide him through this maze often works in still another location.

Such situations are clearly intolerable, yet the Federal Government—which ought to be working to reform these confused systems—actually is responsible for much of the confusion in the first place.

I believe that we can take a major step toward remedying such problems by establishing a new Department of Human Resources which would unify major Federal efforts to assist the development of individual potential and family well-being. This Department would be subdivided, in turn, into three major administrations: Health, Human Development and Income Security.

This new Department would incorporate most of the present Department of Health, Education, and Welfare with the following significant additions: a number of food protection, food distribution and nutrition programs from the Department of Agriculture, the College Housing program from the Department of Housing and Urban Development, the independent Railroad Retirement Board, various programs from the Office of Economic Opportunity (including nutrition, health, family planning, alcoholism, and drug rehabilitation efforts), and the Manpower Administration, the Women's Bureau, the Unemployment Insurance Program and a number of other employment service and training activities from the Department of Labor.

The Department of Economic Affairs

One of the first things most students learn about economics is that the material progress of our civilization has resulted in large measure from a growing division of labor. While a single family or a single community once provided most of its own goods and services, it now specializes in providing only a few, depending increasingly on a far-flung, intricate network of other people and other organizations for its full economic well-being.

The only way the Federal Government can deal effectively with such a highly interdependent economy is by treating a wide range of economic considerations in a comprehensive and coordinated manner. And—as our Gross National Product moves beyond the trillion dollar level and as our productive system, which now accounts for approximately 40 percent of the world's wealth, encounters new challenges from other nations—it is becoming even more important that Federal economic policies be carried out as effectively as possible.

But again, the organization of the Government works against the systematic consideration of economic complexities. The step by step evolution of our Federal machinery has created a series of separate entities—each handling a separate part of the economic puzzle. Some of these entities are relatively autonomous units within departments. Others are independent agencies. But perhaps the most dramatic evidence of our frag-

mented approach to the economy is the existence of four major executive departments which handle highly interdependent economic matters: Commerce, Labor, Agriculture, and Transportation.

This situation can seriously impair governmental efforts to respond effectively to economic challenges. One department, for example, may be concerned with the raw materials a given industry receives from the farms, while a second department is concerned with getting these materials to the factory and getting the product to its market. Meanwhile, a third department is concerned with the workers who harvest the crops, run the transportation systems and manufacture the product, while a fourth department is concerned with the businessmen who own the plant where the product is made and the stores where it is merchandised.

Such a division of responsibility can also create a great deal of overlap. The Agriculture Department, for instance, finds that its interest in agricultural labor is shared by the Labor Department, its regard for agricultural enterprise is shared by the Small Business Administration, and its concern for providing sufficient transportation for farm products is shared by the Department of Transportation. The Commerce, Labor and Agriculture Departments duplicate one another in collecting economic statistics, yet they use computers and statistical techniques which are often incompatible.

It has sometimes been argued that certain interest groups need a department to act as their special representative within the Government. In my view, such an arrangement serves the best interests of neither the special group nor the general public. Little is gained and much can be lost, for example, by treating our farmers or our workers or other groups as if they are independent participants in our economic life. Their problems cannot be adequately treated in isolation; their well-being is intimately related to the way our entire economy functions.

I would not suggest these reforms if I thought they would in any way result in the neglect of farmers, workers, minorities or any other significant groups within our country. To the contrary, I propose these reforms because I am convinced they will enable us to serve these groups much better. Under my proposals, the new Department of Economic Affairs would be in a much stronger position really to *do* something about the wide-ranging factors which influence farm income than is the present Department of Agriculture, for example. It could do more to meet the complex needs of workingmen and women than can the present Department of Labor. It would be able to pull together a wider range of resources to help minority businessmen than can the present Department of Commerce.

Federal organization in the economic area has been the target of frequent criticism over the years. During the previous administration alone, two special studies of executive organization recommended that it be substantially altered. I have received a similar recommendation from my Advisory Council on Executive Organization.

I am therefore recommending to the Congress that a new Department of Economic Affairs be established to promote economic growth, to foster economic justice, and to encourage more efficient and more productive relationships among the various elements of our economy and between the United States economy and those of other nations. As this single new Department joined the Treasury Department, the Council of Economic Advisers and the Federal Reserve Board in shaping economic policy, it would speak with a stronger voice and would offer a more effective, more highly integrated viewpoint than four different departments can possibly do at present. The activities of the new Department would be grouped under the following six administrations: Business Development, Farms and Agriculture, Labor Relations and Standards, National Transportation, Social, Economic, and Technical Information and International Economics.

The new Department of Economic Affairs would include many of the offices that are now within the Departments of Commerce, Labor and Agriculture. A large part of the Department of

Transportation would also be relocated here, including the United States Coast Guard, the Federal Railroad Administration, the St. Lawrence Seaway Development Corporation, the National Transportation Safety Board, the Transportation Systems Center, the Federal Aviation Administration, the Motor Carrier Safety Bureau and most of the National Highway Traffic Safety Administration. The Small Business Administration, the Science Information Exchange program from the Smithsonian Institution, the National Institute for Occupational Health and Safety from the Department of Health, Education, and Welfare and the Office of Technology Utilization from the National Aeronautics and Space Administration would also be included in the new Department.

Other Organizational Reforms

Regrouping functions among departments can do a great deal to enhance the effectiveness of government. It should be emphasized, however, that regrouping functions within departments is also a critical part of my program for executive reform. Just as like tasks are grouped together within a given department, so similar operations should be rationally assembled within subordinate units. Such a realignment of functions, in and of itself, would make it much easier for appointed officials to manage their agencies and for both the President and the Congress to see that their intentions are carried out.

Toward this same end, I am recommending to the Congress a number of additional steps for bringing greater managerial discipline into Government. In the first place, I am proposing that the Department Secretary and his office be considerably strengthened so that the man whom the President appoints to run a department has both the authority and the tools to run it effectively. The Secretary would be given important managerial discretion that he does not always enjoy today, including the ability to appoint many key department officials, to delegate authority to them and to withdraw or change such delegations of authority, and to marshal and deploy the resources at his command so that he can readily focus the talent available to him at the point of greatest need.

Each of the new Secretaries would be provided with a Deputy Secretary and two Under Secretaries to help him meet his responsibilities. In addition, each major program area within a department would be headed by a high-level administrator who would be responsible for effectively managing a particular group of related activities. These officials would be appointed by the President and their appointments would be subject to Senate confirmation.

It is my philosophy that we should give clear assignments to able leaders—and then be sure that they are equipped to carry them out. As a part of this same effort, we should do all we can to give the best new management tools to those who run the new departments. There is no better time to introduce needed procedural changes within departments than a time of structural change among departments. We can reap greater benefits if we take advantage of this opportunity by implementing the most advanced techniques and equipment for such tasks as planning and evaluation, data collection, systematic budgeting, and personnel administration.

Finally, I would again stress in this message—as I have in my discussions of revenue sharing—the importance of decentralizing government activities as much as possible. As I have already observed, the consolidation of domestic departments would do a great deal to facilitate decentralization, since it would produce fewer interagency disputes that require resolution at higher levels. It is also true, as many management experts have pointed out, that as the reliability and scope of information expand at higher levels of government, officials can delegate authority to lower levels with greater confidence that it will be used well.

In addition to the consolidation of functions, I am also proposing a reform of the field structures of the Federal Government that would also promote decentralization. Each Department, for example, would appoint a series of Regional Directors who would represent the Secretary with respect to all Department activities in the field. Planning, coordination and the resolution of conflicts could thus be more readily achieved without Washington's involvement, since there would be a "Secretarial presence" at the regional level. Further coordination at lower levels of government would be provided by strengthening the ten Regional Councils which include as members the Regional Directors of various departments in a given area of the country.

In the first months of my administration I moved to establish common regional boundaries and regional headquarters for certain domestic departments. I observed at that time that the Federal Government has never given adequate attention to the way in which its departments are organized to carry out their missions in the field. It is now time that we remedied this pattern of neglect. Even the best organized and best managed departments in Washington cannot serve the people adequately if they have to work through inadequate field structures.

Industry and government both have found that even the largest organizations can be run effectively when they are organized according to rational principles and managed according to sound techniques. There is nothing mystical about these principles or these techniques; they can be used to make the Federal Government far more effective in a great many areas.

As we consolidate and rationalize Federal functions, as we streamline and modernize our institutional architecture, as we introduce new managerial techniques and decentralize Government activities, we will give Government the capacity to operate far more efficiently than it does today. It will be able to do more work with fewer mechanisms and fewer dollars. It will be able to use its work force more productively. This could mean significant savings for our taxpayers. It would emphasize, however, that any reductions in the Federal work force attributable to this proposal would come by normal turnover; no civil servant should lose his job as a result of this plan.

It is important that these reforms be seen by our civil servants not as a threat to their security but as an opportunity for greater achievement. We have worked hard to bring able people into Government employment. Executive reorganization can help the Nation make even better use of their talent and their dedication and it can also make it easier for us to attract more men and women of great vision and competence into public service at the Federal level.

Focusing Power Where It Can Be Used Best

These proposals for reorganizing the Federal Government are a natural complement to my proposals for revenue sharing; there is a sense in which these two initiatives represent two sides of the same coin. Both programs can help us decentralize government, so that more decisions can be made at levels closer to the people. More than that, both programs are concerned with restoring the general capacity of government to meet its responsibilities.

On the one hand, through revenue sharing, we would give back to the States and localities those functions which belong at the State and local level. To help them perform those functions more effectively, we would give them more money to spend and more freedom in spending it. At the same time, however, we must also do all we can to help the Federal Government handle as effectively as possible those functions which belong at the Federal level. Executive reorganization can help us achieve this and by bringing together related activities which are now fragmented and scattered.

A healthy Federal system is one in which we neither disperse power for the sake of dispersing it nor concentrate power for the sake of concentrating it. Instead, a sound Federal system requires us to focus power at that place where it can be used to the greatest public advantage. This means that each level of government must be assigned those tasks which it can do best and must be given the means for carrying out those assignments.

The Central Question

Ever since the first settlers stepped upon our shore more than three centuries ago, a central question of the American experience has been: How do we best organize our government to meet the needs of the people? That was the central question as the colonists set up new governments in a new world. It was the central question when they broke from their mother country and made a new nation. It was the central question as they wrote a new Constitution in 1787 and, at each critical turning point since that time, it has remained a dominant issue in our national experience.

In the last forty years, as the Federal Government has grown in scope and complexity, the question of how it should be organized has been asked with even greater intensity and relevance. During this time, we have moved to formulate responsive answers to this question in an increasingly systematic manner. Searching studies of Government management and organization have been made under virtually every national administration since the 1930s and many needed reforms have resulted.

What is now required, however, is a truly comprehensive restructuring of executive organization, one that is commensurate with the growth of the Nation and the expansion of the government. In the last twenty years alone our population has increased by one-third and the Federal budget has quintupled. In the last two decades, the number of Federal civilian employees has risen by almost 30 percent and the domestic programs they administer have multiplied tenfold. Three executive departments and fourteen independent agencies have been tacked on to the Federal organization chart during that brief span.

Yet it still is the same basic organization chart that has set the framework of governmental action for decades. While there have been piecemeal changes, there has been no fundamental overhaul. Any business that grew and changed so much and yet was so patient with old organizational forms would soon go bankrupt. The same truth holds in the public realm. Public officials cannot be patient with outmoded forms when the people have grown so impatient with government.

Thomas Jefferson once put it this way: "I am certainly not an advocate for frequent and untried changes in laws and constitutions," he wrote, "but...laws and institutions must go hand in hand with the progress of the human mind. As that becomes more developed, more enlightened, as new discoveries are made, new truths disclosed, and manners and opinions change with the change of circumstances, institutions must advance also, and keep pace with the times."

"Institutions must advance." Jefferson and his associates saw that point clearly in the late 18th century, and the fruit of their vision was a new nation. It is now for us—if our vision matches theirs—to renew the Government they created and thus give new life to our common dreams.

RICHARD NIXON

FUNDS FOR EDUCATION

Following is the text, as made available by the White House, of President Nixon's April 6 message to Congress on revenue sharing for education.

TO THE CONGRESS OF THE UNITED STATES:

A very substantial part of what American government does is directed to the future and to the creation of a suitable legacy for generations to come. In this sense, government reflects a central purpose of the basic family unit and seeks to serve that purpose: as we move to condition the future, we move also to prepare our children to take their place in that future. In this task, all levels of government recognize the Nation's responsibility for educating its youth.

Primary responsibility, of course, rests with State and local governments, as it should. The Federal Government can help provide resources to meet rising needs, but State and local education authorities must make the hard decisions about how to apply these resources in ways that best serve the educational needs of our children. To enable State and local authorities to do this more effectively, I am proposing today a new system of special revenue sharing as a means of providing Federal financial assistance for elementary and secondary education.

This message is the last of six special revenue sharing proposals which I have put forward over the past two months. Combined with the administration's $5 billion general revenue sharing plan and welfare reform proposals, special revenue sharing—as a new and more flexible approach to Federal aid—would fundamentally reform the fiscal roles and relationships of American federalism. The other five special revenue sharing proposals have been in the areas of urban community development, rural community development, transportation, manpower training and law enforcement assistance.

The plan I am putting forward today for Education Revenue Sharing brings together more than 30 Federal aid categories and deals with one of the Nation's most complex systems for providing public services. There are 46 million students presently enrolled in public schools in America, with more than five and a half million more in non-public schools. There are more than 117,000 schools and nearly 18,000 public school districts, each with its own unique conditions and each with its own problems.

Federal expenditures for elementary and secondary schooling over the past decade are projected to increase from $0.9 billion in fiscal year 1961 to $5.5 billion in fiscal year 1972. Yet there are serious problems with the way in which this aid is provided.

The Present System

Under the present piecemeal system of Federal aid, education grants are available to local schools under 38 separate authorizations for "instruction," 37 separate authorizations for low-income students, and 22 separate authorizations for reading instruction. The confusion is so great that some school districts have had to hire separate staffs charged solely with cutting through the maze of applications, guidelines, regulations and reporting requirements which are an intrinsic part of the present grant system.

There are other problems:

• The time, energy and imagination needed to bring educational reform is frequently drained off into what is essentially non-productive effort to qualify for Government grants. Yet, at the same time, rigid qualifications for grants frequently stifle creative initiative. In the end, a system which ought to promote innovation instead discourages it. And because Federal programs are resistant to change, we see money being spent on programs which may have outlived their usefulness, or that simply are ineffective, while funds for new ideas cannot be obtained.

• Educational planning is made difficult because of the fragmentation of grants. Under the present system, a community must make a series of separate applications to a series of Federal officials. There is no assurance that every proposal will be funded, or that any proposal will be funded. Consequently, the present fragmented procedures virtually eliminate any possibility of preparing a comprehensive, coordinated program.

• There is little accountability under the present system; if a program fails it is difficult to assess responsibility. Although it is the common response to blame Washington if something does not function according to design, such an exercise is usually futile given the cumbersome nature of the Federal bureaucracy.

• There is little flexibility in the present system. Individual grants are often too narrowly defined and designed to achieve the things Washington wants, while at the same time allowing little latitude to meet individual community needs.

• There has been little useful evaluation of how Federal aid programs under the present system help children learn more effectively, or of how they provide the children with equal educational opportunities. The diversity of the country and the large number and great variety of Federal aid programs have made it impossible for those at the Federal level to measure the success or failure of their efforts, and so we resort to judging effectiveness by how much we spend rather than by how much we accomplish.

My proposal for special revenue sharing for education is designed to overcome these problems by substituting a basic new approach to providing Federal assistance. To help formulate this proposal, the Office of Education held ten regional hearings to discuss the specifications for Education Revenue Sharing, and my proposal has benefitted from the views of educators and those interested in education all across the Nation.

Education Revenue Sharing

Education Revenue Sharing would revitalize the relationship between the Federal Government and State and local governments. It would stimulate creativity and new initiatives at State and local levels. My proposal would establish a new instrument of Federal assistance which would bring together more than thirty major Office of Education programs representing approximately $2.8 billion in grants in the 1972 budget, and provide for an increase of $200 million in total funding in the first year.

These funds would provide support for educational activities in broad areas where there are strong national interests in strengthening school programs. The national priority areas included are compensatory education for the disadvantaged, education of children afflicted by handicapping conditions, vocational education, assistance to schools in areas affected by Federal activities, and the provision of supporting services.

This new Federal aid instrument would have the following important features:

Automatic Distribution of Funds. Funds would be distributed automatically on the basis of a statutory formula which takes account of the total school age population in each State, the number of students from low-income families, and the number of students whose parents work or live on Federal property. No State would receive less money under Education Revenue Sharing than it receives under the present grant system. In addition, authority for advance funding would be requested to facilitate careful planning free from the vagaries of the present practice of delayed appropriations.

No Federal Approval of State Plans. States would no longer be required to submit exhaustive plans for extensive Federal review or Federal approval, but would simply develop and publish a plan in line with State and local needs so as to permit all concerned citizens to become involved with the allocation of these Federal resources. States would also appoint an advisory council broadly representative of the public and the education community, in order to further insure that all interests are heard. This new system would substitute genuine citizen participation for routine bureaucratic sign-off.

Broad Definition of Purposes. The areas of Federal assistance would be broadly defined in keeping with national interests.

• The provision of equal educational opportunities to all of our children is a key national priority. As I pointed out a year ago, the most glaring shortcoming in American education today is the lag in essential learning skills among large numbers of children of poor families. The largest Federal program in education—Title I of the Elementary and Secondary Education Act—was designed to meet the special educational needs of these children. The Education Revenue Sharing Act would provide that over one-half of the $3.0 billion proposed for the first year be used for providing compensatory education for disadvantaged children. These funds would be passed through directly

to local school districts which enroll large concentrations of these children.

• The specific needs of handicapped children are and would continue to be a matter of concern to the Federal Government. When time is so critical to the training and social development of these youngsters, any delay in the funding of their education can have irreparable consequences. Nevertheless, in the present circumstances, delay is common. I propose to change this. Funds would be allocated directly to the States and the procedures for obtaining these funds would be simplified.

• For many years, the Federal Government has provided assistance for training in industry, agriculture and the crafts in our Nation's schools. This training is vital to the Nation's economy. But the needs in these areas are constantly changing. Vocational education of tomorrow may bear little resemblance to today's form, but its task will be the same: to demonstrate to American youth the worth and dignity of work, and to help them to obtain the specific skills that other forms of education cannot supply. As with my proposal for Manpower Revenue Sharing, States and local educational authorities would be authorized to determine how best to use Federal funds for vocational education in order to meet the needs of particular communities and individual workers.

• An ongoing responsibility of local public schools is to provide education for Federally connected children. The Federal Government rightly provides aid to help meet the financial burden of children who live on Federal property—hence property which provides no taxes for education. To offset the loss of local school taxes, Education Revenue Sharing would provide a direct pass-through to local school districts enrolling such children. For those students whose parents only work on Federal property, and live on locally taxable land, funds would also be provided. In this case, however, the funds would be distributed to the States which would determine the degree of financial need created by those circumstances and allocate funds accordingly.

• The Federal Government currently offers an array of programs designed to purchase specific educational materials or services. These programs range from the provision of textbooks and other library resources to the support of guidance and counseling services. Education Revenue Sharing would continue this aid but would pull together programs from at least fourteen separate statutory provisions into one flexible allocation under which States can decide how best to meet local education needs.

Greater Flexibility. Under this proposal for Education Revenue Sharing, States and local school districts would be given far greater flexibility than is presently the case in deciding how funds should be spent in serving the national priority areas. In addition to the broader definition of national purpose, States would have the authority to transfer up to thirty percent of funds —except those which are passed through directly to local schools —from one purpose to another. This would enhance flexibility in the application of funds for education, and permit the States to make substantial adjustment in their educational plans as their educational needs require.

Other Features. As with my previous special revenue sharing proposals, Education Revenue Sharing would preserve all existing safeguards against infringements of civil rights by assuring that these funds would be subject to Title VI of the Civil Rights Act of 1964.

Non-public schools bear a significant share of the cost and effort of providing education for our children today. Federal aid to education should take this fully into account. This proposal would do that by considerably broadening the authority for extending aid to students in non-public schools. Non-public school students would be counted in the reckoning of population for purposes of allocation, and all forms of educational services would be available to them.

As an important precondition to the receipt of Federal funds for education of the disadvantaged, I propose a requirement for States to certify that services provided in all schools within a given school district from State and local funds must be fully comparable. This is a considerable improvement over the present law. It would assure that Federal funds for compensatory education programs would actually be spent on services beyond those provided for all children, and thus for the first time would truly guarantee that these funds would be used to help equalize learning opportunity for the disadvantaged.

The Federal Role in Education

The proposal I am putting forward today reflects what this administration considers to be the appropriate Federal role in elementary and secondary education. This Federal role is three-fold: (1) the allocation of financial resources on a broad and continuing basis to help States and local school districts meet their responsibilities, (2) the provision of national leadership to help reform and renew our schools to improve performance, and (3) the concentration of resources to meet urgent national problems during the period when they are most intense.

Education Revenue Sharing would strengthen the first by providing a new and expanded system of Federal aid to our schools. It should be noted in this connection that my proposals for general revenue sharing and welfare reform would also both provide and free additional fiscal resources which States and localities could devote to the rising costs of education. At the present time, State and local governments spend forty percent of their revenues for education. Under general revenue sharing, which would distribute a fixed portion of the Federal tax base to the States and localities to use as they determine, education would most certainly be a major beneficiary. These funds would total $5 billion in the first full year of operation. Similarly, the administration's proposals to reform the Nation's failing welfare system would free the States of a significant portion of fast-growing welfare costs at the same time that it would provide a better and more stable home environment for millions of children.

To strengthen the Federal leadership role in reforming and renewing our Nation's schools, I proposed a year ago the creation of a National Institute of Education to bring to education the intensity and quality of research and experimentation which the Federal Government has, for example, devoted to agricultural and medical research. The National Institute of Education would serve as a focal point for identifying educational problems, developing new ways to alleviate these problems, and helping school systems to put the results of educational research and experimentation into practice.

As an example of the concentration of Federal resources to meet urgent national problems during a period of intense need, I proposed in May 1970 an Emergency School Aid Act to provide $1.5 billion over a two-year period to help meet the special problems of desegregating our Nation's schools. Progress in school desegregation has been accelerating. The Emergency School Aid Act would help local communities expedite and adjust to this change, while maintaining and improving the quality of education in affected schools.

Taken together, the National Institute, the Emergency School Aid Act and Education Revenue Sharing represent a bold new approach to fulfilling the Federal role in education and to meeting the educational needs of the 1970s.

Conclusion

The education of our children transcends partisan politics. No one benefits from failures in our system of education, and no one can fail to benefit from improvements in the means by which education in America is given all the assistance proper at the Federal level. The effort to provide that proper assistance, the effort to encourage reform where reform is needed, and the effort to extend to all American children the advantage of equal educational opportunity have all been a concern of this administration as, indeed, they have been of other administrations. These efforts continue.

I believe we must recognize that the Federal Government cannot substitute its good intentions for the local understanding of local problems, for local energy in attacking these problems, and for local initiatives in improving the quality of education in America. We must also recognize that State and local authorities need Federal resources if they are to meet their obligations and if they are to use the peculiar advantages of State and local knowledge, responsibility, and authority to their fullest potential. Education Revenue Sharing accommodates the Federal role in national education to both these realities, and it lays the foundation for a new and more productive Federal-State relationship in this area of vital national concern, just as the previous revenue sharing proposals have afforded similar possibilities in their areas of specific concern.

I consider each of these proposals vitally important in and of itself. But in the aggregate, the importance of revenue sharing is greater than the sum of the parts which comprise this series of legislative proposals. For we are seeking nothing less than a new definition of the relationship between Federal Government and State and local governments—one which answers the needs of the present and anticipates the needs of the future.

RICHARD NIXON

DISTRICT OF COLUMBIA

Following are excerpts, as made available by the White House, from President Nixon's April 7 message to Congress on the District of Columbia:

Crime Reduction

...My 1972 budget requests, together with those of the District government, provide for:

• Full-year funding for Washington's 35 new U.S. Attorneys and 13 new U.S. District judgeships, which were approved by the Congress in a 1971 supplemental appropriation.

• Upgrading the efforts of the Executive Protective Service in protecting the foreign embassies in the District.

• Maintenance of police strength at 5,100 men with additional training to improve force effectiveness.

• Implementation of the new court reform legislation.

• Improved care and custody for the growing institutional population, and expansion of the community-based correctional program.

I urge the Congress to contribute to the momentum of our winning battle against crime in the Nation's Capital by approving these requests.

Helping the District Help Itself

..."Revenue sharing" of a sort has been a way of life in the District of Columbia for many years, as it properly should be in view of the Federal presence in the District. My budget requests for fiscal year 1972 call for Federal payments of $153 million to the District government—an increase of more than 20 percent over the currently authorized level. And General Revenue Sharing, when enacted, would bring the city an additional $23 million share during the first year. Welfare reform, besides extending new dignity and tangible benefits to the District's welfare recipients, would lead to further large savings for the city government.

Beyond the fiscal relief which these national reform proposals would afford Washington, there are several areas where the Federal interest in the District warrants special financial support. These include the metropolitan rapid rail mass transit system (METRO); improved water quality facilities and other public works construction projects; and public higher education.

Federal Guarantees for Metro Revenue Bonds

Excavations for METRO's subway tunnels and stations already dot the District. When it goes into operation at the beginning of 1974 it will be the Nation's most modern mass transit system. It should do much to unify the metropolitan

Washington community, to improve the qualify of life by reducing congestion and pollution in the area, and to stimulate the metropolitan economy by the increased labor mobility it will provide. I am confident that disagreements over implementation of the 1968 and 1970 Highway Acts—now tying up needed METRO funds—can be resolved, and I have urged all of the parties involved to give priority to meeting these legislative obligations.

To remove another major obstacle now confronting METRO, I am today proposing that the Federal Government guarantee the revenue bonds of the Washington Metropolitan Area Transit Authority so as to expedite their sale. Severe inflation in the construction industry has combined with unexpected delays in the METRO development timetable to create a $450 million gap in the financial plan originally advanced by WMATA, and to impair the marketability of the METRO revenue bonds. By guaranteeing these securities, we can help WMATA sell all its originally planned bonds so that METRO construction can go forward at once. The bonds would become taxable as a condition of the guarantee, providing a revenue flowback to the Treasury from the interest paid on them. This flowback in turn would permit the Federal Government to cover 25 percent of the Authority's anticipated interest costs on the bonds, enabling the issuance of $300 million in additional bonds. Federal assistance would thus help WMATA close two-thirds of its $450 million revenue gap, in keeping with the two-thirds Federal and one-third local cost sharing arrangement that has prevailed for METRO funding in general.

Clean Water

Washington's efforts to improve its public services and to enhance the urban environment are doubly deserving of Federal support—not only for the sake of the city and the people themselves, but for the sake of the whole Nation as well. This applies to the city's hopes of showing the Nation the way in urban mass transit, and it applies equally to the ecological and esthetic imperatives of purifying our waters....

AID REORGANIZATION

Following is the text, as made available by the White House, of President Nixon's April 21 message to Congress concerning the reorganization of U.S. foreign assistance programs.

TO THE CONGRESS OF THE UNITED STATES:

On September 15, 1970, I proposed a major transformation in the foreign assistance program of the United States. My purpose was to renew and revitalize the commitment of this Nation to support the security and development objectives of the lower income countries, and thereby to promote some of the most fundamental objectives of U.S. foreign policy.

Today, I report to you on the progress of the last seven months in effecting that transformation and ask the Congress to join me in taking the next creative step in our new approach —the reform of the United States bilateral assistance program.

To achieve such reform, I am transmitting two bills—the proposed International Security Assistance Act and International Development and Humanitarian Assistance Act— and announcing a number of actions which I intend to take administratively. Taken together, they would:

• Distinguish clearly between our security, development and humanitarian assistance programs and create separate organizational structures for each. This would enable us to define our own objectives more clearly, fix responsibility for each program, and assess the progress of each in meeting its particular objectives.

• Combine our various security assistance efforts (except for those in Southeast Asia which are now funded in the Defense budget) into one coherent program, under the policy direction of the Department of State. This would enable security assistance to play more effectively its critical role in supporting the Nixon Doctrine and overall U.S. national security and foreign policy in the 1970s.

• Create a U.S. International Development Corporation and a U.S. International Development Institute to replace the Agency for International Development. They would enable us to reform our bilateral development assistance program to meet the changed conditions of the 1970s.

• Provide adequate funding for these new programs to support essential U.S. foreign policy objectives in the years ahead.

The Importance of Foreign Assistance

U.S. foreign assistance is central to U.S. foreign policy in the 1970s in three ways:

First, we must help to strengthen the defense capabilities and economies of our friends and allies. This is necessary so that they can increasingly shoulder their own responsibilities, so that we can reduce our direct involvement abroad, and so that together we can create a workable structure for world peace. This is an essential feature of the Nixon Doctrine.

Second, we must assist the lower income countries in their efforts to achieve economic and social development. Such development is the overriding objective of these countries themselves and essential to the peaceful world order which we seek. The prospects for a peaceful world will be greatly enhanced if the two-thirds of humanity who live in these countries see hope for adequate food, shelter, education and employment in peaceful progress rather than in revolution.

Third, we must be able to provide prompt and effective assistance to countries struck by natural disaster or the human consequences of political upheaval. Our humanitarian concerns for mankind require that we be prepared to help in times of acute human distress.

The Need for Reform

We cannot effectively pursue these objectives in the 1970s with programs devised for an earlier period. The world has changed dramatically. Our foreign assistance programs—like our overall foreign policy—must change to meet these new conditions.

In my September special message to the Congress I spelled out the major changes in the world which require new responses. Let me summarize them here:

• Today the lower income countries are increasingly able to shoulder the major responsibility for their own security and development and they clearly wish to do so. We share their belief that they must take the lead in charting their own security and development. Our new foreign assistance programs must therefore encourage the lower income countries to set their own priorities and develop their own programs, and enable us to respond as our talents and resources permit.

• Today the United States is but one of many industrialized nations which contribute to the security and development of the lower income countries. We used to furnish the bulk of international development assistance; we now provide less than half. The aid programs of other countries have grown because they recognize that they too have a major stake in the orderly progress which foreign assistance promotes, and because their capabilities to provide such assistance have grown enormously since the earlier postwar period.

• Today the international institutions can effectively mesh the initiatives and efforts of the lower income countries and the aid efforts of all of the industrialized countries. We can thus place greater reliance on such institutions and encourage them to play an increasing leadership role in the world development process.

Our ideas on the reforms needed in the world of the 1970s have evolved significantly since I received the Report of my

Task Force on International Development, chaired by Mr. Rudolph Peterson, and since my special message of last September, as the result of our own deliberations and our further consultations with the Congress, the business community and many other sectors of the American public, and our friends abroad. Before spelling out a new blueprint for our bilateral assistance program, however, I wish to report to you on the gratifying progress achieved since last September in reorienting our assistance policies.

Progress Toward Reform

First, the Congress in December passed supplemental assistance legislation for FY 1971 which represented a major step in implementing the security assistance component of the Nixon Doctrine. This legislation authorized additional funds for military assistance and supporting economic assistance for countries in which the U.S. has major interests and which have convincingly demonstrated the will and ability to help themselves—including Israel and Jordan in the Middle East and Cambodia, Vietnam and Korea in East Asia.

Such support is necessary to carry out one of the central thrusts of the Nixon Doctrine—moving us from bearing the major responsibility for the defense of our friends and allies to helping them achieve an increasing capability to maintain their own defense. This increase in security assistance enables us to continue to reduce our direct presence abroad, and helps to reduce the likelihood of direct U.S. military involvement in the future.

Second, the international development institutions have continued their progress toward leadership in the international development process. For example:

• The World Bank continues to increase the size and improve the effectiveness of its operations. It also has decided to broaden the scope of its lending beyond the traditional financing of projects to the provision of funds to support overall development programs in appropriate circumstances, and it is developing an improved internal evaluation and audit system.

• The United Nations Development Program has initiated a reorganization to improve its administration. In time this will enable it to assume a leading role in coordinating the international technical assistance effort.

• The World Health Organization has effectively guided and coordinated the worldwide effort to cope with the present cholera epidemic in Africa.

Third, the industrialized countries have now agreed on comparable systems of tariff preferences for imports from the lower income countries. The preferences plan is a major step in the crucial international effort to expand the export earnings of these countries, and hence to reduce their reliance on external aid. The European Community has indicated that it plans to put its tariff preferences into effect on July 1, and Japan has announced that it will do so before October 1.

Fourth, there has been satisfying progress toward achieving the untying of bilateral development loans on a fully reciprocal basis. This action will enhance the value of economic assistance to recipient countries, and eliminate the political frictions which tied aid now causes. Virtually all of the industrialized countries have agreed to the principle of untying. Details of a system offering suppliers of all participating countries a fair and equitable basis for competition are now being worked out in the Organization for Economic Cooperation and Development.

Fifth, I have established a Council on International Economic Policy, which I chair, to coordinate all aspects of U.S. foreign economic policy, including development assistance. It will provide top-level focus for our policies in this area, and accord them the high priority which they require in our foreign policy for the 1970s.

I am heartened by this progress, but much more remains to be done:

• I again urge the Congress to vote the additional funds which I have requested for the Inter-American Development Bank and the Asian Development Bank.

• We will shortly transmit legislation to authorize the U.S. contribution to the doubling of the resources of the International Development Association, the soft-loan affiliate of the World Bank, which stands at the center of the network of international financial institutions, and I urge the Congress to approve it.

• We are working with others to help establish a soft-loan window for the African Development Bank.

• We will shortly transmit legislation to authorize U.S. participation in the system of generalized tariff preferences for developing countries, and I urge Congress to approve it.

The New U.S. Bilateral Assistance Program

The next major step is the reform of the U.S. bilateral assistance program, incorporated in the proposed International Security Assistance Act and International Development and Humanitarian Assistance Act.

Our new bilateral assistance program must achieve several objectives. It must:

• Clearly identify our distinct aid objectives: security assistance, development assistance and humanitarian assistance.

• Be truly responsive to the initiatives of the lower income countries themselves and encourage them to play the central role in solving their own security and development problems. In the area of development assistance, this means working within a framework set by the international institutions to the maximum extent possible.

• Be concentrated in countries of special interest to the United States, and in projects and programs in which the United States has a special ability to be of help.

• Recognize the improved economic capacity of many of the lower income countries in establishing the terms of our assistance.

• Assure improved management.

• Reduce substantially the number of U.S. Government officials operating our assistance program overseas.

Let me now spell out the details of our new approach, based on these principles.

Security Assistance. I have repeatedly stressed the essential role played by our military and related forms of assistance in supporting the foreign policy of the United States and our own security interests. The primary purposes of this assistance have been, and will continue to be, the preservation of peace through the deterrence of war, and the support of efforts by allied and friendly countries to move toward self-sustaining economic growth and social progress. To abandon our responsibilities would risk magnifying the world's instability in the short run, and impairing its peaceful development for the longer run, and therefore increase the threat to our own security both now and in the future.

The new course on which we are set, however, encourages others to take on greater responsibilities themselves. Our new security assistance program will seek to strengthen local defense capabilities by providing that mix of military and supporting economic assistance which is needed to permit friendly foreign countries to assume additional defense burdens themselves without causing them undue political or economic costs. If we are to move toward reducing our own physical presence, the effectiveness of our security assistance program will become of ever more crucial importance.

In Asia, this new strategy has already encouraged the nations of the area to assume greater responsibility for their own defense and provided a basis for a major reduction in our military presence. The funds which have been provided to assist the Government of South Vietnam have been essential to the progress of Vietnamization, and helped insure continued U.S. troop withdrawals. We have helped Cambodia to mobilize its manpower and other resources in defense of its independence and neutrality. We are providing Korea with equipment to improve and modernize its defenses and we are withdrawing some of our own troops.

Our friends and allies know that it is no longer possible nor desirable for the United States to bear the principal burden of their defense. A clear lesson of the 1960s is that deterrence against local aggression, or against subversion supported from outside a country's borders, cannot be achieved without a strong contribution by the threatened country itself. We can meet our security assistance objectives effectively only if we link our efforts closely with those of our friends and thereby build the foundations for peace in partnership with them.

To help do so, and also in recognition of the improved economic capability of many of the countries receiving security assistance, I propose today significant changes in our authorities to provide military assistance to our friends and allies.

Our military assistance programs have suffered from undesirable rigidity. The only choice has been between grant assistance and sales on hard credit terms. Many of those nations that need our assistance are unable to meet the hard credit terms —so grant assistance has been the only course open for us to help meet their essential security needs. But as the lower income nations begin to develop an ability to shoulder the costs of their defense, we need to be able to assist them in doing so even though they cannot immediately assume the entire burden. Sales on concessional credit terms would permit earlier participation by some recipient countries in the financing of their essential defense needs and would thus engage their own assessment of priorities for the allocation of their resources at an earlier stage of development than is now possible.

To fill the existing gap between grant assistance and sales on relatively firm commercial terms, the International Security Assistance Act that I propose today includes authorization to finance sales of military equipment on concessional terms. Grant assistance will remain necessary for some nations whose financial resources are simply not adequate to meet their defense needs. But our objective is to move countries, as quickly as possible within the context of international security requirements and their own economic capabilities, along the spectrum from grants to concessional sales to the harder terms we have required for sales under the present act and finally to outright cash arrangements. We will also stress the transition from Government sales to those made directly by private industry to the extent feasible. By making these changes we would help countries move from dependence on the United States to independence in the creation and financing of their own security programs. We would not intend to provide concessional credits to countries able to meet the terms of the present program.

I am also asking, under the new act, greater flexibility to transfer funds among the various security assistance programs. Such flexibility is particularly important, for example, in this period of transition in Southeast Asia, where our troop withdrawals are freeing up substantial amounts of military equipment formerly used by our troops. I am asking that the ceiling on the amount of surplus equipment which can be granted to our friends and allies be increased; this will save us money as well as permit us to better help those of our friends who need it. In the long run, sound management of security assistance demands that there be enough flexibility to transfer funds among various programs in order to insure that the proper mix is used to meet our specific objectives in each instance.

For these international security assistance programs, I request authorization of $1,993 million for FY 1972: $778 million for supporting economic assistance, $705 million for grant military assistance, and $510 million for military credit sales.

These security assistance programs are at the core of our relations with certain key friendly countries. They critically affect our ability to meet our bilateral and collective security commitments. They are central to the achievement of major objectives of U.S. national security and foreign policy.

I therefore intend to direct by administrative action a reorganization of our security assistance program to meet more effectively the objectives of the Nixon Doctrine. Various components of security assistance—military assistance, military credit sales, grants of excess military stocks, supporting economic assistance, and the public safety program—have been fragmented in different pieces of legislation and managed through a series of different administrative arrangements. My proposals would bring these programs under one legislative act to assure that each is viewed as part of a coherent overall program. Military assistance for Vietnam, Laos and Thailand will continue to be funded in the Defense budget because these country programs are subject to the uncertainties of active hostilities and are intimately linked to the logistical support systems of our own force in Southeast Asia.

To assure effective policy control and management of this new security assistance effort, I would direct that a Coordinator for Security Assistance be established at a high level in the Department of State. I would also direct that the supporting economic assistance program be administered by the Department of State. The Department of Defense will continue to have primary responsibility for administering our military assistance and sales programs, and for relating these programs to overall U.S. national defense planning.

These new arrangements would be a significant step in the direction of improving the management of our security assistance program. They would therefore represent a significant step toward achieving greater accountability to the Congress and the public as well.

This new security assistance program would, I am confident, serve our national interest in the 1970s in a number of important ways. It would:

• Enable us to meet U.S. commitments more effectively and at lower cost;

• Strengthen the self-defense capabilities of nations to whose security the U.S. is committed by treaty, by special political ties, or by essential U.S. interests;

• Help to reduce the need for, and likelihood of, U.S. military involvement overseas;

• Foster increased local initiative and self-sufficiency;

• Promote constructive political relations with foreign governments;

• Support U.N. peacekeeping operations;

• Reduce potential frictions by lowering the U.S. profile abroad.

I am also requesting in the International Security Assistance Act authority for $100 million for the President's Foreign Assistance Contingency Fund for FY 1972. This would permit the administration, with due notification to the Congress, to meet worldwide contingencies—in the security, development and humanitarian areas—in ways compatible with our national interests. It is particularly important to have available uncommitted funds which can be used on short notice, when sudden crises in the international community require us to act promptly and decisively.

Development Assistance. The United States continues to have special national interests in particular lower income countries. We continue to have special capabilities in particular functional areas. We continue to need an effective bilateral development assistance program.

In order to advance such a program, I therefore propose legislation which would authorize the creation of two new development assistance institutions. Together with the two created by the last Congress, they would replace the Agency for International Development and enable us to develop a new approach based on the principles outlined above.

The two I now propose to create are:

• An International Development Corporation (IDC) to provide loans to finance development projects and programs in the lower income countries.

• An International Development Institute (IDI) to seek research breakthroughs on the key problems of development and to administer our technical assistance programs.

These would join two created by the last Congress:

• The Overseas Private Investment Corporation (OPIC) to promote the role of private investment in the development process.

• The Inter-American Social Development Institute (ISDI) to provide special attention to the social development needs of Latin America.

The U.S. International Development Corporation. The new IDC would administer our bilateral lending program. The authorities which I seek for it, and the operating style which I would direct it to pursue, would mark a major change in the U.S. approach to development assistance.

The IDC would make loans in response to initiatives from the lower income countries, rather than develop projects or programs on its own. It would have flexibility to tailor its loan terms to the needs of particular lower income countries, requiring harder terms from the more advanced and extending easier terms to the less advanced. Today's program has limited flexibility in this regard. Its lending volume to any particular country would be based on demonstrated self-help performance, and the quality of the projects and programs which that country presented to it. It would not seek to determine annual country lending levels in advance as is done at present.

The IDC would operate to the maximum extent feasible within a framework set by the international financial institutions. It would look to them to provide evaluations of the overall development prospects of particular countries, which would be a major consideration in its decisions to lend, rather than itself carrying out the extensive "country programming" which is now done. Within that context it would participate in non-project lending and international efforts to alleviate the debt burdens of particular lower income countries. It would participate for the United States in the international consortia and consultative groups, managed in most cases by the international financial institutions, through which the bulk of our bilateral assistance will flow.

The IDC would concentrate its activities in countries and regions where the U.S. has a major foreign policy interest in long-term development. For example, it would establish guidelines to assure that an equitable share of its resources is provided to the countries of the Western Hemisphere. But precisely because our interest is in the long-term development of these nations, the IDC would use its funds to pursue such interests rather than to seek merely short-term political gains.

The IDC would provide loans on the basis of both sound business standards and the pursuit of sound development purposes. The terms of its loans would be determined in large part by the financial situation of the borrowing country, rather than on the standard terms now offered to all borrowers. It would avoid loans to countries where the analysis of international financial institutions, and its own views, suggest an inadequate policy framework in which the loans could effectively promote development. The IDC would not be solely a lender of last resort as AID is required to be today, often financing the riskiest projects and programs.

The Corporation would work with and through the private sector to the maximum extent possible. It would give high priority to projects and programs which promote private initiative in the lower income countries, and to this end would seek to increase U.S. lending to local development banks and other financial intermediaries. I recommend that it also have authority to lend directly to private entities in the lower income countries.

The IDC would be governed by a Board of Directors consisting of outstanding private citizens as well as government officials, thus bringing the private sector directly into its decision-making process.

With this clear identification of specific instruments and programs with the specific objectives they are designed to achieve, we should not need to tie the hands of our managers—of the Corporation or any of our other new institutions—with the kinds of foreign policy and administrative restrictions which apply to the present program. Administrators should be held accountable for achieving program objectives. This is a central requirement of the businesslike approach which the new structure is designed to foster.

To ensure the necessary continuity and stability of operations to permit this businesslike approach, and building on the initiative of the Congress in 1969 to provide a 2-year authorization for foreign assistance, I request that the Corporation be given a 3-year authorization. I recommend an authorization of $1.5 billion of directly appropriated funds. I propose also that the IDC be provided with authority to borrow, in the private capital market or from the U.S. Treasury, up to a total of $1 billion during its initial 3-year period. This would help channel private capital more directly into the development process and bring private sector judgments directly to bear on the performance of the IDC. I recommend that it be authorized to use repayments of capital and interest on past U.S. development loans, which are now running at about $250 million annually.

A Corporation based on these principles would enable us to reduce substantially the number of U.S. government personnel involved in development lending overseas. By responding primarily to initiatives from the lower income countries, we would reduce the need for Americans to chart foreign programs and priorities. By relying increasingly on the international institutions for information and analytical work, we would reduce our own requirement for staff in both Washington and the field. By reducing the statutory restrictions on the program, we would be able to concentrate available staff on effective program management.

I am confident that a U.S. International Development Corporation based on these principles would regenerate our development lending program. It would provide major support to the development objectives of the lower income countries. It would enable us to play our full role effectively among the industrialized countries in promoting the development process. It would thereby provide major support for important U.S. national objectives in the 1970s.

The U.S. International Development Institute. The new IDI would administer a reformed bilateral technical assistance program and enable us to focus U.S. scientific, technological and managerial know-how on the problems of development.

The Institute would engage in four major types of activities:

• It would apply U.S. research competence in the physical and social sciences to the critical problems of development, and help raise the research competence of the lower income countries themselves.

• It would help build institutions in the lower income countries to improve their own research capabilities and to carry out a full range of developmental functions on a self-sustaining basis. I would expect it to place particular emphasis on strengthening agricultural and educational institutions.

It would help train manpower in the lower income countries to enable them to carry out new activities on their own.

• It would help lower income countries, particularly the least developed among them, to finance advisers on development problems.

Like the Corporation, the Institute would finance projects in response to proposals made by the lower income countries themselves. It would not budget funds in advance by country, since it could not know in advance how many acceptable projects would be proposed by each. It would look to these countries to select candidates to be trained under its program. Its research activities would be located in the lower income countries, rather than in the United States, to the greatest extent feasible. With its stress on institution building, it would seek to ensure that each program could be carried on after U.S. assistance is ended.

Most importantly, the Institute would seek to assure that all projects which it helps finance are considered essential by the lower income country itself. To do so, the Institute would require that the recipient country make a significant contribution to each as evidence that it attaches high priority to the project and is prepared to support it financially after U.S. assistance ends. We would finance a project for only a definite and limited period of time, and would want assurance that the host country would then carry it on. In the past, all too many technical assistance projects have been undertaken which were of more interest to Americans than to the recipient countries, and had little or no lasting impact. Our new program is designed to ensure that this does not happen in the future.

The international organizations are less advanced in research and technical assistance than in development lending. The Institute would thus be unable to function as fully within an international framework at this time as would the Corporation. However, it would work to help improve the capabilities of these organizations, especially the United Nations Development Program, and would seek to cooperate with them whenever possible. In fact, one of its objectives would be to help create an international framework for technical assistance comparable to the framework which has developed over the past decade for development lending.

By the very virtue of its separate existence, the Institute would be free to concentrate its efforts on the application of research and technology to the problems of development—a key feature of our new bilateral program which would distinguish it markedly from the present approach. The Institute would also concentrate its resources on the few most critical problem areas of development. Such concentration is necessary if it is to achieve the "critical mass" necessary to make real breakthroughs where they are most needed, and to attract the top cadre of experts and managers who can achieve such breakthroughs.

The areas of concentration would evolve in response to the requests of the lower income countries and management's assessment of where we can contribute most. They would undoubtedly shift over time. Experience suggests that limiting population growth, increasing agricultural production and training manpower would be among the concentration areas at first. Unemployment and urbanization problems could be early additions to the list.

While the Institute would provide grant financing, it would vary the effective terms of its assistance by varying the shares of the total cost of particular projects that the recipient must finance itself—ranging from a small percentage in the least advanced countries to most of the cost in the most advanced. In addition, the Institute should have authority to provide advisers on a completely reimbursable basis to countries which no longer need concessional aid at all. At the other end of the development spectrum, the IDI would be conscious of the special problems of the least developed countries—most of which are in Africa—which will continue to need the more traditional types of technical assistance since they have traveled less distance along the road to economic self-sufficiency.

The Institute would be managed on a businesslike basis, and it would carry out its projects largely through the private sector. I propose that it be governed by a Board of Trustees including outstanding citizens from the private sector. It would stress evaluation of past projects to determine their payoff and to help guide future project development; there has been too little followup in these programs in the past. We would seek top flight technical managers, development specialists and scientists for the small staff of the Institute. This new approach would permit a major reduction in the number of U.S. government personnel operating abroad.

To achieve these goals, the IDI should have financial continuity. I therefore propose that the Congress authorize an appropriation of $1,275 million for a 3-year period.

In short, the International Development Institute would provide a new dimension to our foreign assistance effort. It would enable us to focus some of our finest national resources—our capabilities in management, research and technology—on the critical bottleneck problems of development. Its style of operation should enable us to forge a new and more mature partnership with the lower income countries, with the rest of the industrialized world, and with our own private sector. It holds promise of becoming one of the most significant additions to our national capability to engage meaningfully in the world of the 1970s.

Overseas Private Investment Corporation and Inter-American Social Development Institute. The new International Development Corporation and International Development Institute would join two development assistance institutions already created by the Congress: the Overseas Private Investment Corporation and the Inter-American Social Development Institute.

OPIC is already at work promoting the role of private investment in the international development process. The record of economic development shows that successful growth is usually associated with a dynamic private sector, and we therefore look to private investment—primarily domestic but foreign as well—to play an increasing role in the development process. It must do so, since no government or public agency has the resources or technical skills which are necessary to meet the vast needs of the lower income countries.

OPIC's guarantees and insurance of U.S. private investment in lower income countries which seek such investment are already serving effectively the interests of both the U.S. investor and the host countries. Its early activities suggest that an independent corporation, directed by a joint public-private Board of Directors, can effectively manage a development assistance program; it thus augurs well for the structures which I propose today for the Development Corporation and Development Institute.

OPIC is operating within one of the most sensitive areas—private foreign investment—of the inherently sensitive overall relationship between aid donors and aid recipients. It is therefore essential that OPIC assist only sound projects which are responsive to the particular development needs of each country.

And it is clearly for each country to decide the conditions under which it will accept private foreign investment, just as it is for each investor to decide what conditions are adequate to attract his investments. We as a Government ask only that the investments of our citizens be treated fairly and in accordance with international law. In nearly all cases they have been. However, unjust acts by a country toward an American firm cannot help but adversely affect our relationship with that country. As President, I must and will take such acts into account in determining our future assistance and overall policy toward such a country.

The Inter-American Social Development Institute has also begun to develop its programs, which seek to promote the social development of the Latin American and Caribbean people. Working mainly through private organizations and international institutions, it represents a new innovative channel in seeking to promote solutions to basic economic and social problems in these areas. I propose that it be renamed the Inter-American Foundation, to characterize more accurately its proposed style of operation.

Humanitarian Assistance. U.S. humanitarian assistance programs cover a wide spectrum of human needs: disaster relief and rehabilitation; famine; refugee and migration relief and assistance. They aim to help people around the world recover from unfortunate situations by which they have been victimized. In the past year alone, such help has been extended to refugees from civil war in Nigeria and Jordan, earthquake victims in Peru, flood victims in Romania and Tunisia, and cyclone victims in Pakistan.

These activities rely heavily for program implementation on private voluntary agencies. In the past year alone, U.S. voluntary agencies registered with the Advisory Committee on Voluntary Foreign Aid contributed $370 million of their own resources in over 100 countries.

At present, humanitarian assistance programs are carried out through numerous offices in the U.S. Government. I propose to centralize the responsibility for coordinating all humanitarian assistance programs under a new Assistant Secretary of State. We would thereby assure a coherent effort to carry out this vital and literally life-saving aspect of our foreign assistance policy. This new approach would also improve our capability to respond quickly and effectively through better contingency planning, additional stockpiling and training, and the maintenance of closer and better coordinated relationships with the United Nations, other donor countries, and the private voluntary agencies.

Coordination

I have outlined the overriding need to separate our overall foreign assistance program into its three component parts: security assistance, development assistance, and humanitarian assistance. I have indicated that we would pull together all parts of our security assistance and humanitarian assistance under central management, so that each can function effectively as a total program within the context of U.S. foreign policy. And I have also proposed the creation of two new institutions, to go along with the two created by the last Congress, to carry forward our development assistance program in the 1970s.

There is thus a need for new mechanisms to assure effective coordination of our new foreign assistance program.

First, there must be effective coordination among the several components of the new development assistance program. This would be done through my appointing a single Coordinator of Development Assistance, responsible directly to the President, as Chairman of the Boards of the IDC, IDI, and OPIC.

The Coordinator would also chair an executive coordinating committee composed of the chief executive officers of each of these institutions and ISDI. He would be available for congressional testimony on our overall bilateral development assistance policy and the operations of the several institutions. Both the Congress and I could look to him as the administration's chief spokesman on bilateral development assistance policy and programs.

Second, the Secretary of State will provide foreign policy guidance for all components of our new foreign assistance program. His representatives would be members of the boards of each of the development institutions, and he would have direct responsibility for both security and humanitarian assistance. In each country our Ambassador, as my personal representative, will of course be responsible for coordination of all of our assistance programs.

Third, foreign assistance issues which raise broader questions of foreign economic policy will be handled through my new Council on International Economic Policy.

Finally, coordination among the three major components of our assistance program, and between them and our overall national security policy, would be handled through the National Security Council. We will thus establish strong management, coordination, and policy guidance over all of our foreign assistance programs.

Conclusion

This Nation can no more ignore poverty, hunger and disease in other nations of the world than a man can ignore the suffering of his neighbors. The great challenge to Americans of this decade, be they private citizens or national leaders, is to work to improve the quality of life of our fellow men at home and abroad.

We have a unique and unprecedented opportunity. We do not have all the answers to the questions of poverty, nor adequate resources to meet the needs of all mankind. We do possess the greatest scientific and technological capacity, and the most prosperous and dynamic economy, of any nation in history. More importantly, we have, as a vital element of the American character, a humanitarian zeal to help improve the lives of our fellow men.

We are therefore a nation uniquely capable of assisting other peoples in preserving their security and promoting their development. By doing so, we accomplish three major objectives:

• We strengthen international cooperation for a peaceful world.

• We help to relieve the poverty and misery of others less fortunate than ourselves.

• We help to build firm foundations of friendship between this Nation and the peoples of other nations.

I have seen for myself just how important is our aid in helping nations preserve their independence, and in helping men achieve the dignity of productive labor instead of languishing on crowded streets. I have seen its importance to children whose chances for a rewarding life have been increased because they have adequate nutrition, schools and books. It is right that we, the richest nation in the world, should provide our share of such assistance.

And such help, in addition to being right for its own sake, also creates strong bonds.

I recognize that whenever an American firm is nationalized without prompt, fair, and effective compensation; whenever an anti-American demonstration takes place; or whenever a leader of a developing country criticizes the United States, many question the effectiveness of our aid.

But the headline reporting the occasional anti-American act overlooks the many countries which do thank us for providing them the means to preserve their own security; and it also overlooks the countless number of villages where farmers do appreciate our helping provide the know-how and the tools necessary to grow larger crops, the school children who cherish the education our assistance makes possible, and the people everywhere who recognize our help in eliminating disease.

For these people, our aid is a source of encouragement. And they, not those who demonstrate or destroy, are the real revolutionaries—for they, in quietly attempting to preserve their independence and improve their lives, are bringing about a quiet revolution of peaceful change and progress. They are working hard to build the foundations for a better tomorrow and they recognize that we have helped provide them with the tools to do the job.

But while such appreciation is gratifying, foreign assistance has a more basic purpose. Foreign assistance is quite clearly in our interest as a nation. We are a people whose sons have died, and whose great statesmen have worked, to build a world order which insures peace and prosperity for ourselves and for other nations. We are aware that this world order cannot be sustained if our friends cannot defend themselves against aggression, and if two-thirds of the world's people see the richer third as indifferent to their needs and insensitive to their aspirations for a better life. To these people it is critical that this be a generation of peace, and our foreign policy is directed at helping to make it so; and for the impoverished it is equally important that it be a generation in which their aspirations for a better life, improved health conditions, and adequate food supply can be realized—a generation of development, a generation of hope.

Foreign policy is not a one-way street. It requires that other nations understand our problems and concerns, but it also requires that we understand theirs. We cannot ask the lower income countries of the world to cooperate with us to solve the problems which affect our vital interests unless we cooperate with them to help solve the problems critical to their vital interests—the problems affecting their security and development, and thus affecting the quality of life of their people.

The legislation I propose today, along with the corollary administrative actions which I will take, will permit this Nation to carry out the major reforms which are necessary to improve the effectiveness of our foreign assistance program and to fit it to our new approach.

I believe that this new approach is of major importance in promoting the national security and foreign policy interests of the United States in this decade and beyond. I believe that it is sound, and will blend as effectively as possible our special strengths with those of other nations and institutions. It is an approach through which we can focus the energies and resources of this great Nation on the security and development problems of those peoples living in poorer nations who wish to improve their lives, but lack the resources and the expertise to do so. I believe that this program is worthy of your support.

I therefore reaffirm my commitment, and the commitment of this administration, to seek an effective U.S. foreign assistance program for the 1970s. It is our objective to work for peace, not only in our time but for future generations, and we can make no better investment toward that end than to participate fully in an international effort to build prosperity and hope for a better tomorrow among all nations. I urge the Congress to join with me in making the reforms I propose today so that together we can achieve these great goals.

RICHARD NIXON

LEGAL SERVICES

Following is the test of President Nixon's May 5 message to Congress proposing a new legal services program.

TO THE CONGRESS OF THE UNITED STATES:

In the long, uphill struggle to secure equal rights in America, the Federal program of legal services for the poor is a relative newcomer to the cause. Yet it has already become a workhorse in this effort, pulling briskly and tirelessly at the task as the Nation moves ahead.

The legal services program began six years ago as a small experiment within the Office of Economic Opportunity. It grew swiftly, so rapidly that today more than 2000 lawyers work for the poor in some 900 neighborhood law offices. No less than a million cases a year are now processed by these dedicated attorneys, with each case giving those in need new reason to believe that they too are part of the "the system."

A large measure of credit is due the organized bar. Acting in accordance with the highest standards of its profession, it has given admirable and consistent support to the legal services concept. The concept has also had the support of both political parties.

The crux of the program, however, remains in the neighborhood law office. Here each day the old, the unemployed, the underprivileged, and the largely forgotten people of our Nation may seek help. Perhaps it is an eviction, a marital conflict, repossession of a car, or misunderstanding over a welfare check— each problem may have a legal solution These are small claims in the Nation's eye, but they loom large in the hearts and lives of poor Americans.

A New Direction

The Nation has learned many lessons in these six short years. This program has not been without travail. Much of the litigation initiated by legal services has placed it in direct conflict with local and State governments. The program is concerned with social issues and is thus subject to unusually strong political pressures.

Even though surrounded by controversy, this program can provide a most effective mechanism for settling differences and securing justice within the system and not on the streets. For many of our citizens, legal services has reaffirmed faith in our government of laws. However, if we are to preserve the strength of the program, we must make it immune to political pressures and make it a permanent part of our system of justice.

For two years, this administration has studied means of delivering improved, high quality legal services to those in need, as well as the question of what the proper role and structure of the legal services program should be. In 1969, we upgraded the status of legal services, recognizing it as a separate program within the Office of Economic Opportunity. Because of its importance, I also specifically asked the President's Advisory Council on Executive Organization (The Ash Council) to examine the question, and last November the Council recommended that the Government create a special corporation for the program. The role of legal services lawyers was also considered by the recent White House Conference on Youth, and a task force there expressed strong concern that the independence of these attorneys be maintained.

Today, after carefully considering the alternatives, I propose the creation of a separate, nonprofit Legal Services

Corporation. The legislation being sent to the Congress to accomplish this has three major objectives: First, that the corporation itself be structured and financed so that it will be assured of independence; second, that the lawyers in the program have full freedom to protect the best interests of their clients in keeping with the Canons of Ethics and the high standards of the legal profession; and third, that the Nation be encouraged to continue giving the program the support it needs in order to become a permanent and vital part of the American system of justice.

Independence for the Corporation

True independence for a corporation created by the Government demands a governing body drawn from a wide spectrum and safeguarded against partisan interference after its appointment. I believe that we can best meet these requirements by appointing the board of directors for the Legal Services Corporation on the following bases:

• The members of the board should be appointed by the President, by and with the advice and consent of the Senate.

• The board should consist of eleven members, no more than six of whom may be of the same political party.

• A majority should be members of the bar of the highest court of a jurisdiction, and none should be a full-time employee of the United States.

• Members should be appointed for three-year terms and serve no longer than nine years consecutively.

• The board chairman should be elected by the members from among their number and serve a term of one year.

• No board member should be involuntarily removed except by a vote of at least seven members, and only for reasons of malfeasance, persistent neglect, or inability to perform. Political pressures cannot be a basis for removal.

These provisions, all painstakingly designed to insulate the board from outside pressures, find an apt precedent in the corporation created four years ago to promote freedom and initiative in non-commercial broadcasting. In establishing the Corporation for Public Broadcasting. the Congress was once again dealing with a sensitive area of our national life, and it chose much the same course that I am recommending today.

The primary mission of the Legal Services Corporation should be the review and approval of applications for funds submitted by neighborhood law offices, special units of private law firms, and other attorneys who seek to provide legal assistance to the poor. The decision in the case of each individual grant or contract should be made by the corporation's president—an official employed by the board—based upon guidelines established by the board.

To advise the board of the Legal Services Corporation, I propose that an advisory council also be established with its membership including eligible poor clients and representatives of the organized bar.

As a further means of assuring its independence, I recommend that grants made by the corporation to neighborhood offices and other recipients not be subject to veto by governmental officials. It is important, however, that State and local officials be given ample notice of new grants. Therefore, I propose that the corporation be required to notify the Chief Executive Officer of the State, Commonwealth, District of Columbia or possession at least 30 days prior to approving a grant or contract for that area, so that full consideration could be given to the views of that executive. Thus the legitimate concerns of the jurisdiction involved could be taken into account before proceeding, but the corporation would retain its independence.

As yet another guarantee of that independence, and also to assure continuity and facilitate long-range planning, I propose that funding by the Congress be appropriated on a three-year basis.

Independence for the Lawyer

While it is important to insulate the corporate structure so that public funds can be properly channeled into the field, it is even more important that the lawyers on the receiving end be able to use the money ethically, wisely and without unnecessary or encumbering restrictions.

The legal problems of the poor are of sufficient scope that we should not restrict the right of their attorneys to bring any type of civil suit. Only in this manner can we maintain the integrity of the adversary process and fully protect the attorney-client relationship so central to our judicial process.

At the same time, it would be a waste of our resources and a dilution of the legal services program if these same lawyers were also to become involved in criminal suits, since legal representation in criminal cases is already available to the poor under many other programs. Counsel for the indigent has been held by the Supreme Court to be a constitutional requirement in felony cases. States now provide for such counsel, and the Federal Government has made substantial sums of money available for criminal representation. Thus I propose that legal services lawyers be prohibited from criminal representation.

For this same reason, legal services attorneys who are given fulltime grants or contracts should devote their entire professional efforts to representation of eligible clients, and should not be permitted to engage in the outside practice of law. Certain lobbying activities, as well as partisan political action, should also be proscribed. The latter two activities would be another dilution of resources, and would have the further disadvantage of placing the Legal Services Corporation itself squarely in the political arena, where it does not belong—and thus inviting those political pressures from which its independence is designed to insulate it. On the other hand, these limitations should not impair the right of the legal services attorney to prepare model legislation or to respond to the inquiries of legislators. Such actions are traditionally within the scope of the attorney's right to represent a client and must be preserved.

Strength for the Future

In discussing the broad contours of this program, we must not overlook the challenges ahead. The Nation can be proud that we have come so far already. Under this administration alone, the legal services caseload has increased some 97%—from approximately 610,000 cases in fiscal year 1969 to an estimated 1,200,000 cases in fiscal year 1971—and the budget allocations have increased during this period by approximately one-third. Yet today, perhaps four out of every five legal problems of the poor still go unattended. The challenge to us is thus a significant one, and if we are to succeed in so delicate an undertaking we must devise a program which will have the full support not only of the Congress and the executive branch, but of the people as well.

The full financial support of the government is clearly needed in this endeavor. I propose that upon the date of incorporation, all of the funds then appropriated for legal services activities in the Office of Economic Opportunity, including those for research and training, be transferred to the Legal Services Corporation, so that it can undertake existing Office of Economic Opportunity obligations.

To help us broaden the attack on our unmet needs, I am also proposing two new initiatives:

• First, I propose that specific authorization be given for grants to individual lawyers. This will increase the opportunity for the private bar to participate in legal services and will enable the corporation to channel greater resources into rural areas.

• Second, I propose that the Legal Services Corporation be authorized to identify the principal legal problems of the poor involving the Federal Government and then work with appropriate governmental agencies in trying to solve them. Hopefully, this effort might in many cases eliminate the need for poor persons to seek redress in our overcrowded courts. It would also conserve the resources of the corporation without denying to any lawyer the right to bring a suit which he deems necessary.

The Federal program of providing legal services to Americans otherwise unable to pay for them is a dramatic symbol of this Nation's commitment to the concept of equal justice. It is a program both new and unparalleled by any other system of justice in the world. I urge the Congress to join with me in adopting this proposal to give it new strength for the future.

RICHARD NIXON

WILDERNESS PRESERVATION

Following are excerpts from President Nixon's April 28 statement on wilderness preservation as made public by the White House:

I am today transmitting to the Congress fourteen new wilderness proposals. If approved, they would expand our Wilderness System by some 1.8 million acres, exceeding the total of all other additions since its creation. They involve parts of nine States, including four—Utah, Louisiana, Ohio and Virginia—which now have no protected Wilderness Areas at all.

My new proposals would add to the National Wilderness Preservation System land in the following locations: Sequoia and Kings Canyon National Parks, and Farallon National Wildlife Refuge, California; North Cascades National Park and adjacent recreation areas, Washington; Isle Royale National Park, Michigan; Shenandoah National Park, Virginia; Chamisso National Wildlife Refuge, Simeonof National Wildlife Refuge, and Izembek National Wildlife Range and Aleutian Islands National Wildlife Refuge, Alaska; West Sister Island National Wildlife Refuge, Ohio; Breton National Wildlife Refuge, Louisiana; Florida Keys National Wildlife Refuge, Florida; and Cedar Breaks National Monument, Arches National Monument, and Capitol Reef National Monument, Utah. I am also recommending an amendment to the wilderness proposal for the Okefenokee National Wildlife Refuge in Georgia, first submitted to the 90th Congress, so that it would take in 347,000 acres rather than the 319,000 acres originally proposed.

I urge the Congress to act quickly in favor of these new proposals as well as the ones already pending before it. We owe it both to ourselves and to future generations to safeguard as much of primitive America as we can—and time is not on our side.

The protection of wilderness is unusual among public projects in that it costs the taxpayer practically nothing. No government purchase of land is involved, only additional discipline in the use of land already owned. Administrative and management expense is tiny, for man enters these preserves only as nature's guest. He leaves his mechanized transportation behind, and while in the wilderness he builds nothing and extracts nothing.

Of course there are often attractive commercial opportunities in potential wilderness areas; mining, lumbering, recreational development, and others. Wilderness protection, putting these opportunities out of reach, may impose a sort of hidden wilderness tax in marginally higher costs of the goods and services of certain affected industries. That is why the Wilderness Act provides for full public hearings and a careful evaluative process. It recognizes that a sensible land use balance must be struck—that America continues to value development and growth as well as unspoiled nature.

But whatever the extent of the costs and sacrifices incurred when we do set aside appropriate wilderness areas, if they are weighed in the balance against the value of our dwindling virgin lands—priceless, finite, and fragile—it is clear that wilderness is a spectacular bargain for the American people.

Creation of a comprehensive, continent-wide Wilderness Preservation System is a major goal within the drive for environmental protection and quality of life to which we are dedicated. By establishing the new Wilderness Areas I am proposing today we could take a long step toward that goal. Of course, this step and the many others that will logically follow—for nearly 53 million acres of potential Federal wilderness remain for review and study—will call for teamwork.

PROPOSALS FOR ADEQUATE SUPPLY OF CLEAN ENERGY

Following is the text, as made available by the White House, of President Nixon's June 4 message to Congress outlining his proposals for an adequate supply of clean energy for the future.

TO THE CONGRESS OF THE UNITED STATES:

For most of our history, a plentiful supply of energy is something the American people have taken very much for granted. In the past twenty years alone, we have been able to double our consumption of energy without exhausting the supply. But the assumption that sufficient energy will always be readily available has been brought sharply into question within the last year. The brownouts that have affected some areas of our country, the possible shortages of fuel that were threatened last fall, the sharp increases in certain fuel prices and our growing awareness of the environmental consequences of energy production have all demonstrated that we cannot take our energy supply for granted any longer.

A sufficient supply of clean energy is essential if we are to sustain healthy economic growth and improve the quality of our national life. I am therefore announcing today a broad range of actions to ensure an adequate supply of clean energy for the years ahead. Private industry, of course, will still play the major role in providing our energy, but government can do a great deal to help in meeting this challenge.

My program includes the following elements:

To Facilitate Research and Development for Clean Energy:
• A commitment to complete the successful demonstration of the liquid metal fast breeder reactor by 1980.
• More than twice as much Federal support for sulfur oxide control demonstration projects in Fiscal Year 1972.
• An expanded program to convert coal into a clean gaseous fuel.
• Support for a variety of other energy research projects in fields such as fusion power, magnetohydrodynamic power cycles, and underground electric transmission.

To Make Available the Energy Resources on Federal Lands:
• Acceleration of oil and gas lease sales on the Outer Continental Shelf, along with stringent controls to protect the environment.
• A leasing program to develop our vast oil shale resources, provided that environmental questions can be satisfactorily resolved.
• Development of a geothermal leasing program beginning this fall.

To Assure a Timely Supply of Nuclear Fuels:
• Begin work to modernize and expand our uranium enrichment capacity.

To Use Our Energy More Wisely:
• A New Federal Housing Administration standard requiring additional insulation in new federally insured homes.
• Development and publication of additional information on how consumers can use energy more efficiently.
• Other efforts to encourage energy conservation.

To Balance Environmental and Energy Needs:
• A system of long-range open planning of electric power plant sites and transmission line routes with approval by a State or regional agency before construction.
• An incentive charge to reduce sulfur oxide emissions and to support further research.

To Organize Federal Efforts More Effectively:
• A single structure within the Department of Natural Resources uniting all important energy resource development programs.

The Nature of the Current Problem

A major cause of our recent energy problems has been the sharp increase in demand that began about 1967. For decades, energy consumption had generally grown at a slower rate than the national output of goods and services. But in the last four years it has been growing at a faster pace and forecasts of energy demand a decade from now have been undergoing significant upward revisions.

This accelerated growth in demand results partly from the fact that energy has been relatively inexpensive in this country. During the last decade, the prices of oil, coal, natural gas and electricity have increased at a much slower rate than consumer prices as a whole. Energy has been an attractive bargain in this country—and demand has responded accordingly.

In the years ahead, the needs of a growing economy will further stimulate this demand. And the new emphasis on environmental protection means that the demand for cleaner fuels will be especially acute. The primary cause of air pollution, for example, is the burning of fossil fuels in homes, in cars, in factories and in power plants. If we are to meet our new national air quality standards, it will be essential for us to use stack gas cleaning systems in our large power and other industrial plants and to use cleaner fuels in virtually all of our new residential, commercial and industrial facilities, and in some of our older facilities as well.

Together, these two factors—growing demand for energy and growing emphasis on cleaner fuels—will create an extraordinary pressure on our fuel supplies.

The task of providing sufficient clean energy is made especially difficult by the long lead times required to increase energy supply. To move from geological exploration to oil and gas well production now takes from 3 to 7 years. New coal mines typically require 3 to 5 years to reach the production stage and it takes 5 to 7 years to complete a large steam power plant. The development of the new technology required to minimize environmental damage can further delay the provision of additional energy. If we are to take full advantage of our enormous coal resources, for example, we will need mining systems that do not impair the health and safety of miners or degrade the landscape and combustion systems that do not emit harmful quantities of sulfur oxides, other noxious gases, and particulates into the atmosphere. But such systems may take several years to reach satisfactory performance. That is why our efforts to expand the supply of clean energy in America must immediately be stepped up.

RESEARCH, DEVELOPMENT GOALS FOR CLEAN ENERGY

Our past research in this critical field has produced many promising leads. Now we must move quickly to demonstrate the best of these new concepts on a commercial scale. Industry should play the major role in this area, but government can help by providing technical leadership and by sharing a portion of the risk for costly demonstration plants. The time has now come for government and industry to commit themselves to a joint effort to achieve commercial scale demonstrations in the most crucial and most promising clean energy development areas—the fast breeder reactor sulfur oxide control technology and coal gasification.

Sulfur Oxide Control Technology. A major bottleneck in our clean energy program is the fact that we cannot now burn coal or oil without discharging its sulfur content into the air. We need new technology which will make it possible to remove the sulfur before it is emitted to the air.

Working together, industry and government have developed a variety of approaches to this problem. However, the new air quality standards promulgated under the Clean Air Amendments of 1970 require an even more rapid development of a suitable range of stack gas cleaning techniques for removing sulfur oxides. I have therefore requested funds in my 1972 budget to permit the Environmental Protection Agency to devote an additional $15 million to this area, more than doubling the level of our previous efforts. This expansion means that a total of six different techniques can be demonstrated in partnership with industry during the next three or four years.

Nuclear Breeder Reactor. Our best hope today for meeting the Nation's growing demand for economical clean energy lies with the fast breeder reactor. Because of its highly efficient use of nuclear fuel, the breeder reactor could extend the life of our natural uranium fuel supply from decades to centuries, with far less impact on the environment than the power plants which are operating today.

For several years, the Atomic Energy Commission has placed the highest priority on developing the liquid metal fast breeder. Now this project is ready to move out of the laboratory and into the demonstration phase with a commercial size plant. But there still are major technical and financial obstacles to the construction of a demonstration plant of some 300 to 500 megawatts. I am therefore requesting an additional $27 million in Fiscal Year 1972 for the Atomic Energy Commission's liquid metal fast breeder reactor program—and for related technological and safety programs—so that the necessary engineering groundwork for demonstration plants can soon be laid.

What about the environmental impact of such plants? It is reassuring to know that the releases of radioactivity from current nuclear reactors are well within the national safety standards. Nevertheless, we will make every effort to see that these new breeder reactors emit even less radioactivity to the environment than the commercial light water reactors which are now in use.

I am therefore directing the Atomic Energy Commission to ensure that the new breeder plants be designed in a way which inherently prevents discharge to the environment from the plant's radioactive effluent systems. The Atomic Energy Commission should also take advantage of the increased efficiency of these breeder plants, designing them to minimize waste heat discharges. Thermal pollution from nuclear power plants can be materially reduced in the more efficient breeder reactors.

We have very high hopes that the breeder reactor will soon become a key element in the national fight against air and water pollution. In order further to inform the interested agencies and the public about the opportunities in this area, I have requested the early preparation and review by all appropriate agencies of a draft environmental impact statement for the breeder demonstration plant in accordance with Section 102 of the National Environmental Policy Act. This procedure will ensure compliance with all environmental quality standards before plant construction begins.

In a related area, it is also pertinent to observe that the safety record of civilian power reactors in this country is extraordinary in the history of technological advances. For more than a quarter century—since the first nuclear chain reaction took place—no member of the public has been injured by the failure of a reactor or by an accidental release of radioactivity. I am confident that this record can be maintained. The Atomic Energy Commission is giving top priority to safety considerations in the basic design of the breeder reactor and this design will also be subject to a thorough review by the independent Advisory Committee on Reactor Safeguards, which will publish the results of its investigation.

I believe it important to the Nation that the commercial demonstration of a breeder reactor be completed by 1980. To help achieve that goal, I am requesting an additional $50 million in Federal funds for the demonstration plant. We expect industry—the utilities and manufacturers—to contribute the major share of the plant's total cost, since they have a large and obvious stake in this new technology. But we also recognize that only if government and industry work closely together can we maximize our progress in this vital field and thus introduce a new era in the production of energy for the people of our land.

Coal Gasification. As we carry on our search for cleaner fuels, we think immediately of the cleanest fossil fuel—natural gas. But our reserves of natural gas are quite limited in comparison with our reserves of coal.

Fortunately, however, it is technically feasible to convert coal into a clean gas which can be transported through pipelines. The Department of the Interior has been working with the natural gas and coal industries on research to advance our coal gasification efforts and a number of possible methods from accomplishing this conversion are under development. A few, in fact, are now in the pilot plant stage.

We are determined to bring greater focus and urgency to this effort. We have therefore initiated a cooperative program with industry to expand the number of pilot plants, making it possible to test new methods more expeditiously so that the appropriate technology can soon be selected for a large-scale demonstration plant.

The Federal expenditure for this cooperative program will be expanded to $20 million a year. Industry has agreed to provide $10 million a year for this effort. In general, we expect that the Government will continue to finance the larger share of pilot plants and that industry will finance the larger share of the demonstration plants. But again, the important point is that both the Government and industry are now strongly committed to move ahead together as promptly as possible to make coal gasification a commercial reality.

Other Research and Development Efforts. The fast breeder reactor sulfur oxide controls and coal gasification represent our highest priority research and development projects in the clean energy field. But they are not our only efforts. Other ongoing projects include:

• Coal Mine Health and Safety Research. In response to a growing concern for the health and safety of the men who mine the Nation's coal and in accordance with the Federal Coal Mine Health and Safety Act of 1969, the Bureau of Mines research effort has been increased from a level of $2 million in Fiscal Year 1969 to $30 million in Fiscal Year 1972.

• Controlled Thermonuclear Fusion Research. For nearly two decades the Government has been funding a sizeable research effort designed to harness the almost limitless energy of nuclear fusion for peaceful purposes. Recent progress suggests that the scientific feasibility of such projects may be demonstrated in the 1970s and we have therefore requested an additional $2 million to supplement the budget in this field for Fiscal Year 1972. We hope that work in this promising area will continue to be expanded as scientific progress justifies large scale programs.

Coal Liquefaction. In addition to its coal gasification work, the Department of the Interior has underway a major pilot plant program directed toward converting coal into cleaner liquid fuels.

• Magnetohydrodynamic Power Cycles. MHD is a new and more efficient method of converting coal and other fossil fuels into electric energy by burning the fuel and passing the combustion products through a magnetic field at very high temperatures. In partnership with the electric power industry, we have been working to develop this new system of electric power generation.

• Underground Electric Transmission. Objections have been growing to the overhead placement of high voltage power lines, especially in areas of scenic beauty or near centers of population. Again in cooperation with industry, the Government is funding a research program to develop new and less expensive techniques for burying high voltage electric transmission lines.

• Nuclear Reactor Safety and Supporting Technology. The general research and development work for today's commercial nuclear reactors was completed several years ago, but we must continue to fund safety-related efforts in order to ensure the continuance of the excellent safety record in this field. An additional $3 million has recently been requested for this purpose to supplement the budget in Fiscal Year 1972.

• Advanced Reactor Concepts. The liquid metal fast breeder is the priority breeder reactor concept under development, but the Atomic Energy Commission is also supporting limited alternate reactor programs involving gas cooled reactors, molten salt reactors and light water breeders.

• Solar Energy. The sun offers an almost unlimited supply of energy if we can learn to use it economically. The National Aeronautics and Space Administration and the National Science Foundation are currently re-examining their efforts in this area and we expect to give greater attention to solar energy in the future.

The key to meeting our twin goals of supplying adequate energy and protecting the environment in the decades ahead will be a balanced and imaginative research and development program. I have therefore asked my Science Adviser, with the co-operation of the Council of Environmental Quality and the interested agencies, to make a detailed assessment of all of the technological opportunities in this area and to recommend additional projects which should receive priority attention.

MAKING AVAILABLE THE ENERGY RESOURCES OF FEDERAL LANDS

Over half of our Nation's remaining oil and gas resources, about 40 percent of our coal and uranium, 80 percent of our oil shale, and some 60 percent of our geothermal energy sources are now located on Federal lands. Programs to make these resources available to meet the growing energy requirements of the Nation are therefore essential if shortages are to be averted. Through appropriate leasing programs, the Government should be able to recover the fair market value of these resources, while requiring developers to comply with requirements that will adequately protect the environment.

To supplement the efforts already underway to develop the fuel resources of the lower 48 States and Alaska, I am announcing today the following new programs:

Leasing on the Outer Continental Shelf—An Accelerated Program. The Outer Continental Shelf has proved to be a prolific source of oil and gas, but it has also been the source of troublesome oil spills in recent years. Our ability to tap the great potential of offshore areas has been seriously hampered by these environmental problems.

The Department of the Interior has significantly strengthened the environmental protection requirements controlling offshore drilling and we will continue to enforce these requirements very strictly. As a prerequisite to Federal lease sales, environmental assessments will be made in accordance with Section 102 of the National Environmental Policy Act of 1969.

Within these clear limits, we will accelerate our efforts to utilize this rich source of fuel. In order to expand productive possibilities as rapidly as possible, the accelerated program should include the sale of new leases not only in the highly productive Gulf of Mexico, but also some other promising areas. I am therefore directing the Secretary of the Interior to increase the offerings of oil and gas leases and to publish a schedule for lease offerings on the Outer Continental Shelf during the next five years, beginning with a general lease sale and a drainage sale this year.

Oil Shale—A Program for Orderly Development. At a time when we are facing possible energy shortages, it is reassuring to know that there exists in the United States an untapped shale oil resource containing some 600 billion barrels in high grade deposits. At current consumption rates, this resource represents 150 years supply. About 80 billion barrels of this shale oil are particularly rich and well situated for early development. This huge resource of very low sulfur oil is located in the Rocky Mountain area, primarily on Federal land.

At present there is no commercial production of shale oil. A mixture of problems—environmental, technical and economic—have combined to thwart past efforts at development.

I believe the time has come to begin the orderly formulation of a shale oil policy—not by any head-long rush toward development but rather by a well considered program in which both environmental protection and the recovery of a fair return to the Government are cardinal principles under which any leasing takes place. I am therefore requesting the Secretary of the Interior to expedite the development of an oil shale leasing program including the preparation of an environmental impact statement. If after

reviewing this statement and comments he finds that environmental concerns can be satisfied, he shall then proceed with the detailed planning. This work would also involve the States of Wyoming, Colorado and Utah and the first test lease would be scheduled for next year.

Geothermal Energy. There is a vast quantity of heat stored in the earth itself. Where this energy source is close to the surface, as it is in the Western States, it can readily be tapped to generate electricity, to heat homes, and to meet other energy requirements. Again, this resource is located primarily on Federal lands.

Legislation enacted in recent months permits the Federal government, for the first time, to prepare for a leasing program in the field of geothermal energy. Classification of the lands involved is already underway in the Department of the Interior. I am requesting the Secretary of the Interior to expedite a final decision on whether the first competitive lease sale should be scheduled for this fall—taking into account, of course, his evaluation of the environmental impact statement.

NATURAL GAS SUPPLY

For the past 25 years, natural gas has supplied much of the increase in the energy supply of the United States. Now this relatively clean form of energy is in even greater demand to help satisfy air quality standards. Our present supply of natural gas is limited, however, and we are beginning to face shortages which could intensify as we move to implement the air quality standards. Additional supplies of gas will therefore be one of our most urgent energy needs in the next few years.

Federal efforts to augment the available supplies of natural gas include:

• Accelerated leasing on Federal lands to speed discovery and development of new natural gas fields.

• Moving ahead with a demonstration project to gasify coal.

• Recent actions by the Federal Power Commission providing greater incentives for industry to increase its search for new sources of natural gas and to commit its discoveries to the interstate market.

• Facilitating imports of both natural and liquefied gas from Canada and from other nations.

• Progress in nuclear stimulation experiments which seek to produce natural gas from tight geologic formations which cannot presently be utilized in ways which are economically and environmentally acceptable.

This administration is keenly aware of the need to take every reasonable action to enlarge the supply of clean gaseous fuels. We intend to take such action and we expect to get good results.

IMPORTS FROM CANADA

Over the years, the United States and Canada have steadily increased their trade in energy. The United States exports some coal to Canada, but the major items of trade are oil and gas which are surplus to Canadian needs but which find a ready market in the United States.

The time has come to develop further this mutually advantageous trading relationship. The United States is therefore prepared to move promptly to permit Canadian crude oil to enter this country, free of any quantitative restraints, upon agreement as to measures needed to prevent citizens of both our countries from being subjected to oil shortages, or threats of shortages. We are ready to proceed with negotiations and we look to an early conclusion.

TIMELY SUPPLIES OF NUCLEAR FUELS

The Nation's nuclear fuel supply is in a state of transition. Military needs are now relatively small but civilian needs are growing rapidly and will be our dominant need for nuclear fuel in the future. With the exception of uranium enrichment, the nuclear energy industry is now in private hands.

I expect that private enterprise will eventually assume the responsibility for uranium enrichment as well, but in the meantime the Government must carry out its responsibility to ensure that our enrichment capacity expands at a rate consistent with expected demands.

There is currently no shortage of enriched uranium or enriching capacity. In fact, the Atomic Energy Commission has substantial stocks of enriched uranium which have already been produced for later use. However, plant expansions are required so that we can meet the growing demands for nuclear fuel in the late 1970s—both in the United States and in other nations for which this country is not the principal supplier.

The most economical means presently available for expanding our capacity in this field appears to be the modernization of existing gaseous diffusion plants at Oak Ridge, Tennessee; Portsmouth, Ohio; and Paducah, Kentucky—through a Cascade Improvement Program. This program will take a number of years to complete and we therefore believe that it is prudent to initiate the program at this time rather than run the risk of shortages at a later date. I am therefore releasing $16 million to start the Cascade Improvement Program in Fiscal Year 1972. The pace of the improvement program will be tailored to fit the demands for enriched uranium in the United States and in other countries.

USING OUR ENERGY MORE WISELY

We need new sources of energy in this country, but we also need to use existing energy as efficiently as possible. I believe we can achieve the ends we desire—homes warm in winter and cool in summer, rapid transportation, plentiful energy for industrial production and home appliances—and still place less of a strain on our overtaxed resources.

Historically, we have converted fuels into electricity and have used other sources of energy with ever increasing efficiency. Recent data suggest, however, that this trend may be reversing—thus adding to the drain on available resources. We must get back on the road of increasing efficiency—both at the point of production and at the point of consumption, where the consumer himself can do a great deal to achieve considerable savings in his energy bills.

We believe that part of the answer lies in pricing energy on the basis of its full costs to society. One reason we use energy so lavishly today is that the price of energy does not include all of the social costs of producing it. The costs incurred in protecting the environment and the health and safety of workers, for example, are part of the real cost of producing energy—but they are not now all included in the price of the product. If they were added to that price, we could expect that some of the waste in the use of energy would be eliminated. At the same time, by expanding clean fuel supplies, we will be working to keep the overall cost of energy as low as possible.

It is also important that the individual consumer be fully aware of what his energy will cost if he buys a particular home or appliance. The efficiency of home heating or cooling systems and of other energy intensive equipment are determined by builders and manufacturers who may be concerned more with the initial cost of the equipment than with the operating costs which will come afterward. For example, better thermal insulation in a home or office building may save the consumer large sums in the long run—and conserve energy as well—but for the builder it merely represents an added expense.

To help meet one manifestation of this problem, I am directing the Secretary of Housing and Urban Development to issue revised standards for insulation applied in new federally insured homes. The new Federal Housing Administration standards will require sufficient insulation to reduce the maximum permissible heat loss by about one-third for a typical 1200 square foot home—and by even more for larger homes. It is estimated that the fuel savings which will result each year from the application of these new standards will, in an average climate, equal the cost of the additional insulation required.

While the Federal Government can take some actions to conserve energy through such regulations, the consumer who seeks the most for his energy dollar in the marketplace is the one who can have the most profound influence. I am therefore asking my Special Assistant for Consumer Affairs—in cooperation with industry and appropriate Government agencies—to gather and publish additional information in this field to help consumers focus on the operating costs as well as the initial cost of energy intensive equipment.

In addition, I would note that the Joint Board on Fuel Supply and Fuel Transport chaired by the Director of the Office of Emergency Preparedness is developing energy conservation measures for industry, government, and the general public to help reduce energy use in times of particular shortage and during pollution crises.

POWER PLANT SITING

If we are to meet growing demands for electricity in the years ahead, we cannot ignore the need for many new power plants. These plants and their associated transmission lines must be located and built so as to avoid major damage to the environment, but they must also be completed on time so as to avoid power shortages. These demands are difficult to reconcile—and often they are not reconciled well. In my judgment the lesson of the recent power shortages and of the continuing disputes over power plant siting and transmission line routes is that the existing institutions for making decisions in this area are not adequate for the job. In my Special Message to the Congress on the Environment last February, I proposed legislation which would help to alleviate these problems through longer range planning by the utilities and through the establishment of State or regional agencies to license new bulk power facilities prior to their construction.

Hearings are now being held by the Interstate and Foreign Commerce Committee of the House of Representatives concerning these proposals and other measures which would provide an open planning and decision-making capacity for dealing with these matters. Under the administration bill, long-range expansion plans would be presented by the utilities ten years before construction was scheduled to begin, individual alternative power plant sites would be identified five years ahead, and detailed design and location of specific plants and transmission lines would be considered two years in advance of construction. Public hearings would be held far enough ahead of construction so that they could influence the siting decision, helping to avoid environmental problems without causing undue construction delays. I urge the Congress to take prompt and favorable action on this important legislative proposal. At the same time steps will be taken to ensure that Federal licenses and permits are handled as expeditiously as possible.

THE ROLE OF THE SULFUR OXIDES EMISSIONS CHARGE

In my environmental message last February I also proposed the establishment of a sulfur oxides emissions charge. The emissions charge would have the effect of building the cost of sulfur oxide pollution into the price of energy. It would also provide a strong economic incentive for achieving the necessary performance to meet sulfur oxide standards.

The funds generated by the emissions charge would be used by the Federal Government to expand its programs to improve environmental quality, with special emphasis on the development of adequate supplies of clean energy.

GOVERNMENT REORGANIZATION—AN ENERGY ADMINISTRATION

But new programs alone will not be enough. We must also consider how we can make these programs do what we intend them to do. One important way of fostering effective performance is to place responsibility for energy questions in a single agency which can execute and modify policies in a comprehensive and unified manner.

The Nation has been without an integrated energy policy in the past. One reason for this situation is that energy responsibilities are fragmented among several agencies. Often authority is divided according to types and uses of energy. Coal, for example, is handled in one place, nuclear energy in another—but responsibility for considering the impact of one on the other is not assigned to any single authority. Nor is there any single agency responsible for developing new energy sources such as solar energy or new conversion systems such as the fuel cell. New concerns—such as conserving our fossil fuels for non-fuel uses—cannot receive the thorough and thoughtful attention they deserve under present arrangements.

The reason for all these deficiencies is that each existing program was set up to meet a specific problem of the past. As a result, our present structure is not equipped to handle the relationships between these problems and the emergence of new concerns.

The need to remedy these problems becomes more pressing every day. For example, the energy industries presently account for some 20 percent of our investment in new plant and equipment. This means that inefficiencies resulting from uncoordinated government programs can be very costly to our economy. It is also true that energy sources are becoming increasingly interchangeable. Coal can be converted to gas, for example, and even to synthetic crude oil. If the Government is to perform adequately in the energy field, then it must act through an agency which has sufficient strength and breadth of responsibility.

Accordingly, I have proposed that all of our important Federal energy resource development programs be consolidated within the new Department of Natural Resources.

The single energy authority which would thus be created would be better able to clarify, express, and execute Federal energy policy than any unit in our present structure. The establishment of this new entity would provide a focal point where energy policy in the executive branch could be harmonized and rationalized.

One of the major advantages of consolidating energy responsibilities would be the broader scope and greater balance this would give to research and development work in the energy field. The Atomic Energy Commission, for instance, has been successful in its mission of advancing civilian nuclear power, but this field is now intimately interrelated with coal, oil and gas, and Federal electric power programs with which the Atomic Energy Commission now has very little to do. We believe that the planning and funding of civilian nuclear energy activities should now be consolidated with other energy efforts in an agency charged with the mission of insuring that the total energy resources of the nation are effectively utilized. The Atomic Energy Commission would still remain intact, in order to execute the nuclear programs and any related energy research which may be appropriate as part of the overall energy program of the Department of Natural Resources.

Until such time as this new Department comes into being, I will continue to look to the Energy Subcommittee of the Domestic Council for leadership in analyzing and coordinating overall energy policy questions for the executive branch.

Conclusion

The program I have set forth today provides the basic ingredients for a new effort to meet our clean energy needs in the years ahead.

The success of this effort will require the cooperation of the Congress and of the State and local governments. It will also depend on the willingness of industry to meet its responsibilities in serving customers and in making necessary capital investments to meet anticipated growth. Consumers, too, will have a key role to play as they learn to conserve energy and as they come to understand that the cost of environmental protection must, to a major extent, be reflected in consumer prices.

I am confident that the various elements of our society will be able to work together to meet our clean energy needs. And I am confident that we can therefore continue to know the blessings of both a high-energy civilization and a beautiful and healthy environment.

PRESIDENT'S MESSAGE ON DRUG CONTROL PROGRAMS

Following is the complete text of President Nixon's June 17 message to Congress requesting additional funds for drug control programs for fiscal 1972.

TO THE CONGRESS OF THE UNITED STATES:

In New York City more people between the ages of fifteen and thirty-five years die as a result of narcotics than from any other single cause.

In 1960, less than 200 narcotic deaths were recorded in New York City. In 1970, the figure had risen to over 1,000. These statistics do not reflect a problem indigenous to New York City. Although New York is the one major city in the Nation which has kept good statistics on drug addiction, the problem is national and international. We are moving to deal with it on both levels.

As part of this administration's ongoing efforts to stem the tide of drug abuse which has swept America in the last decade, we submitted legislation in July of 1969 for a comprehensive reform of Federal drug enforcement laws. Fifteen months later, in October, 1970, the Congress passed this vitally-needed legislation, and it is now producing excellent results. Nevertheless, in the fifteen months between the submission of that legislation and its passage, much valuable time was lost.

We must now candidly recognize that the deliberate procedures embodied in present efforts to control drug abuse are not sufficient in themselves. The problem has assumed the dimensions of a national emergency. I intend to take every step necessary to deal with this emergency, including asking the Congress for an amendment to my 1972 budget to provide an additional $155 million to carry out these steps. This will provide a total of $371 million for programs to control drug abuse in America.

A New Approach to Rehabilitation

While experience thus far indicates that the enforcement provisions of the Comprehensive Drug Abuse Prevention and Control Act of 1970 are effective, they are not sufficient in themselves to eliminate drug abuse. Enforcement must be coupled with a rational approach to the reclamation of the drug user himself. The laws of supply and demand function in the illegal drug business as in any other. We are taking steps under the Comprehensive Drug Act to deal with the supply side of the equation and I am recommending additional steps to be taken now. But we must also deal with demand. We must rehabilitate the drug user if we are to eliminate drug abuse and all the anti-social activities that flow from drug abuse.

Narcotic addiction is a major contributor to crime. The cost of supplying a narcotic habit can run from $30 a day to $100 a day. This is $210 to $700 a week, or $10,000 a year to over $36,-000 a year. Untreated narcotic addicts do not ordinarily hold jobs. Instead, they often turn to shoplifting, mugging, burglary, armed robbery, and so on. They also support themselves by starting other people—young people—on drugs. The financial costs of addiction are more than $2 billion every year, but these costs can at least be measured. The human costs cannot. American society should not be required to bear either cost.

Despite the fact that drug addiction destroys lives, destroys families, and destroys communities, we are still not moving fast enough to meet the problem in an effective way. Our efforts are strained through the Federal bureaucracy. Of those we can reach at all under the present Federal system—and the number is relatively small—of those we try to help and who want help, we cure only a tragically small percentage.

Despite the magnitude of the problem, despite our very limited success in meeting it, and despite the common recognition of both circumstances, we nevertheless have thus far failed to develop a concerted effort to find a better solution to this increasingly grave threat. At present, there are nine Federal agencies involved in one fashion or another with the problem of drug addiction. There are anti-drug abuse efforts in Federal programs ranging from vocational rehabilitation to highway safety. In this manner our efforts have been fragmented through competing priorities, lack of communication, multiple authority, and limited and dispersed resources. The magnitude and the severity of the present threat will not longer permit this piecemeal and bureaucratically-dispersed effort at drug control. If we cannot destroy the drug menace in America, then it will surely in time destroy us. I am not prepared to accept this alternative.

Therefore, I am transmitting legislation to the Congress to consolidate at the highest level a full-scale attack on the problem of drug abuse in America. I am proposing the appropriation of additional funds to meet the cost of rehabilitating drug users, and I will ask for additional funds to increase our enforcement efforts to further tighten the noose around the necks of drug peddlers, and thereby loosen the noose around the necks of drug users.

At the same time I am proposing additional steps to strike at the "supply" side of the drug equation—to halt the drug traffic by striking at the illegal producers of drugs, the growing of those plants from which drugs are derived, and trafficking in these drugs beyond our borders.

America has the largest number of heroin addicts of any nation in the world. And yet, America does not grow opium—of which heroin is a derivative—nor does it manufacture heroin, which is a laboratory process carried out abroad. This deadly poison in the American lifestream is, in other words, a foreign import. In the last year, heroin seizures by Federal agencies surpassed the total seized in the previous ten years. Nevertheless, it is estimated that we are stopping less than 20 percent of the drugs aimed at this Nation. No serious attack on our national drug problem can ignore the international implications of such an effort, nor can the domestic effort succeed without attacking the problem on an international plane. I intend to do that.

A Coordinated Federal Response

Not very long ago, it was possible for Americans to persuade themselves, with some justification, that narcotic addiction was a class problem. Whether or not this was an accurate picture is irrelevant today, because now the problem is universal. But despite the increasing dimensions of the problem, and despite increasing consciousness of the problem, we have made little headway in understanding what is involved in drug abuse or how to deal with it.

The very nature of the drug abuse problem has meant that its extent and seriousness have been shrouded in secrecy, not only by the criminal elements who profit from drug use, but by the drug users themselves—the people whom society is attempting to reach and help. This fact has added immeasurably to the difficulties of medical assistance, rehabilitation, and government action to counter drug abuse, and to find basic and permanent methods to stop it. Even now, there are no precise national statistics as to the number of drug-dependent citizens in the United States, the rate at which drug abuse is increasing, or where and how this increase is taking place. Most of what we think we know is extrapolated from those few States and cities where the dimensions of the problem have forced closer attention, including the maintenance of statistics.

A large number of Federal Government agencies are involved in efforts to fight the drug problem either with new programs or by expanding existing programs. Many of these programs are still experimental in nature. This is appropriate. The problems of drug abuse must be faced on many fronts at the same time, and we do not yet know which efforts will be most successful. But we must recognize that piecemeal efforts, even where individually successful, cannot have a major impact on the

drug abuse problem unless and until they are forged together into a broader and more integrated program involving all levels of government and private effort. We need a coordinated effort if we are to move effectively against drug abuse.

The magnitude of the problem, the national and international implications of the problem, and the limited capacities of States and cities to deal with the problem all reinforce the conclusion that coordination of this effort must take place at the highest levels of the Federal Government.

Therefore, I propose the establishment of a central authority with overall responsibility for all major Federal drug abuse prevention, education, treatment, rehabilitation, training, and research programs in all Federal agencies. This authority would be known as the Special Action Office of Drug Abuse Prevention. It would be located within the Executive Office of the President and would be headed by a Director accountable to the President. Because this is an emergency response to a national problem which we intend to bring under control, the Office would be established to operate only for a period of three years from its date of enactment, and the President would have the option of extending its life for an additional two years if desirable.

This Office would provide strengthened Federal leadership in finding solutions to drug abuse problems. It would establish priorities and instill a sense of urgency in Federal and federally-supported drug abuse programs, and it would increase coordination between Federal, State, and local rehabilitation efforts.

More specifically, the Special Action Office would develop overall Federal strategy for drug abuse prevention programs, set program goals, objectives and priorities, carry out programs through other Federal agencies, develop guidance and standards for operating agencies, and evaluate performance of all programs to determine where success is being achieved. It would extend its efforts into research, prevention, training, education, treatment, rehabilitation, and the development of necessary reports, statistics, and social indicators for use by all public and private groups. It would not be directly concerned with the problems of reducing drug supply, or with the law enforcement aspects of drug abuse control.

It would concentrate on the "demand" side of the drug equation—the use and the user of drugs.

The program authority of the Director would be exercised through working agreements with other Federal agencies. In this fashion, full advantage would be taken of the skills and resources these agencies can bring to bear on solving drug abuse problems by linking them with a highly goal-oriented authority capable of functioning across departmental lines. By eliminating bureaucratic red tape, and jurisdictional disputes between agencies, the Special Action Office would do what cannot be done presently: it would mount a wholly coordinated national attack on a national problem. It would use all available resources of the Federal Government to identify the problems precisely, and it would allocate resources to attack those problems. In practice, implementing departments and agencies would be bound to meet specific terms and standards for performance. These terms and standards would be set forth under inter-agency agreement through a Program Plan defining objectives, costs, schedule, performance requirements, technical limits, and other factors essential to program success.

With the authority of the Program Plan, the Director of the Special Action Office could demand performance instead of hoping for it. Agencies would receive money based on performance and their retention of funding and program authority would depend upon periodic appraisal of their performance.

In order to meet the need for realistic central program appraisal, the Office would develop special program monitoring and evaluation capabilities so that it could realistically determine which activities and techniques were producing results. This evaluation would be tied to the planning process so that knowledge about success/failure results could guide the selection of future plans and priorities.

In addition to the inter-agency agreement and Program Plan approach described above, the Office would have direct authority to let grants or make contracts with industrial, commercial, or non-profit organizations. This authority would be used in specific instances where there is no appropriate Federal agency prepared to undertake a program, or where for some other reason it would be faster, cheaper, or more effective to grant or contract directly.

Within the broad mission of the Special Action Office, the Director would set specific objectives for accomplishment during the first three years of Office activity. These objectives would target such areas as reduction in the overall national rate of drug addiction, reduction in drug-related deaths, reduction of drug use in schools, impact on the number of men rejected for military duty because of drug abuse, and so forth. A primary objective of the Office would be the development of a reliable set of social indicators which accurately show the nature, extent, and trends in the drug abuse problem.

These specific targets for accomplishment would act to focus the efforts of the drug abuse prevention program, not on intermediate achievements such as numbers of treatments given or educational programs conducted, but rather on ultimate "payoff" accomplishments in the reduction of the human and social costs of drug abuse. Our programs cannot be judged on the fulfillment of quotas and other bureaucratic indexes of accomplishment. They must be judged by the number of human beings who are brought out of the hell of addiction, and by the number of human beings who are dissuaded from entering that hell.

I urge the Congress to give this proposal the highest priority, and I trust it will do so. Nevertheless, due to the need for immediate action, I am issuing today, June 17, an Executive Order establishing within the Executive Office of the President a Special Action Office for Drug Abuse Prevention. Until the Congress passes the legislation giving full authority to this Office, a Special Consultant to the President for Narcotics and Dangerous Drugs will institute to the extent legally possible the functions of the Special Action Office.

Rehabilitation: A New Priority. When traffic in narcotics is no longer profitable, then that traffic will cease. Increased enforcement and vigorous application of the fullest penalties provided by law are two of the steps in rendering narcotics trade unprofitable. But as long as there is a demand, there will be those willing to take the risks of meeting the demand. So we must also act to destroy the market for drugs, and this means the prevention of new addicts, and the rehabilitation of those who are addicted.

To do this, I am asking the Congress for a total of $105 million in addition to funds already contained in my 1972 budget to be used solely for the treatment and rehabilitation of drug-addicted individuals.

I will also ask the Congress to provide an additional $10 million in funds to increase and improve education and training in the field of dangerous drugs. This will increase the money available for education and training to more than $24 million. It has become fashionable to suppose that no drugs are as dangerous as they are commonly thought to be, and that the use of drugs entails no risk at all. These are misconceptions, and every day we reap the tragic results of these misconceptions when young people are "turned on" to drugs believing that narcotics addiction is something that happens to other people. We need an expanded effort to show that addiction is all too often a one-way street beginning with "innocent" experimentation and ending in death. Between these extremes is the degradation that addiction inflicts on those who believed that it could not happen to them.

While by no means a major part of the American narcotics problem, an especially disheartening aspect of that problem involves those of our men in Vietnam who have used drugs. Peer pressures combine with easy availability to foster drug use. We are taking steps to end the availability of drugs in South Vietnam but, in addition, the nature of drug addiction, and the peculiar aspects of the present problem as it involves veterans, make it imperative that rehabilitation procedures be undertaken immediately. In Vietnam, for example, heroin is cheap and 95 percent pure, and its effects are commonly achieved through smoking or

"snorting" the drug. In the United States, the drug is impure, consisting of only about 5 percent heroin, and it must be "mainlined" or injected into the bloodstream to achieve an effect comparable to that which may have been experienced in Vietnam. Further, a habit which costs $5 a day to maintain in Vietnam can cost $100 a day to maintain in the United States, and those who continue to use heroin slip into the twilight world of crime, bad drugs, and all too often a premature death.

In order to expedite the rehabilitation process of Vietnam veterans, I have ordered the immediate establishment of testing procedures and initial rehabilitation efforts to be taken in Vietnam. This procedure is under way and testing will commence in a matter of days. The Department of Defense will provide rehabilitation programs to all servicemen being returned for discharge who want this help, and we will be requesting legislation to permit the military services to retain for treatment any individual due for discharge who is a narcotic addict. All of our servicemen must be accorded the right to rehabilitation.

Rehabilitation procedures, which are required subsequent to discharge, will be effected under the aegis of the Director of the Special Action Office who will have the authority to refer patients to private hospitals as well as VA hospitals as circumstances require.

The Veterans Administration medical facilities are a great national resource which can be of immeasurable assistance in the effort against this grave national problem. Restrictive and exclusionary use of these facilities under present statutes means that we are wasting a critically needed national resource. We are commonly closing the doors to those who need help the most. This is a luxury we cannot afford. Authority will be sought by the new Office to make the facilities of the Veterans Administration available to all former servicemen in need of drug rehabilitation, regardless of the nature of their discharge from the service.

I am asking the Congress to increase the present budget of the Veterans Administration by $14 million to permit the immediate initiation of this program. This money would be used to assist in the immediate development and emplacement of VA rehabilitation centers which will permit both inpatient and outpatient care of addicts in a community setting.

I am also asking that the Congress amend the Narcotic Addict Rehabilitation Act of 1966 to broaden the authority under this Act for the use of methadone maintenance programs. These programs would be carried out under the most rigid standards and would be subjected to constant and painstaking reevaluation of their effectiveness. At this time, the evidence indicates that methadone is a useful tool in the work of rehabilitating heroin addicts, and that tool ought to be available to those who must do this work.

Finally, I will instruct the Special Consultant for Narcotics and Dangerous Drugs to review immediately all Federal laws pertaining to rehabilitation and I will submit any legislation needed to expedite the Federal rehabilitative role, and to correct overlapping authorities and other shortcomings.

Additional Enforcement Needs. The Comprehensive Drug Abuse Prevention and Control Act of 1970 provides a sound base for the attack on the problem of the availability of narcotics in America. In addition to tighter and more enforceable regulatory controls, the measure provides law enforcement with stronger and better tools. Equally important, the Act contains credible and proper penalties against violators of the drug law. Severe punishments are invoked against the drug pushers and peddlers while more lenient and flexible sanctions are provided for the users. A seller can receive fifteen years for a first offense involving hard narcotics, thirty years if the sale is to a minor, and up to life in prison if the transaction is part of a continuing criminal enterprise.

These new penalties allow judges more discretion, which we feel will restore credibility to the drug control laws and eliminate some of the difficulties prosecutors and judges have had in the past arising out of minimum mandatory penalties for all violators.

The penalty structure in the 1970 Drug Act became effective on May 1 of this year. While it is too soon to assess its effect,

I expect it to help enable us to deter or remove from our midst those who traffic in narcotics and other dangerous drugs.

To complement the new Federal drug law, a uniform State drug control law has been drafted and recommended to the States. Nineteen States have already adopted it and others have it under active consideration. Adoption of this uniform law will facilitate joint and effective action by all levels of government.

Although I do not presently anticipate a necessity for alteration of the purposes or principles of existing enforcement statutes, there is a clear need for some additional enforcement legislation.

To help expedite the prosecution of narcotic trafficking cases, we are asking the Congress to provide legislation which would permit the United States Government to utilize information obtained by foreign police, provided that such information was obtained in compliance with the laws of that country.

We are also asking that the Congress provide legislation which would permit a chemist to submit written findings of his analysis in drug cases. This would speed the process of criminal justice.

The problems of addict identification are equalled and surpassed by the problem of drug identification. To expedite work in this area of narcotics enforcement, I am asking the Congress to provide $2 million to be allotted to the research and development of equipment and techniques for the detection of illegal drugs and drug traffic.

I am asking the Congress to provide $2 million to the Department of Agriculture for research and development of herbicides which can be used to destroy growths of narcotics-producing plants without adverse ecological effects.

I am asking the Congress to authorize and fund 325 additional positions within the Bureau of Narcotics and Dangerous Drugs to increase their capacity for apprehending those engaged in narcotics trafficking here and abroad and to investigate domestic industrial producers of drugs.

Finally, I am asking the Congress to provide a supplemental appropriation of $25.6 million for the Treasury Department. This will increase funds available to this Department for drug abuse control to nearly $45 million. Of this sum, $18.1 million would be used to enable the Bureau of Customs to develop the technical capacity to deal with smuggling by air and sea, to increase the investigative staff charged with pursuit and apprehension of smugglers, and to increase inspection personnel who search persons, baggage, and cargo entering the country. The remaining $7.5 million would permit the Internal Revenue Service to intensify investigation of persons involved in large-scale narcotics trafficking.

The steps would strengthen our efforts to root out the cancerous growth of narcotics addiction in America. It is impossible to say that the enforcement legislation I have asked for here will be conclusive—that we will not need further legislation. We cannot fully know at this time what further steps will be necessary. As those steps define themselves, we will be prepared to seek further legislation to take any action and every action necessary to wipe out the menace of drug addiction in America. But domestic enforcement alone cannot do the job. If we are to stop the flow of narcotics into the lifeblood of this country, I believe we must stop it at the source.

International

There are several broad categories of drugs: those of the cannabis family—such as marihuana and hashish; those which are used as sedatives, such as the barbiturates and certain tranquilizers; those which elevate mood and suppress appetite, such as the amphetamines; and, drugs such as LSD and mescaline, which are commonly called hallucinogens. Finally, there are the narcotic analgesics, including opium and its derivatives—morphine and codeine. Heroin is made from morphine.

Heroin addiction is the most difficult to control and the most socially destructive form of addiction in America today. Heroin is a fact of life and a cause of death among an increasing number of citizens in America, and it is heroin addiction that must command priority in the struggle against drugs.

To wage an effective war against heroin addiction, we must have international cooperation. In order to secure such cooperation, I am initiating a worldwide escalation in our existing programs for the control of narcotics traffic, and I am proposing a number of new steps for this purpose.

First, on Monday, June 14, I recalled the United States Ambassadors to Turkey, France, Mexico, Luxembourg, Thailand, the Republic of Vietnam, and the United Nations for consultations on how we can better cooperate with other nations in the effort to regulate the present substantial world opium output and narcotics trafficking. I sought to make it equally clear that I consider the heroin addiction of American citizens an international problem of grave concern to this Nation, and I instructed our Ambassadors to make this clear to their host governments. We want good relations with other countries, but we cannot buy good relations at the expense of temporizing on this problem.

Second, United States Ambassadors to all East Asian governments will meet in Bangkok, Thailand, tomorrow, June 18, to review the increasing problem in that area, with particular concern for the effects of this problem on American servicemen in Southeast Asia.

Third, it is clear that the only really effective way to end heroin production is to end opium production and the growing of poppies. I will propose that as an international goal. It is essential to recognize that opium is, at present, a legitimate source of income to many of those nations which produce it. Morphine and codeine both have legitimate medical applications.

It is the production of morphine and codeine for medical purposes which justifies the maintenance of opium production, and it is this production which in turn contributes to the world's heroin supply. The development of effective substitutes for these derivatives would eliminate any valid reason for opium production. While modern medicine has developed effective and broadly-used substitutes for morphine, it has yet to provide a fully acceptable substitute for codeine. Therefore, I am directing that Federal research efforts in the United States be intensified with the aim of developing at the earliest possible date synthetic substitutes for all opium derivatives. At the same time I am requesting the Director General of the World Health Organization to appoint a study panel of experts to make periodic technical assessments of any synthetics which might replace opiates with the aim of effecting substitutions as soon as possible.

Fourth, I am requesting $1 million to be used by the Bureau of Narcotics and Dangerous Drugs for training of foreign narcotics enforcement officers. Additional personnel within the Bureau of Narcotics and Dangerous Drugs would permit the strengthening of the investigative capacities of BNDD offices in the U.S., as well as their ability to assist host governments in the hiring, training, and deployment of personnel and the procurement of necessary equipment for drug abuse control.

Fifth, I am asking the Congress to amend and approve the International Security Assistance Act of 1971 and the International Development and Humanitarian Assistance Act of 1971 to permit assistance to presently proscribed nations in their efforts to end drug trafficking. The drug problem crosses ideological boundaries and surmounts national differences. If we are barred in any way in our effort to deal with this matter, our efforts will be crippled, and our will subject to question. I intend to leave no room for other nations to question our commitment to this matter.

Sixth, we must recognize that cooperation in control of dangerous drugs works both ways. While the sources of our chief narcotics problem are foreign, the United States is a source of illegal psychotropic drugs which afflict other nations. If we expect other governments to help stop the flow of heroin to our shores, we must act with equal vigor to prevent equally dangerous substances from going into their nations from our own. Accordingly, I am submitting to the Senate for its advice and consent the Convention on Psychotropic Substances which was recently signed by the United States and 22 other nations. In addition, I will submit to the Congress any legislation made necessary by the Convention including the complete licensing, inspection, and control of the manufacture, distribution, and trade in dangerous synthetic drugs.

Seventh, the United States has already pledged $2 million to a Special Fund created on April 1 of this year by the Secretary General of the United Nations and aimed at planning and executing a concerted UN effort against the world drug problem. We will continue our strong backing of UN drug-control efforts by encouraging other countries to contribute and by requesting the Congress to make additional contributions to this fund as their need is demonstrated.

Finally, we have proposed, and we are strongly urging multilateral support for, amendments to the Single Convention on Narcotics which would enable the International Narcotics Control Board to:

- require from signatories details about opium poppy cultivation and opium production—thus permitting the Board access to essential information about narcotics raw materials from which illicit diversion occurs;
- base its decisions about the various nations' activities with narcotic drugs not only as at present on information officially submitted by the governments, but also on information which the Board obtains through public or private sources—thus enhancing data available to the Board in regard to illicit traffic;
- carry out, with the consent of the nation concerned, on-the-spot inquiries on drug related activities;
- modify signatories' annual estimates of intended poppy acreage and opium production with a view to reducing acreage or production; and
- in extreme cases, require signatories to embargo the export and/or import of drugs to or from a particular country that has failed to meet its obligations under the Convention.

I believe the foregoing proposals establish a new and needed dimension in the international effort to halt drug production, drug traffic, and drug abuse. These proposals put the problems and the search for solutions in proper perspective, and will give this Nation its best opportunity to end the flow of drugs, and most particularly heroin, into America, by literally cutting it off root and branch at the source.

Conclusion

Narcotics addiction is a problem which afflicts both the body and the soul of America. It is a problem which baffles many Americans. In our history we have faced great difficulties again and again, wars and depressions and divisions among our people have tested our will as a people—and we have prevailed.

We have fought together in war, we have worked together in hard times, and we have reached out to each other in division—to close the gaps between our people and keep America whole.

The rheat of narcotics among our people is one which properly frightens many Americans. It comes quietly into homes and destroys children, it moves into neighborhoods and breaks the fiber of community which makes neighbors. It is a problem which demands compassion, and not simply condemnation, for those who become the victims of narcotics and dangerous drugs. We must try to better understand the confusion and disillusion and despair that bring people, particularly young people, to the use of narcotics and dangerous drugs.

We are not without some understanding in this matter, however. And we are not without the will to deal with this matter. We have the moral resources to do the job. Now we need the authority and the funds to match our moral resources. I am confident that we will prevail in this struggle as we have in many others. But time is critical. Every day we lose compounds the tragedy which drugs inflict on individual Americans. The final issue is not whether we will conquer drug abuse, but how soon. Part of this answer lies with the Congress now and the speed with which it moves to support the struggle against drug abuse.

RICHARD NIXON

TEXT OF PRESIDENT'S MESSAGE ON PUBLIC WORKS VETO

Following is the text, as made available by the White House, of President Nixon's message on his June 29 veto of the public works bill (S 575), which cleared Congress on June 15.

TO THE CONGRESS OF THE UNITED STATES:

Expansion of job opportunities for those presently unemployed is one of this Administration's highest priorities. Measures to expand job opportunities must be effective; they must hold real promise of providing the jobs when they are needed, where they are needed, for the persons who most need them.

In recent weeks, the Congress has acted on two measures which seek to achieve the same goal of job creation through two quite different approaches.

One meets the test. Another does not. I hope the two houses of Congress will soon vote final passage of the Emergency Employment Act of 1971 (S 31), on which the Conference Committee has now completed its report, which would create new job opportunities in the public sector. However, I am returning without my approval S 575, which among its other provisions would attempt to deal with unemployment through a $2-billion program of accelerated public works.

The Administration has been working closely with congressional leaders on the Emergency Employment Act of 1971 in an effort to ensure its adoption in a form permitting states and localities to move quickly, and on a sound and responsible basis, to create new job opportunities in the public sector. In the form agreed to by the conference committee, it would do so. Like the provision for 200,000 public service jobs in the welfare reform bill passed by the House, it would mark a useful addition to the existing programs—including Operation Mainstream and the Administration's own Public Service Careers program—which are currently providing public service job opportunities for the unemployed.

In December of last year I disapproved a manpower measure passed by the Congress, because in the form in which it was passed it would have created dead-end jobs amounting to a system of permanent subsidized public employment. However, I have made it clear that the Administration considers that our unmet needs in the public sector provide an opportunity to combat joblessness by bringing unemployed men and women into the labor force in selected areas and appropriate circumstances. We have stressed one key point: that these created jobs must be *transitional*—that is, they must be a bridge to permanent, productive jobs, not a substitute for them.

The action taken thus far this year by the Congress on the Emergency Employment Act of 1971 deals effectively with these concerns. Public employment is defined as "transitional." It is targeted on locally-supported jobs of proven need. Moreover, the bill, as it has been agreed to in conference, would be limited to two years and would be triggered when national unemployment exceeds 4.5 percent.

I am particularly gratified that the Emergency Employment Act as currently drawn extends special consideration to recent veterans. The level of unemployment among veterans who have served their country so well and so bravely is unconscionable. The Emergency Employment Act would be an installment on repaying the debt that we owe them.

Furthermore, leaders in both bodies of the Congress have indicated that, as soon as action on the Emergency Employment

Act of 1971 is completed, they will move with dispatch to hold hearings, and then make every effort to obtain favorable action, on broader manpower reform legislation this year. They will include in these deliberations the Administration's proposal for Manpower Special Revenue Sharing.

In terms of its capacity for generating new jobs quickly, the accelerated public works approach—as embodied in S 575—at best comes out a poor and distant second. Among its deficiencies are these:

• Construction projects have notoriously long lead times. Experience under the original Public Works Acceleration Act of 1962 demonstrates that spending—and hence job creation—under this bill would not become fully effective for at least 18 months at which time further stimulation would be unnecessary and inflationary. Only about 10 percent of the funds would be likely to be spent within the next 12 months. It therefore would not even make a real start on delivering on its implied promise of jobs now, when jobs are needed.

• It would have little effect in reducing joblessness in the areas where it is now most concentrated. The Vietnam veteran, the unskilled youth, and other persons unemployed because of lack of training or opportunity would have little chance of securing a job on one of these projects.

• Rather than helping the broad spectrum of the presently unemployed, the impact of the bill would focus primarily on the construction industry which already has experienced rapid cost inflation. In no other industry have wage increases been higher. Increases in that industry have affected collective bargaining elsewhere, thus further fueling inflation in the overall economy.

• Because the accelerated public works program has been conceived of as an emergency measure, with an implied promise of quick approvals and a broad scattering of the benefits, insistent demands could be expected for marginal, hurriedly planned, environmentally damaging and uncoordinated projects.

• Finally, false hopes would be created in many communities, and this Administration does not wish to be a party to these misleading impressions. The previous Accelerated Public Works program resulted in applications for nearly double the amount of funds available despite early efforts to discourage requests. On the basis of these expectations, communities deferred locally funded projects. Therefore, the net economic impact in many communities was, actually, a delay in needed public works projects.

In addition to accelerated public works, S 575 also extends —by Title II—the Public Works and Economic Development Act of 1965 until June 30, 1973, and extends—by Title III—the Appalachian Regional Development Act to June 30, 1975. I agree that our present economic development programs should be extended while the Congress is considering my revenue sharing proposals. But most importantly, the Congress must act immediately to insure that there is no gap in service to the people in Appalachia and in the economically depressed areas served by EDA. In this connection, I am pleased to note that the House has already provided for the temporary continuance of these programs until new legislation can be enacted. I urge the Senate to do likewise.

I know the problems of these areas. I met with the Appalachian Governors last year for a full half day to discuss the best ways in which we could meet the needs of the people of Appalachia. When I met with the Governors of Virginia, West Virginia and Kentucky last week, I emphasized that even if I would have to veto the Accelerated Public Works bill, I support the Appalachian program 100 percent.

The Appalachian Regional Commission has been a very useful experimental development program which can be improved upon and can serve in many respects as a model for a national program. This is essentially what I have done in proposing to the Congress Rural and Urban Community Development Revenue Sharing. The record of the Appalachian Regional Commission goes a long way in proving that state and local governments do have the capacity to make revenue sharing work.

The revenue sharing proposals will insure that states and localities will get their fair share of the funds automatically without having to play grantsmanship games. Furthermore, those proposals would eliminate federal red tape and local share repuirements. State and local officials could more quickly provide public projects which are most responsive to local needs. The gap between federal resources and local needs would be bridged in a way that would strengthen state and local responsibilities and decision-making. These proposals deal with problems which simply will not yield to the old approaches, no matter how they are reworked or expanded. I again urge upon the Congress the early enactment of my revenue sharing programs.

Meanwhile, as a means of providing additional jobs now, the public service jobs approach as it has emerged in the Emergency Employment Act of 1971 is clearly a better answer than the Accelerated Public Works program.

Public sector jobs are labor-intensive: a high proportion of federal appropriations under that bill would flow into direct wages and salaries for new employees. In community service activities such as environmental protection, health and sanitation, unemployed persons can be put to work rapidly. No long lead time is required for complicated engineering studies.

On the other hand our experience during the early 1960s clearly shows that accelerated public works is a costly and time-consuming method of putting unemployed persons to work. Even the bill's strongest proponents recognize that public works programs are not people-intensive, but money-intensive.

The job of the Administration, indeed of any administration, is to search out the best ways to deal with the problems and needs of the nation. We need more jobs. A bill to do this directly and now, when the jobs are needed, is clearly the best answer.

RICHARD NIXON

MINORITY ENTERPRISE TEXT

Following is the text, as made available by the White House, of President Nixon's Oct. 13 message to Congress on encouraging minority enterprises.

TO THE CONGRESS OF THE UNITED STATES:

Approximately 35 million Americans are of Black, Spanish-speaking, or Indian ancestry—about 1/6 of our total population. Yet these same minority Americans presently own only about 4% of America's businesses. And these businesses, in turn, account for less than 1% of our Nation's gross business receipts.

In my statement on school desegregation of March 24, 1970, and again in my statement on equal housing opportunity last June 11, I committed this administration to the untiring pursuit of a free and open society, one which gives all citizens both the right and the ability to control their own destinies. I emphasized that such a society should be diverse and pluralistic, affording all of its members both a range for personal choice and the mobility which allows them to take advantage of that range of choice. Both in law and in practice, I argued, we owe every man an equal chance at the starting line and an equal opportunity to go as high and as far as his talents and energies will take him.

Throughout our history, one of the most effective ways in which we have advanced these goals has been by expanding the opportunity for property ownership and independent business activity. On many occasions our Founding Fathers spoke eloquently about the close relationship between property rights and human rights, and the wisdom of their words has been abundantly demonstrated throughout our national experience.

One of the most effective means now available for advancing the cause of human dignity among minority Americans is by expanding managerial and ownership opportunities for minority entrepreneurs.

On March 5, 1969, in one of my first executive orders as President, I established two new mechanisms for promoting expanded minority business activities: an Office of Minority Business Enterprise within the Department of Commerce to coordinate and oversee all Federal efforts in this field and to stimulate private sector initiatives; and an advisory Council for Minority Business Enterprise to study this complex subject and recommend further action. Since that time, both of these units have been diligently carrying out these assignments. The further steps which I am announcing today have grown in large measure from their suggestions and their experience.

The Record to Date

The record of this administration in promoting minority enterprise is a record of which we are proud. The aggregate total of Federal business loans, guarantees and grants to minority enterprises and purchases from them has increased almost three-fold over the last three fiscal years—from nearly $200 million in Fiscal Year 1969 to an estimated $566 million in Fiscal Year 1971. Federal purchases involving minority businesses alone have increased more than eleven-fold—from $13 million in Fiscal Year 1969 to $142 million in Fiscal Year 1971. Our program to stimulate minority banking, which began just one year ago this month, has surpassed its goal of generating $100 million in new deposits in minority banks; firm commitments have been received for more than $35 million from the Federal Government and $65 million from the private sector.

In addition, the Small Business Administration has licensed 39 Minority Enterprise Small Business Investment Companies (MESBICs), with an aggregate capitalization in excess of $10 million. When Federal monies available to these 39 MESBICs are fully utilized, they should be able to generate some $150 million additional dollars in overall financing for minority business ventures. Moreover, a number of new MESBICs are now in the process of formation. At the same time, the Opportunity Funding Corporation, which has received $7.4 million from the Office of Economic Opportunity, is also developing new projects which will stimulate minority ownership.

Other promising developments include new legislation which provides crime insurance at reasonable rates to minority businessmen, new legislation which assures the availability of surety bonds to minority contractors, and new regulations which require affirmative action to increase minority subcontracting under all Federal prime contracts and increased minority business participation in all Federally financed housing projects.

The Government has also stepped up the collection and dissemination of information critical to the development of minority enterprise, including the first census ever taken of minority-owned businesses. Meanwhile, an Inter-Agency Committee on Minority Business Enterprise has been formed in Washington and a series of Minority Business Opportunity Committees have been set up across the Nation.

Government efforts have also helped stimulate the private sector to provide increasing assistance for minority enterprise—including resources such as equity and debt capital, franchise offerings and other business openings, management services and technical assistance, and a range of market opportunities. For example, there are nearly three times as many minority-owned franchises and more than six times as many minority auto dealerships today as there were 2 years ago.

The Challenges Which Remain

In a wide variety of ways, then, we have been working to give disadvantaged groups a greater stake in the American economy. But, as the Advisory Council on Minority Enterprise concluded in its recent report, there are still "enormous economic inequities" which challenge the will and the resourcefulness of our Nation. The elimination of those inequities must be a national objective of high priority in the 1970s. Accordingly, I am today calling on the Congress to join with the administration in a still more intensive and far-reaching effort to foster business development among minorities.

This program should be guided by several important principles. It should be a comprehensive and pluralistic effort, one that moves forward on many fronts, since the barriers to minority enterprise are varied and numerous. It should also be a flexible approach, one that maximizes local control, since local realities are diverse and changeable. Our program should encourage the private sector to join with Government in creating an economic environment conducive to the development of minority businesses.

Another important principle is that we should carry out this program without overpromising or raising false hopes. There is no automatic road to economic success for any group in our society. A sound program which enables more Americans to share in the rewards of entrepreneurship will find them sharing in the risks and the responsibilities of entrepreneurship as well.

An Expanded Budget

With these considerations in mind, I am calling today for a significant expansion of our minority enterprise budget. In addition to the $3.6 million appropriation which we originally requested for the Office of Minority Business Enterprise in Fiscal Year 1972 we have asked the Congress to budget an additional $40 million—bringing the total budget for the current fiscal year to $43.6 million. I repeat that request today—and in order to provide for continued expansion of the minority enterprise program, I intend to propose that OMBE be given a budget for fiscal year 1973 of $63.6 million. Altogether, we are asking for a new two-year program of $100 million.

What would this money be used for? Primarily, these funds would provide for an expanded program of technical assistance and management services. Approximately 10 percent of these new funds would be used at the national level—to strengthen minority business and trade organizations, to generate broad private programs of marketing and financial assistance, to develop training programs, and to foster other national efforts. The remaining 90% of the new money would be spent on the local level—supporting a variety of efforts to identify, train, advise or assist minority businessmen and to put them in touch with one another and with non-minority businessmen who can provide them with additional help.

In talking about encouraging expanded ownership, we are talking about an impulse which is already strong among minority groups in this country. The desire to gain a bigger piece of the action is already there; it is not something that depends on government stimulation. What government must do, however, is to help eliminate the artificial obstacles to expanded ownership —including the complex array of regulations and forms and bureaucracies which often stand between minority entrepreneurs and the resources which are available to help them.

This is why we are emphasizing the development of local centers which can bring together a vast array of training, advice and information for minority businessmen. Such centers can help them put together in an effective way the many elements which are necessary to build a successful business. We hope to develop more than 100 of these centers over the next three years.

I would emphasize that the money we are requesting for OMBE does not include grants, loans, guarantees, and purchases with minority businessmen by many other Federal agencies. Such direct aid, however, will also be expanded. We have, in fact, budgeted for $700 million in minority loans, grants guarantees and purchases in the current fiscal year, an advance of half a billion dollars—more than three-fold increase—over 1969.

Bolstering the MESBICs

In addition to expanded budgets, I am also submitting to the Congress legislation to strengthen our growing program for Minority Enterprise Small Business Investment Companies. This legislation would:

(1) Lower the level of private financing required to qualify for financing from the Small Business Administration on a three for one basis. At present, a MESBIC must raise $1 million before it can obtain Federal dollars on a three for one basis rather than the two for one basis that otherwise applies. I propose that the qualifying figure for three for one assistance be cut in half.

(2) Provide increased equity to MESBICs in the form of preferred stock to be purchased by the SBA in place of part of the debt instrument purchased by the SBA under current law. This will reduce the debt load presently carried by MESBICs and stimulate added investments to create larger and more vigorous MESBICs.

(3) Lower the interest rate on SBA loans to MESBICs to three points below the normal rate set by the Treasury Department during the first five years of the loan.

These provisions should greatly increase the resources which are available to minority businesses through the MESBIC program.

Better Coordination

I am also issuing today an executive order giving the Secretary of Commerce—and, through him, the Office of Minority Business Enterprise—increased authority over all Federal activities in the minority enterprise field. This order gives the Secretary a clear mandate to establish and carry out Federal policy concerning minority enterprise and to coordinate the related efforts of all Federal departments and agencies. It also directs the departments and agencies to develop systematic data collection processes concerning their minority enterprise programs and to cooperate in expanding the overall Federal effort. The substantive provisions of Executive Order 11458 of March 5, 1969, are also carried over into the new order.

Unfinished Business

In addition to these new initiatives, I again urge action on a number of older proposals. Among these is my suggestion that a new Assistant Secretary for Minority Enterprise be created in the Department of Commerce—an important step in giving greater cohesion and greater emphasis to Federal involvement in this area.

Other important legislation includes Senate Bill 544, which would alter tax laws so as to ease the burden on small, marginal businessmen. I also urge passage of the Small Business Amendments Act of 1971. Finally, I again ask the Congress to enact the Indian Business Development Program Act, the Indian Financing Act, and the Washington, D.C. Development Bank Act of 1971.

Conclusion

The best way to fight poverty and to break the vicious cycle of dependence and despair which afflicts too many Americans is by fostering conditions which encourage those who have been so afflicted to play a more self-reliant and independent economic role.

This goal will not be achieved overnight for there is no easy way to eliminate the barriers which now prevent many who are members of minority groups from controlling their fair share of American business. Yet the long range health of our economy—and, indeed, of our entire society—requires us to remove these barriers as quickly as possible. Both morally and economically, we will not realize the full potential of our Nation until neither race nor nationality is any longer an obstacle to full participation in the American marketplace.

RICHARD NIXON

TEXT OF PRESIDENT'S MESSAGE ON PRIVATE PENSION PLAN

Following is the text, as made available by the White House, of President Nixon's Dec. 8 message to Congress on private pension plans.

TO THE CONGRESS OF THE UNITED STATES:

Self-reliance, prudence and independence are qualities which our Government should work to encourage among our people. These are also the qualities which are involved when a person chooses to invest in a retirement savings plan, setting aside money today so that he will have greater security tomorrow. In this respect, pension plans are a direct expression of some of the finest elements in the American character. Public policy should be designed to reward and reinforce these qualities.

The achievements of our private pension plans are a tribute to the cooperation and creativeness of American labor and management. Over 4 million retired workers are now receiving benefits from private plans and these benefits total about $7 billion annually. More than $140 billion has been accumulated by these plans to pay retirement benefits in the future. But there is still much room for expanding and strengthening our private pension system.

Three groups in our society have a tremendous direct stake in the growth and improvement of private pensions. The first is made up of that 50 percent of American wage earners who are not in private group plans at the present time and who have no tax incentive for investing in retirement savings as individuals. The second group includes those who are enrolled in group plans which provide benefits for their retirement needs which they regard as insufficient or which do not ensure that the benefits which are accumulating while they work will actually be made available when they retire. If we meet the problems of these two groups today, we will also be taking a giant stride toward improving the quality of life tomorrow for an important third segment of our population to which they will eventually belong: the retired Americans whose independence and dignity depend in large measure on an adequate post-retirement income.

Older persons have spoken eloquently about the need for pension reform, especially at the White House Conference on Aging, which was recently held in Washington. It is clear that our efforts to reform and expand our income maintenance systems must now be complemented by an effort to reform and expand private retirement programs.

The five-point program I present today includes three new legislative proposals, a renewed endorsement of an earlier proposal, and a major study project which could lead to further legislation.

1. Employees who wish to save independently for their retirement or to supplement employer-financed pensions should be allowed to deduct on their income tax returns amounts set aside for these purposes.

Today only 30 million employees are covered by private retirement plans. This fact alone demonstrates the need to encourage greater private saving for retirement.

Under present law, both the contributions which an employer makes to a qualified private retirement plan on behalf of his employees and the investment earnings on those contributions are generally not subject to taxes until they are paid to the employee or to his beneficiaries. The tax liability on investment earnings is also deferred when an employee contributes to a group plan, though in this case the contribution itself is taxable. But when an employee saves independently for his own retirement, both his contribution and the investment earnings on such savings are currently subject to taxes.

This inequity discourages individual self-reliance and slows the growth of private retirement savings. It places an unfair burden on those employees (especially older workers) who want to establish a pension plan or augment an employer-financed plan. To provide such persons with the same opportunities now available to others, I therefore ask the Congress to make contributions to retirement savings programs by individuals deductible up to the level of $1500 per year or 20% of income, whichever is less. Individuals would retain the power to control the investment of these funds, channeling them into bank accounts, mutual funds, annuity or insurance programs, government bonds, or into other investments as they desire. Taxes would also be deferred on the earnings from these investments.

This provision would be especially helpful to older workers who are most interested in retirement. The limitation I propose would direct benefits primarily to employees with low and moderate incomes, while preserving an incentive to establish employer-financed plans. The limit is nevertheless sufficiently high to permit older employees to finance a substantial retirement income. For example, a person whose plan begins at age 40, with contributions of $1,500 a year, could still retire at age 65 with an annual pension of $7,500, in addition to social security benefits.

This proposed deduction would be available to those already covered by employer-financed plans, but in this case the upper limit of $1,500 would be reduced to reflect pension plan contributions made by the employer. An appropriate adjustment would also be made in the case of individuals who do not contribute to the Social Security system or the Railroad Retirement System.

2. Self-employed persons who invest in pension plans for themselves and their employees should be given a more generous tax deduction than they now receive.

Under present law, self-employed persons may establish plans covering themselves and their employees. However, deductible contributions are limited annually to $2,500 or 10 percent of earned income, whichever is less. There are no such limits to contributions made by corporations on behalf of their employees.

This distinction in treatment is not based on any difference in reality, since self-employed persons and corporate employees often engage in substantially the same economic activities. One result of this distinction has been to create an artificial incentive for the self-employed to incorporate; another result has been to deny benefits to the employees of those self-employed persons who do not wish to incorporate which are comparable to those of corporate employees.

To achieve greater equity, I propose that the annual limit for deductible contributions by the self-employed be raised to $7,500 or 15 percent of income, whichever is less. This provision would encourage and enable the self-employed to provide more adequate benefits for themselves and for their workers.

3. A minimum standard should be established in law for the vesting of pensions—i.e., for preserving pension rights of employees even though they lose their jobs before retirement.

A basic problem in our present pension system is the situation of the worker who loses his pension when he is discharged, laid off, resigns or moves to another job. A person who is discharged just before retirement, for example, sometimes finds that the retirement income on which he has been relying—and which has been accumulating for many years—simply is no longer due him.

Preservation of the pension rights of employees who leave their jobs—vesting—is essential to a growing and healthy private pension system. A pension is fully vested when an employee is entitled to receive all benefits accumulated up to

a certain date regardless of what happens in the period between that date and his retirement. Despite encouraging increases in the degree of vesting, the pensions of more than two-thirds of all current participants in private pension plans are not now vested. Even among older employees, whose need for vesting is most acute, many pensions are not now vested. Forty percent of participants age 45 or older, 34 percent of participants age 50 or older, and 26 percent of participants age 55 or older do not have vested pension rights.

This problem can be corrected by requiring that pensions be fully vested at an appropriate specified point in a worker's career. But how should that point be determined? If it were set at too early a point, so that too many younger workers were vested, it could create a considerable burden for employers and reduce the level of benefits for retiring workers. On the other hand, if too long a wait were allowed before vesting begins, then many older workers would receive little if any assistance. Both of these pitfalls can be avoided, however, through a carefully drawn formula which provides a shorter waiting period before vesting begins for older workers.

The formula that I propose to the Congress is based upon what I shall call the "Rule of 50." Under this standard, every pension would be considered half vested when an employee's age plus the number of years he has participated in the pension plan equals 50. The vesting process would begin with this jump to half-vested status. After this point has been reached, an additional ten percent of the pension would be vested every year—so that the pension would be fully vested five years later.

Under this standard, which must apply to workers who are 30 years of age or older, anyone joining a plan when he is 30 years old would find that his pension would begin to vest at age 40, when his years of participation (10) plus his age (40) would equal 50. The pension of an employee joining at age 40 would begin to vest at age 45, and that of an employee joining at age 50 would begin to vest immediately. And in each case, the degree of vesting would increase from 50 percent to 100 percent over the subsequent five-year period.

This plan gives older workers the advantage of more rapid vesting, a fact which could limit somewhat new employment opportunities for older workers. To help alleviate this danger, I recommend that a three-year waiting period be allowed before a new employee must be permitted to join a pension plan, and also that employees hired within five years of retirement need not fall under this vesting rule. These safeguards would ensure that older workers are not disadvantaged by this program.

This "Rule of 50" would raise the share of participants in private pension plans with vested pensions from 31 percent to 46 percent. Even more importantly, among participants age 45 and older the percentage with vested pensions would rise from 60 percent to 92 percent. Overall, the number of employees with vested rights would increase by 3.6 million, of whom 3 million would be age 45 and older.

To avoid excessive cost increases in pension plans which might lead to reduction of benefits, this new law would apply only to benefits earned after the bill becomes effective. The average cost increase for plans with no vesting provision now would be about 1.8 cents per hour for each covered employee.

4. The Employee Benefits Protection Act which I proposed to the Congress in March of 1970 should promptly be enacted into law.

This legislation was designed to protect American workers against abuses by those who administer pension funds. As I pointed out when I first made this proposal, "the control of these funds is shared by employers, unions, banks, insurance companies, and many others." Most of these funds are honestly and effectively managed. But on occasion, some are not. By requiring administrators to manage such funds exclusively in the interest of the employee beneficiaries, the proposed law would provide a Federal remedy against carelessness, conflict of interest, and a range of corrupt practices.

The proposed law would also broaden reporting and disclosure requirements and strengthen investigatory and enforcement powers. There would be no interference, however, with State laws which now regu.ate the insurance, banking and securities fields.

It was 21 months ago that I asked the Congress "to give urgent priority to the Employee Benefits Protection Act." I described it then as an action which "further expands my program to protect the American worker as he works, when he is out of work, and after his working career is over." I now renew my request for action in this field—and am resubmitting this legislation in slightly revised form so that it will be even more effective. I urge that the Congress act promptly. There is no excuse for further procrastination.

5. I have directed the Departments of Labor and the Treasury to undertake a one-year study to determine the extent of benefit losses under pension plans which are terminated.

When a pension plan is terminated, an employee participating in it can lose all or a part of the benefits which he has long been relying on, even if his plan is fully vested. The extent to which terminations occur, the number of workers who are affected, and the degree to which they are harmed are questions about which we now have insufficient information. This information is needed in order to determine what Federal policy should be on questions such as funding, the nature of the employer's liability, and termination insurance.

Even the best data now available in this field is itself incomplete and questionable. It was gathered for the period from 1955 to 1965 and it indicates that less than one-tenth of one percent of all workers then covered by pension plans were affected by terminations in any given year. It should also be noted that some workers who are affected by terminations may not actually lose their benefits. The wrong solution to the terminations problem could do more harm than good by raising unduly the cost of pension plans for the many workers who are not adversely affected by terminations.

Nevertheless, even one worker whose retirement security is destroyed by the termination of a plan is one too many. It is important, therefore, that the nature and scope of this problem be carefully and thoroughly investigated. I have directed the Departments of Labor and the Treasury to complete their study within one year.

The proposals which I offer today would enhance substantially the retirement security of America's work force. Those who are not members of group pension plans and those who have only limited coverage would be encouraged to obtain individual coverage on their own. The self-employed would have an incentive to arrange more adequate coverage for themselves and their employees. All participants would have greater assurance that they will actually receive the benefits which are coming to them. And they could also be far more certain that their pension funds were being administered under strict fiduciary standards.

There is sometimes a tendency for Government to neglect or take for granted the "little man" in this country, the average citizen who lives a quiet, responsible life and who constitutes the backbone of our strength as a nation. "He can take care of himself," we say, and there is a great deal of truth in that statement. The self-reliance of the average American is an extremely important national asset.

The fact that a man is self-reliant, however, does not mean that Government should ignore him. To the contrary, Government should do its part to cultivate individual responsibility, to provide incentives and rewards to those who "take care of themselves." Only in this way can we be sure that the self-reliant way of life will be a continuing and growing part of the American experience.

My pension reform program would help do this. It builds on traditional strengths which have always been at the root of our national greatness.

The private pension system has contributed much to the economic security of American workers. We can be proud of its growth and its accomplishments. The proposals I offer will strengthen and stimulate its further development.

I hope this program will receive the prompt and favorable consideration of the Congress. For it can do a great deal to protect the rights of the average American during his working years and to enhance the quality of his life when he has retired.

RICHARD NIXON

TEXT OF PRESIDENT'S BROADCAST STATEMENT ON VIETNAM

Following is the text, as made available by the White House, of President Nixon's April 7 nationally televised statement on the withdrawal of additional U.S. forces from Vietnam.

Good evening my fellow Americans. Over the past several weeks you have heard a number of reports on T.V., radio and in your newspapers on the situation in Southeast Asia.

I think the time has come for me as President and as Commander in Chief of our Armed Forces to put these reports in perspective, to lay all the pertinent facts before you and to let you judge for yourselves as to the success or failure of our policy.

I am glad to be able to begin my report tonight by announcing that I have decided to increase the rate of American troop withdrawals for the period from May 1 to December 1. Before going into details, I would like to review briefly what I found when I came into office, the progress we have made to date in reducing American forces, and the reason why I am able to announce a stepped-up withdrawal without jeopardizing our remaining forces in Vietnam and without endangering our ultimate goal of ending American involvement in a way which will increase the chances for a lasting peace in the Pacific and in the world.

When I left Washington in January of 1961, after serving eight years as Vice President under President Eisenhower, there were no American combat forces in Vietnam. No Americans had died in combat in Vietnam.

When I returned to Washington as President eight years later, there were 540,000 American troops in Vietnam. Thirty-one thousand had died there. Three hundred Americans were being lost every week and there was no comprehensive plan to end the United States involvement in the war.

I implemented a plan to train and equip the South Vietnamese; to withdraw American forces; and to end American involvement in the war just as soon as the South Vietnamese had developed the capacity to defend their country against Communist aggression. On this chart, on my right, you can see how our plan has succeeded. In June of 1969, I announced a withdrawal of 25,000 men; in September, 40,000; in December 50,000; April of 1970—150,000. By the first of next month, May 1, we will have brought home more than 265,000 Americans, almost half of the troops in Vietnam when I took office.

Now another indication of the progress we have made is in reducing American casualties. Casualties were five times as great in the first three months of 1969 as they were in the first three months this year, 1971. South Vietnamese casualties have also dropped significantly in the past two years. One American dying in combat is one too many. Our goal is no American fighting man dying anyplace in the world. Every decision I have made in the past and every decision I make in the future will have the purpose of achieving that goal.

Let me review now two decisions I have made which have contributed to the achievements of our goals in Vietnam that you have seen on the chart.

The first was the destruction of enemy bases in Cambodia. You will recall at the time of that decision, many expressed fears that we had widened the war; that our casualties would increase and our troop withdrawal program would be delayed. I don't question the sincerity of those who expressed these fears. But we can see now they were wrong. American troops were out of Cambodia in 60 days; just as I pledged they would be. American casualties did not rise. They were cut in half. American troop withdrawals were not halted or delayed. They continued at an accelerated pace.

Now let me turn to the Laotian operation. As you know, this was undertaken by South Vietnamese ground forces with American air support against North Vietnamese troops which had been using Laotian territory for six years to attack American forces and allied forces in South Vietnam. Since the completion of that operation, there has been a great deal of understandable speculation—just as there was after Cambodia—whether it was a success or a failure, a victory or a defeat. But, as in Cambodia, what is important is not the instant analysis of the moment, but what happens in the future.

Laotian Operation

Did the Laotian operation contribute to the goals we sought? I have just completed my assessment of that operation and here are my conclusions:

First, the South Vietnamese demonstrated that without American advisers they could fight effectively against the very best troops North Vietnam could put in the field.

Second—the South Vietnamese suffered heavy casualties. But, by every conservative estimate the casualties suffered by the enemy were far heavier.

Third, and most important, the disruption of enemy supply lines, the consumption of ammunition and arms in the battle has been even more damaging to the capability of the North Vietnamese to sustain major offensives in South Vietnam—than were the operations in Cambodia ten months ago.

Consequently tonight—I can report that Vietnamization has succeeded. Because of the increased strength of the South Vietnamese, because of the success of the Cambodian operation; because of the achievements of the South Vietnamese operation in Laos I am announcing an increase in the rate of American withdrawals. Between May 1 and December 1 of this year, 100,000 more American troops will be brought home from South Vietnam. This will bring the total number of American troops withdrawn from South Vietnam to 365,000. That is over two-thirds of the number who were there when I came into office, as you can see from this chart on my left. The Government of South Vietnam fully supports the decision I have just announced.

Now, let's look at the future:

As you can see from the progress we have made to date and by this announcement tonight, the American involvement in Vietnam is coming to an end. The day the South Vietnamese can take over their own defense is in sight. Our goal is a total American withdrawal from Vietnam. We can and will reach that goal through our program of Vietnamization if necessary.

We would infinitely prefer to reach it even sooner—through negotiations. I am sure most of you will recall that on October 7 of last year in a national T.V. broadcast, I proposed an immediate cease-fire throughout Indochina; the immediate release of all prisoners of war in the Indochina area; an all Indochina Peace Conference; the complete withdrawal of all outside forces; and a political settlement. Tonight I again call on Hanoi to engage in serious negotiations to speed the end of this war. I especially call on Hanoi to agree to the immediate and unconditional release of all prisoners of war throughout Indochina. It is time for Hanoi to end the barbaric use of our prisoners as negotiating pawns and to join us in a humane act that will free their men as well as ours.

Announcing a Date

Let me turn now to a proposal which at first glance has a great deal of popular appeal. If our goal is a total withdrawal of all our forces, why not announce a date now for ending our involvement? Well, the difficulty in making such an announcement to the American people is that I would also be making that announcement to the enemy. And it would serve the enemy's purpose and not our own.

If the United States should announce that we will quit regardless of what the enemy does, we would have thrown away our principal bargaining counter to win the release of American prisoners of war; we would remove the enemy's strongest incentive to end the war sooner by negotiation; and we will have given enemy commanders the exact information they need to marshal their attacks against our remaining forces at their most vulnerable time.

The issue very simply is this: Shall we leave Vietnam in a way that—by our own actions—consciously turns the country over to the Communists? Or shall we leave in a way that gives the South Vietnamese a reasonable chance to survive as a free people? My plan will end American involvement in a way that would provide that chance. The other plan would end it precipitately and give victory to the Communists.

In a deeper sense, we have the choice of ending our involvement in this war on a note of despair or on a note of hope. I believe as Thomas Jefferson did, that Americans will always choose hope over despair. We have it in our power to leave Vietnam in a way that offers a brave people a realistic hope of freedom. We have it in our power to prove to our friends in the world that America's sense of responsibility remains the world's greatest single hope for peace.

And above all, we have it in our power to close a difficult chapter in American history, not meanly, but nobly—so that each one of us can come out of this searing experience with a measure of pride in our Nation, confidence in our own character, and hope for the future of the spirit of America.

I know there are those who honestly believe that I should move to end this war without regard to what happens to South Vietnam. This way would abandon our friends. But even more important, we would abandon ourselves. We would plunge from the anguish of war into a nightmare of recrimination. We would lose respect for this Nation, respect for one another, respect for ourselves.

I understand the deep concerns which have been raised in this country, fanned by reports of brutalities in Vietnam. Let me put this into perspective.

I have visited Vietnam many times, and speaking now from that experience and as Commander in Chief of our Armed Forces, I feel it is my duty to speak up for the two and a half million fine young Americans who have served in Vietnam. The atrocity charges in individual cases should not and cannot be allowed to reflect on their courage and their self-sacrifice. War is a terrible and cruel experience for a nation and it is particularly terrible and cruel for those who bear the burden of fighting.

But never in history have men fought for less selfish motives—not for conquest, not for glory, but only for the right of a people far away to choose the kind of government they want.

While we hear and read much of isolated acts of cruelty, we do not hear enough of the tens of thousands of individual American soldiers—I have seen them there—building schools, roads, hospitals, clinics—who, through countless acts of generosity and kindness, have tried to help the people of South Vietnam. We can and we should be very proud of these men. They deserve not our scorn but they deserve our admiration and our deepest appreciation.

The way to express that appreciation is to end America's participation in this conflict, not in failure or in defeat, but in achievement of the great goals for which they fought—a South Vietnam free to determine its own future and an America no longer divided by war but united in peace.

That is why it is so important how we end this war. By our decision we will demonstrate the kind of people we are, and the kind of country we will become.

That is why I have charted the course I have laid out tonight. To end this war—but to end it in a way that will strengthen trust for America around the world, not undermine it; in a way that will redeem the sacrifices that have been made, not insult them; in a way that will heal this Nation, not tear it apart.

I can assure you tonight with confidence that American involvement in this war is coming to an end.

But can you believe this? I understand why this question is raised by many very honest and sincere people. Because many times in the past in this long and difficult war, actions have been announced from Washington which were supposed to lead to a reduction of American involvement in Vietnam. Over and over these actions resulted in more Americans going to Vietnam and more casualties in Vietnam.

Tonight I do not ask you to take what I say on faith. Look at the record. Look again at this chart on my left. Every action taken by this Administration, every decision made, has accomplished what I said it would accomplish. They have reduced American involvement. They have drastically reduced our casualties.

Campaign Pledge

In my campaign for the Presidency, I pledged to end American involvement in this war. I am keeping that pledge. And I expect to be held accountable by the American people if I fail.

I am often asked what I would like to accomplish more than anything else while serving as President of the United States. I always give the same answer—to bring peace—peace abroad, peace at home for America. The reason I am so deeply committed to peace goes far beyond political considerations or my concern about my place in history, or the other reasons that political scientists usually say are the motivations of Presidents.

Every time I talk to a brave wife of an American POW, every time I write a letter to the mother of a boy who has been killed in Vietnam, I become more deeply committed to end this war, and to end it in a way that we can build a lasting peace.

I think the hardest thing that a President has to do is to present posthumously the nation's highest honor, the Medal of Honor, to mothers or fathers or widows of men who have lost their lives, but in the process have saved the lives of others.

We had an award ceremony in the East Room of the White House just a few weeks ago. At that ceremony I remember one of the recipients, Mrs. Karl Taylor, from Pennsylvania. Her husband was a Marine sergeant, Sergeant Karl Taylor. He charged an enemy machine gun single handed and knocked it out. He lost his life. But in the process the lives of several wounded Marines in the range of that machine gun were saved.

After I presented her the Medal, I shook hands with their two children, Karl, Jr.—he was eight years old—and Keven, who was four. As I was about to move to the next recipient, Kevin suddenly stood at attention and saluted. I found it rather difficult to get my thoughts together for the next presentation.

My fellow Americans, I want to end this war in a way that is worthy of the sacrifice of Karl Taylor, and I think he would want me to end it in a way that would increase the chances that Kevin and Karl, and all those children like them here and around the world, could grow up in a world where none of them will have to die in war; that would increase the chance for America to have what it has not had in this century—a full generation of peace.

We have come a long way in the last two years toward that goal. With your continued support, I believe we will achieve that goal. And generations in the future will look back at this difficult, trying time in America's history and they will be proud that we demonstrated that we had the courage and the character of a great people.

Thank you.

WELFARE REFORM

Following is the President's letter of March 13 to the chairman and ranking minority member of the House Ways and Means Committee urging action on the Administration's welfare reform-proposal.

As you know, I have been following closely the House Ways and Means Committee deliberations on the welfare reform bill, HR 1. I appreciate your continued support of the basic principles of the proposal and your determination to obtain early enactment. There is no doubt in my mind that the Nation earnestly wants and needs the reforms in welfare that we seek. The present system is a demoralizing disgrace and must be changed. There is no time to lose.

From the earliest days of the 92nd Congress, we in the Administration have expressed our willingness to consider Committee proposals that would further strengthen HR 1 and facilitate congresssional passage. At this time, I want to reaffirm my support of proposals made by Department officials in this spirit, especially those that strengthen the employment and work incentive provisions of HR 1.

I believe it is incumbent upon the Federal Government to make the link between employment and basic income support as strong as possible. Unlike proposals for a "guaranteed annual income" which other have advocated, my welfare reform program has always included strong work incentives and requirements. I emphatically believe that those recipients who can become self-supporting should be provided both the incentive and the means to work their way to independence. At the same time, we must be certain that the responsibility for effecting this transition from support to self-sufficiency is clearly fixed and that the necessary resources are provided. I believe that HR 1, strengthened in the ways suggested below, will meet this charge.

1. *Public service employment.* The Administration has proposed public service employment for recipients for whom no other work or training is available. In the first year, 200,000 jobs would be provided at a net cost of $495 million. These would not be dead-end jobs; rather, they would be administered in a way to facilitate movement into competitive and permanent employment with significant advancement potential.

2. *Fixing responsibility for the "working poor" and those with employment potential.* Administration of these groups by the Department of Labor would *establish clear accountability* for training, employment and provide movement from the rolls of Family Assistance recipients who are "working poor" or are found to have employment potential. Those who are presently unemployed would also get appropriate development services (for example, job counseling, referral, training, day care for their children). Those who cannot work would receive services more suited to their particular needs. Initially, the Administration proposed mandatory registration of these groups with manpower agencies. The outlines of our new proposal being considered by your Committee would go even further:

The working poor (families headed by an individual presently working, but at wages below the poverty level) would be distinguished from the traditional welfare population. In the same way, those with employment potential but presently unemployed, would receive similar special attention. Manpower training and upgrading programs could then be focused on these groups and carefully tailored to their needs.

The fact that training and employment assistance will be provided by the manpower agencies of government will serve as possitive steps to move individuals into the world of work.

3. *Increased penalty for refusal to register for or accept work or training.* The Administration has proposed an increase in the panalty for those who refused appropriate work or training. This provision stipulates a reduction of benefits equivalent to the full payment for an adult family member who refuses work or training opportunities. We have also recommended the reduction of any State supplementation for such refusal.

4. *Strengthened anti-fraud provisions.* The Administration also believes it is essential to have a strong base for the

detection and prosecution of persons purposefully defrauding the welfare system. Thus, we urge your consideration of specific inclusion in HR 1 of Section 208 of the Social Security Act that clearly defines fraud, corresponding fines, and other punishment.

5. *Cashing-out Food Stamps.* The Administration has encouraged action by your Committee in cooperation with the House Agriculture Committee to cash-out the Food Stamp Program for families. The result would eliminate overlapping and duplication between these two programs.

The Administration will continue to work closely with the Committee on these and other matters. I hope this assistance will be of value to the Committee in its efforts to reform welfare. All of us agree that this is one of the most urgent items on our domestic agenda.

Sincerely,

Richard Nixon

REVERSION OF OKINAWA TO JAPAN

Following is the President's message Sept. 21 to the Senate transmitting for advice and consent to ratification the agreement between the United States and Japan on the Ryukyu Islands and the Daito Islands.

TO THE SENATE OF THE UNITED STATES:

I am transmitting for the Senate's advice and consent to ratification the Agreement between the United States of America and Japan concerning the Ryukyu Islands and the Daito Islands, signed at Washington and Tokyo on June 17, 1971. The Agreement was negotiated in accordance with the understandings I reached with Prime Minister Sato during my meetings with him in November 1969.

I transmit also, for the information of the Senate, the following related documents:

Agreed Minutes,
Memorandum of Understanding concerning Article III,
Exchange of notes concerning the Voice of America facility in Okinawa,
Exchange of notes concerning submerged lands,
Letter from Minister for Foreign Affairs Kiichi Aichi to Ambassador Meyer concerning treatment of foreign nationals and firms,
Memorandum of Understanding on air services to and through Okinawa;
and the Arrangement concerning Assumption by Japan of the Responsibility for the Immediate Defense of Okinawa.

The enclosed report from the Secretary of State describes the Agreement and the related documents.

When Prime Minister Sato arrived in Washington on November 19, 1969, I observed that "whether peace survives in the last third of the century will depend more on what happens in the Pacific than in any other area of the world." I took that particular occasion to emphasize this fact to the American people and to the world because of my strong feeling then, as now, that Japan, as one of the major powers in the Pacific area, will play a central role in determining what happens in that vital region.

Japan's phenomenal economic growth represents a most significant development for us and for the other nations of the Pacific. Japan is now the third largest producer in the world and has developed with us the greatest transoceanic commerce in the history of mankind. The potential for cooperation between our two economies, the world's most productive and the world's most dynamic, is clearly immense. For this among other reasons, Japan and the United States have a strong mutual interest in the peace and security of the Pacific area. This interest is recognized in our Treaty of Mutual Cooperation and Security, which both our countries recognize as a keystone of our security relationships in that part of the world. I think all Americans also realize that a close and friendly relationship between Japan and the United States is

vital to building the peaceful and progressive world both of us want for all mankind. The problems involved in strengthening the fabric of peace in Asia and the Pacific will undoubtedly be challenging. But if Japan and the United States go separate ways, then this task would be incomparably more difficult. Whatever differences may arise between our nations on specific policy questions, it is essential that the basic nature of our relationship remain close and cordial.

When Prime Minister Sato came to Washington in 1969, there was still one great unsettled issue between the United States and Japan arising out of World War II: the Okinawan question. Almost one million Japanese on Okinawa were still living under foreign administration nearly 25 years after the end of the Second World War. This situation subjected the entire relationship with our major Asian ally to strain. It was clear that our continued administration of Okinawa was incompatible with the mature relationship which both we and Japan recognized as the only possible basis for lasting cooperation between nations, especially between two great world powers such as the United States and Japan.

The Prime Minister and I therefore agreed that our two Governments would immediately enter into consultations concerning specific arrangements for accomplishing the early reversion of Okinawa to Japan. We determined that it was essential for this to be done without detriment to the security of the Far East, including Japan. We further agreed that the consultations should be concluded as quickly as possible with a view to accomplishing the reversion during 1972, provided that agreement could be reached on the terms and conditions of the reversion and that the necessary legislative support in both countries could be secured.

In undertaking these negotiations, the United States recognized, as a matter of basic principle, that it was consistent with neither our national character nor our national interest to continue to administer a territory which has been historically connected with Japan and whose people desire to rejoin their mother country. Japan recognized that the presence of United States forces in the Far East constituted a mainstay for the stability of the area, and that the security of countries in the Far East was a matter of serious concern for Japan. More specifically, Japan recognized that United States forces in Okinawa played a vital role in the present situation in the Far East and agreed that the United States would retain, under the terms of the Treaty of Mutual Cooperation and Security, such military facilities and areas in Okinawa as required in the mutual security of both countries.

After intensive negotiations, agreement was reached on the terms and conditions for reversion and the Agreement which I now commend to the Senate was signed on June 17, 1971.

This Agreement is founded upon the common security interests which are reflected in the United States-Japan Treaty of Mutual Cooperation and Security signed in 1960 and in the Communique which Prime Minister Sato and I jointly issued on November 21, 1969. The Agreement stipulates that, even after reversion, the Mutual Security Treaty and related arrangements, such as the Status of Forces Agreement of 1960, will apply to Okinawa without modification. The same will be true of the Treaty of Friendship, Commerce and Navigation, signed in 1953.

The new Agreement provides that after reversion Japan will grant the United States the use of facilities and areas in the Ryukyus in accordance with the Mutual Security Treaty of 1960 and its related arrangements, such as the Status of Forces Agreement. This means that the United States will continue to have the use of bases in Okinawa necessary for carrying out our mutual security commitments to Japan and for maintaining peace in the Far East. Under this Agreement, these facilities will be provided to us on the same terms as those now available to us in Japan. After reversion, a sovereign friendly government will give us permission to maintain these facilities in the Ryukyus, as in Japan, in recognition of mutual security interests. This is the only sound basis for longterm cooperation and I am convinced that it will enable us effectively to protect our own security interests.

The Agreement and related arrangements also deal with other important matters. They provide for appropriate payment to the United States for assets to be transferred to the Government of Japan and for certain costs which will be involved in connection with reversion. They provide protection for United States business and professional interests in Okinawa after reversion. They transfer to Japan responsibility for the immediate defense of the Ryukyus, which will result in substantial savings for the United States, in terms of both budget and foreign exchange.

In summary, then, I am strongly convinced that this Agreement is in the best interests of both countries. It meets United States security needs and it places our relationship with our major Asian ally on a more sound and enduring basis. It fulfills long-held aspirations of the Japanese people, including the people of Okinawa, for the reunification of these islands with Japan.

I believe the return of Okinawa to Japanese administration will be one of the most important accomplishments of our postwar policy in the Far East. It should enhance the prospects for peace and stability in that area, and it is essential to the continuation of friendly and productive relations between the United States and Japan. I therefore urge that the Senate give its early and favorable consideration to this Agreement so that reversion can take place during 1972.

Richard Nixon

BUSING OF SCHOOLCHILDREN

Following is the Aug. 3 statement by the President on the busing of schoolchildren to achieve racial balance.

The Justice Department is today announcing the Government's decision to take an appeal on limited constitutional grounds in the case of the *United States* v. *Austin Independent School District,* involving school desegregation.

The Attorney General advises me that he must appeal the District Court's decision that the school board's plan to bus children periodically for interracial experiences eliminates the dual school system, because that decision is inconsistent with recent rulings of the United States Supreme Court. The Justice Department is not appealing to impose the HEW plan. In the process of the appeal, the Justice Department will disavow that plan on behalf of the Government.

I would also like to restate my position as it relates to busing. I am against busing as that term is commonly used in school desegregation cases. I have consistently opposed the busing of our Nation's schoolchildren to achieve racial balance, and I am opposed to the busing of children simply for the sake of busing. Further, while the executive branch will continue to enforce the orders of the court, including court-ordered busing, I have instructed the Attorney General and the Secretary of Health, Education, and Welfare that they are to work with individual school districts to hold busing to the minimum required by law.

Finally, I have today instructed the Secretary of Health, Education and Welfare to draft and submit today to the Congress an amendment to the proposed Emergency School Assistance Act that will expressly prohibit the expenditure of any of those funds for busing.

Richard Nixon

ECONOMIC POLICY

Following is the text of President Nixon's Sept. 9 address to a joint session of Congress.

I come before this Joint Session to ask the cooperation of the Congress in achieving a great goal: A new prosperity without war and without inflation.

In this century, Americans have never before had a full generation of peace.

In the past 40 years we have had only two years with real prosperity, without war and without inflation.

As a result of major initiatives in the field of foreign policy, I believe that as America is bringing to a conclusion the longest and most difficult war in its history we can look forward with confidence to a generation of peace.

Yet we confront this irony: as the dangers of war recede, the challenges of peace increase.

It is customary for a President to ask the Congress for bipartisan support in meeting the challenge of war.

Today, I ask bipartisan support in meeting the challenge of peace.

Three Problems

In achieving our goal, we find ourselves confronted at the outset by three problems.

The first is a legacy of war. Two million men have been cut back from our armed forces and defense plants because of our success in winding down the war in Vietnam. As part of the transition from a wartime to a peacetime economy, we now have to find jobs for these men—jobs producing for peace instead of for war.

The second problem is also a legacy of war. We must stop the rise in the cost of living.

The third problem is a legacy not of war, but of peaceful progress in the world over the past 25 years—progress which has altered dramatically the balance in the economic relationships between the United States and the other great trading nations of the world. As a result, we now are challenged to protect the value of the dollar, and to learn once again to be competitive in the world.

Action

Twenty-five days ago I took action to attack these problems, and to advance the goal of a new prosperity without war and without inflation.

I ordered a 90-day freeze on prices and wages.

I ordered a $4.7 billion cut in Federal spending, to allow for tax cuts to create new jobs.

On the international front, I ordered a temporary 10 percent surcharge on products imported from abroad, and I ordered the convertibility of the dollar into gold suspended.

In taking these actions, I knew there were great risks. There were dire predictions of massive resentment and non-cooperation at home, and of turmoil and retaliation abroad. But let us look at what has happened.

Here at home, we can be proud of the fact that millions of Americans showed themselves willing to give up wage increases and price increases that would have benefitted some of the people, in order to stop the rise in the cost of living for all of the people.

Abroad, we find that adjustments are being made and actions are being taken to set up a new monetary system within which America can compete fairly once again. Instead of continued talk about the weakness of the American dollar, we find in the world a new understanding of the strength of the American economy.

The reaction of the American people to the new economic policy has been unselfish and courageous. The reaction of our trading partners abroad has been measured and constructive. I am confident that the Congress will respond in a similar spirit, as it has to so many other great challenges in the past. This is a time to set aside partisanship. Let us join together in placing the national interest above special interests.

Three Tax Proposals

I ask the Congress to consider as its first priority—before all other business—the enactment of three tax proposals that are essential to the new prosperity. These three measures will create 500,000 new jobs in the coming year.

First, I urge the Congress to remove the 7 percent excise tax on automobiles, so that the more than 8 million people in this country who will buy new American-built cars in the next year will save an average of $200 each. This is a sales tax, paid by the consumer. Its removal will stimulate sales, and every 100,000 additional automobiles sold will mean 25,000 additional jobs for America's workers.

Second, I urge the Congress to adopt a Job Development Credit to encourage investment in machinery and equipment that will generate new jobs. This credit, first advocated by a Democratic President enacted by a Democratic Congress in the 1960s, was enormously effective then in creating new jobs. It will be just as effective in creating new jobs today. It will be an incentive to business to hire more workers, it will enable wage earners to work more productively, and it will make American products more competitive in the world's markets.

Third, I urge the Congress to create more consumer purchasing power by permitting the planned $50 increase in the personal income tax exemption scheduled for 1973 to take effect next January 1, one full year ahead of schedule. For a family of four, this could mean an additional $200 increase in tax-exempt income, beginning less than four months from now.

Taken together, these proposals would reduce taxes now paid by individuals by $3.2 billion, and would provide $2.7 billion in incentives to companies to invest in job-producing equipment.

Budget Restraints

Another vital area in which I ask the cooperation of the Congress is budget restraint. Tax cuts to stimulate employment must be accompanied by spending cuts to restrain inflation.

Among the spending cuts I have ordered are the following:

I have ordered a postponement of scheduled pay raises for Federal employees.

I have ordered a 5 percent reduction in government personnel.

I have ordered a 10 percent cut in foreign economic aid.

Because the Congress has not yet enacted two of my principal legislative proposals—welfare reform and revenue sharing—I have recommended that their effective dates be postponed, three months for revenue sharing and one year for welfare reform. This adjustment recognizes that there is no longer sufficient time to get the administrative machinery in place by the previously scheduled dates.

In the coming year, the Congress will face many temptations to raise spending and cut taxes in addition to the recommendations I have made. In the short run, these always are popular measures. But as we look at the realities of the budget at this time, we must face up to this hard fact: any additional spending increases not accompanied by tax increases—and any additional tax cuts not accompanied by spending cuts—will be certain to start us again on a spiral of higher prices.

To spend more than we can afford or to tax less than we can afford is the sure route to prices higher than we can afford. There are two other matters on which I seek the cooperation of the Congress. The first concerns the immediate future, and the second the long-range future.

Phase II

The 90-day freeze on wages and prices that I announced on August 15 was a temporary measure, to hold the line while the next phase of stabilization was discussed. I am announcing today that the freeze will not be extended beyond 90 days.

But I assure the Congress and the American people that when this first temporary and necessarily drastic action is over, we shall take all the steps needed to see that America is not again afflicted by the virus of runaway inflation.

The system of wage and price stabilization that follows the freeze will require the fullest possible cooperation not only between the Executive and Legislative branches, but also by all Americans. I have invited representatives of the Congress, of business, of labor and of agriculture to meet within the next few days for the purpose of helping plan the next phase, and they have accepted. In addition, I have directed the members of the Cost of Living Council to continue meeting with representatives of all other interested groups.

As we consider what follows the freeze, let us bear in mind that prosperity is a job for everyone—and that fighting inflation is everybody's business. I shall welcome the cooperation of the Congress in achieving these goals.

Let us also remember that nothing would be more detrimental to the new prosperity in the long run than to put the Nation's great, strong free enterprise system in a permanent strait-jacket of government controls.

Regimentation and government coercion must never become a way of life in the United States. Price and wage stabilization, in whatever form it takes, must be only a way-station on the road to free markets and free collective bargaining in a new prosperity without war.

The longer-term matter on which I seek the cooperation of the Congress centers on this fact: we must set as our goal an economy that within ten years will provide 100 million jobs.

To meet that goal, we need new tax incentives for the creation of additional jobs.

We need new programs to ensure that America's enormous wealth of scientific and technological talent is used to its fullest.

New Challenges

Later today, the Congress will pay its tribute to three Americans back from the moon.

Theirs was a magnificent achievement—a stunning testament to their personal skill and courage, and also to what American technology can achieve.

Let us find the means to ensure that in this decade of challenge, the remarkable technology that took these Americans to the moon can also be applied to reaching our goals here on earth.

In the next session of the Congress, I shall present new proposals in both these areas: tax reform to create jobs, and new approaches toward ensuring the maximum enlistment of America's technology in meeting the challenges of peace.

Achieving these goals will be in the vital interest of the United States not just for the next year, not just for the next decade, but for the balance of this century. I look forward to working with the Congress in ensuring that they are achieved.

As we consider these new economic policies, it is important that we consider the stakes.

America has entered a new era in its economic relationships with the rest of the world.

For a quarter of a century now, since the end of World War II, America has borne the principal burden of free world defense, of foreign aid, of helping old nations back onto their feet and new nations to take their first, sometimes faltering steps. We have laid out nearly $150 billion in foreign aid, economic and military. We have fought two costly and grueling wars. We have undergone deep strains at home, as we have sought to reconcile our responsibilties abroad with our own needs here in America.

In this quarter-century America has given generously of itself and its resources—and we have done this because we are America, and America is a good and generous nation.

In the years ahead, we will remain a good and generous nation—but the time has also come to give a new attention to America's own interests.

New Era

Fifteen years ago a prominent world statesman commented to me that world trade was like a poker game in which the United States held all the chips, and that we had to spread them around so that others could play. What he said was true in the 1940s. It was still partially true in the 1950s and the 1960s. It is no longer true today. We have generously passed out the chips. Now others can play on an equal basis—and we must play the game as we expect and want them to do. We must play the best we know how. The time has passed for the United States to compete with one hand tied behind its back.

This new era is a time of new relationships in the world; of a changed balance of economic power; of new challenges to our leadership, and to our standard of living.

We should not be resentful of these changes. They mean that more of the world's people are living better than before. They help make the world a better and more stable and a safer place for all of us. But they also present us with a new set of challenges—the challenges of peace.

The time has come for the United States to show once again the spirit that transformed a small nation, a weak nation of three million people on the precarious edge of an untamed continent, into the world's strongest and richest power.

In this new era, we must find the roots of our national greatness once again.

In order to meet the challenges of peace, we must have a healthy America—a strong America.

Goals

We need a healthy and a productive economy in order to achieve the great goals to which we are so firmly committed:

- To help those who cannot help themselves.
- To feed the hungry.
- To provide better health care for the sick.
- To provide better education for the children.
- To provide more fully for the aged.
- To restore and renew our natural environment.
- To provide more and better jobs and more and greater opportunity for all of our people.

To accomplish these great goals requires many billions of dollars. We cannot accomplish them without a healthy economy. We cannot accomplish them without the revenues generated by the work of more than 80 million Americans. And we cannot accomplish these goals if we make the mistake of disparaging and undermining "the system" that produces America's wealth—of casting it in the false light of an oppressor and exploiter of human beings.

The much-maligned American "system" has produced more abundance, more widely shared, and more opportunity for more people than any other system, any time, any place. That system is what makes it possible for us to help the poor and feed the hungry, and clean up our environment, and meet all the other great goals we have set for ourselves as a nation. As we correct what is wrong, let us always speak up for what is right about America.

To be a healthy nation, a strong nation, we must also restore the health of our government institutions.

That is why I again urge the Congress to act in this session on the sweeping reorganization of the Executive Branch which I have proposed, in order to make it more efficient, more manageable, more responsive to the needs and wishes of the people. Every day that goes by increases the urgency of this basic reform.

That is why I again urge the Congress to act in this session on the far reaching program of revenue sharing which I have proposed, to help revitalize our State and local governments and to ease the crushing rise in the burden of property taxes.

That is why I again urge the Congress to act in this session on welfare reform—so that going on welfare will not be more profitable than going to work—so that we can bring under control a system that has become a suffocating burden on State and local taxpayers, and a massive outrage against the people it was designed to help.

The postponements I have recommended in the funding of these programs have been made necessary by past legislative delays. Let us make sure there need be no further delays.

American Spirit

All of these programs—all of our new economic programs—will mean nothing unless the American spirit is strong and healthy.

In recent weeks I have traveled back and forth across the country—to Maine and New Hampshire, New York, Idaho, Wyoming, California, Texas, Ohio, Illinois—and I can say with confidence that on the farms, in the cities, in the towns, in the factories throughout this Nation the spirit of the American people is strong and healthy.

A strong and healthy spirit means a willingness to sacrifice, when a short-term personal sacrifice is needed in the long-term public interest.

A strong and healthy spirit means a willingness to work.

Hard work is what made America great. There could be no more dangerous delusion than the notion that we can maintain the standard of living that our own people sometimes complain about but the rest of the world envies, without continuing to work hard. The "good life" is not the lazy life, or the empty life, or the life that consumes without producing. The good life is the active, productive, working life—the life that gives as well as gets.

No work is demeaning or beneath a person's dignity if it provides food for his table and clothes and shelter for his children. The thing that is demeaning is for a man to refuse to work and then ask someone else who works to pay taxes to keep him on welfare.

Let us recognize once and for all that any work is preferable to welfare.

A strong and healthy spirit means having a sense of destiny.

As we look ahead to five, ten, twenty years, what do we see?

Do we see an America grown old and weary, past its prime, in its declining years? Or do we see an America proud, strong, as vigorous in its maturity as it was in its youth?

We hold the future in our own hands.

We have consulted our fears too much. Now let us be inspired by our faith.

If our forefathers had consulted their fears, we would not be here.

America would never have been discovered.

The West would never have been explored.

Our freedom would never have been defended.

Our abundance would never have been created.

As we renew our faith, let the challenge of competition give a new lift to the American spirit.

A Great Enterprise

A nation becomes old only when it stops trying to be great.

We cannot remain a great nation if we build a permanent wall of tariffs and quotas around the United States. We cannot live behind a wall that shuts the rest of the world out. The world is too small, and the United States is too important a part of that world. If we were not a great power, we would not be the America we know. If we do not stay a great power, the world will not stay safe for free men.

We cannot turn inward, we cannot drop out of competition with the rest of the world, and remain a great nation. Because when a nation ceases to compete, when it ceases to try to do its best, then that nation ceases to be a great nation. America today is number one in the world economically. Let us resolve that we shall stay number one.

General DeGaulle once said that France is never her true self unless she is engaged in a great enterprise.

America can be her true self only when she is engaged in a great enterprise.

To build a full generation of peace is a great enterprise.

To help the poor and to feed the hungry, to provide better health and housing and education, to clean up the environment, to bring new dignity and security to the aging, to guarantee equal opportunity for every American—all these are great enterprises.

To build the strong economy that makes all these possible—to meet the new challenges of peace, and to move to a new prosperity without war and without inflation—this truly is a great enterprise, worthy of our sacrifice, worthy of our cooperation, and worthy of the greatness of a great people.

TEXT OF NIXON'S SPEECH AT UNIVERSITY OF NEBRASKA

Following is the text, as made available by the White House, of President Nixon's Jan. 14 speech at the University of Nebraska.

Mr. President, Mr. Chancellor, Governor Exon, Senator Curtis, Senator Hruska, all of the distinguished guests on the platform, and students, members of the faculty of the University of Nebraska, and I also understand that we have guests here from Nebraska Wesleyan and from Union College, and friends of the University of Nebraska:

I appreciate the honor that has been extended to me to visit this campus, and the opportunity to pick up a raincheck, in effect, because Secretary Hardin two years ago on the 100th anniversary of this great University, invited me to come to the University at the request of the University officials, and because I had another engagement at that time I was unable to do so. I told him then that sometime while I was in office I would come. I wasn't quite sure I could make it. I am glad I could make it this year in view of what has happened.

And that allows me, before making this award, to tell a little story. You will recall that from time to time, because I am somewhat of a football fan, that I have called football coaches or captains after a great victory and a significant game. I read a story in one of the Nebraska papers to the effect that immediately after the Orange Bowl game some of the team were gathered around the phone waiting for the call from the White House. It never got through. As a matter of fact, I was not able to make the call because while I had seen the last quarter of the game, which was very exciting—wasn't that something, that last quarter?—in any event—it shows what the defense means—in any event, when we came to the end of the long day of football that day, I had to go on to another engagement. I checked with the White House operator and asked if it might be possible to get through to the dressing room down in Miami. Usually the President can get through on the telephone. This time the operator said, "Well, it will be just a moment, Mr. President. All the circuits are busy."

She said, "Everybody from Nebraska is calling."

I knew that was the case, and I knew that this great team and the University of Nebraska have pride for the whole State, for all the institutions of this State, whatever they may be, and all the people of this State. I am, therefore, honored to be here to participate in your pride in that team.

Having said that, I want you to know that I have gotten into a little trouble over the past couple of years in picking number one teams. In 1970, I should recall, the 100th anniversary of college football, you will remember that before the bowl games I said that Texas was number one, and since then I have never been able to go to Pennsylvania without a passport.

This year I didn't make that mistake because I sought and got very good advice. I was in Omaha in the last weeks of October. At that time Nebraska was number three in the Associated Press poll. I had already been to Columbus, Ohio, where everybody said Ohio State was number one. I was in Indiana where everybody told me that Notre Dame was number one. I was in Texas where everybody told me that Texas was number one, and I was going to be in California where all Californians thought that Stanford was number one. And in Arizona, Senator Barry Goldwater said that Arizona State was number one.

So with Roman Hruska and Carl Curtis, I said, "What should I do?" They thought a bit and finally Carl spoke up and said, "You know, Mr. President, I would wait until after the bowl games." That was vision, real vision.

So in this year of football, a year of many great teams, a year in which many can perhaps rightfully claim to be number one, to come to Nebraska, a great University and clearly apart from its great records in the field of athletics, to come here to the only major college team that was undefeated, and to make

an award is something that I am very proud to do, proud to recognize this University, to recognize its coach, to recognize its co-captains, to recognize its fine members of the team, and in so doing to present the plaque from the President of the United States.

Consequently, at this time, for the official presentation, I would like to have the coach, Bob Devaney, to step forth.

(Presentation of plaque.)

You ought to run for something in this State.

And now the co-captains, Jerry Murtaugh and Dan Schneiss, if they would step forward to represent the team.

I shall now read the plaque which I understand will be put in one of the lockers. But in any event—(laughter)—the plaque's wording is as follows:

"The University of Nebraska 1970 football team, Champions of the Big Eight Conference. Victor in the 1971 Orange Bowl, and picked by the Associated Press Number One Team of the Nation."

Common Problems

And now if I could come to the other part of my assignment, as was pointed out by your president a moment ago, I wanted to use this opportunity to address the great student body of this University and your guests about some of the problems we have in this Nation, common problems, for younger people and older people as well.

In beginning my remarks, it is quite clear from the feeling in this audience that this is a very exciting time for this University. You are beginning the second hundred years of a very great tradition, and you are beginning it as champions.

You can all take pride in your great team. It is a splendid thing to be champions. But a more splendid thing, I believe, is the process by which a team becomes champion, the long struggle through defeat, through doubt, and then on to victory.

There is satisfaction here, and for all of us there are valuable lessons as well. For as vital as the understanding we gain in the classroom is the deeper understanding of ourselves that comes from competing against others, and competing against ourselves.

In these endeavors, we go beyond awareness of what we are and we discover a higher understanding of what we can be if we know and have the courage and if we have the will.

It is in this way that we learn to believe in our dreams.

Nothing matters more to the future of this Nation than ensuring that our young men and women learn to believe in themselves and believe in their dreams, and that they develop this capacity—that you develop this capacity, so that you keep it all of your lives.

As this great University looks to a new century so does our Nation. In this decade we Americans will celebrate the anniversary of the greatest experiment in liberty the world has ever known. It has succeeded for what in the year 1976 will be 200 years. But like the continued success of this University, the continued success of the American experiment depends on one thing: On the qualities of heart and mind and spirit that our young people bring to both.

This Nation will not run on inertia. It could fail in one generation or it could last another 100 years or another 1,000 years. The answer lies in what you and your generation bring to the task of being an American and what you pass on to others.

These depend, in turn, upon what your Nation gives to you and gives to you now. And if we are to benefit fully from the energies and the ideals of our young people, we must break down the barriers to the exercise of those energies, the pursuit of those ideals.

Vietnam War

Let me discuss one of those barriers that I know is on the minds of many of you here and many all over this Nation.

The war in Vietnam has taken a very heavy toll of our young men. This Administration has no higher priority than to end that war. But to end it in a way that we will have a lasting peace.

For one thing, I want to end it because this Nation has positive priorities, right here at home, that young men and women now occupied in war could turn their hands to in peace. Beyond this, I have some very personal reasons that I would like to end it.

Every week, as President of the United States, I write letters to the parents and the wives and even sometimes the children of men who have given their lives in Vietnam. It is no comfort to me that when I came into office I wrote 300 of those letters a week, and that this week I will write 27. One is too many.

These were precious human lives and what they might have brought to America in peace no one will ever know. But there would have been poets among them and doctors and teachers and farmers. There would have been builders of America.

I want nothing in the world so much as to be able to stop writing those letters.

I know you realize, you who have studied history, that every American generation in this century has known war. I want yours to be the first generation in this century to enjoy a full generation of peace.

I have a plan which we are implementing to obtain that kind of peace. I can tell you confidently today it is succeeding. I believe yours will be a generation of peace. And then the question comes, and this is a bigger question, more profound: What will we do with the peace?

I am not one of those who believe that we will have instant tranquility when we have peace. I was talking to a European statesman a few months ago about the common problems that we had in both of our countries of student unrest, and he said to me, "The problem with your youth is war. The problem with our youth is peace."

What he meant, of course, was that the challenges of peace are as great as the challenges of war and as difficult to meet. There needs to be something more than the mere absence of war in life. Young people need something positive to respond to, some high enterprise in which they can test themselves, fulfill themselves. We must have great goals—goals that are worthy of us, worthy of our resources, our capacities; worthy of the courage and the wisdom and the will of our people. And we do have such great goals at home in America. Consider, for example, the problems of our environment. To subdue the land is one thing. To destroy it is another, and we have been destroying it. And now we must undo what we have done. You must help in this venture. It will require all the dedication you can bring to it—your brains, your energy, your imagination, those special qualities you possess in such abundance—idealism, impatience, and faith. To preserve the good earth is a great goal.

The Cities

Consider the problems of our cities. Through time, cities have been centers of culture and commerce, and nowhere has this been more true than in America. But today, many of our great cities are dying. We must not let this happen. We can do better than this. We must do better than this. Only if the American city can prosper can the American dream really prevail.

Rural America

Consider the problems of rural America. We are a nation not only of cities but of towns and villages and farms. In the soul and substance of rural life in this country the most abiding values of the American people are anchored. Rural America, too, needs our attention. We must create a new rural environment, a new rural prosperity, which will not only stem the migration from rural areas to the cities, but which will bring people back to the heartland of America.

Overpopulation

Consider the problems of overpopulation, the problems of education, the problems brought about by technology, the problems of achieving full and equal opportunity for all of our people, of health; the problems of prosperity, itself; of poverty in a land of plenty. Those are just a few of the challenges that face us.

Generation Gap

We must face them together. There can be no generation gap in America. The destiny of this nation is not divided into yours and ours. It is one destiny. We share it together. We are responsible for it together. And in the way we respond, history will judge us together.

There has been too much emphasis on the differences between the generations in America. There has been too much of a tendency of many of my generation to blame all of your generation for the excesses of a violent few. Let me repeat what I have said over and over again during the past two years.

I believe one of America's most priceless assets is the idealism which motivates the young people of America. My generation has invested all that it has, not only its love but its hope and its faith in yours.

I believe you will redeem that faith and justify that hope. I believe that as our generations work together, as we strive together, as we aspire together, we can achieve together—achieve great things for America and the world.

And so let us forge an alliance of the generations. Let us work together to seek out those ways by which the commitments and the compassion of one generation can be linked to the will and the experience of another so that together we can serve America better and America can better serve mankind.

Our priorities are really the same. Together we can achieve them.

I pledge to you that as you have faith in our intentions, we will do our best to keep faith with your hopes.

Volunteer Service Corps

Let me cite one of the ways in which I propose to give substance to this alliance between the generations. One thing government must do is to find more effective ways of enlisting the dedication and idealism of those young Americans who want to serve their fellow man. Therefore, I will send a special message to the 92nd Congress asking that the Peace Corps, VISTA, and a number of other agencies now scattered throughout the Federal Government, be brought together into a new agency, a new volunteer service corps that will give young Americans an expanded opportunity for the service they want to give, and that will give them what they do not now have offered to them —a chance to transfer between service abroad and service at home.

I intend to place this new agency under the dynamic leadership of one of the ablest young men I have ever known, the Peace Corps Director, Joe Blatchford, and I intend to make it an agency through which those willing to give their lives and their energy can work at cleaning up the environment, combatting illiteracy and malnutrition, suffering and blight, either at home or abroad.

To the extent that young people respond to this opportunity, I will recommend that it be expanded to new fields, new endeavors, for I believe that government has a responsibility to ensure that the idealism and willingness to contribute of our dedicated young people can be put to constructive use.

As we free young Americans from the requirements of the draft and of the war, from the requirements of forced service, let us open the door to volunteer service. And for those who want to serve but cannot devote their full time, the new center for volunteer action will open new opportunities for millions of Americans of all ages to the extent they wish to contribute their time, their talents, their hearts, to building better communities, a better America, a better world.

Right to Vote

Let me turn now to another way in which you can contribute. You all know that in the year 1970 we have taken a step which could have a very dramatic effect on your future and the future of America. We have provided you with the most powerful means a citizen has of making himself felt in a free and democratic society.

You now have the right to vote. Today in a new and exciting and dramatically promising way, you, each of you 18 or over, has a voice in the future of America. The whole history of democracy in this country is a chronicle of the constant broadening of the power to participate. Each new group receiving the franchise has had a beneficial effect on the course of America. Each new group has given freshness and vitality to the purposes of government. And now it is your turn to do the same.

The System

So much is in your hands now. To those who have believed the system would not be moved, I say try it. To those who have thought that the system was impenetrable, I say there is no longer a need to penetrate; the door is open. For each of you, as for each of the rest of us, there are going to be some disappointments. There will be defeats, and the hard logic of life is: for anyone to win someone else has to lose.

For some to know victory, others have to know defeat. This is part of democracy. For it is in the very nature of a free society that no one can win all the time, no one can have his own way all the time, and no one is right all the time. If we suffer a setback or if we lose on an issue, the answer is not to blame the system but to look within ourselves to see how we can strengthen our resolve and intensify our efforts or perhaps to see whether the other fellow just might have been right all the time.

Defeat, therefore, can be an occasion for learning, for weighing the wisdom of our own purposes, examining the strength of our own resources.

I have seen two of Bob Devaney's teams play in the Orange Bowl when they lost. But defeat, instead of disheartening them, brought that experience which later led to victory.

I know that there are those who reject politics, who scorn the political life, and I can assure you that politics attracts its share of bad people but so do all the other professions. This does not reflect on the political system, for politics is a process, not an end in itself, and the process can be as good or as bad as the people that are part of it.

It may be tempting to suppose, like the ostrich, that what we choose not to be involved in will, therefore, not involve us. But we cannot make a separate peace, not one of us can. We are all committed, whether we choose to be or not. You can reject this, you can come to the task of being an American like Nietzche's ropemakers, who "pull out their threads in length and themselves are always going backwards." Or you can accept the commitment. You can accept the challenge. You can accept the high adventure of being an American citizen.

In the end, the history of this time will reflect your choice and it will record that you were the first generation of young Americans to be given this chance. Therefore, I urge you to choose well and to choose carefully.

There is an old excuse: This is a world that I never made.

That won't do any longer. You have now the opportunity, the obligation, to mold the world that you live in, and you cannot escape this obligation.

There is a story of an old and very wise teacher in early Athens. There was no question the teacher could not answer. There seemed to be nothing in life the old man did not understand. And finally, one of his students hit upon a way to defeat the old man's wisdom.

The student determined that he would catch a bird and hold it concealed in his hands. He would ask the old man to guess what he was holding. If the old man guessed it was a bird, then the boy would make him say whether the bird was alive or whether it was dead. And if the teacher guessed that the bird was dead, the boy would open his hands and let the bird go, free and alive. But if the wise man guessed that the bird was alive, then the boy would crush out its life and open his hands to reveal a dead bird.

And so it progressed, just as the boy had planned, until he asked the wise man: "Is the bird alive or is it dead?" And the old man said, "My son, the answer to that question is in your hands."

In your hands now rests the question of the future of this Nation, of its promise of progress and prosperity, of the dream of democracy and the future of freedom, of whether men can continue to be governed by human wisdom. And I believe that these things rest in good hands, and that as we put our hands together, your generation and mine, in the alliance we forge we can discover a new understanding, a community of wisdom, a capacity for action, with which we can truly renew both the spirit and the promise of this great and good land we share together.

MESSAGE ON FEDERAL PAY

Following is the complete text, as made available by the White House, of President Nixon's Sept. 1 message to Congress on federal pay.

On August 15, 1971 I announced a number of new economic initiatives to create new jobs, to hold down the cost of living, and to stabilize the dollar. In this connection, Executive Order 11615 calls for the development of policies, mechanisms and procedures to maintain economic growth without inflationary increases after the end of the 90-day freeze period which the order imposes. It is equally essential that the tax reductions which I recommended to the Congress, to provide a powerful stimulus to the economy, not be inflationary in their impact. A significant reduction in Federal expenditures is needed to provide a balance.

Since continuing emphasis will be placed on the exercise of responsible industrial and labor leadership throughout the Nation in the months to come, I must apply such fiscal restraints as will clearly signify the good faith of the Federal Government as a major employer, and to continue to set an example for the American people in our striving to achieve prosperity in peacetime. I place full reliance on the willingness of Federal employees along with their fellow Americans, to make whatever temporary sacrifices in personal gain may be needed to attain the greater good for the country as a whole.

Therefore, in consideration of the economic conditions affecting the general welfare, I hereby transmit to the Congress the following alternative plan, as authorized and required by section 5305(c)(1) of title 5, United States Code:

Such adjustments in the rates of pay of each Federal statutory pay system as may be required, based on the 1971 Bureau of Labor Statistics survey, shall become effective on the first day of the first applicable pay period that begins on or after July 1, 1972.

I recognize that delaying the scheduled January 1972 increase to July 1972 means that two increases will then become due within a period of approximately three months. Since I am unable to predict whether two increases in such a relatively short time span will have a damaging effect on the economy, I am not prepared to make a decision with respect to the October 1972 increase at this time. After reviewing the economic situation during the first half of 1972, I will give serious consideration to the need for an alternative plan to that scheduled increase. If I conclude that an alternative plan is necessary I will, in accordance with the aforementioned provision of law, submit such a plan to Congress before September 1, 1972. It appears highly unlikely that any such plan would involve a postponement of the October 1972 adjustments beyond January 1973.

Our Nation's public servants are entitled to a fair wage in line with the established policy of comparability with private enterprise; I regret the necessity of postponing pay increases, but our fight against the rising cost of living must take precedence. Of course, success in holding down inflation will benefit the Government worker as well as all Americans.

I urge your support of this postponement.

RICHARD NIXON

TEXT ON FLORIDA CANAL

Following is the text, as made available by the White House, of President Nixon's Jan. 19 statement halting construction on the cross-Florida barge canal.

I am today ordering a halt to further construction of the Cross Florida Barge Canal to prevent potentially serious environmental damages.

The purpose of the Canal was to reduce transportation costs for barge shipping. It was conceived and designed at a time when the focus of Federal concern in such matters was still almost completely on maximizing economic return. In calculating that return, the destruction of natural, ecological values was not counted as a cost, nor was a credit allowed for actions preserving the environment.

A natural treasure is involved in the case of the Barge Canal —the Oklawaha River—a uniquely beautiful, semi-tropical stream, one of a very few of its kind in the United States, which would be destroyed by construction of the Canal.

The Council on Environmental Quality has recommended to me that the project be halted, and I have accepted its advice. The Council has pointed out to me that the project could endanger the unique wildlife of the area and destroy this region of unusual and unique natural beauty.

The total cost of the project if it were completed would be about $180 million. About $50 million has already been committed to construction. I am asking the Secretary of the Army to work with the Council on Environmental Quality in developing recommendations for the future of the area.

The step I have taken today will prevent a past mistake from causing permanent damage. But more important, we must assure that in the future we take not only full but also timely account of the environmental impact of such projects—so that instead of merely halting the damage, we prevent it.

PRESIDENTIAL

NEWS CONFERENCES

CQ

JAN. 4 TELEVISION INTERVIEW

Following are excerpts from the text, as made available by the White House, of the Jan. 4 nationally televised interview of President Nixon by John Chancellor of NBC News, Eric Sevareid of CBS News, Howard K. Smith of ABC News and Nancy H. Dickerson, representing public television.

THE PRESIDENT: Good evening, ladies and gentlemen.

I wish to welcome the distinguished members of our television panel to the White House Library, and also to welcome all of you, who are listening on television and on radio, to this Conversation with the President.

I was thinking when this program was announced that I would have an opening statement as I had, you will recall, six months ago when we met in California. But in view of the record of the 91st Congress and some of the talk that went on at the end, I thought a filibuster would not be appreciated. So, we will go directly to your questions.

MR. CHANCELLOR: Sir, you have lived here in the White House and had this responsibility now for two years and I wonder, Mr. President, how you have changed. We heard some talk and read in the papers during the last campaign about the "Old Nixon," but all of the historical evidence we have indicates that the Presidency changes men.

I wonder what changes in yourself you have observed.

THE PRESIDENT: Well, the changes, Mr. Chancellor, are primarily not physical. Physically, as you probably noted from the doctor's report which, incidentally, a President is required to have once a year, and probably that is a good thing, there have been no significant changes there. So, the job must agree with me.

The changes more are in an understanding of the job. When you come into office, the Presidency, one has ideas as to what he can accomplish. He believes he can accomplish a great deal, even though he may have a Congress that is not part of his own party. Then, after he gets in, he finds that what he had hoped in terms of achieving goals will not be as great as the actual performance turns out to be.

So, I would say that in terms of how I have changed, it is in realizing that while we must set high goals and always seek them, we must not become impatient. We must plow forward, recognizing that in the end we are going to make some progress, if not all of the progress that we had hoped.

I would say, in other words, at this time I am not disappointed in the record of the last two years in terms of some of the things we accomplished. But I have great hopes for the next two years, because I think I know better how to do the job. I think I know better how to deal with the Congress. I think I know better how to work with the Cabinet.

This is perhaps how I have changed. I know more. I am more experienced. I hope I do better.

MR. SEVAREID: Mr. President, to be specific about the last two years, what do you now think of as your primary achievement, specifically, and what is your primary failure or mistake?

THE PRESIDENT: Mr. Sevareid, the primary achievement is, I think, in the field of foreign policy. We have not yet ended the war in Vietnam. I hoped we would have by this time. But we now see the end of America's combat role in Vietnam. The fact that, for example, when we came in, American casualties in the last year of the previous Administration were 14,500 and the casualties this year are 4200. That is still much too high. I will not be satisfied until I do not have to write any letter at all to the next of kin of somebody killed in Vietnam.

But we are on the way out and we are on the way out in a way that will bring a just peace, the kind of a peace that will discourage that kind of aggression in the future, and that will build, I hope, the foundation for a generation of peace. That is our major achievement in, I think, the foreign policy field.

In the disappointment side, I think the greatest disappointment legislatively was the failure to get welfare reform. I believe this would have done more than anything else to deal with the problems of poverty in this country, the problems that many of our cities have and our states have, the problems of minority groups who have particular difficulties, insofar as welfare is concerned.

Finally, if I could add one other, I would not like to limit it to just one, I think the greatest disappointment was in terms of the tragedies of Kent State, Jackson State and the University of Wisconsin. It is true that over the past two years we have seen the war wind down. We have seen our cities not as inflamed as they were previously.

We have seen the amount of violence going down some, but during this Administration to have had three such tragedies as that, left a very deep impression upon me. I trust, as we continue to have success in foreign policy, as we continue to solve the problems that people are interested in, that this kind of violence will begin to recede even more.

MISS DICKERSON: Mr. President, I would like to ask you about one of your specific problems, namely the economy. Now, despite the initiatives that you have taken in the past few weeks, there is still widespread pessimism about unemployment. In fact, in places like California, there is a near panic psychology about joblessness. Your own economic advisors say that the basic trouble is a lack of confidence in the economy.

What do you plan to do to restore people's confidence in the economy before things get any worse than they now are?

THE PRESIDENT: Well, first, I believe that that confidence is being restored. Confidence is something that is a very intangible factor, as you know. It is how people feel at a particular moment. And people who may be confident one month may have a lack of confidence the next month.

But let's look at some of the facts. First, we find that insofar as our efforts to control inflation are concerned, that while the progress has not been as fast as we would have liked, that the Wholesale Price Index is half of what it was a year ago; the Retail Consumer Price Index is turning down—not as much as we would like but turning down. We are beginning to make real progress in fighting inflation.

Second, in terms of the unemployment front, here we find that the rate of unemployment for this year will be approximately 4.9 percent. That is too high, even though we could perhaps point to the fact that over the past 20 years there have been only three peacetime years in which unemployment was less than 5 percent, the years of '55, '56, and '57.

But on that score let me say that I take no comfort in that statistic. I know what unemployment does to somebody. I have seen an unemployed man come into my father's store. I have seen the look in his eye when he can't pay the bill. I have seen the look in his children's eyes when he can't pay that bill. So I want a program which not only will turn down the inflation in which we are now beginning to succeed, but one which will expand the economy, and this gets to the specifics that you have asked for.

What we are going to do first is to have an expansionary budget. It will be a budget in deficit, as will be the budget in 1971. It will not be an inflationary budget because it will not exceed the full employment revenues.

We also, according to Dr. Arthur Burns, will have an expansionary monetary policy, and that will, of course, be a monetary policy adequate to meet the needs of an expanding economy.

Now, in addition to that, we are going to have a program that we will present to the Congress, a program that I believe in terms of Government reform will be the most significant reform that we have had perhaps in a century. I think that this program will also have an indirect effect in restoring confidence in the economy.

If I can make a prediction—I made one last year and many people took me to task about it, about the fact that the stock market might go up and right afterwards it went down. But it did go up. And I made that prediction not because I was expecting people to buy stocks and urging them to do so without consulting a broker whose judgments would be better than mine, but because I had faith in the long-term prospects of the American economy.

This is the prediction: 1971 is going to be a year of an expanding economy in which inflation, the rise in inflation, is going to continue to go down; in which unemployment, which is presently too high, will finally come under control and begin to recede. 1971, in essence, will be a good year, and 1972 will be a very good year.

Having made that prediction, I will say that the purpose of this Administration will be to have an activist economic policy designed to control inflation but at the same time to expand the economy so that we can reduce unemployment, and to have what this country has not had for 20 years, and that is a situation where we can have full employment in peacetime without the cost of war and without the cost of excessive inflation.

MR. SEVAREID: Mr. President, you described what you want to happen with your new economy program in the new year, but what is going to be in it? You have sounded as though there is going to be nothing about controls, prices or wages, or anything of the sort. Is that what we should assume from what you have just said?

THE PRESIDENT: Mr. Sevareid, I do not plan to ask for wage controls or price controls. I have noted, incidentally, that all of you, the four commentators here, have commented upon controls in one way or another. I know Mr. Smith, for example, has talked about the possibility of wage-price guidelines, or wage-price push, and Dr. Arthur Burns has indicated that possibly that might be something that we should turn to.

I have considered all of those options. I have decided that none of them at this time would work, and consequently I feel that the best course is to proceed as I have suggested, with an expansionary budgetary policy, but one that will not exceed full employment revenues, and at the same time with a monetary policy that will be adequate to fuel a growing economy. I believe this will reduce unemployment and also I believe it will do so at a time that inflation will continue to come down. Now, there is still the wage-price push and that is what you are referring to.

MR. CHANCELLOR: Mr. Nixon, your budget is going to be a full employment budget—I understand that is going to be true—which will be deficit spending. In the very good year of 1972, which you have said you hope will happen, will you get unemployment down to four percent, which most people call full employment, which you have just referred to? Will it get down that far?

THE PRESIDENT: That certainly will be our goal, Mr. Chancellor. I am not going to indicate what the number actually will be, because even though I am willing to predict on football games and also the stock market, to say what the unemployment number is going to be a year and a half from now, of course, would be completely irresponsible. But our goal is full employment by the end of 1972.

If I could come back, Mr. Sevareid, to another point that you raised, I also should point out that we do not plan—despite the speculation that you have heard about—I do not plan to ask for new taxes. I have considered the possibility of the value-added tax as a substitution for some of our other taxes, and looking to the future, we may very well move into that direction.

But this year, I do not think it is realistic to propose a new tax, either new taxes or tax reform, because I am going to give the Congress, and particularly the Ways and Means Committee of the House and the Finance Committee of the Senate, a very full plate in other areas requiring their attention, including, for example, welfare reform that I will submit again, and including also, a new health program which will go to those committees, and including also, a new, what we will call, revenue-sharing, going far beyond anything that we have suggested to date.

MISS DICKERSON: Mr. President, I would like to ask you a little bit more about the man who is unemployed, as you mentioned, the man who went into your father's store.

There are an awful lot of those people now and their unemployment insurance is running out, and the idea of expansionary programs doesn't really quite get to them.

How do you convince that man who is out of a job and whose wife has had to go back to work and whose children are leaving college because they don't have any money—how do you convince him right now to keep cool because you think the things are going to be reasonably better in the future?

THE PRESIDENT: Well, one way you cannot convince him, I can say, Miss Dickerson, is simply by what we call jawboning. People are too smart to listen to even the President of the United States and be convinced that things are going to be better the day-after-tomorrow. The way he is convinced is by what happens.

For example, notice the area of Southern California, which you have referred to, the fact that we are going to have by far the biggest year in housing in the history of this country is going to have a rather dramatic effect on employment in Southern California; the fact that in areas like the environment we are going to have expanding programs; the fact that in the proposals that we are making to the Congress, these will have an effect in stimulating the economy.

Now, as this movement occurs, that man who is unemployed will see that the rolls go down. That is the only thing that is going to convince him, not any promises, not any talk.

I can only say that I am convinced that our policies are right. I am committed to an activist policy, and I will assure that man who is unemployed that the President of the United States knows what it means, and I intend to do everything that I possibly can to see that our policies will deal with it and deal with it effectively.

MR. SMITH: We have so much to cover and so little time, I am going to dare to change the subject slightly. Dr. Pat Moynihan sent you the most widely publicized secret memorandum in the world which recommended a policy of benign neglect towards the racial problem. We know about that. We don't know what your answer or reaction was. What did you think about that?

THE PRESIDENT: He got a bad rap out of that, Mr. Smith. Dr. Moynihan is one of the most dedicated men to racial justice and to justice for all people that I have ever known. He was referred to when he was on the White House Staff as the White House liberal. Well, as a matter of fact, we have others who perhaps can also be so categorized. But he was enthusiastic.

He was, for example, the author of the Family Assistance Welfare Reform, which I believe will be, as he has said, the greatest single social reform in the last 40 years, and which, incidentally, is the answer to benign neglect.

When he talked about benign neglect, he was not referring to neglecting black Americans or any Americans. But what he was referring to was not to react to violence, not to react to attacks that might be made, verbal or others, by minority groups, black Americans, extremist groups.

His advice was to act on the problems but to have a policy—and he used the term benign neglect in a philosophical way and then the thing came out and everybody jumped on it and, of course, on me.

But I want to say I am proud that he was a member of our staff for two years. And his legacy, and I promised him the day that he left, the day before Christmas—his legacy will be that we are going to have welfare reform, and that every family in America with children will have a minimum income.

MR. SMITH: He was nearly six feet tall so I know your assessment of him is correct.

Someone, I think, told you earlier about telegrams that come to us and ask us to ask you questions. I would like to put one to you from a telegram. In your last news conference you said you opposed forced integration in the suburbs. Well, if a suburban community should use zoning and land use authority to block housing development for minority groups and, in fact, there are cases where it has happened, would you or would you not apply the Federal Fair Housing Law to prevent that?

THE PRESIDENT: Mr. Smith, what we are talking about here, first, is carrying out the law and then, second, going beyond the law.

I also said in that news conference, as you will remember, that I was pledged to carry out the law, this law and every other law, and that I would carry it out.

The law, as you know, does require that there can be no urban renewal funds, that there can be no Federal housing funds, in any community that has a policy which is discriminatory insofar as fair housing is concerned. But now the law does not now require or, in my opinion, allow the Federal Government to have forced integration of suburbs. There is argument on this point.

I realize, for example—and I do listen to some of your commentaries and I read them all—I know Mr. Chancellor has very strong feelings on this—I believe that that is the best course: We are going to carry out the law. We are going to open up opportunities for all Americans to move into housing, any housing that they are able to afford.

But, on the other hand, for the Federal Government to go further than the law, to force integration in the suburbs, I think is unrealistic. I think it will be counter-productive and not in the interest of better race relations.

MR. CHANCELLOR: Let me ask a question about Vietnam, as though nobody was going to ask that question.

Last month you sent a number of bombers into North Vietnam and we were told that they bombed missile sites and antiaircraft installations because the North Vietnamese had fired on an American reconnaissance plane. But then a few days later, sir, we learned that apparently that opportunity was used to make very heavy bombing raids on supply lines in the Mu Gia Pass and the passes in North Vietnam into Laos.

Now, I am confused because of all of the talk about the understandings with North Vietnam, with the new criteria on the bombing you seem to have put on, and the fact that what many people got out of this one series of raids was that we have quite enlarged the reasons for our going to the North to bomb.

THE PRESIDENT: Mr. Chancellor, I have no desire to resume the bombing of North Vietnam. We do not want to go back to the bombing of the strategic targets in North Vietnam, and we do not want even to bomb military targets unless it becomes necessary to do so, and this is the key point—to protect American forces.

Now, with regard to the understanding, let us see what it is.

First, there was an understanding. President Johnson said so, and Dean Rusk said so, and Clark Clifford said so, and Mr. Harriman said so. There was an understanding that after the bombing halt, unarmed reconnaissance planes could fly over North Vietnam with impunity. We had to insist on that, because otherwise, we would have no intelligence with regard to when they were planning on an attack.

So, when they fire on those planes I have given instructions that we will take out the SAM site or whatever it is that has fired upon them.

We will continue to do so, and if they say that there is no understanding in that respect, then there are no restraints whatever on us, and so we must have that in mind.

Now, the other understanding is one that I have laid down. It is a new one. It is a new one which goes along with our Vietnamization program and our withdrawal program. I pointed out a moment ago what has happened in Vietnam, the fact that our casualties are a third of what they were two years ago, the fact that we have 265,000 out of Vietnam now, and that we can see the end of the American combat role in Vietnam. We can see that coming.

We must realize, however, as Secretary Rogers pointed out in his news conference at the State Department a few days ago, that in May of this year, most American combat

forces, ground combat forces, will have been withdrawn from Vietnam. But there will still be 280,000 there left to withdraw.

Now, the President of the United States, as Commander-in-Chief, holds a responsibility to those men to see that they are not subjected to an overwhelming attack from the North. That is why we must continue reconnaissance, and that is why also, if the enemy at a time we are trying to de-escalate, at a time we are withdrawing, starts to build up its infiltration, starts moving troops and supplies through the Mu Gia Pass and the other passes, then I, as Commander-in-Chief, will have to order bombing strikes on those key areas.

That was one of the reasons for this strike, and it will be done again if they continue to threaten our remaining forces in Vietnam. But only on those military targets, and only if necessary.

MR. SEVAREID: Would it calm the situation and help the prospects of peace if we did have some formal alliance with Israel?

THE PRESIDENT: No, I don't believe so, because I think that what we are doing for Israel is so well known to them, and also incidentally it is quite well known to their neighbors, that it provides the balance that is needed.

We just provided a $500 million aid program for Israel. I say "aid" if they are going to be able to purchase weapons to that extent. We have made it clear time and again that we will help to maintain the balance of power in the area, so that Israel would not be in a position that its neighbors could overwhelm them with their superior manpower or with the forces that they received from the Soviet Union. But I do not believe that a formal alliance would be either necessary or would be in the interest of peace in the area.

MR. SMITH: The thing that bothers me is the tendency toward adventurism in this part of the world by the Russians. They are manning the SAM sites, and last summer—it wasn't widely publicized, but eight Israeli jets were on patrol and they ran into eight Egyptian MIGs, and there was a fight and over the radio they heard they weren't Egyptians, they were Russian-piloted MIGs.

The score was four Russians shot down. But how frightfully dangerous that is. If the Russians had been tempted to retaliate, it would be terribly complicated.

THE PRESIDENT: You will remember in the last five minutes of our conversation a year ago—we didn't get to the Mideast until the last five minutes—but I mentioned this very point, that the key to peace in the Mideast is held by several people: first, the parties involved, the Israelis and the neighbors, primarily the UAR and Jordan. Second, the key to peace is in the hands of the Soviet Union and the United States, Britain and France, the four major powers.

If the Soviet Union does not play a conciliatory peace-making role, there is no chance for peace in the Mideast, because if the Soviet Union continues to fuel the war arsenals of Israel's neighbors, Israel will have no choice but to come to the United States for us to maintain the balance to which Mr. Sevareid referred. And we will maintain that balance.

That is why it is important at this time that the Soviet Union and the United States as well as Britain and France all join together in a process of not having additional arms and additional activities go into that area, because that will only mean that it produces the possibility of future confrontation.

This is the time to talk. Let me say one other thing with regard to talk. I would hesitate to give advice to other nations as they enter such delicate talks, but I am sure of this: These talks will have no chance for success if they are done in a public forum. It is very important that it be done quietly, because every time an offer is made or a suggestion is made, it is talked about in the parliaments of one country or another and on the radio, and you can forget it. If these talks can be quietly conducted, there is a chance for success, and in the end we want to remember that the United States and the Soviet Union and Great Britain and France must all be, and I think will be, in a position to guarantee whatever settlement is made through the United Nations.

MISS DICKERSON: Mr. President, to switch from foreign affairs for a moment to some other areas, I would like to ask you a question that involves whether this Government is really going to be able to govern in the future. It involves how you cut up the economy, how you slice the pie. The cities are crying. Mayors say they can't run them. They don't have enough money to pay their teachers or their firemen. The State Governors say that States are near bankruptcy.

How soon are you going to be able to reverse the flow of money and power and responsibility from Washington back to the States and the cities that you said you wanted to do?

THE PRESIDENT: Miss Dickerson, if we get cooperation from the next Congress, we are going to begin to make a breakthrough in that area in this historic next Congress, the 92nd. That will be the major thrust of my State of the Union Message, how we can take this great Government of ours, and it is a great Government, how we can give the people of this country an opportunity to make decisions with what that Government should be and what it does, and what kind of activities it should be engaged in. That is why when I referred to revenue-sharing a moment ago in answering Mr. Sevareid, I pointed out that we were going to have a program that went far beyond any proposal that we had made to this date and it is one that will be, I believe, widely supported by the Governors, by the Mayors, and I trust by the Congress, because, you know, we tried to make a breakthrough when I submitted this in August of last year. The Congress didn't have hearings on it.

This time we expect to get hearings and this is one area where Mr. Connally can help.

MISS DICKERSON: I know that, sir, but, you know, Dr. Moynihan when he left said one of the criticisms was the impression got around that you really weren't behind some of these programs that you had enunciated, and many of the Senators and Congressmen felt that you hadn't really given your personal push to it and that is why it failed to get any hearings at all.

THE PRESIDENT: Well, Miss Dickerson, in evaluating what a President is behind, of course, that is fair game. It is done with all Presidents and I have no complaints about members of the press and others who do this, or members of my own staff.

But there is nothing that I feel more strongly about than the proposal for welfare reform and the proposal for revenue-sharing, the new one that I will be submitting to the Congress.

One of the reasons is that if we do not have it we are going to have States, cities and counties going bankrupt over these next two or three years and we are going to have massive problems in those areas. I believe as the Congress sees that crisis they will act on it.

Let me give you an example with regard to welfare reform. In 1967 there were 660,000 people on welfare in New York City. In 1971 there were 1,200,000 people on welfare in New York City. It just goes up and up and up.

Now, if anybody wants to defend the present welfare program let them be against ours. We are going to propose it again. We are going to put the Congress—we have a commitment from the Congress to act on it or at least get a vote on it early in the next session. And if we can get revenue-sharing with it this crisis of the cities and local governments—we at least have a start in answer to it.

MR. SMITH: A great deal depends on your getting Congress to act. A Liberal Republican Senator has recently said to me that he was never called to confer with you. A Liberal Congressman said he has trouble seeing you. I compare this with your predecessor having Congressmen and Senators in droves in small groups here every week of his Administration.

Do you think you have nursed your Congressional relations well enough?

THE PRESIDENT: Mr. Smith, in regard to how many droves of Congressmen and Senators have been down here, I think you will find—the record, I think, will be put out in the next two or three days because, as you know, at the end of two years people ask for these statistics—I have seen more Congressmen and Senators than any of my predecessors saw, for a good reason. I didn't have a majority.

You see, in the case, for example, of President Johnson he could call the Leaders down and they could get the program through. In the case of President Kennedy he could do the same thing. In the case of President Eisenhower, whereas he had a Republican Congress only in his first two years, in the last six years he had—he was then the Majority Leader Johnson and Sam Rayburn and they could deliver the Democratic vote. I do not have that situation.

You do not have that kind of Leadership on the Democratic side or, for that matter, on the Republican side in the United States Senate. No fault of the Leaders, but because they are a group of individualists.

But to come more precisely to your question, there is nothing that I mean to devote more of my time to—and in this field of revenue-sharing and in this field of welfare reform which will be in the Ways and Means Committee of the House and the Finance Committee of the Senate—nothing that the new Secretary of the Treasury, Mr. Connally, is going to devote his time to, than getting that through.

I notice, incidentally, because I was interested in your reactions to the Connally appointment, that some wondered what good it would do. Some thought it had something to do with Texas politics in 1972. Let me be quite candid. We need, I need, this country needs John Connally as Secretary of the Treasury and in this Cabinet because he is persuasive, he is strong, and he will be effective in helping us get through the Democratic Congress the kind of measures that we need in this domestic field that we haven't been able to get through over the past two years. I am confident he will do that.

MR. SEVAREID: Mr. President, now that we are in the subject of politics—

THE PRESIDENT: You can still ask questions, but I may not give you the answers.

MR. SEVAREID:—if you had the November election to do over again, what would do differently?

THE PRESIDENT: I never try to second guess elections. Here we get back to Mr. Smith's point of a moment ago, or my answer to his question. After what happened to me in the 1960 elections, when I thought of what could I have done differently to have changed 9,000 votes in Illinois or 8,000 votes in Missouri, or 10,000 votes in South Carolina, or 3,000 votes in New Mexico—I didn't go through that agony then when the national election was involved and frankly, I am not going to go through it now with regard to the '70 elections.

I will only say this: I believe that I had a responsibility, having made certain pledges to the people when I ran for President, to work for the election of Senators, and I campaigned particularly for Senators, as you know, Senators who would support me in those policies. Sometimes we succeeded; sometimes we failed. Now that campaign is over and I am going to work with those that got in despite my opposition and those who went with us as best we possibly can.

I want to also say one other thing, and I want to give credit to the men—you, of course, were generally not on the campaign tour, but representatives—Herb Kaplow was on from NBC and others from your networks, Fitzgerald, and so forth. But they have properly reported that in the 22 States that I visited, I never attacked any of the men, the Senators, that were the incumbents.

I simply went in on the basis of saying that we had a choice between two men, one of whom was pledged to support the President on some basic issue and one of whom honestly felt otherwise, and I asked the people for support. I think that was my responsibility. I would do that again.

MR. SEVAREID: One specific technical matter. Do you regret the rebroadcast of the Phoenix speech about the San Jose incident?

THE PRESIDENT: Yes, I think that was a mistake. As a matter of fact, we apparently felt at that time, that the speech said some things that needed to be said, but having the re-broadcast the night before election is not something that I would have perhaps planned had I been, shall we say, running the campaign. Incidentally, when I am the candidate, I run the campaign.

MR. SMITH: It was a technically bad tape, too. You could hardly be heard.

THE PRESIDENT: Yes, it was technically bad and I do not think it was the right speech to make the night before election. I would have preferred to go on, as you know I usually do, in a quiet studio type of program, talking quietly to the American people about the choice and then letting them make their choice, and if I am in another campaign, that is the way it will be the night before election. We wouldn't run that type of tape again.

MISS DICKERSON: Speaking of your campaigns, you made the kick-off address in New Hampshire in 1968, your first speech I remember.

THE PRESIDENT: You couldn't be that old.

MISS DICKERSON: Oh, yes I am. I was there when you were running for Vice President. You made a speech how the next President had to give this country the lift of a driving dream.

Well, as yet, many people have failed to perceive the lift of a driving dream. I wondered if you could articulate that dream for us briefly and tell us how you plan to specifically get it across to the people in the next two years.

THE PRESIDENT: Miss Dickerson, before we can really get the lift of a driving dream, we have to get rid of some of the nightmares we inherited. One of the nightmares is a war without end. We are ending that war. One of the good things incidentally about the campaign of 1970 was that the war was not an issue. That is good. The American people finally realized that we are ending the war.

When I appeared on the program, you may recall in July with you, at that time, a poll had just been taken of college students, and indicated four million college students, because of their disenchantment with the war and Cambodia and the rest, were going to campaign for the peace candidates in the November election. They didn't.

That doesn't mean that they are for war, but they had in some way become convinced we were sincerely trying to end the war. We are ending it.

Second, we have to quiet this country down at home. We made some progress in that respect—not enough.

Third, we have to make that delicate transition from a war-time to a peace-time economy. The fact that 1,700,000 Americans have been let out of defense plants and out of the armed services has contributed to some unemployment to which we referred. But I think most Americans want this Administration to succeed in achieving not only the end of a war, but a peace that will last—something we haven't had—a peace for a generation—and not only the ending of a war, and a peace that will last, but a new kind of prosperity, an era of opportunity for all Americans.

This is why I believe that we are now right at the break point. The war is beginning to end. We are seeing the economy moving through the difficult period of transition. We see that unemployment, I believe, will move down over the period of 1971—not as fast as we would like, but it is going to go down. Inflation is going to be checked. Then we can move forward in the field of welfare reform, in the field of returning decision-making power to the people of this country, and we can move forward on great programs in the environment.

For example, did you happen to see the cover story in *Life* this week on youth in America. Three-fourths of them, I noticed, said they would not work for a plant that was guilty of polluting the environment. That shows you that this is an issue.

Incidentally, I will give credit to our Democrat friends who are just as interested in it as we, but we are in it and we are pushing.

But if we can get this country thinking not of how to fight a war, but how to win a peace—if we can get this country thinking of clean air, clean water, open spaces, of a welfare reform program that will provide a floor under the income of every family with children in America, a new approach to government, reform of education and reform of health—if those things begin to happen, people can think of these positive things, and then we will have the lift of a driving dream. But it takes some time to get rid of the nightmares. You can't be having a driving dream when you are in the midst of a nightmare.

FEBRUARY 17

Following is the text, as made available by the White House, of President Nixon's Feb. 17 news conference in his White House office, his 14th news conference since taking office and his first since Dec. 10.

THE PRESIDENT: We'll make this on the record today.

The mike is for the purpose of a transcription which will be available, I think, rather soon after we complete the conference because it will be run simultaneously by the stenographers.

Any questions which you want to ask?

SOUTHEAST ASIA

Q: Mr. President, the next logical step in Southeast Asia would seem to be South Vietnamese forces moving into the southern part of North Vietnam for the same reasons that they moved into the Laotian panhandle.

Would our policy rule out support for this type of move, air support for it?

THE PRESIDENT. Well, I won't speculate on what South Vietnam may decide to do with regard to a possible incursion into North Vietnam in order to defend their national security. However, I will restate our policy. I stated that policy on November 3d (1969) and have restated it at least nine different times publicly since that time.

I stated then that at a time we are withdrawing our forces that if I found that the enemy was stepping up its activity through infiltration in a way that would threaten our remaining forces that I would take strong action to deal with the new situation.

On December 10 (1970), as you recall, I reiterated that statement and said that this action would include the use of airpower against the infiltration routes, military complex supply depots.

That is our policy, the policy of the President taking action if he finds that the North Vietnamese are undertaking actions which threaten our remaining forces in South Vietnam.

Q: Mr. President, under that guide, is there any limit to what we might do to protect our forces in South Vietnam?

THE PRESIDENT: We have indicated several limits. For example, we are not going to use ground forces in Laos. We are not going to use advisers in Laos with the South Vietnamese forces. We are not going to use ground forces in Cambodia or advisers in Cambodia as we have previously indicated and we have no intention, of course, of using ground forces in North Vietnam. Those are limitations.

Q: I had reference to our use of airpower.

THE PRESIDENT: I'm not going to place any limitation upon the use of airpower except, of course, to rule out a rather ridiculous suggestion that is made from time to time—I think the latest by Hans Morgenthau—that our airpower might include the use of tactical nuclear weapons.

As you know, Mr. Lisagor, this has been speculated on for a period of 5 years and I have said for a period of 5 years that this is not an area where the use of nuclear weapons, in any form, is either needed or would be wise.

As far as our airpower is concerned, it will be directed against—and I ought to be as precise as I was on December 10—against those military activities which I determine are directed against and thereby threaten our remaining forces in South Vietnam.

Q: Can you tell us, sir—the idea of an incursion into Laos has been under consideration in Saigon on the military level for some years. Why did you decide that now is the time to do it? And second, can you give us some kind of a status report on how it's going and what the prognosis is in terms of the possible enemy resistance, what is it the intelligence suggests?

THE PRESIDENT: Yes. In looking at this situation, I recall, as probably some of you who were there, in 1965, that some of our military people and civilians for that matter, were then saying that the way to stop the North Vietnamese infiltration into South Vietnam was to cut the Ho Chi Minh Trail.

It was not undertaken during the previous administration, as I understand, and, I can speak for this administration, was not undertaken until now for a reason that the South Vietnamese and, for that matter, the United States had enough on our plate in South Vietnam.

Laos would not have been possible had it not been for Cambodia. Cambodia cutting off one vital supply line and thereby practically bringing enemy activity in the southern half of South Vietnam to an end released the South Vietnamese forces, who, by this time, had not only gained confidence in Cambodia but also had additional strength, released them for undertaking what they could not have undertaken even 8 months ago, an incursion on their own into Laos with only U.S. air support.

The decision to do it now or, I think, perhaps, put it this way, the decision not to do it before, is that, one, neither the United States nor the South Vietnamese felt that they apparently had the capability to do it; the second, the decision to do it now was that based on the fact that the South Vietnamese, because of the confidence, the training they gained as a result of their actions in Cambodia, the South Vietnamese felt that they were able to undertake it. Our commanders agreed and, therefore, it was undertaken.

Q: Mr. President, could you discuss with us your evaluation of the possibility of Communist China entering this situation now that it's expanded into Laos or if the South Vietnamese go into North Vietnam?

THE PRESIDENT: Let me refer to the situation as it presently exists rather than the hypothesis of whether the South Vietnamese might go into North Vietnam.

As far as the actions in southern Laos are concerned, they present no threat to Communist China and should not be interpreted by the Communist Chinese as being a threat against them.

As you know, the Communist Chinese have been operating in northern Laos for some time. But this action is not directed against Communist China. It is directed against the North Vietnamese who are pointed toward South Vietnam and toward Cambodia.

Consequently, I do not believe that the Communist Chinese have any reason to interpret this as a threat against them or any reason therefore to react to it.

Q: Mr. President, if I could follow up, could you give us your evaluation of how the Laotian operation is really going militarily and otherwise?

THE PRESIDENT: And incidentally, don't hesitate in this smaller forum to ask for follow-up. To the extent I can cover all the questions, I'll be glad to take them.

As far as the Laotian operation is concerned, the reports that have come from the field I think generally give an accurate picture, except, of course, for the day-to-day tendency to hypo this or that incident into a crisis.

The operation—and I read a complete report from General Abrams this morning—the operation has gone according to plan. The South Vietnamese have already cut three major roads—and we call them "roads," let's say trails—which lead from Tchepone down into Cambodia and, of course, into South Vietnam.

The South Vietnamese have run into very heavy resistance on the road going into Tchepone. We expected that resistance.

Putting it in the context of the earlier reply, the Cambodian action in May and June cut one lifeline, the lifeline from Sihanoukville into the southern half of South Vietnam.

This action would either cut or seriously disrupt the other pipeline or lifeline, the lifeline coming from—down through Laos, the Ho Chi Minh Trail, into the northern half of South Vietnam.

Therefore, we expected the North Vietnamese to fight here. They have to fight here or give up the struggle to conquer South Vietnam, Cambodia, and their influence extending through other parts of Southeast Asia.

Finally, I think it's quite important to note General Abrams' evaluation, which I specifically asked him to give me by cable just a few days ago, his evaluation of how the South Vietnamese are conducting themselves. They are fighting, he said, in a superior way. I use the word that he used. They are proceeding in a way that he believes is in accordance with the plan and holding their own against enemy attack.

And he also pointed up another fact that, of course, has been overridden by the Laotian activity, that the operation in the Chup Plantation led by General Tri is going along in a fashion much better than was expected, with a great number of enemy casualties and, as General Abrams put it, excellent performance on the part of those groups.

Q. Mr. President, it is reported in both the South Vietnamese and, I think, in our statement the operation will be limited in time and scope. Can you define those terms?

THE PRESIDENT: By time, the operation will be limited to the time that is necessary to accomplish the objective. The objective is not to occupy any part of Laos. The South Vietnamese are not there to stay. They are there to disrupt the enemy's lines of communication, their supply lines, their infiltration routes, and then to get out.

Once that is accomplished, if it is accomplished early, they will get out. If it takes a longer time, they will stay in.

There is also another limitation in terms of time. And that is the weather. In the latter part of April or the early part of May, the rains come. And they would have to get out then because then the North Vietnamese also would pose no threat.

In terms of area, space, it is limited to the specific area that you see on the maps here, in terms of cutting across the trails—and it is more than one trail, there are three or four trails—the trails that are the supply lines on which the North Vietnamese operate.

Q: Would you have any further word on troop withdrawals for us at this time or when can you tell us about further troop withdrawals?

THE PRESIDENT: I will make a further announcement on troop withdrawals, as I have indicated, before the May 1st period when the last troop withdrawal period will have expired.

By that time, as you know, 265,000 Americans will have been withdrawn and the further withdrawal announcement will be made then.

I can say today that as a result partially of our success in Cambodia, and based on also the present success of the Laotian operation, that the troop withdrawal program will go forward on schedule.

I should also point out, however, that as far as this year is concerned, even if the Laotian operation had not been undertaken by the South Vietnamese with our air-support, the troop withdrawal program could have gone ahead on schedule.

What this relates to, insofar as American troop withdrawals are concerned, is not this year but next year. Next year will be a year when the Vietnamization program's very success creates the point of greatest danger, because then the number of ground combat troops that we will have in South Vietnam will be lower.

Q: If this is a great success, it could go next year much faster —is that a right inference?

THE PRESIDENT: When I made the announcement about moving into Cambodia, I said that its purpose was to insure our troop withdrawal, to reduce our casualties. And we hope to shorten the war. It has had those effects. Our casualties, even in this past week in which we have moved in with air support in support of the South Vietnamese and have suffered some air losses, were only half of what they were in the same week before Cambodia.

So casualties are down and I should point out that casualties in the first month that we came into office were five times as great as they were in the month of January. One is too many. But that, at least, is progress, in terms of casualties.

In terms of troop withdrawals, the Cambodian incursion insured it and allowed us, as a matter of fact, to set our sights somewhat higher.

The success of this operation guarantees the continued program and gives the prospect of a greater troop withdrawal during the months ahead.

I am not going to speculate, however, as to what the troop withdrawal announcement will be on April 15. That will deal with the situation at that time and, at that time, we will not yet see the end of the Laotian operation.

Q: Mr. President, if I could follow that up, is it possible to say now, without talking about numbers of troops to be withdrawn, when the United States might be able to forgo a ground combat role in South Vietnam?

THE PRESIDENT: There will be an announcement on that score at some point. I am not going to indicate it now.

At this time, when the negotiations are going on at Paris still—when I say negotiations, with no progress—we are not going to remove any incentive for a possible negotiation by announcing what our plans are further down the road.

Q: Mr. President, my question does follow his somewhat. How far can you go in withdrawing U.S. troops without a resolution of the prisoner-of-war issue?

THE PRESIDENT. Well, as I have indicated, and as everyone I am sure would agree, as long as the North Vietnamese have any Americans as prisoners of war, there will be Americans in South Vietnam and enough Americans to give them an incentive to release the prisoners.

Q: Mr. President, could I follow that up. Would you be willing to join with Congress, as Senator Javits has suggested, in a resolution saying that it is our intention to withdraw all troops from South Vietnam?

THE PRESIDENT: Not needed, because you see, in my October speech, as you'll recall, I called for a cease-fire, I called for a political settlement, and I also called for a total withdrawal of all forces if it was mutual.

So, the policy of this Government is for a total withdrawal, provided there is a withdrawal by the other side.

BLACK CONGRESSMEN

Q: Would you explain, Mr. President, why you have not found time to see these 12 black Congressmen who have been asking to see you for about a year?

THE PRESIDENT. I talked to Senator Brooke about that just a few days ago and asked him to speak to some of those who had made this request.

As you know, I have seen a great number of Congressmen and, of course, not only these 12 but all the Members of Congress, by the time I finish the breakfast tomorrow, will have been invited to the White House since the new Congress came here.

Some have not accepted. But Senator Brooke now has been talking with, I understand, Congressman Diggs, whom I know—and I know several of them, several of the older ones at least from previously serving with them—and I think that a meeting is going to be worked out. I hope it is, because I will be glad to talk to them of course.

SUPREME COURT

Q: Mr. President, are you happier with the performance of the Supreme Court this year than you were in '68 while you were campaigning and do you anticipate any appointments this term?

THE PRESIDENT. Well, the second part of the question, of course, would be presumptuous for me to comment upon, because there are no—

Q: There are no resignations on your desk obviously.

THE PRESIDENT: No. No, I think I would know about it if there were. But I have no indication of any intention to resign.

With regard to the Supreme Court's decisions, I don't believe that I should comment upon the wisdom of their decisions. I have great confidence in those that I have appointed to the Court and I have great respect for others who are on the Court, with whom I happen to disagree. But I won't comment on that.

SOVIET SUBMARINE

Q: How concerned are you about the presence of a Soviet nuclear submarine in Cuban waters?

THE PRESIDENT. On December 10th (January 4)*, you may recall, I said that if a nuclear submarine were serviced from Cuba or in Cuba, that this would be a violation of our understanding with regard to the Soviet Union's activities in putting offensive weapons or a base in Cuba.

Now, as far as this submarine is concerned, the question is a rather technical one, whether it is there for a port call or whether it is there for servicing. We are watching it very closely. The Soviet Union is aware of the fact that we consider that there is an understanding and we will, of course, bring the matter to their attention if we find that the understanding is violated.

SUBURBAN INTEGRATION

Q: Mr. President, may I ask you about racial integration in suburban housing, a subject that you've treated twice this year and you've expressed your opposition to forced integration and you've said you'll do what the law requires.

In the meantime, the Third Circuit has handed down a decision which would seem to put an increased burden on HUD to move public housing into the suburbs and a major case has been instituted in Black Jack, Missouri.

The Federal Government has yet to announce its intention in regard to either of those cases. Will you appeal, will you enter the Black Jack case, and what do you see as the overall role of the national administration in this area?

THE PRESIDENT: To try to answer all of the questions, let me come first to the attitude of the administration with regard to the Black Jack case.

The Attorney General and HUD jointly are considering the Black Jack case, and I understand within approximately 30 days will have a recommendation to me as to what action should be taken with regard to compliance with that case.

I will not indicate anything further than that. I will have something more to say when I get the recommendations from the Attorney General and from HUD.

With regard to what you call, and what I have called—I think you did not say this—but what I have called forced integration, let me just spend a moment indicating what I believe is the law in this country and where I think the law's limits are.

First, this administration will enforce the law of the land which provides for open housing. Open cities, open suburbs, open neighborhoods are now a right for every American.

Second, however, this administration will not go beyond the law or in violation of the law by going beyond it by using Federal power, Federal coercion, or Federal money to force economic integration of neighborhoods.

The President was referring to a statement he made on January 4 in his television interview.

Now what we will do, however, and what we are doing is to try to give every American, and particularly Americans in minority groups, black Americans for example, a greater opportunity to exercise a right. A right, for example, to live in any neighborhood means nothing unless you've got a job or a position which pays you enough to afford the house.

That's the position that we have.

SOUTHEAST ASIA

Q: Mr. President, if the Army of South Vietnam sought to cross the DMZ in force, would you be of a mind to restrain such action?

THE PRESIDENT: If the—excuse me, the Army of South or North Vietnam?

Q: South Vietnam.

THE PRESIDENT: Oh, South Vietnam.

Q; If the ARVN sought to cross the DMZ in violation—

THE PRESIDENT: I will not speculate on what South Vietnam may do in defense of its national security. South Vietnam now, as we withdraw, has an ever increasing responsibility to defend itself.

South Vietnam will have to make decisions with regard to its ability to defend itself. I will only speak with regard to what the American action will be.

The American action will be, according to the guideline I laid down a moment ago, the use of airpower where I believe that North Vietnam's action may threaten our forces.

Q: Mr. President, if the Laos operation goes according to your expectations and is as much a success as you hope, is it likely to be followed by any new diplomatic initiative in an effort to get the Paris talks going?

THE PRESIDENT: Well, Mr. Potter, the matter of diplomatic initiatives is something that we've been discussing constantly within the administration. As a matter of fact, I've been talking to the Secretary of State and the Secretary of Defense, Dr. Kissinger, and others, both informally and in formal meetings.

I have nothing to report today, but I do want to say this: that we will continue to pursue the diplomacy for a primary reason, the primary reason being to negotiate some settlement of the POW issue.

As we have to realize that as far as a negotiation affecting a political settlement for South Vietnam is concerned, time is running out for the North Vietnamese if they expect to negotiate with the United States. Because as our forces come out of South Vietnam, it means that the responsibility for the negotiation, increasingly, then becomes that of South Vietnam.

But I can only say that looking to the future, we constantly are reexamining the possibility of any diplomatic initiatives. However, I believe that what I stated in October is a very far-reaching, it's very comprehensive, it's a very fair proposal, and we stand on that at this time.

I do not want to suggest that there are any more concessions coming from our side to North Vietnam. We are not going to make any more concessions. The time is for them to negotiate on the principles that we have laid down.

CONSTRUCTION INDUSTRY

Q: Mr. President, I have a question on the economy. Sir, the construction unions and the industry apparently are not going to be able to come up with a voluntary plan to hold down wage and price increases. What actions will you take?

THE PRESIDENT: Secretary Hodgson is going to report to me Monday when he returns from Miami, where, as you know, he has been meeting with the leaders of the construction industry.

I will not indicate now what action we will take until I get his report. But there will be action. The reason there has to be action in their field, in addition to the reasons that all of you have, in your various columns and reports, have indicated, I would put it very simply as this: The construction industry is a sick industry. It's a sick industry not because of the quality of construction in the United States—it's the highest quality construction in the world—but because it's had too rich a diet.

When you find that wage increases—wage increases have been high in a number of industries—but when they are on an average of 16 percent, what has happened is that that has not helped the workers in the construction industry except those that are employed.

We find that unemployment in the construction industry is double the national average and we also find that the Federal Government has a major stake in this, because, looking at this budget, I have found that $14 billion of our budget in the next fiscal year will go into construction.

Now, with that kind of financial interest in construction, it is essential that the Federal Government use its power to the extent that it can to bring about more reasonable settlements within that industry, wage and price stability.

Having stated that goal, you are all aware of some of the actions that have been discussed. I will consider them all and then make a decision and we'll announce it when it's made.

NORTH VIETNAM

Q: Mr. President, may I ask a question, if I could get back to Vietnam for just one moment? There has been quite a bit of speculation about the possibility of the North Vietnamese coming down through the DMZ.

Would this scrap any obligations that you may have under the bombing ban in the North and would you be in a position then of having to retaliate for any crossing of the DMZ?

THE PRESIDENT: My action in case that happened—and I do not believe it will happen—but my action will be guided by the same principles that I have laid down before I would use the power of the United States, and particularly its power in the air, to the extent that I consider it necessary to protect our remaining forces in South Vietnam.

We have a considerable number of forces, as you know, on the DMZ. The blocking forces along Route 9, before you get to the border of Laos, are primarily American. I will not allow those forces to be endangered by a massive North Vietnamese incursion, if one should be undertaken. I think the very fact that the North Vietnamese know that I intend to take strong action to deal with that incursion means that they are not going to take it. If they do, I can assure you that—I don't want to assure you, I simply want to have the record clear that I would not be bound, of course, by any so-called understandings which they have already violated at the time of the bombing halt.

INTEGRATION POLICY

Q: Mr. President, a few minutes ago in response to Mr. O'Rouke's question, you referred to your views on forced integration, a word which you said you have used before.

I am a little puzzled by the distinction between forced integration and enforcement of the laws which are on the books which you, as you properly said, were pledged to enforce, those laws against discrimination.

Where does this line come between those two concepts in your mind?

THE PRESIDENT: In the one case, the laws on the books deal, as they properly should, with human rights, the rights of an individual to buy a house or an apartment, or rent a house or an apartment without regard—and not be barred because of his racial or religious or other background.

In the other case, what we are talking about is an economic consideration having to do primarily with the zoning.

Now, where this is involved, it seems to me a clear distinction. The law does not allow the Federal Government to use its monetary and other power, coercive power, for the purpose of changing the economic pattern of a neighborhood.

I think what the law does require is that there be open neighborhoods. The law does not require that the Federal Government step in and provide in a neighborhood the type of housing that an individual could afford to move into. That's the difference, as I see it.

CONSTRUCTION INDUSTRY

Q: Mr. President, when Secretary Hodgson went back down to Florida, did he carry any message from you, harsh, gentle or otherwise?

THE PRESIDENT: Secretary Hodgson had a long discussion with me and with other leaders in the administratior prior to his going down. We developed a plan and we also gave him several options which he could discuss with the leaders of the labor unions. He's a very persuasive man.

I am not going to concede that he struck out until he tells me so himself. But if he has, then we will be up to bat.

REVENUE SHARING

Q: Mr. President, have you been disappointed with the reaction in Congress to your revenue sharing plan and what do you feel about the prospects of that right now?

THE PRESIDENT: No, I am not disappointed. All reforms have rough sledding. When we consider reforms, we must remember that they are always opposed by the establishment. And by the establishment, I don't refer to what we used to talk about in 1964, some used to talk about the eastern establishment—I am referring to the establishment of Congress, the establishment of the Federal bureaucracy and also great organizations, labor organizations, farm organizations, business organizations have all gotten used to dealing with government as it is and they are always afraid of change.

As far as the Congress is concerned and the bureacracy is concerned, as I pointed out in the State of the Union, they are very, very reluctant to give up power. We expected a difficult time in getting revenue sharing through.

But let me put it, if I can, in other terms. We have been talking about foreign policy. We in Washington in Government live at the very summit of government. And here we do find opposition, dug-in establishmentarians fighting for the status quo or for just a little change, or for putting more money into existing programs rather than really reforming them.

That's the case here. But that's what is happening at the summit. Down in the valleys, where the people live, you will find there that the people in the frontlines, the leaders in the frontlines, the Governors, the mayors, the county officials, an overwhelming majority of them, are for revenue sharing—both general revenue sharing and the other—an overwhelming majority, and also an overwhelming majority of the people of this country are for revenue sharing.

Now, eventually, then, it will be approved. I am not suggesting exactly in the form we have submitted it, but it will be approved because those of us who are in Washington have to reflect eventually what the majority of the people of this country feel.

And as I look at the situation now, I would say I expected that we would have this kind of opposition. However, I must say that the favorable reaction that we have had at the grass roots and among Governors and mayors and county officials has been greater than I expected, and that will be the decisive factor in getting it through.

Q: What do you visualize with regard to accounting procedures on this—what the GAO role would be—for the States and the county and city governments?

THE PRESIDENT: Well, first, let's distinguish the procedures with regard to civil rights guarantees. Those procedures, of course, will be set up in our revenue-sharing programs and the civil rights laws and requirements will be enforced.

We cannot have programs that are paid for by the tax money of all the people and benefit only some of the people. Second, however, with regard to accounting procedures, I can assure you that despite some speculation on this score we don't intend to set up a huge network of bureaucrats to go down and examine the cities and the counties and the States with regard to whether or not they are properly expending funds.

What we are going to do there is to try to handle each case on an individual basis; naturally, take action where there is a failure to use the funds properly, but not to set up simply more government guidelines.

MIDDLE EAST

Q: Could you take a couple of seconds on the Middle East, because it hasn't been brought up and I think it should be?

THE PRESIDENT: Sure.

Q: Israel seems to be balking on the Jarring proposal. If they continue to balk, would you use your powers of persuasion to get them to accept something along that line?

THE PRESIDENT: I don't think it would be helpful, Mr. Warren, to speculate here that we would use powers of persuasion with Israel or, for that matter, with Egypt or Jordan, on the Middle East.

Let me say this: that I have been encouraged—I am not overly optimistic and not Pollyannaish because this is a terribly·difficult area of the world, as I have pointed out in previous press conferences, with hatreds that go back over centuries and they are not going to be removed very easily, the hatreds, maybe never. But a live-and-let-live relationship may develop. But I have been encouraged by the developments that have occurred so far.

Egypt has been more forthcoming than we had expected and I believe that Israel has been somewhat more forthcoming. I have hopes that when the present cease-fire expires that it will be extended.

I will say that neither side will gain anything by starting the fighting again. It is a war in which either side will be a loser.

So as far as the Mideast is concerned—and I answered it in more detail simply to give you the tone of it—as far as the Mideast is concerned it is a difficult area. There are going to be day-to-day blasts by one side or the other or concessions by one side or the other before an eventual settlement is reached.

But for the United States publicly to move in and indicate what we think ought to be done while these delicate negotiations go on would not help.

SOUTHEAST ASIA

Q: Could I clear up what I think is an important point on Laos? You suggested that the Saigon regime is making the decisions as to what it will do in its own interest, particularly in reference to crossing the DMZ.

Most Americans believe that the decision to go into Laos was made in Washington and decisions like crossing the DMZ would have, necessarily, to be made here as well because of the use of American airpower.

Could you straighten out for us where the line is between the decisions that the Saigon regime will make and that this Government will make?

THE PRESIDENT: Any decision, Mr. Lisagor, that called for American participation would have to be approved in Washington. The decision with regard to Laos was one that was approved in Washington.

I approved the operation and I approved the decision to use American airpower. The operation itself was jointly developed, primarily by the South Vietnamese, but with, of course, very close cooperation and consultation with General Abrams and his staff.

But wherever American participation to any extent is required, you can be sure that that decision will be made here.

Now, when you put it in terms of what would happen in the event the South Vietnamese went into North Vietnam, I am not going to speculate on what they will or will not do. I will only say that any American participation has to be approved here.

If South Vietnam's decision with regard to what they do would depend upon American cooperation, then, of course, it could not be undertaken without our approval.

Reporter: Thank you, Mr. President.

MARCH 4

Following is the text, as made available by the White House, of President Nixon's March 4 televised news conference, his 15th news conference since taking office and his first since Feb. 17.

THE PRESIDENT: Will you be seated, please.

Mr. Cormier.

Q: We understand there are some difficulties that the South Vietnamese Army has encountered in Laos in recent weeks. Is this going to cause you to slow down the rate of American troop withdrawals?

THE PRESIDENT: No. As a matter of fact what has already been accomplished in Laos at this time has insured even more the plan for withdrawal of American troops. I will make another announcement in April as I have previously indicated. The disruption of the supply lines of the enemy through Laos, which has now occurred for three weeks, has very seriously damaged the enemy's ability to wage effective action against our remaining forces in Vietnam which assures even more the success of our troop withdrawal program.

There is one other point that has been assured. I have just had a report from General Abrams today with regard to the performance of the South Vietnamese. You ladies and gentlemen will recall that at the time of Cambodia I pointed out that the South Vietnamese Army had come of age. But then they were fighting side by side with American ground forces. Now in Southern Laos and also in Cambodia, the South Vietnamese on the ground by themselves are taking on the very best units that the North Vietnamese can put in the field.

General Abrams tells me that in both Laos and in Cambodia his evaluation after three weeks of fighting is that—to use his terms—the South Vietnamese by themselves can hack it, and they can give an even better account of themselves than the North Vietnamese units. This means that our withdrawal program, our Vietnamization program is a success, and can continue on schedule, and we trust even ahead of schedule, assuming there is more progress in Laos.

INVASION OF NORTH VIETNAM

Q: This is a question that you addressed yourself to at your last news conference, but I would like to ask it again in view of the fact that President Thieu has publicly said several times that there is a possibility of South Vietnamese forces invading North Vietnam. Would the United States support such an invasion of North Vietnam by the South Vietnamese?

THE PRESIDENT: Mr. Risher, I think it is important to re-state the answer that I gave at the last News Conference, because you will recall that was in the office where only you ladies and gentlemen who regularly cover the White House were present, and the television audience did not hear the answer.

To re-state it completely, let me break it down into its component parts. First, the question is, what will President Thieu in South Vietnam do. The second question is, what will the United States do. And, third, what might we do together? Now, on the first question, President Thieu has stated that he would consider the necessity of invading North Vietnam. Let us look at his position. There are no South Vietnamese in North

Vietnam. There are 100,000 North Vietnamese in South Vietnam and they have already killed over 200,000 South Vietnamese. Therefore, President Thieu has to take the position that unless the North Vietnamese leave South Vietnam alone, he has to consider the possibility of going against the North. That is his position, and I am not going to speculate on what position he might take in the future. In order to defend himself, the right of self-defense, in view of the fact that he is being attacked, he is not attacking North Vietnam.

The second part of the question deals with what we will do. There, as you recall, I stated that American policy is that we will have no ground forces in North Vietnam, in Cambodia or in Laos, except, of course, for rescue teams which go in for American flyers or for prisoners of war where we think there is an opportunity in that case.

On the other hand, I have stated on ten different occasions, usually before Press Conferences in which you ladies and gentlemen have participated, that in two respects we would use air power against the North. One is that we would attack those missile sites that fired at our planes, and we have been doing that. We will continue to do that.

Second, if I determine that increased infiltration from North Vietnam endanger our remaining forces in South Vietnam at a time we were withdrawing, I would order attacks on the supply routes, to infiltration routes, on the military complexes, and I have done that in the past. I shall do so again if I determine that such activities by North Vietnam may endanger our remaining forces in South Vietnam, particularly as we are withdrawing.

Now, the third question is this one—whether or not the United States, through its air power, might support a South Vietnamese operation against North Vietnam. The answer to that is that no such plan is under consideration in this Government.

Q: On the subject of enemy missiles, the North Vietnamese seem to be using more and perhaps a different type of missile shooting American planes supporting the Laos operation.

I wonder if this is of unusual alarm to you and if you have any special retaliation other than bombing that you intend to take?

THE PRESIDENT: We are following that very closely, and it is not unusually alarming. We expect the enemy to improve its capabilities just as we improve ours. We are prepared to take the protective reaction measures which will deal very effectively with them. But I can say it will not be tit for tat.

Mr. Horner.

SYMINGTON—ROGERS—KISSINGER

Q: In view of recent remarks by Senator Symington and Senator Fulbright, can you define for us the roles and relative influence in the formulation of foreign policy of Secretary of State Rogers and of Dr. Kissinger?

THE PRESIDENT: Well, Mr. Horner, you have been around Washington even a little longer than I have and, as I am sure you will agree, this game of trying to divide the President from his Secretary of State or to create a conflict between the Secretary of State and whoever happens to be the President's Adviser for National Security Affairs has been going on for as long as I can remember, and I understand it has been going on long before I got here.

I think Senator Symington's attack upon the Secretary frankly was a cheap shot. I say that not in condemnation of him for making the statement, but I say it only because he knows the relationship between Secretary Rogers and me. He knows that Secretary Rogers is my oldest and closest friend in the Cabinet. I have known him for 24 years.

I not only respect his ability and take his advice in the field of foreign policy; I also ask his advice and often take it in many domestic concerns as well. He is the foreign policy adviser for the President. He is the chief foreign policy spokesman for the President. He participates in every decision that is made by the President of the United States. He will continue to participate in those decisions.

Now, the role of Dr. Kissinger is a different one. He is the White House Adviser to the President. He covers not only foreign policy but national security policy; the coordination of those policies. He also gives me advice just as Secretary Laird gives me advice in matters of Defense. I would say that I respect his advice as well.

As to whether either Secretary Rogers or Dr. Kissinger is the top adviser, as to who is on first, the answer to that, of course, is very simply that the Secretary of State is always the chief foreign policy adviser and the chief foreign policy spokesman of the Administration.

At the same time, the Assistant to the President for National Security Affairs does advise the President, and I value his advice very much.

TROOP WITHDRAWALS

Q: Mr. President, there is some feeling in this city and perhaps around the country that you are trying to prepare the American people for the possibility that between 50,000 and 100,000 American troops will still have to be in South Vietnam by election time next year.

Is that true?

THE PRESIDENT: I really can't tell you what the feeling is in this city. I can tell you what my own plans are.

We are for a total withdrawal of all American forces on a mutual basis. As far as those forces are concerned, I have stated in this press conference that Gene Risher referred to a moment ago, I have stated, however, that as long as there are American POWs—and there are 1,600 Americans in North Vietnam jails under very difficult circumstances at the present time—as long as there are American POWs in North Vietnam we will have to maintain a residual force in South Vietnam. That is the least that we can negotiate for.

As far as our goal is concerned, our goal is to get all Americans out of Vietnam as soon as we can by negotiation if possible and through our withdrawal program and Vietnamization program if necessary.

Now, as to when we will have them out, I will make the announcements in due time. I have another one coming in April, and I will be making other announcements. And I think the record will be a pretty good one when we have concluded.

Mr. Bailey.

Q: Speaking of the potentialities of action against North Vietnam, you were talking on the third point about the possibility of American air support for a South Vietnamese attack. You said that no such plan was under consideration in this government. Can you go any further than that, or is that all you wish to say about it?

THE PRESIDENT: Mr. Bailey, I can say further that no such plan has ever been suggested by President Thieu to us. None has been considered, and none is under consideration.

I am not going to go further than that, except to state what I did state in that press conference where you also were present again, that the test as to what the United States will do in North Vietnam, in any event, will always be not what happens to forces of South Vietnam, but it will be whether or not the President as Commander in Chief considers that North Vietnamese activities are endangering or may endanger the American forces as we continue to withdraw.

It is then and only then that I will use air power against military complexes on the borders of North Vietnam.

Q: Mr. President, sir, if all of the North Vietnamese troops were to be withdrawn from South Vietnam, would we still insist that American troops would not be withdrawn until North Vietnamese troops also left Cambodia and Laos?

THE PRESIDENT: The proposal we have made, Mr. Horst, is, of course, for a Southeast Asia settlement, one in which the North Vietnamese troops—there are 40,000 approximately, as

you know, in Cambodia, there are now approximately, by latest estimate, 90,000 to 100,000 in Laos and, of course, there are 100,000 or so in South Vietnam. It is a one-package situation.

As far as we are concerned, that is the proposal and that is the one that we will stick by in Paris.

CHINA POLICY

Q: In your foreign policy report, you invited better relations with Communist China, which is being interpreted in, Taiwan, I believe, with a little bit of apprehension. Are you actually moving toward a two-China policy?

THE PRESIDENT: I understand the apprehension in Taiwan, but I believe that that apprehension insofar as Taiwan's continued existence and as its continued membership in the United Nations is not justified. You also have noted that in my foreign policy report I said that we stood by our defense commitments to Taiwan, that Taiwan, which has a larger population than two-thirds of all of the United Nations, could not and would not be expelled from the United Nations as long as we had anything to say about it, and that as far as our attitude toward the Communist China was concerned that that would be governed by Communist China's attitude toward us.

In other words, we would like to normalize relations with all nations in the world. There has, however, been no receptivity on the part of Communist China. But under no circumstances will we proceed with a policy of normalizing relations with Communist China if the cost of that policy is to expel Taiwan from the family of nations.

Mr. Lisagor.

PARIS PEACE TALKS

Q: On the Foreign Policy Report, even if the North Vietnamese negotiate seriously in Paris, there will be serious problems left in Laos and Cambodia, and on the battlefield there would be some hard options to be made about deploying allied troops. Will you clarify those statements, because it suggests that we are going to be there a much longer time than your earlier answer did.

THE PRESIDENT: Mr. Lisagor, our goal is a complete American withdrawal from Cambodia, Laos and South Vietnam. As you know, that is the proposal I made on October 7th. I made it, however, on a mutual basis, that we would withdraw, but that the North Vietnamese would withdraw at the same time.

Now, as to what happens after we withdraw, we cannot guarantee that North and South Vietnam will not continue to be enemies. We cannot guarantee that there will not continue to be some kind of guerilla activities in Laos or even in Cambodia. As far as our own goal is concerned, our proposal is clear and we ask the enemy to consider it: A mutual withdrawal of forces, our forces and theirs. If that happens, we will be glad to withdraw, and then these other nations will have to see whether or not they can handle their own affairs.

Mr. Theis.

EXECUTIVE PRIVILEGE

A: Do you see any limit on the exercise of executive privilege?

THE PRESIDENT: The matter of executive privilege is one that always depends on which side you are on. I well recall—and, Mr. Theis, you were covering me at the time when I was a Member of the House—that I raised serious questions as a member of an investigating committee about the executive privilege that was at that time, looking back in retrospect, properly insisted upon by President Truman. And, as President, I believe that executive privilege is essential for the orderly processes of government.

Now, let me just point out, however, what it does not cover. I was very surprised to note the suggestion that the Secretary of

State was not available enough for testimony. I checked it out. Over the past two years, State Department officials have testified 499 times before the House and the Senate. The Secretary of State himself has testified personally 14 times in 1969 and 15 times in 1970. He has had 167 private meetings in addition to all that with individual Senators or in groups of Senators at the State Department or at his home. As a matter of fact, I don't know how he has had time to talk to me with all the time he is talking to the Congress.

RESIDUAL FORCES

Q: Mr. President, you said earlier that there will have to be a residual force staying in South Vietnam as long as the North Vietnamese continue to hold prisoners.

You have also said on previous occasions that you will not hesitate to take any strong action in order to protect whatever troops remain in South Vietnam, whatever of our troops remain in South Vietnam.

Does this, in effect, mean that despite your Vietnamization plan that you will have to have, in a sense, an indefinite commitment to South Vietnam with troops there indefinitely determined only by Hanoi and their actions?

THE PRESIDENT: I would suggest that you ladies and gentlemen always pretty much underestimate what I am capable of doing in terms of withdrawing forces and so forth.

Let me just put it all in perspective, as I can. We have had a great deal of discussion about Laos at the last press conference and I can see that it is still of interest here, and the question of Cambodia still troubles many of you.

I recall at the time that we went into Cambodia, and all of you out there looking on television will remember what I said, I said the purpose of our going into Cambodia was to cut American casualties and to ensure the success of our withdrawal program.

Many of the members of the press disagreed with me. They thought that was not an accurate description of what would happen. They were entitled to that view. Night after night, after I announced the decision to go into Cambodia, on television it was indicated that that decision would have the opposite effect; that it would increase American casualties and that it would mean that it would prolong the war.

Now we can look at it in retrospect. Casualties are one-half of what they were before Cambodia and our withdrawal program has continued and actually we were able to step it up some during the last of 1970.

In Laos, the purpose of the Laotian operation was the same as that of the Cambodian operation. This time no American ground forces, only American air power.

I said then, and I repeat now, that the purpose is not to expand the war into Laos; the purpose is to save American lives, to guarantee the continued withdrawal of our own forces, and to increase the ability of the South Vietnamese to defend themselves without our help, which means, of course, their ability to help our Vietnamization program and our own withdrawal program.

I realize that night after night for the past three weeks on television there is a drum beat of suggestion, not from all but from some commentators. And I can understand why they disagree, from the same ones that said Cambodia wouldn't work, that this isn't going to work.

Well, I had analyzed the thing very carefully when I made the decision. I have had reports all day today from General Abrams and, speaking today, I can say there is some hard fighting ahead, but the decision to go into Laos, I think, was the right decision. It will reduce American casualties. The 200,000 rounds of ammunition, the 2,000 heavy and light guns that have already been captured and destroyed, the 67 tanks that have been destroyed are not going to be killing Americans.

And, most significantly, I checked the flow of supplies down the trails from the area in which the North Vietnamese and the South Vietnamese are engaged. And General Abrams reports

that there has been a 55 percent decrease in truck traffic south into South Vietnam, which means that those trucks that do not go South will not carry the arms and the men that will be killing Americans.

We can all, of course, here in a press conference—we can debate as to whether or not my view of it is right or the rest. I hope for the good of the country mine is, and if it is right, what you say now doesn't make any difference.

I am only suggesting while the jury is still out, remember the purpose of this, like the purpose of Cambodia, is to reduce American forces, to reduce our casualties. And I should point out that that is exactly what this Administration has done. We have kept every promise that we made. We have reduced our forces. We have reduced our casualties. We are going to continue to reduce our forces, and we are getting out of Vietnam in a way that Vietnam will be able to defend itself.

Q: Mr. President, partisans in Turkey have kidnapped four of our flyers and are holding them for $400,000 ransom. Do you think the Turkish Government should negotiate with the terrorists and is there anything that you think that we can or should do in a situation like this?

THE PRESIDENT: Mr. Healy, we have had that situation with several other governments. I would not suggest that the Turkish Government negotiate on this matter because I believe that is a decision that that government must make, having in mind its own internal situation.

Mr. Semple.

MIDDLE EAST

Q: The Arabs have reportedly agreed to sign a peace treaty with Israel in exchange for certain withdrawals by Israel from the territory occupied in 1967. Is it not now time for the Israelis to make some concessions of their own and will you be asking them publicly or privately to do so?

THE PRESIDENT: Mr. Semple, as you well know, because you are sophisticated in this area, the question there is whether or not the United States will impose a settlement in the Mid-East, and the answer is no. We will do everything that we can to urge the parties to talk. And, incidentally, when we talk about the problems in the Mid-East, let it not go unnoted that we have made some progress. There was four years of fighting up until August of last year, and for seven months no guns have fired in the Mid-East. That is progress of a kind.

We hope that the cease fire either by agreement or de facto will be extended. We hope the Israelis and the Egyptians and, for that matter the Jordanians, will continue some kind of discussion. As far as imposing a settlement, however, we can only say that we can make suggestions, but we are going to have to depend upon the parties concerned to reach an agreement.

We, of course, will be there to see that the balance of power is maintained in the Mid-East. We will continue to do so, because if that balance changes that could bring on war, and also we are prepared, as I have indicated, to join other major powers including the Soviet Union in guaranteeing any settlement that is made, which would give Israel the security of its borders that it might not get through any geographical acquisition.

Q: You said earlier about Communist China, at least you were perfectly clear about your position on Communist China seeking entrance in the United Nations. Someone asked you if you would favor a two-China policy, but you were not completely clear about that. Could you say, sir, if Taiwan maintained its position on the Security Council, if it maintained its position in the United Nations, if you would favor seating Communist China.

THE PRESIDENT: That is a moot question at this time, because Communist China or the People's Republic of China, which I understand stirred up people in Taiwan because that is the official name of the country, but Communist China refuses even to discuss the matter. Therefore, it would not be appropriate for me to suggest what we might agree to when Communist China takes the position that they will have no discussion whatever until Taiwan gets out. We will not start with that kind of a proposition. Mr. Warren?

SALT TALKS

Q: A few months back, you were quite optimistic about the successful conclusion of the SALT talks. Are you less optimistic now?

THE PRESIDENT: I am just as optimistic now as I was then about the eventual success. As you will note from our World Policy Report, the two great super-powers now have nuclear parity. Neither can gain an advantage over the other if the other desires to see to it that that does not occur. Now, under these circumstances, therefore, it is in the interest of both powers to negotiate some kind of limitation, a limitation on offensive and defensive weapons. We will be stating a position on that on March 15 when the new talks begin in Vienna. As far as when an agreement is reached, I will not indicate optimism or pessimism. As far as the eventuality of an agreement, my belief is that the seriousness of the talks, the fact that there are great forces, the danger of war, the escalating costs, and the fact that neither power can gain an advantage over the others, I think that this means that there will be an agreement eventually between the United States and the Soviet Union.

Yes, sir?

Q: And defensive weapons?

THE PRESIDENT: I should add that I know that the suggestion has been made that we might negotiate a separate agreement on defensive weapons alone. We respect that proposal. We will negotiate an agreement that is not comprehensive but it must include offensive as well as defensive weapons, some mix.

Mr. Kaplow.

TROOP WITHDRAWALS

Q: Mr. President, I would like to go back for a moment to your first answer in which you said that what has happened in Laos has already assured more troop withdrawals.

Were you saying that on the basis of what you obviously consider a success in the Laotian operation will allow you to withdraw American troops at at least the present rate of twelve and a half thousand men a month for 12 months?

THE PRESIDENT: What I am saying, Mr. Kaplow, is that our troop withdrawal schedule will go forward at least at the present rate. It will go forward for at least the present rate.

And when I make the announcement in April, that, of course, will cover several months in advance. More important, however, is the troop withdrawal schedule for next year because, as you will note in my foreign policy report, at least, the oral report I made, I pointed out that the Laotian operation this year would save American lives, save American lives by destroying or capturing equipment that otherwise might move into I Corps where a number of Americans are located. And that next year it would serve to guarantee the continued success of our withdrawal program.

The more that the disruption of the complex of trails leading from North Vietnam to South Vietnam occurs in the operation now being conducted on the ground by the South Vietnamese in southern Laos—the more that that occurs, the more successful that it is, the greater the possibility that the United States may be able to increase the rate of its troop withdrawal.

I am not prepared to make that decision yet, but we can say at this time the troop withdrawal will continue at its present level. I can say, incidentally, that even since the Laotian operation began, with all the news, 10,000 Americans have come home in this period.

THE PRESS: Thank you, Mr. President.

MARCH 22

Following are excerpts from ABC commentator Howard K. Smith's interview with President Nixon on March 22, 1971:

CONGRESS

MR. SMITH: Don't you think your job would be a lot easier if you carried Congress with you? Senator Fulbright has complained that Congress has absolutely no control over foreign affairs. Two major actions, Cambodia and Laos, were undertaken with little information to and without the advice of Congress. Doesn't he have a point?

THE PRESIDENT: Well, Senator Fulbright has a point with regard to himself, yes. But I should point out that if a majority of the Congress, Mr. Smith, disapproved of what the President was doing in Cambodia or in Laos, the majority of the Congress can act, and it can act by cutting off the funds. The majority of the Congress has not done that.

You may recall that the Supplemental Appropriation Bill of $1 billion at the end of last year was passed by both Houses of Congress. Those votes will be close. There is great debate in the Congress. I respect the Congress. I would like to be able to carry the Congress perhaps better than we have. I would like better understanding in the Congress.

But, on the other hand, it is the responsibility of the President of the United States, particularly when as Commander in Chief he has responsibility for the lives of American men, to make those decisions that are going to save those lives. Cambodia saved the lives of American men.

And may I say, too, that the thousands of North Vietnamese who were casualties in North Vietnam, the hundreds and millions of rounds of ammunition that were destroyed there, the time that was bought there, all of these things—that means that the risk to American lives is substantially reduced, and that is why the support of that operation was worthwhile, in my opinion.

MR. SMITH: The members of Congress obviously feel left out, feel they don't have much control, and a subsidiary complaint made by Senator Fulbright is that Congress has no access to White House aides who have played an ever larger role in advising on foreign affairs. The New York Times said the other day a coup d'etat could hardly deprive the people's elected representatives more completely of their constitutional powers than this gradual process of the White House without accounting taking over foreign affairs. Is there something to that?

THE PRESIDENT: It is an old argument, Mr. Smith. As you know, from having studied many Presidents before this one, it has been raised with regard to virtually every Presidential advisor, and there is nothing to it.

I have Presidential advisors—Dr. Kissinger. I have my prime foreign policy advisors, the Secretary of State, with whom I just talked before coming on this program, and the Secretary of Defense for national security policy, with whom I just talked before coming on this program. Both of them, incidentally, have been testifying this week before the Congress; some in private and some in public session.

As far as a Presidential advisor is concerned, however, he cannot be hauled down before the Congress. Then you are going to have two Secretaries of State. You cannot have that, there being only one.

MR. SMITH: Aside from the fact that you have the responsibility, wouldn't it be simply politically prudent if you invited the Senate Foreign Affairs Committee here every month and had a talk with them and listened to their suggestions and explained your point of view to them informally and gave them a sense of participation?

THE PRESIDENT: I would have to go really further than that. I would have to take the Foreign Affairs Committee and the Armed Services Committee and the Appropriations Committees, all of which, of course, have some significant control over these policies.

At the time of Cambodia, as Senator Fulbright will recall, I did have the whole group down and we discussed some of these matters and I answered questions.

The possibility of having meetings on an informal basis with Committee members is something that I can consider. I see many of them individually.

For example, Senator Aiken, Senator Mansfield—I see him virtually every two to three weeks for breakfast as the Majority Leader. Any Senator who asks to see me usually gets in to see me. It is a question of time.

MR. SMITH: The story keeps recurring that access to you is difficult. Newsweek carries a story this week that Secretary Volpe is having a hard time seeing you, as Mr. Hickel complained he did. In the case of Senators, I will use names. A year ago Senator Javits, Republican, New York, the best vote-getter in the State for your Party, said he had not been consulted by you on anything.

And Senator Dole, increasingly your spokesman, was heard to complain recently that he had been "shunned off" to lesser White House aides. Is that true?

THE PRESIDENT: I think there is no substitute, Mr. Smith, for seeing the man in the Oval Office, and yet while my schedule, as you probably are aware, due to a rather disciplined schedule unless I have a guest, I eat breakfast alone in five minutes, never have guests for lunch—I do that in five minutes, too. I perhaps put more time in the day than any President could put in, and it is because it is my way and not bragging about it.

But in terms of the number of people I see, the number of Senators, the number of Cabinet Officers, the number of appointments, I would say that it is probably a record. But the more you see naturally the more others who don't get in as often want to see you. It is not possible to meet this adequately, but the only way I can figure it out is to cut another hour off of my sleep, but then I wouldn't be as sharp on this program.

MR. SMITH: The kind of thing I am concerned about is I see—this is a prediction—the next two years being dominated by this political theme: The age old conflict between the Executive and Congress, but in sharper form than ever. Resolutions are being prepared in the Senate to try and require your aides to testify and resolutions limiting your powers as Commander-in-Chief.

There is another assault coming from another quarter and I don't know whether you are aware of it. But tomorrow morning Senator Ervin begins hearings on the impounding of funds by you which had been appropriated by Congress. It is said that several billions of dollars that Congress is appropriating for things like dams and so on you have refused to spend, that this violates the Constitution and deprives Congress of its main power, the power of the purse.

THE PRESIDENT: Mr. Smith, when I was a Senator and a Congressman, particularly when I was a Senator and a Congressman with a President in the other party in the White House, I played all of those games, too, with very little success.

These games are going to be played. The efforts will be made, it is true, by Members of the Senate, Members of the House and some of them with the very best of intentions to hamstring the Executive, the President. When it is the proper thing to do, it will be done.

But I think, generally speaking, you will find that in these great battles that have occurred through the years, between the President and the Congress, that sometimes the Congress wins, sometimes the President wins. But where the President's responsibility as Commander-in-Chief of the Armed Forces is concerned, and where the lives of American men are involved, usually the President wins and for good reason. You can have only one Commander-in-Chief.

We get back to this business of why not pass a resolution saying that we will get out of Vietnam by Christmas of this year. It is very easy to pass a resolution. It would be very popular for me, as a matter of fact, to sponsor it.

On the other hand, it is my judgment, as I have already indicated, that such a resolution would not be in the interest

of the security of our own forces, not be in the interest of the negotiations, the possibility of negotiating the release of our prisoners and not in the interest of the United States long run in terms of ending this war in a way that might discourage another war coming.

That is my judgment. I have to fight for that judgment. If the Congress determines to move in another direction, so be it. I don't think it will, though, and I don't think the American people will support the Congress whenever it fights the President in his honest effort to serve as Commander-in-Chief, in that service to protect the lives of American men and to, in addition, conduct policy in a way that will avoid those lives being lost, we hope, at some future time.

POLITICS

MR. SMITH: Mr. President, let me ask you some political questions now, because we are approaching the political year.

As you have acknowledged, the Republican Party is the nation's minority party. No matter how often we reporters pronounce the old FDR coalition dead—the blacks, the poor, labor and so on—every election it seems to pull together enough to keep the Democrats the majority party.

What plans have you got, what strategies do you intend to pursue to try to put the Republican Party back where it was before 1932, the permanent majority party?

THE PRESIDENT: That probably will not happen, Mr. Smith, to either the Republican or the Democratic Party. The Democratic Party is not a majority party either, as you know, because approximately, you could take the pollsters, approximately 42 to 43 percent of the people consider themselves to be Democrats. Then approximately 30 percent consider themselves Republicans and the other 30 percent consider themselves to be Independents.

So, we will never have a time again, in my opinion, in this country when you are going to have a polarization of Democrats versus Republicans. I think you are going to have the Independents controlling basically the balance of power.

Also, when you look at the Democratic Party, you must remember that that 43 percent is somewhat overblown because it has particular weight because of the South. And many southern Democrats, and I can say this looking back at our policies in the field of foreign policy and defense policy, many southern Democrats in the House and Senate are our best support—best supporters of this President, not because he is a Republican, but because they think it is in the best interests of the country.

So, in my view, I do not believe that either the Republican or Democratic Party will have a decisive majority such as the Republican Party had before 1932, such as the Democratic Party had in the period of the Roosevelt years.

What I think will happen is that both parties will vie for building the new coalition, starting with their hard core of hearty supporters and then moving into that group of Independents trying to get a field of the Independent voters and also moving over into the other party and picking up a considerable number of them.

MR. SMITH: Talking about forming a coalition, the first Republican President in our history, he wanted to unite the nations, when he ran for re-election he decided the best thing he could do was choose a Democrat as a running mate. I know you admire Abraham Lincoln. Do you think there are other circumstances in which you will want to imitate him in this respect?

THE PRESIDENT: Mr. Smith, when I went on this program, you remember I told you you could ask me anything, but I would have to determine what I answered.

As you may recall, I said after the election of 1970 that 1970 was a political year and I, therefore, did my job in working for the candidates of my party; that 1971 is non-political, and that I would not engage in political activities in 1971.

I recognize that is an intriguing question. I probably have a very good answer. But I think that I will defer giving any answers at this time. Maybe ask me next year at this time and I will give you an answer.

MR. SMITH: Mr. President, I will tell you a secret: I didn't expect an answer.

In one of your speeches you said you would rather be a one-term President than settle in Vietnam dishonorably. A columnist recently has said that you have told a private person that you might voluntarily become a one-term President if your plans do not succeed by 1972.

Have you given serious thought to voluntarily becoming a one-term President?

THE PRESIDENT: Mr. Smith, let me say, first, I have made no decisions with regard to what I will do in 1972, either for myself or for whoever may be the man who runs for Vice President.

On the other hand, I could say categorically that I have certainly made no decisions indicating that I will not be a candidate in '72, not that I will be or that I will not be.

The idea of what you call voluntary retirement, I would suggest, is quite premature where I am concerned, and I would say that anybody who reads my life would perhaps take that kind of a story with a grain of salt.

APRIL 16

Following is the text, as made available by the Federal Register, of President Nixon's April 16 responses to questions at a panel discussion during the annual meeting of the American Society of Newspaper Editors in Washington, D.C.

THE PRESIDENT: President Noyes, President-elect Mc-Knight,* all of the distinguished guests at the head table, and all of the distinguished delegates and members of the ASNE:

It is a very great privilege for me to appear again before this organization, as the president indicated a few moments ago, for the first time in my new capacity. I also wish to congratulate President Newby Noyes on his service as president of this organization.

I understand you have a one-term tradition. I am not sure that is a good idea—(*Laughter*)—but, nevertheless, I congratulate Mr. McKnight on his election as your new president. I understand that after we finish with this distinguished panel you will have the opportunity to have him sworn in, and then he will make his inaugural speech to which we will all listen.

Tonight, the panel has already been introduced and we will go directly to the questions, because I know there will be many. I understand that Mr. Dickinson, on my right—I always turn right first—(*Laughter*)—Mr. Dickinson will have the first question.

Mr. Dickinson.

PRESIDENT'S WORRIES

WILLIAM DICKINSON (Executive Editor, *The Philadelphia Bulletin*): Mr. President, I suppose that like most of us, you must have times when you wake up at 3 a.m. or 4 a.m. and you lie there in the predawn darkness and you think or even worry a little bit. I wonder, sir, if you would tell us what thoughts or worries at this stage of your Presidency come to mind at a time like that?

THE PRESIDENT: We have six members of the panel, too.

Well, Mr. Dickinson, it is quite true that just like every other person who has problems, the President of the United States does wake up in the middle of the night and he worries about sometimes personal problems but usually about problems of the Nation, with which he has tried to wrestle during the day.

I think more often than not the problems I worry about at night are those involving foreign policy. That seems to be neces-

Newbold Noyes, Jr., Editor of the Washington Star, and O.A. Pete McKnight, Editor of the Charlotte, N.C., Observer.

sary at this time in the Presidency—not that the great domestic problems, the problems of the economy, the problems of race relations, the problems of the younger generation, et cetera, do not often also cause great concern in the middle of the night as well as in the daytime.

But at night, if there is any one subject that more often than not comes across my mind, it is what can I do the next day that will contribute toward the goal of a lasting peace for America and for the world.

That is almost a trite statement. Every President wants that. Every President has worked for it. But we have seen so much in this century—wars ended and then another war coming, wars ended with great hopes of lasting peace and then the foundations laid for another war.

I believe now we are ending American involvement in a war we are in, a very difficult war. But we are going to end it in a way that will contribute to a lasting peace. And then beyond that I believe that we are entering a new era of relations with other superpowers in the world, a new era, for example, in our relations with the Soviet Union and a new era in potential relationships with the People's Republic of China. I don't mean that at 3 a.m. in the morning I make decisions as to what we are going to do about China policy or Soviet policy or the Mideast or Berlin or the rest, but I do know that sometimes the mind is clearer then, the thoughts come through much sharper than they do in the morning.

I have a little habit—I will let you all in on my secrets. You can use it for the p.m.'s, if you don't mind. But I write it down. And sometimes in the morning it doesn't look so good, but sometimes the ideas are pretty good. I haven't answered your question as well as I might except to indicate that I am sure that President Johnson when he was there, President Kennedy when he was in that room, President Eisenhower when he was there, whenever they woke up in the middle of the night, their primary concern must have been peace for America and for the world. It is something we haven't had for a full generation in this century. It is something I think we can have now and that is what we are working for, and that is what we are going to get.

U.S. INVOLVEMENT IN VIETNAM

EMMETT DEDMON (Vice President and Editorial Director, *Chicago Sun-Times* and the *Chicago Daily News*): Mr. President, you mentioned ending our involvement in the war in Vietnam and, yet, the Secretary of Defense said the other day that our Air Force and naval power would remain in South Vietnam.

How do you reconcile those two statements or is there a conflict there in your opinion?

THE PRESIDENT: No, Mr. Dedmon, there really isn't a conflict between the two statements. I said that we would end our involvement in Vietnam. You will recall my speech last Wednesday. I said that our goal is a total American withdrawal from Vietnam.

On October 7 of last year you may recall I said that we not only propose a total American withdrawal but a cease-fire all over Southeast Asia which would, of course, mean no airpower, no American forces there, no use of power in any way.

As far as Mr. Laird's statement was concerned, what he was referring to was that pending the time that we can have a total withdrawal consistent with the principles that I laid down in my speech last week, it will be necessary for the United States to retain air power and to retain some residual forces.

Our goal, however, is a total withdrawal. We do not have as a goal a permanent residual force such as we have in Korea at the present time.

But it will be necessary for us to maintain forces in South Vietnam until two important objectives are achieved: one, the release of the prisoners of war held by North Vietnam in North Vietnam and other parts of Southeast Asia, and two, the ability of the South Vietnamese to develop the capacity to defend themselves against a Communist takeover, not the sure capacity, but at least the chance.

Once those two objectives are achieved, then the total American withdrawal can be undertaken and will be undertaken.

We can achieve them earlier, provided the enemy will negotiate. As you noticed, on October 7 I indicated we will have a total withdrawal in 12 months if they would be willing to mutually withdraw their forces.

And so, in sum, the goal of American policy in Vietnam is a total withdrawal with no residual force. But, as long as the prisoner issue remains unsettled, and as long as they hold prisoners, and as long as the South Vietnamese have not yet developed the capacity to defend themselves to take over from us the defense of their own country—a capacity that they rapidly are developing—we will have forces there.

MR. DEDMON: Mr. President, may I follow up with one more question?

THE PRESIDENT: Yes, I understand—all follow up if you want to.

TROOP WITHDRAWAL GOALS

MR. DEDMON: I realize that you do not wish to state a date at this time at which we will withdraw, and that there was some confusion in the press about what Senator Scott said following a meeting at the White House. Could I ask this question: Is Senator Scott's use of the date January 1, 1973, in your opinion, a practicable goal?

THE PRESIDENT: Mr. Dedmon, that is a very clever way to get me to answer a question that I won't answer. *(Laughter)* I would expect that from an editor as well as from a reporter.

The date, let me say, cannot and must not be related to an election in the United States. Let's begin with that. I don't want one American to be in Vietnam one day longer than is necessary to achieve the two goals that I have mentioned: the release of our prisoners and the capacity of the South Vietnamese to defend themselves against a Communist takeover.

Now, as far as that date is concerned, it will depend upon the circumstances. I have announced a troop withdrawal which takes us through November (December) 1st. In the middle of October (November), I will make another troop withdrawal announcement.

I will then analyze the training of the South Vietnamese forces and particularly their air force at that time. I will then analyze enemy activity and, also, any progress in negotiation, particularly in negotiation with regard to prisoners.

At that time, I will be able to make a further announcement with regard to what our withdrawal will be. But for me to speculate about a date would not help us; it would only serve the enemy, and I am not going to do that even though it might be politically popular to set a date.

I have to do what is right for the United States, right for our prisoners, and right for our goal of a South Vietnam with a chance to avoid a Communist takeover which will contribute to a lasting peace in the Pacific and the world.

CALLEY CASE

EUGENE V. RISHER (White House Correspondent, United Press International): Mr. President, I would like to ask you about the Calley case. Captain Daniel, the prosecutor in the case, has said that by publicly interjecting yourself in it, you have undermined the military system of justice and done a disservice to some of the people that are fighting in Vietnam honorably. Can you respond to this?

THE PRESIDENT: Well, Captain Daniel is a fine officer. And, incidentally, the six members of that court had very distinguished military records.

Five of the six, as you know, Mr. Risher, had served with distinction in Vietnam. I respect the prosecutor. I respect also the judicial process under which they acted and I respect those that served on the court.

I acted as I did because one of my capacities is Commander in Chief of the Armed Forces. There was enormous interest in this case. There was concern expressed throughout the Nation with regard to that decision, going far beyond the innocence or guilt of Captain (Lieutenant) Calley with regard to the charges.

I felt that under the circumstances, I should take two steps that I think are completely consistent with upholding the judicial process of the Armed Forces.

One, it seemed to me that if in civilian cases where an individual is charged with a crime, he can get out on bail, it seemed to me that the least that could be done would be to say that Captain (Lieutenant) Calley, pending the time that an appeal made his sentence final, should not be sent to Leavenworth Prison, but should be confined to his quarters.

I think that was the right decision to make about that man at that time.

The second point had to do with my decision that I announced, as you recall, you and Mr. Cormier, in California on Saturday morning, when I said that I, as President and as Commander in Chief, would exercise the authority which I had in such cases to review the case, that I would not pass the buck to a commission, I would not pass it to the Secretary of the Army, but in this case, because of the great public interest in the case, and because it went beyond simply the innocence or guilt of this one man, that I would review the case personally before final sentence was passed.

Now, as far as Captain Daniel's charge is concerned, I can only say that the action of the President, I think, was proper in terms of releasing him from going to Leavenworth and confining him to quarters on the base, and, second, I think it was proper to indicate that at some point in the judicial process, without impinging upon or impugning that process that I would review the case.

That is what I intend to do. I think it is consistent with the judicial process.

Yes, do you want to follow up? Go ahead.

FRANK CORMIER (White House Correspondent, Associated Press): A follow-up on that.

When John Ehrlichman told us of your decision to make the final review, he said, "Certainly, the widespread public interest in the case is a factor. It is not a determining factor." And he was rather vague as to what the determining factor was, apart from the flood of telegrams and so forth.

Could you enlighten us on that?

THE PRESIDENT: Well, Mr. Cormier, the widespread public interest was a factor in the sense that when people all over the Nation, their Congressmen and their Senators, are stirred up about a particular issue, a President, the President, has a responsibility to do what he can within the law to try to quiet those fears, to try to bring some perspective into the whole matter.

I think a pretty good indication that the action that I took was effective in that respect is that since that action we have seen the fears with regard to the Calley case subside because they know that he is going to get a fair review and a final review by the President of the United States.

Now, as far as the other factors, however, are concerned, it goes to this: As I have already implied in my answer to Mr. Risher, in addition to the innocence or guilt of Captain (Lieutenant) Calley with regard to the specific charges involved, there is the problem of trials for war crimes generally, and there is, of course, debate with regard to what should happen in those trials.

There are many other cases—not many—several other cases like his. Some have already been decided, some are still to be decided. It seemed to me under the circumstances that a Presidential statement at the highest level should be made once this case is completed, should be made setting the whole thing into perspective and without infringing upon his rights, a decision that would let the American people know, and the world know, why such a prosecution did take place and why it was upheld, or why it is not upheld.

I, of course, will not prejudge it at this time before it goes through the judicial process. I think it should be done and that is why I am doing it.

MR. CORMIER: On the other hand, Mr. President, the whole military system of justice was overhauled a very few years ago to try to eliminate, or at least minimize, command influence.

This, I think, is Captain Daniel's main argument, that just by the fact that you, as President of the United States and Commander in Chief, interjected yourself into it months before otherwise necessary, it is going to have a filterdown effect all the way.

THE PRESIDENT: The military system of justice, Mr. Cormier—and I checked this before I acted, with the Secretary of Defense—provides implicitly that the President of the United States at any time has the right to review, at any time has the right to intercede, if he believes that the national interest or the interests of the accused require it.

I felt that under these circumstances, the national interest required it and that is why I acted.

MR. MEYER of the Miami News.

SOUTHEAST ASIA

SYLVAN MEYER (Editor, *Miami News*): I would like to return, sir, to the matter of Southeast Asia.

The withdrawal of our troops from Vietnam—it appears a relatively short-run matter at whatever date it occurs.

Does this mean that we will be abandoning or materially changing our long-range strategic goals, the concepts in that part of the world, and do we regard our interests in that part of the world as having changed substantially because of this war?

THE PRESIDENT: Mr. Meyer, it does not mean that our interests have changed. It does mean that our method of contributing to the achievement of those interests has changed.

That is where what has been called the Nixon Doctrine comes in.

Again, Mr. Cormier and Mr. Risher will remember that when I was at Guam, I explained the Nixon Doctrine in brief.

It provides that where we have a situation as we have in South Vietnam, of a country that is threatened by an aggressive force from the outside, that the United States will try to help that country develop the capacity to defend itself, but that we will not do, if we can possibly avoid it, what we did in Korea and then what we again did in Vietnam—go in, in effect, and do the fighting for them—if we can avoid it.

Under our Vietnamization policy, we are getting out. That is one-half of it. But the other very important half of it is that the South Vietnamese are developing and by the time we get out, will have developed the capacity to defend themselves.

And, so, how that fits into our policy to Southeast Asia, it seems to me, is quite clear. Once we leave South Vietnam, South Vietnam will be strong enough, at least for the foreseeable future, to defend itself.

That will mean that in Indonesia, Malaysia, Singapore, Thailand, with which country, of course, we have a treaty, the Philippines, with which we have a treaty, will also have a greater assurance of stability.

And I think the repercussions will go clear up to Japan, because as we look at the rim-land of Asia, we must remember that in all of the debate at the present time and the great interest understandably, in what has happened with regard to Mainland China this last week, that on the rim-land of Asia live 300 million people. They produce three times as much as Mainland China and whether those people are going to remain free nations, independent nations, depends upon whether they think they have the capability and whether they can develop the capability of self-defense.

The policy of the United States—and this is a very significant change—is to help other nations, to help the Thais, to help the Indonesians, to help the Vietnamese, to help the Japanese, the others, develop the capability of defending themselves except, of course, where a nuclear attack would be involved and then the United States assumes the responsiblity.

PRISONERS OF WAR

OTIS CHANDLER (Publisher, *The Los Angeles Times*): Mr. President, what reason do you have to believe that—I realize that you hope to negotiate for the release of the prisoners of war but, assuming that might not be successful, what reason do you have to believe that the North Vietnamese might not keep our prisoners of war there for some time to come as hostages and to try to force the United States into withdrawing or ceasing all aid after our troops have left Vietnam, ceasing all military and economic aid to South Vietnam?

In other words, using them as hostages way into the future.

THE PRESIDENT: Well, Mr. Chandler, as you know, we have had some pretty bitter experiences with some Communist nations with regard to American prisoners. We have had a very difficult experience with the North Vietnamese who have, without question, been the most barbaric in their handling of prisoners of any nation in modern history. Under the circumstances, however, let's put ourselves in the position of North Vietnam. What is in it for them? What is in it for them is to get the United States residual force, including our airpower, out of that part of the world.

Now, that is a lot for them. That, it seems to me, will be a great incentive when the times comes that they have to make the decision as to whether they are going to retain prisoners or whether they are going to have to continue as they will have to continue to be exposed to an American presence in South Vietnam and to American air strikes which, of course, we will continue in the event that they play that kind of a game with the prisoners.

We have some cards to play, too, and we are going to play them right to the hilt where the prisoners are concerned.

MR. CHANDLER: Does this mean that if you are unsuccessful in negotiating at Paris on the POW question, that we will have to leave troops in there until you are successful?

THE PRESIDENT: Well, Mr. Chandler, it means that, first, we haven't given up on the Paris talks. I would suggest that the moment of truth is arriving with regard to the Paris talks because time will soon run out. As the number of our forces goes down, our stroke at the negotiating table recedes and the South Vietnamese's greatly increases.

So, if they want to negotiate with the United States, the time for negotiation, except for the prisoner issue, of course, is rapidly drawing to a close. But I would say that as far as our presence in South Vietnam is concerned—I am speaking of an American force, of a residual force, and of an air presence—that as long as they do retain prisoners, no American President could simply remove our forces and remove the threat to them.

We have the responsibility, as long as there is one American being held prisoner by North Vietnam, to have some incentive on our side to get that man released, and that is why we are going to retain that force until we get it, and I think it will work in the end.

MR. RISHER.

U.S. AIRBASES IN THAILAND

MR. RISHER: Mr. President, I would like to follow up on this. Does this mean that if Hanoi agreed to release the American prisoners, that we would close down the five airbases that we have in Thailand? Would this be part of the withdrawal?

THE PRESIDENT: No. Mr. Risher, the airbases that we have in the area around Vietnam, of course, are there for reasons other than Vietnam. Vietnam is part of the reason. As you know, we have a treaty with Thailand and those air forces are maintained there, in part, in order to sustain that treaty.

What it does mean, though, is that in terms of the use of airpower, the use of airpower against North Vietnam and its forces, that if at an appropriate time two things have been accomplished—one, the return of our prisoners, and the capability of the South Vietnamese to defend themselves—once those two things are achieved, then the use of that airpower as against North Vietnam would no longer be contemplated and, therefore, our airpower in that respect could be reduced.

I should also point out, incidentally, that we have had a great deal of attention, naturally, paid to the fact that we have withdrawn now almost half of the Americans that were there when we came into office, and that we will be down to 184,000 by November (December) 1 of this year.

Our air strikes, as you know, from having covered this closely from the White House, have also been reduced; our attack air sorties since we came into office have been reduced by 45 percent. They will continue to go down.

But, on the other hand, we must retain that airpower as well as residual forces, as long as we have the prisoner problem and as long as there is still a time needed for the South Vietnamese to develop the capability of self-defense.

ASIAN LIVES

MR. DICKINSON: Just one more question on Indochina. Most of your comments on our Indochina policy have emphasized that it is saving American lives.

What I want to ask is, what about the lives of Asians and the many, many refugees created by the incursions into Laos and Cambodia?

THE PRESIDENT: Well, Mr. Dickinson, let's look at the Asian lives. I think of the 50,000 South Vietnamese civilians who have been murdered by North Vietnamese and VC since this war began. I think of a half a million, by conservative estimates, in North Vietnam who were murdered or otherwise exterminated by the North Vietnamese after they took over from the South.

I visited South Vietnam just after the North Vietnamese took over in North Vietnam. As a matter of fact, I am one of the few people, at least in public life, who has been to Hanoi. I was there in 1953 and then came back in 1956. I visited a refugee camp. A million refugees came from North Vietnam to South Vietnam. And they came there because of the terrible atrocities that were visited upon them by the Government of North Vietnam.

Now, let's talk for a moment to put that in balance. We say, what about the people in Laos? As far as the activities in Laos are concerned, the bombing activities in Laos are concerned, if you will look at that particular area that is totally occupied by the North Vietnamese at this time, the number of civilians could be very, very small. As far as civilian casualties in South Vietnam are concerned from air strikes, they are very, very small, because the war has moved out of South Vietnam. The South Vietnamese now have taken it over. And as far as our activities are concerned, on balance I would say that the United States, by its actions in South Vietnam—and I say I understand the controversy, the difficulty, the moral concern that many Americans have about all wars, and particularly this kind of a war, so difficult to understand—but on balance, I will say this, that if the United States were to fail in Vietnam, if the Communists were to take over, the bloodbath that would follow would be a blot on this Nation's history from which we would find it very difficult to return.

Now, it is not necessary—we are now in a position where we can and, I can confidently say, we are ending American involvement, we are going to end it in a way that will, we believe, give South Vietnam a chance—not guarantee it—to defend itself against a Communist takeover. And I believe that this will save many more thousands of Asian lives that it is contended were lost because of American activities.

PEOPLE'S REPUBLIC OF CHINA

MR. DEDMON: Mr. President, when you last appeared before this convention prior to becoming President, you mentioned that laying the groundwork for future relations with the People's Republic of China would be one of the primary goals of your administration.

In light of recent events, as well as the trade review which you have ordered, it looks like this is one area where you are considerably ahead of schedule.

Do you think that we can anticipate an establishment of diplomatic relations with the People's Republic of China in your first administration rather than your second?

THE PRESIDENT: Mr. Dedmon, since you have been so kind to me, I will be kind to you.

Let the record show—and some of you will remember that time I was here in 1968—that Mr. Dedmon was the one that asked me the question about the People's Republic of China or Mainland China, if you want to call it that, and also let the record show, as you may recall, that at an editorial conference at the Chicago Sun-Times last year you asked me the question again.

The first two times I struck out. The third time we got a hit. That is all we can say.

Let me put it all in perspective, however.

What we have here is the result of a long process that began in my own thoughts even before 1968, the spring of 1968, when I answered that question at this convention. I wrote an article for Foreign Affairs—as a matter of fact, I think your question played off of that article at that time—in which I pointed out that we could not have what will be by the end of the century a billion of the most creative and able people in the world isolated from the world and that whoever was President of the United States had to develop a policy which would bring the isolation of a billion Chinese from the rest of the world to an end.

I also pointed out that that was a long-range goal. The long-range goal of this administration and of the next one, whatever it may be, must be two things: one, a normalization of the relations between the Government of the United States and the Government of the People's Republic of China, and two, the ending of the isolation of Mainland China from the world community.

Those are long-range goals.

Let's begin with what we have done then. We can't go that far that fast in one jump. We cannot do it now. I will not speculate on it now, because it is premature to talk about either of those subjects, either recognition or admission to the United Nations.

But I can point to the goal and what we have done to get toward that goal and what it can mean to the future.

Over a year ago we relaxed, as you know, our travel conditions with regard to going to China, and also we made some relaxation with regard to trade.

Finally, we had a response from the Chinese, as you know, last week. Then, on Wednesday of this week, I announced an additional relaxation with regard to trade restrictions and a relaxation with regard to Chinese who wanted to come to the United States.

Now it's up to them. If they want to have trade in these many areas that we have opened up, we are ready. If they want to have Chinese come to the United States, we are ready. We are also ready for Americans to go there, Americans in all walks of life.

But it takes two, of course. We have taken several steps. They have taken one. We are prepared to take other steps in the trade field and also with regard to the exchange field, but each step must be taken one at a time.

I know that as editors and as reporters, looking for that, you know, that hot lead or headline for the morning, this is not a satisfying answer. But from the standpoint of policy, it is the right answer. Because to try to make a headline by saying that tomorrow we are going to do this or that or the other thing would be misunderstood among many countries of the world where this matter has to be discussed and also might have exactly the reverse reaction with the Chinese.

I think the steady ordered process that we have engaged on now begins to bear fruit. I will just conclude with this one thought:

The other day was Easter Sunday. Both of my daughters, Tricia and Julie, were there—and Tricia with Eddie Cox—I understand they are getting married this June—and Julie and David Eisenhower.

And the conversation got around to travel and also, of course, with regard to honeymoon travel and the rest. They were asking me where would you like to go? Where do you think we ought to go?

So, I sat back and thought a bit and said, "Well, the place to go is to Asia." I said, "I hope that some time in your life, sooner rather than later, you will be able to go to China to see the great cities, and the people, and all of that, there."

I hope they do. As a matter of fact, I hope sometime I do. I am not sure that it is going to happen while I am in office. I will not speculate with regard to either of the diplomatic points. It is premature to talk about recognition. It is premature also to talk about a change of our policy with regard to the United Nations.

However, we are going to proceed in these very substantive fields of exchange of persons and also in the field of trade. That will open the way to other moves which will be made at an appropriate time.

MR. RISHER.

MR. RISHER: I just want to follow up on that if I could. Do you think that this might lead to a resumption of the meetings in Warsaw that were broken up about a year ago, I think?

THE PRESIDENT: Well, Mr. Risher, as you recall those meetings were resumed after we came into office. That, again, was a result of an initiative that we took. And then they were broken off again. We are ready to meet any time they are ready to meet.

I cannot—I don't have any information indicating that they want to resume them at this time, but we certainly have the door open. We are not pressing them, although we would welcome them opening them.

MR. MEYER.

CUBA AND CHILE

MR. MEYER: Mr. President, in view of the long-range attempt to normalize relations with China, and in view of the fact that we seem to be trying to maintain normal relations with Chile in view of the changes in that government, are we thinking also about long-range or short-range normalizing our relations with Cuba?

THE PRESIDENT: Certainly not short-range. As far as long-range, until Cuba changes its policy toward us, we are not going to change our policy toward Cuba. Let me distinguish, Mr. Meyer, because coming from Miami I know you have a big Cuban readership and they are torn—I mean they would like to be able to have some communication with their friends back in Cuba and yet they are concerned about the government, as you well know how strong they feel.

Chile has what is termed a Communist-leaning government, at least. We will call it a Marxist government. Allende is a Marxist, with strong Communist support. As far as Chile is concerned, we don't particularly approve of that type of government. We wouldn't want it here. On the other hand, the Chilean people voted for it. So, as far as our attitude toward Chile is concerned, it will be affected by what Chile's attitude is toward us.

If the Chilean Government does some things internally that is their business and the business of the Chilean people. They voted the government in and they will have to live with it. If, however, they do things in Chile or outside of Chile in their foreign policy that is detrimental to us, then that is our business and we will react accordingly. We are waiting to see what they will do. As long as they treat us properly, we will treat them properly.

Now, let's look at Cuba. As far as Castro is concerned, he has already drawn the line. He is exporting revolution all over the hemisphere, still exporting it. His line is against the United States, not only within Cuba but outside of Cuba.

As long as Castro is adopting an antagonistic, anti-American line, we are certainly not going to normalize our relations with Castro. As soon as he changes his line toward us, we might consider it. But it is his move.

FBI DIRECTOR HOOVER

MR. CORMIER: Mr. President, J. Edgar Hoover very recently seems to have become one of the favorite whipping boys of a number of prominent Americans.

THE PRESIDENT: Yes, I am glad to have somebody else there for a change.

MR. CORMIER: Is there the slightest chance that the criticisms would hasten his retirement?

THE PRESIDENT: No. I think the criticisms, particularly when they are unfair, as many of them have been, and malicious, as many of them have been—and I haven't discussed Mr. Hoover's retirement with him; he has not brought it up with me—but if I know Mr. Hoover, such unfair and malicious criticisms tend to have exactly the opposite effect: not to hasten his retirement but to have him dig in.

I can only say this, that with regard to Mr. Hoover, I would ask the editors of the Nation's papers to be fair about the situation. He, like any man who is a strong man and an able man, who has led this Bureau for so many years, has made many enemies. But we can also be thankful that in the FBI he has developed an organization which is recognized throughout the world as the best law enforcement agency in the world.

He has been nonpolitical. He has been nonpartisan. And despite all of the talk about surveillance and bugging and the rest, let me say I have been in police states and the idea that this is a police state is just pure nonsense. And every editorial paper in the country ought to say that.

MR. CORMIER: Well, Mr. President, earlier this week, I think speaking in Detroit, the Vice President said that he felt the Director should remain on the job as long as he is physically and mentally sound. Is that more or less your attitude?

THE PRESIDENT: Well, Mr. Cormier, I am not going to discuss the situation with regard to Mr. Hoover's tenure in office when the matter has not been raised with me, either by me or by him.

I will only say at this time that I believe it would be most unfortunate to allow a man who has given over 50 years of dedicated service to this country to go out under a cloud, maligned unfairly by many critics.

Now, I don't mean that some criticism of him, of me, of anybody, is not justified. But he is taking a bad rap on a lot of things and he doesn't deserve it.

AMERICAN YOUTH

MR. CHANDLER: Mr. President, I would like to change the subject, if we could, for a moment, to the youth of America, and ask you to give us your reading on the attitude and temperature of America's youth on our campuses.

They apparently have turned away, at least in recent months, from violence and seem to be going about their education, and yet I wonder if there is even deeper despair on their minds than there was when they were practicing violence. Do you have any views on that, sir?

THE PRESIDENT: Well, Mr. Chandler, it always does my heart good when I look down on that beach that you and I share—*(Laughter)*

MR. CHANDLER. We do? I can't surf there any more, sir.

THE PRESIDENT—and see young Americans surfing and enjoying it.

Seriously, the problem of American youth concerns us all, and I suppose that we concerned our parents. But youth today is a more difficult problem. There is more alienation.

Let's spend a moment on it, if I could, analyzing it.

One, all the old values aren't there any more—the faith and religion, family ties, what they hear in the colleges and universities generally is against the system, the system is bad, it pollutes the air, it is wrong to minorities, it is repressive and, of course, if wages war.

All of this concerns youth because youth basically, young people basically, by nature, by definition—we all remember how we were—we tend to be idealistic, hopeful, and we want the world to be better. So, I think that young people, particularly in the sixties, the late sixties, fell into a period of great disillusionment. That disillusionment, of course, was certainly increased by what they heard in school, what they heard sometimes in their churches, maybe sometimes what they heard at home.

Now, let's look to the future. We are removing some of the problems. As we end the involvement in the war, as the draft calls come to an end, which they will, as we have programs to deal with the problems of pollution of air and water—we are not going to solve them immediately, we have programs to deal with it—as we make progress in the problems of minorities, and we are making progress—not enough, not as much as we would like, but we are making a lot of progress—and as we see in perspective, and, if I may say so, what I really believe, what a really great and good country this is, I think we are going to find great numbers of American youth reestablishing their faith in America.

You asked about a moment ago, Mr. Dickinson, the question of "What do you think of when you wake up at 3 o'clock in the morning and what do you really want for this country?"

What I want first and above all, of course, is to end the war that we are in, and to build a lasting peace, through what we are doing in China, the Soviet Union, the SALT talks, the Mideast—there are problems all over the world.

But second, we want to build a new economy and a new prosperity which is not based on war, and third, we want to have a revolution in this country, of government, to make it more responsive, to make government work, to make it cost less. That is why we have revenue sharing and government reorganization.

We want to reform our welfare system and all the rest. Now, I believe that if we can just make some progress on all these fronts, that the millions of young, idealistic Americans will take another look at America and they will say, "Well, maybe this system isn't hopeless. Maybe it is possible that it will work. Maybe the United States is"—which I firmly believe—"the world's best hope for peace and for freedom."

That is what we are. And once American youth sees that and once they see that their idealism can be fulfilled within the system, I think that this enormous frustration that is torn down can turn into creative activity that will build up.

That is what I would like to leave when I leave office, that kind of feeling in American youth.

THE ECONOMY

MR. DICKINSON: Mr. President, the economic activity in the first quarter, despite the rise in the GNP, apparently did not measure up to the expectations of your administration.

Do you have new measures in mind in the battle against unemployment and inflation, or are you going to stick to the present game plan?

THE PRESIDENT: Mr. Dickinson, I have analyzed those figures pretty closely.

While, as you do point out, it did not reach the projections of our own economic target, it was far above the projections of people like Otto Eckstein, who said $22 billion. We went to $28½ billion. But let me be quite objective about it.

We all know that when we look at that, what was the gross largest increase in the GNP in any one quarter in history, that part of that is due to inflation, part of it is due to the comeback, the snapback, from the auto strike.

But why I am optimistic about the economy has to with what went into that figure. Let's look at the real numbers.

Automobile sales: Automobile sales in the first 10 days of this year, GM, the highest on record, the highest in history, in the first quarter, the highest in about 20 years.

Housing starts: Housing starts in the first quarter, the highest in 20 years and the figure just announced today, 1,900,000 in the month of March.

Retail sales: This may not yet be reflected in advertising but it will come. Retail sales: We find that retail sales went up a big 9½ percent. But look at what that retail sale was. It wasn't just the Easter bulge, because Easter was late and it was a cold spring—but it was in those things that really build an economy for the future—appliances, home furnishings, and the rest.

Then to take another number, the stock market: The stock market, we all think, is just something for the rich. But there are 27 million people in the market apart from those that are in institutons—(Laughter)—I understand about 11 months ago a few went into institutions too!—but when we look at those that are affected by the market, approximately 60 million Americans are investors in the stock market, either through insurance companies or funds or directly.

What do we find?

We find that the stock market had the biggest growth in the last 11 months, 50 percent gain. People do not buy stocks because they are pessimistic about the future. What I am saying is this: The consumers in America now have confidence. I believe we are going to see that confidence grow in April, May, June. If that confidence grows, the economy will grow with it.

And I would say that at this time, with the movement not being as fast as we had hoped, but with the movement sharply up in the last week in March and the first two weeks of April, that my predictions of a good year in 1971 and a very good year in 1972 still stand, and I don't think we should change the plan now.

We will continue to wage the battle against inflation by holding spending within the full employment surplus, within the full employment revenue, and we will continue, of course, to do everything that we can with pockets of unemployment, like in Southern California and the Northwest where we have airframe and other unemployment, but I believe that at this time we are going to see a strong second half, particularly, and a very, very strong 1972.

I am speaking, of course, economically.

VICE PRESIDENT'S CRITICISM OF THE PRESS

MR. DEDMON: Mr. President, this is a new question. Inasmuch as this is an editors convention, I think it would be inappropriate not to discuss the criticism which has been made of the press, particularly by the Vice President, who is now not only criticizing our viewpoint but analyzing some of our stories in detail.

I was wondering, quite apart from his prowess as a golfer, if you would care to compare his abilities as Vice President and as editor for the Nation's press.

Do you think that the Vice President is better as a Vice President or as an editor?

THE PRESIDENT: You mean you are looking for an editor? (Laughter)

Mr. Dedmon, I am going to make an offer to these distinguished publishers, editors, and so forth that are here. I have had the privilege of being in your offices and to have been in editorial conferences with every paper represented here.

I would like for all of you to have the Vice President in. See what kind of a man he really is.

The trouble is he only makes news when he hits the press or a golf ball.

Here is a man, yes, he is controversial. He says what he thinks and he says it very hard.

As a matter of fact, I believe that some of his criticisms, if you look at them very objectively, some of the criticisms that he has made in terms of some network coverage and press coverage, you really cannot quarrel with if you examine the whole record.

I believe that the Vice President's national image of simply being a man who is against a free press, who is against all the press, is just not accurate.

The difficulty is that he is now known—the things that he does, his capability in the foreign field, his capability in the domestic field—he is one of the best salesmen we have for revenue sharing because he knows what local government is. He was a Governor and he also was a county official and all over this country he goes out and makes effective speeches.

They get two sticks back with the corset ads. They never get up there in the front page.

So, I guess you don't advertise corsets anymore, though.

MR. DEDMON: No.

THE PRESIDENT: That is different. Nevertheless, I am simply saying this: I am simply saying that this old game—and Frank Cormier and Gene Risher have heard me say this often to the White House press corps—of having the President disagree with his Vice President goes on and on, but I am an expert at it and I am not going to get into it. I defend my Vice President.

Mr. Chandler.

MR. CHANDLER: Mr. President, could I ask a followup question on the Vice President? Do you think seriously, sir, in his attacks on the press, that they have been successful in causing any change, in your opinion, for the better in the press? In other words, have his attacks been successful? Has the press reacted in a positive way, in your opinion and if so, how?

THE PRESIDENT: I suppose that is the dilemma, isn't it, of anyone who dares to criticize the press or the television, that if he does he is probably going to get worse treatment than he thought he was getting before? Of course, I am being very guarded, as you noticed.

I will simply say this, Mr. Chandler: You may recall that back in 1962, immediately after running for Governor of California, after I was out of office and had no visible prospects of success, I had some things to say about the press. I have had nothing to say about it since. That's my answer.

SURVEILLANCE BY GOVERNMENT

MR. RISHER: Mr. President, I would like to get back to Mr. Hoover and the FBI. Is there any credence to the complaints by some Congressmen, as far as you know, that they are under surveillance by the FBI?

THE PRESIDENT: Well, Mr. Risher, let me answer that question in terms of what I know, because I checked this personally. I was in the House, I was in the Senate, and I am very jealous of the right of Senators and Congressmen, and every citizen actually, not to have surveillance when he is engaged in public activities. Particularly, I can assure you, that there is no question in my mind that Mr. Hoover's statement that no telephone in the Capitol has ever been tapped by the FBI is correct. That is correct.

The case you referred to, the Dowdy case, did not involve the tapping of a Congressman's telephone.

The second point that I should make is this: Let's get this whole business of surveillance and the rest into some perspective. First, when we talk about police states, there are 205 million people in this country.

Did you know, even the Nation's editors, sophisticated as you are, that over the past 2 years there were only 300 taps by the FBI through court orders?

Do you know what was accomplished from those taps? There were 900 arrests and 100 convictions, and particularly convictions in the important area of narcotics where millions and millions of dollars worth or narcotics that otherwise would have gone to the young people of America were picked up? That was why those taps were carried on.

Now let's talk about the other area which I think Mr. Risher and the people are more concerned about. They say what about the taps that are not made by court order but that are made for the national security? I checked that, too. The high, insofar as those taps are concerned, were in the years 1961, 1962, and 1963. In those years, the number of taps was between 90 and 100. Now, in the 2 years that we have been in office—now get this number—the total number of taps for national security purposes by the FBI, and I know because I look not at the information but at the decisions that are made—the total number of taps is less, has been less, than 50 a year, a cut of 50 percent from what it was in 1961, '62, and '63. As far as Army surveillance is concerned, once we saw what had happened to the Democratic National Convention, that had even been carried to the surveillance of Adlai Stevenson, who later became a Senator, we stopped them.

I simply want to put this all in perspective by saying this: I believe the Nation's press has a responsibility to watch Government, to see that Big Brother isn't watching.

I don't want to see a police state. I argued the right of privacy case in the Supreme Court and I feel strongly about the right of privacy. But let's also remember that the President of the United States has a responsibility for the security of this country and a responsibility to protect the innocent from those who might engage in crime or who would be dangerous to the people of this country.

In carrying out that responsibility, I defend the FBI in this very limited exercise of tapping.

One final point: You talk about police state. Let me tell you what happens when you go to what is really a police state.

You can't talk in your bedroom. You can't talk in your sitting room. You don't talk on the telephone. You don't talk in the bathroom. As a matter of fact, you hear about going out and talking in the garden? Yes, I have walked many times through gardens in various places where I had to talk about something confidential, and you can't even talk in front of a shrub. That is the way it works.

What I am simply saying is this, my friends: There are police states. We don't want that to happen to America. But America is not a police state, and as long as I am in this office, we are going to be sure that not the FBI or any other organization engages in any activity except where the national interests or the protection of innocent people requires it, and then it will be as limited as it possibly can be. That is what we are going to do.

MR. DICKINSON: Thank you very much, Mr. President, thank you.

APRIL 29

Following is the text, as made available by the White House, of President Nixon's April 29 televised news conference, his 16th since taking office and his first since March 4.

THE PRESIDENT: Good evening. Miss Thomas has the first question tonight.

Q: In view of the anti-war demonstrations or the growing Congressional demand for withdrawal from Vietnam, and the latest statements in Paris, will this influence in any way your Indochina policy?

THE PRESIDENT: Miss Thomas, I stated my Indochina policy at considerable length on April 7th, as you will recall, and I have considered all of the demonstrations and I have considered also the arguments made by others after that statement. I believe that the position I took then is the correct one.

I would not want to leave the impression that those who came to demonstrate were not listened to. It is rather hard not to hear them, as a matter of fact. I would say that demonstrators have come to Washington previously about the war. They came now. I was glad to note that in this case most of the demonstrators were peaceful. They indicated they wanted the war to end now, that they wanted peace. That, of course, if what I want. It is what everybody in this room wants and it is what everybody in this nation wants.

I realize, as a matter of fact, that in this room there are many reporters who disagree with my policy to bring the war to an end in the way that I believe it should be ended, and who probably agree with the views of the demonstrators.

I respect you and them and others who disagree with my policies, but as I looked at those demonstrators on television, and I saw so many who were teenagers, this is the thought that passed through my mind. My responsibility is to bring peace, but not just peace in our time, but peace in their time. I want peace not just for us, but peace for our children, their children.

I am convinced that if we were to do what they were advocating, a precipitate withdrawal before the South Vietnamese had a chance to prevent a Communist take-over, that that would lead to a very dangerous situation in the Pacific and would increase the dangers of war in the future.

On the other hand, I believe that if we continue on the path that I have set forth, one in which we are withdrawing our forces, in which we will be down to 184,000 by December 1st and I will make another announcement on October 15th, I believe that on that path we will end the war. We will bring a peace in Vietnam, which will contribute to peace not just in our time, but in their time.

I think that they will judge me very harshly for the position that I take now. But I think what is important is how they judge the consequences of the decisions that I make now, which I think are in their best interest and in the best interest of our children.

Mr. Cormier.

CHINA POLICY

Q: The Commission on the United Nations that you appointed, headed by your 1960 Vice Presidential running mate, has come out rather strongly for a two-China policy. The last time we saw you you weren't prepared to talk about that. I wonder if tonight you can say how you feel about those proposals?

THE PRESIDENT: Well, Mr. Cormier, that recommendation by that very distinguished Committee, of course, is being given consideration in the high counsels of this Government, and I am, of course, considering it along with recommendations that move in the other direction.

I think, however, that your question requires that I put, perhaps, in perspective much of this discussion about our new China policy. I think that some of the speculation that has occurred in recent weeks since the visit of the table tennis team to Peking has not been useful.

I want to set forth exactly what it is and what it is not.

First, as I stated, I think at one of my first press conferences in this room, the long-range goal of this Administration is a normal situation of our relationships with Mainland China, the People's Republic of China, and the ending of its isolation from the other nations of the world. That is a long-range goal.

Second, we have made some progress toward that goal. We have moved in the field of travel; we have moved in the field of trade. There will be more progress made.

For example, at the present time I am circulating among the Departments the items which may be released as possible trade items in the future and I will be making an announcement on that in a very few weeks.

But now when we move from the field of travel and trade to the field of recognition of the Government, to its admission to the United Nations, I am not going to discuss those matters, because it is premature to speculate about that.

We are considering all of those problems. When I have an announcement to make, when a decision is made—and I have not made it yet—I will make it.

But up until that time we will consider all of the proposals that are being made. We will proceed on the path that we have

been proceeding on. That is the way to make progress. Progress is not helped in this very sensitive area by speculation that goes beyond what the progress might achieve.

I would just summarize it this way: What we have done has broken the ice. Now we have to test the water to see how deep it is.

I would finally suggest that—and I know this question may come up if I don't answer it now—I hope, and, as a matter of fact, I expect to visit Mainland China sometime in some capacity. I don't know what capacity, but that indicates what I hope for the long-term. I hope to contribute to a policy in which we can have a new relationship with Mainland China.

Q: Mr. President, following up on that, your Vice President recently held an off-the-record, midnight session with selected newsmen in which he reportedly differed with your policy on China.

You have said in the past that there are always those who are trying to drive a wedge between the President and the Vice President. Do you think in this case he qualifies as a wedge driver?

THE PRESIDENT: I think it is very hard for the Vice President to be off the record. As far as this particular conference was concerned, the Vice President in his usual very candid way expressed some views with regard to our policy that he expressed previously in meetings that we had in which he participates, the National Security Council and other forums.

However, now that the decision has been made with regard to what our policy is, the Vice President supports that decision. He has so stated since he was quoted on his off-the-record conference and I think you will find the Vice President in all areas where he may disagree, as he should disagree when he has strong convictions with policies, once a decision is made, will publicly support those policies.

I expect him to and he always has.

VIETNAM

Q: Mr. President, sir, I wonder, since you have always said that you inherited this war, what you would think about naming a court of inquiry to look into and see just exactly who got us into this war.

THE PRESIDENT: When I say I inherited this war, I want to point out that I am actually quoting what others say. I am not going to cast blame for the War in Vietnam on either of my predecessors.

The first 16,000 combat men, we know, went there in 1963. The murder of Diem, the opening of the Ho Chi Minh Trail as a result of the settlement of Laos that occurred in 1962—President Johnson was President when more men went in later, but both President Johnson and President Kennedy, I am sure, were making decisions that they thought were necessary for the security of the United States.

All that I am saying now is this: we are in this war and the way the United States ends this war is going to determine to a great extent whether we are going to avoid this kind of involvement in the future.

If we end it in a way that encourages those who engage in aggression to try it again, we will have more wars like this. But, if we end it in a way that I have laid out, one that will end it in a way that the South Vietnamese will have a chance to defend themselves and to choose the kind of government they want in a free election, then we will have a chance to have peace in their time that I referred to a moment ago.

Q: Mr. President, the United States' position has been that North Vietnam has not genuinely offered the release of American prisoners, but rather only to discuss the release of American prisoners.

My question is: does your rejection of setting a deadline for the withdrawal of American troops include the possibility that North Vietnam might in the future offer the actual release of

American prisoners rather than simply the discussion of that question?

THE PRESIDENT: You very well have put the problem that we always are confronted with. You may recall very well that when President Johnson ordered the bombing halt it was with the assumption that the North Vietnamese would negotiate seriously on ending the war. They didn't do it.

So a promise to discuss means nothing from the North Vietnamese. What we need is far more than that. We need action on their part and a commitment on their part with regard to the prisoners.

Consequently, as far as any action on our part of ending American involvement completely—and that means a total withdrawal is concerned—that will have to be delayed until we get not just the promise to discuss the release of our prisoners, but a commitment to release our prisoners because a discussion promise means nothing where the North Vietnamese are concerned.

Q: A rejection is not a categorical rejection of setting a deadline for the withdrawal of American troops.

THE PRESIDENT: We have set forth both in my speech of October 7 and then on April 7 a complete American proposal for negotiation. I am not going in a press conference to depart from those proposals.

Those proposals include a cease fire; they include an exchange of prisoners; they include, as you know, mutual withdrawal of forces in Indochina and a peace conference.

Today in Paris, as you may know, we, along with the South Vietnamese, offered to repatriate—as a matter of fact, we are going to unilaterally repatriate without regard to what the North Vietnamese do to 540 North Vietnamese sick and wounded.

And, in addition to that, we offered to send to a neutral country 1600 North Vietnamese prisoners who have been prisoners for four years or longer. We trust that the North Vietnamese will respond.

We also offered, as you know, to have inspection of our camps, not just by the International Red Cross, but by a third country or any other international organization.

Ambassador Bruce puts the prisoner question by my direct orders at the highest priority. He is directed to discuss it separately, to discuss it with other issues, or discuss it as a part of an overall settlement. We are ready to settle it whenever they are ready to talk about it. And, I will say finally, that under no circumstances will our withdrawal programs abandon our P.O.W.'s. We will be there as long as they have any prisoners in North Vietnam. Mr. Jarriel?

CALLEY CASE

Q: Mr. President, you said that you intervened in the Calley case in the national interest. I wonder if you could define for us in greater detail how you feel the courts-martial verdict endangered the national interest and how you feel it was served by your intervention in the case?

THE PRESIDENT: Mr. Jarriel, to comment upon the Calley case, on its merits, at a time when it is up for appeal would not be a proper thing for me to do. Because, as you also know, I have indicated that I would review the case at an appropriate time in my capacity as the final reviewing officer.

In my view, my intervention in the Calley case was proper for two reasons: One, because I felt that Captain (Lieutenant) Calley should not be sent to Leavenworth while waiting for the months and maybe a year or so that appeal would take. I thought that he should be confined to quarters. I think that was proper to do in view of the fact that under civil cases where we have criminal cases, we grant the right of bail to people that are charged with crimes.

Second, I felt that it was proper for me to indicate that I would review the case because there was great concern expressed throughout the country as to whether or not this was a case involving, as it did, so many complex factors in which Captain (Lieutenant) Calley was going to get a fair trial.

I believe that the system of military justice is a fair system. But as part of that system is the right of the President to review. I am exercising that right. And I think that reassured the country and that is one of the reasons that the country has cooled down on this case. I will review it.

DESEGREGATION

Q: Mr. President, you have often said that in the area of civil rights that the law should be applied equally in the North and in the South. Ten days ago the Supreme Court approved mandatory use of bussing to overcome racial segregation. Do you endorse that decision and do you believe that bussing should be used as a technique to overcome racial segregation based on housing patterns in the North?

THE PRESIDENT: This problem involves some very technical legal distinctions. I will not go into them in detail.

I will, however, say this: I expressed views with regard to my opposition to bussing for the purpose of achieving racial balance and in support of the neighborhood school in my statement of March of last year. I stated those views at that time with the preface that this was an area that the Supreme Court had not yet spoken on and that it was my responsibility, therefore, to speak on it and to give guidance to our Executive agencies.

Now that the Supreme Court has spoken on that issue, whatever I have said that is inconsistent with the Supreme Court's decision is now moot and irrelevant, because everybody in this country, including the President of the United States, is under the law; or, putting it another way, nobody, including the President of the United States, is above the law as it is finally determined by the Supreme Court of the United States.

Now what is the law in this instance? The law is that where we have segregation in schools as a result of Governmental action—in other words, de jure— that then bussing can be used under certain circumstances to deal with that problem. And so we will comply with that situation and we will work with the southern school districts, not in a spirit of coercion, but one of cooperation as we have during the past year in which so much progress has been made in getting rid of that kind of a system that we have had previously.

Second, however, the court explicitly by dictums did not deal with the problem of de facto segregation as it exists in the North and perhaps as it may eventually exist in the South. That matter the court still has not decided on explicitly. It will probably have that opportunity because I noted a California case a couple of days ago from San Francisco which said that bussing would be required to deal with segregation which was a result, not of what a Governmental body did, but as a result of housing patterns coming from individual decisions.

Now, until the court does move in that field, I still will hold to my original positions of March that I do not believe that bussing to achieve racial balance is in the interest of better education. Where it is de jure, we comply with the court; where it is de facto, until the court speaks, that still remains my view.

LAOS-CAMBODIA

Q: Mr. President, in present terms, is it possible that U.S. forces might again be involved in Laos or Cambodian-type operations, and if so, under what conditions?

THE PRESIDENT: Well, it is quite obvious, and you put your finger on it with the assumption of your question that with the number of forces that we now have in Vietnam, the possibility of any further actions like Cambodia of last year, or even actions like Laos this year, are quite remote. When we get down to 184,000 by the end of the year, it will be completely remote, I would say.

At this time, we see no need for any further actions. I should point out as one indication of some effectiveness of previous actions, that the casualties which our television viewers heard on their television programs tonight and they will see in their morning newspapers, were half of what they were this same week last year, a fourth of what they were this same week two years ago, and a seventh of what they were in the same week of 1968. So, progress is being made.

As a result of Laos and as a result of Cambodia, the war is winding down. The Americans are coming home and we will achieve our goal of a total withdrawal. But that goal will be achieved only when we also get our prisoners of war back, and when the South Vietnamese develop the capability to have a chance to defend themselves against a Communist take-over.

Mr. Theis?

TROOP WITHDRAWALS

Q: Mr. President, would you consider setting a troop withdrawal date so far in advance that it might be considered safe from our standpoint such as the end of 1972?

THE PRESIDENT: I see no gain from our standpoint to set a troop withdrawal date by the end of 1972 or the end of 1973 or the middle of 1972, when we get nothing for it.

Once you set a date, in other words, when we say in effect to the enemy, "We quit, regardless of what you do," then we destroy any incentive the enemy might have to negotiate. And there is still some incentive. It gets less as months go on, and as our presence becomes less.

And we destroy, of course, also our bargaining position with regard to POW's. Even more important, once we set a date we give the enemy the information that the enemy needs to launch attacks on our rapidly diminishing forces at their greatest point of vulnerability.

Therefore, the setting of a date is not something that is in our interest. It is only in the enemy's interest.

What I will do is simply say what I have said previously, and I have kept my word throughout on this—we are withdrawing from Vietnam. Our goal is a total withdrawal. We do not plan to have a permanent residual force such as we have practically in Korea at the present time. But I am not going to set a date because I believe that setting a date is not in our interests.

Q: Mr. President, may I ask you a question. Are the conditions for the residual force, you have stated that it will be there until we get our prisoners released—you have also stated that it will be there until the South Vietnamese have at least a reasonable chance to defend themselves. Are both of these conditions for the residual force, one of them or the other? Could you clarify that for us?

THE PRESIDENT: The residual force, I think, first, Mr. Lisagor, with regard to the POW's, will be indefinite. In other words, if the North Vietnamese are so barbaric that they continue to hold our POW's, regardless of what we do with regard to withdrawal, then we are going to keep a residual force no matter how long it takes.

Second, however, with regard to the ability of the South Vietnamese to defend themselves is concerned, we have a very good idea when that will occur. And as soon as that eventuality occurs, we will be able to move on that.

So, I think I am answering your question by saying, in effect, that the two are separable. One will occur before the other, unless the North Vietnamese do move on the POW's.

WAR-MAKING POWERS

Q: Mr. President, the demonstrators last week focused on Capitol Hill, the Congress, rather than the White House. Congress will probably be considering cutting off funds for fighting in Vietnam, or the war powers of the President, limiting the war powers. If you were in the Senate now, how would you vote on those two things?

THE PRESIDENT: I guess it would depend on who was President. Seriously, I understand the concern of the Senate on this, and I have talked, for example, with Senator Mansfield, for whom I have enormous respect. He disagrees with me on our

plans in Vietnam, not in all respects, but believes we should move more quickly. But I believe that limiting the President's war powers, whoever is President of the United States, would be a very great mistake.

We live in times when situations can change so fast internationally that to wait until the Senate acts before a President can act might be that we acted too late.

As far as the Senate is concerned, however, I would like also to correct another impression. I think some of the people on television may have gotten the impression, when they saw some of the demonstrations down at the Senate—and Barry Goldwater's door had red paint on it, I understand, and his office door was locked—that Washington is somewhat in a state of siege.

Well, just let me make one thing very clear: The Congress is not intimidated; the President is not intimidated. This Government is going to go forward.

It doesn't mean that we are not going to listen to those who come peacefully, but those who come and break the law will be prosecuted to the full extent of the law.

In the meantime, however, I, as President, have my obligation to consider what they say and all of the other things that I know, and then to make the decision that I think will be in their interests, as well as the best interests of other people in this country.

JONATHAN ROSE

Q: Mr. President, sir, according to published reports Army Lieutenant Jonathan Rose, who is the son of a former high Eisenhower Administration official, and a Republican Party campaign contributor, is serving on duty here in the White House at your request and has for two years, rather than being assigned to active duty. Now the Pentagon will not tell us why, but I wondered whether you could tell us, sir, what his expertise is that makes him so valuable in the White House?

THE PRESIDENT: First, he is a very excellent lawyer, but we have a number of other competent lawyers—including, of course, the President—in the White House. But there is another reason, I think, in fairness to Mr. Rose—and I am sorry that such a personal thing has to be brought up, but I know he would want the record clarified—he has a physical disability, an injury to his shoulder, which disqualifies him from active combat duty.

Consequently, it was felt that the best service he could perform in a civilian capacity was in the White House. That is why he is there. I am glad that a man with that kind of a disability—there is nothing wrong with his brain—is available in the White House as one of our best young lawyers.

CALLEY

Q: If I may follow up on a question on Lieutenant Calley. I am not a lawyer but I inferred from what you said that in this country men who are convicted of multiple murders get out on bail. Is that actually the case, and if so would you recommend that someone like Manson be out on bail as you seem to imply that Lieutenant Calley should be?

THE PRESIDENT: No. I am not going to go into the specific laws of each State, and they do vary, of course, and not being a lawyer, as you know, according to every State—and some States are much more strict than others—where capital crimes are concerned, there are many States that do not allow any bail at all if they feel that the individual is one who is a danger to society.

What I am simply saying is this: that the real test for granting a bail in any case is whether or not the individual concerned is considered by the judge to be one who will be a danger to society.

Now, Captain (Lieutenant) Calley, let me point out, is not getting out on bail in the usual sense. He is confined to quarters on the base. He is, therefore, not free in the sense of somebody getting out on bails.

I am simply saying that I feel that a man who has a long process of appeal ahead of him, and who is going to be confined to quarters in any event, that this was the right thing to do under these circumstances.

TAIWAN

Q: Mr. President, the State Department has said that the legal question of the future of Taiwan and Formosa is an unsettled question. Would you favor direct negotiations between the Nationalist and Communist Governments to settle their disputes?

THE PRESIDENT: I noted a speculation to the effect from various departments and various sources that the way for these two entities to settle their differences was to negotiate directly. I think that is a nice legalistic way to approach it, but I think it is completely unrealistic. I am only saying at this point that the United States, in a very measured way, while maintaining our treaty commitments to Taiwan, is seeking a more normal relationship with the People's Republic of China.

There is one other point that I think is very important to make.

There has been speculation to the effect that the purpose of our, or one purpose of our normalizing our relations or attempting to normalize our relations with Mainland China is to some way irritate the Soviet Union. Nothing could be further from the truth.

We are seeking good relations with the Soviet Union and I am not discouraged by the SALT talk progress. I can only say that we believe that the interests of both countries would be served by an agreement there. We seek good relations with the Soviet Union. We are seeking good relations with Communist China and the interest of world peace requires good relations between the Soviet Union and Communist China. It would make no sense for the United States and it would not be in the interest of world peace to try to get the two to get at each other's throats, because we would be embroiled in the controversy ourselves.

Q: Mr. President, you spoke of your intention to travel to Mainland China. Is that at the invitation of Chairman Mao?

THE PRESIDENT: I am not referring to any invitation. I am referring only to a hope and an expectation at some time in my life and in some capacity, which, of course, does not put any deadline on when I would do it, that I would hope to go to Mainland China.

Mr. Horner?

VIETNAM VETERANS

Q: Mr. President, would you describe for us, sir, the extent of your participation in the Justice Department's change of mind last week about banning the Vietnam veterans from camping on the Mall?

THE PRESIDENT: First, the Justice Department, Mr. Horner, brought the action in order to establish the principle that camping on the Mall was not something that was considered to be legal.

Having established that principle, there was only 36 hours left in which to remove them and thereby, of course, to engage in a confrontation which could have been, we thought, rather nasty.

Under the circumstances, it seemed to me that since in the negotiations with their lawyer, Mr. Ramsey Clark, it had been clearly indicated that they would leave on Friday night, that the decision having been made and the principle having been established I saw no reason to go in and arrest the veterans and to put them into jail at that time.

Mr. Bailey?

CHINA ALTERNATIVE

Q: Sir, in your first answer on China, you said you were considering suggestions for a two-China policy. Along with the suggestions that move in the other direction, could you expound a little bit on what you mean by that?

What is the range of alternatives?

THE PRESIDENT: Mr. Bailey, what I meant to convey was that both within the Administration and from sources outside the Administration, there are those who favor a two-China policy; there are those who favor universality in the United Nations; there are those who favor a one-China policy, either Mainland China, or Taiwan China.

All of these are positions that are taken. I am not suggesting that they are lively options as far as I am concerned. What I am saying is that this is a very complex problem. I will make the decision after advising with the Secretary of State and my other chief advisors in this field, and when I make it, I will announce it, but I am not going to speculate on it now because I emphasize this is a very sensitive area and too much speculation about it might destroy or seriously imperil what I think is the significant progress we have made, at least in the travel area, and possibly in the trade area, looking to the future.

THE PRESS: Thank you, Mr. President.

MAY 1

Following is the text, as made available by the White House, of President Nixon's May 1 news conference at San Clemente, Calif., his 17th since taking office and his first since April 29.

THE PRESIDENT: Good morning, ladies and gentlemen.

I thought this morning that it would be well to give those who particularly are members of the White House press corps, and others, of course, who are here, who joined us in California, an opportunity to follow up on the press conference we had Thursday.

After that conference I noted that there were only one or two questions out of all the questions that were asked of the 18 or 19, that were in the field of domestic policy. So, consequently, so that you can have a chance to follow up in the domestic field, we will limit this conference to domestic policy questions, any area that you would like to explore in that particular case.

I note that you are all standing. I understand that for the purposes of this conference, to get recognition if you will simply hold your hand up, or speak up, either one, and I will recognize you.

I think Mr. Cormier has the first question.

ECONOMIC OUTLOOK

Q: Mr. President, on the basis of the first quarter GNP figures which were up sharply, Director Shultz saw the basis for a broad expansion, some others in your administration said, "Well, it is too early. One swallow doesn't make a spring."

What is your view on that?

THE PRESIDENT: Well, Mr. Cormier, I think it is well to put all of these economic indicators into some perspective. I don't do it as an expert in economics, but I have heard a lot of experts and this is the way I would evaluate it at this time. First, it is true that the first quarter figures are up. I think we can say that at this time we are in the midst of a strong economic upturn. Housing starts are up. Retail sales are up. Productivity is up. And, just as important, inflation is down.

Now, having said that, however, as we look to the future, I think it is well to bear in mind that every month is not going to reflect the same trends. We will have zigs and zags in a free economy. That is the only thing certain about a free economy, that it does not move on a certain path. All that I am sure of is what I stated at a press conference perhaps 2 or 3 months ago when I said that I believe that this would be a good year economically, 1971, and 1972 would be a very good year.

We have projected high goals for the economy and we are adopting policies for the purpose of achieving those goals. We have two dangers, I should point out. One, inflation. While inflation was down, the rate of inflation, it is still a danger, and we must fight it on particularly two fronts: the wage-price front, where we must have decisions made that are responsible, and do not create inflationary pressures, and second, on the governmental front, where it is very important that we not exceed the full employment revenues, and that will make it necessary for me on occasion, perhaps, to veto those irresponsible spending proposals by the Congress where they go beyond the full employment revenues which are, as you know, a very, very high number, and which provide for an expansionary budget.

The other area in which we still have problems ahead is unemployment. Unemployment always hangs high in any kind of recovery or upturn. It is the last number—unemployment is the last number—in a downturn to be reflected in going up, and it is the last number in an upturn to be reflected in going down.

We, however, believe that the long-term effect of our policies will be to bring unemployment down. I would particularly refer, while we are in California, to the fact that unemployment is at this time highly regional in its impact. California is considerably above the national average; so is the State of Washington. One of the major reasons for that is that California and the State of Washington, and Oregon to an extent also, the whole West Coast, has been highly dependent upon defense contracts and also on aerospace industry.

Since we have approximately, now, 2 million men, since this administration has come into office, who have been let out of the Armed Services, and also have left defense jobs, this has had its greatest impact in California. That is why decisions that I will make in the future, and decisions of this administration insofar as future Government contracts, as they deal with our turn from a wartime to a peacetime economy, California and the Pacific Northwest will get special consideration.

That is the way, of course, that the law is properly adjusted. It just doesn't mean that we regionally are favoring one part of the country over another, but this part of the country has suffered the most from the turn from a wartime to a peacetime economy, and now it is necessary, as we move in certain areas, to look at California and the Pacific Northwest, as well as other pockets where they have suffered primarily from the change in defense spending. Mr. Risher.

ANTI-WAR DEMONSTRATORS

Q: Mr. President, you said that you will not be intimidated by the anti-war demonstrators in Washington, but can you tell us if you consider that these demonstrators serve a useful purpose or a legitimate purpose, or whether you will meet with any of them when you return to Washington?

THE PRESIDENT: I have no plans to meet with any of them, Mr. Risher. I am quite aware of their position. They have, along with many others—some of those who represent their views in the Senate have strongly expressed their position to me. I respect their views. I respect their right to disagree with my position.

But I believe my position is right, and I think in the long run they are going to reach that conclusion, too, because they don't want just what is so easy for a man in terms of leadership, that quick political movement that would say "Peace now," without regard to peace in the future. And it is peace, not just in our time, but peace in their time, these young people, that I am constantly emphasizing.

Now, with regard to the demonstrators, when I say that I will not be intimidated, and that the Congress will not be intimidated, I am simply stating the American principle that while everybody has a right to protest peacefully, that policy in this country is not made by protests. Those who make policy must, of course, listen and then they must weigh all the other facts and then do what they think is right.

And also, when I say that we will not be intimidated, I should point out that while the demonstrations a week ago were peaceful demonstrations for the most part, this week we have had some incidents at several departments where it was necessary to arrest those who were breaking the law.

If this kind of illegal conduct continues next week, as some say it will, we are prepared to deal with it. We will arrest those who break the law. The right peacefully to demonstrate, or let me put it another way, the right to demonstrate for peace abroad, does not carry with it the right to break the peace at home, and we are going to see to it that anybody who comes to Washington to demonstrate peacefully is protected in that right, and that it is recognized.

But, on the other hand, we are going to see to it that the thousands of Government workers who have a right to go to work peacefully are not interferred with by those militants, those few militants, who in the name of demonstrating for peace abroad presume that they have the right to break the peace at home.

TAX DEPRECIATION AUTHORITY

Q: Mr. President, Senator Muskie of Maine has sent to the newspapers copies of a memorandum to the White House of last December by the Treasury Department which raises strong doubt that you have the authority to order some of the changes in tax depreciation which were announced when we were out here in January.

Senator Muskie says the memorandum by Deputy Assistant Secretary of the Treasury Nolan shows that the administration was knowingly violating the law. As you know, this whole matter of this $3 billion tax depreciation change has become rather controversial. I wonder if you would tell us your thinking in ordering this change, and whether specifically you ever saw the Nolan memorandum or took any notice of it in your consideration.

THE PRESIDENT: Well, first, so that we may understand that in all these conferences, and I have said this to other members of the White House press corps, but I want the members of the California press corps to know the position that I follow—I, of course, will never comment on any political comments that are made in a conference that I hold as President of the United States. So a release that a presidential candidate or a Senator sends to the paper, I will not comment on that.

But I will comment on your question, which goes to, as I understand, the whole proposition of the order that I did issue with regard to the depreciation. The answer is that within the Government and among lawyers there is and was a difference of opinion as to what authority the President had to provide for depreciation allowances.

The Nolan memorandum and, as a matter of fact, memoranda from others, were also brought to my attention, indicating what that authority was.

I, as President, and as I may say, too, formerly one who practiced a good deal of tax law, I consider that I had the responsibility then to decide what the law is, and my view is that while they had expressed a different view, that the correct legal view and the right view from the standpoint of the country was to order the depreciation allowances.

Now, the reason that we ordered it is this: The reason is that at this time it is vitally important to move this economy from a wartime to a peacetime basis. In order to move it from a wartime to a peacetime basis, we must provide incentives for business to write off faster on a depreciation basis those kinds of expenses that appropriately can be written off, and that means more jobs.

Now, any Senator or any critic who wants to oppose a program that is going to mean more jobs for Americans, peacetime jobs rather than wartime jobs, has a right to take that position.

I don't agree with them.

UNEMPLOYMENT

Q: On the matter of jobs, House Speaker Carl Albert has urged that you call a national conference on unemployment.

Are you considering doing that?

THE PRESIDENT: Well, I believe that many of the critics of our economic policy should listen to their top economist, Mr. Paul Samuelson. You may recall Mr. Samuelson, who is a very fine economist and one who has been rather pessimistic about the economy up to this point, made a statement recently to the effect that he thought those who were criticizing the administration on the economy might find that they might not have an issue next year.

Now, I am not making any predictions about what is going to happen each month, but I do believe that we are on the right track as far as the economy is concerned.

I do believe that what we are doing has now checked the rise in the unemployment. There may be zigs and zags, up and down, but the long-range goal of the administration is one that is achievable. I will also point out that this is an activist administration, as my answer to Mr. Oberdorfer's question a little while ago indicated; where I think that action can be taken to stimulate the economy we are going to take it. And if I find, as we look at the April figures and then the May figures and the June figures, that this economy is not moving as fast as it should move to deal with the unemployment problem, then we will act.

We will act on the tax front and other fronts. I do not see anything to be gained by calling a conference on the problem. We are quite aware of it, and I can only say that we are doing something and achieving something that was not achieved in the 8 years while we were not in Washington. That is that we are achieving an economy that is strong, and we trust one in which we will have a strong economy and a prosperous economy, but without having it at the cost of war.

We want to remember we did not have low unemployment except at the cost of war in the 8 years between 1961 to 1969. It is that that this administration is working on.

NEWSMEN'S NOTES AND FILMS

Q: Mr. President, in the background of this question is the effort of a congressional subcommittee to subpoena film which was made for but never used in a news documentary.

THE PRESIDENT: By CBS.

Q: By CBS, and also NBC. Also in the background of the question, of course, is various pressures and counterpressures which some of us believe to see from your own administration.

In December 1969, the Republican U.S. Senate Policy Committee issued the following statement as a matter of their policy. The question is whether you agree or disagree with this, and also I would like to get your comments on this general area of subpoenaing newsmen's notes and unused film. The Policy Committee statement was, "Whether news is fair or unfair, objective or biased, accurate or careless, is left to the consciences of the commentators, producers and network officials themselves. Government does not and cannot play any role in its presentation."

THE PRESIDENT: Let me address myself first to the quotation. I think the quotation states a principle that most Americans would support. However, I do not believe that that means that network commentators or newspaper reporters, as distinguished from editorial writers—who, of course, have a right to every bias and should express such bias—are above criticism, and they shouldn't be sensitive about it.

Now, when you go, however, to the question of subpoenaing the notes of reporters, when you go to the question of Government action which requires the revealing of sources, then I take a very jaundiced view of that kind of action unless it is strictly—and this would be a very narrow area—strictly in the area where there was a major crime that had been committed and where the subpoenaing of the notes had to do with information dealing directly with that crime.

As you know, that is provided for in many States at the present time. But as far as the subpoenaning of notes is concerned, of reporters, as far as bringing any pressure on the networks, as a government is concerned, I do not support that.

I believe, however, that each of us, as a public figure, has a right to indicate when we think the news coverage has been fair or unfair. Generally speaking, I also feel that I do not have to say much about that because, regardless of what I say, you are going to say anything you want about me, and it usually may not be very good.

WIRETAPS

Q: Mr. President, regarding the use of wiretaps in domestic security matters—

THE PRESIDENT: The kind that you don't have with subpoenas, in other words?

Q: Right, without court orders. The Attorney General has stated the policy on that and he has been criticized by Congressman Emanuel Celler of New York, who says that this could lead to a police state. Would you connect on the threat of a police state in the use of this type of activity?

THE PRESIDENT: Well, I have great respect for Congressman Celler as a lawyer and as, of course, the dean—as you know, he is the dean of all the Congressmen in the House, a very distinguished Congressman. However, in this respect I would only say, where was he in 1961? Where was he in 1962? Where was he in 1963?

Today, right today, at this moment, there are one-half as many taps as there were in 1961, '62, and '63, and 10 times as many news stories about them. Now, there wasn't a police state in 1961 and '62 and '63, in my opinion, because even then there were less than 100 taps and there are less than 50 today, and there is none, now, at the present time.

All of this hysteria—and it is hysteria, and much of it, of course, is political demagoguery to the effect that the FBI is tapping my telephone and the rest—simply doesn't serve the public purpose. In my view, the taps, which are always approved by the Attorney General, in a very limited area, dealing with those who would use violence or other means to overthrow the Government, and limited, as they are at the present time, to less than 50 at any one time, I think they are justified, and I think that the 200 million people in this country do not need to be concerned that the FBI, which has been, with all the criticism of it—which has a fine record of being nonpolitical, nonpartisan, and which is recognized throughout the world as probably the best police force in the world, the people of this country should be thankful that we have an FBI that is so greatly restricted in this respect.

This is not a police state. I have been to police states. I know what they are. I think that the best thing that could happen to some of the Congressmen and Senators and others who talk about police states is to take a trip—I mean a trip abroad, of course (Laughter)—and when they go abroad, try a few police states.

This isn't a police state and isn't going to become one.

I should also point this out: Where were some of the critics in 1968 when there was Army surveillance of the Democratic National Committee—at the convention, I mean? We have stopped that.

This administration is against any kind of repression, any kind of action that infringes on the right of privacy. However, we are for, and I will always be for, that kind of action that is necessary to protect this country from those who would imperil the peace that all people are entitled to enjoy.

CONSIDERATION OF A TAX CUT

Q: Mr. President, Director Shultz, of the Office of Management and Budget, said a couple of weeks ago that the performance of the economy in the first quarter did not come up to your high goals.

If the performance continues in this way for the next few months, are you considering a cut in taxes, or some other action?

THE PRESIDENT: First, with regard to the goals that we set, while the performance in the first quarter did not reach that goal, it was, nevertheless, a very strong first quarter, and I am not going to venture a guess as to what the second quarter will be.

I will say this, that this administration is prepared to act in the event that we feel that the economy is not moving as well as it should. But at the present time, particularly based on the March figures—because when you break out the first quarter, when you break March out from February and January—you find that it was a very strong March.

If the economy continues at its present level, at its present rate, the rate that we had in March and as it seems to be moving in April, or has moved in April—we won't get the figures for April for about another week—then I see no need for the kind of action you suggest. If on the other hand, the economy does not move strongly, we will act.

LOAN GUARANTEES FOR LOCKHEED

Q: Mr. President, getting to the question of the depressed defense industry in California, are you prepared to go to Congress and ask for loan guarantees for Lockheed, for the Tri-Star air bus?

THE PRESIDENT: I have seen, incidentally, some speculation after my meeting with former Prime Minister Wilson, on that point. I was delighted to learn in my conversation with Mr. Wilson that he had had dinner with Senator Humphrey, the night before, and that Senator Humphrey, who had opposed the SST, had indicated that he now would support the administration in the event that we did go to the Congress for the necessary guarantee for Lockheed.

We are going to make the decision on that either Tuesday or Wednesday of next week. Secretary Connally is in charge, and he will make his recommendations to me. I will only say this, that Lockheed is one of the Nation's great companies. It provides an enormous employment lift to this part of the country, and I am going to be heavily influenced by the need to see to it that Southern California, after taking the disappointment of not getting the SST, which would, of course, have brought many, many jobs to this part of the country, that California does not have the additional jolt of losing Lockheed. That gives you an indication of where I am leaning.

On the other hand, if the Secretary of the Treasury comes in and gives me strong arguments to the contrary, I will look in the other direction.

STEEL NEGOTIATIONS

Q: Mr. President, I assume you think that the uncoming negotiations in steel could have a significant impact on the economy. What, if anything, are you doing to see, first, whether a strike can be averted, and secondly, whether a settlement can be reached that you would consider to be noninflationary?

THE PRESIDENT: Well, Mr. Kaplow, to indicate that the Government is going to move in now to impose a steel settlement would mean there would be no negotiation. The parties would just quit negotiating. At this time, the companies, the steel companies, and the unions are negotiating. The Government stands ready to be of assistance at any time in the negotiating process in order to avoid a strike, if that can be done. I will only say this with regard to the stakes involved in this settlement: Let's look at the U.S. steel industry. Twenty years ago, when I first was a Senator from California, the United States produced 50 percent of all steel in the world.

Today we produce 20 percent.

Last year, for example, steel's profits were 2 ½ percent. That is the lowest of any major industry.

Looking at it from a competitive standpoint, Japan 20 years ago produced 5 million tons of steel, last year produced 100 million tons of steel, and by 1974 will produce more steel than the United States of America.

What does all this mean to us? It means that this settlement, a wage-price settlement, must reflect the competitive realities in the world, or we are going to find U.S. steel—and I am speaking of all the companies—we are going to find that the United States steel industry which has been the backbone of our economy, and is the backbone of any strong industrial economy, is going to be noncompetitive in the world.

This gives an indication of how we feel about it. But right at this time we must wait to see what industry and labor will eventually agree upon.

MARIJUANA LAWS

Q: Mr. President, many of us are rather concerned that a large percentage of our young people are breaking the law constantly by smoking marijuana. As you know, your own White House Conference on Youth voted to legalize marijuana. I know you have thought about this problem. I wonder if you would give us some of your thoughts on it.

THE PRESIDENT: Well, Mr. Pierpoint, as you know there is a Commission that is supposed to make recommendations to me about this subject. In this instance, however, I have such strong views that I will express them. I am against legalizing marijuana. Even if the Commission does recommend that it be legalized, I will not follow that recommendation.

Now, with regard to the penalties on marijuana, that is a matter which I do think is open to a national recommendation with regard to more uniform standards. In some States they are extremely strict, and in other States they are quite lax. I believe that a penalty in some instance can have a detrimental effect in achieving our goal. But I do not believe that legalizing marijuana is in the best interests of our young people, and I do not think it is in the best interests of this country.

LOCKHEED MANAGEMENT

Q: Mr. President, let me follow up on this possible action for Lockheed. It seems a lot of its problems are from mismanagement in the military sector, and now these management problems in the commercial 1011 sector.

Mr. Packard, at the Pentagon, has indicated they could continue operating these defense programs even if they were in bankruptcy.

Where are you going to draw the line about helping these multi-billion-dollar corporations that end up in shaky financial condition because of mismanagement?

THE PRESIDENT: Well, it is rather easy to belabor a company as big as Lockheed—as you know, it is the biggest airframe producer in the world—belabor it for its mismanagement.

There has been a lot of mismanagement in military contracts, as you know. In mu view, however, looking at this precise case, the air bus problem did not come as a result of Lockheed's mismanagement. It was because of the failure of Rolls Royce in Britain.

Under those circumstances, it seems to me that this particular contract is one that should be looked at separately, and I will certainly—when I make this decision Tuesday or Wednesday, whatever day we finally get together on it—I will have in mind all these considerations.

But we are not going to damn the whole company for some areas of mismanagement, for some mistakes. We need a strong airframe producer like Lockheed in southern California, and if we can save the company, and frankly, help it toward better management, we will do so.

CALLEY

Q: Mr. President, to go to the Calley case for a minute, you said Thursday night that you felt that the military system of justice in this country was a fair system, but don't you admit the possibility that your repeated expressions of sympathy for Lieutenant Calley, and your decision to review the case, will inevitably have the consequence of influencing the judges, the military judges, who are going to be reviewing this case up the line, and don't you admit that it is a possibility, at least, that this would actually thwart the system of military justice?

THE PRESIDENT: Well, I should point out that what is important is that I am the final reviewing officer. As far as I am concerned, I am going to review the case. I am going to review it fairly, having in mind what the trial court has found, and also what the other reviewing authorities say.

I am not trying to influence the reviewing authorities. I am simply indicating, as they all know, and the law so provides, that as Commander in Chief, I will exercise my right to review.

CIVIL RIGHTS ACTIONS

Q: Mr. President, many black Americans seem to think that your administration is anti-equal rights. My question is, what are you doing to counter that impression, and what do you consider to be your most important action in advancing the cause of civil rights?

THE PRESIDENT: When we consider the many things we have done in this area, we could refer, for example, to the food stamp program, which, of course, benefits, as you know, many disadvantaged Americans and many black Americans. For example, the increment that we have asked for this year is twice as much as the program, the whole program, was when we came into office.

In other words, we are dealing with the problem of hunger in America which affects black Americans and many other disadvantaged Americans.

Second, we are making very great strides, significant strides, in the field of minority enterprise. They have not been well advertised, but they are known among those who have businesses, who didn't have them before and didn't have that chance.

Third, we are providing opportunities in government that have not been provided before.

Fourth, and this is an area that I think needs to be emphasized, let's look at the matter of the dual school system.

When we consider today that even before the Supreme Court decision that was handed down last week, 38 percent of all black children in the South now go to majority white schools as compared to 28 percent of all black children in the North going to majority white schools, we can see that a very quiet but significant revolution has taken place in this country, and it is to the great credit of the far-seeing, law-abiding black and white leaders of the South that this has taken place.

They now have another difficult problem, complying with the Supreme Court decision, and I believe compliance will take place because we are going to follow our same tactic of cooperation rather than coercion.

As far as the entire problem is concerned, I have met with black leaders, with black Congressmen, and with various representatives of the black community, and will continue to do so, and with representatives of other parts of our society, because we have got to move forward not only with black Americans, we have very significant problems—we in California know it—in the Mexican-American community.

I found, for example, looking at some statistics recently, that with regard to poverty, for example, that the problem of Mexican-Americans in the Los Angeles area is even worse than that of black Americans. So we have got to zero in on that problem as well.

Reporter. Thank you, Mr. President.

JUNE 1

Following is the text, as made available by the White House, of President Nixon's June 1 televised news conference, his 18th since taking office and his first since May 1.

THE PRESIDENT: Mr. Risher has the first question.

Q: Mr. President, Chairman Brezhnev recently indicated a willingness to negotiate troop withdrawals from Europe. Do you plan to take him up on this?

THE PRESIDENT: We have completed within our own government our study of the question of balanced mutual force reductions. Secretary Laird has had some consultations last week on this matter with the NATO defense chiefs and Secretary Rogers is conducting consultations at the present time with the Foreign Ministers of the various NATO countries. When those consultations have been completed, then the United States and our allies will move forward to discuss, negotiate, with the Soviet Union and other countries involved with regard to mutual, balanced force reductions.

EUROPEAN MEETING

Q: Mr. President, we not only have the prospect—maybe this is in the future—of the mutual reduction of force, but we have the Berlin question, the SALT talks, the dollar problem in Europe. Do you foresee meeting with the leaders of Europe on their own soil within the foreseeable future?

THE PRESIDENT: Mr. Cormier, I plan no trip to Europe and no meetings with European leaders in the near future. If such plans do develop, of course, I will announce them. And if it becomes necessary, as a result of developments in the question of mutual force reductions or arms limitation that such meetings occur, I will, of course, go any place that I think would serve the interests of our goal of reducing the dangers to peace in the world, and, of course, reducing the burden of armaments.

DRUG ADDICTION

Q: Mr. President, what are you going to do about the tens of thousands of American soldiers who are coming back from Vietnam with an addiction to heroin?

THE PRESIDENT: I think it is well for us first to put the problem of drug addiction in Vietnam in perspective. It is not simply a problem of Vietnam veterans; it is a national problem. It is a national problem that primarily focuses on young people. When Mr. Finch and Mr. Rumsfeld came back from Europe they pointed out it was a problem not only of young people who were in the Armed Services but of young people who were tourists in Europe.

Consequently, what we need is a national offensive on this problem and one which, of course, will particularly take into account the immediate problem in Vietnam. The problem in Vietnam is aggravated by the fact that heroin can be purchased there at a much lower price than it can in the United States and, therefore, when men are exposed to it, they are able to obtain it. The habit is one that they can afford to have.

What we are going to do, therefore, is to step up our national program on four fronts: First, the front of getting at the sources. This means working with foreign governments where the drugs come from, including the Government of South Vietnam, where they have, of course, a primary responsibility.

It means also, of course, prosecuting those who are the pushers. It means, in addition to that, a program of treating the addicts, and that, incidentally, insofar as veterans are concerned, means treating them where they are addicted to heroin or hard drugs before releasing them, giving them the opportunity. And, finally, it requires a massive program of information for the American people with regard to how the drug habit begins and how we eventually end up with so many being addicted to heroin, a hard drug, which virtually is a point of no return for many.

In that respect, that is one of the reasons I have taken such a strong position with regard to the question of marijuana. I realize this is controversial. But I can see no social or moral justification whatever for legalizing marijuana. I think it would be exactly the wrong step. It would simply encourage more and more of our young people to start down that long, dismal road that leads to hard drugs and eventually self-destruction.

I am going to be meeting, incidentally, Thursday of this week, with the Secretary of Defense, the three Service Secretaries, the three heads of the Armed Services, and get a direct report from them on the programs they have initiated at my suggestion and at the suggestion and request of the Secretary of Defense in the drug field.

We consider it a problem of the highest priority, and we are going to give it the highest priority attention at all levels, not just with regard to veterans, where it is a special problem, but nationally, where it is one that concerns us all.

VIETNAM IMMORALITY

Q: Mr. President, much of the debate about Vietnam seems to have shifted from the question of practicality of policy to the questions about morality of U.S. involvement. Some of the people have been demonstrating against the war have contended that your Administration is responsible for war crimes, not only speaking of certain face-to-face encounters between U.S. soldiers and civilians, but speaking of the policy of massive bombing in large areas in Southeast Asia.

How do you respond to the suggestions that the bombing constitutes immoral, criminal conduct?

THE PRESIDENT: Well, my views with regard to war are well known. I grew up in a tradition where we consider all wars immoral. My mother, my grandmother on my mother's side, were Quakers, as I have often pointed out to this Press Corps, and very strongly disapproved of my entering World War II. As far as Vietnam is concerned, like all wars, it involves activities that certainly would be subject to criticism if we were considering it solely in a vacuum.

But when we consider the consequences of not acting, I think we can see why we have done what we have. To allow a take-over of South Vietnam by the Communist aggressors would only result in the loss of freedom of 17-million people in South Vietnam; it would greatly increase the danger of that kind of aggression and also the danger of a larger war in the Pacific and in the world. That I believe. That is why I have strongly supported ending this war, ending our involvement as we are, withdrawing Americans, but ending it in a way that we do not turn the country over to the Communists, ending it in a way that we give the South Vietnamese a reasonable chance to defend themselves against Communist aggression. And that is why I believe that kind of an ending will contribute to the peace that we all want.

SALT AGREEMENTS

Q: Mr. President, if there should be agreements on both defensive and offensive weapons with the Soviet Union, do you plan to submit both of those agreements to the Senate in a treaty form, or only the agreement on defensive weapons, leaving the other to an understanding?

THE PRESIDENT: Mr. Lisagor, this is a matter which you have raised, along with other reporters that cover the White House, in some of the background briefings, and I am sure that all of you know that it is not possible for me, and it would not be appropriate for me, to discuss this matter in any way that would jeopardize the agreement itself.

We cannot tell at this time what form the agreement will take. With regard to defensive weapons, the ABM, it is a simpler matter because we are talking only about one weapons system. Therefore, it might be subject to a treaty.

With regard to the offensive limitations that we are talking about, it is not as simple a matter, because here we have several weapons systems. We have missiles. We have bombers. We have nuclear submarines. And the understanding, the commitment that has been made at the highest level, deals only with some of those systems. Consequently, what would come out with regard to offensive weapons may or may not be at the treaty level. It might be at an understanding level at this point, and be at a treaty level at a later point.

I would like to be more precise than that, but that is an accurate statement of what we expect.

EMPLOYMENT OF WOMEN

Q: Mr. President, women make up more than 50 percent of the population, but it seems that men have a lot of the top Government jobs. Out of the top 10,000 Federal supervisory posts, only 150 are filled by women, and in 2-1/2 years you have appointed only 200 women to Federal jobs, 62 of them in one single arts commission.

What are your goals of bringing more qualified women into Government and promoting them, and how do you personally feel about Women's Liberation?

THE PRESIDENT: After that question, I am not going to comment upon Women's Liberation. But I will comment about the problem about women in Government jobs.

This Administration is proud of its record insofar as putting women in top positions of responsibility. We have women, as you know, as not just members of commissions, but one is the Chairman of the Maritime Commission, and I have just appointed a woman as Chairman of the Tariff Commission. These are breakthroughs. There will be more. They were appointed to these positions not because they were women, but because they were the best qualified people for those jobs.

There are many women who are the best qualified people for jobs in Government, and wherever we can get women to take those jobs, they will be appointed.

I have asked my staff—and particularly in this case we have Miss Franklin working on this—to give me any recommendations that they possibly can that will bring qualified women into Government, because finding qualified people is very difficult and we don't want to rule out such a great source of qualified people as the women provide.

SOVIET-EGYPTIAN TREATY

Q: Mr. President, what effect will the Soviet-Egyptian treaty have on your efforts to get a peaceful settlement in the Middle East?

THE PRESIDENT: The Soviet-Egyptian treaty will have effect only in terms of how it might affect the arms balance. In the event that this will be followed by an introduction of more weapons into the Middle Eastern area, it can only mean a new arms race and could greatly jeopardize the chances for peace. We trust that that is not the case.

It is too early to appraise the treaty in terms of what it could mean, in terms of introducing arms into the area.

As far as we are concerned, we continue to support the truce which is now in its tenth month. We continue to work for an agreement, either an interim agreement if necessary; of course, a comprehensive one if possible.

And we are not going to allow this treaty to discourage us insofar as seeking that agreement is concerned. We seek normal relations with all of the countries in the area, including the UAR. We believe that the chances for an agreement are still there. Whether the Soviets follow up with large-scale arms shipments into the area will determine whether or not it increases the chances for peace or sharply increases the chances for war.

McCLOSKEY

Q: Mr. President, a Republican Congressman who is a Marine Corps veteran from your own state, Paul McCloskey, has been going around the country talking against your Vietnam policies and has plans for running against you in the primaries next year. Do you welcome this as a challenge or does it make you the least bit nervous?

THE PRESIDENT: I realize that there are probably many political questions in the minds of reporters, and, of course, many of our listening audience. I, however, have decided as a matter of policy that a Presidential press conference is not a proper forum to comment on any partisan political matters or political questions.

Consequently, I will not comment on that and I will not comment on any other political questions.

PRISONERS-OF-WAR

Q: Mr. President, what does a refusal of all but a handful of sick and disabled prisoners that South Vietnam planned to return to the north do to the chances for exchange of such prisoners?

THE PRESIDENT: Mr. Horner, you will remember that we went through somewhat the same thing in Korea many years ago when the Korean prisoners, many of them, refused to go back. As far as this is concerned, there are a few, less than 20, who have agreed to go back, and of course, they will be returned.

We hope that the refusal of the others to go back will not deter the North Vietnamese at least to consider some kind of action on their part with regard to sick and disabled prisoners.

WITHDRAWAL DATE

Q: Mr. President, I certainly appreciate your giving me the opportunity to follow up on Mr. Horner's question. Some of the wives—by no means all—but some of the wives of the prisoners of war held by North Vietnam are critical of you and your policies concerning their husbands, saying specifically, among other things, that you should set a date for withdrawal of all U.S. troops in Vietnam contingent upon release of all prisoners; that, if North Vietnam doesn't respond, that you lose nothing by that.

The question is, first, generally, would you respond to that criticism, and then specifically, what is it you will lose by setting a date contingent upon release of all prisoners?

THE PRESIDENT: I discussed that matter with Ambassador Bruce when he was here. I asked him what success he had had in raising this question with the North Vietnamese. As you know, they have even put out stories to the effect that if we would set a date certain way in the future, they would be willing to move on the prisoner issue. It always comes back to the same thing. If we end our involvement in Vietnam and set a date, they will agree to discuss prisoners, not release them.

Now, we have been around this track before. I should point out that when President Johnson agreed to the bombing halt in October of 1968, he do so with the understanding that there was going to be progress in negotiations, that there was going to be discussions and for two and a half years we have had discussions in Paris and no progress.

Now, as far as we are concerned, we at this time are not going to make any kind of agreement with regard to prisoners that is not going to be followed by action or concurrent with action; from the standpoint of the North Vietnamese we have as yet no indication whatever that they would be willing to release prisoners in the event that we took certain steps.

MAY DAY DEMONSTRATION

Q: Mr. President, it has been about a month now since the May Day demonstrations. In that period, several people have raised questions as to whether the police handled it properly, and also the charges against something more than 2,000 people arrested on that Monday have been dropped.

I wonder with that perspective of the month whether you think the police handled it properly, and the broad constitutional question involved of protecting individual rights in a difficult situation of control.

THE PRESIDENT: Mr. Kaplow, yes, I believe the police in Washington did handle the question properly with the right combination of firmness and restraint in a very difficult situation.

Let us separate the question into what we are really dealing with.

First, there are demonstrators. The right to demonstrate is recognized and protected, and, incidentally, has been recognized and protected by the Washington police. Thousands of demonstrators have come down here peacefully and have not been, of course, bothered. They have been protected in that right.

But when people come in and slice tires, when they block traffic, when they make a trash bin out of Georgetown and other areas of the city, and when they terrorize innocent bystanders, they are not demonstrators, they are vandals and hoodlums and law breakers and they should be treated as law breakers.

Now, as far as the police were concerned, they gave those who were in this particular area, and who were engaging in these activities, approximately 15,000 in all, an opportunity to disperse. They did not. They said they were there to stop the Government from operating.

I have pledged to keep this Government going. I approve the action of the police in what they did. I supported it after they did it. And in the event that others come in, not to demonstrate for peace but to break the peace, the police will be supported by the President and by the Attorney General in stopping that kind of activity.

This Government is going to go forward, and that kind of activity which is not demonstration, but vandalism, law-breaking, is not going to be tolerated in this Capital.

SOUTHEAST ASIA VISIT

Q: Mr. President, there has been persistent speculation that you may also visit Southeast Asia this year. If you can tell us anything about that it would be welcome, but specifically, are you ruling out a visit to South Vietnam in advance of the Presidential elections there this fall?

THE PRESIDENT: Mr. Theis, I have no plans to visit South Vietnam before the Presidential elections. As far as any other travel to Southeast Asia is concerned, I have no present plans. Naturally, I will give all of you advance notice because I know you have to have shots before you go to Southeast Asia.

CIVIL RIGHTS

Q: Mr. President, in the past week in Birmingham you praised Southern progress for the blacks. And you held in contempt those Northerners who you said used a double standard on civil rights. However, the Civil Rights Commission has in effect accused your Administration of the same thing. In its May 10th report, for instance, it says that the Department of HUD appears to be withdrawing from the battle for fair and desegregated housing.

Do you have a response to that report?

THE PRESIDENT: Mr. Morgan, I have read the report of the Civil Rights Commission and I respectfully disagree with it in two areas: One, where they say that this Nation, the American people, do not have a commitment to the cause of civil rights. I believe that is an unfair charge. I do not question the sincerity of the members of the Commission. I don't think they should question the sincerity of the great majority of the American people on this issue, particularly in view of the great progress that has been made.

With regard to the housing question, I should point out that the Supreme Court has spoken out on that issue in two recent cases, the Lackawanna case and the California case. As a result of those two cases, it is now possible for us to issue a comprehensive statement on housing which will be in compliance with the Supreme Court cases.

The Attorney General and the Secretary of HUD are completing their memoranda. They will be submitted to me later this week. The statement will be issued the first of next week. This will set forth this Administration's position on the housing question, which will be in complete compliance with the law, as interpreted by the Supreme Court.

MAY DAY - 2

Q: Mr. President, regarding the mass arrests, I wonder—you seem to have thought that closing down the Government and keeping it running, in other words, was so important that some methods such as suspending constitutional rights was justified.

Was it that important? Do you think it was?

THE PRESIDENT: I think when you talk about suspending constitutional rights that this is really an exaggeration of what was done. What we were talking about here basically was a situation where masses of individuals did attempt to block traffic, did attempt to stop the Government. They said in advance that is what they were going to do. They tried it and they had to be stopped. They were stopped without injuries of any significance. They were stopped, I think, with a minimum amount of force and with a great deal of patience.

And I must say that I think the police showed a great deal more concern for their rights than they showed for the rights of the people of Washington.

MAY DAY - 3

Q: Mr. President, if I may follow up, if that is true, then why are the courts releasing so many of the cases and so many of the people have been arrested? If they were lawfully and properly arrested, why are the courts letting them out?

THE PRESIDENT: It is because, of course, Mr. Ter Horst, as you know, that arrest does not mean that an individual was guilty. The whole constitutional system is one that provides that after arrest an individual has an opportunity for trial. In the event that the evidence is not presented which will convict him, he is released. I think that proves the very point that we have made.

MAY DAY - 4

Q: Mr. President, they are not being released on the grounds that guilt isn't proved. They are being released on the grounds that they weren't properly arrested.

THE PRESIDENT: It seems to me that when we look at this whole situation that we have to look at it in terms of what the police were confronted with when those who contended they were demonstrators, but actually were law-breakers, came into Washington.

They were confronted with what could have been a very difficult crisis. They dealt with it. They dealt with it, it seems to me, with very great restraint and with necessary firmness.

I approve of what they did, and in the event that we have similar situations in the future, I hope that we can handle those situations as well as this was handled. I hope they can be handled that well in other cities so that we do not have to resort to violence.

VIETNAM EQUIPMENT

Q: Mr. President, sir, I wonder what you are going to do about the supply of goods in Vietnam. I understand we have enough telephone poles over there for 125 years and acres of trucks and other communications equipment.

Will that be brought back, and where will it be put?

THE PRESIDENT: At the present time, my main concern is to bring back the men from Vietnam. After that we will think about the goods.

CHINA POLICY

Q: Mr. President, since April you have been considering policy studies of the China question, easing trade with China, and representation at the United Nations. Can you say where these stand now, please?

THE PRESIDENT: With regard to the United Nations question, a significant change has taken place among the members of the United Nations on the issue of the admission of Mainland China. We are now analyzing that situation in consultations with the Republic of China on Taiwan and with third countries.

After we have completed our analysis, which I would imagine would take approximately six weeks, we will then decide what position we, the Government of the United States, should take at the next session of the United Nations this fall, and we will have an announcement to make at that time with regard to that particular problem.

A number of various options are open to us.

With regard to trade, various agencies have now completed their review of the situation and have submitted their recommendations to me. On June 10th, I will make an announcement releasing a wide variety of items which previously have been banned. These are all non-strategic items in which trade can be conducted with Mainland China.

Let me put all of this in context by saying that there are only two areas where we have moved. They are significant, however, in themselves. In the area of opening the door to travel and opening the door to more trade, we have made significant moves. I think, however, we should realize we still have a long way to go.

As I recall, there is a Chinese proverb to the effect that a journey of a thousand miles begins with a single step. We have taken two steps, but the important thing is that we have started the journey toward the eventual, more normal relationship with Mainland China, and eventually, and this is vitally important, ending its isolation and the isolation of 700 million people from the rest of the people of the world. This we think is a goal well worth pursuing.

VIETNAM DRAFTEES

Q: Mr. President, when do you plan to stop sending draftees to Vietnam?

THE PRESIDENT: The question of whether we can stop sending draftees has been considered, and I find that we are unable to do so at this point. I think, however, the question is going to be a moot one in due time, since as you know, as we stand here at this time, over half of those who were in Vietnam when I came into office have now come home.

By December 1st, two-thirds of those who were there when I came into office will have come home. On November 15th I will make another announcement with regard to a further withdrawal.

Under those circumstances, it would seem that the number of draftees that will be called into service for Vietnam would be very, very small in number.

CREDIBILITY

Q: Mr. President, in view of your continually reducing the troops in Vietnam, bringing more American troops home all the time, how do you account for the fact that two major public opinion polls now show that about two-thirds of the American public believe they are not being told the truth with regard to the war?

THE PRESIDENT: I am not surprised by the polls. I think the people—and the war has been going on for a long time—are tired of the war. We are an impatient people. We like to get results.

On the other hand, if all the problems that I have in this Government could be as easily solved as this one, I would be very happy, because the answer to whether or not the American people believe that I am ending the American involvement in war is in the fact. We have already brought home half. We will have brought home two-thirds, and we are going to bring all home, and bring them home—and this is what is vitally important—in a way that will not be inconsistent with two other objectives: In a way that will secure the release of our prisoners of war; and also in a way that will give the South Vietnamese a chance to avoid a Communist takeover, and thereby contribute to a more lasting peace.

That fact, the very fact that we accomplish that goal, will end the credibility gap on that issue once and for all.

INTERNATIONAL LABOR ORGANIZATION

Q: Mr. President, may I ask a question on the ILO? As you know, there is a considerable uncertainty about the position of the American Government with respect to membership in the International Labor Organization, the ILO. To remove this uncertainty, could you tell us, does the United States seriously intend to continue its membership in the ILO; and secondly, if it does, will the Administration leadership apply its energies on Capitol Hill to get the appropriations necessary to pay our dues with the ILO?

THE PRESIDENT: Mr. Meany talked to me about the ILO. As you know, he has very strong feelings and reservations about our membership in the ILO. However, we have decided to continue our membership. We will attempt to get the dues in arrears paid by the Congress. We will have to have considerable support in order to accomplish that.

But also, we are going to see to it that American labor, and free labor throughout the world, gets a better voice in the ILO than it has had previously.

The reason that Mr. Meany, a top free world trade union leader, opposes the ILO is because free trade unions have received a very bad deal in ILO meetings, and we are going to have to have better treatment in that way or American support for the ILO is going to go right down the drain.

THE PRESS: Thank you, Mr. President.

AUGUST 4

Following is the text, as made available by the White House, of President Nixon's Aug. 4 impromptu news conference, his 19th since taking office and his first since June 1.

THE PRESIDENT: Ladies and gentlemen, I wanted to begin this with a brief resume of the conversation I have just had with the Secretary of State, because I know the subject will probably come up in any event.

This is in regard to the Pakistan refugee situation, to recap what we have done. Insofar as the refugees, who are in India are concerned, we have provided $70 million to date for the refugees and we are prepared to provide more. That, incidentally, is more than all the rest of the nations of the world put together, so it is a substantial amount.

As far as those in East Pakistan themselves are concerned, whereas you know there are prospects of famine, in the event that the crop reports are as bad as they seem to be, at this time we have 360,000 tons of grain ready for shipment there. We have also allotted $3 million for the chartering of ships for the purpose of getting the grain into the overcrowded ports.

As a further step, the Secretary of State has worked out with my very strong approval a plan to go to the United Nations next week to talk to the responsible and appropriate members of the United Nations, including the U.N. High Commissioner in that office, to see what additional steps can be taken on both fronts to help the refugees in India from East Pakistan, and also to help those who are in East Pakistan and are presently confronting famine situations.

With regard to a problem that was addressed by the House yesterday, we do not favor the idea that the United States should cut economic assistance to Pakistan. To do so would simply aggravate the refugee problem because it would mean that the ability of the Government of Pakistan to work with the U.N., as it presently has indicated it is willing to do so in distributing the food supplies, its ability to create some stability would be seriously jeopardized.

We feel that the most constructive role we can play is to continue our economic assistance to West Pakistan and, thereby to be able to influence the course of events in a way that will deal with the problem of hunger in East Pakistan which would reduce the refugee flow into India, and which will, we trust, in the future look toward a viable political settlement.

We are not going to engage in public pressure on the Government of West Pakistan. That would be totally counterproductive. These are matters that we will discuss only in private channels.

CHINA TRIP

Q: Mr. President, can you tell us any more about your forthcoming trip to China, when it is likely to occur, and can you give us your assessment of what effect you think this will have on ending the war in Vietnam?

THE PRESIDENT: As far as the timing is concerned, I cannot add to what I said in the original announcement. It will be before May 1. The time will be worked out sometime within the next two to three months, I would assume, and a considerable amount of preparatory activity must take place, setting up the agenda, setting up the numbers in the official party.

These are matters, of course, that must be discussed and worked out before the time of the visit is finally announced.

Second, and I know a number of you are interested in who is going, that is a matter still to be decided. It was raised by Dr. Kissinger and by Premier Chou En-lai in their conversations, and will be worked out by mutual agreement.

As far as our party is concerned, it will be a small working party. The only ones that presently are definitely going are, of course, the Secretary of State and Dr. Kissinger and myself. Beyond that, whatever others will be added will be determined by mutual agreement between the parties concerned.

Now, as to the effect the visit will have and the conversations will have on Vietnam, I will not speculate on that subject. I will only say that as the joint announcement indicated, this will be a wide-ranging discussion of issues concerning both governments. It is not a discussion that is going to lead to instant detente.

What it really is, is moving, as we have moved, I believe, in the situation with regard to the Soviet Union, from an era of confrontation without communication to an era of negotiations with discussion. It does not mean that we go into these meetings on either side with any illusions about the wide differences that we have. Our interests are very different, and both sides recognize this, in the talks that Dr. Kissinger had, very extended talks he had with Premier Chou En-lai. We do not expect that these talks will settle all of those differences.

What is important is that we will have opened communication to see where our differences are irreconcilable, to see that they can be settled peacefully, and to find those areas where the United States, which today is the most powerful nation in the world, can find an agreement with the most populous nation in the world which potentially in the future could become the most powerful nation in the world.

As we look at the peace in the world for the balance of this century, and for that matter the next century, we must recognize that there cannot be world peace on which all the peoples in the world can rely, and in which they have such a great stake, unless there is communication between and some negotiation between these two great superpowers, the Peoples Republic and the United States.

I have put this in general terms because that is the understanding of the Peoples Republic, Premier Chou En-lai, and it is our understanding that our agenda will be worked out at a later point; before the trip it will be very carefully worked out so that the discussions will deal with the hard problems as well as the easy ones.

We expect to make some progress, but to speculate about what progress will be made on any particular issue, to speculate, for example, as to what effect this might have on Vietnam, would not serve the interests of constructive talks.

VIETNAM NEGOTIATIONS

Q: Can I ask a related policy question on Vietnam?

THE PRESIDENT: Sure.

Q: There have been some suggestions, including some indirect hints from China, that a negotiating forum involving an Asian conference to be held in Asia, primarily with Asian participants, but the United States as well, might be a better forum for negotiating a settlement in Vietnam. Can you speak to that?

THE PRESIDENT: Mr. Bailey, the question of whether there should be an all-Asian conference, with the Government of the Peoples Republic participating, as you know, has risen several times over the past few months, and was raised before our announcement was made.

As far as we are concerned, we will consider any proposal that might contribute to a more peaceful situation in the Pacific and in the world. However, at this point there is no understanding between the United States and the Peoples Republic as to whether or not out of this meeting should come that kind of proposal.

Let me say on that score, there were no conditions asked for on either side, and none accepted. There were no deals made on either side, or accepted, none offered and none accepted. This is a discussion which will take place with both sides knowing in advance that there are problems, but with both sides well prepared. This is the secret of any successful summit meeting.

As you know, parenthetically, I have always taken somewhat of a dim view of summitry when it comes in an unprepared form. But both sides will be well prepared, well in advance, on all points of major difference, and we will discuss any points of difference that could affect the peace of the world.

SOVIET VISIT

Q: Mr. President, is there any diplomatic reason you might not visit the Soviet Union before going to Peking? That was suggested.

THE PRESIDENT: In view of the announcement we have made on our visit to Peking, that will be the first visit that I will make. Obviously, it takes a great deal of time to prepare a visit and to attempt now to visit—and the Soviet Union, I am sure, feels exactly the same way—to attempt to rush around and have a summit meeting in Moscow before we go to Peking would not be in the interest of either country.

I would add this point, too: When Foreign Minister Gromyko was here, we discussed the possibility of a possible summit meeting, and we had a very candid discussion. He agreed and said that his government leaders agreed with my position, which was that a meeting at the highest level should take place and would be useful only when there was something substantive to discuss that could not be handled in other channels.

With regard to the Soviets, I should also point out that we are making very significant progress on Berlin. We are making good progress on SALT. Discussions are still continuing on the Mideast, although there I will not speculate about what the prospects for success are in view of the fact that Mr. Sisco is presently in the area exploring with the governments concerned

what the possibilities of some interim settlement looking toward a final settlement may be.

Having mentioned these three areas in which we are negotiating with the Soviet Union, I will add that if the time comes, as it may come, and both sides realize this, then the final breakthrough in any of these areas can take place only at the highest level, and then there will be a meeting. But as far as the timing of the meeting before the visit to Peking, that would not be an appropriate thing to do.

SALT

Q: I was thinking of such a thing as a settlement on the SALT talks.

THE PRESIDENT: Mr. Theis, when I said there was good progress being made on SALT, it is still a very technical and sticky problem for both sides, because it involves our vital interests. Let me emphasize that in SALT, both sides are asked to make an agreement which limits that. This is not unilateral. We, on our part, will be having very severe limitations with regard to our defensive capability, the ABM. They, on their part, will have limitations on their offensive capability, their buildup of offensive missiles.

Neither side can make those decisions lightly, without very, very basic discussions, but the fact that we have at the highest level committed ourselves to working toward an agreement simultaneously this year on both those issues, and the fact that since the talks at Helsinki began that we have made progress, gives hope that we are going to make an arrangement.

But to speculate that maybe we are going to get that done before we go to Peking, I think, would be ill-advised.

VIET CONG PROPOSALS

Q: Mr. President, why have you not accepted the Viet Cong proposals after all these weeks of probing, or given some formal reply?

THE PRESIDENT: I have noted some criticism in the press about the fact that Ambassador Bruce had to leave August 1st. Incidentally, I am most grateful that he stayed an extra month, because his doctor got hold of me and said he should have left July 1st. In any event, his having left August 1st, and Mr. Porter not being able to arrive until the latter part of August, there has been some speculation, and I understand this, criticism in the press and the Senate and the House that the Administration is not interested in negotiating a settlement, that we are not considering the various proposals that have been made by the VC and North Vietnamese.

Now, just so the members of the press will not get out on a limb with regard to predicting what we are or are not doing, let me make one statement and then I will go no further.

We are very actively pursuing negotiations on Vietnam in established channels. The record, when it finally comes out, will answer all the critics as far as the activity of this Government in pursuing negotiations in established channels. It would not be useful to negotiate in the newspapers if we want to have those negotiations succeed.

I am not predicting that the negotiations will succeed. I am saying, however, that as far as the United States is concerned, we have gone and are going the extra mile on negotiations in established channels. You can interpret that any way you want, but do not interpret it in a way that indicates that the United States is missing this opportunity or that opportunity, or another one, to negotiate.

VIETNAMESE ELECTIONS

Q: Mr. President, one of the points being mentioned in the comments on the negotiations is the election in South Vietnam this fall. Is that a factor that does have some bearing on the pace of the negotiations?

THE PRESIDENT: It has certainly in terms of the North Vietnamese. As you know, the stumbling block for them in negotiations really is the political settlement. As they look at the election this fall, they feel that unless that election comes out in a way that a candidate they can support, or at least that they are not as much against as they are President Thieu, but unless it comes out that way, it will be very difficult for them to have a negotiated settlement.

With regard to the elections, let me emphasize our position. Our position is one of complete neutrality in these elections. Under Ambassador Bunker's skillful direction, we have made it clear to all parties concerned that we are not supporting any candidate; that we will accept the verdict of the people of South Vietnam.

I have noted, for example, that President Thieu has invited observers to come from other nations to witness the election. I hope observers do go. I think they will find, I hope they will find, as they did when they observed previous elections in Vietnam, that by most standards they were fair.

As far as observers from this country are concerned, we have, of course, several members of the Senate and others that have indicated a desire to go. We, of course, have no objection to that. We want a fair election and we, of course, have some observers on the scene in the person of the Ambassador and his staff who will watch that election.

ECONOMIC PROBLEMS

Q: Mr. President, the last time you gave some stock market advice to us, it turned out pretty well. What would you do now, buy or sell?

THE PRESIDENT: With regard to the stock market, I suppose my advice should not be given much weight because I am not in the market. It is so easy to make predictions where your own assets are not involved.

I will say this: I would not sell the United States economy short at this point. And long term, I would not be selling my investments in the American economy whether it is in stocks or real estate or what have you; selling them in a panicky way.

The stock market has come up, even at its present level of 850, 230 points since I made that prediction. I can only say that my long-range prediction for this economy is still what I said at the first of this year.

At the first of this year, when the very same people had written—and I have read the news magazines and business magazines, and not, of course, any of the columns you had written this week—but I heard all the rest this week, and the gloomy predictions about the economy and it is going down and there is nothing good about it. I read them also for November of last year; exactly the same gloominess and same words, and so forth.

I said then, and I think all of you were present then, I thought 1971 would be a good year for the economy, and 1972 would be a very good year. I stand by that. When we look at the first half of this year, it is not what people said about the economy; it is what they do about it that counts.

GNP is up a record $52 billion. Retail sales now in June, and the first indications as far as July are concerned, it will stay at this level, are at record highs. Consumer spending is at a record high. Construction, particularly in housing, are near record highs. Inventories—and this is another indication of what will happen to the future for those who may be thinking of investing their money in businesses—inventories are abnormally low in view of the high level of retail sales.

What this tells me is that there is a lot of steam in the boiler in this economy, and you cannot continue to have high retail sales and low inventories without eventually starting to rebuild. Therefore, my projection for the balance of this year is that the economy will continue to move up as it has moved up in the first half.

That doesn't mean that there will not be aberrations in the monthly figures. It does mean, however, that the economy

has a great deal of strength in it. This is a period when it is absorbing almost 2 million people who have been let out of defense plants and the Armed Forces and is absorbing that with a lower rate of unemployment than was the case in 1961, 1962, 1963, which were the last three peacetime years before Vietnam when the unemployment rate, as you recall, averaged 6 percent.

INCOMES POLICY

Q: Mr. President, in that connection, to continue that, does that mean that you are still resolutely opposed to any incomes policy or, specifically, wage-price controls?

THE PRESIDENT: I think, Peter, it is well to identify incomes policies and wage-price controls for what they are and what they are not, because, as a matter of fact—and this gives me an opportunity to set the record straight with regard to some greatly blown up differences that I am supposed to have with my very good friend Arthur Burns, and perhaps you were too polite to ask that direct question—

ARTHUR BURNS

Q: Well, I will ask it.

THE PRESIDENT: I thought that would be the follow-up, so I anticipated it. Let me get at it this way:

Arthur Burns, in terms of monetary policy and in terms of fiscal policy, has followed a course that I think is the most responsible and statesmanlike of any Chairman of the Federal Reserve in my memory. In other words, you have seen an expansionary monetary policy, and that is one of the reasons we have had an expansionary economy in the first six months of this year.

He has also stood firmly with this Administration in its responsible fiscal policy, resisting, for example, spending above what the economy would produce at full capacity. He has strongly supported me in those efforts.

That brings me to an area where he has taken a very unfair shot. Within this Administration, the Office of Budget and Management, on a reorganization plan two months ago, recommended that the Chairman of the Federal Reserve, because he basically is our central banker, should be raised to the same status of the central bankers abroad. I enthusiastically approved the idea. However, when the matter was raised with Dr. Burns by my associates, he indicated that neither he nor any other individual in a high position in Government should take a salary increase at a time that the President was going to have to take some strong measures, as I am going to take to limit salary increases in other areas of Government, including, for example, blue collar workers.

So, consequently, while there is not any question but that the Federal Reserve position will eventually be raised to the Level I position that was recommended, Arthur Burns and, incidentally, George Shultz, who is also on this list as a recommendation of the Ash Council, Arthur Burns and George Shultz being the responsible men that they were, asked that there not be an example set by them of a pay increase which would make it very difficult for us to deal effectively and responsibly with pay increases in other sectors of the Government. So we find that Burns agrees, that I agree with Burns, let's put it that way, very strongly on his monetary policy, on his fiscal policy, the question he has raised with regard to an incomes policy.

When we talk about an incomes policy, let's see what he is not for. He is unalterably opposed, as I am, to the Galbraith scheme, which is supported by many of our Democratic Senators, I understand, of permanent wage and price controls. Permanent wage and price controls in America would stifle the American economy, its dynamism, its productivity, and would be, I think, a mortal blow to the United States as a first-class economic power.

On the other hand, it is essential that Government use its power where it can be effective to stop the escalation, or at least temper the escalation in the wage-price spiral. That is why we moved on construction, and we have been somewhat successful, from 16 down to 9 percent. That is why we moved to roll back an oil price recently.

As far as the two recent settlements, the one in railroads and the one in steel, on the plus side, the fact that they were settled was positive; the fact, too, that in the case of railroads, they spoke to the problem of productivity by modification of work rules, and the fact that the steel settlement also spoke to the problem of productivity by setting up productivity councils, that was constructive.

On the other hand, I would be less than candid if I were not to say, and I know the leaders of the steel and railroad industry know this, that this kind of settlement where a wage increase leads to a price increase, and particularly in steel, where the industry is already noncompetitive with foreign imports, is not in the interest of America, not in the interest of labor, and not in the interest of industry.

Dr. Burns, without being completely specific, has only suggested the idea should be considered. That is why Secretary Connally said we welcome the move by several Republican Senators to hold hearings concerning wage and price supports. That is why Dr. Burns said we should move to attempt to temper these increases.

The problem here is, how can we move without putting the American economy in a straitjacket? In other words, as Secretary Connally raised the question in his statement this morning, "Are we to have criminal penalties?" Are, for example, the wage-price guidelines to affect all the examples down to the neighborhood filling station or the grocery store or the meat market, as the case might be, or will they affect only major industries?

As far as this Administration is concerned, I can say this: I have asked the Secretary of Labor to bring to my attention every major wage-price negotiation which may be coming up in the future, and I will use the power of this office to the extent it can be effective to see that those negotiations are as responsible as possible.

On September 21st, we will have a meeting of our Productivity Commission, and Subject "A" in that meeting will be this same problem, because as we look at America's trade balances, which have deteriorated over the past 10 years, but as we look at America's competitive position, it is essential that American industry and American labor sit down together and determine whether, at a time when we are in a race, we no longer can be Number 1 simply because we were that big and that strong after World War I, whether we determine we are going to get out of the race or whether we are going to tighten our belts and be responsible in wage-price decisions so that we can continue to be competitive in the world.

That speaks to the problem of an incomes policy, this meeting that we will have. The only question of difference between Arthur Burns, and some Senators have raised this question, is the degree to which, in tackling these individual wage settlments, we have compulsion, we have criminal penalties. I don't think they want compulsion or criminal penalties.

Then the question is: How far will persuasion go. Our record shows that in most countries abroad that have tried it, except for very small countries that are tightly controlled, persuasion alone will work for only three to four months.

So as far as we are concerned, I am glad to consider recommendations for tackling the problem. I will tackle them, and I am serving notice now that we are going to take up the problem with the Productivity Commission. We are going to look at each individual settlement in major industries where there is going to be wage-price negotiations, and use the influence we can to keep them in line, and in addition to that, we will consider a recommendation on wage-price boards. But I will reject it if I find, and I have yet to find any recommendation that did not have this ingredient in it, if I find that it would impose a new bureaucracy with enormous criminal powers, to fasten itself on the American economy. That, I think, would do far more harm than good.

JAWBONING

Q: In the same line to follow up that question, if the settlement in the steel industry and particularly the raise in prices which was recently announced is not good for the country and not good for labor and management, why do you not call in the leaders of the steel industry and use your influence to get them to change the increase in prices and then if necessary other parts of the settlement which are so inimical to the country?

THE PRESIDENT: Calling in the steel industry and getting them to change would not be effective. As you may recall, in one instance earlier this year, we were able to get a steel rollback. That had a temporary beneficial effect. But at a time that the steel industry has negotiated a settlement of this nature, at a time when its profits at 2½ percent are the lowest of any major industry, to tell the steel industry that after they have negotiated a settlement they must roll back their price and run at a loss is simply unrealistic. They are not going to do it.

The longer term answer here is for the steel industry, and this is what we have addressed ourselves to, and the labor to recognize that now that they have had their settlement, now that labor has gotten a good increase, an increase consistent with aluminum and others, now that steel found it necessary to raise prices that this may be good temporarily for both but in the long run it will simply mean less steel sold and less jobs and that is why we are zeroing in on the productivity side because increases in productivity can be the only answer where a wage increase of this kind takes place.

FEDERAL EMPLOYEES

Q: Mr. President, a minute ago you mentioned something about doing something about wages for government employees.

THE PRESIDENT: Yes, one of the problems, difficult problems, I confronted last year and that I will confront again this year, is a recommendation to increase the wages for blue collar workers within the government. I have examined that situation and I have determined that an increase in the blue collar wage scale would not be in the interests of our fighting the inflation battle.

Speaking to the same point, we have a situation with regard to the Congress and some of its appropriations bills. We are trying to keep our budget within the full employment limits for 1972.

The Congress already has exceeded our budget by $5.4 billion. That includes mandatory spending which they have imposed upon us and additions to the appropriations bills. Before they get through with the appropriations process I hope that comes down.

But that will be highly inflationary unless the Congress speaks to that problem more effectively. What I was indicating, in other words, Herb, I am indicating in advance the decision that I do not intend to approve the wage increase relative to the blue collar workers in the government. Under those circumstances, I could not, of course, approve an increase in salaries for people as underpaid basically as Dr. Burns is, considering what he could get on the outside or Dr. Shultz is, considering what he could get on the outside.

Q: How many people are there in the blue collar area?

THE PRESIDENT: I don't have that but it is a significant number. Incidentally, I think it is an equitable decision because they have had some substantial increases in the past. It is a question of whether we just continue for a short time.

WAGE-PRICE GUIDELINES

Q: Sir, you also mentioned guidelines in a manner that suggested that you might accept the concept of numerical guidelines, did you mean to suggest that?

THE PRESIDENT: No. What I meant to say was that my study of the situation indicates that guidelines in this country have always failed. They have never worked. Guidelines in other industrial countries including Canada, for example, and Britain, have worked only for a short time and then have fallen because guidelines basically connote voluntary compliance and voluntary compliance goes on only for a brief time.

Now, as far as what I am saying, it is that our approach at this time is a selective one to take those particular industries that are coming up for bargaining and to use our influence as effectively as we can to see that those settlements are responsible.

Secondly, that as far as a wage price board is concerned, that it would be considered favorably only if the hearings that are going to be taken in this field, only if the hearings can convince me that enforcing an incomes policy could be accomplished without stifling the economy.

It is the problem, in other words, of enforcement, because I come back to this fundamental proposition: I have yet to find except for the extremists on the left, and I don't say this in a condemning way, it is only an observation, but the extremists on the left of the economy spectrum have always favored a totally government-controlled economy.

They believe that. I don't believe it. They believe that we should have permanent wage and price controls and that government should determine what wages should be and what prices should be. I don't believe that. Dr. Burns does not believe that if you have read his speeches over the years. He is a strong opponent of that.

The question is, how can we address ourselves to the problem of wages and prices without having those mandatory criminal penalty features which would lead us to something we all are trying to avoid. This is why this is a matter for discussion.

It is not one yet for decision but I will continue to work on individual settlements as I have said.

WAGE-PRICE BOARD

Q: Mr. President, would it be fair to say, then, that in view of what you said there and what you said earlier that you will consider recommendations of the wage and price board, that you are giving renewed and perhaps more favorable consideration to some form of wage-price board, assuming that they don't have penalties?

THE PRESIDENT: No. I am saying that I shall continue the policy of moving aggressively on individual settlements on a case-by-case basis. Secondly, I will address this particular problem in a meeting with the major leaders of American industry and American labor at the Productivity Commission meeting on September 21. Third, with regard to wage-price boards, I have still not been convinced that we can move in that direction and be effective. However, Secretary Connally, in his statement this morning, raised all the questions that should be raised on that. As far as we are concerned, we have an open mind in terms of examining the various proposals to see if there is a new approach which we may not have thought of.

I have serious doubts that they will find such a new approach, but I do want to indicate that we will examine it because we all agree that the wage-price spiral is a significant danger to this expanding economy. The question is what do we do about it, without going all the way to a totally controlled economy.

INFLATION

Q: Mr. President, Dr. Burns, before the Joint Economic Committee, said he didn't think we were making much progress against inflation. Do you think we are?

THE PRESIDENT: I read Dr. Burns statement quite carefully. What he was saying is what I would say. I would say it with regard to inflation and unemployment. I am never satisfied and never will be satisfied, and anybody in the free economy is never satisfied and should never be satisfied with anything except perfection.

That doesn't mean that we are going to reach perfection. With regard to inflation, I will just point to the numbers,. Inflation, which, of course, was boiling along when we came into office in January of 1969, reached its peak in 1970, six percent. Then the CPI dropped to 4 percent in the first six months of 1969. Now, 4 percent is still too high, but that is progress.

The GNP deflator, which of course goes far beyond the consumer price index, as you know, the GNP deflator covers all, the whole spectrum of the economy, in the first six months of 1971, it was the lowest in three years. That is progress; not enough, but it is progress.

In the last month the CPI was higher than the average it has been for the first five months. We all know that these month-to-month variations are not what counts. My view is that we are making progress against inflation, but it is going to require continued strong policies on the part of the Administration with the cooperation of the Congress in limiting our budget expenditures to full capacity or full employment revenues. That is the battle we will continue to wage and it will also need cooperation from labor and management on limiting the wage price spiral.

On the unemployment front, we have a somewhat similar problem. In the last three peacetime years before the Vietnam War expenditures began to hypo the economy, 1961, 1962, and 1963, unemployment in those years averaged six percent. We, at this point, have brought unemployment below six percent, not as much as we would like. It reached its peak in January. It was 6.2. What the figures will be for this month you will known on Friday. I don't know what they are myself. I will read this as you do and that is the way it should be.

But in any event, the unemployment curve is down. Six point two was the high and we are now below six percent. I believe that it will continue, with monthly aberrations, on a downward course through the balance of the year.

I believe that as we go into 1972, I still stick with my prediction that we shall see unemployment continue to move downward and that 1972, for that year, will be a very good year.

I would point out one final thing on the unemployment facts. As I have often pointed out, as of this morning, I looked at the numbers, over 2 million Americans have been let out of the armed services and out of defense plants since we started to wind down the war in Vietnam.

If they were in the services or in the defense plants at the present time, unemployment would be 4.3. But the other side of that coin is that casualties when we came in were 300 a week. This week, last week, they were 12.

I just think the price is too high to pay. We believe that our goal of a new prospect of low unemployment but with peace and not at the cost of war is one that Americans are willing to work toward.

We are going to achieve that goal. Getting back to the stock market question, I will simply say this: Everybody else has been prophetic about the future. I think the prophets who presently say that the American economy is on the skids, that we have made no progress on inflation, that the economy is not moving up, who ignore the $52 billion increase in GNP, who ignore the increase in retail sales, who ignore the strong, positive elements in the economy, I think by the end of this year that they are going to look bad so I will go out on the limb to that effect but by the end of this year I might look bad.

Let's just hope that they do rather than myself because all of us are involved.

VIETNAM CASUALTIES

Q: On the casualties, Mr. President, do you think that the figures of 12 per week in that category, are they an aberration or does your policy envision them to continue to decline during this year?

THE PRESIDENT: No, they are not an aberration. They are the result, frankly, of first an American withdrawal.

American forces in Vietnam today, as you can tell from reading the reports, are in defensive positions. We are frankly just defending the area in which we have responsibility and there are less of them.

Consequently, our casualties go down for that reason. Secondly, they are down for another reason. The enemy doesn't have the punch it had because another point to look at is that South Vietnamese casualties are also substantially down from what they were. What has happened is that the two operations, Cambodia and Laos, so very severely disrupted the enemy's ability to wage offensive actions that for both Americans and South Vietnamese the level of fighting is down.

There again will be aberrations up and down, I would assume. Nobody can predict that. But the war is being wound down and as far as Americans are concerned, we trust it will continue to go down.

THE PRESS: Thank you, Mr. President.

OCTOBER 12

Following is the text, as made available by the White House, of President Nixon's Oct. 12 impromptu news conference, his 21st since taking office and his first since Sept. 16.

THE PRESIDENT: Be seated, please.

Ladies and gentlemen, I have an announcement which is embargoed until 12:00 noon Washington time and 7:00 o'clock Moscow time. In order for you to have a chance to file before the 12 o'clock deadline, I have asked Mr. Kempster, who has the right to end the conference, to break it off at five minutes to twelve. Between that time and the time that I read this announcement, of course, I will take questions on this announcement or any other subject you would like to have covered.

The announcement is as follows:

The leaders of the United States and the Soviet Union in their exchanges during the past year, have agreed that a meeting between them would be desirable once sufficient progress had been made in negotiations at lower levels.

In light of the recent advances in bilateral and multilateral negotiations involving the two countries, it has been agreed that such a meeting will take place in Moscow in the latter part of May 1972.

President Nixon and the Soviet leaders will review all major issues, with a view toward further improving their bilateral relations and enhancing the prospects of world peace.

We will go to your questions.

MOSCOW, PEKING VISITS

Q: Mr. President, what relationship does this have to your visit to China?

THE PRESIDENT: The two are independent trips. We are going to Peking for the purpose of discussing matters of bilateral concern there and I will be going to the Soviet Union for the purpose of discussing matters that involve the United States and the Soviet Union. Neither trip is being taken for the purpose of exploiting what differences may exist between the two nations.

Neither is being taken at the expense of any other nation.

The trips are being taken for the purpose of better relations between the United States and the Soviet Union and better relations between the United States and the Peoples Republic of China. And any speculation to the effect that one has been planned for the purpose of affecting the other would be entirely inaccurate.

Q: Mr. President, why announce a trip of this nature so far in advance?

THE PRESIDENT: It is vitally important, both in the case of this trip and the trip to the Peoples Republic of China—which, as you know, we announced far in advance. The date yet to be selected. Dr. Kissinger will work out that date on his

trip, which will take place in the next two or three weeks—but it is vitally important that the meeting accomplish something.

It is therefore important that the preparation for the meeting be adequate in every respect and in the discussion that I had with Mr. Gromyko when he was here and discussions prior to that time, that were had at other levels with regard to the setting up of this trip, it was felt that May of 1972 would be the time when progress on a number of fronts, in which we are presently involved with the Soviet Union, would have reached the point that a meeting at the highest level could be effective.

ARMS TALKS

Q: Mr. President, do you expect to be able to sign an agreement on strategic arms when you go to Moscow next May?

THE PRESIDENT: As you will recall, we, at the highest level in May, indicated that our goal would be to try to achieve an agreement on strategic arms this year. We are making progress towards that goal. We will continue to move toward achieving that goal, either at the end of this year or as soon thereafter as we possibly can.

If the goal can be achieved before May of 1972, we will achieve it and that, incidentally, is also the view of the Soviet Union.

I will not speculate as to failing to achieve that goal. If it is not achieved, certainly that would be one of the subjects that would come up.

Q: Mr. President, what would you expect other items on the agenda to be in addition to anything that is concluded at the SALT Talks?

THE PRESIDENT: I have already indicated we will review all major issues. Now today what the issues will be is quite premature. For example, the question that has just been raised with regard to the SALT Talks is one that may be behind us at that point.

Both governments are working toward that end. And then the question would be, what do we do in arms control going beyond simply the limitation of strategic weapons at this point and the same would be true of the Mideast, which is a possible subject. The same is true in a number of other areas where presently the Soviet Union and the United States are having negotiations.

The fact that we are going to have a meeting in May does not mean that the negotiating tracks that we are engaged on with the Soviet Union, in a number of areas, are now closed or that we are going to slow down.

We are going to go forward in all other areas so that in May we can deal with unfinished business.

CUBA

Q: Would this include Cuba, Mr. President?

THE PRESIDENT: The question as to whether peripheral areas—and I mean by "peripheral areas", areas that do not directly involve the Soviet Union and the United States—would be involved would depend on the situation at that time.

For example, Cuba is one possibility. The question of Southeast Asia is another. As far as Southeast Asia is concerned, I would emphasize there, again, however, that, completely without regard to this meeting, and completely without regard to the meeting that will take place with the Chinese leaders at an earlier date, we are proceeding both on the negotiating track and on the Vietnamization track to end American involvement in Vietnam. We trust that we will have accomplished that goal, or at least have made significant progress toward accomplishing that goal, by the time this meeting takes place.

BACKGROUND TO SOVIET SUMMIT

Q: Can you tell us the mechanics, sir? How did the meeting come about? Did their Ambassador come here? Was it hot-lined, and can you tell us, sir, when the ball started rolling toward this meeting?

THE PRESIDENT: The ball started rolling toward this meeting, I think, in my first press conference when, you recall, the inevitable question came up, "Are we going to have a summit with the Soviet Union?"

I pointed out then I did not believe a summit would serve a useful purpose unless something was to come out of it. I do not believe in having summit meetings simply for the purpose of having a meeting. I think that tends to create euphoria. It raises high hopes that are then dashed, as was the case with Glassboro. We are not making that mistake.

Both in our meeting with the Chinese which is being very carefully planned, as evidenced by Dr. Kissinger's trip to help prepare the final agenda and arrangements, in our meeting with the Soviet Union we have agreed to a summit meeting only on the basis that we would have an agenda in which there was a possibility of making significant progress, and also on which items would be on the agenda on which progress could best be made, and in some instances might only be made by decisions at the highest level.

Now, I stated that, or at least made that point, in several press conferences, including my first one. In the spring of last year there was some discussion with the Soviet Union at lower levels with regard to the possibility of a summit. There was further discussion of the possibility of a summit when I met with Mr. Gromyko in the fall of last year when he was here with the United Nations.

Those discussions have continued on and off, not at my level, but on other levels, until Mr. Gromyko arrived for his visit with me on this occasion. On this occasion he brought a formal invitation.

Let me say on the Soviet side that they agreed basically with my principle, which is also theirs, that a summit meeting should be held only when both sides are prepared to discuss matters of substance, and it is because both of us have been waiting for the time that we felt there were matters on which major progress could be made that the summit meeting is being held at this time, rather than at an earlier time.

I should also point out the very significant areas in which we have made progress in Soviet-American relations, both on our part and their part. We have felt unless we were able to make progress in this era of negotiations rather than confrontation and other areas, that a meeting at the summit might be simply an impasse; but when we look back over the record of the last 2½ years, significant progress has been made.

We have had a treaty with regard to the seabeds. We have had one with regard to biological weapons. We have had an agreement coming out of the SALT talks with regard to the hot line and accidental war and, of course, most important of all—and I think this is the item that, for both us and for them, led us to conclude that now was the time for a summit meeting—we have had an agreement on Berlin. The Berlin negotiations, of course, are not completely wrapped up; but on the part of the Soviet Union and the United States and, of course, the other two powers involved, this agreement had historic significance.

In view of the progress that we have made, Mr. Gromyko, speaking for his government, and I, speaking for ours, agreed on the occasion of his visit that this was the time for a summit meeting.

Q: Mr. President, this then was the reason you announced you would go to Peking before May? You had this May date in mind at that time?

THE PRESIDENT: No, Mr. Theis, when we announced that we would be going to Peking, we did not have an understanding with the Soviet Union that we were going to have a visit to the Soviet Union. However, I should point out that as far as the announcement with regard to the Soviet summit is concerned, that the Government of the Peoples Republic of China was informed that this announcement would be made today, and is aware of the date of the Soviet visit that I had mentioned, the latter part of May.

I should also point out that the government in Peking is aware of the fact that we will be working toward agreement on a date with them, which will be prior to the meeting with the Soviet leaders.

Q: Mr. President, with which Soviet leaders do you expect to have your most significant talks, Kosygin, Brezhnev, or Podgorny, or all three of them or two of them?

THE PRESIDENT: Generally speaking, in the Soviet system, the talks that take place will, of course, cover all three, but the Chairman, in this case Mr. Brezhnev, is the man with whom I would expect to have very significant talks. I would expect certainly to have significant talks also with Kosygin and perhaps Mr. Podgorny.

But in the Soviet system, as I pointed out—and the same is also true of the Peoples Republic system—in any Communist system, the Chairman of the Communist Party is the man who is the major center of power.

Q: Mr. President, at the time the Red China trip was announced, I believe we were told it was going to be before May first because you didn't want to get it involved in domestic political politics. I wonder how this differs, since this is after May 1, as far as domestic political politics is concerned?

THE PRESIDENT: We have this just as close to May 1 as we possibly could. This was the best date that the Soviet Union and we could agree upon, and it will come, as I said, in the latter part of May.

We both deliberately agreed that it should not come—which would generally have been their first choice, because June or July is a better time to go to Moscow than May, I understand—we agreed for the reasons that we have mentioned, that it should be in May.

VIETNAM WITHDRAWAL

Q: Mr. President, you said that it is your goal to end the American involvement in South Vietnam or at least make significant progress toward that by the time you meet in Moscow.

Is it your goal that you can end at least the American ground combat involvement by that time?

THE PRESIDENT: I will have another announcement on Vietnam in November. That announcement will speak to that question and other announcements after that will also speak to that question.

I will not speculate further on that. The American presence in Vietnam, both in terms of our residual forces, the ground combat forces to which you refer, and the use of our air power, will be maintained to meet the objectives that I have often times spelled out, including among others, the return of our POW's, and the ability of the South Vietnamese to take over the responsibility themselves. But I would strongly urge the members of the press not to speculate as to what I am going to say in November.

PHASE TWO

Q: Mr. President, a question on Phase 2, sir. Are you prepared to give the Tripartite Board complete autonomy in order to gain labor's cooperation?

THE PRESIDENT: A meeting is taking place at this moment, and perhaps may be nearing conclusion, in which the AFL-CIO Council is discussing their participation in the Tripartite Board, and the question as to the extent of their cooperation with our efforts to control inflation.

I believe, first, that Secretary Connally answered your question, and that is our position, in his press conference. As far as any further discussion with regard to the role that labor will play, and the relationship of the board to the Cost of Living Council, I think it would be well to wait until their meeting has been concluded.

If they make a statement today, I will issue a statement from here commenting upon that specific matter, if it is raised.

Q: Could you tell us what consultations were had with the NATO allies or Japan on the two visits?

THE PRESIDENT: All were informed.

SUPREME COURT

Q: Mr. President, can you tell us when you may make a nomination or nominations for the Supreme Court and is Senator Byrd of West Virginia on the list of those you are considering?

THE PRESIDENT: He is definitely on the list and I will make the nominations next week, both.

Q: Both?

THE PRESIDENT: Both.

Q: Sir, you are going to have a woman on there, aren't you? (Laughter)

THE PRESIDENT: I would simply add that I don't rule out Senator Byrd and I certainly don't rule out a woman for consideration.

Incidentally, the speculation with regard to the court, I know, is naturally a subject of very great interest, but I can assure you that the dope stories that a man is certain to get it and then a dope story this morning, he is out of the running, both are wrong.

Senator Byrd, as a result of several of his colleagues recommending him, is one that is being considered. And I will also say in answer to Miss McClendon's question that at at least two women are under consideration at this time.

KISSINGER TRIP

Q: Mr. President, to clarify your expectation on the Moscow visit, it would be equally your expectation to have significant talks with Chairman Mao in Peking rather than meetings with Chou En-lai or ceremonial meetings with the Chairman?

THE PRESIDENT: The question as to what kind of meetings will take place in Peking will be worked out by Dr. Kissinger when he is there. There will, of course, be meetings with Chou En-lai. I would assume there would be meetings with the Chairman. However, in each system, the Soviet system and the Chinese system, the question as to which individual should cover which subject varies and, of course, I will be prepared to meet with whatever leader in the Soviet Union or whatever leader in the Peoples Republic of China has the responsibility for the particular subjects we have in mind.

For example, take the Soviet. It may well be that Chairman Brezhnev may have the responsibility in certain political or foreign policy areas. It might be that Prime Minister Kosygin would have responsibility in trade areas. I am not trying to say what they have decided, but we are prepared, and both governments know we are prepared, for me to meet with the head of government or the Chairman of the Party, or any other that they designate who has responsibility.

I should also point out that the Secretary of State will accompany me to both Moscow and Peking. Dr. Kissinger will accompany me and it will be a small working group, and meetings will take place not only between the President and various leaders on their side, but between the Secretary of State and the people designated by them on their side.

We expect to have a very busy, working visit, not a ceremonial visit. Ceremony, I should indicate, will be at an absolute minimum in both the Soviet Union and in the Peoples Republic.

I emphasize again, the purpose of both visits is not simply cosmetics. We are not taking a trip for the sake of taking a trip. The purpose of these visits is at the very highest level to attempt to make progress in negotiating in areas where there are very significant differences. Differences between us and the Peoples Republic. Differences between us and the Soviet Union.

I should emphasize, too, that in pointing out the progress we have made with the Soviet Union, that Mr. Gromyko and I agreed that we still have very great differences. We do not expect all those differences to be resolved, but there is one thing in which we agree at this point and that is that the interest of neither country would be served by war.

If there is another world war, if there is war between the super powers, there will be no winners. There will be only losers.

I think we can both agree that neither major power can get a decisive advantage over the other, an advantage which would enable it to launch a pre-emptive strike or an advantage because it was able to launch a pre-emptive strike which might enable it to engage in international blackmail.

It is because we have reached the point that the competition in terms of escalating arms race cannot gain an advantage, and both of us emphasize this in our meeting, it is for that reason that now the time has come to negotiate our differences, negotiate with regard to our differences, recognizing that they are still very deep, recognizing, however, that there is no alternative to negotiation at this point.

TEXTILE AGREEMENTS

Q: Mr. President, are we going to have textile agreements this week in advance of the October 15th deadline which, reportedly, the Administration has set down for mandatory quotas?

THE PRESIDENT: At the present time very intensive talks are going on with the Japanese on the textile question. We are hopeful that those talks will produce a mutual agreement. In the event there is not a mutual agreement, and in the event that by October 15th there is either not an agreement or a process underway which points to the negotiating of an agreement, then the United States will move unilaterally.

EUROPEAN SECURITY

Q: In connection with the agenda for the Moscow talks, what is the position of the United States at present on the question of a European Security Conference, and specifically, is it the U.S. position that we will not agree to a European Security Conference until there is a final agreement on Berlin and first-stage agreement on SALT?

THE PRESIDENT: The European Security Conference is a matter that has been very widely discussed between our two governments. As a matter of fact, it was one of the suggestions for discussion, I think it is proper to reveal, when I met with Mr. Gromyko. I note the press has so speculated, and the press, in this case, is correct.

With regard to the European Security Conference, you are correct in saying that, until the Berlin matter is wrapped up, the discussions with regard to the possibility of a European Security Conference would not serve a useful purpose. After it is wrapped up, then we shall go forward with preliminary discussions to see whether or not a European Security Conference could serve a useful purpose.

Both governments agree, with regard to the European Security Conference, that it, like a summit conference, should not be held until there are areas where there can be substantial chances for agreement. The Secretary of State will have the primary responsibility, after the Berlin settlement is totally wrapped up, to explore with our allies, as the Soviet Union will be exploring with theirs, whether or not the European Security Conference should be held, and if it should be held, when it should be held.

I should also point out, because it does raise the other questions, I mentioned in answer to an earlier question, that our allies had been informed and that Japan had been informed. Prior to the visit to the Soviet Union, there will, of course, be extensive consultation with our allies on matters which affect them. For example, mutual balanced force reduction, the European Security Conference, matters of this sort, if they are to come up at a summit conference, will, of course, be discussed with our allies, just as we expect the Soviet Union to discuss it with their allies.

VIETNAM ELECTIONS

Q: Now that the South Vietnamese election returns are official, will you be sending your congratulations to the winner, and do you have any comments on those elections?

THE PRESIDENT: On September 16th I indicated my view about the elections, and I stand by that view. I believe, as the Secretary of State pointed out in his television appearance Sunday, that we have to keep this matter in perspective. We would have preferred, just as we would prefer in all countries of the world, a contested election somewhat along the lines that would meet our standard.

On the other hand, the situation in South Vietnam has been that they have made great progress toward representative government there. There has been a very lively opposition in both the National Assembly and in the Senate.

As far as President Thieu is concerned, he is aware of my statement of September 16th, and I will be sending a representative, of course, to his inauguration. Let me say in that respect that if the United States followed the practice of not sending representatives to inaugurations unless the President or the Prime Minister was there as a result of a contested election, we would only have one-third as many delegations to send, and we wouldn't want to do that.

THE PRESS: Thank you, Mr. President.

NOVEMBER 12

Following is the text, as made available by the White House, of President Nixon's Nov. 12 impromptu news conference, his 22nd since taking office and his first since Oct. 12.

THE PRESIDENT: Won't you be seated, ladies and gentlemen.

Ladies and gentlemen, I have an announcement of a substantially increased troop withdrawal from Vietnam. When I entered office on January 20, 1969, there were 540,000 Americans in Vietnam and our casualties were running as high as 300 a week.

Over the past three years, we have made progress on both fronts. Our casualties, for example, for the past five week have been less than 10, instead of 300 a week, and with regard to withdrawals, 80 percent of those who were there have come home— 365,000.

I have now had an opportunity to appraise the situation as it is today. I have consulted with my senior advisors and I have an up-to-date report from Secretary Laird.

Based on those consultations and consultations with the Government of South Vietnam, I am now able to make this announcement. Over the next two months, we will withdraw 45,000 Americans. I will make another announcement before the first of February. As far as that second announcement is concerned, before the first of February, the number to be withdrawn—the rate that is—as well as the duration of the announcement, will be determined by three factors.

First, by the level of enemy activity and particularly by the infiltration route and its rate because if the level of enemy activity and infiltration substantially increases, it could be very dangerous to our sharply decreased forces in South Vietnam.

Second, the progress of our training program, our Vietnamization program in South Vietnam, and third, any progress that may have been made with regard to two major objectives we have, obtaining the release of all our POW's wherever they are in Southeast Asia and obtaining a cease fire for all of Southeast Asia.

Those three criteria will determine the next announcement, both its duration and its rate.

Now, I will be glad to take questions on this announcement or any other subject, domestic or foreign, you would like to make.

LAOS AND CAMBODIA

Q: Mr. President, to be clear on the cease fire, that includes Laos and Cambodia as well as South Vietnam?

THE PRESIDENT: That is our goal, Mr. Lisagor, yes, sir. As you know, we offered that in my talks of last year in October. We have been continuing to offer it. We would, of course, believe that attaining that goal would bring peace to the whole area which is what we want and of course would greatly reduce the need for a very heavy American aid program that presently we have for particularly Cambodia.

PRISONERS OF WAR

Q: Mr. President, do you have any reason for encouragement on the release of prisoners of war from any source?

THE PRESIDENT: No reason for encouragement that I can talk about publicly. I can say, however, that we are pursuing this subject as I have indicated on several occasions in a number of channels and we have not given up. We will never give up with regard to our prisoners of war. That is one of the reasons why an announcement is being made for a shorter period rather than a longer period, because the moment that we make an announcement that is too long, it means that whatever negotiating stroke we might have is substantially reduced.

INFILTRATION

Q: Mr. President, what has been the most recent trend towards the infiltration by the enemy and do you have figures for that and also, what rate would have to be maintained for you to carry out your optimum plan?

THE PRESIDENT: We would have to examine that situation at the time. The infiltration rate has come up some as it always does at this time of year. However, it is not as high now, just as the casualties are not as high now and the level of enemy activity as it was last year. We want to see, however, what the situation is in December and January, which, as you all know, are the key months when infiltration comes along, because that will determine what the activity will be in April, May, June and July on the battlefield.

FEB. 1 TROOP CEILING

Q: Mr. President.

THE PRESIDENT: Yes, Mr. Bailey.

Q: To be clear, what is your new February 1 troop ceiling or are you doing it the way you have done it before by setting a new troop ceiling at the end of the withdrawal period?

THE PRESIDENT: It will be a new troop ceiling for the end of the withdrawal period. I think we would have to cover that later. The 45,000 should be taken off of the present ceiling. We are reducing the ceiling by 45,000.

Now, incidentally, I should say, too, that in terms of the withdrawal, I think it would be proper to inform the press on this matter. We are going to withdraw 25,000 in December and 20,000 in January. Obviously we would like to get a few more out before Christmas and we were able to do this after Secretary Laird made his report.

Q: In this present situation you are announcing a two or three months—

THE PRESIDENT: Two months.

Q: Two months withdrawal, whereas the last time it was seven or eight months, I believe. How does this situation, in terms of the negotiating need that you spoke of, differ from the other one and can you tell us if you now, as a result of this two month withdrawal, foresee an end to the United States combat role in Vietnam?

THE PRESIDENT: Well, first, the situation is very different because, as we get down in numbers, each withdrawal has a much more dramatic effect on the percentage that we had there; 45,-000 as against, for example, 184,000, which is the present troop ceiling, is a lot different from 25,000 as against 539,000 or 540,000, which was our first withdrawal program.

So, consequently, it is essential as we get closer to the end if we are going to maintain any negotiating leverage, that the withdrawal periods, in my opinion, be somewhat shorter.

With regard to the other questions that we have on this— does that cover that point?

Q: Yes, sir. About that combat role, though.

THE PRESIDENT: Well, the combat role, let us understand, based on the casualties, as far as the offensive situation is concerned, is already concluded. American troops are now in a defensive position. They, however, will defend themselves, and what casualties we have taken—they are very small—will be taken in that defensive role.

You will find, as you analyze the battlefield reports, as I do from time to time, that the offensive activity, search and destroy, and all the other activity that we used to undertake, are now being undertaken by the South Vietnamese.

We will take the far left. (Laughter)

OFFENSIVE AND DEFENSIVE ROLES

Q: Mr. President, have you sent or are you sending orders to the forces in South Vietnam regarding the offensive and defensive role? Could you outline that for us?

THE PRESIDENT: That is a matter which is worked out by General Abrams in the field, and it is one that has just gradually come about. No orders need to be given for that purpose. And, incidentally, that is possible due to the fact that the South Vietnamese have gained the capability to handle the situation themselves.

Also, there is another reason. As we get to 184,000, and at the end of this period 45,000 less than that, what offensive capabilities we have are very, very seriously limited.

NEGOTIATIONS

Q: Mr. President, you said there was no movement on the prisoners of war issue. Is there anything at all to report on negotiations either through Paris or through some other means?

THE PRESIDENT: I would respond to that only by saying that we have not given up on the negotiating front. This announcement is somewhat of an indication that we have not given up on the negotiating front. I, however, would not like to leave the impression that we see the possibility of some striking breakthrough in negotiations in the near future.

But we are pursuing negotiations in Paris and through whatever other channels we think are appropriate.

PROGRESS ON PRISONERS

Q: One might infer from what you said previously that there has been progress on the prisoner question privately. Would that be a correct inference to draw?

THE PRESIDENT: No, it would not be a correct inference to draw. I wish it were, because this issue should, of course, as we all, I think, be separated from the issue of the combat role of Americans and our withdrawal program. It is a humanitarian issue. We have not, as yet, had any progress in our talks with the North Vietnamese in getting them to separate that issue from the rest.

On the other hand, we have not given up on the negotiating track, and we are going to continue to press on that track because that is the track on which we eventually are going to have success in getting our prisoners back.

Q: There has been no progress, either publicly or privately, on getting release of our prisoners?

THE PRESIDENT: I do not want to give any false encouragement to those who are the next of kin or who are close relatives of our prisoners. I can only say, however, that we, on our part, have taken initiatives on a number of fronts here. So the possibility of progress in the future is there. As far as the enemy's position is concerned, it is still intransigent.

AMERICAN AIR POWER

Q: Mr. President, from the conditions that you know now in Vietnam and Southeast Asia, can you foresee in the near future a substantial diminution of American air power use in support of the Vietnamese?

THE PRESIDENT: Well, air power of course, as far as our use of it is concerned, will continue to be used longer than our ground forces, due to the fact that training Vietnamese to handle the aircraft takes the longest lead time, as we know, and we will continue to use it in support of the South Vietnamese until there is a negotiated settlement or, looking further down the road, until the South Vietnamese have developed the capability to handle the situation themselves.

As far as our air power is concerned, let me also say this: As we reduce the number of our forces, it is particularly important for us to continue our air strikes on the infiltration routes. If we see any substantial step-up in infiltration in the passes, for example, which lead from North Vietnam into Laos and, of course, the Laotian trail which comes down through Cambodia into South Vietnam—if we see that, we will have to not only continue our air strikes; we will have to step them up.

That is why I have been quite categorical with regard to that situation, because as the number of our forces goes down, their danger increases, and we are not going to allow the enemy to pounce on them by reason of our failure to use air power against increased infiltration, if it occurs.

VISITS TO PEKING AND MOSCOW

Q: Mr. President, do you expect to discuss methods, possibily, to help alleviate the situation in Indochina in your visit to Peking and to Moscow?

THE PRESIDENT: I do not think it would be helpful to indicate at this time what we will discuss with regard to Indochina when our visits to Peking and Moscow take place. We are hopeful and continue to be hopeful that we can make progress on handling this problem ourselves, and that it may not have to be a problem that will have to be discussed in those areas.

Incidentally, I think it would not be well to speculate as to what, if anything, either Peking or Moscow can or will do on this matter. All that I can say is that we are charting our own course, and we will find our own way to bring it to a halt.

We will, of course, welcome any assistance; but we are not counting on it from either source.

NORTH VIETNAM STRENGTH

Q: Is it not true that at this particular poing the North Vietnamese are probably at their weakest they have been since the war, and is this because of floods and lack of resources?

THE PRESIDENT: The major reason they are the weakest since the war is because of Cambodia and Laos, and the floods, of course, have hurt them, too.

Miss Thomas?

1968 PROMISE

Q: In connection with your answer on negotiations, is what you are saying that perhaps you might not be able to keep your 1968 promise to end the war which I believe was your campaign pledge rather than just ending America's role in the war?

THE PRESIDENT: I would suggest that I be judged at the time of the campaign, rather than now on that. I would also suggest that every promise that I have made I have kept to this date and that usually is a pretty good example of what you might do with regard to future promises.

RESIDUAL FORCE

Q: Mr. President, we read much speculation that you plan to keep a residual force, 40,000 or 50,000 men in Vietnam until the prisoner of war issue is settled completely and all prisoners are out. Is that still valid?

THE PRESIDENT: Well, Mrs. Cornell—(Laughter)

Q: Touche. (Laughter)

THE PRESIDENT: First, if the situation is such that we have a negotiated settlement, naturally that means a total withdrawal of all American forces. It also not only means a total withdrawal of American forces in South Vietnam, it means a discontinuation of our air strikes and also withdrawal of forces stationed in other places in Southeast Asia or in the Asian Theater that are directly related to the support of our forces in Vietnam.

That is, in other words, what is involved if we can get a negotiated settlement. If we do not get a negotiated settlement, then it is necessary to maintain a residual force for not only the reason—and this is, of course, a very primary reason—of having something to negotiate with, with regard to our prisoners, but it is also essential to do so in order to continue our role of leaving South Vietnam in a position where it will be able to defend itself from a Communist take-over.

Both objectives can be fulfilled, we believe, through a negotiated settlement. We would prefer that. If they were not fulfilled through a negotiated settlement, then we will have go to another route and we are prepared to do so.

AMNESTY

Q: Mr. President, do you foresee granting amnesty to any of the young men who have fled the United States to avoid fighting in a war that they consider to be immoral?

THE PRESIDENT: No.

SALT NEGOTIATIONS

Q: Mr. President, you met this afternoon with our SALT negotiating team which is returning to Vienna. Earlier this year you expressed the hope that some kind of agreement could be made. Do you foresee some kind of SALT agreement before the end of the year?

THE PRESIDENT: We have made significant progress in the arms limitation talks. The progress, for example, with regard to the hot line and the progress with regard to accidental war is quite significant. Also, we have made significant progress in the discussion on limitation of defensive weapons and we are beginning now to move into discussions on offensive weapons.

Whether we are able to reach agreement by the end of the year, I think, is highly improbable at this point. I say highly improbable—not impossible. It depends on what happens.

Our goal is—and I discussed this at great length with Mr. Gromyko when he was here—our goal is, of course, at the highest level to urge our negotiators to try to find a common basis for agreement. But it must be a joint agreement. We cannot limit defensive weapons first and then limit offensive weapons. Both must go together. It will happen.

I would say this: I believe we are going to reach an agreement. I believe we will make considerable progress toward reaching that agreement before the end of the year. I think reaching the agreement before the end of the year is probably not likely at this time, but great progress will be made and I think by the end of the year we will be able to see then that our goal can be achieved.

PHASE TWO

Q: Mr. President, are you satisfied with the guidelines laid down by the Pay Commission and the Price Board and are you concerned about the effect of a likely bulge of increases in wages and prices after the freeze and public confidence on Phase 2?

THE PRESIDENT: Well, the possibility of some bulge, of course, has always been there, as you know, so when I announced the freeze it was widely speculated that once the freeze was off and once we then moved to guidelines, that there would be therefore some increase in wage rates and some increase also in prices. The freeze could not be kept on indefinitely.

However, I think the decisions of both the Pay Board and the Price Board have been very sound. They did not, in some instances, perhaps, reach the goals some would have liked. I think some businessmen thought the wage increases should have been in the neighborhood of three to four percent. That would have been a very good thing from their standpoint perhaps. It would have been totally unrealistic. It would have broken the Board wide open.

I think 5.5 percent is an achieveable goal. That would be a substantial reduction insofar as the wage-price push for 1971, as compared to 1960, 1969, and 1968.

As far as prices are concerned, the guidelines that have been laid down would cut the rate of inflation approximately in half. That is real progress.

One other point I should make. I noticed that many of you very properly have written about the uncertainty with regard to Phase 2. That is inevitable. It is inevitable in any free economy. We can have total certainty only with total control of the economy. But with a totalitarian economy we have no freedom as far as our economy is concerned and we would destroy the major advantage the United States has in its competitive position in the world, in other words, the free enterprise system.

I believe that this answer of the Pay Board and the Price Commission is a very realistic one. I believe it will succeed and one of the major reasons I believe it will succeed is the enormous public support that we had not only during the 90-day period, but that we continue to have for the period after the freeze. That public support will make this work.

VIETNAM WITHDRAWAL

Q: Mr. President, could I be quite clear on the withdrawal?

THE PRESIDENT: You mean perfectly clear, right. (Laughter)

Q: Is the 45,000 to be taken from the 184,000, sir? Does it come from the December 1 target figure?

THE PRESIDENT: Yes, that is right. You take your ceiling of December 1 and take 45,000 from that and you get where we will be on February 1. Let me point out incidentally that we are always slightly below that ceiling, as you know, with regard to actual withdrawals. But we have set as the ceiling for February 1 the 45,000 from 184,000, but we will probably be below that at that time by a few hundred or maybe even a few thousand.

DATE FOR CHINA TRIP

Q: Mr. President, have you set a date to go to China yet?

THE PRESIDENT: I have nothing to announce on that at this time.

THIEU REACTION

Q: Mr. President, if we can assume that President Thieu was informed at least of the withdrawals, can you tell us what his reaction was?

THE PRESIDENT: Complete approval. President Thieu, along with General Abrams, and General Binh and the others who work together in the combined Joint Chiefs over there, have been, just as Secretary Laird has reported, enormously impressed with the speed of the training program and the ability of the South Vietnamese to defend themselves.

It has gone faster than we had thought, and also, as was pointed out by one of the earlier questioners here, the level of enemy activity has not been as great as it was, due to the fact that the enemy doesn't have the punch it had. Cambodia took a great deal out of the enemy's punch. Laos took a great deal out of its punch. And in addition to that, these torrential floods have made it difficult for the enemy to be as effective in its attacks as it was previously.

That does not mean, however, looking to the future, that we must not be on guard. That is why I said we are going to watch this infiltration route and rate very, very carefully in the critical months of December and January before making another withdrawal announcement.

AID FOR CAMBODIA

Q: Mr. President, in your most recent foreign aid bill, you requested a total of $341 million in military and economic aid for Cambodia. The head of the government of Cambodia has just renounced democracy as a viable form of government, which some people think has analogy to earlier developments in Vietnam. What assurance can you give the American people that we are not sliding into another Vietnam in Cambodia?

THE PRESIDENT: We didn't slide into Vietnam. That is the difference. In Vietnam, conscious decisions were made to send Americans there to become involved in combat. I am not criticizing the decision; I am reflecting what the situation was.

It was not a question of sliding in; but was a question of decisions being made, first, to send American combat troops in. Those were first made by President Kennedy, the first troops that went in; and then the decisions to bomb in the North. Those were made by President Johnson, and the increases in forces.

Let's look at Cambodia. We have made a conscious decision not to send American troops in. There are no American combat troops in Cambodia. There are no American combat advisers in Cambodia. There will be no American combat troops or advisers in Cambodia.

We will aid Cambodia. Cambodia is the Nixon Doctrine in its purest form. Vietnam was in violation of the Nixon Doctrine. Because in Cambodia what we are doing is helping the Cambodians to help themselves, and we are doing that rather than to go in and do the fighting ourselves, as we did in Korea and as we did in Vietnam. We hope not to make that mistake again if we can avoid it.

STOCK MARKET

Q: Mr. President, in May of 1970, when stocks hit their biggest low of the year, you gave counsel to buy. Now that we have reached the biggest low in 1971, what is your counsel today to the American investor?

THE PRESIDENT: Don't sell. (Laughter)

I would like to comment on that particular matter, because if my advice had been taken, you would have done reasonably well then, as you know. As I said in Detroit, whether it is investments in stocks or bonds, or, for that matter, in real property, which is my only source of investment, if I may paraphrase what one of the television commercials I have heard often enough, I am bullish on America. However, I would strongly advise somebody who invests to invest on the long term; not the short term.

On the long term, 1972 is going to be a good year. When we see, for example, inflation cut in half, which is our goal, when we see employment beginning to rise,—it rose over a million during the period of the freeze—and when we see something else, when we see our economy now being built on the basis of peace rather than war, this is a time when people looking to the future, planning to hang on, could, it seems to me, well invest in America with the hope that their investments will prove well.

1968, for example, was a very bad time to buy, and yet it appeared to be like the best of times. Stocks were high. Unemployment was low. Everybody thought that we had high prosperity, but prosperity was based on 300 American casualties a week, 500,-000 Americans in Vietnam, twenty-five to thirty billion dollars being spent on a war in Vietnam and on a burgeoning rate of inflation.

At that time, therefore, I would not have advised, and I trust many brokers did not advise their clients to buy, because when prosperity is based on war and inflation, you are eventually going to have a setback.

The new prosperity that we are working toward—and we may have some rocky times; we have had some and we may have some more—but looking toward the year 1972, as I appraise the situation, the new prosperity, based on jobs in peacetime, on peace production primarily, and based on a checked rate of inflation, will be a much sounder prosperity and, therefore, a better time to invest in America.

THE PRESS: Thank you, Mr. President.

INDEX

CQ